*"Islam is inherently synonymous with justice and compassion.
Without them, Islam is irrelevant."*

To my beloved wife Fauziah,
whose support and patience mean everything to me..

To all my teachers,
who have taught, guided and imparted their knowledge to me that made it
possible for me to come up with this piece of work with God's permission.
May God count all of you among those who will be blessed with His grace and
mercy on the Day of Judgment.

Table of Contents

Surah (Chapters)

Introduction

The Glorious Qur'an is God's divine book of guidance for all mankind. And The Contemporary Qur'an is an English translation of the Glorious Qur'an written in simple modern English for the reading pleasure of everyone who understands English.

Apart from helping Muslims and new converts see the Qur'an's message clearer, The Contemporary Qur'an also addresses the most fundamental question asked by non-Muslims about the Qur'an and Islam which typically is: "How do you prove that the Qur'an is God's literal words and how can I be convinced that Islam is the true religion to follow, especially when it is being widely associated with terrorism and violence?"

The following approaches were taken to address this question :

1. In the book's Foreword section, I discussed about my own experience in seeking the truth and how I applied simple logic to show that Islam stands out from other religions.

2. Through irrefutable historical and scientific evidence that have been proven by recent advancements in science and technology, I impressed on how impossible it is for the Qur'an to be authored by a mortal, especially an illiterate who lived in the plain desert of Arabia during the 7th century, which serves as proof that the Qur'an is truly a book of divine revelation; and I also briefly explained how its linguistic beauty in Arabic is a miracle that can never be rivaled until the end of time.

3. In reference to the issue of terrorism that is being relentlessly propagated by the media causing widespread Islamophobia, I pointed out the relevant passages in the Qur'an and offered commentaries to prove this notion wrong. It is important to first and foremost take note that these passages must be read and understood in the right context where war and fighting is allowed only as an act of retaliation and self defense against the enemy's aggression and must cease when the enemy ends its hostility. Through the comments I offered, readers should be able to see and appreciate that Islam is a universal religion of peace where racial supremacy and extremism have no place near it. In fact, Islam is respectful and tolerant of other faiths, and places unequivocal emphasis on its command to uphold justice and fairness for everyone, regardless of race and religion. Islam ordains that everyone is equal in the sight of God in this world and deserves fair treatment. A true religion must have this all-inclusiveness universal feature because God cannot be God if He practices racial discrimination, encourages intolerance among His creations, and promotes aggression. Those who violate this may escape legal retribution in this world but will surely suffer dire consequences in the afterlife.

4. I also endeavored to make non-Muslims see that there is actually nothing wrong with the teachings of Islam even though many of its followers and nations are besieged with woeful conditions such as poverty, and political and social instability. The problem is not with the religion itself, but with its adherents' flawed understanding and practice of Islam. There are many Muslims who regard Islam as nothing more than a religion that is steeped in rituals which lead them to over-emphasize the practice of many meaningless unauthentic rituals that are not prescribed by Islam but are instead products of culture and tradition that have been blindly inherited from earlier generations. Because of this, they become ritual-centric and preoccupy themselves with many unprescribed acts of worship until they unwittingly lose sight of Islam's bigger picture and neglect the more important responsibilities that have been commanded by God to fulfill such as to be ever compassionate to others, to uphold justice at all times, and to pursue sound knowledge relentlessly. Worse still, many choose to elect bad leaders to power because they are simply gullible and cannot discern between truth and falsehood. These bad leaders would in turn worsen the condition through widespread corruption and stealing because of their insatiable greed and excessive love for worldly pleasures, thus impoverishing their own people. Some of these countries would end up beholden to foreign powers with ulterior agendas for the financial aid and other assistance that they receive, thus worsening their condition further. These people forget that they will not live forever and all the wealth that they illegitimately amass will not be of any help when they face God to answer for all their wicked and cruel deeds. The painful truth is: Muslims who are ignorant of Islam's true teachings are Islam's worst enemy who are responsible for destroying themselves and the *ummah* (i.e. entire community of Muslims bound together by ties of Islam). They are the ones who give a bad name and image to Islam.

The Qur'an is truly a book of divine guidance for mankind which should not be ignored. It awakens our higher consciousness and addresses the real concerns and challenges faced by every individual and society at all times. It is a book that we turn to when we want God to speak to us and be reminded about the reason of our existence so that we can stay true in His path. It is also a book that forces us to contemplate deeply about how we should live our life in this world and fare eternally in the next life to emerge victorious. This book which you are holding in your hand hopes to serve you in addressing these.

There is no compulsion in religion, for truth stands clearly distinct from falsehood. Through this book, I hope to continue the legacy of our beloved Prophet (may peace be upon him) in spreading God's divine words of truth to those who have never been exposed to the Qur'an and Islam correctly. I pray that many will join me to spread this book as far and wide as possible to all corners of the world in fulfilling a part of our duty as God's emissary to promote universal justice and peace to all mankind.

Foreword

All praise be to God, the Lord and Sustainer of all the worlds Who revealed the Noble and Glorious Qur'an as guidance for all mankind to attain true success both in this world and in the life to come. May peace and His blessings be upon Prophet Muhammad who was chosen as His final Messenger to convey His message of truth that brings good news to those who accept and a stern warning to those who reject it.

This is the third edition of my humble work in translating the Glorious Qur'an in English. The first edition was published in May 2014 and the second edition in January 2021. This third edition now comes with more footnotes than the second one and they also highlight the verses that negate the allegations of terrorism in Islam and the widespread baseless perception of Islamophobia (verses 2:190, 5:8. 5:32 and 60:8). Other than this, the two main features that were already included in the second edition, namely the use of the word "God" in place of "Allah" and the Biblical names of the Prophets are maintained so that non-Muslim readers can better relate the content of this book with their Scripture and take note of what both these books share in common. The goal of this book is to make it easy for uninitiated English readers to grasp the essence and underlying message of the Glorious Qur'an, realign their thoughts, perception and paradigm about Islam correctly, and apply its true teachings in their lives with full appreciation and wisdom.

But be mindful that this book which you hold in your hand now is not the actual Glorious Qur'an. Instead, it is only a manifestation of an attempt to present the meaning of the Qur'an and its charm in simple modern English. Any translation of the Qur'an in other languages can never be completely accurate due to the range of meanings of what an Arabic word offers depending on its context. Only God alone knows the true and precise meaning of His own words. Translations of the Qur'an are merely thoughts and interpretations of its translators based on the knowledge they have acquired through their study and research.

With regard to my translation method, I adopted the contextual approach by paraphrasing the text instead of translating them literally to bring out their meaning clearer. As a result, readers will find many verses that are interspersed with additional words and expressions that I placed in parentheses for coherent narration and also to provide clarity in presenting their meaning according to the best of my understanding and interpretation, while endeavoring to still maintain the true spirit of the text. In addition, I also grouped together several verses in single paragraphs so that they can be better understood from the contextual and thematic perspective to avoid readers from losing sight of the underlying message if each verse were to be read independently from their preceding and succeeding passages.

Foreword

This translation is named The Contemporary Qur'an for three main reasons. Firstly because the Qur'an's content is always relevant until the end of time. Hence, it must be read and understood in the context of how its message can be related with the modern and contemporary setting that we live in today and be correctly guided by its divine teachings Secondly because the translation uses modern English and is expressed in quite a simple manner. And finally because wherever applicable, the interpretation takes into account relevant historical and scientific facts that have been made available by recent advancements in science and technology. The approach is aimed to evoke a sense of awe in both the Muslim and non-Muslim readers alike who do not understand Arabic, towards the abundant wondrous signs of God's immense power and greatness that is imprinted in every corner of the universe and within the human body too (verses 41:53 and 51:21-22) that serve as irrefutable proofs of the Qur'an's divinity.

On a personal note, my journey to seriously study the Qur'an and Islam started with a spiritual awakening during the mid-80's when I was studying Economics in the United States. I was approached by a Christian missionary then, who tried to proselytize Christianity to me in a situation where I knew very little about my own faith - Islam, the religion that I was born in by virtue of my parents' faith. What he did shook me because I could not defend my religion except for telling him that I only believe in the One Universal Almighty God Who is Inidvisible. It is He Who created this entire universe and is not associated with any partner, and that only He alone deserves all worship.

It was at that moment when I realized that I must take the initiative to learn, understand and practice my religion correctly if I wanted to be a true Muslim instead of merely following it blindly. I also realized that it was wrong for me to take Islam for granted just because I inherited it from my parents and the culture and tradition that I grew up in. I should be a Muslim by choice, not by default because being a Muslim means nothing if we do not understand and practice it correctly with true conviction. Faith is not the same as culture. Faith must be based on divine guidance whereas culture is a set of widely practiced tradition and accepted norm of a society invented by man. Ultimately, We shall all have to face God one day and be accountable for all our actions because we are given free will to decide what we want to believe and practice. So I set on a journey to fulfill this by studying and researching to find the true religion to follow if I was born in a non-Muslim family and did not know anything about Islam. I decided to unlearn Islam by leaving all the baggage I knew about this religion behind in order to relearn it from a fresh start. I did this to be really sure if Islam is indeed the true religion that the Almighty God has prescribed for all mankind to follow. I figured that a true religion cannot be complicated. It must make sense and come with clear and logical concepts that are easy to understand. Hence, my journey began.

For a start, I divided people into two main groups of those who believe in the existence of God and those who do not. I easily struck out the latter because I fall into the category of those who cannot imagine how this universe could ever come into existence with such perfect laws that govern its entire operations in utmost precision without a Supreme Power behind it to regulate all these harmoniously. They simply cannot perfectly fall into place by chance. Its simple analogy is like if we see a fresh trace of foot prints on the ground in the forest, surely We shall come to a logical conclusion that there was someone in the forest who walked in that path before us even if we do not see him. We know that he was there because there was a clear sign of his presence from the foot prints. In the same way too, we conclude and affirm God's existence by observing and studying His signs of creations from the biggest to the minutest that are abundant everywhere - in every corner of the vast universe and within ourselves too (41:53). These signs are there for us to research, explore, reflect and ponder about how they came into existence and who is regulating and harmonizing their operations and functions perfectly. Hence, only those with sound knowledge and pure heart will stand in awe of God's mighty power and unrivalled greatness, and are fearful of His wrath if He is defied and rejected (35:28). Denying His existence is simply illogical to say the least. It is like saying we came into this world without a mother.

With this most basic question out of the way, the next step was to find out which is the true religion of God to follow. In exploring this, my mind simply cannot accept any religion or faith that involves idol worshipping, deification of ancestors, and belief systems that do not come with religious Scriptures to prove their divinity. I figured that God cannot simply leave us on our own without guidance to understand the purpose of our creation. Any responsible creator, inventor or producer of something must provide an operation manual to teach users how to use his product. Therefore, it does not seem right if the Creator of mankind did not provide a manual to teach and guide us how to lead our lives correctly according to the purpose of our creation. Since He has honored only the human specie with the faculties of reason and intellect that place us way above all His other creations (see verses 17:70, 95:4-6 and their footnotes), surely He must also give us some form of guidance on how to use this gift correctly within certain parameters that would not damage it. Both these faculties have very powerful potentials that can be used to either cause unimaginable havoc and damage to this planet, or provide great service to humanity. Therefore, it simply does not make sense to not worship and submit to The One Who Created and granted us this powerful gift, but instead choose to worship lifeless objects or creations that are weak and cannot teach us anything, and have to depend on something else for their existence and survival. Taking this stand would naturally result in the elimination of every religion on the face of earth except for the three Semitic religions namely Judaism, Christianity and Islam that claim to offer divine Scriptures as guidance. Consequently, the ensuing task would be to find out which of these three religions offers the true Scripture that is authentically divine for mankind to follow.

Looking deeper into them, it is obvious that Judaism cannot be the answer because it is not a universal religion. There is no racial equality in Judaism. Even though it is monotheistic, it is essentially an ethnic based religion for the Jews alone which glorifies them as God's chosen race in spite of their constant rebellion against Him. How can a religion of truth be ethnocentric and not promote racial equality? Certainly God cannot be unfair to favor only a group of people that belongs to a certain race. What kind of God practices double standard? By striking out Judaism from my list, what was left to explore and consider was whether Christianity or Islam is the true religion to follow.

Essentially, the main difference between these two religions is : Christianity does not stand on pure monotheism even though the church claims it does, while Islam is truly monotheistic in a very strict way. Hence, all one needs to do is to look into the claims and arguments put forward by both sides to see the logic in following a religion that is based on the concept of Trinity with three co-equal Gods embodied as one and yet still insists that it is a monotheistic religion, or the other that is based on pure monotheism which makes it absolutely clear that there is only One God Who deserves all worship.

Poring through the Bible for many years, I must say that I am still lost about its dominant theme. The Old Testament basically talks about the history of the Children of Israel and its monotheistic concept, while the New Testament contradicts this by trying very hard to deify Jesus but without any direct mention that Jesus claimed himself to be God who must be worshipped. In fact, the concept of Trinity is not even mentioned anywhere in the Bible but must be accepted according to how the church has set it out to be because discussions about this subject based on rational reasoning is unpermitted. But if Jesus is indeed God, why does it have to be this way? Why is this not spelled out clearly in the Bible? Why did Jesus not openly announce that he is God and then command people to worship him? Is this not the logical thing to do if he is really God, and should this not be the most dominant theme that the Bible must highlight unambiguously? Why all the drama and mystery instead?

Furthermore, Christians themselves openly admit that all the books that make up the Bible are not God's literal words but were instead authored by people who they claim were inspired by God. I find this claim strange and cannot accept it with a logical mind because there is no possible way to determine that all these authors were infallible and divinely inspired to pen down God's message to mankind especially when no one has any inkling of their identities. How can those who are believed to have written Scriptures on behalf of God be in a condition of complete anonymity? A case to point is about the number of books that are compiled in the Bible. The Roman

Catholics have 73 books in their Bible while the Protestants have 66 books after they expunged 7 books out from the Roman Catholic's Old Testament. How could it be that the Catholics believe the authors of these 7 books were divinely inspired while the Protestants on the other hand decided they were not? How is it also possible that the Catholics and Protestants apply different standards and criteria in determining the infallibility of the authors? I find this unsettling because the Bible surely cannot claim and prove itself to be divine this way.

On the contrary, the Qur'an presents itself as God's literal words and gives out a very clear unequivocal statement in all its 114 chapters that there is no other god but the Almighty God alone Who deserves all worship, and Muhammad bin Abdullah of Makkah is His final Prophet and Messenger whose teachings every Muslim must follow since he alone was the one who received God's divine revelation on behalf of all mankind. This theme and message is dominantly mentioned all over the Qur'an from cover to cover. No one can ever miss this. It is what the Qur'an clearly spells out. No ambiguous hints and clues. No mystery. Those who believe in this are called believers and those who don't are called disbelievers. Each will receive different treatment in the Hereafter. It is as clear as crystal.

Other than this, the Qur'an also presents many irrefutable historical and scientific facts that were not known before the 20th century as proof of its divinity with the advent of science and technology. With this, people who live in the modern and contemporary setting today are able to relate and appreciate the Qur'an's miracle from a scientific perspective. This is how God makes the Qur'an's infallibility remain relevant forever and easy to grasp by non-Arabic speaking laymen, both Muslims and non-Muslim alike, who are unable to appreciate the linguistic beauty of the Qur'an in its original Arabic.

But those who lived during the time of the Prophet in the 7th century did not need any scientific fact and evidence to convince them of the Qur'an's truth. All of them - both believers and disbelievers alike - were mesmerized and captivated by the unrivaled linguistic excellence and beauty of the Qur'an, so much so that they unanimously concluded it cannot originate from a mortal. Sadly, even though the Arab pagans admitted this, they still continued to oppose the message that the Qur'an presented due to pride and arrogance. To this, God challenged them on three separate occasions to produce a recitation that could rival the Qur'an, which no one could. The first challenge was to produce a whole book like the Qur'an (verse 17:88). When this could not be met, the second challenge came for them to produce just ten chapters of similar merit as the Qur'an (verse 11:13). And when this still could not be met, the final challenge came for them to produce only a single chapter that could match the Qur'an (verse 2:23) in the face of the fact that all they needed to do was to rival the shortest chapter in the Qur'an (i.e. *Al-Kautsar*, the 108th chapter) which comprises only three verses.

The findings of my research point to a very clear conclusion that Islam is the undisputed religion to follow. Not only are the Qur'an's scientific evidence irrefutable, but the knowledge that I gained through countless religious classes that I have attended throughout the many years behind me also taught the amazing miracle of the Qur'an from its linguistic perspective. The usage of specific Arabic words in the Qur'an that cannot be found in other languages and their application in certain contexts to bring out their specific meaning with pin-point accuracy is truly mind boggling.

During the 23 years of the Qur'an's revelation, the consistency of its language style, presentation and choice of words clearly demonstrate that this Book cannot possibly be authored by any mortal, especially when the person who recited it was illiterate. This was what truly dumbfounded the disbelievers throughout the 23-year period. In the end, all they could do was to only accuse the Prophet as a sorcerer who had the ability to bewitch people with his spellbinding eloquence. How these revelations were recited by the Prophet is very much like the email that we are very familiar with today. Once we hit the "Send" button, there is practically no way to retract and edit its content. It is as it is. Likewise, once the Prophet recited the words and verses that were sent down to him from God through Angel Gabriel, his scribes would quickly write these on whatever objects they could find and then orally "viral" them to the rest of their other companions for memorization without any possibility of editing. If there was any error in these messages that was discovered later, this would certainly cause a huge problem to the Qur'an's veracity and put its claim of infallibility and divinity in jeopardy. But this was never the case at all. Not even once. Chapter 111 demonstrates a clear example of this.

With the question about the Qur'an's veracity and Islam's truth resolved, my mind then turned to another burning question that had always been haunting me for such a long time and needed to be urgently addressed : "If Islam is indeed the true religion for all mankind and is the solution to all kinds of personal and social problems, why then is the vast majority of Muslims all over the world in such a pathetic and woeful state today, helplessly experiencing calamities of gigantic proportions that force many to flee to non-Muslim countries to seek for a better life? Why are we so disunited, weak, oppressed, corrupt, and in a nutshell manifesting virtually almost all the negative traits and attributes of human character? Why is this happening especially when all of us believe in the same One Almighty God Who is the ultimate Creator and Master of all the worlds, bear witness that Prophet Muhammad (may peace be upon him) is His final Messenger, and even have in our hands the Glorious Qur'an which we believe without an iota of doubt is a Book which contains His literal words that is divinely infallible to guide us aright? And why is it also that Muslims seem so incapable of stepping up to our duty to become God's emissary on earth serving as exemplary leaders, exhibiting the best intellect and conduct in the most natural manner that would make Islam so appealing and attractive to everyone, and actively vie among one another to make this world a better place for everyone to live in?"

For a long time, no one could give me a satisfactory answer. But by the grace of God, I found the answer in verses 3:112, 6:123, 4:135 and 5:8 in the Qur'an. In essence, the *ummah* (i.e. entire community of Muslims bound together by ties of Islam) is being afflicted with this calamity because most of us are indifferent and do not care to stand-up against injustice. We seem to think that this has very little or nothing to do with religion. This paradigm is prevalent mainly in cultures that are steeped in a feudal mindset which still exists even in the modern world that we live in today where we are being taught to never go against our leaders and to just ignore their wrongdoings. Instead, we are being told to only focus on practicing the religious rituals that have been infused with centuries-old meaningless customs and traditions that we blindly inherit from earlier generations so much so that we are unable to separate religion from custom. We are being conditioned to believe that by practicing these rituals, We will earn God's pleasure and become eligible to enter Paradise, regardless of whether or not we understand what we are doing. Verse 2:170 depicts this mindset and scenario.

We end up like this because we have never been taught of our Prophet's strict warning to shun innovative practices in matters of worship that he neither taught nor practiced, and that those who do so are actually committing a grave sin. As such, we are ignorant of the fact that these seemingly good deeds in our sight carry no value in God's sight and are therefore rejected [Sahih Muslim, no. 1718]. This is precisely why we have close to two billion adherents of Islam in this world today who can recite the Qur'an in Arabic like parrots but at the same time perform all sorts of meaningless religious rituals because we do not truly understand the meaning of what is being recited, let alone apply its virtues and correct teachings in our lives even as we become adults and continue to age. As a result, instead of focusing on the qualitative aspects of the obligatory and other prescribed acts of worship that are authentic, most of us become very ritual-centric and are fixated on the quantitative aspect of our rituals, especially the supererogatory or voluntary ones where most of them are not authentically prescribed by Islam.

Islam is a clear religion based on logical and practical concepts that are relevant at all times. There is nothing mystical about this religion. The path for those who hope and seek to elevate themselves to higher spiritual stations to get closer to God by over-performing supererogatory acts of worship that are not authentically prescribed by Islam needs to be critically examined. The stark truth is many among us fail to practice Islam with the best quality as mentioned in verses 18:7 and 67:2 because of our obsession with quantity. As a result, many among us are being led astray to perpetrate or condone injustice, corruption and disorder on earth (verse 6:123) without any feeling of guilt and remorse while religiously performing all sorts of rituals at the same time, thinking that everything is fine because we cannot connect these two together. Many Muslims simply fail to understand that the duty to serve humanity with justice and fairness regardless of race and religion is as equally important as performing our obligatory religious rituals and practices. There is a major breakdown in understanding the importance of implementing this virtue with utmost priority and the unnecessary emphasis on performing supererogatory ritual practices that the majority of us are more interested in. And because of this, we forget that the way to earn God's pleasure is by striving earnestly to become His best emissary on earth by fulfilling the purpose of our creation (verse 2:30), which is to worship Him alone by strictly following the *sunnah* (i.e. teachings and practices) of the Prophet and to serve humanity by ensuring that justice and compassion must always prevail. This gross oversight needs to be urgently addressed so that Muslims can free themselves from the calamity and humiliation that has besieged the *ummah* as warned in verse 3:112.

Worshipping the One and Only God and upholding justice go hand in hand. One cannot stand without the other. According to an authentic *hadith* (i.e. Prophetic saying), it was reported that God Almighty said: 'O My servants! I have forbidden injustice for Myself and among you. So do not be unjust and cruel.'" [Sahih Muslim, no. 2577]. It is clear that God abhors injustice and has forbidden it to ever be associated with Him and prohibits His servants from playing any part in it (see verse 11:113). Essentially, Islam is inherently synonymous with justice and compassion. Without them, Islam is irrelevant. Therefore, it is the job of every Muslim to put this in place and guard it jealously (see verse 4:135 and its footnote). This fundamental concept of Islam must be clearly understood by every Muslim. In fact, this is the wholeness of Islam that I invite everyone to embrace wholeheartedly. Through this book, I hope to awaken us from our complacency and lack of attention regarding Islam's unequivocal emphasis to uphold justice and exercise compassion at all times alongside the worship rituals that we are obligated to perform in strict accordance with the Prophet's *sunnah* (i.e. traditions and practices).

It is important to know that no amount of self-engrossed rituals that one does during his lifetime will free and absolve him from the sins of injustices and wrongdoings that he has inflicted on others. Sins that are committed towards God that do not affect others, including acts of ascribing divinity to false deities besides Him (verse 4:48) can be readily forgiven through sincere repentance before death as long as it is not done in the eleventh hour of his dying moment (see verses 4:18 and 10:90-91). But sins that involve wrongdoings upon others can only be atoned by forgiveness from those who have been wronged [Sahih Bukhari, no. 2449]. In another *hadith*, the Messenger of God (peace be upon him) once asked his companions, "Do you know who is a bankrupt?" Someone answered, "A bankrupt among us is the one who neither has any dirham with him nor wealth." Answered the Prophet in return, "(No.) The bankrupt from my *ummah* is the one who will come on the Day of Resurrection with (merits from) his prayers, fasts and charities that he gave out but he would find himself bankrupt on that day because he hurled abuses, made calumnies, consumed wealth unlawfully, shed blood, and harmed others (during his time on earth). The merits from the good deeds that he has earned will be credited into the account of those who suffered at his hand. And if his good deeds fall short to clear the account, then the sins of those he had wronged will be loaded into his account. In the end, he will be thrown into the Hellfire (because all his good deeds have vanished due to the injustices that he committed)." [Sahih Muslim, no. 2581]. Chapter 107 of the Qur'an also emphatically tells us that all our rituals will go to waste if we ill-treat others. And in verse 11:113, we are sternly warned to never condone and be a party to any act of injustice committed by others if we do not want to be caught by the flames of the Hellfire. All these show how strict and serious Islam is in its stand against injustice where the threat of Hellfire is not only leveled against those who commit injustice but also to those who condone it whether directly or indirectly.

Muslims must learn to balance their worship rituals to establish an excellent vertical relationship with God at a personal level together with establishing an excellent horizontal relationship with other fellow humans at the social level (verse 3:112) by concurrently fulfilling their duty to uphold justice and fight oppression. How strange it is when the Prophet and his companions went to many battles to fight oppression and injustice perpetrated by the disbelievers in the past, but today we find Muslims who are in power oppressing and impoverishing other fellow Muslims with support from many others who condone these wrongdoings through unholy alliances, or through ballot boxes, or through whatever other forms there are because of their inability to discern between right and wrong due to their corrupt *fitrah* (i.e. man's pure natural disposition and value system, see verses 7:172, 30:30, 54:5 and 91:10) and ignorance in Islam's unequivocal emphasis on social justice. By neglecting social justice, Islam is grossly misrepresented because it gives the impression that Islam is an impractical religion that is made up of rituals alone that are not relevant and applicable to address the real problems happening in this world concerning injustice and gross violation of basic human rights whereas this was what the Prophet and his companions had actually stood-up for in defending the sanctity of Islam during their time.

Sadly, what we are seeing in many parts of the world today are rampant cases of injustice involving many Muslim leaders who get away by plundering billions of dollars from their nation's coffers and from the people who they are supposed to serve. Even worse, many religious scholars and preachers choose to condone these wrongdoings by turning a blind eye on them, thus incurring God's curse Who equates their behavior like dogs and donkeys (see verses 7:175-176 and 62:5). In fact, they audaciously go as far as manipulating the Qur'an's verses and prophetic sayings to justify support for despotic leaders and rulers for the sake of their selfish worldly gains much like what the Jewish priests in the past did (see verses 2:42, 2:159 and 3:71). Consequently, a great majority of Muslims are being misled into the trap of Satan which makes them see their evil deeds as right and fair-seeming (see verses 15:39 and 2:212).

Until this is corrected, the *ummah* will continue to live in humiliation (verse 3:112) which will only get worse with each passing day. This is God's true promise of what will surely happen when we neglect and fail to uphold social justice, continue to condone corruption, honor its evil perpetrators (verse 6:123) and allow double standard practices to prevail where the rich and powerful are accorded privileges and are treated differently from the common folks. The following *hadith* serves as a stern warning about the inevitable destruction of any society or nation that allows unjust double standard practices to prevail : "O people! Your predecessors were destroyed because a person of high social status among them would be spared from punishment when he stole. But when an ordinary and weak one among them committed theft, he was severely punished." [Sahih Muslim, no.1688]. At the same time, it will also not be easy to attract non-Muslims to Islam because the bad image that result from this betrays Islam's pure and sound theological concept of strict monotheism and the good behavior that is supposed to emerge from this pure faith. We must realize that non-Muslims do not read the Qu'ran to understand Islam. Instead, they read the actions and behavior of Muslims to form their image, opinion and perception of Islam.

To get out from this predicament, Muslims must return to Islam's true teachings by balancing the ritual obligation to worship our Creator and concurrently serve humanity by striving against oppression and upholding justice for everyone. In fighting oppression and injustice, we are not enjoined to bear arms in revolt and worsen the dire situation that our nations are already in. Instead, we are taught to operate in a civilized manner within the prescribed laws of our respective lands to bring about the necessary institutional reforms that would beget justice and fairness for everyone. This can be accomplished by courageously living up to the following *hadith* : "Whoever among you sees evil, let him change it with his hand (i.e. through authority). If he is unable to do so, then with his tongue (i.e. through speech and/or writing). If he is still unable to do so, then with his heart (by detesting and not condoning it), and that is the weakest level of faith." [Sahih Muslim, no. 49]. But in order to live up to this *hadith*, Muslims must first of all be able to recognize and detest everything that constitutes and represents evil and injustice. This can only happen if we earnestly strive to purify our *fitrah* and strive to attain *taqwa* first (see verse 29:45 and its footnote) so that what is right and wrong can be clearly discerned according to God's standard and sound moral values. It is impossible to fight evil when one cannot recognize it especially for those who are associated with it because those whose *fitrah* is corrupt can never be able to distinguish between good and evil. See verse 54:5 and its footnote.

And as God's emissaries and trustees on earth, Muslims must strive to always exhibit the best conduct and behavior with the highest level of integrity that represents the true values and teachings of Islam. Speaking about this, I cannot resist from citing the Japanese who are generally far better than most Muslims in this aspect especially after their defeat in World War II that has humbled them. Other than integrity, their discipline in cleanliness and punctuality is extraordinary. If they get their faith right and submit to the Almighty God, they can easily earn a spot among the best examples of Muslims to emulate in our present era. Coming back to point, Muslims must demonstrate that Islam offers practical solutions to the mess that the world is in instead of being counted as part or cause of the problems. We need to be confident of Islam's universal practicality and its compatibility with modernity. To make this work, its principles and ideals need to be correctly understood and interpreted, and then reapplied to formulate new responses to the political, scientific and cultural challenges of our modern life.

God did not give humans the faculties of intellect and reason for nothing. They must be put to good use to formulate appropriate responses to successfully deal with contemporary challenges as proof of Islam's claim that it is an ever relevant religion of truth until the end of time. And this must be done carefully without compromising Islam's immutable monotheistic belief while concurrently practicing its rituals in strict accordance with the authentic tradition of God's final Messenger that are free from elements of innovations to safeguard its originality and purity from any form of corruption. Verses 3:31, 33:21 and 53:2-4 tell us in a very clear term that we must follow the Prophet's *sunnah* (i.e. practices) and emulate his excellent conduct if we truly love God, want to gain His pleasure and emerge victorious both in this world and the next. There is no need to do more than what he has taught us because they have no value in God's sight [Sahih Muslim, no. 1718] and will only blur our focus on the more important social obligations that we have been commanded to fulfill, which is to ensure social justice to prevail in our society at all times without different standards and sets of rules that discriminate the weak from the powerful, and the poor from the rich (verses 4:135 and 5:8).

A true religion must promote universal peace and justice. Violence can never be a part of it (verse 5:32). Hence, there is no logic for the One and Only universal God Who emphatically commands justice to be upheld at all times to be regarded as the same God who is also telling a group of people to commit violence on others at the same time. This should not make sense to anyone with sound reason and it would be a real shame if he allows himself to be intoxicated with the baseless hype of Islamophobia that propagates this lie. But then again, Islamophobes are ignorant about Islam's true teachings and have no interest to find out the truth by themselves. As such, it is the responsibility of Muslims to patiently educate them about Islam in the best possible way and manner (verse 16:125) just as how the Prophet did 1,450 years ago while facing the hostile Arab pagans of Makkah. And if they reject the message, leave them alone (verse 7:199). But if God opens their heart to see the truth and subsequently accept Islam, you will see them become a dear friend (verse 41:34) and perhaps even a staunch defender of Islam compared to the billions of hereditary Muslims on the planet who take their religion for granted because they regard Islam merely as a culture and tradition instead.

But the fact is, the urgency to demonstrate Islam as a sensible and universally practical religion cannot be emphasized enough especially in current circumstances where it is being widely regarded as a backward religion that is closely associated with violence, which is causing widespread Islamophobia despite the fact that nowhere in the Qur'an can a single verse be found instigating its adherents to perpetrate violence on others of different faith. On the contrary, Muslims are being emphatically commanded to always uphold justice for everyone regardless of race and religion; and be kind, courteous and compassionate to others especially to those who are not hostile towards Islam. See verses 60:8, 5:8, 11:113 and 107:4-7. Notwithstanding this however, Islam does allow fighting but only as retaliation against aggression by others and must end when the enemy ceases its hostility and transgression as mentioned in verses 22:40 and 2:190-193. In fact, all retaliatory actions must be proportionate to the wrong that is committed by the enemy without going overboard (verse 16:126) because God dislikes extremism and strictly forbids it (verses 2:190).

The truth is, those with evil agendas who cause corruption, disorder and violence on earth as they cruelly trample over the rights of others are the real terrorists that the world should focus on and deal with, including those who condone and are complicit in these evil acts regardless of whatever their religion or faith is. The clearest example of this is the illegal occupation of Palestine by the Zionists of Israel and their unending transgressions against the Palestinians since 1948. This has been taking place for far too long with unwavering support from Zionist Christians all over the world that are met with mute response from Muslim leaders who worship lusts as their god (verses 25:43, 45:23 and 79:38) and sell their souls to the devil in exchange for worldly gains (verse 5:52). They think their wealth will allow them to live forever (verses 104:2-3) hence making them oblivious to the repercussions that they will face in the next life with great regret (verses 69:28-29) just like those who reject God.

During the time of the Prophet, some Jews who were deadly envious and jealous of him for being chosen by God as His final Messenger went to the extent of betraying their monotheistic religion by making a pact with the polytheist Arab pagans of Makkah to destroy Islam that stands firm on the strict belief of monotheism (verse 5:79-81) just like what the Jews believed in. Ironically, the same is happening today but in the other way round where it is the Muslim leaders who ally themselves with evil forces that are scheming against Islam (see verse 5:57) and commit crime against humanity. Instead of upholding justice and fight against evil as commanded by God, they embrace and establish close ties with Zionist terrorists and then turn a blind eye to the atrocities that are inflicted by these terrorists on the Palestinians who are being cruelly driven out of their lands and homes for the Zionists to illegally seize and occupy. See the footnotes of verses 5:20-21, 7:137 and 17:2-8.

Even though these evil perpetrators and their allies may escape legal retribution on earth for the sufferings that they inflict on others, they will never be able to escape God's justice in the next life. This is precisely why an eternal afterlife must exist because it is the only way for true justice to be served where everyone will be fairly judged and requited for everything that we do during our short stay on earth (verses 34:3-5 and 49:13). If the corrupt rich and powerful can do anything they please with total impunity without ever being made accountable for their evil deeds, then life would have no meaning because the rights, honor and dignity of those who were born poor and have to endure all kinds of sufferings including oppression and injustice will never get a chance to be redeemed. What is the point for them to endure all the hardship and continue living if they will never see justice and be rewarded for their patience and faith in God? The cruelty and unfairness in this world must have a closure where true justice will finally prevail and be served by God in the afterlife.

Most of us may not be able to fully comprehend why God would allow evil forces to inflict pain and suffering upon innocent children, women and men. The fact is violent conflicts between truth and falsehood have been going on since time immemorial. Incidentally, verses 85:4-8 and 2:214 were revealed in Makkah and Madinah respectively to console the Prophet's companions while they too were experiencing hardship and sufferings inflicted by the enemy for embracing the truth. The hardship serves as a means for victims of injustice to be rewarded with the highest station in Paradise. It is also for those who are spared from this great test of hardship to earn their merits and God's pleasure and subsequently be greatly rewarded in the afterlife too if they stay firm to their faith and strive in every possible way within their means to ease the plight of their oppressed brethren in humanity. By the same token too, those who commit injustice and oppression and then die before they repent and be forgiven by those whom they have wronged will surely find themselves in the lowest depth of the Hellfire.

Verses 2:156, 2:214 21:35 and 29:2-3 remind us that God will surely put all of us through a big test of faith to make evident those among us who have true faith in Him and those who do not. The ultimate reward of Paradise does not come easy and cheap. Just as love for our spouse, children and family requires many sacrifices as we go through life with them, so is our faith in God too. Lip service does not count for anything. The ultimate challenge while in the midst of the trials that we are tested with is to endure them with great patience and to always maintain pure thoughts of God and be grateful to Him for all the blessings and favors that He has graced us with. Take up our troubles to God through prayer beseeching His help, for God indeed loves those who are steadfast in their patience (verse 3:146). He has promised that He will always be with those who turn to Him for help with perseverance (verses 1:5, 2:154 8:46), and has reserved a great reward for them in the next life without measure (verse 39:10). This is without doubt the greatest triumph that one can ever hope and aspire to achieve!

Admittedly, to be patient when faced with calamity and trouble is easier said than done. But herein lies the real test. Many among us tend to blame God for being unfair when we are tested with misfortune, death of our loved ones, and all kinds of tribulations because we are ignorant of the fact that God has actually forewarned us about this. We wrongly think that we are entitled to a wonderful life on earth, forgetting that real life actually begins after we leave this world. Our temporary stay on earth is only a test to prepare us for the next life which is eternal in nature and we should therefore count our blessings for not being tested like those who are forced to endure oppression and atrocities. This should make us realize that the trials we are being put through are not worth complaining and be too sad about. How bad can they be compared to what those who constantly live in fear of being attacked and brutalized by evil oppressors are going through? Rightfully, we should be grateful for God's immeasurable favors and express this gratitude through patience and full submission to Him in humility and serving humanity to the best of our ability.

In ending this note, words simply cannot express my gratitude to Almighty God for giving me the strength, inspiration and *taufeeq* (i.e. the ability and opportunity) to initiate and diligently complete this work which took 6 years in total. May peace and His blessings be upon His Prophet, and may He forgive all my shortcomings and mistakes, and accept this humble work as a means for me to gain His pleasure. May He guide all of us aright and grace us with His mercy on the Day of Judgment. Indeed, from God we came, and to Him shall we finally return with our deeds. Let us all strive to earn His pleasure by making the earth a better place for everyone. Aameen..

Muhammad 'Abdul Mannan
August 2021, Malaysia

The Main Themes of the Qur'an

1. The Qur'an is a book that no one should ignore. It contains God's literal words that serve as guidance for all mankind. Its unrivaled linguistic excellence in Arabic and the prophecies it foretold during the 7th century in the plain desert of Arabia that have only been proven true recently through the advent of science and technology serve as proof of its divinity. There are many verses in the Qur'an where God challenges man to use reason to ponder over these evidence in order to be intellectually convinced of the Qur'an's truth.

2. The Qur'an's most dominant message from cover to cover is about God's Oneness (i.e. absolute monotheism) and that everyone will be resurrected on the Day of Judgment to be made accountable for all their deeds. God is truly Most Gracious and Most Merciful. He is the Creator of the heavens and the earth and everything that exists in between. He is the One Who gives life and then takes it away from every living being. He is also the One Who everyone originated from and will ultimately return to when our temporary stay in this world expires. Therefore, it does not make sense for anyone to worship anything else besides Him, associate partners with Him, or outrightly reject His existence. In essence, only He alone deserves all worship.

3. God gave the same message of absolute monotheism to all His Prophets and Messengers to convey to their respective people and nations in the ancient past. Prophet Muhammad (may peace and blessing be upon him) is God's last and final Messenger to all mankind. Those who choose to submit to God are commanded to follow and emulate the Prophet's *sunnah* (i.e. examples, practices and good conduct) that are all based on the teachings of the Qur'an as the only way to God.

4. Human beings are God's most perfect creation. We are placed on earth as His emissaries and trustees to administer it well so that goodness and prosperity are equitably shared among all mankind and His other creations. At the same time, we are commanded to invite people to submit to God through reason, wisdom and kindness. We are also commanded to always uphold justice among fellow humans regardless of race and religion, and to stand firm against oppression. There is no compulsion when inviting people to submit to the One and only God because truth stands clear from falsehood. People are given freedom to make their own choice and will be held accountable for it. Those who defy Him either by rejecting His existence or by worshipping false gods besides Him will be dealt with by Himself on the Day of Judgment. But as far as life in this world is concerned, everyone is commanded to treat each other with respect, honor and dignity at all times. Notwithstanding this, we are also commanded to defend ourselves against aggression by others. Retaliation is allowed but only within the limits prescribed by God Who does not approve of extremism. Fighting must stop when the enemy ceases its hostility.

5. In the Qur'an, God gives good news of Paradise to those who sincerely submit to Him and strive hard to remain steadfast in His path, and stern warning of suffering in the Hellfire to those who ignore His warnings and defy Him. This is clearly presented through the many stories cited in the Qur'an about the recalcitrant communities of ancient times and the Prophets who were sent to guide them but faced rejection.

6. The Qur'an speaks about the disbelievers in Makkah who were hostile towards the Prophet and his followers because they were against the new social order brought by Islam which teaches belief in absolute monotheism alone is not sufficient to earn God's pleasure. Faith must also be accompanied with unequivocal stand against social injustice and oppression, and to hold everyone equal before the rule of law without discrimination. This is very much against the pagan Arabs' tradition and way of life where the concept of "might is right" and blind loyalty to tribal supremacy - or racism as it is known today - had prevailed for centuries. The Qur'an also speaks about the Arab hypocrites of Madinah who were Islam's enemy from within due to their envy and jealousy towards Prophet Muhammad who was elected as the leader of the nascent nation centered in Madinah after migrating there with his followers from Makkah in the 13th year of his Prophethood. The hypocrites worked closely with the three main Jewish tribes that have been living in Madinah for centuries and also shared the same feeling of jealousy and animosity towards the Prophet. With regard to these Jews, God severely rebuked them for opposing the Prophet and Islam especially because they knew about his Prophethood from their Scriptures but decided to still oppose him simply because he was an Arab instead of a Jew. And finally, the Qur'an also speaks about the Christians who took Prophet Jesus (may peace be upon him) as God's son and partner in divinity and were actively promoting this erroneous belief to the pagan Arabs at that time. All these serve as lessons and reminders about similar challenges that Muslims will continue to face until the end of time, and to not follow the selfish and rebellious behavior of the disbelievers who rejected and opposed the truth out of sheer arrogance and ignorance.

7. Finally, the Qur'an points out that life in this world is nothing but a test of faith and to also make evident who among us are the best in our deeds and conduct. Everyone will taste death. Real life which is eternal in nature actually begins after death. So be ever mindful of the day when everyone will be made accountable and requited for his own deeds where no soul will be made to bear the burden of another. Hence, no one should ever expect his burden of sin to be borne by others and that he can escape punishment if he dies before repenting and be forgiven by those whom he has wronged. No amount of wealth will be of any use to anyone at that time to ransom himself from the grievous punishment that awaits him. The only currency that is accepted on that day is faith and piety towards God together with good deeds and conduct towards others during our temporary stay on earth.

A Brief Account of the Prophet's Life

PART I

At Makkah

The Prophet's birth

Muhammad, son of Abdullah, son of Abdul Muttalib, from the tribe of Quraysh, was born in Makkah in the year 570 of the Common Era. His father died before he was born, and he was protected first by his grandfather, Abdul Muttalib; and after his grandfather's death, by his uncle, Abu Talib. As a young boy he traveled with his uncle in the merchants' caravan to Syria, and some years afterwards made the same journey in the service of a wealthy widow named Khadijah.

His marriage

So faithfully did he transact the widow's business, and so excellent was the report of his behavior which she received from an old servant who had accompanied him, that she married her young agent afterwards; and the marriage proved a happy one, though she was fifteen years older than he was. Throughout the twenty-six years of their life together, he remained devoted to her. And when he took other wives after her death, he always mentioned her with the greatest love and reverence. This marriage gave him rank among the notables of Makkah, while his conduct earned for him the title *Al-Amin*, the "trustworthy."

The Makkans claimed descent from Abraham through Ishmael, and tradition stated that their house of worship - the Ka'bah, had been built by Abraham for the worship of the One Supreme God. It was still called the House of God, but the chief objects of worship there were a number of idols; which were called daughters of God and intercessors.

The *Hunafa*

The few who felt disgust at this idolatry, which had prevailed for centuries, longed for the religion of Abraham and tried to find out what had been its teaching. Such seekers of the truth were known as *Hunafa* (or *Hanif* for singular) a word originally meaning "those who turn away" (from the existing idol-worship), but coming in the end to have the sense of "upright" because such persons held the way of truth to be right conduct. These *Hunafa* did not form a community. They were the agnostics of their day, each seeking truth by the light of his own inner consciousness. Muhammad son of Abdullah became one of these. It was his practice to retire from his family for a month of every year to a cave in the desert for meditation. His place of retreat was Hira, a desert hill not far from Makkah, and his chosen month was Ramadan, the · month of heat.

The first revelation

It was there one night, toward the end of his quiet month, that the first revelation came to him when he was forty years old. He was asleep when he was suddenly awakened by a commanding voice that said, *"Read!"* to which he replied, *"I cannot read."* The voice again said, *"Read!"* and he replied, *"I cannot read."* Then for the third time the voice commanded, *"Read!"* and he asked, *"What should I read?"* The voice said:

Read! In the name of your Lord Who created (everything).
He (is the One Who) has created man from a (leech-like) clinging zygote.

Read! For your Lord is the Most Bountiful;
the One Who taught (man) the use of pen;
(and) taught man what he knew not. [96: 1-5]

The vision of Mount Hira

When he awoke, the words remained as if inscribed upon his heart. He went out of the cave on to the hillside and heard the same awe-inspiring voice said, *"O Muhammad! You are a Messenger of God, and I am Gabriel."* Then he raised his eyes and saw the Angel, in the likeness of a man, standing in the sky above the horizon. And again the dreadful voice said, *"O Muhammad! You are a Messenger of God, and I am Gabriel."* The Prophet stood quiet still, turning away his face from the brightness of the vision, but wherever he turned, there always stood the Angel confronting him. Thus he remained for a long while until the Angel finally vanished, when he quickly returned in great distress to his wife Khadijah. She did her best to reassure him, saying that his conduct had been such that it would not be likely God would let any harmful spirit come to him. Then she took him to her cousin Waraqa ibn Naufal, a very old man who knew the Scriptures of the Jews and Christians. Upon hearing the story, he declared his belief that the heavenly Messenger who came to Moses of old had come to Muhammad, and that he was chosen as the Prophet of his people.

His distress of mind

To understand the reason of the Prophet's diffidence and his extreme distress of mind after the vision of Mount Hira, it must be remembered that the *Hunafa*, of whom he had been one, sought true religion in the natural and regarded with distrust any association with spirits of which men avid of the unseen such as sorcerers and soothsayers and even poets, boasted about in those days. Moreover, he was a man of humble and devout intelligence, a lover of quiet and solitude, and the very thought of being chosen out of all mankind to face mankind, alone - with such a Message - terrified him at first.

Recognition of the Divine nature of the call he had received involved a change in his whole mental outlook that was sufficiently disturbing to a sensitive and honest mind, and also the forsaking of his quiet way of life. But with the continuance of the revelations and the conviction that they brought, he accepted the tremendous task imposed on him, and became filled with an enthusiasm of obedience which justifies his proudest title of "The Servant of God."

First converts

For the first three years of his mission, or rather less, the Prophet preached only to his family and his intimate friends, while the people of Makkah as a whole regarded him as one who had become a little mad. The first of all his converts was his wife Khadijah, the second his first cousin Ali, whom he had adopted, the third his servant Zayd, a former slave. His old friend Abu Bakr also was among those early converts.

Beginning of persecution

At the end of the third year, the Prophet received the command to "arise and warn," (74:2) whereupon he began to preach in public, pointing out that the wretched folly of idolatry was totally against the natural laws of day and night, of life and death, of growth and decay, which manifest the power of God and attestation of His sovereignty. It was then, when he began to speak against their gods, that the Quraysh became actively hostile, persecuting his poorer disciples, mocking and insulting him. The one consideration which prevented them from killing him was fear of the blood-vengeance of the clan to which his family belonged. Strong in his inspiration, he went on warning, pleading and threatening, while the Quraysh did all they could to ridicule his teaching, and deject his followers.

The flight to Abyssinia

The converts of the first four years were mostly humble folk unable to defend themselves against oppression. So cruel was the persecution they endured that the Prophet advised all who could possibly contrive to do so to emigrate to a Christian country, Abyssinia. And still in spite of persecution and emigration, the little company of Muslims grew in number, which seriously alarmed the Quraysh.

As guardians of the Ka'bah, the Quraysh ranked the idol-worship at that site as first among their vested interests. And so during the season of the pilgrimage, they posted men on all the roads to warn the visiting tribes against the madman who was preaching in their midst. They tried to bring the Prophet to a compromise, offering to accept his religion if he would so modify it as to make room for their gods as intercessors with God, offering to make him their king if he would give up attacking idolatry; and, when their efforts at negotiation failed, they went to his uncle Abu Talib, offering to give him the best of their young men in place of Muhammad, to give him all that he desired, if only he would let them kill Muhammad and have done with him. Abu Talib refused.

The *Sahifah* or Deed of Ostracism

The exasperation of the idolaters was increased by the conversion of Umar, one of their stalwarts. They grew more and more embittered until things came to such a pass that they decided to ostracize the Prophet's whole clan, and idolaters who protected him as well as Muslims who believed in him. Their chief men caused a document to be drawn up to the effect that none of them or those belonging to them would associate with any clan who continued to trade with the Prophet and his followers. This they all signed, and it was deposited in the Ka'bah. Then, for three years, the Prophet was shut out with all his kinsfolk in their stronghold which was situated in one of the gorges which run down to Makkah. Only at the time of pilgrimage could he go out and preach, or did any of his kinsfolk dare to go into the city.

Destruction of the *Sahifah*

After some time, some kinder hearts among the Quraysh grew weary of the boycott of old friends and neighbors. They managed to have the document which had been placed inside the Ka'bah brought out for reconsideration; when it was found that all the writing had been destroyed by white ants except the words *Bismika Allahumma* (i.e. In Your name, O God). When the elders saw that marvel, the ban was removed, and the Prophet was again free to go about the city. But meanwhile the opposition to his preaching had grown rigid. He had little success among the Makkans, and an attempt which he made to preach in the city of Ta'if was a failure. In short, his mission was a failure, judged by worldly standards. His only consolation was when at the season of the yearly pilgrimage, he came upon a little group of men who heard him gladly.

The men from Yathrib

These men came from Yathrib, a city more than two hundred miles away, which has since become famously known as Al-Madinah (i.e. the City par excellence). At Yathrib, there were Jewish tribes and learned rabbis, who had often spoken to the pagans of a Prophet soon to come among the Arabs, with whom, when he came, the Jews would destroy the pagans as the past tribes of 'Aād and Tsamud had been destroyed for their idolatry. When the men from Yathrib saw Muhammad, they recognized him as the Prophet whom the Jewish rabbis had described to them. On their return to Yathrib they told what they had seen and heard, with the result that at the next season of pilgrimage a deputation of twelve men came from Yathrib purposely to meet Muhammad - the Prophet.

First treaty of Al-'Aqabah

These men swore allegiance to him in the first treaty of Al-'Aqabah. The oath they took being that they would believe in one God, abstain from theft, fornication and killing children. They then returned to Yathrib with a Muslim teacher in their company, and soon there was not a house in Yathrib wherein there was not mention of the Messenger of God.

Second treaty of Al-'Aqabah

And so at the time of pilgrimage in the following year, seventy-three men from Yathrib came to Makkah and became Muslims after they spoke with him and accepted the divine message of God's Oneness which he conveyed. Consequently, they vowed allegiance to the Prophet and invited him to their city. This incident once again took place at Al-'Aqabah, where they swore to defend him as they would defend their own wives and children. It was then that the *Hijrah*, the flight or emigration to Yathrib, was decided.

Plot to murder the Prophet

Soon the Muslims in Makkah who were in a position to emigrate to Yathrib began to sell their property and to leave unobtrusively, but the Quraysh had wind of what was going on. They hated Muhammad in their midst, but dreaded what he might become if he escaped from them. It would be better, they considered, to destroy him now. The death of Abu Talib about two to three years earlier had removed his chief protector; but still they had to reckon with the vengeance of his clan upon the clan of the murderer. To avert this potential problem, they cast lots and chose a slayer out of every clan. All these men were to attack the Prophet together and simultaneously as one man, so that each clan would have a hand in his killing. Thus his blood would be on all Quraysh and the Prophet's own clan would not be able to demand effective retribution.

The *Hijrah* (622 CE)

The last of the able Muslims to remain in Makkah were Abu Bakr, Ali and the Prophet himself. Abu Bakr, a man of wealth, had bought two riding camels and retained a guide in readiness for the flight. The Prophet only waited for God's command. It finally came on the night when the plan to murder him was to take place. But the Prophet knew of their plot and substituted Ali in his place because he knew they would not injure Ali. Then as he left the house, he cast a handful of dust in the direction of the would-be murderers as he passed by them and their sight was "as if covered with a veil". He then went to Abu Bakr's house and called him, and the two of them went together to a cave in the desert hills and hid there until the hue and cry had passed. In the meantime Abu Bakr's daughter and his herdsman brought them food and news every day. Once a search party came quite near them in their hiding-place, which alarmed Abu Bakr; but the Prophet said, *"Do not grieve (and fear), for God is with us."* (9:40). Then, when the coast was clear, Abu Bakr had the riding-camels and the guide brought to the cave one night, and they set out on the long ride to Yathrib. Finally, after traveling for many days by unfrequented paths, they reached Yathrib.

Such was the *Hijrah*, the flight or emigration from Makkah to Yathrib, which counts as the beginning of the Muslim era. The thirteen years of humiliation, of persecution, of seeming failure, of prophecy seemed unfulfilled, were over. The ten years of success, the fullest that has ever crowned one man's endeavor, had begun. The *Hijrah* makes a clear division in the story of the Prophet's mission, which is evident in the Qur'an. Until then he had been a preacher only. Thenceforth, he was the ruler of a State, at first a very small one, which grew in ten years to the empire of Arabia.

In accomplishing this, the kind of divine guidance which he and his people needed after the *Hijrah* was not the same as that which they had received before. The Madinan chapters differ, therefore, from the Makkan chapters. The latter gave guidance to the individual soul and to the Prophet as warner, while the former gave guidance to a growing social and political community and to the Prophet as an example, lawgiver and reformer.

Classification of Makkah chapters

For classification, the Makkan chapters are here subdivided into four groups:

- The Very Early chapters are those revealed before the beginning of the persecution.
- The Early chapters are those revealed between the beginning of the persecution and the conversion of Umar.
- The Middle chapters are those revealed between the conversion of Umar and the destruction of the deed of ostracism.
- The Late chapters are those revealed between the raising of the ban of ostracism and the *Hijrah*.

PART II

At Madinah

Background of Madinah

Into the older Arab town of Yathrib, Jews arrived as refugees in the 2nd century AD in the wake of the Jewish-Roman wars. There were three prominent Jewish tribes that inhabited the city up to the 7th century AD, namely Bani Qurayza, Bani Nadir, and Bani Qaynuqa.

The situation changed after the arrival of two new Arab tribes named Bani Auws and Bani Khazraj from Yemen. At first, these tribes were clients of the Jews, but later they revolted and became independent. Toward the end of the 5th century, the Jews lost control of the city to Bani Auws and Bani Khazraj and became their clients instead.

Eventually Bani Auws and Bani Khazraj became hostile to each other and by the time of the Prophet's *Hijrah* to Madinah in 622 AD, they had been fighting for 120 years and were the sworn enemies of each other. The Jewish tribes of Bani Nadir and Bani Qurayza were allied with the Auws, while the Qaynuqa sided with the Khazraj. Their last and bloodiest battle was the Battle of Bu'ath that was fought a few years before the Prophet's arrival. The outcome of the battle was inconclusive and the feud continued. Abdullah ibn Ubayy, who was the chief of one of the Bani Khazraj's clans, had refused to take part in the battle, which earned him a reputation for equity and peacefulness. Until the arrival of the Prophet, he was the most respected inhabitant of Yathrib.

To solve the ongoing feud, concerned residents of the city met secretly with the Prophet in Aqabah, inviting him and his small band of believers to come to Yathrib, where the Prophet could serve as an impartial mediator between the factions while his community could freely practice its faith.

The arrival of the Prophet together with around 70 of his followers from Makkah - who were known as the *Muhajiruns* (i.e. the Emigrants) - transformed the religious and political landscape of the city completely. The longstanding enmity between the Auws and Khazraj tribes was dampened as many of the two Arab tribes and some local Jews embraced *Islam*. The Prophet was agreed upon as the new leader of the city-state Yathrib that was renamed

Madinah. The Muslim converts native to Madinah of whatever background - pagan Arab or Jewish - were called *Ansar* (i.e. the Patrons or the Helpers).

Among the Prophet's first actions was the construction of the first mosque in an area called Quba in Madinah. He then set about the establishment of a pact, known as the Charter of Madinah, between the local pagan Arab tribes of Madinah, the Jews, the Christians, the Muslim emigrants from Makkah (i.e. the *Muhajirun*), and the local Muslims of Madinah (i.e. the *Ansar*) which committed all parties to mutual cooperation under his leadership. The Charter effectively established the first Islamic state and formed the basis of the future caliphate. The document was drawn up with the explicit concern of bringing to an end the bitter inter-tribal fighting between the Auws and Khazraj. To this effect, it instituted a number of rights and responsibilities for the Muslim, Jewish, Christian and pagan communities of Madinah bringing them within the fold of one community.

Briefly, the Charter established the community's security, religious freedoms, the role of Madinah as a *Haram* or sacred place (barring all violence and weapons), the security of women, stable tribal relations within Madinah, a tax system for supporting the community in time of conflict, a system for granting protection of individuals, a judicial system for resolving disputes, and also regulated the paying of blood money in lieu of equal retribution (2:178 and 5:45). In addition, the agreement also included boycotting Quraysh, abstention from extending any support to them, assistance of one another if attacked by a third party, and defending Madinah in case of a foreign attack.

The Jews and Hypocrites

But the reality is, almost all the Jews who lived in Madinah and in the surrounding areas of the city rejected his Prophethood and the divine message that he tried very much to convey; and so, dealing with them was never easy for the Prophet. Their idea of a Prophet was one who would give them dominion, not one who would make the Jews follow him as brothers of every Arab who might happen to believe as they did. His quick rise to power in Madinah shook the pre-existing power relations that existed there, and escalated the resentment and jealousy among these Jewish tribes and also among some of the non-Jewish elites who were seeing their power waning. When the Jews found that they could not use the Prophet for their own ends, they tried to shake his faith in his mission by casting doubts about the Qur'an and seducing his followers to abandon him. At the same time, they also conspired secretly with the Quraysh idolaters of Makkah to restrict the Muslims from gaining more power so that they could protect their selfish interest and maintain their privileges, despite the Charter that they had all agreed to abide by earlier. All the three main Jewish tribes in Madinah were involved in this evil work.

Bani Nadir : Like other Jews of Madinah, Bani Nadir bore Arabic names but spoke a distinct dialect of Arabic. They earned their living through agriculture, money lending, and trade in weapons and jewels, maintaining commercial relations with Arab merchants of Makkah. Their fortresses were located half-a-day's march to the south of Madinah. The people of Bani Nadir were wealthy and lived in some of the best lands in Madinah.

Bani Qurayza : Just like Bani Nadir, Bani Qurayza also lived in an area south of Madinah, and earned their living through agriculture and trade. During the first few months after the Prophet's arrival in Madinah, Bani Qurayza was involved in a dispute with Bani Nadir, and the more powerful Nadir rigorously applied the law of *Al-Qisaas* (equal retribution) against the Qurayza while not allowing it being enforced against themselves. Further, the blood money paid for killing a man of the Qurayza was only half of the blood-money required for killing a man of the Nadir, placing the Qurayza in a socially inferior position. The Qurayza called on the Prophet as arbitrator, who delivered verses 42-45 of the chapter of *Al-Maa'idah* (5) and judged that the Nadir and Qurayza should be treated alike in the application of *Al-Qisaas* and raised the assessment of the Qurayza to the full amount of blood money.

Soon afterwards, the Prophet came into conflict with Bani Nadir when he ordered the execution of one of the Bani Nadir's chiefs - Ka'b ibn Ashraf, for his act of treason; and after the Battle of Uhud, found the entire Bani Nadir guilty of contravening the Charter and plotting against his life. The tribe was subsequently expelled from the city. While this conflict was taking place, Bani Qurayza remained passive because of their dissatisfaction with Bani Nadir over the blood money issue mentioned above.

Bani Qaynuqa : The Bani Qaynuqa tribe was living in two fortresses in the south-western part of Madinah, where the city's marketplace was. They earned their living through commerce and craftsmanship, including goldsmithery, and were closely allied with the local Arab tribe of Khazhraj. Of the three Jewish tribes, Bani Qaynuqa was the most hostile against the Prophet and his followers.

The Hypocrites and their Leader : Abdullah ibn Ubayy, also called ibn Salul in reference to his mother, was a chief of one of Bani Kahzraj's clan and the most leading men in Madinah before the *Hijrah*. His tribe had been embroiled in an intense conflict with the other major Arab tribe of the city - Bani Auws, for more than a century. But during his time, he used every effort to end the strife and achieved a partial reconciliation between the two factions, which resulted in both these tribes recognizing his leadership. He occupied a high status in pre-Islamic Madinan society and his supporters aimed for him to become "King of Madinah".

However, this aim was not realized due to the arrival of the Prophet in 622 AD, when some citizens of Madinah looked towards another arbitrator to help solve the tribal conflict that was never completely resolved. And so, the Prophet - whose preaching had made him famous beyond his home town of Makkah - was called in. The arrival of a man who spoke in the name of God naturally eclipsed Ibn Ubayy's influence, and this provoked his jealousy. But because most of the Arab population in Madinah converted to *Islam* and embraced the Prophet's teaching, Ibn Ubayy followed suit because he felt that it would be safer for him to join than to stand out against it.

Being second only to Prophet Muhammad, Ibn Ubayy became a figurehead for those Arabs of Madinah who openly or secretly, sneered at the Prophet's teaching and complained of the confusion and the danger the *Muhajirun* had brought to Madinah. These people were not altogether convinced of the political wisdom in supporting Prophet Muhammad, so they paid lip-service to *Islam* and concealed treachery in their hearts. Because of his repeated conflicts with the Prophet, the Qur'an labeled Ibn Ubayy a *Munafiq* (i.e. hypocrite), hence the "leader of the *Munafiqun*" by virtue of the leadership role that he played among his people. He died in 631 AD, about nine years after the Prophet's arrival in Madinah.

The Qiblah

Until then, the *Qiblah* (i.e. the place toward which the Muslims turn their face in prayer) had been Jerusalem. The Jews imagined that the choice implied a leaning toward Judaism and the Prophet therefore stood in need of their instruction. However, not too long after that, he received the divine command to change the *Qiblah* from Jerusalem to the Ka'bah at Makkah (2:144, 149, 150). A great part of the chapter of *Al-Baqarah* (2) relates to this Jewish controversy.

The first expeditions

The Prophet's first concern as ruler was to establish public worship and lay down the constitution of the State; but he did not forget that the Quraysh had sworn to make an end to *Islam*. However, he did not launch any military campaign against them until about nine months after his arrival in Madinah when the first verse granting permission for Muslims to go to war was revealed: *"Permission (to fight) is given to those against whom war is being wrongfully waged. Most certainly, God has the power to grant them victory."* (22 : 39)

Thereupon, several small expeditions went out, led either by the Prophet himself or by some other among his *Muhajirun* followers for the purpose of reconnoitering and of dissuading other tribes from siding with Quraysh. These are generally represented as warlike, but considering their weakness and the fact that they did not result in fighting, they can hardly be regarded as war. It is noteworthy that in those expeditions, only the *Muhajirun* were employed, never the *Ansar*.

The campaign of Badr

In the month of Ramadan 2 *Hijrah,* the Makkan merchants' caravan was returning from Syria as usual by a road which passed not far from Madinah. As its leader Abu Sufyan approached the territory of Madinah, he heard of the Prophet's design to capture the caravan. At once he sent a camel-rider to Makkah, who arrived in a worn-out state and shouted frantically from the valley to Quraysh to hasten to the rescue, unless they wished to lose both wealth and honor. A force of 1,000 was soon on its way to Madinah to face the Muslim army and rescue Abu Sufyan's caravan.

The army of Quraysh had advanced more than half-way to Madinah before the Prophet set out with only 313 men who were ill-equipped to face a well-armed force three times their number, which the Muslims knew nothing about, except the Prophet himself, who had some news of it through divine inspiration which he kept to himself. All three parties - the army of Quraysh, the Muslim army and the caravan - were heading for the water of Badr. Abu Sufyan, the leader of the caravan, heard from one of his scouts that the Muslims were near the water, and turned back to the coast-plain. Because of this, the parties that were finally present at the water of Badr were just the Muslims and the army of Quraysh alone. It was only at this time when the rest of the Muslim army discovered that they were clearly outnumbered and materially lacking to handle the Quraysh, but decided in all their valor that they would proceed to face their enemies, regardless of the outcome. In truth, this was an encounter that was divinely set by God in His infinite wisdom (8:42-44).

By the grace of God, the battle ended in a great victory for them and this gave the Prophet new prestige among the Arab tribes. But thenceforth, a new feud had opened between Quraysh and the Islamic State in addition to the old religious hatred - a feud that now involved blood. A great part of the chapter of *Al-Anfaal* (8) refers to this battle and gave warning of much greater struggles yet to come.

After the Battle of Badr, one of the Bani Nadir's chiefs in Madinah - Ka'b ibn Ashraf, went to the Quraysh to lament the loss at Badr and to incite them to take up arms to regain lost honor. He even went so far in flattery of Quraysh as to declare the religion of the pagan Arabs superior to *Islam* (4:51) His act was in clear contravention of the Madinah Charter which prohibited his tribe from extending any support to the tribes of Makkah, namely Bani Quraysh. Because of this treacherous act, the Prophet ordered the execution of Ka'b. This brought much shock and fear to Bani Nadir and managed to silence them for a while.

The Expulsion of Bani Qaynuqa

At the same time, tensions quickly mounted between the growing numbers of Muslims and the other Jewish tribes. Bani Qaynuqa for instance, began displaying their animosity towards the Prophet and his followers openly, and felt no qualms in contravening the terms of the Madinah Charter which they had agreed to abide by earlier. In his effort to advise and remind them of their obligation to the Charter, the Prophet approached Bani Qaynuqa, gathering them in the marketplace and addressing them as follows, *"O Jews! Beware, lest God bring on you the like of the retribution which he brought on Quraysh. Accept Islam, for you know that I am a Prophet sent by God. You will find this in your Scriptures and in God's covenant with you"*; to which they replied, *"O Muhammad! You seem to think that we are your people. Do not deceive yourself just because you have vanquished a contingent of Quraysh who have* no knowledge of warfare; in fact, you were fortunate to get the better of them. By God, if you fight us, you will find that we are real men, and that you have not met the like of us." Their answer clearly contained a challenge and a threat, despite the fact that they had accepted the Prophet's leadership earlier according to the terms of the Charter. Thereupon, verses 3:10-13 of the Qur'an were revealed to the Prophet following this exchange of words.

It was reported that not too long after this incident, a member of the Bani Qaynuqa tribe tied the hem of the garment of a Muslim woman who was in their marketplace in such a way that when she stood up, she was uncovered. When she screamed, a Muslim man came to her defense, and in the ensuing commotion killed the Jew who outraged her modesty. The Jews in turn attacked the Muslim and killed him, and the Muslim's family then called on the rest of the Muslims to help them against the Jews. This unrest escalated to a chain of revenge killings and intense enmity grew between the Muslims and Bani Qaynuqa. The act of aggression and open hostility was a clear breach of security, which convinced the Prophet that it was impossible to live with Bani Qaynuqa in peace.

The Prophet then besieged Bani Qaynuqa's fortress in the month of Zulqa'edah (about two months after the Battle of Badr) for 15 days before they surrendered. At the time of the siege, the Qaynuqa had a fighting force of 700 men, 400 of whom were armored. The Prophet had initially wanted to kill them but later yielded to the plea of Abdullah ibn Ubayy who was an old ally of the Qaynuqa. And so, Bani Qaynuqa was finally expelled from Madinah but some members of the tribe chose to stay in Madinah and convert to *Islam*.

Because of this interference and other episodes of his discord with the Prophet, ibn Ubayy earned for himself the title of the leader of hypocrites (i.e. *Munafiqun*) as mentioned in the Qur'an. Some of the commentators of the Qur'an transmitted the opinion that the following verse was revealed concerning ibn Ubayy's close friendship with the Jews of Bani Qaynuqa, "*O you who believe! Do not take the Jews and the Christians as allies and protectors (lest you would be tempted and inclined to imitate their corrupt faith and way of life). They are allies of one another. So whoever among you allies himself with them will indeed become one of them. Behold! God does not give guidance to those who transgress.*" (5:51).

Bani Qaynuqa left Madinah for the Jewish colonies in the Wadi al-Qura, north of Madinah; and from there to Der'a in Syria, west of Salkhad. In the course of time, they assimilated with the Jewish communities pre-existing in that area, strengthening them numerically. Meanwhile in Madinah, the Prophet confiscated the property of Bani Qaynuqa, including their arms and tools, and divided them among his followers who had emigrated with him from Makkah, taking for the Islamic state a fifth share of the spoils for the first time.

The Battle of Mount Uhud

In the month of Syawal of the following year (i.e. 3 *Hijrah*, or 635 AD), an army of three thousand came from Makkah to avenge their defeat in Badr seeking to destroy Madinah. The Prophet's first idea was merely to defend the city, a plan of which Abdullah ibn Ubayy strongly approved. But the men who had fought at Badr believed that God would help them against any odds and thought it a shame that they should linger behind walls. The Prophet, approving of their faith and zeal, gave way to them, and set out with an army of one thousand men toward Mt. Uhud, where the enemy were encamped. Ibn Ubayy was much offended by the change of plan. He thought it unlikely that the Prophet really meant to give battle in conditions so adverse to the Muslims, but when the Prophet really did, Ibn Ubayy was unwilling to take part in the battle as a show of protest against the decision. So he withdrew with his men, which comprised about one-fourth of the Muslim army.

Despite the heavy odds, the battle on Mt. Uhud would have been an even greater victory for the Muslims than that at Badr except for the disobedience of a band of fifty archers whom the Prophet set to guard a pass on the hillside of Mt. Uhud against the enemy's cavalry. Seeing their comrades victorious, these men left their post, fearing to lose their share of the spoils. The cavalry of Quraysh led by Khalid al-Walid then rode through the gap and fell on the exultant Muslims. The Prophet himself was wounded and the cry arose that he was slain, until someone recognized him and shouted that he was still living, a shout to which the Muslims rallied. Gathering round the Prophet, they retreated, leaving many dead on the hillside.

On the following day the Prophet again sallied forth with what remained of the army, so that the Quraysh might hear that he was in the field and might perhaps be deterred from attacking the city. The stratagem succeeded, thanks to the behavior of a friendly Bedouin, who met the Muslims and conversed with them and afterwards met the army of Quraysh. Questioned by Abu Sufyan, he said that the Prophet was in the field, stronger than ever, and thirsting for revenge for yesterday's affair. On that information, Abu Sufyan decided to return to Makkah.

The killing of Muslims and expulsion of Bani Nadir

The reverse of Badr which they had suffered on Mt. Uhud lowered the prestige of the Muslims with the Arab tribes and also with the Jews of Madinah. Tribes which had inclined toward the Muslims now inclined toward Quraysh. The Prophet's followers were attacked and murdered when they went abroad in little companies. One of his envoys - Khubayyb, was captured by a desert tribe and sold to Quraysh, who tortured him to death in Makkah publicly.

And as for the disbelieving Jews, they could now hardly conceal their hostility against the Prophet and his followers despite their treaty. This deep feeling of intense animosity and hatred had led Bani Nadir to plot an assassination attempt on the Prophet while he was on a visit to their place, breaking the laws of hospitality and their own sworn alliance. In the course of doing so, they caused the death of some Muslims during a skirmish. As a result, the Prophet besieged them in the month of Rabi'ul Awal 4 *Hijrah* (i.e. about five months after the Battle of Uhud) and demanded they surrender their property and leave Madinah within ten days.

At first, they decided to comply, but a group of hypocrites from Madinah sent a message to them pledging support to fight alongside them if they were attacked by the Muslims. But in the end, Bani Nadir were forced to surrender after the siege came into its 14th day when the promised help failed to arrive, and when Prophet Muhammad ordered the burning and felling of their palm-trees. The exigencies of the siege necessitated the destruction of these properties so that the enemies' supplies would be cut off. The unexpected turn in their fortunes indeed disheartened Bani Nadir and their hearts were struck with terror. Finally, they capitulated and destroyed their own homes before they left

Under the conditions of surrender, Bani Nadir could only take with them what they could carry on camels with the exception of weapons. Most of them found refuge in Khaybar, while others emigrated to Syria. After their expulsion, the Prophet confiscated their land and divided it between his companions who had emigrated with him from Makkah. The chapter of *Al-Hashr* (59) was revealed in relation to this episode with Bani Nadir.

The Battle of the Trench

In the month of Syawal of 5th *Hijrah* (627 AD, about 19 months after the expulsion of Bani Nadir), the idolaters made a great effort to wage a war against *Islam* in the Battle of the Trench. The Quraysh with all their clans together with the Bani Nadir tribe that was expelled from Madinah earlier and some desert tribes - namely Bani Ghatafan, Bani Assad and Bani Sulaym - formed a confederation and mustered an army of 10,000 men to ride into Madinah.

The Prophet (following the advice from one of his companions, Salman the Persian) caused a deep trench - a novelty in Arab warfare - to be dug along the northern front of the city to act as a barrier to the enemies' cavalry, as the rest of Madinah was surrounded by rocky mountains and trees impenetrable to large armies. Every capable Muslim in Madinah including the Prophet contributed to digging the massive trench in six days. They also harvested all their crops early, so that the confederate armies would have to rely on their own food reserves for survival.

The confederate armies arrived soon after - unaware of the Muslim's unconventional war tactic - and besieged Madinah. As anticipated, they were stopped by the trench and found the Muslims rigidly entrenched, making it impassable for their cavalry. Both armies then gathered on either side of the trench and spent two or three weeks exchanging insults in prose and verse, backed up with arrows fired from a comfortable distance.

The confederates then attempted several simultaneous attacks to improve their dire condition, in particular by trying to persuade the Bani Qurayza tribe to attack the Muslims from the south. A leader of the exiled Jewish tribe of Bani Nadir was dispatched to Madinah to seek the support of Bani Qurayza against the Muslims.

So far, Bani Qurayza had tried their best to remain neutral, and was very hesitant about joining the confederates since they had made a pact with the Prophet earlier. But the Bani Nadir representative managed to persuade them that the Muslims would surely be overwhelmed. The sight of the vast confederate armies, surging over the land with soldiers and horses as far as the eye could see, eventually swung Bani Qurayza's support in favor of the confederates.

News of Bani Qurayzah's renunciation of the pact was brought to the Prophet and he became anxious of their conduct. He realized the grave potential danger Bani Qurayza posed, especially since they possessed quite a large stock of weaponry. The Prophet attempted to hide his knowledge of Bani Qurayza's activities but rumors of a massive assault on the city of Madinah from Qurayza's side soon spread, which severely demoralized the Muslims. They found themselves in greater difficulties with the passing of each day. Food was running short, and nights were colder. The lack of sleep made matters worse. So tense was the situation that, for the first time, the canonical daily prayers were neglected by the Muslim community. Only at night, when the attacks stopped due to darkness, could they resume their regular worship. In short, the situation became serious and fear was everywhere. The chapter of *Al-Ahzab* (33) : 10-22 relates this account.

By the grace of God, someone among the confederates who was secretly a Muslim, managed to sow distrust between Quraysh and their Jewish allies which resulted in both parties to hesitate in their action. Then came a bitter wind from the sea, which blew for three days and nights so terribly that not a tent could be kept standing, not a fire lighted, and not a pot boiled. The confederates were in utter misery. Finally, one night the leader of Quraysh decided that the torment could be borne no longer and gave the order to retire. When the Ghatafan tribe awoke next morning, they found the Quraysh had gone and they too took up their baggage and retreated. The almost month-long siege had finally ended in a fiasco and the defeat caused the Makkans to lose their trade and much of their prestige.

The siege turned out to be a "battle of wits" in which the Muslims tactically overcame their opponents while suffering very few casualties. Efforts to defeat the Muslims failed, and *Islam* thenceforth became influential and gained true prominence in the region.

Punishment of Bani Qurayza

Subsequently, after the confederates were defeated, Bani Qurayza was left alone to face the Muslims and quickly retreated to their fortress and towers for refuge, which led to a 25-day siege by the Muslims that finally ended in the tribe's surrender (33:26-27). They were charged with treason but refused to submit to the Prophet's judgment. Instead, they asked the Auws tribe - of which they were adherents - to intervene on their behalf. The Prophet granted their request.

But the judge - Sa'd ibn Mua'dth (leader of the Auws tribe), upon whose favor they had counted, had just experienced and seen how the two Jewish tribes that had been allowed to leave Madinah previously had instigated the other tribes living around Madinah and summoned the united front of ten thousand men against the Muslims in the Battle of the Trench. He was also aware how treacherously this last Jewish tribe had behaved right on the occasion when the city was under attack from outside and threatened the safety of the whole of its population. Therefore, he commanded the leaders of Bani Qurayza to gather and asked them what the punishment was for a traitor to their own religion. They bowed their heads and stated that according to the Torah, the punishment is death. So, on the order of Sa'd ibn Mua'dth, the men were executed, while the women and children were enslaved and their properties distributed among the Muslims. The sentence was duly carried out.

When the Muslims entered Bani Qurayza's strongholds, they found that these treacherous people had collected 1,500 swords, 300 coats of mail, 2,000 spears and 1,500 shields in order to join the war. If God's help had not reached the Muslims, all this military equipment would have been used to attack Madinah from the rear right at the time when the Quraysh idolaters were making preparations for a general assault on the Muslims after crossing the trench. After this disclosure, there remained no doubt that the decision of Sa'd ibn Mua'dth concerning those people was absolutely correct.

The Bani Mustaliq Expedition

In the month of Sha'ban 6 *Hijrah* (about 9 months after the Battle of the Trench), the Prophet set out on an expedition with a force of seven hundred men against Bani Mustaliq, an Arab tribe that lived in the Qudaid region located on the coast between Makkah and Madinah. Bani Mustaliq was a strong ally of the Quraysh and was not hesitant to demonstrate their hostility at every available opportunity. During the time in which the Quraysh were making preparations for the Battle of the Trench, Bani Mustaliq had supported the confederates by setting up a military post at the watering place called Muraysi' and incited neighboring tribes to join them attack Madinah. Hence, the

Prophet's expedition at this point of time was for the purpose of punishing Bani Mustaliq for the role they played in that Battle and to neutralize them once and for all, while also serving as a warning to other neighboring tribes that they should never consider taking any aggressive action against *Islam* in future.

The battle was a swift one, resulting in about seven hundred members of the Bani Mustaliq tribe taken as prisoner and a large amount of spoils that included 2,000 camels and 5,000 sheep being acquired. Among the captives was Juwayriya bint Harith, daughter of the defeated Bani Mustaliq tribe's chief Harith ibn Abu Dirar. Upon her acceptance of *Islam*, the Prophet released her and proposed marriage to her. This marriage eased the hostilities that ensued due to the battle. By virtue of Bani Mustaliq now becoming the Prophet's relations through marriage, all the prisoners were released. Such was the effect of this attitude of the Muslims on the Bani Mustaliq that all of the captives, including Juwayriya's father - Harith, immediately embraced *Islam*.

In another related incident, Abdullah ibn Ubayy and many of his followers also participated in this battle, and their evil intention to cause trouble to the Muslim hosts during this occasion was recorded in verse 9:47 of the Qur'an. On the return from the campaign, tension arose between the *Muhajirin* and the *Ansar* when a Bedoiun servant of Umar pushed an ally of the Khazraj at a well where they were drawing water. Ibn Ubayy wasted no time in taking advantage of this tense situation by saying, *"They (i.e. the Muslims) have outnumbered us and shared our land. Remember that if you fatten your dog, it will eat you."* Then he added further, *"Once we return to Madinah, surely the most worthy of honor will drive the most contemptible ones out of our city."* Verse 8 of the chapter of *Al-Munafiqun* (63) was revealed in relation to this incident.

When that talk was reported to the Prophet, Umar asked for permission to have Ibn Ubayy killed but the Prophet turned down his proposal on the grounds that it was unbecoming of a Prophet to be accused of killing his people. The Prophet forestalled any fighting that was about to erupt at that scene by immediately continuing their march nonstop until noon the following day. Exhausted after such a long and arduous journey, the soldiers did not have the strength even to speak when reaching their resting place, and fell asleep immediately. In this way, the tension that had arisen only a day before was completely dissipated.

The slander against A'ishah

This extremely painful incident took place on the Prophet's return from the expedition against Bani Mustaliq. The Muslim army had to halt for a night at a place, a short distance from Madinah. In this expedition, the Prophet was accompanied by his wife, A'ishah. As it so happened, A'ishah went out some distance from the camp to attend to the call of nature. When she returned, she discovered that she had dropped her necklace somewhere and went out again to search for it. On her return, she found to her great grief that the army had already marched away with the camel she was riding, her attendants thinking that she was in the litter as she was then thin, very young and light of weight. In her helplessness she sat down and cried until sleep overcame her.

Safwan bin Mu'attal, a *Muhajirin*, who was coming in the rear recognized her as he had seen her before the verse enjoining the veil was revealed, and brought her on his camel to Madinah without saying a single word to her, himself walking behind the animal. The hypocrites of Madinah led by Abdullah ibn Ubayy, sought to make capital out of this incident and spread a malicious scandal against A'ishah and unfortunately some of the Muslims also became involved in it. On arrival in Madinah, the Prophet held counsel with his companions, who pronounced different opinions ranging from divorce to retention.

The incident almost roused a fight between the Auws and Khazraj, but the Prophet's intervention silenced both parties. A'ishah, unaware of the rumors being circulated, fell ill and was confined to bed. On recovering, she heard of the slander and took permission to go and see her parents seeking authentic news. She then burst into tears and stayed for two days and one sleepless night ceaselessly weeping. The Prophet visited her in that situation, and after testifying to the Oneness of God he told her, *"If you are innocent, God will acquit you, otherwise, you have to beg for His forgiveness and pardon."*

She stopped weeping and asked her parents to speak for her, but they had nothing to say, so she herself took the initiative and said *"If I tell you I am innocent, which God knows that I am surely innocent, you will not believe me; and if I were to admit something of which only God knows that I am innocent of, you will believe me. Therefore, I have nothing to make recourse to except these words of Prophet Jacob: 'Patience (is indeed a virtue and it) is most fitting (for me). It is to God alone that I turn for help in this misfortune that you have described."* (12:18).

She then turned away and lay down for some rest. At that decisive moment the revelation came acquitting A'ishah of all the slanderous talk fabricated in this concern. A'ishah, of course, was wholeheartedly joyful and praised God thankfully. God's Words in this regard went as follows, *"Verily, those who would falsely accuse others (of being unchaste) are indeed a group from among you. (For you who are thus wronged,) do not regard it as something bad for you. Nay, (in fact) it is something good for you (if you exercise patience and place your trust in God for He will surely reward you well). As for the slanderers, each one of them will be accounted for the sin that he has earned; and (on top of it is) an awesome suffering that awaits the one who took on himself the lead among them."* (24:11)

The main persons involved in the slander affair, namely Mistah bin Athatha, Hassan bin Thabit and Hamnah bint Jahsh, were all flogged with eighty stripes, in accordance with the following decree, *"As for those who accuse chaste women (of fornication) and cannot produce four witnesses, flog them with eighty lashes; and do not accept their testimony ever after; for they are certainly among those who are defiantly disobedient."* (24:4).

But the main person who took the principal part (i.e. Abdullah ibn Ubayy) was not flogged. This was either because the corporal punishment would compensate the chastisement in store for him in the Hereafter, which he does not deserve its merit; or in the same public interest for which the Prophet had prevented Umar from killing him previously. Subsequently, Ibn Ubayy became the butt of reproach and humiliation among his people after his real intention was exposed to all the public.

Almost a month later, the Prophet and Umar bin Al-Khattab were engaged in the following talk, *"Don't you see Umar, if I had had him (i.e. Abdullah ibn Ubayy) killed as you wanted so on that day, a large number of dignitaries would have furiously hastened to fight for him. Now, on the contrary, if I ask them to kill him, they will do so out of their own free will."* Umar replied, *"I swear by God that the Prophet's judgment is more sound than mine."*

Al-Hudaibiyah

In the same year, the Prophet had a vision in which he found himself entering the holy place at Makkah unopposed (48:27); therefore, he determined to attempt the *'Umrah* (i.e. minor pilgrimage). In addition to a number of Muslims from Madinah, he called upon the Bedouin Arabs, whose numbers had increased since the miraculous defeat of the confederate tribes, to accompany him; but most of them did not respond (48:11). Attired as pilgrims and taking with them the customary offerings, a company of 1,400 men journeyed to Makkah in the month of Zulqa'edah of 6th *Hijrah* (628 AD), 3 months after the Bani Mustaliq expedition.

As they drew near the holy valley, they were met by a friend from the city, who warned the Prophet that the Quraysh had put on their leopard skins (i.e. the badge of valor) and had sworn to prevent his entering the sanctuary; their cavalry was on the road before him. On that, the Prophet ordered a detour through the mountain gorges before they came down into the valley of Makkah and encamped at a spot called Al-Hudaibiyah. From there, he tried to open negotiations with Quraysh, explaining that he came only as a pilgrim. The first messenger he sent towards the city was maltreated and his camel hamstrung. He returned without delivering his message. The Quraysh on their side sent an envoy who was threatening in tone and very arrogant. But it was also he who, on his return to the city, said, *"I have seen Caesar and Chosroes in their pomp, but never have I seen a man who is so honored by his comrades as Muhammad is."*

The Treaty of Hudaibiyah

On the part of the Prophet, he sought for a messenger who would impose respect. Uthman ibn Affan was finally chosen because of his kinship with the powerful Umayyad family. While the Muslims were awaiting his return the news came that he had been murdered. It was then that the Prophet, sitting under a tree (48:18) in Al-Hudaibiyah, took an oath from all his comrades that they would stand or fall together. After a while however, it became known that Uthman had not been murdered. A troop which came out from the city to harass the Muslims in their camp were captured before they could do any hurt (48:24) and brought before the Prophet who forgave them on their promise to renounce hostility.

Then proper envoys came from Quraysh. After some negotiation, the truce of Al-Hudaibiyah was signed. For ten years there were to be no hostilities between the parties. The Prophet was to return to Madinah without visiting the Ka'bah, but in the following year he could perform the pilgrimage with his comrades, and the Quraysh promised to evacuate Makkah for three days to allow of his doing so. Deserters from Quraysh to the Muslims during the period of the truce were to be returned; not so deserters from the Muslims to Quraysh. Any tribe or clan who wished to share in the treaty as allies of the Prophet might do so, and any tribe or clan who wished to share in the treaty as allies of Quraysh might do so.

There was dismay among the Muslims at these terms. They asked one another, *"Where is the victory that we were promised?"* It was during the return journey from Al-Hudaibiyah that the chapter *Al-Fath* (48) or "The Victory" was revealed. The truce proved, in fact, to be the greatest victory that the Muslims had until then achieved. War had been a barrier between them and the idolaters, but now both parties met and talked together, and *Islam* was suddenly given the space to spread more rapidly. In the two years which elapsed between the signing of the truce and the fall of Makkah, the number of converts was greater than the total number of all previous converts. The Prophet traveled to Al-Hudaibiyah with 1,400 men. Two years later, when the Makkans broke the truce, he marched against them with an army of 10,000.

The campaign of Khaybar

While in Khaybar, Bani Nadir who had settled down there after their expulsion from Madinah, did not cease in their effort to cause trouble to the Muslims when they grouped together with some other Jewish tribes that were already residing there. And so, in the month of Muharram 7 *Hijrah* (about 2 months after the Treaty of Hudaibiyah), the Prophet led a campaign against Khaybar, the stronghold of the Jewish tribes in North Arabia which had become a hornets' nest of his enemies. This was especially so when Bani Nadir, still unrepentant from their expulsion from Madinah, had participated in the Battle of the Trench a year earlier to attack Madinah and get rid of the Prophet.

Although the Jews put up fierce resistance, the lack of central command and preparation for an extended siege sealed the outcome of the battle in favor of the Muslims. When all but two fortresses were captured, the Jews negotiated their surrender. The terms required them to hand over one-half of the annual produce to the Muslims, while the land itself became the collective property of the Muslim state.

Pilgrimage to Makkah

In the month of Zulqa'edah of the same year (i.e. 7 *Hijrah*) the Prophet's vision was fulfilled; he visited the holy place at Makkah unopposed. In accordance with the terms of the truce, the idolaters evacuated the city, and from the surrounding heights watched the procedure of the Muslims. At the end of the stipulated three days the chiefs of Quraysh sent to remind the Prophet that the time was up. He then withdrew, and the idolaters reoccupied the city.

The Battle of Mut'ah

The Treaty of Hudaibiyah that was signed earlier initiated a truce between the Muslims in Madinah and the Quraysh of Makkah. Following this, Badhan - the Sassanid governor of Yemen, had converted to *Islam* and as a result of this, many southern Arabian tribes also followed suit and joined the rising power in Madinah. Consequently, the Prophet was free to focus on the northern Arab tribes in Syria who were under the protection of the Byzantines. Subsequently, he sent an emissary to the governor of Busra Al-Hariri in Syria to invite him to *Islam*, but the emissary was murdered by a Ghassanid chief in Balqa, Jordan.

As a result, the Prophet dispatched 3,000 of his troops to the area in the month of Jamadil Awal 8 *Hijrah* (about 6 months after his return from performing the *'Umrah* in Makkah) for a quick expedition to attack and punish the tribes in Balqa. This was the largest Muslim army raised against a non-Makkan confederate force and the first to confront the Byzantines. The army was led by Zayd ibn Haritha, the second-in-command was Jafar ibn Talib and the third-in-command was Abdullah ibn Rawahah. The leader of the Ghassanids is said to have received word of the expedition and prepared his forces; and requested for aid from the Byzantines at the same time. It was reported that the Byzantine emperor Heraclius gathered a combined force of Roman soldiers and Arab allies approximately between 100,000 to 200,000 strong.

When the Muslim troops arrived at the area to the east of Jordan and learnt of the size of the Byzantine army, they wanted to wait and send for reinforcements from Madinah. Abdullah ibn Rawahah reminded them of their desire for martyrdom and questioned the move to wait when what they desired was awaiting them, so they continued marching towards the waiting army. The Muslims engaged the Byzantines at their camp by the village of Musharif and then withdrew towards Mu'tah in Balqa. It was here that the two armies fought. During the battle, all three Muslim leaders fell one after the other as they took command of the force. Subsequently, Khalid ibn al-Walid took command.

Khalid ibn Al-Walid reported that the fighting was so intense and seeing that the situation was hopeless, prepared to withdraw. He continued to engage the Byzantines in skirmishes, but avoided pitched battle. One night he completely changed his troop positions and brought forth a rearguard that he had equipped with new banners; all this was intended to give the impression that reinforcements had arrived from Madinah. He also ordered his cavalry to retreat behind a hill during the night, hiding their movements, and then to return during daytime when the battle resumed, raising as much dust as they could. This also was intended to create the impression that further reinforcements were arriving. The Byzantines believed in the fictitious reinforcements and withdrew, thus allowing the Muslim force to safely retreat to Madinah. The campaign ended in a draw but it nevertheless impressed the Byzantines with the Muslims' unmatched valor, when their 3,000 did not hesitate to join battle against Byzantines' large number.

Truce broken by Quraysh

In the same year, the Quraysh broke their truce with the Muslims by attacking a tribe that was in alliance with the Prophet and massacring them even in the sanctuary at Makkah. Afterwards they were afraid because of what they had done and quickly sent Abu Sufyan to Al-Madinah to ask for the existing treaty to be renewed and its term prolonged. They hoped that he would arrive in Madinah before the news of the massacre. But a messenger from the injured tribe had been before him; and so, Abu Sufyan's attempt to pacify the Muslims was fruitless.

Conquest of Makkah

The Prophet then summoned all the Muslims capable of bearing arms and marched to Makkah in the month of Ramadan 8 *Hijrah*, 4 months after the Battle of Mut'ah, as consequence to the breached Treaty of Hudaibiyah. The Quraysh were simply overawed. Their cavalry put up a show of defense before the town, but were routed without bloodshed; and the Prophet entered his native city as conqueror. The inhabitants expected vengeance for their past misdeeds. The Prophet proclaimed a general amnesty. Only a few known criminals were proscribed, and most of those were in the end forgiven. In their relief and surprise, the whole population of Makkah hastened to swear allegiance. The Prophet caused all the idols in the sanctuary to be destroyed, saying: *"Truth has come; darkness has vanished away;"* (17:81) and the Muslim call to prayer was heard in Makkah.

Battle of Hunayn

The conquest of Makkah astounded both the Arabs and other tribes, who realized that they were doomed and had to submit. However, some of the fierce and proud Bedouin tribes of Arabia - namely the Hawazin, Thaqif and Bani Hilal - did not submit to *Islam* and favored resistance instead. The Battle of Hunayn was fought between the Muslim forces against these recalcitrant Bedouin tribes, in a valley on one of the roads leading from Makkah to Ta'if.

When they learnt from their spies that the Muslim forces had departed from Madinah to begin an assault on Makkah, they began mobilizing their forces. They had apparently hoped to attack the Muslims while they besieged Makkah, and encamped themselves in the valley of Hunayn. However, the Prophet uncovered their intentions through his own spies in the camp of the Hawazin, and marched to Hunayn just two weeks after the conquest of Makkah in the month of Syawal 8 *Hijrah* with a force of 12,000 men.

Of this number, 10,000 men were from Madinah and the other 2,000 were recruits from the newly converted Makkans. This new army was the largest force ever assembled in Arabia to that date. Hence, in contrast with the past, they prided themselves on their large number of soldiers and became overly optimistic. This euphoria led some of them to announce, *"Look at our numbers! Surely, we cannot be defeated this time."* But this statement was soon proven wrong when they encountered serious difficulties at the hands of their enemies even though they were thrice as numerous.

To their bewilderment, arrows suddenly began to shower intensively on the Muslim army when they arrived at Hunayn, and the enemy's battalions launched a simultaneous fierce attack against them on the ground, which left them with no choice but to retreat in a state of disorder and confusion. It was only after the Prophet instructed his uncle -Abbas, to hail the panic stricken

Muslim army with his loud voice to return to the battlefield while the Prophet prayed, *"O God! Send down Your Help!"* that the Muslims rallied and regrouped.

The Prophet then picked up a handful of earth and hurled it at the enemy, saying, *"May your faces be shameful."* Suddenly, their eyes became thick with dust and they began to retreat in utter confusion while the Muslim forces advanced and overpowered them. The battle finally ended in a decisive victory for the Muslims, who also captured enormous spoils, but not before they were severely tested and nearly succumbed to defeat.

This incident was recorded by the following verse in the Qur'an as it called on the attention of the Muslims and admonished them of their wrong attitude and behavior so that they may draw an important lesson from it : *"Verily, God granted you His support on many battlefields, but not in the Battle of Hunayn when you took pride in your numerical strength, for it availed you nothing. For all its vastness, the earth seemed too narrow for you (on that day), and you turned back fleeing. Then (finally), God sent down His tranquility upon His Messenger and upon those who are steadfast in their faith in Him. And (as an act of His grace), He sent down forces that you could not see to punish those who opposed the truth (so that you could vanquish them). Such is the requital of those who reject the truth. Yet after all this, God still turns in mercy to whomsoever He wills (among the believers) after they (realized their error and) repented, for God is Most Forgiving, Most Compassionate."* (9:25-27)

Conquest of Ta'if

The Battle of Ta'if was a continuation from Hunayn when the Hawazin and Thaqif soldiers - who retreated from the battlefield and sought refuge in the fortress of this city - were immediately pursued by the Muslims. Upon arrival, the Muslim army besieged the fortress and used catapults against it, but without much success. Seeing this, the Prophet then ordered the vineyard of the city to be cut down and burnt, as he saw no other way to force the people of Ta'if to surrender. He offered amnesty to those who surrendered themselves to *Islam* but only twenty people surrendered and became his followers. The siege went on for close to a month and some soldiers were becoming restless with the indecisive outcome.

Consequently, the Prophet commanded his troops to return to Makkah and vowed to return to Ta'if after the sacred months, in which fighting was forbidden, were over. During this period, the inhabitants of Ta'if sent a delegation to Makkah pleading with the Prophet to let them continue worshipping their goddess Al-Lat for a period of three years. The Prophet naturally refused the proposal and said that he would only accept their surrender if they agreed to accept *Islam* immediately and let the Muslims destroy those idols. Eventually, they consented to the Prophet's terms. And so after surrendering, they allowed the idol of Al-Lat to be destroyed along with all of the other signs of the city's previous pagan existence.

The Tabuk expedition

Ever since his *Hijrah* from Makkah to Madinah about 9 years earlier, the Prophet was violently opposed by one Abu Amir, a prominent member of the Khazraj tribe in Madinah, who had embraced Christianity many years earlier and enjoyed a considerable reputation among his compatriots and among the Christians of Syria. From the very outset he allied himself with the Prophet's enemies, the Makkan Quraysh, and took part on their side in the battle of Uhud in 2 *Hijrah*. Shortly thereafter, he migrated to Syria and did everything he could to induce the Emperor of Byzantine - Heraclius, to invade Madinah and crush the Muslim community.

And so when Makkah was taken over by the Muslims, and when prominent chiefs of the Arabian peninsula began embracing *Islam*, Heraclius found justification in Abu Amir's instigation and decided to launch a surprise attack on the Muslims, as he felt his empire to be in grave danger on account of the extraordinary influence and expansion of *Islam*.

Upon hearing that the Byzantine army was being mustered once again, and this time to invade the Arabian peninsula instead of defending their extended territories as in the case of the Mut'ah campaign the year before, the Prophet called on all the Muslims to support him in a great campaign to march to Tabuk in Syria in the month of Rajab in 9 *Hijrah* (630 AD, about 9 months after the Battle of Hunayn and the Conquest of Ta'if) . He was aware to some extent of the capability and experience of the enemy and was sure that besides necessitating spiritual capital (i.e. faith in God and fighting for the sake of God), victory in this battle also depended on a big army that requires large expenditures. Keeping this fact in view, he sent men to Makkah as well as to the areas adjoining Madinah to invite Muslims to fight in the path of God and also to ask well-to-do Muslims to provide for the expenses of war by making payment of *zakat*. Soon after the proclamation was made, about 30,000 men declared their readiness to participate in the battle and gathered in the camping ground of Madinah.

The Battle of Tabuk was the best occasion on which the self-sacrificing persons and the pretenders and hypocrites could be recognized, because general mobilization was ordered when the weather was very hot and the great distance between Madinah and Tabuk would surely compound the journey's difficulties. In addition, the business community of Madinah was also ready to harvest the palm-dates at that time. As such, refusal of some of them to take part in the battle on various pretexts cast off the veil from their real faces and Qur'anic verses condemning their actions were revealed in chapter *At-Taubah*.

The Muslim army arrived Tabuk in the beginning of the month of Sha'ban 9 *Hijrah*. However, no trace of the Roman army could be seen there. It appears that the commanders of the Roman army became aware of the numerical strength of the Muslim soldiers. In addition, the legendary valor and unparalleled self-sacrifices which the Romans had already experienced from a small sample of the Muslim army in the Battle of Mu'tah required no further reminder. Hence, they considered it expedient to recall their army within the frontiers of their own territories. By doing so they practically wished to deny that they had mobilized forces against the Muslims, and wanted to give the impression that they had never thought of launching an attack and that any such report was mere gossip, and thus wished to prove their impartiality regarding the events taking place in Arabia.

At this juncture the Prophet assembled his esteemed officers, and acting on the established Islamic principle of consultation, asked for their views as to whether they should advance into the territory of the enemy or return to Madinah. As a result of military consultations, it was decided that the army of *Islam* which had suffered innumerable hardships on performing the journey to Tabuk should return to Madinah to revive its strength. Furthermore, by performing this journey the Muslims had achieved their major aim, which was to scatter the Roman army. The Romans were intimidated enough that for quite a long period, they did not think of launching an attack and during that period, the security of Arabia from the northern side was ensured.

The Prophet was aware that the rulers who inhabited the frontier areas of Syria and the Arabian peninsula were all Christians and wielded considerable influence among their people. So, it was possible that one day the Roman army might utilize these local powers to attack Arabia with their assistance. It was therefore necessary for the Prophet to conclude non-aggression treaties with them to acquire better security. This intention was duly accomplished. As a consequence of this tedious journey, the Prophet did not come face-to-face with the enemy and no fighting took place, but a number of benefits were attained.

Firstly, this expedition enhanced the prestige of the army of *Islam* and the Prophet was enabled to impress his greatness and strength on the hearts of the people of the Arabian peninsula and the frontiers men of Syria. Consequently the friends as well as the enemies of *Islam* came to know that its military power had grown so much that it could face the biggest powers of the world, and this intimidated them. As for the Arab Bedouin tribes whose penchant for crime and rebellion had become second nature to them, they began restraining themselves for fear of the repercussions that they would have to face from the Muslim army if they continued indulging in this bad habit. Hence, upon the Prophet's return to Madinah, representatives of many tribes which had not surrendered until then began coming to Madinah and making declarations regarding their submission to the new Islamic Government and their acceptance of *Islam*, so much so that the 9th year of *Hijrah* was called The Year of Deputations.

Secondly, on having concluded various agreements with the frontiers-men of the Arabian peninsula and Syria, the Muslims ensured the safety of this region, and were satisfied that the chiefs of these tribes would not co-operate with the Roman army.

Thirdly, as a result of this journey, the Prophet made the future conquest of Syria easier. He made the commanders of the army acquainted with the difficulties of this region and taught them the method of warfare against the big powers of that time. Hence, the first region which the Muslims conquered after the demise of the Prophet was the territory of Damascus and Syria. Furthermore, by general mobilization of this expedition, the true believers were clearly distinguished from the hypocrites and profound understanding was created among the Muslims.

The Tabuk expedition was also the last military campaign in which the Prophet took part before his demise.

Declaration of Disavowal

Although Makkah had been conquered and its people were now Muslims, the official order of the pilgrimage had not been changed; the pagan Arabs performing it in their manner, and the Muslims in their manner. It was only after the pilgrims' caravan had left Madinah for Makkah in the month of Zulqa'edah in 9 *Hijrah* (4 months after the Tabuk Expedition) for the Muslims to perform their first *Hajj* (i.e. major pilgrimage) and when *Islam* was dominant in North Arabia, that the Declaration of Disavowal (9:1-12) as it is called, was revealed. The Prophet then hurriedly dispatched a messenger to send a copy of this revelation to Abu Bakr, who was leading the pilgrimage, with the instruction that Ali was to read it to the multitudes at Makkah. Its purport was that after that year, only Muslims were allowed to make the pilgrimage, with the exception being made for certain pagan tribes who already had a treaty with the Muslims and had never contravened it nor supported anyone against them. Such were to enjoy the privileges of their treaty for the term thereof, but when their treaty expired, they would be treated just as other idolaters who were barred from entering Makkah. That proclamation marked the end of idol-worship in Arabia.

The Farewell Pilgrimage

In the 10th year of the *Hijrah*, the Prophet went to Makkah as a pilgrim for the last time - his "pilgrimage of farewell", it is called - when from Mount 'Arafat he preached to an enormous throng of pilgrims. He reminded them of all the duties that *Islam* enjoined upon them, and that they would one day have to meet their Lord, who would judge each one of them according to his work and deeds. At the end of the discourse, he asked, *"Have I not conveyed the Message?"* And from that multitude of men who a few months or years before had all been conscienceless idolaters, the shout went up, *"O God! Yes!"* And to this, the Prophet replied, *"O God! Be You a witness to this!"*

Illness and death of the Prophet

It was during this last pilgrimage that chapter *An-Nasr* (110) or "Divine Help" was revealed, and the Prophet received inspiration that death was approaching him. Soon after his return to Madinah he fell ill. The news of his illness caused dismay throughout Arabia and anguish to the folk of Madinah,

Makkah and Ta'if. At early dawn on the last day of his earthly life, he came out from his room beside the mosque at Madinah and joined the public prayer, which Abu Bakr had been leading since his illness. There was great relief among the people, who supposed him well again.

But later in the day, the rumor grew that he was dead. Umar threatened those who spread the rumor with dire punishment, declaring it a crime to think that the Messenger of God could die. He was storming at the people in that strain when Abu Bakr came into the mosque and overheard him. Abu Bakr went to the chamber of his daughter Aisha, where the Prophet lay. Having ascertained the fact, he kissed the dead man's forehead and went back into the mosque. The people were still listening to Umar, who was saying that the rumor was a wicked lie, that the Prophet could not be dead. Abu Bakr went up to Umar and tried to stop him by a whispered word. Then, finding he would pay no heed, Abu Bakr called to the people, who, recognizing his voice, left Umar and came crowding round him. He first gave praise to God, and then said, "*O people! Behold! As for him who worships Muhammad, know that Muhammad is dead. But as for him who worships God, know that God is alive and will never die.*" He then recited the following verse of the Qur'an:

"*(O believers! Verily,) Muhammad is no more than a Messenger of God, and many Messengers have certainly came and gone before him. If he dies or is slain, will you turn back on your heels (and give up your faith)? Know that whoever gives up his faith will cause no harm to God in any way, and God will only reward those who are grateful to Him.*" (3:144).

It was as if the people had not known that such a verse had been revealed until Abu Bakr recited it. Reality began to finally sink in to everyone who heard it. As for Umar, he was quoted to have said, "*Right after I heard Abu Bakr recite that verse, I felt as though my feet were cut from beneath me and I fell to the ground, for I knew that God's Messenger was dead. May God bless and keep him!*"

The Prophet died on Monday, 12th Rabi'ul Awwal in the 10th year of Hijrah (8th June 632 AD), in Madinah at the age of 63, in the house of his wife Aisha and was buried where he died.

Prophet Muhammad was the fountainhead of Muslim life and no other person in history occupied a position in relation to his people as he did. The number of the campaigns which he led in person during the last 10 years of his life, from his base in Madinah, was 27 - in which 9 involved hard fighting - and the number of the expeditions which he planned and sent out under other leaders was 38. He personally controlled every detail of organization, judged every case and was accessible to every supplicant.

In those 10 years, he destroyed idolatry in Arabia; raised woman from the status of a chattel to complete legal equality with man; effectually stopped the drunkenness and immorality which had until then disgraced the Arabs; made men in love with faith, sincerity and honest dealing; transformed tribes who had been for centuries content with ignorance into a people with the greatest thirst for knowledge; and welded together a community of believers transcending their allegiance to tribe, race or nationality.

And the glue that had cemented this process was the Qur'an and his *Sunnah* (i.e. the Prophet's way of life, which includes his sayings and actions that are used as the reference in Islamic law as these represent the practical aspects of the Qur'an) which he left behind as a legacy that went on to continuously shape and influence the lives of millions of people and the course of world history.

You Must Know This Man

You may be an atheist or an agnostic; or you may belong to any one of the religious denominations that exist in the world today. You may be a communist or a believer in democracy and freedom. No matter what you are, and no matter what your religious and political beliefs, personal and social habits happen to be, you must make an attempt to know This Man!

He was by far the most remarkable man that ever set foot on this earth. He preached a religion, founded a state, built a nation, laid down a moral code, initiated numberless social and political reforms, established a dynamic and powerful society to practice and represent his teachings, and completely revolutionized the worlds of human thought and action for all times to come.

His name is Muhammad, and he accomplished all these wonders in the unbelievably short span of 23 years.

Muhammad was born in Arabia in the year 570 of the Common Era and when he died after 63 years, the whole of the Arabian peninsula had changed from paganism and idol-worship to the worship of One God; from tribal quarrels and wars to national solidarity and cohesion; from drunkenness and debauchery to sobriety and piety; from lawlessness and anarchy to disciplined living; and from utter moral bankruptcy to the highest standards of moral excellence. Human history has never known such a complete transformation of a people or a place before or since.

The Encyclopedia Britannica calls him "the most successful of all religious personalities of the world". Bernard Shaw said about him that if Muhammad were alive today, he would succeed in solving all those problems which threaten to destroy human civilization in our times. Thomas Carlyle was simply amazed as to how one man, single-handedly, could weld warring tribes and wandering Bedouins into a most powerful and civilized nation in less than two decades. Napoleon and Gandhi were never tired of dreaming of a society along the lines established by this man in Arabia 14 centuries ago. And Michael H. Hart in his book entitled "The 100: A Ranking of the Most Influential Persons in History" (New York, 1978, p. 33) wrote, "My choice of Muhammad to lead the list of the world's most influential persons may surprise some readers and may be questioned by others, but he was the only man in history who was supremely successful on both the religious and secular levels."

Indeed no other human being ever accomplished so much, in such diverse fields of human thought and behavior, in so limited a space of time, as did Muhammad. He was a religious teacher, a social reformer, a moral guide, a political thinker, a military genius, an administrative colossus, a faithful friend, a wonderful companion, a devoted husband, a loving father - all in one. No other man in history ever excelled or equaled him in any of these difficult departments of life.

The world has had its share of great personalities. But these were one-sided figures who distinguished themselves in only one or two fields such as religious thought or military leadership. None of the other great leaders of the world ever combined in themselves so many different qualities to such an amazing level of perfection as did Muhammad.

The lives and teachings of other great personalities of the world are shrouded in the mist of time. There is so much speculation about the time and the place of their birth, the mode and style of their life, the nature and detail of their teachings, and the degree and measure of their success or failure, that it is impossible for humanity today to reconstruct accurately and precisely the lives and teachings of those men.

Not so for this man Muhammad. Not only was he born in the fullest blaze of recorded history, but every detail of his private and public life, of his actions and utterances, has been accurately documented and faithfully preserved to our day. The authenticity of the information so preserved is vouched for not only by faithful followers but also by unbiased critics and open-minded scholars.

At the level of ideas, there is no system of thought and belief - whether secular or religious, social or political - which could surpass or equal *ISLAM*, the "system" which Muhammad propounded. In a fast-changing world, while other systems have undergone profound transformations, *Islam* alone has remained above all change and mutation, and retained its original form for the past 1,400 years. What is more, the positive changes that are taking place in the world of human thought and behavior, truly and consistently reflect the healthy influence of *Islam* in these areas.

Further, it is not given to the best of thinkers to put their ideas completely into practice, and to see the seeds of their labors grow and bear fruit, in their own lifetime. Except of course Muhammad, who not only preached the most wonderful ideas but also successfully translated each one of them into practice in his own lifetime. At the time of his death, his teachings were not mere precepts and ideas straining for fulfillment, but they had actually become the very core of the life of tens of thousands of perfectly trained individuals - each one of whom was a marvelous personification of everything that Muhammad taught and stood for. At what other time or place and in relation to what other political, social, religious system, philosophy or ideology did the world ever witness such a perfectly amazing phenomenon?

Indeed no other system or ideology, secular or religious, social or political, ancient or modern, could ever claim the distinction of having been put into practice in its fullness and entirety even once in this world, either before or after the death of its founder. Except of course *ISLAM* - the religion preached and practiced by Muhammad - which was established as a complete way of life by the teacher himself, before he departed from this world. History bears testimony to this fact and the greatest skeptics have no option but to concede this point.

In spite of these amazing achievements and the countless absolutely convincing and authentic miracles performed by him and the phenomenal success which crowned his efforts, he did not for a moment claim to be God, or God's incarnation, or Son of God, but only a human being who was chosen and ordained by God to be a teacher of truth to mankind and a complete model and pattern for their actions.

He was nothing more and nothing less than a human being. But he was a man with a noble and exalted mission, and his unique mission was to unite humanity in the worship of The One and Only God and to teach them the way to honest and upright living in accordance with the laws and commands of the Creator of the heavens and the earth and all that is between them. He always described himself as a Messenger and Servant of God, and so indeed every single action and movement of his, proclaimed him to be.

A world which has not hesitated to raise to Divinity individuals whose very lives and missions have been lost in legend and who, historically speaking, did not accomplish half as much, or even one-tenth, as was accomplished by Muhammad, should stop to take serious note of this remarkable man's claim to be God's Messenger to mankind.

Today, after the lapse of a little more than 1,400 years, the life and teachings of Muhammad have survived without the slightest loss, alteration or interpolation. Today, they offer the same undying hope for treating mankind's many ills that they did when Muhammad was alive. This is an honest claim and an inescapable conclusion forced upon us by a critical and unbiased study of history.

The least you should do as a thinking, sensitive, concerned human being is to stop for one brief moment and ask yourself: Could it be that these statements, extraordinary and revolutionary as they sound, are really true? Supposing they really are true and you did not know this man Muhammad, or hear about his teachings, or did not know him well and intimately enough to be able to benefit from his guidance and example. Isn't it time then you responded to this tremendous challenge and made some effort to know him? It will not cost you anything, but it may well prove to be the beginning of a completely new era in your life.

Who is Allah?

Some of the biggest misconceptions that many non-Muslims have about *Islam* have to do with the word "Allah." For various reasons, many people have come to believe that Muslims worship a different God than Christians and Jews. This is totally false, since "Allah" is simply the Arabic word for "God" - and there is only One God.

Let there be no doubt - Muslims worship the God of Adam, Noah, Abraham, Moses, David and Jesus - peace be upon them all. However, it is certainly true that Jews, Christians and Muslims all have different concepts of Almighty God. For example, Muslims - like Jews - reject the Christian beliefs of the Trinity and the Divine Incarnation. This, however, does not mean that each of these three religions worships a different God - because, as we have already said, there is only One True God. Judaism, Christianity and *Islam* all claim to be "Abrahamic Faiths", and all of them are also classified as monotheistic. However, *Islam* teaches that other religions have, in one way or another, distorted and nullified a pure and proper belief in Almighty God by neglecting His true teachings and mixing them with man-made ideas.

First of all, it is important to note that "Allah" is the same word that Arabic-speaking Christians and Jews use for God. If you pick up an Arabic Bible, you will see the word "Allah" being used where "God" is used in English. This is because "Allah" is a word in the Arabic language equivalent to the English word "God" with a capital "G". Additionally, the word "Allah" cannot be made plural, a fact which goes hand-in-hand with the Islamic concept of God.

It is interesting to note that the Aramaic word "El", which is the word for God in the language that Jesus spoke, is certainly more similar in sound to the word "Allah" than the English word "God." This also holds true for the various Hebrew words for God, which are "El" and "Elah", and the plural or glorified form "Elohim." The reason for these similarities is that Aramaic, Hebrew and Arabic are all Semitic languages with common origins. It should also be noted that in translating the Bible into English, the Hebrew word "El" is translated variously as "God", "god" and "Angel"! This imprecise language allows different translators, based on their preconceived notions, to translate the word to fit their own views. The Arabic word "Allah" presents no such difficulty or ambiguity, since it is only used for Almighty God alone. Additionally, in English, the only difference between "god", meaning a false god, and "God", meaning the One True God, is the capital "G". Due to the above mentioned facts, a more accurate translation of the word "Allah" into English might be "The One and Only God" or "The One True God."

More importantly, it should also be noted that the Arabic word "Allah" contains a deep religious message due to its root meaning and origin. This is because it stems from the Arabic verb *ta'allaha* (or *alaha*), which means "to be worshipped." Thus in Arabic, the word "Allah" means "The One who deserves all worship." This, in a nutshell, is the Pure Monotheistic message of *Islam*.

Suffice to say that just because someone claims to be a "monotheistic" Jew, Christian or Muslim, that does not keep them from falling into corrupt beliefs and idolatrous practices. Many people, including some Muslims, claim belief in "One God" even though they have fallen into acts of idolatry. Certainly, many Protestants accuse Roman Catholics of idolatrous practices in regard to the saints and the Virgin Mary. Likewise, the Greek Orthodox Church is considered "idolatrous" by many other Christians because in much of their worship they use icons. However, if you ask a Roman Catholic or a Greek Orthodox person if God is "One", they will invariably answer: "Yes!" This claim, however, does not stop them from being "creature worshipping" idolaters. The same goes for Hindus, who consider their gods to be "manifestations" or "incarnations" of the One Supreme God.

It should also be mentioned here that there are many who misconstrue "Allah" as some Arabian "god", and that *Islam* has no common roots with the other Abrahamic religions (i.e. Christianity and Judaism). To say that Muslims worship a different "God" because they say "Allah" is just as illogical as saying that French people worship another God because they use the word "Dieu", that Spanish-speaking people worship a different God because they say "Dios" or that the Hebrews worshipped a different God because they sometimes call Him "Yahweh." This type of reasoning is certainly ridiculous!

With this explanation, it is hoped that the erroneous perception and confusion that one may have regarding "Who is Allah" can be put to rest and perhaps trigger an interest for people to learn about *Islam* and the true message that it propounds. Hopefully too, people may then discover that there is indeed a universal religion in the world that teaches people to worship and love The One True Supreme God – The One Who created mankind and everything that is in the heavens and the earth and all that is in between them, and the One Who all creatures will one day ultimately return to for reckoning and judgment.

Additional note on the word 'Lord'.

The word "Lord" in English has several related meanings. The original meaning is "master" or "ruler", and in this sense it is often used to refer to human beings, such as "the lord of the mansion" or "Lord so-and-so" (in the United Kingdom for example). The word Lord with a capital "L" is used in the lexicon of *Islam* to refer to the One and Only God - Allah, the Creator and Sustainer of all the worlds. In *Islam*, there is no ambiguity about the meaning of this word. While it is true that one may occasionally use the word lord (whether capitalized or not) to refer to a human being, in Islamic discourse the reference of this term is always clear from the context. Whereas for Christians, Hindus and other polytheists, the word Lord with a capital 'L' may refer to God, to Jesus or to some other imagined deity; but for Muslims, there can be no plurality of meaning. Allah alone is the Lord, and the Lord is Allah - not any other being.

1. Al-Fātiḥah
[The Opening : 7 verses]

This chapter is called is *Al-Fatihah* or The Opening because the Holy Qur'an opens and starts with it. It is called by other names as well such as "Mother of the Qur'an" because it embodies the essence of the Qur'an, or the "Most Repeated Seven Verses" (see verse 15:87) because its seven verses are repeated in every unit (*rak'ah*) of both the compulsory and optional prayers. Prophet Muhammad (may peace and blessings be upon him) said that it is the greatest and most superior chapter of the Qur'an (Sahih Bukhari, no. 5006) because it contains a sublime prayer in such succinct and concise form that declares the absolute Oneness of God and man's duty to worship Him Alone. It also reminds man of his dependence on Him in all affairs, his accountability to Him on the Day of Judgment, the need for seeking His guidance to the correct way of life and conduct, and beseeching His favor to be saved from pitfalls.

¹ In the name of God, the Most Gracious, the Most Compassionate.

² All praise and thanks is due to God alone, Lord of all the worlds.

³ The Most Gracious, the Most Compassionate.

⁴ The Master of the Day of Judgment.

⁵ You alone do we worship and to You alone do we turn for help.

⁶ Guide us to the straight path;

⁷ the path of those upon whom You bestowed Your favors; and not the path of those who incur Your wrath and those who are astray.

2. Al-Baqarah
[The Cow : 286 verses]

T his chapter is called *Al-Baqarah* or The Cow in reference to the account of the cow mentioned in verses 67 - 71 describing the deviation of the Children of Israel from the original teachings of Moses. It is the longest chapter of the Qur'an which also includes its longest verse (i.e. 282). Most of this chapter was revealed at the initial Madinan period of the Prophet's life, while the other parts were revealed at later dates at Madinah. It contains the most sublime verse (i.e. 255) known as *Ayat al-Kursi* or "The verse of the Foot-rest". The chapter's concluding verse forms a very fervent and appropriate prayer to be made by man to God. *Al-Baqarah* starts with emphasizing that this Qur'an is beyond doubt a Book sent down by God for the guidance of the God-fearing who are always mindful of his or her Creator and yearns salvation. It then describes the respective characteristics of believers, disbelievers and hypocrites, the creation of man, the conduct of the Children of Israel in relation to the Prophets who were sent to them with special reference to the struggles of Prophets Moses and Jesus, the objections raised by the people of earlier revelation (i.e. the Jews and Christians) to Prophet Muhammad and his mission, and the replies thereto. It also refers to the mission of Prophet Abraham and his building of the Ka'bah together with his son Ishmael. Further, it contains injunctions and rules regarding a number of important matters like fasting in the month of Ramadan, pilgrimage, *jihad* (fighting in the way of God), matters concerning the formation and regulation of family - the basic unit of society, such as marriage, divorce and rules regarding inheritance together with rules regarding foods and drinks, prohibition of gambling and taking of usury (*riba*), and treatment of the orphans and the needy.

In the name of God, the Most Gracious, the Most Compassionate.

The Message Spelled Out

¹ *Alif Lām Mīm.* ² This is the Book, (a writ of divine revelation). Let there be no doubt that this is the guidance for those who are mindful of God (and yearn for salvation). ³ They are those who believe in the existence of what is unseen, and who are steadfast in their prayer, and spend in charity out of what We have provided for them as sustenance.

⁴ They are also the ones who believe in this revelation *ᵃ* that has been sent down to you (O Muhammad), and the revelations that were sent before you (to other Messengers), and they firmly believe in the existence of the life to come. ⁵ They are on true guidance from their Lord, and they are the ones who will

---

ᵃ The Qur'an.

ultimately be victorious.

[6] Indeed, as for those who persist in denying the truth, it is the same whether you warn them or not, they will still refuse to believe. [7] God has set a seal on their hearts and on their hearing; and on their vision is a veil. And a great punishment awaits them.

[8] And among the people, there are some who say, "We believe in God and in the Last Day," but they are not true believers. [9] They seek to deceive God and those who believe but they do not deceive anyone except themselves, yet they do not realize it. [10] In their hearts is a disease and God has increased their disease, and they will have painful punishment for their persistent lying.

[11] And when it is said to them, "Do not spread corruption (and cause disorder on earth)", they reply, "Indeed, we mean well and seek to set things right." [12] But beware! It is they who are actually the ones who spread corruption (and cause disorder on earth), and yet they do not realize (the damage that they have caused and done).

[13] And when it is said to them, "Believe as the others have believed," they reply, "Should we believe like those fools?" In fact, it is they who are actually the fools but they do not know this. [14] And when they meet those who believe, they say, "We believe (just like you do)!" But when they are alone with their evil companions, they say, "We are actually on your side. We only pretended to be like them whereas we were in fact mocking them."

[15] God will throw their mockery back on them and leave them alone in their transgression. As such, they will continue to wander to and fro like the blind. [16] Those are the ones who trade away guidance for error. Their bargain surely did not profit them, nor are they guided to the right path.

[17] Their example is like the one who kindles a fire. And as it lit up all around him, God took away their light and left them in darkness, unable to see anything. [18] Deaf, dumb, and blind - they will not return to the right path.

[19] Or another example is that of a dark storm-cloud in the sky charged with thunder and lightning. They press their fingers to their ears at the sound of each stunning thunderclap for fear of death; but God encompasses these deniers of truth from all sides (and there is no escape for them). [20] The lightning terrifies them as if it was going to snatch away their eyesight. Whenever it flashes, they walk in its light; and when darkness covers them, they stand still. And if God so willed, He could have certainly taken away their hearing and their sight completely. Indeed, God has power over everything.

²¹ O mankind! Worship your Lord, the One Who created you and those before you, so that you may always be in the state of being mindful of Him (and live a righteous life). ²² He is the One Who has made the earth a resting place for you, the sky a canopy and then sent down rain from it so that fruits may grow as provision for you. So do not then claim that there is any power that could rival God when you know (the truth).

²³ And if you are in doubt about this Book which We have revealed to Our servant (Muhammad), then produce a single chapter like it and call upon whatever supporters you have other than God to bear witness (and assist you in this task) if you insist you are right. ²⁴ But if you fail, as you most certainly will, then be mindful of the Fire - whose fuel is of men and stones - that awaits all those who deny and reject the truth.

²⁵ To those who believe and do good deeds, give them good news that they will reside in gardens which rivers flow from right beneath them. Whenever they are offered fruits therefrom as provision, they will say, "This is like what was given to us before!"; for they will be provided with something similar (that will make them recall such delightful past). They will also have chaste and pure spouses who will remain (together with them) in there forever.

²⁶ Indeed, God does not disdain using the parable of a mosquito or something even less significant (to teach people a lesson). For those who believe, they know that it is the truth from their Lord. Whereas those who disbelieve (and reject God's revelation) will ask, "What does God mean by this parable?" (Behold!) Many will be confounded and sent astray by such parable, while many will also be enlightened and rightly guided by it. (Verily,) God confounds and leads none astray, except those who defiantly disobey Him. ²⁷ (They are) those who break their bond with God after it has been established, and those who cut asunder the ties of relationships which God has commanded to be held together, and those who cause corruption and disorder on earth. It is they who are the actual losers.

²⁸ How could you bring yourself to deny and defy God? Is He not the One Who gave you life when you were initially lifeless, and is He also not the One Who will cause you to die and then bring you back to life again (on the Day of Resurrection), and is He not the One Whom you will ultimately return to (one day)?

²⁹ Verily, it is He Who created all that is in the earth for you. Moreover, His (supremacy) is firmly established over the (vast) heaven which He had fashioned it into seven heavens (earlier). And it is He alone Who has full and perfect knowledge of everything.

Man as God's Emissary on Earth

³⁰ (Now take heed of the occasion) when your Lord said to the Angels, "Behold! I am going to place an emissary on earth (who will inherit and administer it." The Angels) asked, "Why would You want to place someone there who will cause disorder and shed blood while we (continuously declare and) glorify Your perfection with (limitless) praises and (unceasingly) proclaim Your sanctity? God answered, "Verily, I know what you do not know!"

³¹ And so God (created Adam and gave him the gift of intellect and the ability to reason, and also) taught him the attributes of all things. Then He presented those things to the Angels and said, "Tell Me about them if you know. ³² Glory be to You (Who are Most Perfect O God!" replied the Angels). "We know nothing except only what You have taught us. Indeed, You (alone) are perfect in knowledge and wisdom."

³³ Then God said, "O Adam! Tell them (what you know) about the things (that I have taught you)." And when Adam did so, God said to the Angels, "Did I not tell you that it is I (alone) Who know all the unseen (secrets of the) heavens and the earth, and I know everything that you reveal and conceal?"

³⁴ And so, when We ordered the Angels, "Prostrate to Adam (as a mark of respect of My perfect creation)!"ᵃ all of them did, except *Iblis*, who refused in his self-glory and arrogance, and thus became a rejecter of truth (and a rebellious transgressor).

³⁵ Then We said to Adam, "Live with your wife in this garden and eat freely from its bountiful food as you both wish, but do not come near this tree or you will both become wrongdoers (and bring injustice upon yourselves)." ³⁶ But Satan (tempted them with the tree and) caused them both to slip and be removed from their erstwhile state. And so We said, "Get down (both of you from this state of blessedness and innocence. Verily, take heed and learn from this lesson that) some of you will always be enemies (and cause trouble) to one another (out of greed and jealousy). Dwell on earth from now on. That is where you will have your place to stay and provision for a specified term (before I return you all to Me and make you accountable for all your deeds)."ᵇ

ᵃ This does not refer to the act of prostration in its literal sense. See verses 22:18 and 55:6. In the specific context of this verse, it carries a symbolic meaning of showing respect.
ᵇ It is a gross misconception to believe that God was angry with Adam and his wife and severely rebuked them for eating the forbidden fruit in the garden of Paradise. This idea is actually based on the Jewish and Christian's narrative in the Bible's Book of Genesis where both Adam and his wife were expelled from Paradise as punishment for

³⁷ Thereupon, Adam received words (of guidance) from his Lord (and repented); so his Lord turned towards him (in mercy and forgave him). Verily, God is the Acceptor of Repentance, the Most Compassionate. ³⁸ And so We said, "(Now) get down (from here) all of you (to dwell on earth until an appointed time before I return you to Me). And when My guidance comes to your (descendants), whoever follows it will have nothing to fear nor grieve." ³⁹ "But those who reject and deny Our signs and revelations will be the Fire's inmates where they will remain forever."

---

their disobedience. Subsequently, some among those who came after Jesus used this narrative to invent a new religion that they named Christianity with the Doctrine of Original Sin as one of its main cores. Essentially, the doctrine teaches that because of Adam's disobedience to God, innocence is lost and all subsequent human beings are born in a state of sin which can only be atoned by believing that Jesus died on the cross to save mankind from their sins, and only those who subscribe to this faith are eligible to go to heaven. In truth, Adam's disobedience was a natural act of a mortal who would sometimes experience a lapse of judgment, despite the intellectual superiority and other fine qualities that God has bestowed upon him over His other creations (see verse 31 and also 95:4). Committing the error of eating the forbidden fruit was actually part of Adam's destiny that he was bound to fulfill because this would serve as the reason for him to be sent to this world, fully equipped with the necessary attributes and capabilities to perform his predestined role as God's emissary on earth (see verse 30) after learning this very important lesson. This was actually a test which God had prepared for Adam. What God had actually wanted to see was how Adam would respond to his mistake - would he deeply regret his lapse of judgment and turn to God to seek forgiveness, or act in arrogance and defiance? As it turned out, Adam reacted with great remorse for his unintended error. He passed his test, unlike Satan who was deadly jealous of Adam's superior qualities over him that led him to arrogantly disobey God and vowed to mislead every progeny of Adam until the end of time (see verse 15:39). And so, Adam and his wife were forgiven by God - The Most Gracious and Most Merciful Lord, and this incident marked the right time for him to leave Paradise to fulfill his destiny as the father of all mankind on earth. Only through this way could Adam's descendants be entrusted with their predestined responsibility as God's emissary to rule the earth by upholding justice and bring a life of quality and ease to all mankind, while always maintaining an excellent relationship with God and with fellow humans concurrently (see verse 3:112 and the corresponding footnote). This is how verse 51:56 should be understood too - man must serve and worship God Almighty alone to the best of his ability by striving to become God's successful emissary on earth in fulfilling the purpose of his creation. And because God knows that man must be properly guided to undertake this monumental task, Prophets were sent from time to time to provide the necessary guidance for man to stay on the right course, shun evil temptations and not become a follower of Satan. To perform their tasks, some Prophets were given Scriptures and some were just inspired by God without Scriptures.

Glimpses of Israelite History

[40] O children of Israel! Remember My favors that I have bestowed upon you. So fulfill your promise to Me and I shall fulfill Mine to you. And stand in awe of Me alone. [41] Believe in what I have revealed (to My final Messenger - Muhammad), which confirms (the message in) the earlier Scriptures that are already in your possession. Do not be foremost among those who deny its truth, and do not trade away My signs and revelations for a petty price (to seek a trifling gain of this fleeting world). Always be mindful of Me (and keep your duty to Me diligently). [42] Do not mix truth with falsehood, nor knowingly conceal the truth (to satisfy your evil motives). [43] Establish (and be steadfast in) your prayer; spend in charity; and bow down with those who bow down (to Me in worship).

[44] (O children of Israel!) Does it make sense for you to tell others to be righteous while you neglect it, and yet (proudly claim to be the people of earlier revelation and even) have the Scripture in your hands to read and study? Do you not have common sense?

[45] (Hence), seek God's help through perseverance and prayer (if you wish to be rightly guided in His path). This is indeed difficult, except for those who are humble (in spirit and are always mindful of God); [46] (and) those who believe in certainty that they will (ultimately) return and meet their Lord (to face judgment).

[47] O children of Israel! Remember those special favors and blessings that I have graced upon you, and how I raised (and honored) you above the rest of mankind (before this). [48] So be mindful (and guard yourselves) against the Day (when everyone will be made fully accountable for their own deeds. That is the Day) when no soul will be able to avail another, no intercession will be accepted, no ransom will be taken and none will be helped (and rescued).

[49] (O children of Israel! Do you not remember the time) when We saved you from Pharaoh and his people who afflicted you with horrible torment, slaughtered your sons and spared your women? And (surely) in that was a severe trial from your Lord (for you to take heed). [50] And (do you not remember) when We parted the (Red) Sea for you, took you to safety and then drowned Pharaoh and his people right before your very eyes? [51] (Do you also not remember the time) when We appointed for Moses forty nights (on Mount Sinai), then you built (and worshipped a golden statue of) a calf after that and became evildoers (who committed a wicked transgression)? [52] Even then, We still forgave you so that you would (repent and) be grateful (for the favors We graced upon you).

⁵³ (Now, call to mind) when We gave Moses the Book *ᵃ* (during the time We communed with him on Mount Sinai) which contained the criterion (of right and wrong) so that you may be rightly guided. ⁵⁴ (And remember how dismayed Moses was when he returned to his people and found them worshipping the statue they built.) He said, "O my people! Indeed, you have brought gross injustice upon yourselves by building and worshipping this (golden statue of a) calf (during my absence). Turn in repentance to your Creator and slay (the culprits) among you. That will be best for you in His sight." And (in dispensing His grace,) God accepted your repentance (after you had executed His command). Verily, God alone is the Accepter of Repentance, the Most Compassionate.

⁵⁵ (But among you, there were some who refused to obey this command and retorted,) "O Moses! We shall never believe you (and will not follow what you have instructed) until we clearly see God with our own eyes." Thereupon, We seized you with a sudden thunderbolt while you were gazing. ⁵⁶ Then We revived you (back to life) after you were dead (as a sure sign of Our greatness) so that you would be grateful.

⁵⁷ (And do you also not remember when) We dispensed Our grace to you by providing shades of clouds over you as comfort, and sent down *Al-Manna ᵇ* and quails (for your sustenance while you were wandering in the desert)? We said, "Eat from the good things that We have provided you." (In spite of these bounties, they were still ungrateful and arrogant.) Verily, these transgressors (certainly) did not wrong Us; instead, they only wronged themselves (and harmed their own souls).

⁵⁸ And (recall too O children of Israel) when We said, "Enter this town and eat freely from its abundance. But make your way through the gates in humility first and announce, 'O Lord, we repent!', and (only after this) shall We forgive your sins and amply reward those who excel in good deeds." ⁵⁹ Instead, the wrongdoers among you (made a mockery of Our command by manipulating and) changing the words from what We had commanded. And so We sent down a scourge from heaven (in the form of a plague) that inflicted these wrongdoers (as requital) for their defiant disobedience.

⁶⁰ (O children of Israel! Do you not remember the time) when you pleaded with Moses to pray to Us for water (when you were wandering in the desert)? So We said to Moses, "Strike the rock with your staff!" Thereupon, twelve springs gushed forth from it and each tribe was assigned their drinking station. (Then Moses said), "Eat and drink of what God has provided. (Be grateful to God and) do not act wickedly on earth as those who cause disorder."

ᵃ The Torah.
ᵇ A sweet type of food.

 61 (But because of your ungrateful attitude), you continued to demand, "O Moses! We cannot continue living like this, enduring only one kind of food. *ª* So call on your Lord to give us a variety of food which the earth produces such as green herbs, cucumbers, garlic, lentils, and onions (that we used to enjoy before this)." Moses replied, "Why would you want something that is inferior in exchange of something better, (which is the safety and freedom that God has granted you)? If that is what you really want, then go back to Egypt (where you used to live in shame as slaves). You will certainly find what you are asking for over there." And so, humiliation and misery were struck upon them as they incurred God's wrath and condemnation. This was the consequence of their persistent denial of God's message, their unjust slaying of His Prophets, and their disobedience and transgression (against His commandments).

62 Verily, those who believe (in this Qur'an), as well as the Jews, the Christians, and the Sabians (who had correctly followed the teachings of the true Messengers of their times) - who believed in the Oneness of God and in the Last Day, and did righteous deeds; they will be justly rewarded by their Lord and they will have nothing to fear nor grieve.

63 (O children of Israel! Remember) when We accepted your solemn pledge (to become true believers) and exalted Mount (Sinai) towering above you saying, "Hold firmly to what We have given you *ᵇ* and follow the commandments in it, so that you will always be mindful of God (and guard yourself against evil)." **64** But even after that, you turned away from your pledge. And had it not been for God's favor (and guidance that He continued to) graciously bestow upon you, you would surely have found yourselves among the losers (who will be damned in the Hellfire permanently).

65 Surely you are well aware of the story about those among you who violated the Sabbath-law. (We wanted to test their obedience by prohibiting them from going out to seek their livelihood on every Saturday. Instead, they defiantly disobeyed Our rule and went out fishing in the sea on that day.) And so We said to them, "Be apes - despised (and rejected)!" **66** So We made their fate as a warning example for people of their time and for all times to come, as well as an admonition to all who are mindful of God.

67 (O children of Israel! Do you not remember the story of the cow which God had commanded you to sacrifice? Recall) when Moses said to his people, "God commands you to sacrifice a cow!" They retorted, "Are you ridiculing us?" Moses answered, "I seek God's protection from being among those who are (arrogantly) ignorant." **68** (Hearing this,) they said, "If so, request from

---

ª *Al-Manna* and the quails.
ᵇ The Torah.

your Lord to give us more details about the cow." Moses replied, "God says the cow should neither be too old nor too young but of an age in between. Now do what you are commanded!" [69] They said in return, "Request your Lord again to let us know what color should it be." Moses replied, "God says the cow should be of a bright yellow color, pleasing to the eyes of the beholder."

[70] (Still dissatisfied), they (continued to) ask (Moses further), "Request your Lord to clarify the exact type of cow it should be because all cows look alike. If God wills, (He could make it easy for us so that) we shall be rightly guided." [71] Moses answered, "God says the cow should have never been used to plough the earth or water the crops. (It must also be) a healthy animal and free from blemish." They responded, "Now we are clear about what you have asked from us." Finally they sacrificed the cow after (offering many excuses and) nearly refused to carry out the order.

[72] (O children of Israel! Do you also not remember the incident) when you killed a man and began casting the blame upon one another as to who killed him? But God exposed what you tried very hard to conceal. [73] We commanded, "Strike the dead body with a piece of the slaughtered cow!" (Behold! The dead man briefly came to life again to announce who had actually killed him.) That was how God brought the dead back to life to show you His signs so that you will use reason (to know that nothing can be hidden from God and how simple it is for Him to restore life whenever He wills).

[74] But even after witnessing this, your hearts became hard like rocks or perhaps even harder. Whereas (unlike your hearts), there are some rocks that gush out from streams, there are some that split open and water comes out of them, and there are also some that tumble down due to their awe and fear of God. And truly, God is not unaware of what you do.

[75] (Therefore O believers), do you still hope that they will believe in what you are preaching when some of them have already heard and understood the word of God, and yet (still dare to) manipulate it (to satisfy their own evil motives) even when they knew (that what they were doing was wrong)?

Covenants Breached All the Time

[76] (Beware that) when they meet the believers, they say, "We too believe (in what you believe)", but when they are alone with their own kind, they say, "Did you tell Muhammad and his followers about what God revealed to us (in

the Torah regarding the final Messenger)? *ᵃ* Have you no sense that (if they knew about this) then they would be able to use it as an argument against you in the court of your Lord later?" ⁷⁷ Do these people not know that God is fully aware of what they conceal and what they reveal?

⁷⁸ And among them are some illiterates who (are ignorant and) have no knowledge of their Holy Book.*ᵇ* They depend on empty hopes and (are guided by mere conjecture). So they do nothing but guess. ⁷⁹ Woe to those who (manipulatively) write the Book with their own hands and then claim, "This is from God!" (to satisfy their own selfish and wicked motives) then trade it away for (the sake of) a trifling gain. Woe to them for what their hands have written, and woe to them for what they earn (from this evil work)!

⁸⁰ (And in asserting their perverted arrogance,) they audaciously say, "The Hellfire will not touch us except for only a few days." Ask them (in return O

ᵃ This verse is in direct reference to the Jews of Madinah during the time of the Prophet who did not accept Jesus as their Messiah and were waiting for the right Messiah to arrive. What is mentioned in the verse is alluded to the Book of Deuteronomy 18:15-18 from the Torah that is believed to be God's literal words conveyed by Moses to the Children of Israel, "... *I shall raise up for them a Prophet like you (i.e. Moses) from among their brothers. And I shall put My words in his mouth, and he will speak to them all that I command him.*" Most of the Jews in Madinah who were in direct contact with Prophet Muhammad knew that the person who is being prophesied here is him due to the many similarities that he shared with Moses and they could clearly witness the signs of his Prophethood through his conduct and teachings. Some notable Jewish scholars in Madinah such as 'Abdullah ibn Salam and Ka'b ibn Malik accepted the prophecy and embraced Islam, but a great majority of the Jews refused to accept due to their envy and jealousy towards Muhammad who came from the lineage of Ishmael - the patriarch of Arabs, instead of Isaac - the patriarch of Jews, even though both of them were brothers. The prophecy also cannot be referred to Jesus because Moses was a plain mortal whereas Christians believe that Jesus is God who incarnated Himself as man. Even the birth and "death" of Jesus too was completely unnatural, unlike Moses. In fact, the name *Muhammadim* which clearly refers to *Muhammad* is mentioned in the Book of Song of Solomon 5:16 in the Hebrew Bible but is translated as "He is altogether lovely" in the English Bible. This is not far off from its actual meaning in Arabic which is "The one who is frequently praised". It would be natural to expect someone who is regarded as "altogether lovely" to be adored and praised frequently. Rightfully, the name of a person should be left alone in its original language to maintain its originality instead of translating it to another different language. Had this been the case, then Prophet Muhammad's name would have surely been found printed in every single copy of the Bible on this planet for everyone to see, thus confirming the Bible's own prophecy of his coming as the final Messiah.
ᵇ The Torah.

Prophet), "Have you obtained a promise from God regarding this matter which He will not repudiate? Or, are you attributing to God something of which you have no knowledge?" [81] Behold! (Let it be clear that) those who commit evil and become engulfed in sin will be the Fire's inmates. They will remain in there forever. [82] But those who truly believe in God and do righteous deeds are the residents of Paradise. They will remain in there forever.

[83] And (remember) when We accepted this solemn pledge from (you, O) children of Israel, that, "You will worship none but God; be good to your parents, relatives, orphans and destitute; speak to people with kindness; be steadfast in your prayer; and spend in charity." But except for a few, most of you turned away in disobedience. Verily, you are truly an obstinate lot!

[84] And (remember too) when We took your solemn pledge that you will not shed blood among yourselves nor drive your own people out of their homes. You confirmed and acknowledged this promise, and bore witness to it. [85] Yet there you are - slaying your own people, expelling a group among you from their homes, and complementing each other in sin and enmity. And if those you had persecuted come to you as captives, you traded them for ransom whereas their expulsion was unlawful for you to begin with. Do you only believe in some parts of the Book and reject those that do not serve your selfish desires? What then would be the requital for people who behave like this other than disgrace in this world and a grievous torment on the Day of Resurrection? Verily, God is never once unaware of what you do.

[86] Such are the people who acquire (a trifling gain of) this fleeting world in exchange (for the eternal victory and pleasure) of the life to come. Hence, neither their suffering will be lightened nor will they be helped (and rescued on that dreadful Day).

[87] Indeed, We (have dispensed Our grace to you, O children of Israel, by revealing and) giving the Torah to Moses and sent after him other Messengers in succession (to guide you to Our path). We also gave Jesus, the son of Mary, clear evidence (and signs of the truth) and strengthened him with holy inspiration (so that you will be convinced of the truth). Yet, whenever a Messenger came to you with a message that did not suit your (evil and selfish) desires, you gloried in your arrogance (and rejected him). Some of them you accused as impostors while some you would slay.

[88] And yet (these wicked infidels still have the audacity to) boast (to you O Prophet), "Our hearts are (already full of knowledge and securely) wrapped, (and we shall not accept what you are telling us)." Behold! God condemns them for their refusal to accept the truth. Verily, so little is what they believe!

[89] And now, when the final Book (of divine revelation) from God [a] is being brought to them confirming the message in the earlier Scriptures that are already in their possession (regarding the coming of the final Messenger who will triumph over infidels), they rejected him when he finally came, even though they recognized his clear signs in spite of the fact that they used to pray for victory against the infidels. (Verily, it is they who are in fact the true infidels) and God's curse is on those who defiantly reject the truth!

[90] Evil is what they have sold their souls for. They (foolishly) rejected the revelation that God has sent down because of their deep jealously (and grudge) against whom God has chosen as His servant (from among the Arabs instead of Jews) to receive His grace. For this, they have incurred (the burden of God's condemnation and) His wrath upon wrath. Verily, a humiliating punishment awaits them (in the life to come).

[91] And when they are asked to believe in the revelation that God is sending down now, they reply, "We only believe in what God has sent to us earlier!" [b] and they reject whatever that comes after that even though it is the truth that confirms the message in the earlier Scripture that is already in their possession. So ask them, "Why then did you kill some Prophets before this who God had chosen (among yourselves) if you truly believe (in the Torah)?"

[92] Verily, Moses came to you with (many) clear signs (of the truth). Yet you still acted wickedly by worshipping the (golden statue of a) calf (that you built) while he was away (to commune with God).

[93] (O children of Israel! Remember) when We accepted your solemn pledge (to become true believers) and exalted Mount (Sinai) above you saying, "Hold firmly to the commandments that We have given, listen carefully (and obey them)". But they replied, "(Indeed) We have heard but we disobey!" (They became like this because) their hearts were imbued with a feeling of great love for the (golden statue of the) calf as a result of their (persistent) defiance against God. So say (to them O Prophet), "Evil indeed is what your faith commands you to commit, if you have any faith at all!"

[94] Say (to them further), "If the (eternal) home of the Hereafter with God is indeed for you alone to the exclusion of all other people, then wish for death if you are true in your claim!" [95] But surely they will never wish for death because they are aware of the sins that their hands have committed (and the consequences that they will have to face in the life to come). God knows everything about those evildoers (have done).

---

[a] The Qur'an.
[b] The Torah.

⁹⁶ (O believers!) You will surely find that these are the greediest people who cling to the life of this world, even greedier than the idol worshippers (of Makkah). Each one of them wishes to be given a life of a thousand years even though the grant of such a life will not save them from the punishment (in the life to come). Verily, God sees all that they do.

⁹⁷ (O Prophet!) Tell them that whoever is an enemy of Gabriel who brought down the Qur'an into your heart by God's permission that confirms the truth of the earlier Scriptures as guidance and good news to those who believe, (then behold!) ⁹⁸ (Know that) whoever is an enemy to God, His Angels, His Messengers including Gabriel and Mikhael; then indeed God will be a (fierce) enemy to (him and to) everyone (else) who denies the truth.

⁹⁹ Indeed (O Prophet), We have sent down to you clear signs and revelations (as guidance for mankind to attain salvation) and none can deny their truth except those who willfully choose to become defiantly disobedient. ¹⁰⁰ Is it not always the case that every time when they make a solemn pledge, some of them would (renege and) cast it aside? The truth is, most of them are (obstinate) infidels!

¹⁰¹ And even now when a Messenger from God has come to them to confirm the truth that is already in their possession, a group from those who were given the Scripture (earlier) would cast this Book of God ᵃ behind their backs as if they knew nothing about it; ¹⁰² and (instead) followed what the evil ones (had fabricated and) used to practice during Solomon's reign even though Solomon never denied the truth (and was never involved in any practice of disbelief). Whereas, it was the evil ones who denied the truth by teaching people witchcraft and sorcery, and also by teaching a certain knowledge which was revealed to Haarut and Maarut - the two Angels in Babylon. But both of them never taught anything to anyone without first declaring, "Verily, we have been merely sent to you as a trial, (and the knowledge that we have could be a temptation to evil); so do not compromise your faith (by turning what you learn from us into witchcraft and sorcery)." In spite of this warning, there were some who learnt from both these Angels what could be used to cause discord between a man and his wife, but they can harm no one except only by God's permission. Indeed, what they learned (and practiced) would only harm their own souls and render no benefit. They knew very well that whoever acquires this (evil art) would have no share (of good) in the life to come. Evil indeed is what they have traded with for their own souls. If only they knew (the grievous suffering that awaits them)!

¹⁰³ If they had believed (in God's revelations) and been mindful of Him, then surely they would know that God's reward is far better (than anything

---

ᵃ The Qur'an.

else). If only they really knew (and understood this well)!

Jewish Efforts to Undermine Islam

[104] O you who believe! (Be mindful that when you approach the Prophet to seek his attention). Do not say "*Raa'ina*" *[a]* (like those Jews do with a twist of their tongues to imply a bad meaning), but say "*Unzurna*" instead,*[b]* and then pay attention (to him). Remember that grievous suffering awaits those who (deride the Prophet and) deny the truth.

[105] (O Prophet!) Know that neither those who are bent on rejecting the truth among the people of earlier revelation nor among the idol worshipping pagans would like to see any good ever sent down to you by your Lord. But God singles out for His grace to whomsoever He wills. (Verily,) God is limitless in His great bounty.

[106] (O children of Israel!) We do not annul or abrogate any sign or message,*[c]* or consign it to oblivion except that We substitute it with something better or similar.*[d]* Do you not know that God has power over everything? [107] Are you oblivious (and have forgotten) that God has absolute dominion over the heavens and the earth? (Surely you know that) there is none to protect and help you except Him. [108] Or do you intend to ridicule the Messenger who is being sent to you (now) just as how Moses was ridiculed before? (Remember!) Whoever trades away belief for disbelief has indeed strayed from the straight path (and will surely be requited with a stern punishment).

[109] (O believers! Know that) even after the truth has become clear to them, many among these followers of earlier revelation still wish to lead you back to disbelief after you have embraced faith, out of their deep-seated envy and jealousy. Forgive them and forbear until God brings forth His decree. Indeed, God has power over all things. [110] (In the meantime,) establish (and remain steadfast in) your prayer and render the purifying dues (punctually). Whatever good deeds you send forth for yourselves, you will find it safe with God. Indeed, God sees all that you do.

[111] And (how strange it is that) these deniers of truth (who wish to lead you back to disbelief have the audacity to) claim, "None will ever enter Paradise unless he be a Jew or a Christian." Such are their wishful fancies. Say to them, "Bring your proof if what you say is true!" [112] The fact is, only he

---

[a] *Raa'ina* means "Listen to us."
[b] *Unzurna* means "Have patience with us."
[c] The earlier revelations namely the Torah, Psalms and Gospel.
[d] The Qur'an.

who surrenders himself entirely to God and excels in good deeds will be rewarded by his Lord, and they will have nothing to fear nor grieve.

[113] (Is it not ironic that) the Jews say the Christians have no basis for their faith, while the Christians (on the other hand) say the Jews have no basis for their faith (too)? Yet, they both recite the Scriptures (that were revealed to them). Likewise, those (idol worshipping pagans) who have no knowledge of the Scriptures also say the same as what the Jews and Christians say. Verily, God will be their Judge on the Day of Resurrection regarding their dispute.

[114] Now, who could be more unjust and wicked than those who forbid the mention of God's name in His places of worship and strive for their ruin? It is not proper for such people to enter into these places except with deep humility and fear (of God. Verily,) humiliation will befall them in this world and grievous punishment awaits them in the life to come.

[115] To God belongs the east and the west. Whichever direction you turn to, there is God's (presence and) countenance. Behold! God is All-Embracing and All-Knowing.

[116] And yet some people assert, "God has taken a son (for Himself)!" Glorified is He (above all the imperfections and the blasphemous accusations that they say against Him). Nay! To Him belongs all that is in the heavens and in the earth, and all are humbly obedient to Him. [117] (He is) the Originator of the heavens and the earth; and when He decrees a matter, He need only say, "Be!" and it is.

[118] Only those who are devoid of knowledge ask, "Why does God not speak to us directly or send a (miracle to us as a sure) sign?" The same demand was made by those before them too. Verily, the hearts (and minds) of those who reject the truth are alike. Indeed, We have already made all the signs clear to those whose faith is firm (and are endowed with inner certainty). [119] Behold! We have sent you with the truth (O Prophet), and made you the bearer of good news and a warner (to all mankind). Verily, you will not be held accountable for those who (reject it and willfully) destine themselves as the inmates of the Blazing Fire.

[120] (O Prophet!) Be mindful that never will the Jews nor the Christians be pleased with you until you follow their faith. Say (to them), "Behold! God's guidance is the only true guidance (and this is sufficient for me and those who follow me)." And if you follow their (errant views and yield to their wishful) fancies after the knowledge has come to you, (then know that) there will be none to protect or help you from God's (wrath). [121] (As for) those to whom We have given the Book (of divine revelation) and read it as it ought to be read (without distorting its meaning), it is they who are the true believers. Whereas

those who (choose to deny its truth and) reject it, they are the sure losers.

[122] O children of Israel! Remember those special favors and blessings that I have graced upon you. I have indeed raised (and honored) you over the rest of mankind (before this). [123] Therefore, be mindful and guard yourselves against the Day when no soul will be able to avail another, no ransom will be taken, no intercession will benefit anyone, and none will be helped (and rescued).

Universal Faith

[124] (O Prophet! Now narrate the story) about Abraham who fulfilled his Lord's commands (in true obedience) when his Lord tested him by saying, "Behold! I shall make you the leader of mankind." (And) Abraham asked, "What about my descendants?" God replied, "My covenant does not include those who commit injustice and transgression."

[125] And when We made the (sacred) House [a] as a place of resort and sanctuary for mankind, We said, "Take the place where Abraham once stood, as a place of prayer." Then We commanded Abraham and Ishmael, "Purify My House for those who circumambulate it, those who seclude themselves for devotion and prayer, and those who bow down and prostrate (in worship)."

[126] And (take heed) when Abraham supplicated, "O My Lord! Make this land [b] secure and grant its people who believe in You and in the Last Day, fruitful sustenance." God replied, "As for those who deny the truth, I shall also provide for them in this life to enjoy (My bounties) for a short while. But in the end, I shall drag them to the torment of Hellfire." How wretched it is for their journey to end!

[127] And as Abraham and Ishmael raised the foundations of the (sacred) House, they prayed, "Our Lord! Accept this as a (noble) deed from us. Indeed, You are the One Who hears all and knows all. [128] Our Lord! Make both of us submit to You (wholeheartedly) and make from our descendants a community that will submit to You (in true devotion). Show us our worship rites, accept our repentance (and forbear our shortcomings). Verily, You are the only Accepter of Repentance, the Most Compassionate. [129] O our Lord! Raise among them a Messenger who will recite (and convey) Your words (of truth), teach them the content of Your Book and (also help them acquire) wisdom so that (their belief and faith in You) will (always) be pure. Verily, You alone are the Almighty, and the All-Wise."

---

[a] The Ka'bah.
[b] Makkah.

¹³⁰ Only a fool would turn away and forsake the religion of Abraham. Indeed We have chosen and raised him high in this world, and in the life to come he will rank among the righteous. ¹³¹ (This is because) when his Lord said to him, "Submit yourself to Me!", Abraham answered, "I hereby submit myself (wholeheartedly) to You alone, O Lord of all the worlds!"

¹³² And Abraham commanded his children to do the same, and so did Jacob (too). They said, "O my children! Behold! God has granted you the purest faith and chose it for you as your way of life. So do not allow death to overtake you except while you are in the state of complete submission to Him."

¹³³ (O children of Israel!) Were you present when death approached Jacob and witnessed (the occasion) when He asked his sons, "What will you worship after I am gone?" They replied, "We shall worship your God - the God of your forefathers : Abraham, Ishmael and Isaac - Who is the One True God. It is Him alone Whom we fully submit ourselves to."

¹³⁴ That was (the story of) the community who came and left before you. For them is what they earned and for you is what you earn. And you will not be asked about what they have done.

¹³⁵ (Notwithstanding this,) the Jews and Christians (still continue to) say, "Be Jews or Christians, and you will then be rightly guided." Say (to them), "Nay! (By no means will we ever follow you!) We follow only the faith of Abraham the upright monotheist (who was truly devoted to God), and he was not of those who associated partners with God."

¹³⁶ Proclaim (O believers!), "We believe only in God and in what is revealed to us, and in what was revealed to Abraham, Ishmael, Isaac, Jacob and their descendants, and in what was given to Moses and Jesus, and in what was given to all the Prophets by their Lord. We make no distinction between any of them, and to Him alone have we submitted ourselves (in complete obedience)." ¹³⁷ So if they believe in the way you believe, then indeed, they will be rightly guided. But if they turn away, then they are (surely entrenched) in dissension. And sufficient is God (alone) to protect you from them. Verily, He hears all and knows all.

¹³⁸ (Tell them, "Our faith and way of life take its) hue from God! And who is better at giving hue (to our life) other than God? And it is Him alone do we worship." ¹³⁹ Say (to them further), "Why do you want to argue with us about God when He is our Lord and your Lord (too)? Verily, for us are our deeds, and for you are your deeds. And to Him alone are we devoted. ¹⁴⁰ Or are you claiming that Abraham, Ishmael, Isaac, Jacob and their descendants were either Jews or Christians?" Ask them (O Prophet), "Who knows better - is it

you or God? And who could be more wicked than the one who hides the testimony he receives from God (to serve his evil motives)? Behold! God is never once unaware of what you do."

¹⁴¹ That was (the story of) the community who came and left before you. For them is what they earned and for you is what you earn. And you will not be asked about what they have done.

Change of Direction

¹⁴² The foolish among the people will say, "What has turned Muhammad and his followers from the direction of prayer which they used to face before?"ᵃ Say (to them), "To God belong the east and the west. He guides whomsoever He wills to the straight path."

¹⁴³ And so, We have made you become a (just and) balanced community so that you will bear witness to the truth (of God's message) over all mankind, and the Messenger will also bear witness to this truth over you; (and so that your way of life will serve as an example to all mankind just as the Messenger is to you). We changed the direction of the prayer which you used to face in order to make evident those who are the true followers of the Messenger from those who (are in doubt and) would revert to their erroneous ways. Indeed, it was a great test except for those whom God has guided aright (because of their firm grasp of the truth). And God would surely not let your faith be in vain. Indeed, God is Full of Kindness towards mankind, He is the Most Compassionate.

¹⁴⁴ Verily, We see that you often turn your face towards the sky (O Prophet. And as a clear sign of Our grace and mercy), We shall make you turn in prayer towards a direction that pleases you. So turn your face towards the direction of the Sacred Mosque. ᵇ And wherever you all may be, turn your faces in prayer towards its direction. And indeed, those who were granted earlier revelation know well that this (commandment) comes in truth from their Lord, (yet they still reject it). And God is not unaware of what they do.

¹⁴⁵ And even if you bring every possible proof to those who have been granted earlier revelation, they would still not follow your direction of prayer. And neither will you follow their direction of prayer, nor will they even follow each other's direction. If you (ever) follow their (errant views and yield to their) fancies after all the knowledge that has come to you, then you will certainly be among those wrongdoers (who are being unjust to their own souls). ¹⁴⁶ Those to whom We granted earlier revelation know (the truth in)

ᵃ From Jerusalem to Makkah.
ᵇ The Ka'bah.

this (command) just like they recognize their own children. But some of them deliberately conceal the truth while they know it (to serve their own evil motives). [147] Truth (cannot be suppressed as) it comes from your Lord. So do not ever be among those who fall into doubt.

[148] And for every community is a direction it faces (to worship God). So vie with one another in good deeds (and worship Him alone). Wherever you are, God will bring all of you together, for only He has the power to do anything He Wills. [149] So from wherever you come forth, turn your face in prayer towards the Sacred Mosque. Behold! This commandment comes in truth from your Lord and He is never once unaware of what you do.

[150] Hence, from wherever you come forth, turn your face in prayer towards the Sacred Mosque. And wherever you all may be (O believers), turn your face towards it too, so that no one will have any argument against you, except the wrongdoers among them. Hence, do not fear them, but fear (and obey) Me alone and I shall bestow upon you the full measure of My blessings so that you may be rightly guided; [151] just like how We have sent to you a Messenger from among yourselves to recite (and convey) Our words (of truth), purify your corrupt faith (and cleanse your soul), teach you (about the content) of the Book, (impart) wisdom (to you through his examples and sayings), and to teach you about what you do not know. [152] So remember Me, and I shall remember you. Be grateful to Me and never defy Me.

Acquiring Real Strength

[153] O you who believe! Seek help through patience and prayer. Indeed, God is with those who are patient. [154] And do not say that those martyred in the cause of God are dead. Nay! They are alive but you do not realize it.

[155] And most certainly We shall test your patience with fear and hunger; and loss of wealth, lives, and the fruits (and crops that you labor). But give good news to those who endure (these adversities) with patience; *a* [156] those who when misfortune afflicts them, they say, "Indeed, to God we belong and surely to Him we shall return." [157] Such are the people on whom their Lord's blessings and grace are bestowed, and they are the ones who are rightly guided.

Setting the Record Straight

[158] Indeed, *Safa* and *Marwah* *b* are among the symbols of God. Anyone

---

a See verses 2:214, 21:35, 29:2-3
b The two hills within the vicinity of the Sacred Mosque.

who visits the Sacred Mosque to perform (actual) pilgrimage or *'Umrah,*^a would do no wrong to walk to and fro between them. And whoever does more good (than he is obliged to), behold! God is Most Appreciative, All-Knowing.

¹⁵⁹ But for those who suppress and conceal the clear proofs and guidance after We sent them down and made clear in this Book, upon them will be God's curse and the curse of all who are entitled to curse; ¹⁶⁰ except those who repent and mend their ways, and openly declare (the truth). Then from those, I shall accept their repentance. Verily, I alone am the Acceptor of Repentance, the Most Compassionate.

¹⁶¹ Behold! As for those who are bent on denying the truth and die as disbelievers, upon them is the curse of God, the Angels and all (righteous) men. ¹⁶² They will remain in this state forever (and) neither will their punishment be lightened nor will they be granted respite. ¹⁶³ And indeed, your God is the One and Only God; there is no god except Him, (and He is) the Most Gracious, the Most Compassionate.

Regret

¹⁶⁴ Indeed, in the creation of the heavens and the earth and the alternation of the night and the day; and the ships that sail in the sea carrying what is useful for people; in the rain that God sends down from the sky giving life to the earth after it had been lifeless, that cause all kinds of living creatures to multiply and scatter on it; and in the movement of the winds and the clouds that float between the sky and the earth - surely in all these are signs (from their Creator) for people who use their reason (and intellect to ponder).

¹⁶⁵ And yet there are some who take others as God's equal. They love these false gods as they should love God, whereas the true believers love God even more. If only the evildoers could now see the punishment (that they will face on the Day of Judgment, they will surely concede) that to God alone belongs all power and might. And He is indeed (stern in retribution and) severe in punishment.

¹⁶⁶ (On that day,) those who had been (falsely adored) and followed will disown their followers, and these followers will see the punishment (that awaits them) with all their ties (and hopes) severed. ¹⁶⁷ And they will say, "If only we had one more chance to return to the world, we will surely disown them as they disown us today (and we shall certainly mend our ways)." Through this way, God will make them see their (evil) deeds which will cause them bitter regret (and sorrow). And they will never come out of the Fire.

---

^a Minor-pilgrimage.

Ruling on Food

¹⁶⁸ O mankind! Eat from whatever is on the earth that is lawful and good, and do not follow the footsteps of Satan. Indeed, he is your clear enemy. ¹⁶⁹ He is (always) inciting you to commit evil and indecency, and to say things about God that you have no knowledge of.

¹⁷⁰ And when it is said to them, "Follow what God has revealed," they reply, "Nay! We shall only follow the ways of our forefathers." (Is this what they still wish to do) even when their forefathers understood nothing and were devoid of guidance? ¹⁷¹ The parable of those who are bent on denying the truth is like (an animal) that hears the shepherd's call but understands nothing except for the (empty sound of) shouts and cries. They are deaf, dumb, and blind, and they do not understand anything.

¹⁷² O you who believe! Eat from the good and clean things that We have provided for you as sustenance, and render thanks to God if it is truly Him that you worship. ¹⁷³ He has only forbidden you to consume carrion, blood, the flesh of swine, and that over which any name other than God is invoked (while slaughtering the animal). But whoever is compelled by absolute necessity to consume them - neither coveting it nor exceeding his immediate need - then he will incur no sin. Verily, God is Most Forgiving, Most Compassionate.

¹⁷⁴ Behold, those who conceal (or manipulate) any part of the revelation that God has sent down and trade it away for a trifling gain, they will swallow nothing but fire into their bellies. And on the Day of Resurrection, God will neither speak to them nor cleanse them of their sins and they will have grievous punishment.

¹⁷⁵ They are the ones who trade away good guidance in exchange for error, and forgiveness for suffering. How (admirable) is their endurance of the Fire! ¹⁷⁶ Their doom is because (they deliberately seek causes to reject) God's Book that was sent down with the truth. Indeed they are in extreme dissension because they (persistently) dispute God's message.

¹⁷⁷ True piety and righteousness is not whether you turn your face towards the east or the west, but righteousness is to believe in God, the Last Day, the Angels, the Book, and the Prophets; and to spend from what you cherish very much for your kin, for the orphans, for the destitute, for the (stranded) travelers, for the beggars, and for the freeing of human beings from bondage (all out of love for God. Righteousness also includes) establishing and being steadfast in prayer; rendering purifying dues (punctually); fulfilling promises when made; being patient in misfortune and adversity, and at the time of peril. Such are those who have proved themselves true, and such are the ones who

are always mindful of God (and fear Him even though He is unseen).

Social Justice and Fasting

[178] O you who believe! Equal retribution [a] is ordained for you in cases of murder - a free man for a free man, a slave for a slave, and a woman for a woman. But if the guilty party is pardoned by the representing kin of the aggrieved party, then a suitable compensation should be made to them in fairness and goodly manner. This is a concession and mercy from your Lord. Whoever transgresses the limits after this will face grievous punishment.

[179] O you who are endowed with insight and wisdom! There is security of life for you in equal retribution so that you may be mindful of God (and learn self-restraint).

[180] It is ordained upon you that when death approaches, those of you who leave behind some wealth will make a bequest in favor of your parents and other near of kin with due fairness. This duty is binding on all who are mindful of God. [181] Whoever changes the bequest after hearing it, then the burden of sin will certainly lie on him. Indeed, God hears all and knows all. [182] But if one has reason to fear that the testator has committed an error or a deliberate mistake and acts to bring about a reconciliation and settlement among the parties involved, then there is no blame or sin on him. Verily, God is Most Forgiving, and Most Compassionate.

[183] O you who believe! Fasting is ordained upon you as it was ordained upon those before you so that you will (learn self-restraint and) achieve the state of being ever conscious and mindful of God. [b]   [184] So fast on the

---

[a] *Al-Qisās.*

[b] The Qur'anic term for "being in the state of ever conscious and mindful of God" is *Taqwa*, where one does not become a slave to his vain desires and lusts but earnestly strives to please God and avoid from incurring His displeasure. It also involves the act of striving to establish a well balanced and excellent relationship with God and other fellow humans concurrently, regardless of race and religion. Fasting is a means that has been prescribed by God for Muslims to heighten their consciousness in attaining the goal of *Taqwa*, and the month of Ramadhan has been divinely chosen as the training camp for this purpose. Being in the state of *Taqwa* is not exclusively limited to Ramadhan alone. Rather, *Taqwa* is a state of condition where one should strive to live his life even outside of Ramadhan with the virtues that he has succeeded to attain while fasting during Ramadhan. Fasting is not only about enduring hunger and thirst from dawn to dusk. But it is a means to help a believer to spiritually overhaul himself to attain *Taqwa* by guarding his speech, sight, hearing and all other senses through self-restraint from indulging in all sorts of negative activities that will pollute and corrupt his

prescribed number of days. But whoever among you is ill or on a journey, then he may fast the same number of days at a later time. And upon those who can fast (but find it a strain too hard to bear due to old age or grievous illness) may compensate for it by feeding a needy person (for each missed day). And whoever does more good (than he is bound to), that is better for him. Nevertheless, to fast is better for you if you knew.

¹⁸⁵ The month of *Ramadhan* is the month in which the Qur'an was revealed as guidance for all mankind with clear teachings showing the right way together with the criterion (to distinguish between truth and falsehood). So whoever witnesses the new moon of Ramadan should fast the whole month. But whoever is ill or on a journey should make up for the lost days by fasting on other days later. God wishes ease for you, not hardship; so that you will complete the prescribed period while glorifying God and be grateful to Him for having rightly guided you (and bestowing His favors upon you).

¹⁸⁶ And when My servants ask you about Me (O Prophet), tell them that I am truly near and I answer to the prayer of every (devoted) supplicant who calls upon Me (directly). So let them respond to Me (in obedience) and believe in Me, so that they may be rightly guided.

¹⁸⁷ It is permitted for you to be intimate with your wives during the night

---

fitrah (i.e. the purity of his soul). The following Prophetic sayings (i.e. *hadith*) exemplifies the fact that fasting is meaningless in the sight of God if one's conduct with other fellow humans is offensive and hurtful as this would defeat the goal of achieving *Taqwa* : (1) "There are people who fast but get nothing from their fast except hunger (and thirst). And there are those who stand for prayer at night but get nothing from their prayer except a sleepless night." [Sunan Ibn Majah, no. 1690]. (2) A man asked the Prophet, "O Messenger of God! There is a certain woman who prays a lot at night, gives charity and fasts a great deal during the day. But she offends her neighbors and others with her sharp tongue." The Messenger of God replied, "Her place is in hell!" Then the man said, "O Messenger of God! There is another woman who is well-known for how little she fasts and prays (outside of her obligatory requirement). She gives charity from the dried yoghurt that she makes and she (has a pleasant demeanor which) does not offend others." The Messenger of God replied, "Her place is in Paradise." [Adab al Mufrad by Imam al Bukhari, no. 119]. In essence, Islam is not about physically performing obligatory and supererogatory rituals correctly from the technical aspect alone. But it is also about getting it right from the spiritual aspect that relates to the conscious state of our heart and soul as God's true humble servants who must be kind, fair, considerate, respectful and courteous to other fellow humans and all other God's creations too as we concurrently fulfill our ritual obligations. Without this, the acts of worship rituals lose their merit and are rendered meaningless. See chapter 107.

of fasting. They are like garment for you as you are for them. God is aware that you have been deceiving yourselves (regarding this matter by imposing abstinence upon yourselves during the night of fasting and then violating it afterwards), and He has turned to you in His mercy and pardoned you (for this self-imposed baseless rule). Hence, you are now free to approach your wives (at night during *Ramadhan*) and seek what God has ordained for you. (You may also) eat and drink until you can discern the white streak of dawn against the blackness of night. Then resume your fast until nightfall. But do not approach your wives during your (devotional) retreat in the mosques. These are the bounds set by God, so do not come near them. Through this way does God make His signs and revelations clear to mankind so that they will be ever mindful of Him (and observe His prescribed limits).

¹⁸⁸ Do not devour each other's wealth wrongfully, nor use it to bribe judges to misappropriate a portion of other people's wealth while you clearly know that it is sinful.

The Sacred Months, Fighting and Pilgrimage

¹⁸⁹ They ask you about the new moons (O Prophet). Say, "They are signs for people to measure and mark fixed periods of time, including the pilgrimage." (Tell them also that), "Righteousness does not mean that you enter your houses from their back doors (when you return from pilgrimage) but righteousness is to always be mindful of God (and performing noble deeds). So enter your houses by their (proper) doors. Always be mindful of God (and keep your duty to Him diligently) so that you will be successful.

¹⁹⁰ Fight in the cause of God only those who wage war against you, but do not be extreme (in your retaliation). Indeed, God dislikes extremists. *ᵃ* ¹⁹¹ Slay those aggressors wherever you find them, and drive them away from wherever they drove you away; for persecution (and injustice) is worse than killing (those who commit acts of transgression. But) do not fight them near the Sacred Mosque unless they attack you first. Should they attack you (there), then slay them. Such will be the requital of those who are hostile in their opposition of the truth. ¹⁹² But if they desist (and cease their aggression), then (leave them alone, for) God is indeed Most Forgiving, Most Compassionate. *ᵇ*

ᵃ Islam does not approve of extremism and terrorism (see verse 16:126) but make no mistake that Islam allows fighting for self defense against tyranny, injustice and aggression (see verse 22:40 and its footnote). All verses about fighting that are found in the Qur'an and the sayings of the Prophet (i.e. *hadith*) must be read and understood purely in this context alone and nothing else. And fighting must stop when the enemy ceases its aggression as mentioned in verses 192 and 193.
ᵇ See verse 8:61.

¹⁹³ (Continue) fighting against them until there is no more persecution (and injustice), and until worship can be (freely) devoted to God (without fear and hindrance). But if they cease (in their aggression), then there should not be hostility (from your side too) except against those who (continue to) oppress.

¹⁹⁴ (Fighting in) the sacred month is (only permissible to defend against aggression that is committed against you during) the sacred month. For any violation that is committed, there is equal retribution.[*] Therefore, if anyone commits aggression and attacks you (during this time), retaliate with the same force. But remain conscious of God (and do not exceed the limits that He has set), and know that God is with those who are always mindful of Him.

¹⁹⁵ And spend generously for the cause of God and do not let your own hands throw you into ruin (by being stingy). Persevere and be steadfast in doing good. Behold, God loves those who excel in good deeds.

¹⁹⁶ Complete the (actual) pilgrimage and *'Umrah* ^a for the sake of God. But if you are prevented from doing so, then offer whatever sacrificial animal you can (afford and) obtain with ease. Do not shave your heads until the offerings have reached their place of sacrifice. But if any of you are ill or suffers from an ailment of the scalp (that necessitates shaving), he should compensate by fasting, or giving charity, or sacrificing (an animal for its meat to be given to the poor). And when you are in safety, whoever takes advantage of performing the *'Umrah* before the (actual) pilgrimage will make whatever sacrificial offering he can easily afford. Whoever lacks the means will fast three days during the pilgrimage and seven more days on returning home - that is, ten days in all. This applies to those whose household are not resident in the vicinity of the Sacred Mosque. Always be mindful of God (and keep your duty to Him diligently). Know well that He is severe in retribution.

¹⁹⁷ Pilgrimage will take place in the appointed months that are well known.^b Whoever undertakes to perform pilgrimage in those months will abstain from lewdness, wicked conduct and quarrelling. Whatever good you do, God is well aware of it. And make provision for yourselves; and verily, the best of all provisions is God-consciousness and piety. So, be ever mindful of Me, O you who are endowed with insight and wisdom!

¹⁹⁸ There is no sin upon you to seek the bounty of your Lord during pilgrimage (by continuing your business activities). And when you surge downward from Mount Arafat (in multitude towards Muzdalifah), remember God at the Sacred Monument ^c (by glorifying Him) as the One who guided

---

^a Minor-pilgrimage.
^b *Syawal, Zulqa'edah* and *Zulhijjah.*
^c *Mash'aril-Haraam.*

you after you were indeed astray before this. [199] Then surge onward from the place where all other pilgrims surge, and pray for God's forgiveness. Verily, He is Most Forgiving, Most Compassionate.

[200] And after you have fulfilled your sacred duties, (continue to) remember God (by glorifying Him) as you dearly remember your forefathers. In fact, remember God with keener and greater remembrance. Of the people among you, there are some who pray, "Our Lord! Grant us success in this world." (Such are the ones who will have a share in this world) but no share in the rewards of the life to come. [201] And there are others who pray, "Our Lord, grant us what is good in this world and what is good in the life to come and protect us from the torment of the Fire." [202] Such are the ones who will have their share (of reward) in return for what they have earned (from their good deeds). And God is swift in reckoning.

[203] Remember God (and glorify Him) during the appointed days (while performing pilgrimage). Whoever hastens his departure (from Mina) after two days incurs no sin, and whoever stays longer incurs no sin too, as long as he is ever mindful of God (and observes the pilgrimage rules). So be ever mindful of God (and strive to fulfill your duty to Him). Remember that you will all be ultimately gathered to Him (someday).

The Nature of Islamic Society

[204] Among people, there is a kind of man whose speech and views on the life of this world greatly fascinates you. He (is skillful in argument and) cites God to witness what is in his heart, yet he is your most contentious adversary. [205] And when he leaves you, he sets out to cause disorder in the land destroying crop and livestock, whereas God (whom he claims to be his witness) does not love disorder. [206] And whenever it is said to him, "Be mindful of God (and fear Him)", his pride and arrogance gets incited and drives him to commit more sin. Hence, sufficient for him is the Hellfire. How wretched it is as a resting place! [207] But there is also a kind of man who would readily give himself away to please God. And God is indeed full of kindness to His servants.

[208] O you who believe! Submit yourselves to God whole-heartedly, and do not follow the footsteps of Satan. He is without doubt your clear enemy. [209] And if you (still) falter and slip back after all evidence of truth has come to you, then be aware that God is Almighty, All-Wise.

[210] Are these people (who are indifferent towards their Lord) waiting for God to come and reveal Himself to them in the shadow of clouds together with the Angels (before they would take heed of His message? If this took place),

then all matters would have been decided (and the doors to repentance would have been tightly shut because it would mean that the Day of Judgment would have already arrived). Verily, to God will all matters return for decision (and judgment).

²¹¹ Ask the children of Israel, how many clear signs have We given to make them see the truth? And whoever substitutes these favors and blessings from God (with falsehood) after receiving them, then behold! Verily, God is severe in retribution.

²¹² (Indeed,) the life of this world has been made appealing and alluring to those who reject the truth. Hence, they (become arrogant and) scoff at those who believe (in God and refrain themselves from the indulgence in sinful pleasures). But those who are (always) mindful of God will rank high above those disbelievers on the Day of Resurrection. (On that day), God will grant His bounties and blessings to whomsoever He wills without measure.

²¹³ Humanity was once a single community (sharing the same pure faith of monotheism. Then people began to differ when some among them invented false religions to satisfy their perversions after being hoodwinked by Satan). Thereupon, God sent Prophets as bearers of good news and stern warnings, and with them He sent the Book in truth *a* to judge between people in matters wherein they differed. Yet after clear evidence of truth came to them, they still continued to differ out of mutual jealously and rivalry. And by His grace, God guided only those who believe (in Him) to the truth regarding those disputes. Verily, God guides whom He wills towards the path that is straight (if they are receptive to the truth and want to be guided).

²¹⁴ (O believers!) Do you think that you will easily enter Paradise before being tested like those before you? They were afflicted with adversity and hardship until they were so shaken that even their Messenger and the believers with him cried out, "When will God's help come?" Surely, God's help is ever near (for those who are patient and firm in their faith).

²¹⁵ (O Prophet!) They ask you about what they should spend in charity. Say, "Anything good you spend of your wealth should (first) go to your parents and the near of kin, to the orphans and the destitute, and to the travelers (who are in need). Verily, God is well aware of whatever good you do."

---

a Divine revelations.

What We Like is Not Necessarily Good

²¹⁶ Fighting is ordained for you even though you might hate it. It may well be that you hate something that is good for you and love something that is bad for you. Indeed, only God knows (what is good and bad for you) whereas you do not.

²¹⁷ They ask you about fighting in the sacred months. Say to them, "Fighting in those months is a grave sin; but hindering people from God's path to make them disbelieve in Him, (preventing access to) the Sacred Mosque and expelling people from it is even a greater sin in the sight of God, for oppression (and injustice) is worse than killing (those who commit acts of transgression)." They will not cease to fight with you until they can force you to renounce your faith. And (remember that) whoever among you turns away from his religion and dies as a disbeliever, all their deeds will most certainly become worthless in this world and in the life to come. It is they who will be the inmates of the Fire and they will remain in there forever. ²¹⁸ Indeed, those who have become believers and those who have forsaken their homeland and strived hard for God's cause are the ones who may look forward to God's (bountiful) grace. And God is Most Forgiving, Most Compassionate.

²¹⁹ (O Prophet!) They ask you about intoxicants and gambling. Say, "There is grave sin in both of them as well as some benefit for people. But their sin and evil outweigh the benefit." And they ask you about what they should spend in charity. Say, "Any surplus you can spare." Through this way, God makes clear His revelations to you so that you may (reflct and) ponder about them; ²²⁰ in relation to (the affairs of) this world and (the consequences in) the Hereafter.

They also ask you about (how to deal with) orphans. Tell them, "Improving their condition (and dealing with them fairly) is best (for you and them). And if you wish to jointly manage (their inherited properties with yours, that is permitted since) they are your brethren (in faith), as long as you protect their interests diligently). God knows who means harm and who means well for their welfare. Had God so willed, He could impose hardship on you (through strict rules and you would find this difficult to manage). Verily, God is Almighty, All-Wise."

Women and Rulings on Divorce

²²¹ (O believers!) Do not marry idolatresses unless they embrace true faith. Any believing slave-woman is certainly better than an idolatress even though the idolatress is pleasing to you. And do not give your women in marriage to idolaters unless they embrace true faith. Any believing slave is certainly better

than an idolater even though the idolater is pleasing to you They invite (you) to the Fire (and eternal disgrace) whereas God invites (you) to Paradise and forgiveness by His grace. He makes His revelations clear to people so that they will take heed and be mindful.

²²² They ask you about menstruation. Tell them, "It is an impure condition, so do not have sexual intercourse with women during their menstruation and do not approach them (sexually) until they are clean again. After they have cleansed themselves, you may approach them in the proper manner as God has ordained." Indeed, God loves those who turn to Him in repentance, and He loves those who keep themselves (clean and) pure.

²²³ Your wives are like your farmland. You may approach your farmland as you please (within the boundaries set by God) and perform (good deeds) for (the benefit of) your soul. Always be mindful of God and know for certain that you are destined to meet Him. So give good news to those who believe (O Prophet).

²²⁴ (O believers!) Do not allow your oaths in God's name to prevent you from doing good, from being mindful of God and from making peace between people. Verily, God hears all, knows all. ²²⁵ God will not call you to account for what is unintentional in your oaths but He will make you responsible for what you intended in your hearts. And God is Most Forgiving, Most Forbearing.

²²⁶ Those who vow abstention from their wives will have a waiting period of four months. If they change their mind and retract, then (know that) God is indeed Most Forgiving, Most Compassionate. ²²⁷ But if they resolve on divorce, then remember that God hears all, knows all.

Divorce, Remarrying and Care for Infant

²²⁸ Divorced women will refrain themselves (from remarrying) for a period of three monthly courses (of menstruation cycles). It is unlawful for them to conceal what God might have created in their wombs, if they believe in God and the Last Day. During this period, their husbands are entitled to take them back if they desire reconciliation. Although men have a degree (of right) over their wives (for the responsibilities that they carry as the head of the household), women will, in a reasonable manner enjoy equitable and similar rights to those of their husbands. (Both should always remember that) God is indeed Almighty, All-Wise.

²²⁹ Divorce is (only permissible) twice, whereupon a woman may either be retained in fairness or released with kindness. It is unlawful for you to take back from women anything that you have given them (as bridal dues), unless

both (partners) have reason to fear that they may not be able to keep within the bounds set by God. If you (as arbiters) have reason to fear this, then there is no sin upon either of them if she gives something as compensation to her husband (in order to free herself from the marriage). These are the bounds set by God, so do not exceed them. Those who exceed the bounds set by God are (certainly) wrongdoers.

²³⁰ If he divorces her (for the third time), then she is not lawful for him to remarry until she marries a different man. And if the latter divorces her, then there is no sin on the earlier husband to remarry her, if they both believe that they will be able to keep within the bounds set by God. Such are the bounds set by God, which He makes clear for people of knowledge.

²³¹ And when you divorce women and they reach their waiting term,ᵃ either retain them honorably or release them honorably. Do not retain them out of malice in order to harm them, for this would surely cause you to exceed the bounds set by God. Whoever does so will only bring injustice to his own soul. So do not take God's revelations lightly. Remember the favors and blessings that God has blessed you with, and what He has revealed to you from the Book and wisdom to teach you. Be ever mindful of God (and fear Him). Know that He has full knowledge of everything.

²³² And when you have divorced women and they have reached the end of their waiting term, do not prevent them from marrying their (prospective) husbands if they have consented to each other honorably. This is an instruction for those among you who believe in God and the Last Day (to take to heart) - it is more dignifying and purer for you. Verily, God knows (what is good for you) whereas you do not.

²³³ The (divorced) mothers will breastfeed their children for two whole years if they wish to complete the nursing term; and it is incumbent upon the father to provide for their maintenance and clothing in a fair manner (but) no one should be burdened with more than his capacity. Neither a mother nor a father will be made to suffer on account of their child. The same duty rests upon the (father's) heir (if the child is an orphan). If both (parents) decide by mutual consent and consultation to wean the child, there will be no blame on them. Nor will there be any blame if you wish to entrust your children to wet-nurses to breastfeed them, provided you (compensate the wet-nurses fairly and) ensure the safety of the child that you are handing over. ᵇ Be ever mindful of God (and keep your duty to Him), and be reminded that He sees all that you do.

ᵃ *'Iddah.* See also chapter 65.
ᵇ See verses 65:6-7

²³⁴ If any of you die and leave widows behind, they should refrain (from remarrying) for a period of four months and ten days. And when they complete their specified term, then there is no blame on their legal guardian regarding what they may do with themselves as long as it is in a reasonable and appropriate manner. And God is fully aware of all that you do.

²³⁵ You will incur no sin if you give an indication of courtship to the widowed women or harbor the intention quietly to yourselves. God knows that you might entertain such intentions concerning them. But do not make any secret promise with them, except that you speak to them in an honorable manner; nor resolve on the marriage contract before the prescribed waiting term is fulfilled. Be reminded that God knows what is in your mind, so beware of Him; and know that God is Most Forgiving, Most Forbearing.

²³⁶ You will also incur no sin if you divorce women before consummating your marriage or before you specify your (bridal dues) obligation (to them). Make provision for them in a fair manner - the rich according to his means and the less privileged according to his means. Such provision is an obligation on those who excel in good deeds. ²³⁷ And if you divorce them before consummating your marriage but after specifying your (bridal dues) obligation, then give them half of what you have promised unless they waive it, or he - in whose hand holds the marriage contract - waives it. To forgo what is due to you is closer to piety. Do not forget to be kind (and generous) to one another. Indeed, God sees all that you do.

²³⁸ Guard strictly your (obligatory) prayer, especially the middle prayer. ª And stand in devout obedience before God. ²³⁹ And if you are in danger, then you may pray while walking or riding. But when you are safe, remember God (by celebrating His praises abundantly) for teaching you what you did not know.

²⁴⁰ In advance of death, those of you who will leave widows behind should make a bequest for them to receive a year's maintenance and residence. But if they leave (the residence of their own accord), there will be no blame on their legal guardians for what they do with themselves as long as it is within their rights. And (remember that) God is Almighty, All-Wise.

²⁴¹ Divorced women will be given reasonable provision according to what is considered fair. This is an obligation upon those who are mindful of God (and fear Him). ²⁴² In this way does God make clear His revelations to you so that you may use reason (to ponder and understand).

ª In reference to the afternoon prayer - 'Asr.

God's Limitless Bounty

²⁴³ (O Prophet!) Are you not aware of those who fled their homelands in the thousands for fear of death, whereupon God said to them, "Die!" then He restored them to back to life? Indeed, God grants limitless bounty to mankind, but most people are ungrateful. ²⁴⁴ So fight for the cause of God and know that God hears all, knows all.

²⁴⁵ Who among you will lend to God a good loan (by spending in His cause) which He will repay it many times over? Verily, (remember that) it is God alone Who can withhold and grant provision in abundance, and it is to Him you will all be returned.

The Israelites Get a King

²⁴⁶ Have you not heard the story about the elders among the children of Israel after the time of Moses? They said to their Prophet, ᵃ "Appoint for us a King so that we may fight (against Goliath ᵇ) for God's cause." (Samuel) replied, "I worry that if this leader is brought to you, you will disobey him and refuse to fight when you are commanded." They answered, "How could we refuse to fight in God's cause when we have really been (unjustly oppressed and) driven out of our homes along with our children (and some of our families are held as captives)?" But when a King was then appointed for them and they were ordered to fight, most of them refused except a few. Verily, God knows everything about these evildoers.

²⁴⁷ And so Prophet (Samuel) said to them, "Behold! It was God, (and not me) who appointed Saul ᶜ to be your King." They replied, "How can he be our King when we are better-off and more deserving than him? Samuel answered, "Saul was chosen (to rule) over you because God has granted him vast knowledge, (prowess) and (great) strength. Verily, God grants dominion and authority to whomsoever He pleases. His bounties are indeed infinite and He is All-Knowing."

²⁴⁸ Said Prophet (Samuel further), "Behold! The sign of his (rightful) appointment as a King is that he will come to you with a chest, ᵈ where you will find remnants (of God's divine writ in the form of relic Scriptures) in it. These are Angel-borne heritage left behind by the family of Moses and the family of Aaron that will give you peace and tranquility (if you read and

---

ᵃ Believed to be Prophet Samuel, or Samwil in Arabic.
ᵇ Jalut in Arabic
ᶜ Thalut in Arabic.
ᵈ Ark of the Covenant.

earnestly abide by them). Surely, in this is a sign (of God's grace) for you if you are true believers."

²⁴⁹ And when Saul marched forth with his troops, he announced, "Behold, God will test you with a river. Anyone who drinks from its water will cease to be my follower. And whoever refrains from it, except only for a sip or so from the hollow of his hand, will (be forgiven and) continue to fight on my side." (And when they arrived at the river, most of them drank much from it, except a few.) So when Saul and those who had kept faith with him crossed the river (to fight Goliath and his large army), those who had drunk said, "We have no strength left in ourselves to fight against Goliath and his army today." But the ones who kept faith and knew with certainty that they were destined to meet God, said, "How many times in the past did a small group successfully defeat a mighty host of army by the grace of God? Verily, God is with those who (endure adversity with) patience!"

²⁵⁰ When they marched forth to face Goliath and his troops, they prayed, "Our Lord! Shower us with patience and make our steps firm. Grant us victory over the people who deny the truth." ²⁵¹ And thereupon, by God's will, they defeated the enemy and Goliath was killed by David. And (after the passing of Saul,) God gave the kingdom to David and taught him the necessary knowledge (and wisdom to rule justly). Verily, if God had not enabled mankind to defend themselves against one another, there would surely be disorder on earth and corruption would certainly prevail. Indeed, God's infinite bounties are graciously dispensed to all the worlds.

²⁵² These are God's revelations that We convey and recite them to you (O Prophet), to set forth the truth. Verily, you are surely among Our chosen Messengers.

Faith

²⁵³ Those are the Messengers! We gave precedence to some above the others. To some God spoke directly, and some He raised in rank. We gave Jesus, the son of Mary, clear signs and strengthened him with holy inspiration. If God had willed, those who came after these Messengers would not have differed and fought against one another after clear proofs had come to them, but they did. Among them were some (who accepted Our message and) became believers while most rejected it. Had God willed, they would not have fought against one another. But God does as He pleases (and gave man intellect, reason and free will to decide for himself).

²⁵⁴ O you who believe! Spend (in Our way) out of what We have provided you before a Day comes when there will be no bargaining, nor any friendship

and intercession. Those who deny (Our revelations) are indeed (evil) wrongdoers (who will face severe consequences on that Day).

²⁵⁵ God! There is no god except Him (and only He alone deserves all worship). He is the Ever-Living, the Sustainer and Protector of all that exists. Neither slumber nor sleep touches Him. To Him belongs all that is in the heavens and the earth. Who is there that can intercede with Him (on behalf of another) except by His permission? He knows everything that lies open before all His creatures and all that is hidden from them, whereas they understand nothing of His knowledge except what He wills. ª (His domain encompasses everything that even the majesty of) His *Kursi* ᵇ alone spreads over the and the earth, and no fatigue ever befalls Him in guarding and preserving them both. Indeed, He is truly Exalted, the Most Supreme. ᶜ

²⁵⁶ Let there be no compulsion in religion, for truth stands clearly distinct from falsehood. ᵈ Whoever rejects false gods and believes in the One and Only Almighty God has certainly grasped the firmest handhold (and has nothing to fear). God hears all, knows all. ²⁵⁷ (Verily,) God is the Guardian and Protector of the believers. He leads them out of darkness into light. As for those who refuse to accept the truth, their patrons are false gods who lead them out of light into darkness. They are the inmates of the Fire and will remain in there forever.

Causing Life and Death

²⁵⁸ Are you not aware of the one who argued with Abraham about his Lord simply because God had granted him kingship? ᵉ Abraham said, "My Lord is the One Who grants life and causes death." He replied, "I too can give life and cause death." Abraham said, "Verily, God makes the sun to rise in the east. Can you then make it to rise in the west instead?" And so the disbeliever became dumbfounded. Indeed, God does not guide people who (deliberately) do wrong and are unjust.

²⁵⁹ Or, are you not aware of the one ᶠ who said to himself when he passed

---

ª See verse 35:28 and its corresponding footnote.
ᵇ Foot-rest.
ᶜ This verse which is known as *Ayatul Kursi* is one of the most, if not the most, sublime and significant verses in the Qur'an. It essentially summarizes God's unrivaled power and majesty where absolutely nothing can ever be comparable to Him.
ᵈ See verse 18:29
ᵉ This is a possible allusion to King Nemrod of Mesopotamia.
ᶠ Possible allusion to Prophet Ezra or Uzair in Arabic who lived sometime between 450 to 550 BC.

by a township which had been overturned on its roof (and fallen into utter ruin), "How can God bring this town back to life now that it is dead?" Thereupon God caused him to be dead for a hundred years. Then He brought him back to life, and asked, "How long have you remained here?" Answered the man, "Only a day or (maybe) less than a day." God said, "Nay! You have remained here for a hundred years. Just look at your food and drink - none of it has changed. And look at your donkey. (It has perished and its remains are only of decayed bones)." And surely We did this as a sign for mankind (to be mindful of Us). And then, God said to him, "Now look at the bones and witness how We reassemble them and cover them again with flesh." When it had all become clear to him, he said, "I know now that God has power over all things."

²⁶⁰ And (take heed also of the occasion) when Abraham said, "My Lord! Show me how You give life to the dead." God asked, "Do you not have faith (in Me)?" "Indeed, I do", said Abraham, "but I only wish to set my heart fully at rest." (And so) God said, "Take four birds and tame them. Then (cut them into pieces and) place a part of them on each mountain. After that, call them back and you will see them come to you in haste. Know that God is Almighty, All-Wise."

Spending in the Cause of Truth

²⁶¹ The parable of those who spend their wealth in the way of God is like a grain that sprouts seven ears, each bearing a hundred grains. And God multiplies the return to whomsoever He wills. Truly, God's bounties are infinite and He is All-Knowing. ²⁶² Those who spend their wealth for the sake of God and do not destroy their deeds with reminders of their generosity (to gain praises) or with hurtful words (that would injure the feelings of the recipient), will get their reward from their Lord. And they will have nothing to fear nor grieve. ²⁶³ A kind word and forgiveness is better than a charitable deed followed by hurtful remarks. Indeed, God is All-Sufficient, Most Forbearing.

²⁶⁴ O you who believe! Do not make your charities worthless by flaunting your benevolence or by injuring (the feelings of the recipients). These are the actions of those who spend their wealth only for show and praise and neither believe in God nor in the Last Day. Their parable is like a slippery rock covered with a thin layer of soil which gets washed away by rainfall, leaving it just a bare stone afterwards (free from the soil that covered it earlier). Such people will not gain any reward which they thought they had earned (from their seemingly good deeds). Verily, God does not guide disbelievers.

²⁶⁵ And the parable of those who spend their wealth out of a genuine desire to please God and out of their own inner certainty is like a garden on a

hillside. When heavy rain falls on it, it yields up twice its normal harvest. And even if it does not receive a heavy rain, a drizzle is sufficient. Verily, God sees all that you do.

²⁶⁶ Would any of you like to have a garden of date-palms and grapevines for him with rivers flowing underneath and therein grows all kinds of fruits, then he is overtaken by old age and has children who are still weak (to look after themselves); and then a fiery whirlwind strikes it and burns it down? This is how God makes His signs (and revelations) clear to you so that you may ponder.

²⁶⁷ O you who believe! Give charity (to others) out of the good things (We have enabled) you to earn and also out of what We have brought forth for you from the earth. Do not choose inferior things to give away as charity which you yourselves would not accept without turning your eyes in disdain. Know that God is All-Sufficient, Immensely Praiseworthy. ²⁶⁸ Satan threatens you with poverty and encourages you to commit indecency, whereas God promises you His forgiveness and bounty. Verily, God's bounties are infinite and He knows everything. ²⁶⁹ He grants wisdom to whomsoever He wills. Whoever is granted wisdom, he has surely been granted (privilege and) goodness in abundance. But none takes heed of this except those with insight and wisdom.

²⁷⁰ Whatever charity you give or vow (to give) are known to God. Those who do wrong (by withholding charity or spending in the way of Satan) will have none to help them (from God's wrath). ²⁷¹ If you give charity openly, that is good. But if you give it to the needy secretly, that is even better for you. He will absolve (some of) your sins from your misdeeds. And God is fully aware of all that you do.

²⁷² (O Prophet!) It is not your (task and) responsibility to compel people to follow guidance. Instead, it is God Who guides whomsoever He wills (that submits to Him in true sincerity and devotion). Whatever charity you give is for your own good, provided you do it (for God's sake) seeking His (pleasure and) countenance. And whatever you give in good cause will be repaid to you in full and you will not be wronged.

²⁷³ (Give charity) to the needy who are preoccupied in the service of God and are unable to move around freely in the land (to earn their livelihood). The ignorant may perceive them as self-sufficient because their self-respect refrains them (from asking for help). But you will be able to recognize them from their conduct of not asking help from others insistently. Whatever good you give is certainly known to God. ²⁷⁴ Those who spend their wealth (for the sake of God) by night and day either secretly or openly will have their reward with their Lord. They will have nothing to fear nor grieve.

The Evil of Usury

²⁷⁵ Those who gorge themselves on usury will not be able to rise up (on the Day of Resurrection) except like the rising of a person who is confounded by the touch of Satan. That is because they say, "Trading is no different than usury", whereas God has permitted trade but has forbidden usury. Whoever, after receiving this warning from his Lord refrains from it, may retain his past gains and it will be for God to judge him. But those who persist will be the inmates of the Fire and they will remain in there forever. ²⁷⁶ God deprives usury from all blessings but blesses charitable deeds with manifold increase. And God does not love anyone who is stubbornly ungrateful and engrossed in sin. ²⁷⁷ Indeed, those who truly believe (in Him), do good deeds, are steadfast in their prayer and spend in charity, they will have their reward from their Lord and they will have nothing to fear nor grieve.

²⁷⁸ O you who believe! Be ever mindful of God (and fear Him). Give up and forefeit any ursury that remains due to you if you are true believers. ²⁷⁹ If you do not, then be warned that God and His Messenger hereby declare war against you. But if you repent, then you will be entitled to (the return of) your principal without causing others and yourself to suffer losses. ²⁸⁰ And if (the debtor) is in difficulty, grant him time until ease. But if you (waive the debt entirely as a) gift of charity, it will be better for you, if you knew (the reward that God has in store for such magnanimous deed)!

²⁸¹ (O mankind!) Fear the day when you will all return to God. Every soul will be paid in full for what it has earned and no one will be wronged.

Safeguards for Financial Transactions

²⁸² O you who believe! When you contract a debt with one another for a fixed term, put this in writing. Have a scribe write it down between you with impartiality. The scribe who is given the gift of literacy by God should not refuse to write (as he is under obligation to do so). Let him who incurs the liability ^a dictate, fearing God - his Lord, and not diminishing anything from the settlement. And if the debtor is of limited understanding, or if he is weak or unable to dictate, then let his guardian dictate with impartiality. And call for evidence two witnesses from among your men. And if two men are not available, then one man and two women of your choice should bear witness so that if one of the women errs or forgets, the other may remind her. The witnesses must not refuse to give evidence when they are called upon. And do not loathe writing every contractual provision together with the time at which it falls due whether the amount is small or large. That is more equitable in the

---

^a The debtor.

sight of God, more reliable to serve as evidence, and more likely to prevent doubts from arising between you later. However, if it is a commercial transaction concluded on the spot among yourselves (that does not involve any element of debt), then no offence is committed if you do not write it down. (But it would be better to) have witnesses when your transaction is finalized (to help resolve any dispute that may arise later). And do not let either the scribe or the witnesses suffer any harm (at your hand). If you do, then you will be guilty of (crime and) sinful conduct. Be ever mindful of God (and keep your duty to Him diligently), for it is He who teaches you what you do not know and He has perfect knowledge of everything.

²⁸³ If you are traveling and cannot find a scribe, then the goods in hand may be pledged (as security against the debt). But if the creditor trusts the debtor, then (there is no need for security) and the debtor who is entrusted (with the debt) must fulfill the trust (by repaying it). May he fear (and be mindful of) God - his Lord! Do not conceal any testimony. He who does so clearly has a sinful heart. And God has perfect knowledge of everything that you do.

²⁸⁴ To God belongs all that is in the heavens and the earth. Whether you reveal or conceal your (evil) intentions, God will bring you to account (if you act upon it). But He forgives whomsoever He wills (that turns to Him in repentance) and punish whomsoever He wills (that stubbornly rejects the truth. Remember that) God has power over all things.

One Divine Message

²⁸⁵ The Messenger believes in what has been revealed to him by his Lord, and so do the believers. They all believe in God, His Angels, His Books, and His Messengers, making no distinction between any of His Messengers. And they say, "O Lord, we hear and we obey (Your command). So grant us Your forgiveness, our Lord. Indeed, to You is our final return."

²⁸⁶ God does not burden a soul with more than it can afford. In its favor will be whatever good it does, and in its loss will be whatever evil it does. (And so, the believers pray,) "Our Lord! Do not punish us if we forget or err. Our Lord! Do not burden us as You burdened those before us. Our Lord! Do not burden us with what we cannot bear. Pardon us, forgive our sins, and have mercy on us. You are our only Protector. So grant us victory over those who are bent on rejecting the truth (and commit injustice)."

3. Āli 'Imrān
[The Family of Joachim : 200 verses]

The name of this chapter takes after the household of Joachim the father of Mary - the virgin mother of Jesus, mentioned in verse 33 in relation to the story about the birth of Jesus and his Prophethood. Joachim is known as Imrān in the Qur'an. Arguments presented by the Qur'an in refuting his divinity as claimed by the Christians, occupies a big part of this chapter. In addition, this chapter also deals with (i) the articles of faith, namely the evidences and arguments regarding monotheism, the Prophethood of Muhammad and the truth of the Qur'an; (ii) the battles of Badr and Uhud and the lessons to be learnt from them, and (iii) the instructions and rules regarding *jihad* (fighting in the way of God), *hajj* (pilgrimage), *zakah* (tithe or purifying dues), and the illegality of *riba* (usury). The concluding verses of the chapter call for reflection in the creation of the heavens and the earth and contain a very appropriate prayer to be made by man to God, just like the end of chapter *Al-Baqarah*. The very last verse mentions the requisites of success in struggle for the truth, particularly the need for patience and perseverance.

In the name of God, the Most Gracious, the Most Compassionate.

Concepts Outlined

[1] *Alif Lām Mīm.* [2] God! There is no god except Him (and He alone deserves all worship). He is the Ever-Living, the Sustainer and Protector of all that exists.

[3] He has sent down this Book *a* to you with the truth (O Prophet), confirming (the same message) that was revealed when He sent down the Torah and the Gospel; [4] before this as guidance for people. He is indeed the One Who sent down the criterion (to distinguish truth from falsehood). Verily, those who are bent in denying God's signs and revelations will endure severe punishment (in the Hereafter). And God is Almighty, All-Able of Retribution.

[5] Indeed, nothing on earth and in the heaven is hidden from God. [6] He is the One Who fashions and shapes you in the wombs as He wills. There is no god except Him, the Almighty, the All-Wise.

Clear and Allegorical Verses

[7] It is He Who has revealed to you this Book containing verses that are

---

a The Qur'an.

absolutely clear and precise that form the essence of the Book, and others that are allegorical. Those whose hearts have swerved from the truth are keen to pursue the allegorical verses to create confusion through their misguided and false interpretations, whereas none grasps its (true and final) meaning except God. But those who are (firmly) grounded in knowledge say, "We believe in the entire Qur'an (even though we may still not completely understand its allegorical verses yet), for all of them are indeed from our Lord." None takes this seriously except those who are endowed with insight and wisdom. [8] (They pray to God by saying,) "Our Lord! Do not let our hearts deviate from the truth after You have guided us, and grant us mercy from Yourself. Indeed, You alone are the Bestower (of bounties without measure). [9] Our Lord! Indeed, You will gather mankind on a Day which there is no doubt about it. Verily, God never fails to fulfill His promise."

[10] As for those who reject the truth, neither their riches nor their children will in the least avail them against God. It is they who will be the fuel of the Fire; [11] just like the people of Pharaoh and those before them who denied and rejected Our signs and revelations. And so God seized them for their sins (and arrogance). And God is indeed severe in retribution. [12] So say to those who reject the truth, "Soon you will be vanquished and herded to Hell - an evil resting place!"

[13] Indeed there was a sign for you (to take heed) when the two armies met (on the battlefield of Badr). One was fighting for God's cause, and the other opposing Him. The believers saw their enemies with their very eyes as being (at least) twice their own number. But God strengthens with His help to whomsoever He wills (that wholeheartedly strives and fights in His cause). Surely there is a lesson in this for those with insight.

[14] Alluring in the eyes of men is the love for worldly pleasures that they desire - women and sons; heaped-up hoards of gold and silver; horses of high mark; and wealth of cattle and well-tilled land. These are (merely the short-lived) comforts for the fleeting life of this world. Whereas the most excellent place of return is surely with God. [15] Say (to them O Prophet), "Shall I inform you of something better than all these? For those who are ever-mindful (of God), their Lord will give them gardens which rivers flow from right beneath them and they will remain in there forever. And they will be with their pure spouses, all blessed by God. And God is All-Seeing (and All-Aware) of His servants.

[16] (They are) those who say, "Our Lord! Indeed, we have believed (and accepted the faith), so forgive our sins, and save us from the torment of the Fire." [17] They are the ones who are patient in adversity, always true to their word, truly devoted in their worship, spend in the cause of God, and pray for

forgiveness (from their innermost hearts) before dawn.

Concepts Clarified

[18] Behold! God (Himself) bears witness that there is no other god except Him, and so do the Angels and all who are endowed with knowledge and stand firm on justice - that there is none who is worthy of worship except Him, the Almighty, the All-Wise. [19] Verily, the (only true) religion in the sight of God is *Islam.* [a] Those who were given the earlier Scriptures did not dispute among themselves regarding the true religion until the revealed knowledge (of the Qur'an) was brought to them. (They fell into dispute) because of the envy and jealousy (that some shared) among themselves (towards you O Prophet). [b] Verily, whoever denies the truth of God's revelations - (beware! Know that) God is swift in reckoning!

[20] So if they argue with you, then say, "I have submitted myself (totally) to God and so have those who follow me." And ask those who were given the earlier revelations and also those unlettered (idolaters who have no revealed Scripture of their own), "Have you submitted yourselves (to God)?" If they submit, then surely they will be rightly guided. But if they turn away, then your duty is only to convey the message (and remind them). Verily, God is ever watchful over all His servants.

[21] Indeed, those who deny the truth of God's signs and revelations, unjustly kill their Prophets and those who stand up for justice, give them news of a grievous punishment (that they will never be able to escape from). [22] Those are the ones whose deeds have become worthless in this world and in the life to come too, and they will have none to help them (from the torment of the Blazing Fire).

[23] Have you not seen those who were given a share of the Scriptures? They are now invited to the Book of God [c] to settle their disputes but a party of them turned away in defiance. [24] That is because they say, "Never will the Fire touch us except for only a few days." Indeed, the false beliefs which they invented have deceived them and (caused them to betray) their (true) faith. [25] How then will they fare when We gather them altogether to witness the Day which there is no doubt (about its coming)? On that Day, every soul will be

---

[a] *Islam* means total submission to God; and by doing so, one will attain peace.

[b] The split between believers and disbelievers came after the Qur'an was revealed because of the disbelievers rejection of Muhammad's Prophethood and the new social order that he propagated alongside the belief in the Oneness of God.

[c] The Qur'an.

paid in full for what it has earned and none will be wronged.

²⁶ Say (O Prophet), "O God, Lord of all dominions! You grant dominion and control to whoever You will and take it away from whoever You will. You honor whoever You will and disgrace whoever You will. In Your hand is all that is good. Indeed, You have absolute power over everything. ²⁷ You cause night to enter into day and day into night, and You bring forth the living out from the dead and the dead out from the living. And You give provision to whoever You will without measure.

²⁸ Let not the believers take those who reject the truth as patrons (and allies) instead of their fellow believers. Whoever does so will cut-off himself from God's (help) unless it is to safeguard himself against the fear (of tyranny). And God warns you to beware of Him; for indeed, to God alone will all of you be returned. ²⁹ Say, "Whether you conceal what is in your hearts or reveal it, God knows everything. And He knows all that is in the heavens and in the earth. God has absolute power over everything." ³⁰ On the Day when every soul will find itself confronted with whatever good and evil it has done, it will wish that the time between itself and that Day were far apart. God warns you to beware of Him; and God is Most Kind towards His servants.

³¹ Say (to them O Prophet), "If you love God, then follow me, God will love you and forgive your sins.ᵃ   And God is Most Forgiving, Most Compassionate." ³² Say (further), "Obey God and His Messenger." But if they turn away, then indeed, God does not love those who disbelieve.

The Birth and Prophethood of Jesus

³³ God chose and raised Adam and Noah, and the family of Abraham and the family of Joachim ᵇ above all mankind. ³⁴ They were the descendants of one another. Verily, God hears all and knows all.

³⁵ (O Prophet! Narrate to them the story) when Joachim's wife said, "My Lord! Indeed, I vow to You that what is in my womb will be devoted to Your service. So accept this vow from me. Indeed, You alone are the One Who hears all and knows all."

³⁶ And so when she gave birth to a girl (instead of a boy), she said, "My Lord! Indeed I have given birth to a girl" - but God knew better what she had

---

ᵃ See verse 33:21 and its corresponding footnote.
ᵇ Known as Imrān in the Qur'an, but not the same Imrān or Amram (in Hebrew) who is the father of Moses, Aaron and Miriam that lived about 1600 years before Jesus.

delivered : A boy would surely not be able to play the role that the girl was destined for - "and I have named her Mary. *ᵃ* Surely, I seek refuge for her in You, and also for her descendants from Satan, the accursed." ³⁷ So her Lord graciously accepted the girl, blessed her with a pleasant upbringing and entrusted her to the care of Zachariah.*ᵇ* Whenever Zachariah visited her in the prayer chamber, he found her with some provision. He asked, "O Mary! Where did this come from?" She said, "This is from God! Indeed, God gives provision to whomsoever He wills without measure."

³⁸ Thereupon Zachariah prayed to his Lord, "O Lord! Grant me too, out of Your grace, a noble child. Indeed, You hear every prayer." ³⁹ And as he stood praying in the prayer chamber, the Angels called out to him saying, "God sends good news to you O Zachariah, of (a son to be named) John *ᶜ* who will confirm the true words of God. He will be noble, chaste and a Prophet from among the righteous."

⁴⁰ And so Zachariah said, "My Lord! How can I have a son when I have certainly reached old age and my wife is barren?" The (Angel) answered, "Such is God - He does what He wills!" ⁴¹ Zachariah said, "O my Lord! Grant me a sign (as confirmation of this miracle)" The (Angel) said, "Your sign will be that you will not speak with anyone for three days except through gestures. Remember your Lord unceasingly and glorify His perfection in the evening and in the morning."

⁴² And behold! The Angels said, "O Mary! Indeed, God has chosen you, purified you, and exalted you above (all) the women of the worlds. ⁴³ O Mary! Be obedient to your Lord. Prostrate and bow down with those who bow down (to God) in worship."

⁴⁴ This is an account of something unseen that We reveal to you (O Prophet.) You were not present with them when they cast lots to decide who among them should take charge of Mary; nor were you present while they were disputing about it with one another.

⁴⁵ (And so) the Angels said, "O Mary! Indeed, God gives you good news through a word from Him (about a son) who will be known as The Messiah - Jesus son of Mary. He will be held in honor in this world and also in the life to come, and be among the company of those who are brought close to God. ⁴⁶ And he will speak (about the truth) to people while he is in the cradle and as a grown man, and he will be among the righteous."

ᵃ Maryam in Arabic.
ᵇ Zakariya in Arabic
ᶜ Yahya in Arabic.

⁴⁷ She said, "My Lord, how will I have a child when no man has ever touched me?" The (Angel) answered, "Such is God - He creates what He wills. When He decrees something, suffice for Him to only command, 'Be' and it is! ⁴⁸ And He will teach your son the revelation and wisdom, and the Torah and the Gospel; ⁴⁹ and make him a Messenger to the children of Israel, saying, 'Indeed, I have brought you a sign from your Lord. I shall fashion for you out of clay the likeness of a bird. I shall breathe into it and by God's permission, it will become a living bird. I shall heal the blind and the leper, and bring the dead back to life by God's permission. I shall inform you about what you eat and what you store up in your homes. Surely, there is a sign (of truth) for you in all these if you are true believers."

⁵⁰ "And (I have been sent) to confirm (the message of truth) that came before me in the Torah and to make lawful for you some things that used to be forbidden. I have come to you with a sign from your Lord. Hence, be ever mindful of God and obey me. ⁵¹ Indeed, God is my Lord and your Lord, so worship Him alone. This is the straight path."

⁵² When Jesus became aware of their refusal (to acknowledge the truth), he asked, "Who will be my helpers in the cause of God?" His disciples replied, "We are your helpers in God's cause. We believe in God. So be our witness that we have fully submitted ourselves to Him. ⁵³ Our Lord, we believe in what You revealed and we follow the Messenger. Count us among those who bear witness (of the truth)." ⁵⁴ But the disbelievers (among the children of Israel) plotted and schemed (against Jesus). God planned too (and brought their scheming to nothing). Verily, God is the best of all planners.

⁵⁵ Behold! God said, "O Jesus! Indeed, I shall end your term (on earth) and exalt you to Me (in rank and honor), and purify you from (the malicious lies invented by) those who refuse to accept the truth. And I shall place those who follow you above those who reject the truth until the Day of Resurrection. In the end, it is to Me you will all be returned and I shall judge between all of you about what you used to differ.⁵⁶ Then as for those who are bent on denying the truth, I shall inflict on them severe punishment in this world and in the life to come. And they will have none to help them; ⁵⁷ whereas for those who believe and do righteous deeds, He will grant them their reward in full. And God does not love those who are unjust."

⁵⁸ (Indeed O Muhammad!) What We recite to you here is among the signs (of your Prophethood) and a wise reminder (for mankind). ⁵⁹ Verily, in the sight of God, the nature of Jesus is similar to Adam whom He created out of soil and then said to him, "Be!" and he was. ⁶⁰ (Verily,) truth is from your Lord. So do not be among those who fall into doubt.

⁶¹ (O Prophet!) If anyone should dispute with you about this truth after all the knowledge has come to you, then say to them, "Come! Let us call our sons and your sons, our women and your women, ourselves and yourselves. Then, let us humbly pray and invoke God's curse upon who among us are the liars." ⁶² Indeed, this is the true narration. And there is no other god except the only One God. And indeed, God is Almighty, All-Wise. ⁶³ And if they turn away, then indeed, God has full knowledge of those who spread corruption.

⁶⁴ Say, "O People of earlier revelation! Let us come to a common understanding that we shall worship none but God, that we shall not associate partners with Him, and that we shall not take one another for Lords besides God." And if they turn away, then say, "Bear witness that we have fully submitted ourselves to God (alone)."

The Heirs of Abraham's Faith

⁶⁵ O people of earlier revelation! Why do you argue about Abraham when both the Torah and the Gospel were not revealed until (long) after him? Have you no sense? ⁶⁶ This is the type of people you are - always arguing in matters that you know very little about. Why must you now argue about what you know nothing (other than what you make up from your own misguided conjecture)? Indeed, God knows everything, while you do not.

⁶⁷ Verily, Abraham was neither a Jew ᵃ nor a Christian but he was an upright monotheist who submitted himself only to God alone. He (turned away from all that is false and) was not from among those who associated partners with God. ⁶⁸ Indeed, the people who have the best claim to Abraham are surely those who follow his ways, as does this Prophet (now) ᵇ and all those who believe (in his creed). Indeed, God is surely the Guardian of the believers.

Hatred, Jealousy and Hypocrisy

⁶⁹ A party of the people of earlier revelation wish to lead you astray (because of their jealousy and hatred towards you). But they mislead none except themselves and they do not realize it.

⁷⁰ O people of earlier revelation! Why do you reject God's (divine) signs

---

ᵃ The Jews originated as an ethnic and religious group from the descendants of Jacob who was also known as Israel. He was the son of Isaac and the grandson of Abraham. Therefore, Abraham was not a Jew because the Jewish people did not exist during his time.
ᵇ Muhammad.

(and revelation to Muhammad) while you are witnesses to their truth? ⁷¹ O people of earlier revelation! Why do you mix truth with falsehood and hide this when you know (what you are doing is wrong)?

⁷² Some people of earlier revelation say (to one another, "Pretend to Muhammad's followers that you) believe in what has been revealed by declaring this at the beginning of the day. Then renounce this faith at the end of the day so that they will (become doubtful and) return to their old faith." ⁷³ (They also say among themselves,) "Do not trust anyone except the one who follows your faith." Tell them (O Prophet), "Indeed, true guidance comes from God. Do you fear if someone other than yourselves may be given knowledge just like what was given to you earlier, and they would be in the position to challenge you before your Lord (on the Day of Judgment)? Behold! Know that all bounties belong to God alone and He grants it to whomsoever He wills. Verily, God is Infinite, All-Knowing; ⁷⁴ and He chooses for His grace whomsoever He wills. Indeed, God is limitless in His great bounty."

⁷⁵ Among the people of earlier revelation, there are some who will return all the treasures that you entrust them with. Yet there are also some who will not give back a single coin until you demand and insist, because they say, "It is not a sin for us to usurp the rights of the unlettered people." *^a* They (have no qualms to) fabricate lies against God even though they know (it is sinful). ⁷⁶ Surely, whoever fulfills his promise (to God) and guards himself (against evil), indeed God loves those who are ever mindful of Him (and strive to keep their duty to Him diligently). ⁷⁷ Verily, those who trade away their promise with God and their oaths for a trifling gain (of this fleeting world) will have no share (of anything good) in the life to come. God will neither speak to them, nor cast a look on them on the Day of Resurrection, nor will He cleanse them of their sins. For them is a grievous suffering.

⁷⁸ And indeed, some among them twist their tongues when quoting the Scripture to make you think what they say is from the Scripture whereas it is not. They (audaciously) claim that it is from God whereas it is not. They (despicably) lie about God while they know (it is wrong).

⁷⁹ It is not conceivable that anyone to whom God has given the Scripture, wisdom and Prophethood would ever say to people, "Worship me instead of God!" Instead, he would say, "Be devoted to God (and spread the truth of His message) because you have been teaching the Scripture and studying them (diligently)." ⁸⁰ Nor would he command you to take the Angels and the Prophets as your Lords. How could he tell you to become disbelievers after you have submitted yourselves to God?

---

^a The Jews of Madinah call the non-Jews (or Gentiles) unlettered or illiterate people.

⁸¹ And behold, God accepted this pledge (from the followers of earlier revelations) through the Prophets, "This is the Scripture and wisdom which I give you. And when a Prophet comes to you (later) confirming the truth that is already in your possession, you will believe and help him." So God asked, "Do you affirm and accept My covenant on this condition?" They answered, "Yes, we affirm and accept!" God said, "Then bear witness (to what you have pledged), and I am with you among the witnesses too." ⁸² Whoever turns away after that, they are truly (rebellious and) disobedient.

⁸³ Do they seek a faith other than in Almighty God when whatever is in the heavens and the earth has willingly or unwillingly submitted to Him, since it is to Him they will all be returned? ⁸⁴ Say, "We believe in God and what has been sent down (as revelation) to us, and in what was sent down to Abraham, Ishmael, Isaac, Jacob and their descendants, and also in what was given by their Lord to Moses and Jesus and all the Prophets. We make no distinction between any of them and to Almighty God alone do we fully submit ourselves." ⁸⁵ (Verily,) he who seeks a religion other than *Islam, ͣ* it will not be accepted from him and he will be among the losers in the life to come.

⁸⁶ How will God guide those who chose to reject faith after they had accepted it and bore witness that the Messenger is true, especially after clear evidence had been brought to them? Verily, God does not guide those who are unjust. ⁸⁷ For such people, the requital (for their arrogance) is Hell and the curse of God, the Angels and all (righteous) men. ⁸⁸ They will remain (in that state) forever. Neither will their suffering be lightened, nor will they be granted respite; ⁸⁹ except those who repent and mend their ways afterwards. Then surely, God is Most Forgiving, Most Compassionate.

⁹⁰ But those who return to disbelief after having accepted true faith and then grow more stubborn in their rejection of the faith, never will their (claimed) repentance be accepted. They are the ones who have truly gone astray. ⁹¹ Indeed, those who oppose the truth and die as disbelievers, all the gold that is enough to fill the earth will never be accepted as ransom to save them from the grievous torment that awaits them, and they will find no helpers (to rescue them on the Day of Judgment).

One God, One Faith

⁹² You will never attain true piety unless you spend on others out of what you dearly love and cherish, and God has full knowledge of what you spend.

ͣ Complete submission to the will of Almighty God alone.

⁹³ All food was initially lawful to the children of Israel except what Israel*ᵃ* forbade for himself (and was subsequently followed by his descendants as a tradition) before the Torah was revealed (without any mention of this). So (challenge those Jews by) saying, "Bring the Torah and recite a passage from it (that decreed this prohibition) if what you claim is true." ⁹⁴ And whoever (continues to) fabricate a lie after this and attributes it to God, such people are indeed evildoers (who have committed injustice). ⁹⁵ Say (to them O Prophet, "Indeed,) God has spoken the truth. Follow then, the creed of Abraham the upright monotheist, who turned away from all that is false, for he was not one of those who associated anything with God."

⁹⁶ Behold! The first House of God ever built for mankind is the one at Bakka,*ᵇ* a blessed site and a source of guidance for all mankind. ⁹⁷ In it you will find clear messages (of God's grace) and the station of where Abraham once stood (to conduct his worship). Whoever enters it will find inner peace (and a sense of security). Pilgrimage to this House is a duty owed to God by everyone who is able (and has the means) to undertake it. Whoever disbelieves and disobeys this commandment should know that God does not need anything from anyone.

⁹⁸ Say, "O People of earlier revelation! Why do you refuse to acknowledge the truth of God's signs and revelations? Do you not realize that He is a witness to everything you do?" ⁹⁹ Say (further), "O People of earlier revelation! Why do you prevent those who believe from God's path, seeking to make it appear crooked when you know that it is the truth? God is never once unaware of what you do."

¹⁰⁰ O you who believe! If you obey some of those people of earlier revelation, they will turn you into disbelievers after you have attained faith. ¹⁰¹ And how can you sink into disbelief when God's revelations are being recited to you (directly) while His Messenger is in your midst? Whoever holds firmly to God's (revelations), he will surely be guided to the straight path.

¹⁰² O you who believe! Be ever conscious of God with all the consciousness that is due to Him, and do not allow death to overtake you unless you have truly submitted yourselves to Him. ¹⁰³ Hold firmly to God's rope altogether and do not be divided among yourselves. Remember God's favor to you when you were once enemies to one another and then He brought your hearts together by His grace and turned you into brothers. And (remember) when you were once at the edge of a fiery pit before He saved you from it. This is how God reveals His clear signs to you so that you may be

---

ᵃ Jacob or Yaqub in Arabic.
ᵇ This is the ancient name of Makkah.

rightly guided (and remember Him much).

¹⁰⁴ And let there arise among you a group of people inviting to all that is good (through knowledge and wisdom) urging (one another to defend and practice) what is right, and forbidding what is wrong. It is they who will attain true success. ¹⁰⁵ Do not follow the example of those who became divided and fell into conflict with one another after all evidence of truth has come to them. A severe punishment awaits such people. ¹⁰⁶ On that Day, some faces will shine (with happiness) and some faces will become dark (with grief). Those whose faces have darkened (will be told), "Did you deny the truth after you had embraced it earlier? Taste then this punishment for having sunk into disbelief!" ¹⁰⁷ But as for those whose faces will radiantly shine on that Day, they will be within God's grace *ᵃ* and will remain in there forever..

¹⁰⁸ These are the revelations of God that We recite to you in truth (O Prophet). And God wills no injustice to all His creatures. ¹⁰⁹ To God belongs all that is in the heavens and in the earth, and to Him (alone) will all things finally return.

¹¹⁰ (O companions of the Prophet!) You are the best community that has ever been brought forth for (the good of) mankind - you urge (to defend and practice) what is right and forbid what is wrong, *ᵇ* and you believe in God. Had the people of earlier revelation attained to (this kind of) faith, it would have surely been better for them. (But only a few) among them are believers while most of them are defiantly disobedient. ¹¹¹ They will never be able to harm you except a little annoyance. Even if they come out to fight you, they will only turn their backs towards you (and flee). They will not get any help.

¹¹² They will be struck with humiliation wherever they are unless (they bind themselves) in a bond with God and also with men.*ᶜ* They have certainly

---

ᵃ Paradise.
ᵇ The same exhortation is repeated in verse 114. Unfortunately, many Muslim communities and societies conservatively apply this exhortation by typically limiting their focus to prohibit free and unrestricted social interaction among non *mahram* male and female adults (i.e. men and women who have no religious restriction to enter into marriage) to prevent fornication (verse 17:32), but neglect to address the evils of social injustice, oppression and corruption that would destroy their societies for many generations. This verse must be read in connection with verse 112 to understand its full context. Simply put, by being apathetic towards injustice, God will punish these societies with humiliation. See verse 6:123 and its footnote.
ᶜ This is one of the most fundamental concepts in Islam that has been grossly overlooked and neglected. It clearly outlines every individual's duty to strive in building and guarding an excellent vertical relationship with God while concurrently maintaining

incurred God's wrath upon themselves and will be afflicted with misery because they persisted in denying God's revelations and even killed some Prophets unjustly. All because of their disobedience and continued transgression. [113] (But) not all of them are alike. Among the people of earlier revelation, (you will find) some who are upright. They recite the verses of God in the depths of the night and prostrate themselves in worship. [114] They believe in God and in the Last Day and encourage (others to defend and practice) what is right and forbid what is wrong, and they hasten in doing good deeds. Such

---

an excellent horizontal relationship with fellow humans through mutual respect, and by ensuring that justice must prevail at all times. Failure to balance these two bonds of relationship successfully will result in humiliation. Those who think they can get away by over-zealously adopting a ritual-centric life alone without fully understanding and embracing their underlying meaning and purpose may run into the likelihood of not feeling any sense of guilt and remorse when they usurp and violate the rights, honor and dignity of others (see chapter 107), or by being complicit in the evils perpetrated by others (verse 11:113). These people will face dire consequences on the Day of Judgment. In relation to this, Abu Huraira reported that the Messenger of God once asked a group of us, "Do you know who is a bankrupt?" Someone answered, "A bankrupt among us is the one who neither has any *dirham* with him nor wealth." Answered the Prophet in return, "(No.) The bankrupt from my *ummah* is the one who will come on the Day of Resurrection with (merits from) his prayers, fasts and charities that he gave out but he would find himself bankrupt on that day because he hurled abuses, made calumnies, consumed wealth unlawfully, shed blood, and harmed others (during his time on earth). The merits from the good deeds that he has earned will be credited into the account of those who suffered at his hand. And if his good deeds fall short to clear the account, then the sins of those he had wronged will be entered into his account. In the end, he will be thrown into the Hellfire (because all his good deeds have vanished due to the injustices that he committed)." [Sahih Muslim, no. 2581]. On the other hand, those who exhibit good conduct and treat others well but refuse to submit to their Creator will also face serious consequences on the Day of Judgment. Majority Muslim societies and nations exhibit problems depicted by the former scenario while non-Muslim societies and nations exhibit the latter. In the former, we see problems of rampant corruption and social injustices that impoverish and cause hardship to its masses because most of its people see Islam as a religion that is limited to rituals alone, hence they become apathetic and blind towards injustice and corruption committed by their leaders. In the latter we see societies and nations that achieve great material progress but are besieged with spiritual emptiness and moral decadence that often lead to widespread collapse in family institutions and high suicide incidences. Islam is all about successfully balancing both the vertical and horizontal relationships with God and His creations respectively. Prophet Muhammad was sent by God as grace and mercy to all the worlds (verse 21:107) to teach and guide mankind to achieve this balance. See also verses 4:135 and 5:8 together with their corresponding footnotes.

people are among the righteous; [115] and they will not be denied (the reward) for whatever good deeds they do. And God knows those who are mindful of Him (and strive hard to keep their duty to Him diligently).

[116] Indeed, as for those who reject the truth, neither their wealth nor their children will ever avail them against God. They are the inmates of the Fire and will remain in there forever. [117] The parable of what they spend in the life of this world is like a frosty wind that strikes the harvest of a people who have sinned against themselves and destroyed their own deeds. It is not God Who is unjust to them, but it is they who have brought injustice upon themselves.

[118] O you who believe! Do not take for intimate friends those who are not of your kind (that are against the truth). They will not spare any opportunity to ruin you as they love to see you in distress. Their vehement hatred is clearly evident from what they say, and what they conceal in their hearts is far worse. We have certainly made the signs clear to you, if (only) you (would) use reason (to understand and take heed). [119] Behold! It is you who are prepared to love them but they will not reciprocate even though you believe in all the Books. [a] When they meet you, they assert, "We believe (as you believe)" but when they are alone, they bite their fingertips in rage against you. Say to them (O Prophet, "May you) perish in your rage!" Verily, God has full knowledge of what is in their hearts. [120] When good fortune comes your way, it grieves them. But if misfortune befalls you, they rejoice. If you remain steadfast and are always mindful of God, their plot will not harm you in any way. Indeed, God encompasses everything they do.

Lessons for All Muslim Generations

[121] (O Prophet! Remember the day) when you set out from your home in the early hours of the morning to assign the believers to their battle posts. [b] Verily, God hears all and knows all; [122] when the two parties [c] among you had suddenly become fainthearted (as a result of a scheme by the hypocrites who reneged in their pledge to fight alongside you). But God protected them (by strengthening their hearts and forgiving their temporary lapse). Verily, it is in God that the believers must place their trust (to attain success and victory).

[123] (O believers!) God had indeed helped you in Badr when you were weak. Hence, be ever mindful of God (and keep your duty to Him diligently)

---

[a] The Torah, Psalms, Gospel, and the Qur'an.
[b] This is in reference to the battle of Uhud to face the idolaters of Makkah who were seeking revenge for their defeat in the battle of Badr.
[c] The clans of *Bani Harithah* and *Bani Salamah*.

so that you will (always) be grateful (for all the favors and mercy that He has bestowed upon you).

[124] (O Prophet! The courage and spirit of the believers were certainly regained and revived) when you said to them, "Is it not enough for you that your Lord sent down three thousand Angels to help you (in Badr)? [125] Surely, if you are patient (in adversity) and are always mindful of Him, your Lord will reinforce you (further) with five thousand (swooping) Angels with marks (of distinction if the infidels attack you)."

[126] And God did not convey this message to you (O believers), except as good news so that your hearts will take comfort from it and (be truly certain that) there is no help except from God, the Almighty, the All-Wise. [127] (He also sent this aid) to help cut-off a part of the disbelievers' army and frustrate them so that they would retreat in utter disappointment.

[128] (O Prophet!) It is not for you to decide whether He will accept their repentance or punish them, for they are surely evil wrongdoers. [129] And to God belongs all that is in the heavens and in the earth. He forgives whomsoever He wills (that turns to Him in repentance) and punishes whomsoever He wills (that rejects the truth). And God is Most Forgiving, Most Compassionate.

[130] O you who believe! Do not gorge yourselves on usury, multiplying your money many times over (causing difficulty to others). Be mindful of God (and fear His wrath) so that you may be truly successful. [131] Guard yourselves against the Fire which is prepared for those who reject the truth; [132] and obey God and the Messenger so that you may be graced with His mercy. [133] Hasten towards the forgiveness of your Lord, and a Paradise that is as vast as the heavens and the earth prepared for those who are ever mindful of God (and continuously strive to fulfill their duty to Him diligently). [134] They are those who spend (generously in His cause) whether in prosperity or hardship. They are those who also restrain and subdue their anger, and (readily) forgive others. Verily, God loves those who (are magnanimous and) excel in good deeds.

[135] They are also those who remember God and pray for the forgiveness of their sins whenever they commit a gross indecency or any wrong against themselves. Verily, who is it that can forgive sins other than God? And they do not knowingly persist in doing wrong [136] The reward for such people is forgiveness from their Lord and gardens which rivers flow from right beneath them and they will remain in there forever.. How excellent is the reward for those who labor!

A High Price for Paradise

¹³⁷ God's universal law (of cause and effect) has certainly prevailed before you (and will always prevail forever). So journey upon the earth to see and learn about the natural consequences of those who stubbornly denied (and rejected) truth. ¹³⁸ This (revelation) is a clear declaration for mankind, and a guidance and lesson for those who are mindful of God (and strive to fulfill their duty to Him diligently). ¹³⁹ So do not be disheartened and grieve (over the trials that you face while you strive in God's way), for you are bound to rise high if you truly put your faith in God (and His Messenger).ᵃ

¹⁴⁰ If you suffer an injury, know that those (who fought against you) also suffered similar injuries too. We make such alternation (of victory and defeat) in the affairs of men to make evident those who are the true men of faith and also to select martyrs from among you. God does not love those who commit injustice. ¹⁴¹ (God does this) so that He may purify those who believe and destroy those who are bent on opposing the truth.

¹⁴² Or do you think that you can enter Paradise before God makes evident who among you fought hard in His cause and remained steadfast? ¹⁴³ Verily, you used to wish for death in (God's cause) before you came face to face with it. So (why are of you hesitant to fight now after) you have finally seen it with your own eyes?

¹⁴⁴ (O believers! Verily,) Muhammad is no more than a Messenger of God, and many Messengers have certainly came and gone before him. If he dies or is slain, will you turn back on your heels (and give up your faith)? Know that whoever gives up his faith will cause no harm to God in any way

---

ᵃ This footnote is the explanation for verses 137-139. The law of "cause and effect" comes under God's universal law of nature which is called *Sunatullah*. It applies to all earthly beings. In simple terms, what goes around comes around. Those who are evil will never be able to escape punishment. Wealth and power may buy temporary immunity in this world for someone who rejects the truth and commits injustice, but he will never be able escape death and the grievous suffering that awaits him in the next life. Likewise, those who are steadfast in God's path will be generously rewarded in the next life if they patiently endure the tests of worldly tribulations with firm and unwavering faith (see verses 29:2-3). In essence, how we lead our lives during our temporary stay in this world will determine how we end up permanently in the next world. Some among us will receive part of our good and bad share in this world, while some may be spared but will receive their full share of requital later, greatly compounded. Either way, this verse is to remind us that every cause or action has a specific and predictable effect, and every single one of us is subjected to this *Sunatullah*. In essence, we reap what we sow.

and God will only reward those who are grateful to Him. [145] No soul will ever die except by God's permission at an appointed time. Whoever desires the reward of this world, We shall grant him thereof. And whoever desires the reward of the life to come, We shall grant him thereof. And We shall (only) reward those who are grateful to Us (with the best reward in the life to come).

[146] How many Prophets have fought together with many devout men alongside them? But they never lost heart for what they had to suffer for God's cause, neither did they weaken (in will) nor succumb (to temptations). And God loves those who are firm and steadfast (in His cause). [147] And not were their words except that they said, "Our Lord! Forgive our sins and our excesses in our affairs. Make our feet firm and grant us victory over those who disbelieve (and are bent on rejecting the truth)." [148] So God granted their due reward in this world while the best reward awaits them in the life to come. And God loves those who (are righteous and) excel in good deeds.

Forgiveness of a Disastrous Error

[149] O you who believe! If you obey those who disbelieve, they will (corrupt your faith and) turn you back on your heels, and you will surely become losers. [150] But no! God is your Protector and He is the Best of all Helpers. [151] We shall cast terror in the hearts of those who are bent on opposing the truth because they associated partners with God - something which He has never granted any authority (or permission for this). And their refuge will be the Fire. What a wretched place of return for these evil wrongdoers!

[152] And indeed, God fulfilled His promise to you when you were slaying your foes with His permission (in the battle of Uhud) until you faltered and fell into dispute about the (Prophet's) command. You disobeyed after God brought you in sight (of the spoils) which you intensely desired. Among you are some who desire (the temporary gains of) this world just as there are some who desire (the everlasting rewards of) the life to come. Then He denied you victory (by preventing you from defeating your foes) to put you to test. Thereafter, He forgave you (and effaced your sins), for God is indeed limitless in His bounty to those who believe and have faith in Him.

[153] (O Believers! Call to mind) when you fled and ran uphill without casting a glance at anyone while the Messenger was calling you from behind. Thereupon, God repaid you with distress upon distress so that you would not grieve (and lament) over (the spoils) that had escaped you, nor over (the disaster) that had befallen you. And God is aware of all that you do.

[154] Then, after this distress, He sent down upon you a sense of security - a slumber that overcame some of you (followed by inner calm); while others who cared only for themselves were stirred to anxiety by their own fancies. Instead of seeing the truth, they had (unjust and foolish) suspicions about God like the pagans in the times of ignorance (after seeing that many believers were killed in this war unlike in Badr). And so they asked, "Did we have any power of decision in this matter? Say (to them O Prophet), "Surely, all affairs rest with God." But they hide in their hearts what they dare not reveal to you. (In fact, what they had actually meant to tell you was,) "If we had any say in this matter instead of merely following you, none of us would have been killed here." Say (to them), "Even if you had remained in your homes, those for whom death was decreed would certainly have gone forth to the place of their death. Indeed, it was God's will to test your faith (by decreeing this battle) so that what was really in your hearts was purged (for others to see). Indeed, God has full knowledge of the secrets that you conceal in your hearts."

[155] As for those of you who turned their backs on the day when the two armies met (in Uhud), it was Satan who caused them to slip because of their misdeeds. But God has forgiven them (and effaced their sins when they repented and returned to the battlefield). Indeed, God is Most Forgiving, Most Forbearing.

[156] O you who believe! Behave not like the disbelievers who speak of their brothers who died during their journey or while engaged in war as follows: "Had they remained with us, they would not have died or been killed." God will cause such thoughts to become a source of bitter regret and anguish in their hearts. Verily, it is God who decides and grants life and death, and He sees everything that you do. [157] And if you get killed (while fighting) in God's cause or die (during your journey to the battlefield), His forgiveness and mercy on you is far better than all the wealth that those (who stayed behind) could amass (during their lifetime). [158] And whether you die or get killed, only to God alone will you be ultimately gathered.

The Prophet's Message of Compassion

[159] (O Prophet!) It was by the grace of God that you dealt gently with your companions and followers. Had you been harsh or hard-hearted, they would have surely deserted you. So pardon them and ask God's forgiveness for them. Take counsel with them in matters (of public concern) and when you have come to a decision upon a course of action to take, place your trust in God. Verily, God loves those who place their trust in Him. [160] If God helps you, nothing can ever overcome you. But if He forsakes you, then who is it that can help you besides Him? In God then, let the (faithful) believers place their trust.

[161] It is not conceivable that any Prophet would deceive (and illegally take anything from the spoils of war for himself). Anyone who does so will bring along with him on the Day of Resurrection what he has illegally taken; and (on that Day) every soul will be repaid in full for whatever he has done and none will be wronged.

[162] Can he who strives to gain God's pleasure be compared to the one who has incurred God's wrath and whose final place of return is in the Hellfire, which is a truly wretched destination? [163] In God's sight, these two are certainly on (entirely) different ranks. Verily, God is All-Seeing and Most Observant of everything that they do. [164] Certainly, God bestowed a great favor upon the faithful believers when he raised among them a Messenger - reciting to them His verses, purifying their corrupt faith (and cleansing their souls), teaching them about the Book, and (imparting) wisdom (to them through his examples and sayings) whereas they were clearly astray before.

Priorities Defined

[165] And when you (O believers) were afflicted with grief (from the loss in Uhud as a result of your disobedience to the Prophet) whereas you had (victoriously) inflicted disaster upon your enemy (in Badr previously with an injury that was) twice as great, is it fair for you to ask, "How did this calamity befall us now?" Say (to them O Prophet), "It is from your own doing." Verily, God has full power over everything.

[166] The misfortune which befell you when the two armies met in Uhud was by God's permission to mark the true believers and make them evident. [167] It was also to make evident the hypocrites (who live among you. Such were the people) when it was said to them, "Come! Let's fight in the cause of God!" or, "Defend yourselves!", they answered, "If only we knew that it would (really) come to a fight, we would have indeed followed you." Indeed, they were nearer to disbelief (and apostasy) on that day than to belief and faith for saying with their mouths what was not in their hearts. Behold! God is fully aware of what they conceal. [168] Such are the ones who, as they sat (at home), said of their brothers, "Had they listened to us, they would not have been killed." Tell them, "If what you say is true, then prevent and ward-off death from yourselves (when it comes to you)."

[169] And do not think of those who are slain in the way of God as dead. Nay! They are alive in the sight of their Lord (in a different realm) and they are given provision. [170] They rejoice in (the martyrdom) which God has bestowed upon them out of His bounty. They receive good news about those who have not yet joined them (in their bliss) but are left behind (dedicated in

their fight against the enemies of God) without fear and grief (because of their utmost faith in God). [171] Indeed, they rejoice in the blessings and bounty from God and (in the promise) that God will not let the reward for those who truly believe in Him go waste.

[172] As for those who responded to the call of God and His Messenger (to advance to Hamra al-Asad and face the idolaters of Makkah in the aftermath of Uhud) even after injury and misfortune had just befallen them, a magnificent reward awaits those who persevered in doing good and are ever mindful of God. [173] They are the ones who, when asked and warned by other people, "Do you not fear your enemies that have mustered a great force against you?", grew more firm in their faith and replied, "God's help is All-Sufficient for us. Verily, He is The Best Protector and Disposer of all affairs." [174] As a result, they returned (from the battlefield) unharmed with blessings and bounty from God, for they had striven to please God. Indeed, God is limitless in His great bounty and grace. [175] Verily, it is Satan who instills fear of his allies into you. So fear them not. Instead, fear (and be mindful of) Me alone if you truly believe in Me.

[176] (O Prophet!) Do not be grieved by the actions of those who are quick to reject the truth. Their (arrogant defiance) can do no harm to God. In fact, God does not intend to give them any share (of victory and happiness) in the life to come. A great punishment awaits them instead. [177] Remember! Those who trade away faith in exchange for denial and disbelief will in no way harm God. For them is a grievous punishment. [178] Those who are bent on opposing the truth should not think that when We postpone their punishment, it is good for them. In fact, We grant them respite so that they will add more to their sins. (In the end,) they will suffer a humiliating punishment.

[179] (O you who deny the truth!) It is not God's plan to abandon the believers to your way of life. And to that end, He will set apart the bad from the good (for the believers to discern). And it is not God's wish to give you any insight into the secrets of the unseen. Instead, God chooses from among His Messengers whom He wills (to intimate such knowledge). So believe in God and (all) His Messengers. If you believe and are always mindful of Him (and strive hard to keep your duty to Him diligently), you will be given a magnificent reward.

Main Issues Re-emphasized

[180] And let not those who are stingy in spending in God's cause think that it is good and clever to withhold the bounty that God has blessed them with

(from sharing some of it with others). Nay! It is actually bad for them. God will hang all the wealth that they hoard like a necklace around their necks on the Day of Resurrection. It is God Who will (finally) inherit the heavens and the earth, and He is fully aware of everything that you do.¹⁸¹ Certainly, God has heard the words of those who said, "Indeed, God is poor and we are rich." We shall certainly record everything they said together with their unjust killings of the Prophets. And on the Day of Judgment, We shall say to them, "Taste now the punishment of the Blazing Fire!" [182] Such is the requital for your own misdeeds (and arrogance. Remember that) God is never unjust to His servants.

[183] As for those who claim, "Indeed, God has ordained that we should not believe in a Messenger until he brings to us a sacrifice that is consumed by fire", ask them (O Prophet), "If what you claim is true, then why did you kill the Messengers before me who came to you with all evidence of the truth and with the same sign (that you are asking from me now)?" [184] (So do not despair) if they reject you (O Prophet)! They did the same to other Messengers who came before you with clear signs (and evidence) together with Scriptures (of divine wisdom) and enlightening revelation.

[185] Every soul will taste death and your reward will only be paid in full on the Day of Resurrection. Whoever is kept away from the Fire and is admitted into Paradise will indeed attain the greatest triumph, for the life of this world is nothing but (a deception and brief) enjoyment of self-delusion. [186] You will surely be tested in your wealth and your souls. And you will certainly hear many hurtful remarks from those to whom revelation was granted before your time and also from those who ascribe partners to God. But if you remain steadfast in true faith and maintain your consciousness of God, that would be the best resolution in your affairs.

[187] And (take heed of the occasion) when God accepted a solemn pledge from those who were granted earlier revelation and were then commanded, "Make My revelations clear to mankind and do not conceal them." Instead, they cast this pledge behind their backs and exchanged it for a trifling gain. How vile was their bargain! [188] Those who rejoice in their misdeeds and love to be praised for the good deeds that they have not done should not think that they will escape punishment. A grievous torment awaits them (in the life to come). [189] To God belongs the dominion of the heavens and the earth, and it is God Who has full power over everything.

Attitude of the Believers

[190] Indeed, in the creation of the heavens and the earth and the alternation

of night and day, there are signs (to ponder) for those who are endowed with insight and wisdom. [191] (They are) those who remember God while standing, sitting, and lying on their sides, and they reflect on the creation of the heavens and the earth, then cry out, "O our Lord! You have surely not created all this without purpose. *ᵃ* All glory belongs to You alone (Who are truly free from all imperfections)! So keep us safe from the torment of the Fire.

[192] Our Lord! Whomsoever You cast into the Fire will indeed be in eternal disgrace and there will be none to help and rescue the wrongdoers. [193] Our Lord! Indeed we have heard someone calling to true faith saying, 'Believe in your Lord!', and we have believed. O our Lord! Forgive us. Erase and remove our sinful deeds, and let us die the death of the truly virtuous. [194] Our Lord! Grant us what You have promised through Your Messengers and save us from the shame on the Day of Resurrection. Indeed, You never fail to fulfill Your promise." [195] And so their Lord responded to them, "Indeed, I shall not let the good deeds of those among you, whether male or female, to go waste. (Both are equal in reward,) for you are all the offspring of one another. Those who emigrated (to forsake the domain of evil) and were driven out from their homes, and those who suffered persecution in My cause, fought for it and were killed - I shall certainly erase and remove their sinful deeds and admit them into gardens which rivers flow from right beneath them as a reward from God. Verily, only with God rests the most excellent reward."

[196] Do not be deceived by the free movement (and prosperity) of the disbelievers (who seem to be able to do as they please) on earth (while you are being restricted by their oppression). [197] Their enjoyment is brief and their ultimate home is in the Hellfire. How wretched it is as a resting place! [198] Whereas those who are always mindful of their Lord (and strive to fulfill their duty to Him diligently) will be given gardens which rivers flow from right beneath them and they will remain in there forever.. This will be their welcome from God and (surely) what is with God is the best for those who are truly virtuous.

[199] And indeed, among the followers of earlier revelation, there are those who truly believe in God and in what has been revealed to you (O Prophet), and what was revealed to them (earlier). They humble themselves before God and do not trade away God's revelations for a trifling gain. They will have their reward with their Lord. Indeed, God is swift in reckoning!

[200] O you who believe! Be steadfast and patient (in adversity and in doing good deeds). Be ever ready (to strive in the cause of God) and remain conscious of Him so that you may ultimately be victorious.

ᵃ See verses 35:28 and 41:53 with their corresponding footnotes.

4. An-Nisā'

[Women : 176 verses]

L ike most Madinan chapters, this one too lays down important rules, particularly for the regulation and conduct of domestic and family affairs as well as for state and society as a whole. A good deal of it, however, contains rules regarding women and family, where the name of this chapter takes after. It delineates the rights of women and female orphans under the care of their guardians, and specifies their rights regarding inheritance, income and marriage, thereby rescuing them from their exploited condition under the social system during the era of *jahiliyyah* (i.e. pre-Islamic period) which had prevailed for ages. With family being the basic unit of society, the primary organization for man's happy living, rules regarding marriage and conjugal relationships, the question of divorce, the status of women within the family and society, the permissibility or otherwise of marriage between a man and a woman because of affinity, consanguinity, and uterine or foster relationships are all laid down in this chapter.

In the name of God, the Most Gracious, the Most Compassionate.

Fair Inheritance for All

¹ O mankind! Be ever mindful of your Lord, the One who created you from a single soul, *ᵃ* then from that soul He created its mate and dispersed from them a multitude of men and women. So be conscious of God (and fear Him), through Whom you claim (your mutual rights from one another) and (honor) the ties of kinship. Verily, God is Ever-Watchful over you.

² Hence, render to the orphans their property when they are able to handle it themselves and do not substitute worthless things (of your own) for the valuable ones (that belong to them). Do not consume their possessions by mixing it up with your own. Indeed, this is a great sin. ³ If you have reason to fear that you might not be able to treat the orphans with fairness (with regard to administering their possessions equitably according to God's commandments, then do not marry them). Instead, marry other women of your choice (that are lawful to you), even up to two, three or four. *ᵇ* But if you fear

---

ᵃ Adam.

ᵇ In the pre-Islamic era, it was customary for men to marry women without limit. Islam put a limit to this and placed fair and equitable treatment to all the wives as a condition for men who wish to marry more than one. Do not misinterpret this by alleging that Islam promotes polygamy. Allowing polygamy by placing a limit up to four wives with fair treatment to all when there was no limit previously is not the same as freely

that you might not be able to treat them with equal fairness, then marry only one (from among you) or (from among) those whom you rightfully possess. This will be more appropriate and make it less likely for you to commit injustice. ⁴ Give the women whom you marry their bridal dues graciously (as an obligation). But if they remit to you a portion of it on their own accord, then you may enjoy it with pleasure and ease.

⁵ And do not entrust to those who are weak (of judgment) their wealth and possessions which God has placed in your custody as the source for their sustenance until they reach maturity and gain sound judgment. Instead, manage their possessions (honestly so that they will not be deprived of their rightful sustenance). Clothe them reasonably and speak to them with kindness.

⁶ When the orphans who are under your care reach the age of marriage, test them (to see if they are capable of sound judgment). If you find them to be mature in mind, then hand over to them their possessions. Do not (betray them by) consuming their possessions wastefully in haste before they grow up. If the guardian is rich, he should abstain (from taking any compensation from the orphan's possessions). But if he is poor, then he is allowed to take some remuneration in a fair manner. When you hand over the orphans their possessions, let there be witnesses on their behalf (even though) God alone is sufficient as a Reckoner.

⁷ Both men and women will have a share in what their parents and kinsfolk leave behind, whether little or much. They are legally entitled to their shares as ordained by God. ⁸ If the relatives, orphans or needy are present at the time of the distribution of inheritance, give them something out of it (as a gesture of benevolence), and speak to them kindly. ⁹ Let those who are entrusted to distribute and dispose the inheritance have the same fear in their minds if they were to leave behind children who are still weak (to look after themselves). Hence, (fear and) be mindful of God and speak the truth (while discharging this responsibility). ¹⁰ Behold! Those who wrongfully misappropriate the possessions of orphans are in fact swallowing fire into their bellies. (And in the life to come,) they will enter a blazing flame!

¹¹ This is God's command upon you concerning the inheritance of your children : Each male will have the equivalent share of two females. But if there are two or more females, they will have two-thirds of the estate. If there is only one daughter, then she will have half. And for your parents, to each one of them is one-sixth of what is left, if you have a child. But if you do not have

---

promoting polygamy. Ultimately, a husband who treats his wife unfairly will be answerable to God on the Day of Judgment, what more if he has more than one wife and fails to treat them fairly.

a child and your parents are the sole heirs, then for your mother is one-third. But if you have siblings, then for your mother is one-sixth. (In all cases, the distribution is) after the fulfillment of bequests and debts. Verily, between your parents and children, you do not actually know who is more beneficial to you. (So follow this) decree from God. Indeed, God is All-Knowing, All-Wise.

¹² You will inherit one-half of your wives' estate if they have no child. But if they have children, then for you is one-fourth of the estate after the fulfillment of bequests and debts. But if you pass away, your wives will inherit one-fourth of your estate if you do not have any child. But if you have children, your wives will receive one-eighth of your estate after the fulfillment of bequests and debts. And if a man or woman whose estate is to be inherited has no parent or child but only a brother or sister, then for each of them is one-sixth. But if they are more than two, then they will all share one-third of the estate after the fulfillment of bequests and debts with no harm (and injustice) done to anyone. This is a commandment from God. Verily, God is All-Knowing, Most Forbearing.

¹³ These are the bounds set by God. Whoever obeys God and His Messenger will be admitted into gardens which rivers flow from right beneath them and they will remain in there forever. And that is great success! ¹⁴ But those who disobey God and His Messenger, and transgress the bounds of God, they will be cast into the Fire and will remain in there forever. And for them is a humiliating punishment.

Perfect Social Morality

¹⁵ If any of your women are guilty of lewdness, bring against them four (reliable) witnesses from among you. And if they testify (and find the offenders guilty as charged), keep them under house arrest until they die or until God opens for them a way out (of this later).ᵃ ¹⁶ And if two men among

---

ᵃ This verse was revealed during the early stages of Islam with regard to the punishment prescribed for women who were caught red-handed by four witnesses while engaging in lewd acts prior to the revelation of verse 24:2. However, the mentioned punishment was never carried out during Islam's rule because the condition to have four witnesses of the act could never be fulfilled. This goes to show that Islam is not all about punishment. Rather, it places the safeguarding of human dignity above everything, so much so that if anyone accuses a woman of committing any immoral sexual act without being able to produce four eye-witnesses, he will be flogged 80 times instead for the punishment of calumny and slander as dictated in verse 24:4. This is to deter people from injuring the dignity of others. Logically, in order to produce four eye-witnesses of such immoral acts, those who committed it would have to be performing the act in public, which is unlikely to take place in any decent society.

you are guilty of lewd acts, punish them both. But if they repent and mend their ways, then leave them alone; for God is The Acceptor of Repentance, The Most Compassionate.

¹⁷ God accepts repentance only from those who do evil out of ignorance and then repent soon after. And it is they whom God will (turn in His Mercy to and) forgive, for God is All-Knowing, All-Wise. ¹⁸ Repentance will not be accepted from those who continue to do evil deeds until their dying hour and then say, "Behold, I repent now!", nor from those who die as non believers. *ᵃ* It is for these whom We have prepared a grievous punishment.

¹⁹ O you who believe! It is not lawful for you to inherit women against their will or ill-treat them. (Do not also) make them return a part of the (bridal dues) that you have given them unless they are guilty of a proven shameful act. Treat them with kindness (and do not act in haste to punish or divorce them) even if you dislike them. It is possible that you might only dislike something in which God has placed much good (and a great blessing).

²⁰ And if you wish to take a new wife as a replacement for the one whom you have divorced and have given her a large sum of wealth, do not take back anything from what you have given her. Would you take it away by slandering her (or by employing inappropriate means), thus committing a manifest sin? ²¹ How could you take it away after you have given yourselves to one another and after she has received a most solemn pledge from you (to protect her when you took her hand in marriage before)?

²² (O believers!) Do not marry those women whom your fathers have previously married, except what has already passed prior to this commandment. This is indeed a shameful, despicable, and evil practice. ²³ Forbidden to you for marriage are your mothers, your daughters, your sisters, your father's sisters, your mother's sisters, daughters of your brothers, daughters of your sisters, foster mothers who have breastfed you, your foster sisters, mothers of your wives, and stepdaughters under your guardianship from those wives with whom you have consummated your marriage. But there is no sin on you in marrying your stepdaughters if you have not consummated your marriage with their mothers (whom you have divorced). And also forbidden are wives of your own sons, and you are also forbidden to have two sisters as your wives at the same time, except what has already passed before this commandment. Indeed, God is Most Forgiving, Most Compassionate.

²⁴ And all married women (are forbidden for you) except those whom you rightfully possess (as captives of war). This is God's decree, binding upon

---

ᵃ God does not accept eleventh-hour repentance. See verses 4:48 and 10:90-91.

you. Lawful to you are all women other than these, provided you seek them with your wealth in a legal marriage and not for fornication. So give bridal dues as an obligation to those with whom you desire to enjoy marriage. It is permissible (to vary the bridal dues) by way of a mutual agreement after having set its obligation (earlier). God is indeed All-Knowing, All-Wise.

 ²⁵ And those among you who cannot afford to marry free (and chaste) believing women, then you may marry believing girls from those whom you rightfully possess - God knows best the state of your faith (and theirs) - for indeed, you are of one another. Marry them then, with the consent of their guardians and give them their bridal dues in an equitable manner; provided they are honorable and chaste, not fornicators, nor keeping anyone as secret love companions. If after their marriage, they are guilty of gross immoral conduct, they will be liable to half the penalty of free women. This provision applies to those of you who fear stumbling into sin. But if you are patient (and can abstain from such marriages), that is better for you. Verily, God is Most Forgiving, Most Compassionate.

²⁶ God wishes to make all things clear to you and to guide you in the (virtuous) ways of life of those who have preceded you, and to accept your repentance. Verily, God is All-Knowing, All-Wise. ²⁷ God (truly) wishes to accept your repentance, but those who follow their lusts wish that you deviate far away (from the right path). ²⁸ (Verily,) God wants to lighten your difficulties, for man has been created weak.

Fairness in All Deals

²⁹ O you who believe! Do not devour one another's wealth unjustly. Instead, conduct your businesses (equitably) with mutual consent. And do not kill (and destroy) one another, for God is merciful to you. ³⁰ Whoever does this out of hostility and injustice, We shall cast him into the Fire. And that is easy for God.

³¹ If you avoid the major sins that you have been forbidden, We shall erase and remove (the sins of) your (minor) misdeeds and admit you into a noble entrance. *ᵃ* ³² Do not covet the bounties that God has bestowed to some of you more than others. Men will have a share of what they earn and women will also have a share of what they earn too. Turn to God instead, and ask Him to give you from His bounty. Verily God knows all.

³³ And so for everyone, We have assigned heirs to receive what parents

---

ᵃ Paradise.

and nearest relatives leave behind. As to those whom you have your pledged your hands (in marriage), give them their due portion as well. Verily, God is a witness to everything.

³⁴ Men are protectors (and caretakers) of women because God has bestowed on some of them (more strength) over the others and because they must spend from their wealth and possessions (to support their family). The righteous women are the ones who are devoutly obedient (to God) and guard in the absence of their husbands what God has ordered to be guarded (namely their own chastity and dignity, and their husbands' honor, interests and secrets). As to your wives of whom you fear rebellion (and animosity), advise them (first); then, forsake them in bed (if they remain unmoved by your words); and (finally) strike them lightly (if you must, but only with sincere intention to educate them if the first two approaches fail to achieve their purpose). And if they obey you, then do not seek ways to harm them. Indeed, God is Most High, Most Great.

³⁵ And if you (have reason to) fear that a discord might occur between a (married) couple, appoint one arbiter from his family and another one from hers. If the couple wish to put things right, then God will bring about reconciliation between them. Indeed, God is All-Knowing, All-Aware.

Unfailing Kindness

³⁶ Worship God (alone) and do not associate anything with Him in any way. Do good and be kind to your parents, near relatives, orphans, the destitute, the neighbor who is related to you, the neighbor who is a stranger, the companion by your side, the traveler (who is stranded) and those whom you rightfully possess. Indeed, God does not love those who are arrogant and boastful; ³⁷ (and) those who are stingy and urge others to also be stingy and withhold the bounties which God has bestowed upon them. We have prepared a humiliating punishment for all these deniers of truth; ³⁸ and those who spend their wealth for show and praise. (Indeed, these are the people) who neither believe in God nor in the Last Day. Whoever chooses Satan as his companion has (surely) chosen the most evil soul-mate!

³⁹ What harm could have come to them if they had believed in God and the Last Day, and spent (in God's cause) from what God has provided for them? And God knows everything about them. ⁴⁰ Indeed, God does not wrong (anyone even by as much as) an atom's weight. If someone does a good deed (even by as small as an atom's weight), He will multiply it and bestow out of His grace a great reward.

⁴¹ How then (will the sinners fare on the Day of Judgment) when We bring forward a witness from each community and bring you (O Prophet) as witness against them? ⁴² Those who rejected true faith and disobeyed the Messenger will wish on that Day that they were leveled with the earth because they will not be able to hide a single word from God!

⁴³ O you who believe! Do not approach prayer while you are in a state of intoxication until you know what you are saying; nor (while you are) in a state of impurity until you take a full bath - except when you are traveling (and are unable to do so). If you are sick, or on a journey, or have just satisfied a call of nature, or have had sexual relations with your wife and can find no water (to cleanse yourselves to perform prayer); then purify yourselves with pure dust, ᵃ by wiping it lightly over your faces and hands. Indeed, God is The Absolver of Sins, Most Forgiving.

Worshippers of "Taghut" (i.e. False God)

⁴⁴ Do you not see those who were granted their share of Our divine revelation, now trade it away for error and want you to lose your way too? ⁴⁵ But God knows best about your enemies. Sufficient is God as your Protector, and Sufficient is God as your Helper.

⁴⁶ Among the Jews are those who play and distort words out of their context (to discredit the Prophet and Islam). They say (to him), "We hear", (but in their hearts they mean), "We disobey". (They also say among themselves,) "Just pretend to hear (Muhammad), but do not take heed". (They also say), "*Raa'ina*" which they utter with a twist of their tongues to slander and imply that the (true) faith is false. If they had said, "We hear and we obey", or "Hear us", or "*Unzurna*", that would have been more appropriate and better for them. (Because of their evil mischief,) God has rejected and cursed them. With the exception of only a few, most of them are indeed devoid of faith.

⁴⁷ O people of earlier revelation! Believe in what We have now revealed to Our Messenger which confirms the truth in the Scriptures that you already have in your hands before We obliterate your faces and turn them backwards (to completely wipe out your sense of direction). We shall lay Our curse on these defiant people as We did the Sabbath-transgressors (before). Remember that God's command is always executed. ⁴⁸ Verily, God does not forgive the sin of associating partners with Him (for as long as one remains in this state) but He forgives any lesser sin to whomsoever He wills (that turns to Him and

---

ᵃ *Tayammum.*

make amends and then follows up with good deeds).*a* Whoever associates any partner with God has surely fabricated a grave sin (and must redeem this deplorable act through sincere repentance before he dies). *b*

⁴⁹ Do you not see those who claim purity for themselves? Behold! It is God Who causes whom He wills to grow in purity and none will be wronged even by as much as a hair's breadth (for God is the Most Just). ⁵⁰ Just look at how they invent lies against God. This in itself is clearly a blatant sin!

⁵¹ Do you (also) not see how those who after been granted their share of Our divine revelation earlier (suddenly) believe in baseless superstitions and false gods, and (have the audacity to) tell the disbelieving pagans that they are better guided than the devoted believers who follow the way (of Our Messenger)? ⁵² Those are the ones whom God has cursed. And whoever God curses will find none to rescue him.

⁵³ Do these people (who dare to invent lies against God) think that they have a share in God's dominion? Even if they do, these (misers) would not give anyone anything, not even a speck on a date-seed. ⁵⁴ Or are they jealous of those whom God has given them (something) from His bounty? But did We not grant Our divine revelation and wisdom to the descendants of Abraham, and blessed them with great authority (as promised)? ⁵⁵ Then, some of them chose to believe in Our Messenger and some chose to turn away. And sufficient is Hell as a Blazing Fire (for those who turned away).

⁵⁶ Indeed, those who reject Our signs will soon be cast into the Fire. Every time their skins are roasted, We shall replace them with fresh skins so that they will taste torment permanently.*c* Verily, God is Almighty, All-Wise. ⁵⁷ As for those who believe and do righteous deeds, We shall admit them into gardens which rivers flow right beneath and they will remain in there forever. They will also have chaste spouses and We shall place them under thick cool shade (for comfort).

---

a See verse 47:2.

b However, repentance will not be accepted in the eleventh-hour as mentioned in verses 4:18 and 10:90.

c Modern scientists say that every square centimeter of the human skin contains around 200 pain receptors known as nociceptors that send pain signals to the brain which means that no signal would be carried to the brain if the outer skin is damaged. This scientific fact was revealed more than 1,450 years ago in the Qur'an through this verse which says that the skins of those who will burn in the Hellfire will be replaced with new ones every time they are roasted so that pain will always be felt. This is because fresh news skins come with nociceptors.

Sincerity and True Faith

⁵⁸ Behold (O believers!) God commands you to return whatever that have been entrusted to you back to their rightful owners; and whenever you judge between people, judge with justice and fairness. How excellent is what God teaches you. Indeed, God is All-Hearing, All-Seeing.

⁵⁹ O you who believe! Obey God, obey the Messenger and those with authority among you. If you are in dispute over anything, refer it to God and His Messenger if you truly believe in God and the Last Day. Verily, this is the best (course of action) for you as it yields the best outcome in the end.

⁶⁰ (O Prophet!) Do you not see (the behavior of) those who claim (in false pretense) that they believe in what is being revealed to you now and what was revealed before you? They wish to still take judgment from evil powers *ᵃ* even though they were clearly ordered to reject it. (Indeed,) Satan wishes to mislead them far astray. ⁶¹ And when it is said to them, "Come to God's revelations and the Messenger (for judgment)," you see the hypocrites turning away from you in disgust. ⁶² But what happens when misfortune befalls them because of their own misdeeds? Then, they come to you swearing by God, saying, "We intended nothing except to do good and to bring about harmony." ⁶³ God knows what is in the hearts of these people. So turn away from them and admonish them, and speak to them with penetrating words that may impact their souls.

⁶⁴ We did not send any Messenger except for him to be obeyed, by God's permission. And if only these hypocrites had come to you when they wronged themselves and asked for God's forgiveness, and the Messenger prayed for their forgiveness too, they would have surely found that God is Most Forgiving, Most Compassionate.

⁶⁵ But no! By your Lord, they are not true believers until they let you decide between them in all matters of dispute and find no reluctance in their hearts to accept your decisions in total submission. ⁶⁶ And if We had decreed, "Sacrifice your lives!" or "Leave your homes!", only a handful of them would have done so. And if they had done what they were told, surely it would have been better for them and stronger reassurance (of their faith). ⁶⁷ And We would have certainly given them a great reward of Our own; ⁶⁸ and guided them to the straight way.

⁶⁹ And whoever obeys God and the Messenger, they will be with those on

---

ᵃ The Qur'anic term for evil powers that people obey and pay homage to is *Taghut*.

whom God has bestowed (His) favor - the Prophets, those who never deviated from the truth, the martyrs, and the righteous. How excellent are such people as companions! [70] That is the bounty of God, and sufficient is God as the All-Knower.

Fighting for a Noble Purpose

[71] O you who believe! Always be on guard (against any possible encounter with your enemy. Then as circumstance demands,) either advance in small groups or advance altogether. [72] And indeed, there is such among you who will lag behind. Then if calamity befalls you, he says "Verily, God has favored me because I was not together with them." [73] And if bounty comes to you from God, he would surely say, "Oh! If only I had been with them, I would have surely attained (a share in) a great success" - as if there had been no ties of affection between you.

[74] Let them fight in God's cause - all who are willing to trade the life of this world for the life to come. To anyone who fights in God's cause, whether he be killed or be victorious, We shall grant a great reward.

[75] And why should you refuse to fight in the cause of God to rescue the helpless and oppressed men, women and children who cry, "Our Lord! Take us out of this land whose people are oppressors, and raise for us out of Your grace, a protector and helper." [76] Those who believe, they fight in the cause of God; and those who disbelieve, they fight in the cause of evil. So fight against these allies of Satan. The guile of Satan is indeed weak.

The Cowardice of Hypocrites

[77] (O Prophet!) There are (among you) those who were (so eager to fight before this but were) told, "Restrain your hands (from fighting for the time being) but be constant in your prayer and spend (regularly) in charity instead." Did you not notice them? Then, as soon as fighting (in the cause of God) was finally ordained, a group of them feared men as they should have feared God, or even in greater fear. They said, "Our Lord! Why have You ordered us to fight (now)? Can You not grant us more time?" Tell them, "The enjoyment of this world is only little (and temporary), whereas the (reward in the) life to come is better for those who are always mindful of God (and earnestly strive in His cause). And you will not be wronged even by as much as a hair's breadth."

God is the Wisest and Best Regulator of All Affairs

[78] (O people!) Wherever you may be, death will overtake you even if you secure yourselves in lofty towers. But if any good comes to the (hypocrites), they say, "This is from God!" And if any evil befalls them, they say, "This is from you (O Muhammad)!" Say (to them, "Do not conveniently blame others for your misfortune). Everything is a consequence of God's natural law (of cause and effect)." What is amiss with these people that they do not seem to understand anything?

[79] (Say to them further O Prophet! "Know that) whatever good comes to you is from God and whatever evil befalls you is (from God too Who in this case has willed it as) the consequence of your own doing (that has nothing to do with your unfair blame on me)." And (indeed,) We have sent you as a Messenger (to convey Our message of truth) to all mankind (and to guide them to Our straight path). Sufficient is God as a Witness (to the choice that they will make out of their own free will).

[80] Whoever obeys the Messenger then surely he has obeyed God. And whoever turns away, they should know that We have not sent you as a guardian over them. [81] And they say, "We pledge obedience." Yet when they leave you, some of them meet in the secrecy of the night to plot against you. But God recorded what they plotted. So turn away from them and put your trust in God. And sufficient is God as (the best) Guardian..

[82] (Is it not ironic that) they do not bother to ponder over the Qur'an (and make any attempt to understand it? Verily,) if it had been from other than God, surely they would have found many discrepancies in it.

[83] If any matter regarding public security or threat comes to their knowledge, these hypocrites quickly make it known to all and sundry (without due consideration to its authenticity and ensuing negative implications to the community). If only they had referred it first to the Messenger or to those having authority (and knowledge) among them, (that would be best, for) surely they would be able to find its correct answer from them. (O believers!) Had it not been for God's grace and mercy, all of you with the exception of a few, would have followed Satan (and chaos would certainly reign among you).

Rally to a Good Cause

[84] So fight in the path of God (and be mindful that you cannot compel anyone to follow you). You are accountable for no one except yourself. Nevertheless, urge and rouse the believers (to fight alongside you). God may

curb the might of the infidels (to make it easy for you to defeat them). Indeed, God is greater in Might and severe in Retribution. [85] (Remember that) whoever rallies and intercedes to a good cause will have a share in its (benefits), and whoever rallies to an evil cause will have (a share of) its burden. Verily, God watches and has control over everything.

[86] And (bear in mind that) when someone greets you with a greeting (of peace), let your greetings be better than his, or (at least) return the same. Verily, God keeps account of everything.

Organizing External Relations

[87] God, there is no god except Him. (He) will surely gather you altogether on the Day of Resurrection, there is no doubt in this. Whose words can be more truthful than God's?

[88] (O believers!) What is with you that you are divided into two groups concerning the hypocrites when God Himself has rejected and disowned them because of what they have done? Do you wish to guide those whom God has left to stray (because of their own disobedience)? Verily, you will never be able to guide whoever God leaves to stray. [89] They wish that you will reject faith just as they did so that you will all be alike. So do not take them as your allies until they emigrate (to Madinah) for God's sake. But if they turn their backs (and revert to open enmity), then seize and slay them wherever you find them. And do not take from among them any ally or helper; [90] except those who take refuge with a people with whom you have a treaty, or come over to you because their hearts restrain them from fighting against you and from fighting against their own people. If God had willed, He could have easily given them power over you and they would have fought against you. So if they withdraw and cease hostility against you and offer peace, then God does not permit you to fight them.

[91] You will also find others who wish to obtain security from you as well as from their own people. But every time when there arises an opportunity to cause trouble, they plunge into it. (These are the true hypocrites.) If they do not keep their distance from you or offer peace or cease hostility, then seize them and slay them wherever you find them. Verily, We grant you clear authority against these hypocrites.

Murder of a Muslim

[92] Never should a believer kill another believer except by mistake. (It is ordained that) whoever does so must free a believing slave and pay blood

money to the family of the deceased, except if they forgo it as charity. If the victim is a believer from a people who are hostile to you, then the freeing of a believing slave is sufficient. But if he belonged to a people with whom you have a treaty, then blood money must be paid to his family along with the freeing of a believing slave. Those who do not have the means (to do this), then he must fast for two consecutive months as a way of repentance to God. And God is (indeed) All-Knowing, All-Wise. [93] But whoever kills a believer intentionally, then his retribution is Hell and he will remain in it forever. He will incur the wrath of God who will lay His curse on him. A grave punishment awaits him (in the life to come).

[94] O you who believe! When you go out to fight in the cause of God, make sure who you are fighting. Do not say to the one who offers greetings of peace, "You are not a believer!" (and then proceed to kill him) out of the desire for the fleeting gains of this worldly life, for with God lies abundant gains. Remember that you were once like them before God conferred His favor upon you (by opening your heart to accept His religion of Islam). So investigate carefully (first before acting in haste). Indeed, God is well aware of all your actions.

No Excuse for Not Emigrating

[95] Those among the believers who stayed behind other than the disabled, are not equal to those who strived hard in God's cause with their possessions and lives. God has exalted those who strived hard with their possessions and their lives far above the ones who stayed behind. Even though God's promise of good is for all, He has granted His favor of the highest reward to those who struggle over those who stayed behind. [96] For them are higher ranks, forgiveness and mercy from God. Indeed, God is Most Forgiving, Most Compassionate.

[97] As for those whose souls are taken by the Angels while they are in the midst of sinning against themselves, they will be asked, "What circumstances were you in?" They will answer, "We were oppressed in the land (and were too weak)." The Angels will reply, "Was not God's earth spacious enough for you to emigrate (and free yourselves)?" Hell will (soon) be their (permanent) home. How wretched it is as a (final) destination!

[98] The exception to this is on those helpless men, women and children who have neither the strength nor the means to escape. [99] As for them, there is hope that God may excuse and efface their sins, for God is indeed an Absolver of Sins, The Most Forgiving. [100] Whoever emigrates for the sake of God will find many places of refuge on earth and abundant resources. And whoever leaves his home as an emigrant towards God and His Messenger and is then

overtaken by death, his reward certainly becomes incumbent upon God (to secure it), for God is truly The Most Forgiving, The Most Compassionate.

Prayer While Traveling and During Battle

[101] And when you travel on earth, there is no blame upon you for shortening your prayers, (especially) if you fear the disbelievers may harm you. Indeed, they are your clear enemies.

[102] (O Prophet!) When you are among the believers and about to lead them in prayer on the battlefield, let only a group of them stand up with you while retaining their weapons. After they have prostrated (and completed their prayer), let them go behind you (to provide security) while another group who has not yet prayed will come forward and pray with you together with their weapons, being fully prepared against danger. Take heed that your enemies wish to see you neglect your weapons and belongings so that they can launch a surprise attack on you. However, there is no blame if you lay down your weapons while praying if you are troubled by rain or illness, as long as you are always fully prepared against danger. Verily, God has prepared a humiliating punishment for those who oppose and defy the truth.

[103] When you finish your prayer, remember God much while you are standing, sitting or lying down on your sides. And once you are safe, re-establish the regular prayer. Indeed, prayer is prescribed for the believers at the appointed times.

[104] Do not languish in pursuing the enemy. If you are suffering pain, remember that they are suffering similar pain too. But (the difference is) you have hope to receive reward from God while they have none. Indeed, God knows all and He is All-Wise.

Justice for All

[105] Behold (O Prophet)! We have bestowed upon you this divine revelation, setting forth the truth so that you may judge between people in accordance with what God has taught you. Hence, do not be an advocate for those who betray their trust. [106] Seek God's forgiveness (for your oversight); for He is indeed the Most Forgiving, the Most Compassionate. [107] Do not plead on behalf of those who betray their own souls. Indeed, God does not love the one who is deceitful and persists in sinful ways. [108] They seek to hide (their wrongdoings) from people but they cannot hide (anything) from God. He is with them even when they plot at night saying things that displease Him. And God certainly encompasses everything they do (with His knowledge).

[109] Here you are (O believers)! You may plead and argue for them in this life, but who will do so for them with God on the Day of Resurrection? Who will come to their defence then? [110] Whoever does evil or wrongs his own soul and then seeks God's forgiveness, he will find God as Most Forgiving, Most Compassionate. [111] And whoever commits a sin, he is only committing it against his own soul. (Verily,) God is All-Knowing, All-Wise. [112] Whoever commits a crime and puts the blame on an innocent person will certainly bear the guilt of slander and a flagrant sin.

Beliefs That Degrade Mankind

[113] (O Prophet!) Had it not been for the favor of God and His grace upon you, some of them who were determined to mislead you (could have had their way). But they misled none except themselves and they will not be able to do you any harm. And it is God Who has bestowed upon you His divine revelation and wisdom, and He taught you what you do not know. Indeed, God's favor upon you is immense.

[114] There is no virtue in much of their secret talks except those who (encourage and) command charity, or fairness, or reconciliation among people. Whoever does these seeking the good pleasure of God, We shall in time grant him a great reward. [115] Anyone who opposes the Messenger after guidance has become clear to him and follows other than the way of the believers, We shall leave him in the (erroneous) path that he has chosen and then throw him (to burn) in Hell (in the Hereafter). What an evil (and wretched) destination it is!

[116] Indeed, God does not forgive if you associate partners with Him (and die in this state), but He forgives any lesser sin to whomsoever He wills (that turns to Him in repentance). And whoever associates partners with God has surely gone far astray.

[117] The ignorant idolaters of Makkah invoke female deities besides God (claiming these deities to be His daughters). But they invoke nothing except the rebellious Satan; [118] on whom God has laid His curse, and who said in rebellion, "Of Your servants, I shall indeed take my due share; [119] and I shall certainly lead them astray and inspire them with vain hopes (and desires). And I shall command them to slit the ears of cattle (in idolatrous sacrifice); and to tamper with God's creation." So whoever befriends Satan and takes him as patron instead of God has surely suffered a clear loss. [120] Satan makes promises and inspires vain hopes (and desires) in them, but Satan's promises are nothing except delusion. [121] The (final place of return and permanent) home for such people will be Hell and they will not find any escape from it.

[122] Those who (truly) believe (in God and His Messenger) and do

righteous deeds, We shall admit them into gardens which rivers flow from right beneath them and they will remain in there forever. This is God's true promise. Who can be truer in his words other than God?

[123] (Paradise is) neither (obtained) by your wishful thinking nor those of the prople of earlier revelation. Whoever does evil will be requited accordingly and he will not find any protector or helper besides God. [124] And whoever does righteous deeds - whether male or female - and is a true believer will enter Paradise and will not be wronged (even as much) as the speck of a date-seed.

[125] And who is of better faith than the person who submits himself entirely to God, is magnanimous to others, and follows the faith of Abraham - the upright monotheist, whom God took as a friend? [126] And to God belongs all that is in the heavens and in the earth. And God encompasses everything.

Treat Orphans and Wives Justly

[127] They ask you for the rulings about women (O Prophet). Tell them, "Rulings concerning women (regarding their rights to inheritance) are given by God through what is being recited to you from this Book. (He warns you about the repercussions of your behavior) towards orphan girls (under your care) whom you deprive what has been prescribed for them (because you wish to usurp their inheritance) by marrying them. (He also reminds you) about helpless children and of your duty to treat orphans with fairness. (Verily,) whatever good you do, God surely knows it."

[128] If a woman has reason to fear ill treatment or neglect by her husband, there is no sin if they come to a peaceful settlement, for (peace and) reconciliation is (always the) best. Human souls are ever prone to selfishness but if you do good (to overcome this) and are always mindful of God, (that is best for you). Indeed, God is All-Aware of everything that you do.

[129] You will never be able to treat your wives with equal fairness even if you really wanted to. So do not be totally inclined (towards one of your wives) and leave the others hanging in the state of suspense (between marriage and divorce). And if you put things right and are always mindful of God, then indeed God is Most Forgiving, Most Compassionate. [130] And if they (choose to) separate, God will enrich both of them from His abundance. Verily, God's bounties are All-Encompassing, He is All-Wise.

[131] To God belongs all that is in the heavens and in the earth. We have indeed commanded those who were granted divine revelation before your time as well as yourselves (now) to always be mindful of God (and fear His wrath). Even if you defy Him, know that all that is in the heavens and in the earth are

His (alone) and He is All-Sufficient, Immensely Praiseworthy. ¹³² And (be reminded again that) to God belongs all that is in the heavens and in the earth. Verily, sufficient is God as your Guardian.

¹³³ (Always bear in mind that) if God wills, He can (easily) remove you altogether O mankind, and replace you with others. Verily, God has full power over everything. ¹³⁴ (Hence,) whoever desires only the reward of this world (by denying the existence of the next life, then he is surely short-changing himself); for with God are the rewards of (both) this world and the life to come. Indeed, God hears all, sees all.

The Reality of Hypocrisy

¹³⁵ O you who believe! Stand out firmly for justice as witnesses (to the truth) for the sake of God, even if it is against yourselves, or your parents and relatives. Whether the person concerned is rich or poor, (God's claim takes precedence since) He is nearer to both of them (than you ever are). So follow not the behest of lusts, lest you deviate from justice. If you distort the truth or refuse (to do justice), then know that God is All-Aware of everything you do (and He will surely call you to account for your evil acts on Judgment Day). ᵃ

¹³⁶ O you who believe! Believe in God and His Messenger, and believe in the Book which He revealed to His Messenger and the Scriptures that He revealed in earlier times. Whoever denies God, His Angels, His Books, His Messengers and the Last Day, then surely he has lost his way - straying far away. ¹³⁷ Indeed, those who accept faith, then disbelieve, then return to it, and deny once again and thereafter increase in disbelief, they will not be forgiven by God nor be guided to the right way.

¹³⁸ So give good news to the hypocrites about the grievous punishment awaits them. ¹³⁹ They are the ones who (readily) take infidels as allies in preference to believers. Is it honor that they are (so desperately) seeking from

---

ᵃ This verse should be read in conjunction with verses 3:110, 5:8, 5:32, 11:113, 60:8 and scores of other verses that emphasize God's command to fight against the hypocrisy of unfair double standard practices and to uphold justice at all times which is the hallmark of His true and pure religion. As far as life in this world is concerned, everyone is commanded to treat each other with fairness, compassion, respect, honor and dignity, including those of other faiths (see also verse 49:13). They will be dealt with by God Himself on Judgment Day for choosing to reject Him and to worship false deities instead. Essentially, faith or *Imaan* is abstract, but justice is tangible. The beauty of Islam can be seen, felt and become appealing to everyone, especially to non-Muslims, only when justice is truly practiced.

those infidels? Verily, (know that) all honor belongs to God alone, (so seek this only from Him).

[140] And surely, He has sent down and revealed to you in this Book that whenever you hear people deny the truth of God's signs and revelations and mock them, avoid their company until they engage in a different conversation or you will be no different from them. Verily, God will gather both the hypocrites and the disbelievers together in Hell, (so do not you be one of them). [141] (They are) those who wait and watch what happens to you. If victory comes to you from God, they say, "Were we not on your side?" But if the infidels gain success, they say to them, "Have we not earned your affection by defending you against Muhammad and his followers?" Behold! It is God Who will judge between (all of) you on the Day of Resurrection and He will never allow the infidels to overcome the believers.

[142] Indeed, the hypocrites seek to deceive God without realizing that it is He Who actually outwits them. (They are the ones that) when they rise to pray, they rise reluctantly only for show and praise by others. And they do not hold God in remembrance, except a little. [143] They waver between faith and disbelief, and belong neither to these (believers) nor to those (disbelievers) completely. And whoever God lets go astray (as a result of his own hypocrisy), never will you be able to find a way for him (to receive guidance).

[144] O you who believe! Do not take disbelievers as patrons (and allies) instead of your fellow believers. Do you wish to give God a clear proof (of your defiance)?

[145] Indeed, the hypocrites will be in the lowest depths of the Fire, and never will you find any helper for them; [146] except for those who repent, mend themselves and hold firmly to God, and grow sincere in their devotion to God, then such people will be counted among the believers. And God will give the believers a great reward soon. [147] Why should God punish you (for your past sins) if you (have repented), are grateful and truly believe in Him? (Know that) God is Most Appreciative to those who are grateful, and He is All-Knowing.

One Religion for All Mankind

[148] God does not like the bad deeds (of others) to be exposed in public except when injustice has been done. (Surely) God hears all and knows all. [149] Whether you do good openly or secretly, or pardon an evil (done to you, know that) God is indeed Most Forgiving, infinite in His Power.

[150] Verily, those who disbelieve in God and His Messengers and wish to make a distinction between them to forge a compromise, say, "We believe (in

God and we believe) only in some Messengers and not in all of them"; [151] it is they who are the true disbelievers. And We have prepared a humiliating punishment for them. [152] But those who believe in God and all His Messengers without making any distinction among them, He will soon give them their reward in full. And God is Most Forgiving, Most Compassionate.

[153] (O Prophet!) The people of earlier revelation demand that you bring down a Book from heaven (to prove that you are indeed God's true Messenger). In fact, their forefathers had demanded an even greater (miracle) than this from Moses when they said to him, "Make us see God with our own eyes!" Thereafter, a thunderbolt struck them for their wickedness. (And yet they did not learn any lesson from this when) they took the (golden statue of a) calf for worship after God's clear proofs had come to them. But even after all that, We still effaced their sins and gave Moses clear authority (to lead them to the right path). [154] And (then) We raised Mount Sinai high above them as witness for their solemn pledge (that they will obey Our commandments). On another occasion, We commanded them, "Enter the gate (of Jerusalem,) bowing humbly!" And We also told them, "Do not transgress and break the Sabbath-law!"; and We received from them a firm pledge.

[155] Hence, (We laid Our curse on them) for breaking their pledge, for rejecting God's signs and revelations, for the unjust killing of their Prophets, and for saying, "Our hearts are (full of knowledge and) securely enwrapped. (So, we do not need any guidance from you)." Nay! (In fact) it is God Who has sealed their hearts because of their (persistent) denial of the truth. As a result, they do not believe (in Our signs) except only a few (of them).

[156] And (We also laid Our curse on these obstinate Jews) for their refusal to acknowledge the truth and for their terrible slander against Mary; [157] and also for boasting, "Indeed, we have killed the Messiah - Jesus, son of Mary (who claimed to be) the Messenger of God!" Whereas in fact, they did not kill him and neither did they crucify him, but it was made to appear so to them. In fact, even those who argue for this are actually in doubt about it, with no firm knowledge except only conjecture to follow. And most certainly they did not kill him.

[158] Nay! (They were indeed confounded and lost in manifest error. Verily,) God exalted Jesus to Himself (in rank and honor, and purified him from all the malicious lies that they accused him of). God is Almighty, All-Wise. [159] (In fact,) there is not one among these (stubborn) followers of earlier revelation who, at the moment of his death, disbelieves (in the Prophethood of Jesus). And on the Day of Resurrection, Jesus (himself) will bear witness to the truth against them.

¹⁶⁰ Then, because of the wrongdoing among the Jews and for their hindering of many others from the path of God, We made unlawful for them (some of the) good things that were lawful to them before; ¹⁶¹ and also for their taking of usury while they were forbidden from taking it, and for their wrongful devouring of other people's wealth. And (in the end), We have prepared a grievous punishment for those who defiantly denied the truth among these Jews.

¹⁶² But as for those among them who are firmly rooted in knowledge and also the believers who believe in what has been revealed to you and before you (O Prophet), and those who are steadfast in their prayer and spend in charity, and all who firmly believe in God and in the Last Day - to them We shall indeed grant a great reward.

¹⁶³ Indeed (O Prophet), We sent revelation to you just as We sent to Noah and the Prophets after him. We also sent revelation to Abraham, Ishmael, Isaac, Jacob and his descendants - Jesus, Job, ^{*a*} Jonah, ^{*b*} Aaron and Solomon, and to David We gave the *Zaboor.* ^{*c*}

¹⁶⁴ (We also inspired other) Messengers whom We mentioned (about them) to you previously, as well as other Messengers whom We did not mention to you. ^{*d*} And to Moses, God spoke directly. ¹⁶⁵ We sent all these Prophets as bearers of good news and also as warners (to mankind) so that no one should have any plea against God (regarding their ignorance) after these Messengers came. Verily, God is Almighty, All-Wise. ¹⁶⁶ (O Prophet! Regardless of whether people believe you or not), God bears witness to what He has sent down to you which He revealed with His full knowledge (and wisdom) as witnessed by the Angels even though God's testimony alone is sufficient.

¹⁶⁷ Indeed, those who disbelieve and hinder others from God's path have surely strayed very far. ¹⁶⁸ For those who reject faith and commit injustice, God will neither forgive them nor guide them to any path; ¹⁶⁹ except the path that leads to Hell where they will remain it it forever. And that is easy for God (to accomplish).

¹⁷⁰ O people! The Messenger has now come to you with the truth from

---

^{*a*} Ayyub in Arabic.
^{*b*} Yunus in Arabic.
^{*c*} Psalms.
^{*d*} See also verse 40:78. This is made evident in verses 25:37, 26:105, 26:123, 26:141, 26:160 and 26:176 where more than one Messenger whose identities were not mentioned by the Qur'an were sent to people of some nations.

your Lord. So believe (him; for indeed,) this is surely better for you. But if you reject, then remember that to God belongs all that is in the heavens and in the earth. Verily, God is indeed All-Knowing, All-Wise.

The Truth About Jesus

[171] O followers of the Gospel! Do not exceed the limits of your religion and do not say anything about God except the truth. The Messiah - Jesus, the son of Mary, was no more than a Messenger of God, a soul that He created (and placed in Mary's womb) as the fulfillment of His promise which He had conveyed to her. So believe in God and His Messengers, and do not say "Trinity". Stop this assertion for your own good! Verily, God is One (and indivisible). Glory be to Him (Who is truly free) from the imperfection of having a son. To Him alone belongs everything that is in the heavens and in the earth. And sufficient is He as the Best Protector (for those who reject this falsehood and return to the right path).

[172] The Messiah never disdained to be God's servant, nor do the Angels who are nearest to Him. Those who refuse to worship God (alone) and are drowned in their own arrogance should know that He will gather them all to Him on the Day of Judgment. [173] As for those who believe and do righteous deeds, He will grant them their reward in full and give them more from His bounty. But to those who stubbornly refuse (to believe in His warnings) and are arrogant, He will inflict them with grievous suffering and they will find no one to protect or help them besides God.

[174] O people! Indeed, a convincing proof of truth has come to you from your Lord. Verily, We have sent down to you a clear light *ᵃ* (as guidance to the right way). [175] For those who believe in God and hold fast to Him, He will admit them in His grace and bounty, and will guide them towards Him on a straight path.

[176] They ask you for a legal decision (about inheritance O Prophet). Say to them, "God hereby gives you His ruling concerning someone who dies childless with no surviving parents. If a man leaves a sister, she will inherit one-half of his estate; and if she dies childless, her brother is her sole heir. But if there are two sisters, they will both have two-thirds of the inheritance between them. And if there are male and female siblings, then the male will have the equal of two females' share." God makes His commandments clear to you so that you will not go astray. Verily, God has perfect knowledge of everything.

ᵃ The Qur'an.

5. Al-Mā'idah
[The Table Spread with Food : 120 verses]

This chapter is called *Al-Maa'idah* or The Table Spread with Food on account of the reference in verses 112 - 115 which narrates the request by the disciples of Jesus to bring down this miracle from heaven. The greater part of the chapter was revealed shortly after the Treaty of Hudaibiyah that took place in the year of 7 Hijrah. Like other Madinan chapters, this chapter also contains, among other things, rules and instructions regarding a number of matters such as the duty to fulfill contracts and agreements, rules regarding purification of the body, lawful and unlawful food, inviolability of the Sacred Mosque, the duty to be strictly just and impartial in dealings, prohibition of wine and gambling; and punishment for theft, insubordination and rebellion. Besides such matters, reference is also made to the conduct of the people of earlier revelation, particularly the defiance and disobedience of the Children of Israel to their Prophets and their deviation from the guidance they were given, and to the struggle between the forces of the right and the wrong as typified by Cain's (Qabil) killing of his brother Abel (Habil) mentioned in verses 27 to 31. At the end of the chapter, attention is drawn to the mistake of elevating the status of Jesus as God and in worshipping him as such, by pointing out that he will be brought forward on the Day of Judgment to testify whether he had asked men to worship him, which he will emphatically disavow that he had ever done so.

In the name of God, the Most Gracious, the Most Compassionate.

Contracts and Their Fulfillment

¹ O you who believe! Be true to your obligations and contracts. Lawful to you is the flesh of all four-legged animals that feed on plants, other than those which are hereby mentioned. However, do not violate the prohibition of hunting while you are in the state of pilgrimage (wearing the *Ihram*). Indeed, God decrees what He so wills.

² O you who believe! Do not violate the sanctity of the (pilgrimage) symbols (and rituals) set up by God, nor the Sacred Month, nor the sacrificial animals, nor the garlands that mark out such animals, nor the (safety of) those who are coming to the Sacred House seeking the bounty and good pleasure of their Lord. Only when you are free from pilgrimage obligations are you allowed to hunt. Do not let your hatred of those people who prevented you from the Sacred Mosque lead you into aggression (and hostility); but rather help one another in righteousness and piety, and do not help one another in sin and aggression. Be mindful of God (and fear His wrath), for God is severe in retribution.

³ Forbidden to you are carrion, blood, the flesh of swine; and that over which any name other than God is invoked during the animal's slaughter; and the animal that has been strangled, or beaten to death, or killed by a fall, or gored to death, or savaged by a beast of prey - except that which you may have slaughtered when it is still alive; and forbidden to you are animals that have been slaughtered on idolatrous altars. And forbidden also is the division (of meat) by raffling with arrows (and drawing lots); for all these are acts of grave disobedience and evil. Today, those who deny the truth have despaired (and lost all hope) of defeating your religion. So do not fear them, but fear (and stand in awe of) Me alone. Today, I have perfected your religion for you and have bestowed upon you the full measure of My blessings, *ᵃ* and have chosen *Islam ᵇ* as your religion. And as for him who is forced by hunger to eat what is forbidden with no inclination to commit sin, he will surely find God the Most Forgiving, the Most Compassionate.

⁴ They ask you about what is lawful to them (O Prophet). Say, "Lawful to you are all the good and clean things." This includes what you have taught your trained hunting animals to catch in the manner directed to you by God. So eat what they catch but mention God's name over it first. Be ever mindful of God (and observe the limits that He has set for you), for God is indeed swift in reckoning.

⁵ On this day, all things that are good and clean have been made lawful to you. And is made lawful for you too the food of those who were given revelation before you, as your food is made lawful for them. And the virtuous women from among the believers and the virtuous women from among those who were given revelation before you are also lawful to you when you give them their bridal dues, taking them in honest wedlock, not in fornication, nor as mistresses. Anyone who turns back on his faith will find that all his deeds will be worthless; and in the life to come, he will be among the losers.

⁶ O you who believe! When you stand up for prayer, wash your faces and your hands up to the elbows and wipe your heads and wash your feet until the ankles. If you are in the state of impurity, purify yourselves first. If you are ill, or on a journey, or one of you has just satisfied a call of nature, or you have had sexual relations with your wife and cannot find water (to cleanse yourselves to perform prayer); then take recourse by wiping pure dust,ᶜ lightly over your faces and your hands. God does not intend to impose any difficulty on you but He intends to purify you and bestow upon you the full measure of His blessings so that you may be grateful.

ᵃ See verse 30:30.
ᵇ Complete submission to the One and Only Almighty God.
ᶜ *Tayammum.*

[7] And remember the blessings of God upon you and the covenant that He made with you when you pledged, "We hear and we obey!" Hence, be ever mindful of God (and keep your duty to Him diligently). Verily, God has full knowledge of what is hidden in everyone's heart.

[8] O you who believe! Be steadfast in your devotion to God, bearing witness to the truth with justice. Never allow your hatred of any people to lead you away from justice. Be just and fair, for this is closer to God-consciousness (and piety). [a] Be ever mindful of God (and keep your duty to Him diligently), for He is indeed aware of everything that you do. [9] God has promised those who believe (in His revelation) and do righteous deeds that for them is forgiveness and a great reward. [10] As for those who disbelieve and deny Our revelation, they will be the inmates of the Hellfire. [11] O you who believe! Remember the blessings of God upon you when He restrained the hands of those who sought to harm you. So be ever mindful of God (and fear His wrath); and in God alone let the believers put their trust.

Broken Pledges

[12] And indeed, God had accepted a solemn pledge from the children of Israel and appointed twelve leaders from among them. And God said, "Behold! I am with you if you are steadfast in your prayer, spend (regularly) in

---

[a] This verse should be read in conjunction with verse 60:8 which does not forbid Muslims from being kind, courteous and respectful to non-Muslims who are not hostile and do not wage wars against Muslims. A true Muslim is someone who must be fair, just, kind and compassionate to everyone regardless of race and religion (see also verse 49:13 and its corresponding footnote). In essence, a Muslim is not a true Muslim if he does not uphold justice and instead condones oppression. He will face dire consequences in the Hereafter if he becomes a party to injustice with a very bleak prospect of entering Paradise (verse 11:113). Muslims cannot be unfair and unjust to others and then expect to get away with it unpunished. The two following authentic Prophetic sayings or *hadith* sums it all : (1) "Beware! Any Muslim who oppresses a *Muahid* (i.e. any non-Muslim who lives in a Muslim land under a peace agreement) or violates any of his rights, or takes anything from him without his permission, then I shall be his defender on the Day of Judgment". [Sunan Abu Dawud, No. 3052]. (2) "Any Muslim who kills a *Muahid*, then he (i.e. the Muslim) will not smell the fragrance of Paradise which takes a traveling distance of forty years." [Sahih Bukhari, No. 6914]. These two *ahadith* serve as a stern warning to Muslims to never be unjust to non-Muslims. Such acts will put the guilty Muslim party in such a woeful state in the Hereafter. This verse and *ahadith* clearly imply that racism and terrorism has no place in Islam. If this is understood correctly, Islamophobia has no reason to exist. See also verse 5:32 and its footnote.

charity, believe in My Messengers and assist them, and lend to God a goodly loan - I shall surely erase and remove (the sins of) your bad deeds and admit you into gardens which rivers flow from right beneath them. But whoever among you rejects (and ignores) this pledge, then he has certainly strayed from the right path." ¹³ And because they reneged on their pledge, We cursed them and We caused their hearts to harden for distorting the words of the Scriptures (out of context and deliberately) neglecting some of what they were (always) reminded to uphold. You will always hear of (deceit and) treachery on their part (O Prophet), except for a few. But pardon them and forbear. Indeed, God loves those who are magnanimous (and excel in their deeds).

¹⁴ Likewise, We also took a pledge from those who call themselves Christians, but they too neglected much of what they were told to uphold. So We stirred up enmity and hatred among them until the Day of Resurrection. In time, God will apprise them all about what they have done.

¹⁵ O people of earlier revelation! Indeed, Our Messenger has come to reveal to you much of what you used to conceal and ignore of the Scripture. A light has now come to you from God, and a Book that make things clear. ¹⁶ (Through this,) God will guide those who seek His good pleasure to the ways of peace, and bring them out of the depth of darkness into light by His will, and guide them to the straight path.

¹⁷ Those who (blasphemously) say, "God is the Messiah, son of Mary", are certainly the deniers of truth! Ask (them O Prophet), "Who has the power against God to stop Him if He wishes to destroy the Messiah - the son of Mary, his mother and everyone on earth? And to God alone belongs the dominion of the heavens and the earth and all that is between them. He creates what He wills and has power over everything."

¹⁸ Both the Jews and the Christians say, "We are God's children and His loved ones!" Ask them, "(If that is true,) why then does He punish you for your sins?" Nay! You are just humans from among those He has created. He forgives whomsoever He wills (that turns to Him in repentance) and punishes whomsoever He wills (that stubbornly rejects the truth). And to God alone belongs the dominion of the heavens and the earth and all that is between them, and only to Him will all return.

¹⁹ O people of earlier revelation! Lest you say, "There did not come to us any bearer of good news or a warner" because of the long interval (after We sent Moses and Jesus to you), behold! Indeed the final Messenger is sent to you now bringing good news and also a fierce warning (to guide you to the path of salvation. Therefore, you are in no position to plead ignorance regarding the truth of Our message anymore. Know that) God has power over

everything.

²⁰ And call to mind when Moses said to his people, "O my people! Remember the blessings that God has bestowed upon you when He raised Prophets from among you, made you your own masters and gave you favors that He did not grant to anyone else in the world (before this)." ²¹ And Moses continued, "O my people! Enter the Holy Land *ᵃ* which God has decreed for you and do not turn back or you will become losers." *ᵇ* ²² Answered their leaders, "O Moses, behold! (Ferocious) people with great strength live in that land. We shall not set our foot there until they leave. As soon as they leave, we shall be ready to enter."

ᵃ Canaan, which is the ancient name for Palestine.

ᵇ This verse comes with a specific condition that forbid the children of Israel from breaking their covenant with God by staying true to their faith. When they reneged on their pledge (verses 5:12-13), God sent ferocious conquerors to humiliate and exile them from the land. See verses 7:137 and 17:2-8 and their corresponding footnotes. Before the Islamic empire took control of Jerusalem and Palestine circa 640 AD, the land was under the rule of the Christian Byzantine empire centered at Constantinople. The Jews were severely persecuted during this era and many fled Jerusalem to take refuge in other lands. The Islamic empire then ruled Palestine for close to 1,300 years from 640 AD until after World War 1 in 1922 which saw the collapse of the Ottoman dynasty. This long rule of the Islamic empire by many dynasties was interrupted by two brief periods of Christian rule between 1095 to 1291 when the crusade war took place. Otherwise, Muslims, Christians and Jews generally lived peacefully among one another during this long period of 1,300 years and the land gradually came to have an Arab majority as many Arab tribes migrated there. Trouble started when the Zionist movement founded in 1897 by Theodor Herzl successfully made a pact with Britain that gained control of Palestine after World War 1 in 1923 to hand over the land to the Zionists after World War 2 in 1948 that would rule by renaming it Israel. In truth, the Zionist Jews have no rightful claim on Palestine as their Promised Land based on religious grounds. Zionism is a nationalist secular movement with the sole objective to turn Palestine into the home of diaspora Jews by driving out Arab Muslims using every possible way including violence and oppression from the land that they have inhabited peacefully for more than 1,000 years. This is the root cause of the widespread violence and terrorism that has all along besieged the whole world until today. Many Muslim jihadist groups that resort to terror and violence causing the death of innocent lives suddenly sprung-up out of anger and desperation in retaliation to the atrocities committed by the Zionist terrorists on Palestinians. Admittedly, while the actions of these jihadists are against the true teachings of Islam that forbid the killing of innocent lives (see verse 5:32), one has to really look at the root cause of this problem and remove it in order to end this long conflict that has made the world very fragile and unsafe. The illegal occupation of Israel in Palestine must be put to a stop and the rights of the Palestinians as decent humans must be restored.

²³ Thereupon, two (God-fearing) men *ᵃ* whom God had blessed apart the other cowards, stood up and responded, "(We can seize the land if) we attack directly from the city gate (in surprise). Once we enter it, we shall surely be victorious. Place your trust in God (to give us victory) if you are true believers." ²⁴ But the rest of them said, "O Moses! Indeed, we shall never enter that land as long as those (ferocious) people are there. So go forth and fight - just both you and your Lord alone (without us). We shall stay here and wait." ²⁵ And so Moses said, "My Lord! Indeed, I have no control over anyone except myself and my brother (Aaron). So separate us from those defiantly disobedient people." ²⁶ God responded, "Then indeed, the land will be forbidden to them for forty years. In the meantime, We shall make them wander aimlessly on earth (until they are succeeded by a new and courageous generation). So do not grieve for those defiantly disobedient people."

The First Murder

²⁷ And narrate to them in truth, the story of the two sons *ᵇ* of Adam, when they both offered a sacrifice following a dispute. But the sacrifice was only accepted from one of them. Said (Cain whose sacrifice was rejected, to Abel, out of great envy and jealousy), "Surely I shall kill you!" (Abel) replied, "(Behold!) God only accepts (the sacrifice) from those who are (righteous and) conscious of Him." ²⁸ "Even if you stretch your hand to kill me, I shall not stretch mine to kill you because I fear God, the Lord of all the worlds." ²⁹ "If you proceed to kill me, I wish that you be laden with the burden of my sin as well as yours, and you will certainly be among the inmates of the Fire which is the requital for (unrepentant) wrongdoers."

³⁰ (Ignoring Abel's admonition, Cain's raging) soul prompted him to kill his brother. So he became one of the losers. ³¹ Then God sent a crow scratching into the ground to show him how to bury his brother's corpse. And (Qabil) cried out, "Woe to me! How could I not be able to (think and) do like what the crow did to bury my brother's corpse?" Verily, (Qabil) became very remorseful.

³² Thereupon, We ordained upon the children of Israel (a rule which also applies to everyone) that whoever kills a soul - except as legal retribution for murder or for spreading corruption on earth - it will be as if he has killed all mankind. *ᶜ* And whoever saves a soul, it will be as if he has saved the lives of

---

ᵃ Believed to be Joshua and Caleb.
ᵇ Abel and Cain.
ᶜ This passage underscores Islam's vehement prohibition against violence and terrorism. Those who profess themselves as Muslims but kill others without legal right

all mankind. Yet, even though (one after another of) Our Messengers came to them with clear evidence of the truth, many of them still committed transgressions on earth.

³³ Verily, the requital for those who wage a war against God and His Messenger and spread corruption on earth is that they be killed (if they commit the crime of murder), or crucified (if they commit murder and plunder), or their hands and their feet of opposite sides be cut off (if they commit only plunder), or be banished from the land (if they cause chaos and disorder among you). Such is their disgrace in this world, and more grievous suffering awaits them in the life to come. ³⁴ For those who repent before you apprehend them, spare them from this punishment. And know that God is Most Forgiving, Most Compassionate.

³⁵ O you who believe! Always be mindful and conscious of God, and seek the means to be closer to Him (through the teachings of His Messenger). Strive hard in His cause so that you will attain success. ³⁶ As for those who disbelieve and are bent on opposing the truth, even if they have everything that the earth contains or twice as much to offer as ransom from the punishment (that will befall them) on the Day of Resurrection, it will not be accepted from them and they will have a grievous punishment. ³⁷ They will wish to get out of the Fire but will not be able to. For them is an everlasting punishment.

³⁸ Whoever is guilty of theft - be it male or female - cut off their hand (that was used in the theft) as a punishment for their crime. This is exemplary punishment as ordained by God to serve as deterrent. Verily, God is Almighty, All-Wise. ³⁹ But whoever repents after his wrongdoing and reforms his conduct, God will surely accept his repentance. Verily, God is Most Forgiving, Most Compassionate. ⁴⁰ Do you not know that to God belongs the dominion of the heavens and the earth? He punishes whomsoever He wills (for refusing to accept the truth) and He forgives whomsoever He wills (who turns to Him in repentance). Verily, God has power over everything.

The Right Basis for Judgment

⁴¹ O Messenger! Do not be grieved by those who vie with one another in disbelief, such as those who say with their mouths, "We believe!" but have no faith in their hearts, and the Jews who eagerly listen to lies and words from others who had never met you. They conveniently distort the meaning of the revealed words (to suit their evil fancies) by saying, "If you are given such and

---

commit a grave sin. This unjust act does not represent Islam and cannot be associated with Islam's true teachings. An example of this is like what we see happening in Iraq and Syria where ISIS is wreaking havoc. See also verses 6:151 and 60:8.

such commandment, accept it. But if it is other than that, reject it." If God wills to leave a person tempted with evil (due to his own inclination towards it), there is nothing you can do about it. Such people are the ones whose hearts God does not desire to purify. They will have humiliation in this world and a grievous suffering in the life to come. ⁴² That is because they listen to falsehood and greedily devour (and swallow) all that is evil. So if they come to you for judgment, you may either judge between them or leave them alone. Know that if you ignore them, they will not be able to harm you in any way. But if you judge between them, then do so with fairness. Indeed, God loves those who are just. ⁴³ But why do they come to you for judgment when they already have the Torah with God's judgment in there and still turn away from it? Such people are not believers.

⁴⁴ Indeed, We revealed the Torah (to Moses) with guidance and light by which the Prophets who submitted themselves to God judged the Jews. And the rabbis and the priests (too, judged the Jews by the Torah after those Prophets), for it was to them that the preservation of God's Book was entrusted to and they became witnesses to the truth contained in it. Therefore, O children of Israel! Do not hold men in awe, but stand in awe of Me. And do not trade away My revelations for a trifling gain. (Verily,) those who do not judge by what God has revealed are (clearly) disbelievers. ⁴⁵ And We ordained for them in the Torah that a life is for a life, an eye for an eye, a nose for a nose, an ear for an ear, a tooth for a tooth, and for a wound is an equal retaliation.*ᵃ* But whoever forgoes it out of charity, it becomes an act of atonement for his bad deeds. (Verily,) those who do not judge by what God has sent down (and ordained) are (defiantly) unjust.

⁴⁶ In the footsteps of those earlier Prophets, We sent Jesus - the son of Mary, confirming the Torah that was sent before him. We gave him the Gospel - in it is guidance and light, confirming what was revealed in the Torah earlier as a guide and lesson for those who are mindful (and conscious) of God. ⁴⁷ Let then, the followers of the Gospel judge in accordance with what God has revealed in it. Those who do not judge by what God has revealed are defiantly disobedient.

⁴⁸ (O Prophet!) We sent down the Qur'an to you in truth to confirm whatever that still remains intact in the Scriptures that came before it and as final authority over them. So judge between people by what God has revealed. Do not yield to their vain desires and forsake the truth that has come to you. For each of you (O Jews and Christians), We have prescribed a set of laws and a clear way of life (before this through the Torah and Gospel, which is now superseded by the Qur'an). And if God had willed, He would have made you

---

ᵃ Al-Qisās.

all one single community. But He willed otherwise to test you with what He has given you. So vie with one another in good deeds. Ultimately, you will all return to God and He will show you the truth over those matters that you used to dispute.

⁴⁹ Hence (O Prophet), judge among them in accordance with what God has revealed and do not follow their errant views and vain desires. Beware of them, lest they tempt you away from some parts of what God has revealed to you. If they reject your judgment, then know that it is God's wish to punish them for some of their sins. Indeed, most people are defiantly disobedient. ⁵⁰ (By rejecting divine law,) do they wish to be judged by the laws of pagan ignorance? For those who are certain in their faith, who else could be better than God in judgment?

Delineation of an Essential Relationship

⁵¹ O you who believe! Do not take the Jews and the Christians as allies and protectors (lest you would be tempted and inclined to imitate their corrupt faith and way of life). They are allies of one another. So whoever among you allies himself with them will indeed become one of them. Behold! God does not give guidance to those who are unjust. ⁵² You will see those in whose hearts is a disease (of hypocrisy) would hasten to the Jews and Christians (to obtain their goodwill. They seek to justify their actions by) saying, "We ally ourselves (with the Jews and Christian for protection) in case any misfortune befalls us." But God may well bring about victory or some other event of His own making for the believers. Then, the hypocrites will be smitten with remorse for the hypocrisy which they had secretly concealed within themselves. ⁵³ (At that time,) the believers will say to one another, "Are these the same people who solemnly pledged to God that they would stand beside you?" (As a result of their betrayal,) all their deeds have become worthless and they end up as the greatest losers!

⁵⁴ O you who believe! If you abandon your faith, God will replace you with people He loves and who love Him, in due time. They are humble towards the believers, and stern against all who deny the truth. They will strive hard in God's cause and they do not fear blame from anyone. Such is God's favor which He grants to whomsoever He wills (that constantly turns to Him in true devotion and strive in His cause). Indeed, God's bounties are infinite, and He is All-Knowing. ⁵⁵ Verily, your allies are none but God, His Messenger, and the fellow believers - who are steadfast in their prayer, render their purifying dues (punctually) and bow down humbly in worship (to Him alone). ⁵⁶ Indeed, whoever makes God, His Messenger and the fellow believers as his allies, they belong to the party of God and they will be victorious!

⁵⁷ O you who believe! Do not take those who ridicule and mock your faith among the ones who were given the revelation before you nor the disbelievers as your patrons (and allies). Always be mindful of God (and keep your duty to Him diligently) if you are true believers. ⁵⁸ When you make a call for prayer, they take it in ridicule and amusement. That is because they are people who do not use reason (and are devoid of understanding). ⁵⁹ Ask them, "O people of earlier revelation! "Do you (envy and) resent us just because we believe in God and in what has been sent down to us and also in what was sent down (to you) before this? Indeed, most of you are a defiantly disobedient lot."

⁶⁰ Tell them, "Shall I tell you who in the sight of God deserves an even worse retribution than this disobedient lot? They are those whom God has rejected and incurred His wrath and whom He has turned into apes and pigs because they worshipped false gods. They are those who are worse in rank and have strayed farthest away from the right path." ⁶¹ (These are the people who) when they come to you, they say, "We believe!", whereas they actually come with the intention to deny the truth and also depart in the same state. Verily, God is fully aware of what they conceal in their hearts. ⁶² And you see many of them hastening into sin and transgression and devouring what is forbidden and unlawful. Evil indeed are their deeds! ⁶³ Why do their rabbis and scholars not forbid them from making sinful assertions and devouring what is forbidden? Evil indeed is what they have done.

⁶⁴ The Jews derided, "God's hand is shackled!" (because they accuse God of not having the means to help the poor among the believers). Nay! It is their own hands that are shackled and they will be cursed for the blasphemy that they utter. Behold! God's hands are (always) stretched out and He dispenses His bounty as He wills. (And because We have chosen you O Muhammad - an Arab instead of a Jew - to receive Our final revelation,) they become more stubborn in their rebellion and denial of the truth (as a consequence of their jealousy and deep hatred towards you. As such,) We have cast enmity and hatred among them until the Day of Resurrection. At the same time, whenever they kindled the fire of war (to provoke and encourage the idol-worshipping pagans to attack you), God extinguished it. Verily, they strive to spread corruption (and cause destruction) on earth but God does not like those who spread corruption.

⁶⁵ And if those people of earlier revelation would believe and keep their duty to God diligently, surely We would erase and remove (the sins of) their bad deeds and admit them into Gardens of Bliss. ⁶⁶ And if only they had stood firmly by the Torah and the Gospel and all that had been revealed to them by their Lord, they would indeed be given abundant provision from above and below them. There is a moderate community among them who pursue the right course, but many of them are of evil conduct.

Who Follows Divine Faith?

⁶⁷ O Messenger! Convey everything that has been revealed to you from your Lord. If you ever hold back anything, you will be deemed as not delivering the message at all. (Do not fear and despair, for) God will protect you from (the evil mischief of) the people. Verily, God does not guide those who refuse to accept the truth.

⁶⁸ Say to them, "O people of earlier revelation! You have no ground to stand upon unless you uphold the (true teachings of the) Torah and the Gospel, and what has been sent down to you (now in this Qur'an) by your Lord." (Take heed O Muhammad,) that this Qur'an which has come to you from your Lord will surely increase many of them in rebellion and disbelief. But grieve not over these defiant disbelievers. ⁶⁹ Truly, those who believe (and have faith in this Qur'an), as well as those among the Jews, Sabians, and Christians who (during their time had piously followed the teachings of their Prophets and) believed in the Oneness of God, the Day of Judgment, and do righteous deeds - they have nothing to fear nor grieve.

⁷⁰ Verily, We accepted a solemn pledge from the children of Israel and We sent Messengers to them (for guidance). But every time a Messenger came to them with anything that was not to their liking, (they rebelled.) Some they accused as impostors and some they killed. ⁷¹ And they thought no trial or harm would befall them. So they became blind and deaf (to the truth). But God still turned to them (in His mercy) and yet many of them chose to continue being blind and deaf. (Indeed,) God sees everything that they do.

⁷² And they certainly defied the truth when they said, "The Messiah - son of Mary, is indeed God"; whereas The Messiah had actually said, "O children of Israel! Worship God, Who is my Lord and your Lord." Indeed, whoever ascribes divinity to anything besides the Almighty God will be forbidden from entering Paradise. Instead, his (place of final return and permanent) home will be the Fire and there is no one who can ever rescue and help these evil wrongdoers! ⁷³ Anyone who says, "God is the third of the Trinity" is certainly a denier of truth! There is no god except the One and Only Almighty God. If they do not desist from saying so, a grievous punishment will surely befall those disbelievers among them. ⁷⁴ Why do they not turn to God and ask for His forgiveness? God is Most Forgiving, Most Compassionate (in dispensing His grace to those who are remorseful of their sins and repent).

⁷⁵ The Messiah - son of Mary, was no more than a Messenger just like the others who passed away before him. His mother (was a virtuous woman who) never deviated from the truth. They both ate food (like other mortals). See how We make these signs clear to the followers of Gospel, and then see how they

(ignored the truth and) turned away. [76] Ask them (O Prophet), "Why do you worship something other than God that has no power to do you harm or good when God alone is the All-Hearing, All-Knowing?" [77] Say, "O followers of Gospel! Do not overstep the bounds of truth in your religion, and do not follow the vain desires (and whims) of those who have certainly gone astray before you and misled many. They have all strayed from the right path."

The Evil Nature of the Jews

[78] Those among the children of Israel who were bent on denying the truth (in the past) were cursed (by God) through the tongue of David and Jesus the son of Mary. That was because they rebelled against God and persisted in transgressing (the bounds of what is right). [79] They (condoned injustice and) did not prevent one another from committing wrongdoings. Evil indeed were their deeds. [80] (And instead of repenting and upholding the truth now,) they would rather ally themselves with the idolaters (of Makkah to oppose you O Prophet). Wretched indeed is what their souls have prepared for themselves, for they have certainly incurred God's wrath. They will suffer everlasting punishment. [81] And if only they had truly believed in God, in the Prophet and in what has been revealed to him, they would not have taken those idolaters as allies. But most of them are defiantly disobedient.

[82] (O Prophet!) You will certainly find the most hostile in enmity to the believers are the Jews and the idolaters, while the nearest in affection to the believers are those who say, "Indeed, we are the followers of Christ." That is because among them are priests and monks who do not behave arrogantly. [83] And when they listen to what has been revealed to the Messenger, you see their eyes overflowing with tears because they recognize the truth (which they have been misled from). They say, "Our Lord! We are believers now. So count us among those who bear witness to the truth. [84] And why should we not believe in God and in the truth that has come to us when we have been fervently hoping that our Lord will include us in the company of the righteous?" [85] So God rewarded them for what they said with gardens which rivers flow from right beneath them and they will remain in there forever. Such is the reward for those who excel in good deeds; [86] whereas those who disbelieve and deny the truth in Our signs and revelations will be the inmates of the Hellfire.

Detailed Legislation for Believers

[87] O you who believe! Do not forbid yourselves the good things that God has made lawful for you and do not be excessive (in your consumption). Indeed, God does not like those who exceed their limits. [88] Consume the

lawful and good things that God has granted you as sustenance (moderately) and be mindful of God in Whom you believe (and keep your duty to Him diligently). [89] God will not call you to account for your thoughtless utterances in your oaths but He will call you to account for your deliberate oaths. The penalty for a broken oath is to feed ten needy persons with such food as you normally provide to your own family, or to clothe them, or to free a slave. For those who cannot afford, then fast for three days. That is the atonement for your oaths when you have sworn (and breached them). So be mindful of your oaths and guard them. This is how God makes clear His words to you so that you will be grateful (for all His favors that He has granted you).

[90] O you who believe! Verily, intoxicants, gambling (and games of chance), idolatrous practices (including sacrificial acts intended for anything other than God), and (believing in superstitions such as) divining with arrows (to come to decisions) are truly despicable deeds of Satan. Shun them all so that you may be successful (in this world and in the next life to come). [91] Verily, it is Satan's desire to stir up enmity and hatred among you through intoxicants and gambling, and to turn you away from the remembrance of God and prayer. Will you not then desist (from these despicable acts)? [92] Hence, obey God and obey His Messenger, and always be on your guard (against evil). But if you turn away (from this reminder), then know that Our Messenger's duty is only to clearly convey (the message that has been entrusted to him and he will not be called to account for what you do). [93] Those who have faith (in God) and do good deeds will not be held guilty for (any unlawful food) they consumed (in the past) as long as they are mindful of God and truly believe in Him; and (then continue to) do good deeds, and be mindful of God and believe in Him, and grow even more mindful of Him and are magnanimous (in their conduct). God loves those who excel in good deeds.

[94] O you who believe! God will most certainly test your obedience by making it unlawful to hunt for animals that are well within the reach of your hands and your weapons (while you are in the state of pilgrimage) to distinguish those who truly fear Him unseen. A grievous suffering awaits those who transgress His boundaries after this (clear warning). [95] O you who believe! Do not kill animals while you are in the state of pilgrimage. Whoever kills them intentionally will have to pay a penalty through an offering of a domestic animal equivalent to the one killed, as determined by two just men among you, brought to the Ka'bah. Alternatively, he could either feed a few needy people or fast their equivalent days as his atonement so that he may taste the consequences of his violations. God has forgiven what has taken place in the past but for whoever repeats it, God will inflict retribution on him. Verily, God is Almighty, Lord of Retribution.

[96] Although you are forbidden to hunt on land while you are in the state of

pilgrimage, catch from the sea and its food as provision for you and the travelers is made lawful. So be mindful of God to whom you will all be (finally) gathered. ⁹⁷ God has made the Ka'bah - the Sacred House - (a sanctuary and) establishment for mankind. So are the sacred months and the animals for offering that are garlanded to differentiate them from others. These are all meant to make you know that God is aware of all that is in the heavens and the earth. (Verily,) God has full knowledge of everything. ⁹⁸ Know that God is severe in retribution, but He is also the Most Forgiving, the Most Compassionate Dispenser of Grace.

⁹⁹ (O Muhammad!) Your duty as a Messenger is no more than to convey God's message. And God knows what you reveal and what you conceal. ¹⁰⁰ So tell them, "Evil and good are not equal even though much of the evil may dazzle and please you. So be mindful of God (and fear Him alone) O you who are endowed with insight and wisdom so that you will attain success!"

¹⁰¹ O you who believe! Do not ask about matters which if they were to be made manifest to you might cause you hardship. If you do so while the Qur'an is being revealed, they might indeed be made manifest to you (as laws that will burden you). Verily, God has forgiven (and absolved you from any obligation) regarding this matter. Indeed, God is Most Forgiving, Most Forbearing. ¹⁰² Indeed, (some) people before your time had asked such questions and then denied the truth when the answers were given.

¹⁰³ God did not ordain (for certain kinds of animals to be forbidden for the use of man and slaughter) such as a *Bahiirah,*ᵃ a *Saa'ibah,*ᵇ a *Wasiilah,*ᶜ and a *Haam.*ᵈ This lie is invented by the infidel pagans against God where most of them do not care to use common sense. ¹⁰⁴ When they are told, "Come to what God has revealed and to the Messenger (for guidance)!", they replied, "Sufficient (and good enough) it is for us to (inherit and) follow what we found our forefathers (had practiced)." Is this their stand) even though their forefathers knew nothing and were devoid of guidance?

¹⁰⁵ O you who believe! (Remember that) you are accountable only for yourselves. (So guard yourselves well with God's guidance). Those who have gone astray can do no harm to you if you are rightly guided. To God will you

---

ᵃ A she-camel that has given birth to five offspring of which the last one is a male.
ᵇ A she-camel that has given birth up to ten female offspring.
ᶜ A male goat that came in pair with a female goat in twin-birth.
ᵈ A camel stallion that has fathered ten male offspring.
The ears of these animals would be slit to mark their sacred status so that people would not disturb them.

all ultimately return and He will apprise you about everything that you have done (during your lifetime).

¹⁰⁶ O you who believe! (Take heed that) when death approaches any one of you, let two just men from among yourselves act as witnesses at the time of making your bequest. If you are traveling and the calamity of death overtakes you, it is permissible for you to take non-believers as witnesses if you could not find witnesses of your same faith. And if you doubt their honesty, keep them after prayer and let them both swear by God, saying, "For the sake of God, we shall not sell our testimony for any price, even to a near relative, and we shall not conceal the testimony which we shall be giving. We would indeed be sinners (if we do so)."

¹⁰⁷ But if it is discovered that these two are guilty of the sin (of perjury), then replace them with two other witnesses who are nearest in kin to the deceased from among those with immediate lawful right (in making claims). Let them swear by God, saying, "Our testimony is truer than theirs and we have not transgressed (the limits of what is right. If we did,) then we would surely be among the wrongdoers." ¹⁰⁸ This way, it will be more likely that people will give true testimony because there is cause for them to fear that their oaths will be refuted by others afterwards. So be mindful of God and take heed (of His commands) for God does not guide those who are defiantly disobedient.

About Jesus and The Table Spread with Food

¹⁰⁹ When God gathers all His Messengers on the Day of Judgment, He will ask, "What was the response you received (from the people to whom you delivered My message)?" They will answer, "We have no knowledge (of what is really in their hearts). Verily, only You have the knowledge of all that is hidden and unseen." ¹¹⁰ Then to Jesus, God will ask, "O Jesus son of Mary! Remember the blessings which I bestowed upon you and your mother when I strengthened you with holy inspiration so that you could speak (about the truth) to people while in the cradle and as a grown man; how I taught you the knowledge of the Book and wisdom including the Torah and Gospel; how you were able to make the figure of a bird out of clay and turn it into a live bird by breathing life into it by My permission; how you healed those born blind and the lepers by My permission; how you brought the dead back to life by My permission; how I prevented the children of Israel from harming you when you came to them with evidence of the truth, and when the disbelievers among them said, "This is nothing but clear sorcery!"

¹¹¹ And (remember the time) when I inspired the disciples (of Jesus) to

have faith in Me and in him, they responded, "We believe (in you O God)! And bear witness that we have surrendered ourselves to You." [112] (Then behold,) when they asked, "O Jesus, son of Mary! Can you supplicate to your Lord to send down to us a table spread with food from heaven?" Jesus replied, "Fear and be mindful of God; (trust in Him for your provisions and do not ask for this) if you are true believers, (for it may become a trial for you)." [113] They replied, "We only wish to eat from it so that (our faith will be strengthened and) our hearts will be at peace knowing that you have indeed told us the truth and that we bear witness to it."

[114] (Having understood the sincere intention of his disciples,) Jesus son of Mary supplicated, "O God, our Lord! Send us a table spread with food from heaven so that it will mark an ever-recurring feast for us - for those of us who are here today and for those who will come after us; and as a sign (of miracle) from You. And provide us our sustenance, for You are the Best Provider of Sustenance." [115] And so, God responded, "Behold! I shall send it down to you. But if any of you deny the truth and disbelieve after that, I shall punish him with a torment which I have never (yet) inflicted upon any of My creations."

[116] And (take heed of the Day of Judgment O Christians) when God will ask, "O Jesus son of Mary! Did you ever tell people to worship you and your mother as two other gods besides Me?" And Jesus will answer, "Glory be to You (from all forms of blasphemy O God)! How could I say what I had no right to say? If I had ever said so, You would have certainly known it. You know what is in my heart but I know not what is with You. Indeed, You have full knowledge of all that is hidden and unseen." [117] "Verily, I never said anything other than what You commanded me to say, which is, 'Worship God alone, [a] Who is my Lord and your Lord' and I was a witness over what they did only while I was among them. But when You (gracefully) ended my term (on earth), You were the Ever Watchful over them. You are indeed a Witness over everything. [118] If You punish them (for their transgression, nothing can stop You) - for verily, they are Your servants. And if You forgive them - verily, You alone are Almighty, All-Wise."

[119] And so, God will say, "This is the Day when the truthful will benefit from their truthfulness. For them are gardens which rivers flow from right beneath them and they will remain in there forever." God is pleased with them and they are pleased with Him. That is the greatest success. [120] Verily, to God (alone) belongs the dominion of the heavens and the earth, and all that is between them. aHe has absolute power over everything.

---

[a] See also verse 19:36 and its footnote.

6. Al-An'ām
[The Cattle : 165 verses]

This is one of the long Makkan chapters. It is called *Al-An'aam* or The Cattle after its mention in verses 136 - 138 in relation to some of the polytheistic practices of the pre-Islamic Arabs that developed around the cattle. This title is only symbolical of the folly and falsehood of polytheism, a denunciation of which is the main theme of the chapter. Like most other Makkan chapters, this chapter also concentrates on the fundamentals of the faith, more specifically on monotheism in respect of worship, divine revelation, messengership, resurrection, judgment and reward. These themes are highlighted by drawing attention to the creation of nature and its aspects with reference to the peculiar views, objections and demands of the disbelievers. Attention is also drawn to the struggles of the previous Prophets and Messengers of God to preach and establish the same truth, and the opposition and enmity that they faced for this. Towards the end of the chapter in verses 151 - 152, emphasis is laid on some commandments that constitute the essence of Islamic morality which the previous Prophets and Scriptures equally inculcated.

***In the name of God, the Most Gracious,
the Most Compassionate.***

The Origin of Life

[1] All praise is due to God, the One Who created the heavens and the earth, and made darkness and light. Yet those who disbelieve set up (other deities) as equals to their Lord. [2] He is the One who has created you from clay, then appointed a term for you (to live in this world) and another one that He specified (for your resurrection which He alone knows its time). Yet you are in doubt of this (absolute certainty)! [3] Verily, He is the One and Only God in the heavens and the earth. He knows what you conceal and what you reveal, and He knows what you deserve (in the end for everything that you have done during your temporary stay on earth).

Stubborn Rejection

[4] But whenever a sign or revelation comes to those who disbelieve from their Lord, they turn away from it. [5] Now the truth has come to them (again through His final Messenger), but still they deny it. Soon they will come to know the reality of what they used to ridicule. [6] Do they not see how many generations We have destroyed before them? We made them more established on earth than you, sent down on them abundant rain from the sky and made running rivers flow under their feet (so that they could enjoy Our bounties from the lands that we made fertile). And (when they were persistently

ungrateful), We destroyed them for their sins and raised new generations after them.

⁷ And even if We had sent down to you (O Prophet), a book inscribed on paper for them to touch with their own hands, the disbelievers would still assert, "This is nothing but clear sorcery (and deception!)" ⁸ They ask, "Why did God not send down an Angel to accompany Muhammad?" (Tell them that) if this took place, then it would mean that the Day of Judgment has arrived and all matters (in dispute) would have been settled. Thereupon, they would not be granted any respite (because their fate would have already been sealed).

⁹ And if We had sent down an Angel as Our Messenger, surely We would make him appear as a man and this would certainly make them more confused than they already are. ¹⁰ And indeed, even before your time (O Muhammad), many Messengers were also mocked and ridiculed (for conveying Our message). But those among them who scoffed (at Our Messengers) were in the end overwhelmed by (the punishment) they used to ridicule.

A Commitment to Mercy

¹¹ So say to them, "Travel all over the earth and see what happened in the end to those who denied the truth." ¹² And ask them, "To whom (do you think) belongs everything that is in the heavens and the earth?" Then tell them, "(Surely) to God!" Verily, He has decreed mercy upon Himself (and will not punish you for your misdeeds right away). Instead, He will surely gather you altogether on the Day of Resurrection (to requite you for everything that you have done) - there is no doubt about this. Yet those who have lost their souls still refuse to believe this. ¹³ And to Him belongs everything that dwells in the night and in the day. Verily, He hears all, knows all.

¹⁴ Ask them (O Prophet), "Should I take a protector other than God - the Originator of the heavens and the earth Who gives provision to all while He needs none? Indeed, I have been commanded to be the first (among you) to submit to God and not one of those who associate partners with Him." ¹⁵ "Behold! Never will I ever disobey my Lord, for I fear the torment on that mighty (dreadful) Day (when everyone will be resurrected and judged)." ¹⁶ Verily, whoever is spared from punishment on that Day has indeed received God's grace and mercy. And that is indeed a clear victory!

¹⁷ If God touches you with harm, no one can remove it except Him. And if He touches you with a blessing and good fortune, (no one can take it away from you except Him too). He has power over everything. ¹⁸ And He reigns Supreme over His creatures. He is All-Wise, All-Aware.

Preference to Remain Blind

¹⁹ Ask them, "Is there any greater testimony (other than the Qur'an)? Let God be the witness between me and you (that I am truly His Messenger) whom He has revealed this Qur'an to, so that I may warn you and all whom it may reach (about the danger that awaits those who deny His revelation). Do you truly bear witness that there are other gods besides Him?" Say (to them, "Behold!) I do not bear witness to such thing!" Say (further), "He is indeed the One and Only God (Who deserves all worship), and I am indeed free from whatever you associate Him with." ²⁰ Those to whom We have given earlier revelation recognize (and know for a fact that this Qur'an is God's word of truth just) like they recognize their own sons. But those who have lost their souls refuse to believe (and admit this).

²¹ And who is more unjust than the one who invents a lie against God or rejects His divine signs? Indeed, the evil wrongdoers will not be successful. ²² And on the Day when We gather them altogether, We shall say to those who associated partners (with God), "Where now are those partners whom you (invented and) claimed (to have a share in God's divinity)?" ²³ (In their utter confusion,) they will have nothing to say except, "By God, our Lord! We never meant to associate You with anything!" ²⁴ Just look at how they will lie against themselves and how (the false gods of) their own inventions will leave them in the lurch.

²⁵ And among them are those who pretend that they listen to you (O Prophet, but their prejudices and arrogance have dulled their faculties). Hence, We have placed veils over their hearts that prevent them from understanding (the Qur'an), and deafness in their ears too. So even if they see every sign (of the truth), they will still not believe in it; so much so that when they come to you, they will only argue and say, "What you say are only tales of ancient times." ²⁶ And they forbid others (from listening to the Qur'an) while they themselves distance from it too. By doing so, they destroy none except themselves while they fail to realize it.

²⁷ And if you could see when they are made to stand in front of the Hellfire, they will say, "If only we could be returned to (earthly) life again, we would (surely) not deny and reject our Lord's revelation and shall (certainly) be among the believers!" ²⁸ Indeed, what they had used to conceal during their days on earth will become manifest to them (on that Day). And even if they were sent back, they would certainly repeat the same things which they had been forbidden. Indeed they are liars!

²⁹ And they say (now), "There is nothing beyond our worldly life, and we

shall not be raised from the dead." [30] If you could only witness the scene when they will be brought before their Lord, (behold)! He will ask, "Is this (resurrection now) not the truth?" They will answer, "Yes our Lord, indeed it is!" Thereupon He will reply, "Taste then the punishment for refusing to accept the truth (when you had the chance to do so before)!"

[31] Those who do not believe that they will meet God are indeed the biggest losers. When the Last Hour suddenly comes upon them, they will exclaim, "Woe to us for ignoring the warnings (that were brought to us) about this Hour!" They will be made to bear the burden of their sins on their backs, and evil indeed are the burdens that they will bear. [32] And not is the life of this world except play and (short-lived) amusement, whereas the (eternal) home in the life to come is far better for those who are mindful of God (and pay heed to His reminders). Will you not use reason (to reflect upon this)?

The Dead Cannot Hear

[33] We know too well that what they say saddens you (O Prophet). Yet it is not you that they charge with falsehood, but it is God's revelation that the evil wrongdoers actually reject. [34] Other Messengers were charged with falsehood before your time too, but they patiently endured all those charges and abuse until Our help came. There is no power that can substitute or alter (the outcome of) God's promises. And surely the news of these earlier Messengers has come to you (O Muhammad. Endure then, the adversities patiently).

[35] If their aversion distresses you (so much), then see if you can make a tunnel into the earth or put a ladder to ascend in the sky to bring them a (more compelling) sign. Had God willed, He would have gathered them all to His guidance. (But He grants them reason and free will for them to make their own choices that they will be called to account for, someday). So do not (allow yourself to) be among those who are ignorant (of the truth). [36] Verily, only those who listen (with their sincere hearts) can respond (to the call of truth). As for those (whose hearts are) dead, only God alone can bring them back to life (to receive guidance); and to Him will everyone be finally returned (for reckoning).

[37] And they say, "Why is not a miracle sent down to Muhammad from his Lord (to convince us of his Prophethood)?" Say, "Behold! God has the power to send down any sign if He wants." Yet most people are ignorant (that His signs are already everywhere). [38] Just look at any beast that walks on the earth and at any bird that flies in the air with its wings. Are they not communities of His creations just like you? (Behold! These are some of Our signs and) We have neglected nothing in Our Book. Verily, to their Lord will everyone be

finally gathered. ³⁹ Those who deny Our signs and revelations are indeed deaf and dumb, they live in (the midst of profound) darkness. God lets go astray whomsoever He wills (that refuse to accept the truth) and guides to the straight path whomsoever He wills (that submits to Him in true devotion).

⁴⁰ Ask them, "If there comes to you God's retribution or if the Last Hour approaches you, would you call upon anyone for help other than God? (Answer,) if you are men of truth. ⁴¹ Nay! It is to Him alone Whom you will certainly call upon. And if He so wills, He could easily remove the distress (which caused you to call upon Him); and (at that moment) you will forget everything that you used to associate Him with.

Consequences of Rejection

⁴² Indeed (O Prophet), We sent forth Messengers to people and communities before you (to convey Our divine message). But (as a consequence of their rejection,) We afflicted them with adversities and misfortunes so that they might humble themselves (to Us). ⁴³ But why did they not humble themselves when they were punished? Instead, their hearts grew hardened because Satan made all their sinful acts seemed fair and alluring to them. ⁴⁴ And when they had forgotten what they were reminded of, We opened for them the gates of every kind of (enjoyment and pleasure which led them to stray further). Then while they were rejoicing (in these false pleasures) that they were given, We seized them (without warning) and they were caught dumbfounded and were plunged into utter despair. ⁴⁵ This was how the remnants of the unjust (and evil) people were rooted-out of existence. And all praise and thanks is due to God (alone), the Lord of all the worlds.

⁴⁶ Ask them, "Have you considered that if God took away your hearing and your sight and sealed your hearts, would you be able to get any god other than Almigty God to restore them for you?" Look at how We explain Our signs and revelations (in various ways), yet they still turn away in disdain. ⁴⁷ Ask them further, "Have you ever pondered that if God's punishment comes to you in an unexpected or expected way, can the evil wrongdoers escape from it?" ⁴⁸ Verily, We did not send the Messengers except as bearers of good news and fierce warners. So whoever believes and mends his ways will have no fear nor grief. ⁴⁹ And those who deny Our signs and revelations will be punished for their defiant disobedience.

Accountability and Grace

⁵⁰ Say (to them O Prophet), "I do not say that I possess the treasures of God, nor do I know about the unseen, nor do I claim that I am an Angel.

Instead, I follow only what is revealed to me (and only those whose hearts are opened to receive light would be able to see the truth in what I have been asked to convey). Is the blind same as the one who can see? Will you not (give thought and) ponder (this)?" [51] Hence, warn with this Qur'an all those who dread to be brought before their Lord (on the Day) when they will have no guardian or intercessor other than (God) Himself, so that they will be ever mindful of Him (while they are still alive on earth).

[52] And do not send away those (poor and humble believers) who invoke their Lord in the morning and in the evening seeking His pleasure (whom the arrogant disbelievers demand you to repulse in exchange for their attention to the message that you are conveying). You are in no way accountable for the deeds of those disbelievers, nor are they in any way accountable for yours. (Hence, do not yield to their wishes.) If you send the (poor believers) away,*ᵃ* you will certainly be counted among those who are (wrong and) unjust. [53] This is how We test some of those (who are affluent among you) against others (who are poor) so that they will say, "Does God favor them more than us?" Do they think God does not know who are the grateful ones among them?

[54] And when those who believe in Our revelations come to you, say to them, "Peace be upon you." Verily, your Lord has decreed grace and mercy upon Himself so that if any of you does a bad deed out of ignorance and thereafter repents and lives righteously, he will find God as Most Forgiving, Most Compassionate." [55] This is how clearly We explain Our revelations so that the path of those who are lost in sin is clearly distinct (from that of the righteous).

God's Infinite Knowledge and Wisdom

[56] Say (to them O Prophet), "Indeed, I am forbidden to worship those whom you invoke besides God. I shall not yield to your wishes, for if I do, then I shall be astray and misguided." *ᵇ* [57] Say, "Behold! I take my stand on clear proof from my Lord which you deny. (His punishment) which you mock

---

ᵃ Some of the pagan chieftains at Makkah expressed their willingness to consider accepting Islam on condition that the Prophet would dissociate himself from the former slaves and other humble believers among his followers - a demand which the Prophet rejected. The incident presumably took place after God rebuked the Prophet earlier when he frowned and turned away from Ibn Umm Maktum, the blind man who was repeatedly asking the Prophet to teach him any new revelation without knowing that he was actually interrupting the Prophet's discussion with some chieftains among the Arab pagans. See verse 80:1-2 and 26:111, and their corresponding footnotes.
ᵇ See chapter 109..

and demand to see in haste is not in my power, for the decree rests solely with God. He declares the truth and He is the best of all judges."

⁵⁸ Say (to them further), "If what you so hastily demand to see is within my power, surely the matter would have been (easily) decided between me and you. (But the matter is in the hands of God) and He knows best how to deal with unjust wrongdoers." ⁵⁹ With Him are the keys to the unseen and none knows them except Him alone. He knows what is on the land and in the sea. No leaf falls to the ground without His knowledge, nor is there a single grain in the darkness of the earth, or anything fresh or dry except that they are all clearly registered in His record.

⁶⁰ He is the One who takes your souls while you are asleep at night and He knows the work that you do during the day. Then He raises you again to life each day until the term that He has decreed for you is fulfilled. In the end, it is to Him you will all finally return and He will apprise you about all that you have done. ⁶¹ He reigns Supreme over all His creations and He sends forth Angels to watch over you. And when death comes to anyone of you, Our Angels will take away his soul, and they are never negligent in their duties. ⁶² Verily, every soul is returned to God Who is their true guardian, and all judgment truly rests with Him alone. He is the Swiftest of all Reckoners.

⁶³ Ask them (O Prophet), "Who is the One that saves you from dark calamities of the land and sea when you humbly call upon Him in the secrecy of your hearts promising - 'If He saves us from this distress, we shall most certainly be grateful'?" ⁶⁴ Say, "It is not God (alone) Who can save you from this and from every distress? Then, why do you (have the audacity to) worship others besides Him?"

⁶⁵ Say (to them further), "It is He alone who is All-Capable of afflicting you with suffering from above or from under your feet, or split you into (hostile) factions making some taste the violence of others." (Behold!) See how We demonstrate Our signs (to mankind in various ways) so that they may understand. ⁶⁶ And yet your people still choose to deny the Qur'an now even though it is the truth. So say (to them), "I am not a guardian over you (and I shall not be responsible for your conduct). ⁶⁷ A time is fixed for every news (brought by God's Messengers to be proven true). Soon you will come to know (the truth about what you are arrogantly denying now)."

Point of Separation

⁶⁸ O believers! When you see those who are engaged in useless conversations about Our revelations, turn away from them (in a dignified

manner) until they enter into another conversation. If Satan makes you forget this, then withdraw from the company of these wrongdoers as soon as you remember this reminder. [69] Those who are mindful of God are not in any way accountable for the actions of the disbelievers. But it is their duty to remind the disbelievers to fear God's (wrath and refrain from evil deeds).

[70] And leave alone those (who are deluded by the life of this world) for taking their religion as play and a passing delight. But proclaim (to them) this (truth) - that every soul will be damned by its own sinful deeds and it will find no protector or intercessor for itself except God. And if they seek to offer every imaginable ransom, it will not be accepted. Such are those who will be damned by the sins of their own evil deeds. For them will be a drink of boiling water and a painful punishment because of their persistent defiance of the truth.

Sovereign of All the Worlds

[71] Say (to the believers O Prophet), "Should we invoke besides God something which can neither benefit nor harm us and cause us to turn back to disbelief after God has guided us? Do not be like the one who is misled by Satan, wandering around the land, lost and confused, despite his companions' (effort to save him by) calling him towards (God's) guidance, saying, 'Come to us'!" So remind them (O Prophet), "God's guidance is the only true guidance. Indeed, we are commanded to only devote ourselves to the Lord of all the worlds; [72] and to be steadfast in prayer and always be mindful of Him. And it is He to Whom you will all be finally gathered (on the Day of Judgment)."

[73] It is He who created the heavens and the earth with a true (and meaningful) purpose. And on the Day when He says, "Be!" - it will be (the Day when everyone will be resurrected from their graves and assembled before Him for the reckoning of their deeds). His word is the truth and for Him is the absolute dominion on the Day when the trumpet (of resurrection) is blown. Verily, He has full knowledge of all that is hidden and manifest. And He is truly All-Wise, All-Aware.

Reminder for All Mankind

[74] (Now narrate to them the story of Abraham) when he said to his father - Aazar, "Do you take idols as gods? Indeed, I see you and your people in obvious error and have gone astray." [75] And so We gave Abraham insight into God's mighty dominion over the heavens and the earth so that he would be among those who are certain (in faith). [76] Then, when the night plunged him

(in darkness), he saw a bright star and exclaimed, "This is my Lord!" But when it went down, he said, "I do not like things that can fade away. How can I worship objects of such nature?"

⁷⁷ Then, when he saw the moon rising, he exclaimed, "This is my Lord!" But when it went down, he said, "Indeed, if my Lord does not guide me (to the truth), I shall surely be among the people who would go astray." ⁷⁸ Then when he saw the sun rising (with its brighter shine), he said, "This (must be my Lord because it) is greater (than the star and the moon)." But when it also came down, he exclaimed, "O my people, behold! Indeed, (I hereby declare that) I am free from whatever you associate with God. ⁷⁹ Verily, I have set my face (firmly) as a true monotheist to the One who created the heavens and the earth. And I am not among those who ascribe divinity to anything other than God, (the Lord of all the worlds)."

⁸⁰ And when his people argued with him, he said, "Why do you want to argue with me about God when it is He who has guided me? I do not fear those whom you take for gods besides Him (because no evil can befall me) unless my Lord wills so. Verily, His knowledge encompasses everything. Why do you not want to take heed?" ⁸¹ "And how could I possibly fear the (powerless) idols that you associate with God without any valid authority (and permission) from Him? (Is God not the Ultimate Creator and Master of all things Who deserves our sole worship)? So tell me, who between us has more right to feel secure (from ruin) if you know the answer?"

⁸² (Certainly,) those who believe in God and do not mix their faith with evil acts (by ascribing divinity to others besides Him) are those who are guaranteed security, for they are the ones who are rightly guided. ⁸³ Such was the argument We gave to Abraham against his people. Verily, We exalt whomsoever We please in rank. Indeed, your Lord is All-Wise, All-Knowing.

⁸⁴ (And then) We bestowed upon him Isaac and Jacob, and guided each of them as We guided Noah before. And out of his descendants also were David, Solomon, Job,ᵃ Joseph, Moses and Aaron. And thus We reward those who are truly excellent (in their conduct). ⁸⁵ And other descendants include Zachariah, John,ᵇ Jesus, and Elijah.ᶜ All of them were righteous. ⁸⁶ And also Ishmael, Elisha,ᵈ Jonah ᵉ and Lot. We exalted every one of them over all other people and communities; ⁸⁷ just as We exalted some of their forefathers, descendants

---

ᵃ Ayyub in Arabic.
ᵇ Yahya in Arabic.
ᶜ Ilyas in Arabic.
ᵈ Ilyasa' in Arabic.
ᵉ Yunus in Arabic.

and brothers. We chose them all for Our service and guided them on a straight path.

⁸⁸ Such is God's guidance. He guides whomsoever He wills of His servants (that submits to Him in true devotion). But if they ascribe divinity to others besides Him, then all their good deeds will become worthless. ⁸⁹ It was to them that We gave revelation, wisdom, and Prophethood (and they were firm and steadfast in their faith). And because those (pagans of Makkah) who reject your Prophethood now also deny the truth that you bring, We have entrusted the message to a people who will not disbelieve and reject it (in Madinah). ⁹⁰ Those are the ones whom God has guided. Follow their guidance (if you are wise, O disbelievers). And say to these (stubborn) disbelievers (O Prophet), "No reward do I ask from you for (conveying) this (truth). Behold! It is a reminder to all mankind!"

⁹¹ And those (who deny the truth among the Jews) did not appraise God with true appraisal when they said, "God did not reveal anything to anyone." Ask them, "(If that was the case,) then who revealed the Book (of Torah) that Moses brought as light and guidance for people which you treated as mere parchments? You (hideously manipulated its content by) revealing some and concealing much of it, whereas through it you were taught things that neither you nor your forefathers knew." Ask them, "Was it not God who actually revealed this?" So leave them alone to their play and foolish chatter.

⁹² And this (Qur'an) is another Book that We sent down; full of blessings, confirming (the revelations) that came before it so that you may warn the people of the Mother of Cities ᵃ and those around it. Verily, only those who believe in the next life to come will believe in this (Book), and they are steadfast in guarding their prayer.

⁹³ And who could be more unjust than the one who invents a lie against God, or says, "This was revealed to me!" while nothing was actually revealed to him; or the one who says, "I can reveal like what God has revealed!"? If only you could see when these evildoers are in the agonies of death, (you will realize how severe God's retribution is to those who deny His message). The Angels of death will stretch forth their hands and say, "Discharge your souls! Today, you will be requited with a humiliating punishment for saying lies against God and for having persistently scorned His revelations in arrogance."

⁹⁴ And (on the Day of Judgment), God will say to them, "Indeed, you have come to Us now in a lonely state just as We created you the first time, and you have left behind (all the pleasures and possessions) that We have given you (to

---

ᵃ Makkah.

enjoy) during your stay on earth. We do not see with you today those intercessors and saviors whom you claimed to be God's partners in your affairs. Indeed, all the ties between you (and them) have been severed and those whom you made such claims about have clearly forsaken you!"

The Miracle of Creation

⁹⁵ Indeed, it is God who cleaves the seed and fruit-stone (and then causes it to sprout), thus bringing forth the living from the dead, and the dead from the living. Such is the power and grace of God. So how are you deluded from the truth (and be misled into perversion)? ⁹⁶ He is the One Who causes the dawn to break and He has made the night for rest, and the sun and the moon (to run according to their appointed courses with precision) for the count of time. All this is decreed by the will of the Almighty, the All-Knowing. ⁹⁷ And He is the One Who has set up for you the stars so that you can be guided by them in the midst of the deep darkness of the land and sea. Indeed, We have clearly spelled out the signs (of Our magnificence) for people who have knowledge.

⁹⁸ And He is the One Who created you from a single soul and then gave you (the earth as) a place to stay and a final place to rest (after death). Indeed, We have made Our signs clear to those who understand. ⁹⁹ And He is the One Who sends down rain from the sky, then We bring forth from it vegetation of every kind. From green stalks, We produce thick clusters of grains. And from date-palm and its spathes, come clusters of dates that hang low (and are within reach). And (there are also) gardens of grapes, and olives, and pomegranates, each similar (in kind) yet different (in variety). Look at their fruits as they yield and ripen. Behold! In these are signs for people who believe (in God and His greatness).

¹⁰⁰ And yet those who turn away from the truth take the Jinn as partners to God, even though He is their Creator. They also falsely attribute sons and daughters to Him out of sheer ignorance. Glorified and exalted is He above (all the blasphemy and imperfections) that they attribute (to Him).¹⁰¹ He is the Originator of the heavens and the earth. How can He have a son when He has never had a spouse? It is He Who is the Creator of all things and He has complete knowledge of everything.

¹⁰² That is God, your Lord (Who deserves all worship). There is no other god except Him and He is the Creator of all things. So worship Him alone. He is (indeed) the Guardian and Protector over everything. ¹⁰³ No power of vision can ever grasp and encompass Him, whereas He encompasses all vision. He is the Most Subtle and Courteous to all His creations, yet All-Aware and Well-

Acquainted with everything. [104] Verily, (clear evidence and) enlightenment has now come to you from your Lord (through this Qur'an). Whoever chooses to see (its truth), does so for his own good; and whoever chooses to remain blind, does so at his own peril. (So say to the blind-hearted O Prophet,) "I am (merely a warner and) not your guardian."

[105] And this is how We explain Our signs and revelations (in many facets to make Our message easy to understand. But those who choose to deny the truth refuse to accept it as divine revelation and instead) accuse Our Messenger by saying, "You have learned this (from someone else and memorized it)!" Verily, We make this Qur'an clear for people with knowledge (and understanding). [106] So, follow what is revealed to you by your Lord (O Prophet), and turn away from those who ascribe divinity to anything other than Him. Verily, there is no other god except Him alone. [107] And if God had so willed, they would not have ascribed divinity to anything besides Him (but He bestows mankind with reason and free will for them to attain faith without compulsion). And verily, We did not make you their guardian and neither are you their keeper (who is responsible to manage their affairs).

[108] (O believers!) Do not insult what they invoke besides Almighty God, lest they (retaliate and) insult Him in enmity without knowledge. To each community, We make their deeds fair-seeming (and alluring as how they want it to be). In the end, they will all return to their Lord and He will apprise them about everything they did.

[109] Those (infidels) swear by God most solemnly that if a miracle were shown to them, they would believe (in your Prophethood, O Muhammad). Say to them, "Verily, miracles are in God's power alone." Do you not realize (O believers) that even if one is shown to them, they would still not believe (in the truth? So do not pay attention to them. [110] If they persist,) We shall (continue to) turn their hearts and eyes away (from the truth) just as they had refused to believe in the first instance. Verily, We shall leave them in their blunder (and overweening arrogance), wandering blindly (without guidance).

Man's Inclination to Evil

[111] And even if We had sent down the Angels to them, and if the dead had spoken to them, and if We had gathered every miraculous creation before their very eyes, they would still not believe and accept the truth unless if God so willed. Most of them (choose to) ignore the truth. [112] In the same way, We made evil forces as enemies against every Prophet (and all mankind) from among men and invisible beings who inspire one another with decorative speech meant to delude the mind (and lead them astray). But if your Lord willed (to destroy them), they would (certainly) not be able to do (what they

intended). So leave them alone with all their (false) inventions (if you truly believe in God and wish to be safe). [113] As for those whose hearts do not believe in the (certainty of the) life to come, they will be inclined towards these deceptions. Let them delight and persist in (the erroneous ways) that they have chosen to indulge in, (for they will certainly be requited for all their deeds).

[114] (Ask them O Prophet,) "Should I seek anyone apart from God for judgment when it is He who has sent down this Qur'an to you (as guidance) that clearly spells out the truth in detail?" (Verily,) those to whom We have given this Qur'an (that you are in their midst), know (in their hearts) that this is a true revelation sent down by your Lord (but they choose to deny it out of sheer defiance and arrogance). So, do not be among those who doubt (Our promise of doom for whoever that rejects the truth). [115] Indeed, the words and promises of your Lord (to those who had rejected His message in the past) have been fulfilled in truth and justice. (So beware O you disbelievers!) There is no power that can change His words and promises. He hears all, knows all. [116] And if you (persist to ignore God's Messenger and instead) follow the majority of those on earth (who do not pay heed to his teachings), you will certainly be misled from God's way; for they follow nothing except conjectures and they are merely guessing. [117] Indeed, your Lord knows best who strays from His path and who are rightly guided.

On Permissibility and Prohibition

[118] Eat then, only what is slaughtered in God's name if you truly believe in His revelations. [119] And why should you not eat what is slaughtered in God's name when He has made it distinctly clear what is forbidden, except if you are truly compelled? And indeed, (it is precisely in such matters that) many people are being led astray by their own vain desires without knowledge. Verily, your Lord is fully aware of those who transgress (His bounds).

[120] So, abstain from sinning, whether openly or secretly. Behold! Those who commit sin will be requited for what they have committed. [121] So do not eat anything that is not slaughtered in God's name, for that is surely an act of grave disobedience. Indeed, the evil ones (unceasingly) inspire their allies to dispute and argue with you (to confound and lead you astray). If you obey them, then you too will be counted among those who worship false gods.

Evil Communities Deserve Evil Leaders

[122] Is he who was (initially) dead (in spirit) and then We raised to life by

giving the light (of knowledge and faith) for him to clearly see his way among people, the same as another who is in the depths of darkness from which he can never emerge? This is how the misdeeds of the disbelievers are made fair-seeming (and alluring) to them. [123] As such, We have placed the greatest sinners in every society and nation (and allowed them) to contrive and deceive therein (until its people can distinguish between truth and falsehood, and strive to oppose them by upholding justice). But the fact is, these evil perpetrators contrive against none except their own souls without realizing it (and those who condone and accept their ways are no different). [a]

[124] And whenever Our sign is brought to them (to admonish their errant ways), they arrogantly refute it by saying, "We shall never believe this unless we are given what God's Messengers were given (because we are more entitled to it than Muhammad)." Verily, God knows best upon whom to entrust His message. In time, these evildoers will be afflicted by humiliation and severe punishment from God for their (wicked) schemes.

[125] Whomsoever God wills to guide (for his sincerity in seeking the truth), He will expand his chest to completely submit himself to God, and whomsoever God wills to let go astray (as a consequence of his refusal to accept guidance), He will make his chest tight and constricted as though he is forced to climb up to the skies. That is how God lays filth on those who deny the truth (and persist in their disbelief).

[126] And this is indeed your Lord's path that is straight. We have indeed set forth Our signs in detail for people who (use common sense) to take heed. [127] For them will be the (final) home of peace with their Lord. And He will be their protector as a reward for the good deeds they used to do.

---

[a] Sinful leaders will always contrive evil, commit injustice and wreak havoc to the societies and nations that they have been entrusted to lead. If the majority condones this because their *fitrah* (i.e. natural disposition and value system) is equally corrupt, widespread injustice will surely prevail and these nations will surely suffer hardship. See verse 54:5 and its footnote. In addition, Satan has successfully made their evil deeds fair-seeming and attractive (see verses 15:39 and 2:212) until they see no wrong in what they do. The following *hadith* underscores the severity of God's wrath towards them : Ma'qil bin Yasar al-Muzani reported that he heard the Messenger of God (peach be upon him) said, "Whoever that has been entrusted to manage the affairs of his people and dies in a state where he was dishonest in his dealings over those he ruled, Paradise will be forbidden for him." [Sahih Muslim, No. 142]. Those who condone these vile acts are not spared too. See verse 11:113. To overcome this, there must be a group among them who will continuously strive to uphold justice and oppose evil. They are the ones who are victorious in the sight of God. See verses 3:104 and 3:110.

Judgment According to Deeds

¹²⁸ On the day when God gathers all of them together, He will say, "O you assembly of (evil) Jinn! You have certainly misled a great number of men." And then their allies among men will say, "Our Lord! We have both benefited from each other's company but we have reached the end of our term which You have appointed for us. (We see the error of our ways)." Then God will say, "The Hellfire will be your eternal home from now unless God wills otherwise." Verily, your Lord is All-Wise, All-Knowing. ¹²⁹ That is how We make evildoers as friends of one another (in sharing the punishment of the Hellfire) because (of the evil deeds that) they committed together (during their lifetime).

¹³⁰ (And God will ask,) "O you assembly of (evil) Jinn and (like-minded) humans! Did there not come to you Messengers from among yourselves who narrated (and conveyed) My signs and revelations and warned you about the meeting of this Day?" They will answer, "(Yes they did, and) we bear witness against ourselves (for our errors and stubbornness)." Verily, (they will regretfully realize that) they have been deceived by this worldly life and they (have no choice but to) testify against themselves that they had indeed rejected the truth. ¹³¹ Hence, (know that) your Lord will not (unjustly) destroy any community for its wrongdoings while its people are unaware (of the truth).

¹³² Everyone will be assigned ranks according to their deeds, and your Lord is not unaware of what they do. ¹³³ Your Lord is All-Sufficient, Full of Benevolence. If He wills, He can put you away and make whomsoever He pleases to succeed you just as He raised you from the descendants of other people. ¹³⁴ Indeed, what you are promised will surely come *ª* and you cannot escape from it. ¹³⁵ So tell them (O Prophet), "O my people! Do as you wish, and I too will do what I deem right. In time, you will know who will be rewarded with the ultimate (and permanent) home (of everlasting happiness). Most certainly, those who commit evil will not be successful."

Baseless Self-Imposed Prohibitions

¹³⁶ The idolaters set aside some shares of the crops and cattle that God has created, claiming, "This is for God, and this is for our idols." But the share that they assigned for their idols does not bring them any closer to God, while what they assigned for God goes to their idols (and only brings them closer to evil). Vile indeed is their judgment! ¹³⁷ And this is how the evil partners (that they worship) deceive them into believing that the killing of their children is indeed

---

ª The Day of Judgment.

a goodly act, thus bringing them to ruin and confusing them in their faith. If God had willed, they would not have done so (but He grants them reason and free will for them to make their own choices that they will surely be called to account for). So leave them alone with their (false) inventions.

¹³⁸ And they assert in false belief that certain cattle and crops are forbidden for consumption except to those whom they permit (and assign). Then there are also some cattle which they have prohibited from riding or carrying loads, and there are other cattle that they slaughter but not in God's name. They have (falsely) attributed all these fabrications to Him. Soon He will requite them for their invented lies.

¹³⁹ And they also say, "What is in the wombs of these cattle is exclusively for the consumption of our men and forbidden to our spouses. But if it is stillborn, then everyone has a share in it." God will punish them for everything that they (falsely) attribute to Him. Indeed, He is All-Wise, All-Knowing. ¹⁴⁰ Lost indeed are those who kill their children *ᵃ* in foolish ignorance, forbidding what God has provided (and allowed them to consume), and fabricating lies against Him. They have certainly gone astray and are devoid of true guidance.

¹⁴¹ It is He who creates gardens (with all kinds of plants) - both the cultivated ones and those that grow in the wild - and palm trees, field crops of different variety, olives and pomegranates, similar (in kind) yet so different (in variety and taste). Eat their fruits when they come to fruition and pay its dues on the day of harvest. And do not be wasteful, for God does not love those who are wasteful. ¹⁴² And of the cattle are some reared for work and some for meat. Eat whatever God has provided for you as sustenance and do not follow the footsteps of Satan. He is indeed your real enemy.

¹⁴³ (The followers of Satan claim that any of these) eight animals in (four different) pairs (of male and female is unlawful for consumption). From the pairs of sheep and goat, ask them, "(Of these four animals,) does God forbid you to consume the two males, or the two females, or what is in the wombs of the two females? Answer me (not with superstition but) with real knowledge if you are truthful." ¹⁴⁴ Likewise, (they also declare as unlawful) the pairs of camels and of cows. Ask them (the same question, "Which of these four animals) has God forbidden (you to consume? Is it) the two males, or the two females, or what is in the wombs of the two females? (Whatever their answer is, query them,) "Were you present when God gave this decree?" (If not,) then who can be more unjust (and wicked) than the one who attributes his lying inventions to God and misleads people with false knowledge? Behold! God

---

ᵃ See verses 6:151, 16:58-59 and 17:31.

does not guide those who are evil and unjust.

¹⁴⁵ Say (to them O Prophet), "I do not find in what has been revealed to me anything forbidden to be eaten by one who wishes to eat it, except the meat of carrion, or running blood or the flesh of swine, all of which is unclean; or (that which has become profane) because of the disobedience in slaughtering them in names other than God." But whoever is compelled by necessity to consume them, intending neither disobedience nor exceeding his bare need, you will find your Lord Most Forgiving, Most Compassionate.

¹⁴⁶ As for the Jews, We have forbidden every animal with claws, and the fat of cows and sheep, except the fat that is attached to their backs, intestines or joined with the bone. This is the requital for their rebellion (and disobedience to many of Our commandments, and their numerous broken pledges). Behold! We are (always) true to Our word. ¹⁴⁷ If they deny you, then say, "The grace of your Lord is limitless but His wrath will not be averted from people who are lost in sin."

¹⁴⁸ Those who associate partners with God will say, "Had God willed, neither we nor our forefathers would have associated partners with Him, or make anything (which He does not forbid) to be unlawful." Likewise, their predecessors had also lied until they tasted Our punishment. Ask them, "Do you have any sure knowledge (or proof) that you can bring to support your claim? Verily, you only follow conjecture and do nothing but tell lies." ¹⁴⁹ Say (to them further), "The final word and statement of truth rests with God alone. Had He willed, He could have surely guided all of you (but it is you who refuse to accept the truth)." ¹⁵⁰ Say, "Bring forward your witnesses to prove that God has forbidden what you claim." (Behold!) They will probably attempt to do so (by cheating). So do not testify with them and do not yield to the wishes of those who deny Our signs and revelations, those who do not believe in the life to come and associate partners of equal status with their Lord.

Guiding Rules of Life

¹⁵¹ Say (to them O Prophet), "Come, let me tell you what your Lord has (really) forbidden you from. Never ascribe divinity to anything else besides Him. Be good and kind to your parents, and do not kill your children for fear of poverty." It is We Who provide sustenance for you as well as for them. (So do not ever lose hope of Our grace). "Do not also approach immoralities whether openly or secretly, and do not take the life of any human soul which God has forbidden (and declared sacred) except through legal retribution. ᵃ

ᵃ See verses 17:33, and 5:32 and its footnote.

This is what He has commanded you and expects you to use reason (to willingly obey your Lord's command)."

¹⁵² "(In addition,) do not go near the property of an orphan who has not attained maturity, except with the best (intentions). Be fair in your dealings by giving full measure and weight (in what you sell)." Verily,) We do not burden anyone with more than what he can bear. "And whenever you speak (to testify anything), be just (and truthful) even if it is against your near relatives." (Behold!) You are clearly commanded to fulfill your covenant with God. This is what He commands you to do. Perhaps you will (always) bear this in mind.

¹⁵³ Verily, this is the path leading straight to Me. So (say to them O Prophet), "Follow it, and do not follow other paths, lest they cause you to deviate from God's path. This is what He has commanded you so that you will be ever mindful of Him (and guard yourself against evil)."

¹⁵⁴ To this end, We gave the Torah to Moses (earlier) in fulfillment (of Our favor), and as an explanation of all things and guidance to those (among the children of Israel) who persevered in doing good, and (also as a clear sign of Our) grace so that they will have faith in the meeting with their Lord. ¹⁵⁵ And so, We have revealed this Qur'an (to you now O Prophet, similar to what was given to Moses) as a blessing (to all mankind). So (invite others to) follow it and be ever mindful of God so that you will (all) be graced with His mercy.

¹⁵⁶ (And We revealed this Qur'an to you too, O idol worshipping pagans of Makkah), lest you say, "The Scriptures were revealed only to the two groups before us. *ᵃ* (So do not blame us for having no knowledge of the truth because) we were certainly unaware of what they learned and knew"; ¹⁵⁷ or lest you say, "If only the Scriptures were revealed to us, then surely we would have been better guided than them". Behold! (The Qur'an) is being brought to you now with clear evidence as guidance and grace from your Lord. So who could be more unjust (and wicked) than the one who denies God's revelations and turns away (in disdain)? Verily, We shall requite all those who turn away from Our revelations with the worst punishment because of their persistent rejection.

¹⁵⁸ Are they waiting for the Angels and your Lord to come, or for some of His miraculous signs to appear before they would decide to believe? But on the Day when your Lord's signs finally appear, faith will not benefit those who rejected truth earlier, or those who already believed but did not earn any good through their faith. So say (to them), "Wait (then for the day to arrive).

ᵃ The Jews and Christians.

Indeed, we too, are waiting!"

¹⁵⁹ Indeed (O Prophet), you have nothing to do with those who divide their religion into factions. Behold! Their affairs rest with God and in time He will apprise them about what they have done (and then judge them). ¹⁶⁰ Whoever comes (to God) with a good deed will be given credit for ten similar good deeds, and whoever comes with a bad deed will be requited for only one. Verily, no one will be wronged.

¹⁶¹ Say (to them O Prophet), "Behold, my Lord has guided me to a straight path which is an ever-true religion, the faith of Abraham, an upright monotheist (who turned away from all that is false). Verily, he was not among those who ascribed divinity to anything else besides God." ¹⁶² So proclaim, "Indeed, my prayer, my acts of worship, my life and death are only devoted for God alone, the Lord of all the worlds; ¹⁶³ in Whose divinity none has a share; and this is what I have been commanded (to convey to all mankind). Indeed, I shall always be foremost among those who submit themselves to Him." *ᵃ*

¹⁶⁴ Say also to them, "Should I seek another Lord besides God when He is the Lord of everything? (Verily,) every soul will reap the fruits of its own deeds and no soul will be made to bear the burden of another. (Hence, no one should ever expect his burden of sin to be borne by others). In time, you will ultimately return to your Lord and He will apprise you about everything that you have been disputing among yourselves."

¹⁶⁵ So behold (O people)! It is He who has made you His emissaries on earth and raised some of you in ranks over others so that He may test (who among) you (are best in faith and conduct) through what He has given you. Your Lord is indeed Swift in Retribution, yet He is also Most Forgiving, Most Compassionate (in dispensing His grace).

ᵃ This proclamation was made in reference to those who lived during the time of Prophet Abraham about 2,700 years before the birth of Prophet Muhammad. It should not be confused with the same proclamation made by Prophet Muhammad mentioned in verse 39:12 as to who was foremost to proclaim this between them.

7. Al-A'rāf
[The Heights : 206 verses]

This is another long Makkan chapter. Its main emphasis is on monotheism and the fundamentals of belief such as the truth of the Qur'an and the Prophethood of Muhammad, the resurrection, and reward and punishment in the Hereafter. It draws attention to how the father of mankind - Adam, was deceived by Satan and warns mankind against his machinations and perennial enmity. In the course of administering this warning, God addresses mankind as "O children of Adam" four times in this chapter (with the only other time in chapter 36) to remind that He has sent His Prophets and Messengers from time to time to call mankind to the right way. The chapter also reminds mankind of the Day of Judgment and mentions that on that day, people will fall into three groups : the first group that will be admitted into paradise, a second group that will be hurled into hell and a third group that will occupy a middle position being consigned to neither paradise nor hell before judgment finally falls upon. They are called "the people of Al-A'raaf" where the name of this chapter is taken from. It is also in this chapter that accounts of some of the Prophets and Messengers of God such as Noah, Hūd, Saleh, Lot, Shu'aib [i.e. Jethro] and Moses are given for the first time in some detail, mentioning how the disbelievers from among their respective peoples offered resistance and opposition. In this connection, mention is also made about the trials of the Children of Israel that have been granted numerous blessings, only to be repaid with disobedience and recalcitrance which brought God's displeasure and punishment upon them. The chapter concludes with repeated emphasis on monotheism and on the folly and sin of taking objects and creations as deities.

In the name of God, the Most Gracious, the Most Compassionate.

Opponents' Doom

[1] *Alif Lām Mīm Ṣād.* [2] This is a Book that has been sent down to you (O Prophet). Let there be no doubt in your heart (about its truth) so that you will warn (the disbelievers) and remind the believers with it. [3] (Say to them, "O people!) Follow what has been sent down to you by your Lord and do not take any other patron besides Him." Yet how seldom do you bear this in mind. [4] (Do you know) how many (rebellious) communities that We have destroyed (before you)? Our retribution took them all by sudden at night or at midday while they were resting. [5] And when Our retribution came upon them, they had nothing to plea, except cry, "(Woe to us!) Indeed, we were wrongdoers!"

[6] (On the Day of Reckoning,) We shall question those to whom the Messengers were sent and question the Messengers too (whether they had conveyed Our message in truth). [7] And most certainly, We shall give them a

full account (of what they have done) based on Our sure knowledge, for We were never once absent. ⁸ On that Day, truth will be the criterion in the weighing (of deeds). Those whose good deeds tip the scales will be the successful ones; ⁹ whereas those whose scale is light will be the ones who have lost their souls for unjustly rejecting Our signs. ¹⁰ Verily, it is We Who established you firmly on earth and provided you with the means of livelihood. Yet, very little (and seldom) do you give thanks.

Iblis's Opposition to Man

¹¹ It is We Who created you and gave you shape. Then We ordered the Angels, "Prostrate yourselves before Adam (as a mark of respect of My perfect creation)!" All prostrated except *Iblis*, (who in his self glory and arrogance) refused to prostrate with the others. ¹² God asked, "(O *Iblis*!) What prevented you from prostrating when I commanded you?" Answered *Iblis*, "I am better than him, for You created me from fire whereas him You created from clay." ¹³ And God said, "Get down from this place! It is not for you to be arrogant here. Now begone! For you are truly the most despicable (of all creatures)!" ¹⁴ Said *Iblis*, "(O God!) Grant me respite from your punishment until the Day of Resurrection." ¹⁵ And God replied, "Indeed you will be among those who are granted respite."

¹⁶ (*Iblis* retorted further in defiance,) "Now that You have declared me astray, I shall certainly lie in ambush to deviate everyone from Your straight path. ¹⁷ Then, surely I shall (never cease to) come upon them from the front, and from the back, and from the right, and from the left. And You will find that most of them are ungrateful." ¹⁸ And God said, "Get out of here you despicable outcast! I shall certainly fill the Hellfire with you and all those who follow you."

¹⁹ "And (as for you) O Adam, dwell with your wife in this garden and eat whatever you wish. But do not approach this tree, lest both of you will disobey me and bring injustice upon yourselves." ²⁰ Thereupon, Satan whispered evil suggestions to deceive them into exposing their nakedness that was hidden from them (all the while). And he said, "Your Lord forbade you this tree to prevent you both from (staying in this garden permanently as) Angels or immortals." ²¹ And he swore to (convince) them, "(Trust me). Indeed, I am advising you sincerely."

²² So he (cunningly enticed them and) made them slip (from their promise to God) with his deception. And when they had eaten from the tree, their nakedness became exposed and they began to cover themselves with leaves from the Garden. Then their Lord called out to them, "Did I not forbid you

from approaching this tree and warn that Satan is your clear enemy?" [23] Both of them replied, "O our Lord! We have certainly wronged and sinned against our souls and unless You grant us forgiveness and mercy, we shall certainly be among the losers."

[24] And so God said, "Get down (both of you from this state of blessedness and innocence! Verily, take heed and learn from this lesson that) some of you will always be enemies (and cause trouble to one another). The earth will be your dwelling place from now on, and you will be granted the means for your livelihood there for an appointed time. [25] On it you will live and on it too you will die. And out of it you will then be raised to life again (to face the reckoning of all your deeds)."

Warning Against Satan's Insinuations

[26] O children of Adam! We have sent down to you (the knowledge of making) garments to cover your nakedness and also as adornment; but the garment of God-consciousness and piety is the best of all. These are some of God's signs for people to ponder.

[27] O children of Adam! Do not let Satan deceive you as he deceived your parents, causing them to be expelled from Paradise and stripped from their garments to expose their nakedness. Verily, he and his tribe watch you from where you cannot see them. Indeed, We have made Satans as patrons to those who reject the truth.

[28] And whenever they commit a shameful act, they say, "We found our forefathers doing this and it was God Who commanded us to do this." Tell them, "Behold! God would never command anyone to do any shameful act. Are you attributing to God things of which you have no knowledge?" [29] And say to them, "My Lord commands to do justice (in everything). Set your faces towards Him at every place of worship and then call upon Him (in true devotion). Make the practice of your religion pure and sincere for Him alone. (Remember that it is) Him Whom you will be returned to just as He had created and originated you (in the beginning)." [30] Some among you He guided while others deserved the loss of their way for taking Satan as their patrons and masters in preference to God, thinking that they are being rightly guided.

[31] O children of Adam! Dress well when you attend your places of worship. Eat and drink moderately, for God does not love those who are extravagant (and wasteful). [32] Ask them (O Prophet), "Who has forbidden you the adornment or to eat the good things which God has provided for His servants?" Say, "All these things are for the enjoyment of the believers in the

life of this world (though shared by others)." But on the Day of Resurrection, all good things will be exclusively for the believers alone. This is how We clearly spell out Our signs and revelations to people of (innate) knowledge.

³³ Say (O Prophet), "Verily, my Lord has forbidden shameful deeds - whether apparent or hidden, all types of sin, wrongful oppression, and He has forbidden you to associate any partner with God for which He has never granted any authority to do so; and saying things about God of which you have no knowledge." ³⁴ For every community is an appointed term. When their term arrives, they can neither delay nor hasten it even for a moment.

Just Retribution

³⁵ O children of Adam! If Messengers come from among you conveying My signs (of divine guidance), those who take heed and mend their ways (to live righteously) will have nothing to fear nor grieve. ³⁶ But those who deny Our signs and treat them with arrogance, they will be the inmates of the Fire and remain in it forever. ³⁷ Who can be more unjust (and wicked) than the one who invents a lie against God or denies His signs and revelations? Whatever God has decreed to be their portion in life will be theirs until Our Angels come to them to take their souls, saying, "Where are now those you used to worship besides God?" And their reply will be, "They have forsaken us!" Verily, they will (have no choice but to) testify against themselves that they were indeed among those who disbelieved (and defied the truth).

³⁸ (And then) God will say, "Enter the fire of Hell and join the community of Jinn and men who were before you." As they enter, each group will curse the one before it. And when all are gathered there, the last of them will say about the first, "Our Lord! These are the ones who led us astray. Let their torment be doubled in the Fire." He will answer, "Each one of you deserves double suffering but certainly you had not expected this." ³⁹ And so the first of them will say to the last of them, "You were actually no better than us. Taste then the punishment of your own misdeeds!"

⁴⁰ Verily, the gates of heaven will not be opened for those who deny Our revelations and scorn them with arrogance. Their admission into Paradise will be as impossible as the passing of a camel through the eye of a needle. That is how We requite habitual sinners. ⁴¹ Hell will be their bed while flames will be their blanket. That is how We requite evil wrongdoers.

⁴² No burden do We place on any soul more than what it can bear. For those who believe and do good deeds, they are worthy of Paradise and will remain in it forever. ⁴³ There, We shall remove whatever malice that may be

lingering in their hearts against one another. Rivers will flow right beneath them and they will say (in full humility), "All praise is due to God alone Who guided us to this (victory). Verily, we would have not found the right path if God had not guided us. Indeed, our Lord's Messengers have told us the truth (and our faith in their teachings has truly saved us today)." Then it will be announced to them, "This is the Paradise that you have earned because of (your unwavering faith and) the noble deeds that you have done."

⁴⁴ And the residents of Paradise will call out to the inmates of the Fire, "Indeed, we found our Lord's promise to be true. Did you find your Lord's promise to be true too?" They will answer, "Yes!" Then an announcer will proclaim from their midst, "God's curse is on the arrogant wrongdoers." ⁴⁵ They are the ones who hindered others from God's path, strived to make it appear crooked, and rejected the Hereafter." ⁴⁶ Between the two groups will be a (tall) barrier and on top of it will be men who recognize everyone by their marks (of distinctive features). They will call out to the residents of Paradise, "Peace be upon you!" They have not entered it but are longing to enter it very much.

⁴⁷ And when their eyes turn towards the inmates of the Fire, they will plead in fear, "O our Lord! Do not place us together with those whom You have judged guilty of evildoings!" ⁴⁸ They ask the inmates of the Fire who are recognized by their distinctive features, "Are your riches or arrogant pride unable to rescue you now?" ⁴⁹ (And they ask further,) "Are these people (whose faces are radiant today) the ones whom you had previously sworn that God would not extend any mercy to them?" (Finally, those who are on top of the tall barrier will be told, "You may) enter Paradise now! There is nothing for you to fear and grieve (about anymore)."

⁵⁰ Then, (in deep agony,) the inmates of Fire will plead to the residents of Paradise, "Please give us some water or food which God has provided you." But the residents of Paradise will reply, "God has forbidden both of these from being given to those who had (arrogantly) rejected the truth." ⁵¹ They are the ones who have taken their religion as amusement and play, and who have been deceived by their worldly life. God will say, "Today We shall forget them as they (had deliberately chosen to) forget the meeting of this Day and mocked Our revelations (when they were warned about it before)."

⁵² And certainly, We brought to them a Book that We explained (its content) with knowledge, as guidance and blessing to those who believe. ⁵³ Are they waiting for the fulfillment (of its warning before they will believe it? Verily,) on the Day when that warning is (finally) fulfilled, those who had neglected it will say, "The Messengers of Our Lord did indeed bring forth the truth (but we ignored it). Are there any intercessors who will plead on our

behalf (to save us from the torment of Hellfire that lies before our eyes now)? Or, can we be restored to (earthly) life so that we can perform differently from what we used to do before?" Indeed, they have truly squandered their souls and all false gods that they fabricated before have forsaken them now.

To Whom All Authority Belongs

⁵⁴ Verily, your Lord is the Almighty God Who created the heavens and the earth in six phases, and He is firmly established on His (Supreme) Throne. He overlaps the night with the day that swiftly follows it. The sun, the moon and the stars are all subservient to His command, and He has absolute authority and command over every creation. Blessed is God, the Lord of the worlds! ⁵⁵ Call upon your Lord with humility and in the secrecy of your heart. Indeed, He does not like those who transgress (the bounds He has set). ⁵⁶ Hence, do not corrupt the earth after it has been set right. Call upon Him with fear and hope. Verily, God's grace is ever near to those who excel in good deeds (and are benevolent).

⁵⁷ He is the One Who sends forth the winds as good news in advance of His coming grace. And when it gathers up heavy clouds, We drive them to a barren land and We make the rain fall upon it, bringing forth all kinds of fruits. Likewise shall We bring forth the dead (to life on the Day of Resurrection). Will you not reflect on this? ⁵⁸ Verily, good soil yields rich vegetation by the will of its Lord while barren soil yields nothing but poor vegetation. This is how We explain Our signs and revelations (over and over again in various ways) for (the benefit of) those who are grateful (of Our grace and mercy).

Common Message Conveyed

⁵⁹ Indeed, We sent forth Noah to his people and he said, "O my people! Worship God alone. (Behold!) You have no other god but Him and I fear for you the punishment of a mighty (dreadful) Day (if you ignore my warning)." ⁶⁰ But the leaders of his people answered, "It seems to us that you are obviously lost in error!" ⁶¹ Noah replied, "O my people! There is nothing wrong with me. I am really a Messenger from the Lord of all the worlds. ⁶² I (have been appointed) to convey the message of my Lord and give you sincere advice. Verily, I know something from God that you do not know. ⁶³ Do you deem it strange that a reminder has come to you from your Lord through a man from among you who warns you to fear Him (and avoid evil) so that you will be graced with His mercy?" ⁶⁴ But they denied him. So We rescued him in the Ark, together with those who stood by him, and drowned the others who denied (and rejected) Our signs. They were indeed a people who chose to be blind (to the truth).

⁶⁵ To the people of 'Aād, We sent their brother Hūd, who said, "O my people! Worship God alone. You have no other god except Him! Will you not (take heed of this warning and) fear Him?" ⁶⁶ But the leaders who disbelieved among his people said, "Verily, you look like someone who is immersed in foolishness and we think you must surely be a liar." ⁶⁷ And Hūd replied, "O my people! I am not foolish. On the contrary, I am a Messenger from the Lord of all the worlds. ⁶⁸ I am conveying my Lord's messages to you and I come to you as a trusted adviser."

⁶⁹ Do you deem it strange that a reminder has come to you from your Lord through a man from among you who warns you (to beware of Him)? Remember that He has made you heirs to Noah's people and endowed you with great stature. So, be mindful of God's blessings so that you will attain success." ⁷⁰ They said, "Have you come to tell us to only worship God alone and forsake what our forefathers used to worship? Bring (the doom that) you are threatening us with if you are a man of truth!"

⁷¹ Hūd said, "Your Lord's condemnation and wrath have already befallen you! Do you (still want to) dispute with me about the empty names (of the false gods) that you and your forefathers have invented for worship without any authority (and permission) from God? Wait then (for your doom). Verily, I shall wait with you too." ⁷² And so, by Our grace, We saved Hūd and those who stood by him while We annihilated the last remnants of those who denied (and rejected) Our signs and refused to believe.

⁷³ And to the people of Tsamud, We sent their brother Saleh, who said, "O my people! Worship God alone. You have no other god except Him! Clear evidence of the truth has now come to you from your Lord. This she-camel is God's sign for you. So leave her alone to pasture freely on God's earth. Do not harm her, lest you be seized by a grievous punishment. ⁷⁴ Remember how He made you successors to (the people of) 'Aād, and settled you firmly on earth. You built for yourselves palaces in open plains and carved out homes in the mountains. So remember the blessings of God and do not act wickedly on earth by spreading corruption (and causing disorder)."

⁷⁵ The arrogant leaders of his people then asked the believers among them who were (weak and) powerless, "Do you really believe that Saleh is a Messenger from his Lord?" They replied, "Indeed, we believe in the message (and guidance) that he brings." ⁷⁶ But the arrogant ones said, "We reject what you believe in!" ⁷⁷ Then they slaughtered the she-camel and rebelled against their Lord's commandment, and challenged Saleh, "Bring down the punishment that you are threatening us with, if you are really a true Messenger." ⁷⁸ Thereupon, an earthquake seized them and their bodies sprawled lifeless in the ruins of their homes. ⁷⁹ Then, Saleh turned away from

them and said, "O my people! Indeed, I have conveyed my Lord's message to you and gave you good advice, but you do not like those who give advice."

⁸⁰ We also sent Lot who said to his people, "Why are you committing such lewd and indecent acts *ᵃ* which no one else in the world has committed before you?" ⁸¹ "Indeed, you approach men lustfully instead of women. You are certainly (an evil group of) people who has deliberately transgressed (the bounds of what is just and decent)." ⁸² His people had no answer except to say, "Expel Lot and his followers from your land for (acting as if they are pious and) want to remain chaste!" ⁸³ And so We saved him and his family except his (stubborn) wife who was among those who were left behind. ⁸⁴ And We rained down upon them a shower of stones. (Therefore O people,) will you still not take heed of what happened in the end to those who were lost in sin?

⁸⁵ And to the people of Madyan, We sent their brother Shu'aib who said, "O my people! Worship God alone. You have no other god except Him! Clear evidence of the truth has now come to you from your Lord. Give full measure and weight in all your dealings. Do not (cheat and) deprive people of what is rightfully theirs. Do not spread corruption on earth after it has been set right. This is indeed for your own good if you are true believers."

⁸⁶ "And do not sit in ambush at every road that leads to the truth, threatening and hindering all those who believe in God from His path, and trying to make it appear crooked. Remember how He graced His bounty upon you by multiplying you when you were few in number? So take heed of what happened in the end to those who spread corruption (and caused disorder on earth)." ⁸⁷ "If there are some among you who believe in the message that I bring in the midst of others who deny it, then have patience until God judges between us. Verily, He is the Best of all Judges."

⁸⁸ The arrogant leaders of his people said, "O Shu'aib! We shall certainly drive you and your fellow believers out of our land unless you revert to our ways." Replied Shu'aib, "(Will you still do so) even if we despise (those ways)?" ⁸⁹ "If we return to your misguided religion after God has rescued us from it, we would surely be fabricating a great lie against Him. It is not conceivable for us to turn back unless God, our Lord, wills it. Verily, the knowledge of our Lord encompasses everything and we put our trust in Him." Then they prayed, "Our Lord! Expose the truth between us and our people, for indeed You are the best of those who lay open the truth (for all to see and the best Judge)."

⁹⁰ But the leaders among his people who did not believe said (to their

---

ᵃ Homosexual acts.

people), "If you follow Shu'aib, you will surely end up as losers!" [91] Thereupon, an earthquake seized them and their bodies sprawled lifeless in the ruins of their homes. [92] And those who called Shu'aib a liar were (destroyed) as if they had never lived there. Those who denied and rejected Shu'aib were the true losers. [93] And so, Shu'aib turned away from them and said, "O my people! Indeed, I have conveyed my Lord's message to you and gave good advice. Why should I (be sad and) mourn for those who refused to believe?"

Lessons to Learn

[94] Never have We sent a Prophet to any community except that (he was derided and rejected. So) We seized its people with misfortune and hardship so that they might submit to Us in humility. [95] Then, We replaced their suffering with prosperity until they grew and multiplied, (yet they did not draw any lesson from this. Instead of being grateful to God and humbling themselves,) they said, "Verily, the same (natural) cycle of events were experienced by our forefathers too." So We seized them by surprise while they were in a state of blissful ignorance. [96] If only the people of those communities had believed in God and were mindful of Him, We would have opened upon them blessings from the heaven and the earth. But they (chose to) reject the truth. So We seized them for (their misdeeds and the sins that) they earned.

[97] Did the people of those communities feel secure against the coming of Our punishment while they were asleep at night? [98] Or did they feel secure against its coming in broad daylight while they were busy engaging themselves in worldly play (and amusement)? [99] Or did they really feel secure against God's plan? Verily, only those who would end up as losers (and are doomed to ruin) feel a sense (of false) security from God's plan. [100] Is it not obvious to those who inherited the land after what We did to the former generations, that if We so willed, We could (easily) punish them for their sins and put a seal over their hearts so that they cannot hear (and perceive the truth)?

[101] Such were the communities whose stories we relate to you (O Prophet). All of them had Messengers who were sent to them carrying Our messages with clear evidence of truth but they persisted in their disbelief of what they had been denying. This was why God placed a seal on their hearts (and made them completely oblivious of the truth). [102] And We did not find many men who were true to their promise. Instead, We found most of them truly defiantly disobedient.

A Confrontation With Pharaoh

[103] And after those early people, We sent Moses with Our revealed signs to Pharaoh and the leaders of his people, but they too defied these signs and treated them unjustly. So take heed of what happened in the end to those who are corrupt (and cause disorder on earth). [104] Moses said, "O Pharaoh! Verily, I am a Messenger from the Lord of all the worlds. [105] It does not befit me to say anything about God except the truth. Verily, I have come to you with a clear sign from your Lord (to invite you to faith, but you chose to reject it). So let the children of Israel go with me (in God's path)." [106] But Pharaoh said, "If you have come with a sign to prove that you are God's Messenger, then show it (to me) if you are speaking the truth." [107] After that, Moses threw down his staff and suddenly it turned into a real serpent. [108] Then he drew out his hand (from his garment) and it turned white and shining for all to see.

[109] The leaders from the people of Pharaoh said, "He is indeed a skilled sorcerer; [110] and intends to drive you out from your land." So Pharaoh asked them, "What is your advice to me then?" [111] They answered, "Let him and his brother wait, while we send announcers to all the cities; [112] to summon every skillful sorcerer to you." [113] So the sorcerers were brought to Pharaoh and they asked, "Will we be given a great reward if we defeat Moses?" [114] Pharaoh answered, "Yes! Surely you will be among those who are close to me."

[115] And when the sorcerers and Moses were brought together, they asked Moses, "Who should throw (down their staff) first - you or we?" [116] Moses answered, "You first!" So when they did, they cast a spell upon the eyes of the audience and struck them with awe by showing a great feat of sorcery (when all the staves that they threw down turned into make-believe serpents). [117] Then We inspired Moses to throw down his staff. Behold! It (became a real serpent that) swallowed all the false (serpents). [118] Hence, the truth prevailed and all that Pharaoh and his followers did became futile. [119] They were vanquished right there and became utterly humiliated.

[120] As for the sorcerers, they fell down in prostration (because they knew that what Moses did was not sorcery but a clear evidence of God's might). [121] And they exclaimed, "(Behold!) We now believe in the Lord of all the worlds; [122] the Lord of Moses and Aaron." [123] Pharaoh replied, "How dare you believe in Him without my permission? This must have been a plot which you cunningly devised (behind me) to drive its people out from this city. You will soon know (how terrible is my revenge). [124] I shall surely have your hands and feet cut off on opposite sides and then crucify all of you." [125] But his sorcerers answered, "Verily, only to our Lord will we return. [126] Are you inflicting vengeance on us because we believe in the signs of our Lord that

have come to us? O Lord! Shower us with patience and let us die in the state of full submission to You."

[127] And the leaders of Pharaoh's people asked him, "Will you let Moses and his people go free to commit mischief in the land while they abandon you and your gods?" Pharaoh replied, "(Nay!) We shall kill their sons and spare their daughters. Surely we shall be in control (and prevail) over them." [128] And so Moses said to his people, "Turn to God for help and be patient. Indeed, the whole word belongs to God. He lets whomsoever He wills of His servants to inherit it. The future belongs to those who are always mindful of God (and strive to fulfill their duty to Him diligently)." [129] Answered Moses's followers, "Indeed, we have been oppressed before and after you came. (We do not see how we can be freed from this condition)." Mosa replied, "(If you hold firm to faith and place your trust in your Lord), perhaps He may destroy your enemy and make you successors in the land to see how you will manage your affairs."

[130] And so We inflicted the people of Pharaoh with years (of drought) and shortage of crops so that they will take heed (of Our warnings and come to their senses). [131] But whenever good fortune came to them, they said, "This is what we deserve!", and whenever they were gripped with calamity, they would blame their evil fortune on Moses and those who followed him. Behold! Their misfortune was actually decreed by God (because of their transgressions), but most of them did not realize this. [132] They said to Moses, "Whatever signs you bring to cast your magic spell on us, we still do not believe you."

[133] So We plagued them with flood, locusts, lice, frogs and water that turned into blood - all as clear signs from Us but they persisted in their arrogance. They were a nation of people who were lost in sins. [134] Every time a plague struck them, they would cry, "O Moses! Pray to your Lord for us with what He has promised you. If you remove the plague from us, we shall surely believe you and let the children of Israel go with you." [135] But when We removed the plague from them and gave time to honor their promise, they would (always) break their word. [136] And so We inflicted Our retribution on them and caused them to drown in the sea because they (continuously) denied Our signs and were heedless of them.

[137] (Then at a later time), We made (the descendants of) the people who were (oppressed and) deemed weak to inherit the eastern and western parts of the lands that We blessed. *ᵃ* (Verily,) your Lord's good promise to the children

---

ᵃ The Children of Israel lived prosperously in the land of Palestine during the reign of Solomon from 970 to 931 BC but it was short lived because they reneged their pledge with God and defied Him (verse 5:13). About 350 years later in 586 BC,

of Israel was fulfilled because they patiently (endured Pharaoh's oppression). And as for Pharaoh, We destroyed the great works and fine buildings that he and his people had erected (with such pride).

The Israelite's Relapse Into a State of Ignorance

¹³⁸ And so, We rescued and brought the children of Israel across the sea. Then they came upon a community of people who were devoted to the worship of idols, and said, "O Moses! Make for us a god like the gods they have." Replied Moses, "You are really foolish and ignorant (because you still cannot discern between what is right and wrong). ¹³⁹ Indeed, what these people believe and follow is doomed to destruction, and worthless are all that their practices. ¹⁴⁰ Should I seek a (false) god for you to worship other than Almighty God when it is He who has exalted (your rank) above the rest of all mankind?"

¹⁴¹ And (then Moses reminded them of this word from God : "Do you not remember) when We saved you from Pharaoh and his people who afflicted you with cruel suffering, slaughtered your sons and spared only your women?" Were you not faced with a severe trial from your Lord at that time? *ᵃ*

¹⁴² Then, We summoned Moses for thirty nights on (Mount Sinai) and added ten more to complete the term of forty nights (for communion) with his Lord. (Before leaving,) Moses said to his brother Aaron, "You will be in my place among my people (while I am away). So act righteously and do not follow the path of those who (are evil and) spread corruption."

¹⁴³ When Moses came to Our appointed place and his Lord spoke to him, he asked, "O my Lord! Show Yourself so that I can see You." God answered, "By no means can you see me. But look at the mountain. If it remains firm in its place, then you might be able to see Me." So when his Lord manifested His glory upon the mountain, it crumbled to dust and Moses fell down

---

Nebuchadnezzar of Babylon conquered the land and destroyed the Temple of Solomon in the city of Jerusalem. Many of them were forced into exile in Babylon before they were allowed to return to Palestine by Cyrus the Great of Persia (who is believed to be Dzul-Qarnayn mentioned in verses 18:83-98) when he conquered Babylon in 539 BC and set them free. The Temple was rebuilt soon after but was totally destroyed again for the second time when the Romans invaded Jerusalem in 70 AD. Hundreds of thousands of Jews perished in the siege of Jerusalem and many thousands more were sold into slavery. The destruction of the Temple that occurred twice in history fulfilled the prophecy and warning promised by God to the Children of Israel that was conveyed through Moses. See verses 17:4-8 and the footnotes.
ᵃ See also verses 2:49 and 14:6.

unconscious. When he recovered, he said, "Glory be to You (O God, Who are the Most Perfect)! To You alone do I turn in repentance and I am foremost among those who believe (in You)." ¹⁴⁴ Said God, "O Moses! Indeed, I have chosen (and raised) you over others by giving you My messages and speaking to you (directly). Hold on to what I have given you and be among those who are grateful."

¹⁴⁵ We inscribed all the laws that We ordained to the children of Israel on Tablets with lessons to be learned from all things together with their explanation. And We said, "Take and hold these firmly and command your people to follow them to the best of their ability. Soon, I shall show all of you the home (and fate) of those who are disobedient (for you and your people to take a lesson from it)."

¹⁴⁶ Verily, I shall turn My signs away from all those who are (unjust and) arrogant on earth so that they will not believe in My commandments (even if the signs are clearly presented to them). And even if they may see the path of righteousness, they will choose to not follow it. But if they see a path of error, they will not hesitate to take it. This is because they have denied Our signs (and revelations) and remained heedless of them. ¹⁴⁷ The (good) deeds of those who denied Our signs and the meeting in the life to come will become worthless. Why should they expect to be rewarded for anything other than the wrong that they have done?

¹⁴⁸ And in his absence, the people of Moses's made (a golden statue of) a calf that produced a lowing sound from the jewellery (and ornaments that they carried with them). Did they not see that the statue could neither speak nor provide them any guidance? And yet they took it for worship and became wicked wrongdoers. ¹⁴⁹ And when they felt remorseful about what they had done and realized that they had gone astray, they cried, "If our Lord does not have mercy on us and forgive us, surely we shall end up among the losers."

¹⁵⁰ And when Moses returned to his people, angry and disappointed (over they had done), he said, "Evil is what you have committed during my absence! Have you forsaken your Lord's commandment?" Then he cast aside the Tablets (of the Law), seized his brother by the hair and dragged him towards himself. Cried Aaron, "O son of my mother! Behold, the people overpowered me and almost killed me. So do not let our enemies rejoice over me, nor you count me among the evil wrongdoers." ¹⁵¹ Hearing this, Moses prayed, "O Lord! Forgive me and my brother (for our weaknesses) and accept us in Your grace. Verily, You are the Most Compassionate of all those who show compassion." ¹⁵² (God said,) "Verily, those who took the (golden statue of a) calf for worship will indeed be overwhelmed by their Lord's wrath and humiliation in this life." That is how We requite those who fabricate (lies and)

falsehood. ¹⁵³ But for those who do evil deeds and then repent and become true believers, your Lord is certainly the Most Forgiving, the Most Compassionate.

¹⁵⁴ And when Moses's anger subsided, he picked up the Tablets that were inscribed with guidance and grace for those who were in awe (and fearful) of their Lord. ¹⁵⁵ Then Moses chose seventy men from among his people to pray for forgiveness (on Mount Sinai) at a time that We set. When (they arrived,) they were seized by an earthquake, (and Moses) cried, "O my Lord! Had it been Your will, You could have easily destroyed us all. Would You destroy us for something the foolish among us had done? This is certainly a trial from You by which You let go astray whomsoever You will (that refuse to follow Your guidance), and guide whomsoever You please (that repent and turn to You in devotion). Verily, You are our Protector, so grant us Your forgiveness and mercy. You are indeed the Best of all Forgivers. ¹⁵⁶ And ordain for us what is good in this life and in the life to come, for indeed, we have turned to You (in repentance)." God replied, "I afflict My punishment (only) on those whom I will (for their defiance towards Me) but My grace encompasses everything. And for those who do righteous deeds, spend in charity and believe in Our revelations, I shall indeed ordain (and confer) My mercy upon them."

¹⁵⁷ (They are) those (among the children of Israel) who follow the (last and final) Messenger - the unlettered Prophet whom they will find mentioned in the Torah *ᵃ* that is with them, and also in the Gospel *ᵇ* - who commands

---

ᵃ Muhammad in Hebrew is *Muhammadim*. Refer to the footnote for verse 2:76.
ᵇ Muhammad in Aramaic Hebrew is *Mawhamana*. See footnote for verse 61:6. Essentially, Muslims believe that the original *Injeel* (i.e. Gospel) that recorded God's revelation to Jesus which he then conveyed to his people in his original Aramaic Hebrew language is lost and nowhere to be found since two thousand years ago. What is available now are the 27 books that form the New Testament (NT), all written in Koine Greek with the earliest one being in the year 70CE, or 37 years after the disappearance of Jesus. On top of this, all the actual authors of these 27 books had never met Jesus with the possible exception of Matthew alone according to the Gospel of Matthew 9:9. But this can still be challenged based on the fact that the Gospel of Matthew was not written in Aramaic Hebrew which should have rightfully been the case since it is Matthew's native and spoken language. The analogy of this would be like reading the Qur'an in Persian because there is no original Qur'an scripture in Arabic. How can this be logical and possible to accept when it is a known fact that Prophet Muhammad's native tongue is Arabic and the language of revelation to him was in Arabic too? The veracity of the scripture's content in Persian can never be verified as true if the original scripture in Arabic is not available for reference. The same logic applies to the NT too and because of this, Muslims categorically and unequivocally

them to do what is right and forbids from what is wrong; makes good (and clean) things lawful to them and bad things unlawful; and relieves them from their heavy burdens and shackles that were imposed upon them (before). So those who believe in him, honor him, aid him and follow the light which has been sent down with him, it is they who will triumph.

¹⁵⁸ Say (O Muhammad), "O mankind! Indeed I am the Messenger of God to all of you, to Whom belongs the dominion of the heavens and the earth. There is no other god except Him. It is He alone Who gives life and causes

---

reject the authenticity of the NT and do not regard it as the originally preserved *Injeel* unless the original Aramaic version is available for reference. As such, it would be natural to expect intense debates between Muslim textual critics and Christians that have been going on for centuries regarding the veracity of the Bible. In the case of Prophet Muhammad's mention in the NT, these two verses stand out. They are about what Jesus is believed to have said to his disciples : (1) [John 16:7] "But the fact of the matter is that it is best for you that I go away, for if I don't, then the Comforter won't come. If I do, he will - for I shall send him to you." (2) [John 14:25-26] "I am telling you these things now while I am still with you. But when the Father sends the Comforter instead of me - and by the Comforter I mean the Holy Spirit - he will teach you much, as well as remind you of everything I myself have told you." The focus of the debate here is on who is the Comforter mentioned in these verses? John 14:26 says that the Comforter is the Holy Spirit. However, this claim is contrary to the plain and unambiguous words of John 16:7, wherein Jesus said that his departure is inevitably necessary for the coming of the Comforter. In other words, if the Comforter is the Holy Spirit, then the one who will come to replace Jesus on earth only after he goes away is the Holy Spirit. But this directly contradicts Luke 1:15 which says that John the Baptist was filled with the Holy Spirit even before he was born. Also in Luke 1:35, it is mentioned that the Holy Spirit came to Mary the mother of Jesus when she conceived him, and in Matthew 3:16 which speaks of Jesus receiving the Holy Spirit in the form of a dove when he was baptized. Thus, it is clear that the Holy Spirit had visited some people on earth before Jesus as well as during his own time too. In fact, it is a matter of common knowledge in Christianity that the Holy Spirit was also co-existing with Jesus and it would be sacrilegious to think for a moment that Jesus was without the Holy Spirit. So to what then is the reference in the words, "If I do not go away, the Comforter will not come to you" in John 16:7? Surely not to the Holy Spirit who the Scripture itself admitted that it has already come before and during the time of Jesus? As such, Muslim textual critics point out that the Comforter must be a mortal and only Prophet Muhammad fits into this prophecy. The only way for this to be refuted is if the original *Injeel* or Gospel in Aramaic Hebrew can be produced for reference. Unfortunately, this is not possible because the Scripture is lost without any trace since the past 2,000 years. The word "Comforter" in Koine Greek is discussed further in the footnote for verse 61:6.

death." Believe then, in God and His Messenger - the unlettered Prophet who believes in God and His Words; and follow him, so that you will be rightly guided.

[159] And among the people of Moses, there were some who guided others in the way of truth and established justice. [160] And We divided them into twelve tribes of distinct communities. And when they asked Moses for water (while wandering in the desert,) We inspired him to strike the rock with his staff; whereupon twelve springs gushed forth from it and each tribe was assigned its own drinking station. And We also shaded them with clouds and sent down *Al-Manna* and quails to them, saying, "Eat of the good things which We have provided for you." (But they rebelled, and by doing so,) they did no harm to Us. Instead, they only brought injustice to their own souls.

[161] Then We allowed them to live in (Canaan) *a* and to eat from it whatever they wished but they would first have to plead, "We repent! (So remove from us the burden of our sins)" and enter the gate (humbly) in prostration. By doing so, We would forgive them of their sins and increase the reward for those who excel in their deeds. [162] But the wicked among them mocked and substituted the word which was commanded to them (with something else that carried a foul meaning). And so, We let loose a scourge upon them from heaven as requital for their persistent wrongdoings.

[163] Ask them about the town which was situated by the sea and what happened when they transgressed the Sabbath law. (Behold!) On the day of their Sabbath, fish came to them at the water's surface but this did not happen on other days. That was one of Our tests on them because they were always defiantly disobedient.

[164] And when some of the obedient among them asked (those who tried to restrain the Sabbath transgressors), "Why do you preach to people whom God is about to punish with severe suffering?"; the pious ones answered, "So that we shall have a reason to present to your Lord and be free from blame and at the same time hope that these wrongdoers will be mindful of Him (and desist from evil deeds)." [165] So when they disregarded the reminder, We saved those who had tried to forbid evil, and We seized the wrongdoers with a wretched punishment because of their defiant disobedience. [166] And when they persisted in exceeding the bounds of what they had been forbidden from, We said to them, "Be apes - despised and rejected!"

[167] And (remember) when your Lord proclaimed that He would surely raise people against the Jews who would cruelly afflict them with grievous

---

a The ancient name of Palestine.

torment until the Day of Resurrection (because of their evil deeds). Behold! Your Lord is Swift in Retribution yet He is also The Most Forgiving, The Most Compassionate. **168** And (because of their persistent disobedience), We divided and dispersed them as separate communities all over the earth - some were righteous, and some not. We tested them with both blessings and misfortunes so that they may ponder and mend their ways.

169 After them, succeeded an evil generation who in spite of inheriting the Torah, took for themselves whatever vanities of this lower life (as an excuse to sustain their livelihood. They falsely justified this action by) saying, "We (do this out of necessity and) will surely be forgiven by God." But when more of those vanities came to them again, they continued to greedily gorge (and made more lies against God to continue justifying their misdeeds instead of refraining). Have they not solemnly pledged through the Torah to say nothing but the truth about God? And have they not studied what is in it? Surely (they must know that) life in the Hereafter is far better for whoever that fears God and is ever mindful of Him. (But why did most of them choose to disregard this?) Why will you not think (and take any lesson from this)? **170** As for those who hold firm to the Book and perform their prayer (steadfastly), We shall not let the reward for those who strive to set things right become worthless.

171 (And remind them too O Prophet, of what We said to their forefathers) when We violently shook Mount (Sinai) until it loomed above them like a canopy and they feared it was going to fall on them, "Hold firmly to what We have revealed to you (through Moses) and take heed of what is in it so that you (will always) be mindful of God (and refrain yourselves against evil)."

Bearing Witness

172 (O Prophet! Remind mankind of the occasion) when your Lord brought forth from the loins of the children of Adam their descendants, He asked them, "Am I not your Lord?" They replied, "Yes, we bear witness that You are." *ᵃ* We did this lest on the Day of Resurrection you would say, "We were never made aware of this." **173** Or lest you would say, "Verily, our forefathers

---

ᵃ Every soul is embedded with the *fitrah* (i.e. natural disposition, innate tendency and pure value system) to worship its Creator alone and do good to others as he would like others to treat him. But man will stray from the right path when he does not turn to God's divine revelation for guidance. When this happens, he will take his own lusts as God (see verses 25:43 and 45:23) and end up either worshipping false gods, or completely rejecting the existence of God and the promise of resurrection and Judgment Day. He will also be prone to commit injustice and violate the rights of others.

were idolaters and we are their descendants who came after them. Will you destroy us for the errors that were committed in the past by those who had gone astray?" [174] This is how clearly We explain Our signs so that those (who have sinned will ponder and) return (to Our path).

[175] (O Prophet!) Recite to them the story of the one to whom We gave (the knowledge of) Our signs and revelations but he turned away from them (for the sake of worldly gains). As a result, Satan took hold of him and he ended-up misguided like many others. [176] Had We willed, We could have elevated him with (the revelation of Our signs) but he clung to (the deception of) worldly life and succumbed to his vain desires. His parable like a dog that pants with its tongue lolling whether you approach him in a threatening manner or even if you leave him alone. Such is the parable of those who reject Our signs (and revelations). Tell people this story so that they may ponder. [a] [177] Evil is the example of people who deny Our signs. They have indeed brought injustice to their own souls.

[178] Whoever God guides (because of his faith and piety) is rightly guided, and whoever He lets astray (because of his stubbornness and defiance to the truth) is surely a loser. [179] Certainly, We have created Hell to be filled with many Jinn and people who have hearts they fail to understand (the truth) with, eyes they do not use for sight, and ears they do not use for hearing. They are like cattle; in fact even worse because they are more misguided, for they (choose to be) heedless (of Our clear warnings).[b] [180] Verily, God has the most excellent names, so invoke Him by these names and shun those who distort the meaning of His names, for they will certainly be requited for their misdeeds.

[181] Among those whom We have created are a group of people who guide others to the truth and establish justice accordingly. [182] As for those who deny (and ignore) Our revelations, We shall lead them (to ruin) in ways that they do not expect and realize, step by step. [183] And even though I grant them respite, My (subtle) plan is exceedingly firm. [184] Has it never occurred to them that

---

[a] According to Ibn Kathir who is a renowned Qur'an exegete, this is the story about a pious sage who lived during the time of Moses by the name of Bal'am bin Ba'ura (or Balaam son of Beor as he is mentioned in Jewish Scriptures). He started off as a righteous and godly person but ended up on the wrong side after relenting to incessant requests by King Balak of Moab to pray for the destruction of Moses and the Israelites in exchange for worldly gains. This verse and footnote should be read in conjunction with verse 62:5 and its footnote that share a common theme.
[b] This also applies to those who worship their lusts and vain desires and lead a hedonistic lifestyle as though this is the main purpose of their existence. See verses 25:43 and 45:23

there is no madness in their fellowman *ᵃ* and that he is only a plain warner (who will not be held accountable for their actions)?

¹⁸⁵ Have they also never considered God's mighty dominion over the heavens and the earth and all the things that He has created, and then asked themselves that perhaps their hour of death is already very near? (If not,) in what other statement (or news) will they pay heed after this (Qur'an) to realize and believe (that mankind will surely be resurrected and requited for their deeds)? ¹⁸⁶ Verily, there is no guide for those whom God lets astray (because of their own doing). He will leave them in their overweening arrogance, blindly stumbling to and fro.

¹⁸⁷ (O Prophet!) They will ask you about the Last Hour, "When will it come?" Say, "Verily, it is known only to my Lord. He alone will reveal it at its appointed time. It weighs heavy in the heavens and the earth and will strike suddenly without warning." They ask you as if you could gain insight to this mystery. Say to them, "Indeed, its knowledge rests with my Lord alone, but most people do not (understand and) know this." ¹⁸⁸ Say (further) "I have no power to benefit or protect myself from harm, except what God wills. If I knew about the unseen, I would certainly have acquired many benefits for myself and prevented any harm from touching me. (Behold!) I am just a plain warner and a bearer of good news for those who believe."

The Final Word

¹⁸⁹ It is He who created you from a single soul and made his mate from it so that he might find comfort in her. And when he embraced her, she conceived a light burden that developed gradually. And as it grew heavy, they both invoked God their Lord, (saying,) "If You grant us a righteous child, we shall certainly be among those who are grateful." ¹⁹⁰ But when He gives them a righteous child, they associate false gods with Him for the gift that He has given them. But God is exalted far above whatever they associate with Him. ¹⁹¹ How could they associate Him with those who cannot create anything and are themselves created? ¹⁹² These false gods neither have the ability to help those (who ascribe divinity to them) nor can they help themselves.

¹⁹³ And if you call upon them for guidance, they will certainly not be able to fulfill your prayer. It makes no difference whether you call upon them or remain silent. ¹⁹⁴ Verily (O disbelievers), the false gods that you call upon other than God are created beings like yourselves. So, go ahead and call upon them. Let them answer you if your claims are true.

ᵃ Prophet Muhammad.

[195] Do these (gods that you worship) have feet to walk with, or hands to hold with, or eyes to see with, or ears to hear with? Say (to them O Prophet), "Call on your gods and work out a scheme against me (if you can), and grant me no respite. [196] Behold! God alone is my guardian Who has sent down this Book (as guidance for mankind). And He is the best protector of the righteous."

[197] (On the contrary,) those whom you call besides Him have neither the ability to help you, nor can they help themselves. [198] And if you pray to them for guidance, they do not hear you. Even though you may seem to think that they are looking at you, they do not actually see you.

[199] (O believers!) Be gracious (and do not hold grudges against these confused idolaters). Command (and invite to) what is right and leave alone all those who choose to remain (foolish and) ignorant.

[200] And if an evil urge or temptation is prompted to you by Satan, seek refuge in God. Indeed, He is All-Hearing, All-Knowing. [201] Verily, those who are ever mindful and conscious of God will certainly remember Him and become alert (from complacency) whenever a thought of evil from Satan touches them. [202] But (know that) those who follow of Satan will always help one another in error, and they will never cease (to tempt others to follow them).

[203] (O Prophet!) Whenever you do not bring (and read) to them a new verse, they ask mockingly, ("Do you not have anything new to read to us?) Can you not just create one? Tell them, "(How could I?) Verily I only follow what is revealed to me by my Lord. This Book *ᵃ* brings enlightenment from your Lord, and guidance and blessing only for those who believe (the truth).

[204] And when the Qur'an is recited, pay attention and listen quietly to it so that you will be graced with God's mercy. [205] (Always) remember your Lord within yourself in humility and reverence. (When you recite His Book) in the mornings and evenings, do so in a moderate tone of voice (with your heart attuned to it is meaning). And do not be among the heedless. [206] Behold! (Even the Angels) who are nearest to your Lord are never too proud to worship Him. They (constantly proclaim) and glorify His perfection and prostrate themselves only to Him alone.

ᵃ The Qur'an.

8. Al-Anfāl

[The Spoils of War : 75 verses]

This chapter is named *Al-Anfaal* which means The Spoils of War from a word which is mentioned in its first verse. The chapter was revealed in the context of the Battle of Badr which took place on 17 Ramadan in the 2nd year of Hijrah. The battle marked the first victory of the Muslims against the evil infidel forces of disbelief. The chapter refers to a number of events and aspects of that battle and lays down the rules of conduct for fighting in the way of God and for distributing any spoils that might accrue to the Muslims, and for the treatment of the prisoners of war. It is stressed that victory comes from God alone as a reward for the unflinching faith in Him and in His cause, and not by virtue of superiority in number and arms and ammunitions. In this battle, a small band of some three hundred ill-equipped Muslim infantry inflicted a crushing defeat upon an army of the disbelievers numbering more than a thousand including a sizeable cavalry and equipped with the best arms of the time. The chapter ends by reminding that the believers are of one community, irrespective of their race, color or place of origin. Likewise, the disbelievers are of one community too, irrespective of their race, color or domicile.

In the name of God, the Most Gracious, the Most Compassionate.

The Battle of Badr

¹ They ask you about the spoils of war (O Prophet). Tell them, "All spoils of war belong to God and His Messenger. So remain conscious of God (O believers), keep alive the bonds of brotherhood among yourselves, and pay heed to God and His Messenger, if you are true believers." ² Verily, true believers are those whose hearts tremble with reverence and awe when God is mentioned, and whose conviction is strengthened whenever His verses are recited to them; and they put their trust in their Lord. ³ They are also those who are steadfast in their prayer and regularly spend (in charity) out of what We have provided them. ⁴ Such are the true believers. They will have high standing with their Lord, as well as forgiveness and noble provisions.

⁵ (O Prophet!) Just as (the distribution of war spoils was decreed in truth,) the command from your Lord that you leave your home to fight for justice was a decree in truth too. Some among you were exposed as reluctant believers (because they were averse to this command). ⁶ They argued with you (out of ignorance) as if they were being driven to death with their eyes wide open even though the truth has been made clear to them.

⁷ (O believers!) Remember when God promised you victory over one of

the two enemy hosts - one unarmed and the other fully armed; it was your wish to fight the unarmed host (to gain easy victory). But God decreed (that you fought with the armed host) to prove the truth in His promise and to eliminate the infidels to their roots; **8** so that truth may be accomplished and falsehood nullified (for people to discern), however hateful this might be to those who were lost in sin. **9** (Remember) when you prayed to your Lord for aid, He responded, "I shall reinforce you (with the assistance of) one thousand Angels, one after another." **10** God gave this good news to comfort and reassure your hearts (with hope of victory. Ultimately,) victory comes only from God, The Almighty, All-Wise.

11 (Call to mind) when He made slumber to overtake you which caused you to experience inner calm as an assurance from Him (before the battle). Then He caused rain to descend on you from heaven to purify and free you from Satan's evil whisperings so that your hearts would be strengthened and your steps firm. **12** (Behold, O Prophet!) Your Lord also inspired the Angels (to convey His message to you, saying), "I am with you. So give courage to the believers. Indeed, I shall cast terror (and panic) into the hearts of the infidels. So strike above their necks and strike off from them every fingertip." **13** That is because those who deny the truth have defied God and His Messenger, and whoever does so should know that God is severe in retribution. **14** This is the reality for you (O enemies of God)! So taste it now and know that a more severe torment awaits you in the Hellfire.

15 O you who believe! When you encounter the infidels who are advancing towards you in battle, never turn your backs to them (in flight). **16** Whoever turns his back to them on such an occasion – unless if it is a strategy of war or to join a fighting troop - he will incur God's wrath and his final home will be Hell, a vile destination indeed. **17** (O believers!) Know that it was not you who killed them, but it was God Who did. And it was not you (O Prophet) who cast terror in them by throwing (the handful of sand in their direction), but it was God Who did. Verily, He put the believers through this for an excellent test of faith. Behold! God hears all, knows all. **18** That is how (God bestowed His grace upon true believers and at the same time) weakened the scheme of those bent on rejecting the truth.

19 (O disbelievers!) If you have been seeking for a decisive judgment, it has indeed come to you now. If you cease (from opposing the truth), it will be for your own good. But if you persist, so shall We. (And know that) never will your forces be of any help to you, however great their numbers may be. (Behold!) God is certainly with the believers (who are firm in their faith).

20 O you who believe! Obey God and his Messenger. Do not turn away from Him, now that you have heard His message. **21** Do not be like those who say, "We have heard!" but pay no heed to what they hear. [22] Verily, the worst of all creatures in the sight of God are those who are (willfully) deaf and dumb, and do not use common sense (to understand the truth). [23] Had God perceived any virtue in them, He would have surely endowed them with hearing. But (it would make no difference) even if He made them hear because they would still turn away (and refuse to listen) since they are truly an obstinate lot.

[24] O you who believe! Respond to the call of God and His Messenger whenever He calls you to that which will make your spirit becomes truly alive. Know that God intervenes between man and (the desires of) his heart (to guide him on the right path, only if he wants to be guided). Indeed, it is to Him alone Whom you will all be gathered. [25] And beware of God's trial that does not afflict the wrongdoers alone (but encompasses all). Know that God is severe in retribution.

[26] And remember when you were few (in number) and oppressed in the land, living in fear that you might be captured. Then He sheltered you, strengthened you with His help, and provided you with good things (for sustenance) so that you will be grateful. [27] (Hence) O believers! Do not betray the trust of God and His Messenger, nor knowingly betray what has been entrusted upon you.

[28] And know that your wealth and your children are only a trial and temptation for you. And that it is God with Whom lies your highest reward. [29] O you who believe! If you are ever mindful of God (and strive to fulfill your duty to Him diligently), He will endow you with a Criterion (to distinguish right from wrong and guide you aright). He will also erase and remove your sinful deeds and forgive you. Verily, God is limitless in His great bounty.

In Defiance of The Truth

[30] (Remember) how the infidels plotted against you (O Prophet). They sought to take you captive, kill, or exile you. They planned, and God planned too. Indeed, (little do they know that) God is the best planner of all. [31] And whenever Our verses were recited to them, they say, "Indeed, we have heard all this before. If we wanted, we could certainly compose sayings like these ourselves. They are nothing but fables of ancient times." [32] And they continued, "O God! If this is indeed the truth from You, then rain down stones on us from the sky or inflict some grievous suffering on us (to prove Your might)." [33] But God would not punish them while you are present in their midst, nor would God punish them while they could still ask for His forgiveness.

³⁴ Yet why should God not punish them for hindering others from the Sacred Mosque while they are not its (rightful) guardians? Only those who fear and are mindful of God deserve to be its guardians. But most disbelievers do not know (and understand) this. ³⁵ Their prayer at the House of God is nothing but whistling and clapping of hands. Taste then the punishment (of being defeated in Badr) because of your persistent rejection of the truth.

³⁶ Indeed, those who are bent on denying the truth spend their wealth to hinder others from the path of God and they will continue to do so until it becomes a cause of their regret before they will be finally defeated. Verily, these infidels will surely be gathered together in Hell. ³⁷ Indeed, God will separate the wicked from the good. He will heap the wicked upon one another, group them altogether and then cast them all into Hell. It is they who are the losers. ³⁸ So say to the infidels that if they desist (from their transgressions and follow Our path), their past sins will be forgiven. But if they revert (to their evil ways), tell them to reflect upon the (fate and) natural consequences of those before them.

³⁹ And fight against them until there is no more persecution (and injustice), and until worship can be entirely devoted to God (freely, without fear and hindrance). ⁴⁰ And if they turn away (from your warning), then know that God is your Protector, an Excellent Protector, and an Excellent Helper.

God's Will at Work

⁴¹ (O believers!) Know that whatever you acquire as spoils of war, one-fifth of it belongs to God and His Messenger, his near relatives, the orphans, the destitute, and the (stranded) traveler. This you must observe if you believe in God and in what We sent down upon Our servant *ᵃ* on the Day of the Decision (or Criterion) when the two forces met (in the battle of Badr, where truth was clearly distinguished from falsehood). Verily, God has the power to will anything.

⁴² Recall when you were encamped at the nearer end of the valley (of Badr) while the infidels were at the far end, and the caravan was down below you (along the coast). Had you made prior arrangements to meet them for battle, surely you would have argued among yourselves to set its timing and location. But the encounter was brought about by God for Him to accomplish what He had destined, which is to make truth and falsehood clearly distinguished to those who survived and those who died (in the battle). Behold! God is indeed All-Hearing, All-Knowing.

ᵃ In reference to the Angels that were sent down to help the Prophet in this battle.

⁴³ (Remember too O Prophet) when God showed them to you in your dream as few in number. Had He shown them to you as many, you would have surely been discouraged and disputed among yourselves about what to do. But God saved you from this (chaos). Verily, He has full knowledge of what is in the hearts of everyone. ⁴⁴ And so, when you met in battle, He made them appear few in your eyes just as He made you appear insignificant in their eyes so that God will accomplish what He has destined (out of this battle). And to God do all matters return (for judgment).

⁴⁵ O you who believe! When you face your enemy in combat, stand firm and remember God as much as you can so that you will be successful. ⁴⁶ Obey God and His Messenger and do not fall into disputes, lest you lose courage and weaken in strength. Persevere, for verily God is with those who persevere. ⁴⁷ And be not like those who leave their homes full of arrogance, desiring to be praised, and (with the intention) to hinder others from the path of God. Indeed, God encompasses everything that they do.

⁴⁸ (Behold!) It was Satan who made their sinful acts look appealing and said, "No one can defeat you today, for I shall be there to help you." But when the two forces came within sight of one another, he turned on his heels and fled, saying, "Behold! I shall not be responsible for you. Indeed, I see what you do not see and I fear God." (Verily,) God is severe in retribution.

⁴⁹ (At the same time,) the hypocrites and all those with sickness in their hearts said about the believers, "(With their small number against the big Makkan army,) they must have really been deluded by their faith (to muster enough courage to face their opponents today)." Whereas in reality, those who put their trust in God (will truly find Him as their Helper against evil). God is indeed Almighty, All-Wise.

⁵⁰ And if you could see when the Angels take away the souls of those who opposed the truth, you will indeed see them striking the faces and the backs of those infidels, saying, "Taste the torment of the Blazing Fire!" ⁵¹ This is (the punishment) for what your hands have committed. Indeed, God is never unjust to His servants. ⁵² The same had happened to the people of Pharaoh and also to those who lived before them. They too rejected God's signs (and messages), and were seized by God for their sins. Verily, God is indeed Almighty and severe in retribution.

⁵³ That is because God will not withdraw the blessings which He has graced upon a people until they discontinue their faith. Verily, God hears and knows everything. ⁵⁴ The same had happened to the people of Pharaoh and also to those who lived before them. They too denied God's signs (and messages), so We destroyed them for their sins and drowned them. Indeed,

they were all evildoers.

Delineation of Loyalties

⁵⁵ Verily, the worst living creatures in the sight of God are those who defy Him and refuse to believe (in His message). ⁵⁶ They are those who make treaties with you (O Prophet) and time after time violate their treaties, for they have no fear of God. ⁵⁷ So if you encounter them in combat, (punish them severely to serve as a fearsome example) so that those who come after them may take heed of this lesson and be deterred. ⁵⁸ If you (have reason to) fear betrayal by a people, respond by throwing (the treaty) back at them on equal terms. Verily, God does not like those who betray.

⁵⁹ Do not let the infidels think that they can escape (God's punishment). Indeed, they can never weaken His powers. ⁶⁰ Hence, prepare against them whatever you are able to - of force and cavalry - so that you may strike terror into the hearts of your enemy and the enemy of God, and also others besides them who are unknown to you but known to God. Remember that whatever you spend in the cause of God will be fully repaid and you will not be wronged. ⁶¹ But if they incline towards peace, then you should too (O Prophet); ᵃ and place your trust in God. Verily, He is the One who hears and knows everything.

⁶² But if they intend to deceive you (by their pretense of peace), then God is indeed sufficient for you (to rely on). He is the One Who has strengthened you with His help and given you believers (as your faithful and loyal followers); ⁶³ whose hearts He brought together (and placed affection in them). Even if you had spent all (the treasures) in the earth, you would still not be able to bring their hearts together (by yourself) but God has brought them together (in genuine faith and affection). Verily, He is the Almighty, All-Wise. ⁶⁴ O Prophet! Sufficient is God for you and for the believers who follow you.

⁶⁵ O Prophet! Rouse the believers to fight. If there are twenty steadfast (warriors) among you, they will be able to vanquish two hundred (enemies). And if there are a hundred steadfast among you, they will be able to vanquish a thousand infidels (who are fighting against you), for they are a people devoid of understanding. ⁶⁶ But God has lightened your burden for now because He knows that there is still weakness in you. So if there are a hundred steadfast (warriors) among you, they will be able to vanquish only two hundred (enemies). And if there are a thousand, they will be able to vanquish two thousand, with God's permission. Verily, God is with those who are steadfast.

ᵃ See verses 2:190-193 and 16:126.

⁶⁷ It is not befitting for a Prophet to take prisoners of war until he has battled strenuously (and thoroughly subdued) the land (by overcoming the enemy. Some of the believers among) you may desire the fleeting gains of this world, but God desires for you (the good of) the next life to come. Verily, God is Almighty, All-Wise. ⁶⁸ Had there not been a previous decree from God (which promised to efface the sins of all the believers who had participated in the battle of Badr), a severe penalty would have surely befallen upon all of you for the ransom you took. ⁶⁹ (And since God has forgiven you for your unintentional fault,) you may enjoy what you have gained in war, for it is now made lawful and pure for you. But fear and be ever mindful of God (so that you may be rightly guided). Verily, God is Most Forgiving, Most Compassionate.

⁷⁰ O Prophet! Say to the captives who are in your custody, "If God finds goodness in your hearts, He will give you even better than what has been taken from you, and He will forgive you (of your sins). Verily, God is Most Forgiving, Most Compassionate." ⁷¹ But (do not be surprised) if they intend to betray you since they have betrayed God before. That is why He gave you power over them (and made them your captives). Indeed, God is All-Knowing, All-Wise.

⁷² Verily, those who have accepted faith, emigrated (from their homes to forsake evil), strived hard in the cause of God with their possessions and their lives, and those who gave shelter and helped them - they are all allies of one another. But those who believed and did not emigrate, it is not your duty to protect them from anything until they emigrate. And if they seek your help against religious persecution, then it is your duty to help them, except against people with whom you already have a treaty. Verily, God sees everything that you do.

⁷³ Know that those who reject the truth will always be supporters and allies of one another. Unless you (are closely united and) do the same like them, oppression, (injustice) and widespread corruption will (surely) reign on earth. ⁷⁴ Those who have accepted faith, migrated from their homes (to forsake evil), strived hard in the cause of God, and those who gave shelter and helped them, they are indeed true believers! For them is forgiveness and a noble provision. ⁷⁵ And as for those who subsequently accepted faith, emigrated (from their homes to forsake evil), and strived hard in God's cause alongside you, they are your brothers. However, only those with blood relationship have greater rights and are entitled to inherit from one another in accordance with God's decree. Verily, God has full knowledge of everything.

9. At-Taubah
[Repentance : 129 verses]

This is a late Madinan chapter revealed in the year of 9 Hijrah against the background of the Tabuk expedition by the Prophet and the repeated breach of treaties and agreements by the disbelievers. The Tabuk expedition took place during the height of the summer season when marching to a distant destination like from Madinah to Tabuk that covered a distance of roughly 650km (406 miles). The expedition was difficult and arduous, and presented a real test in patience which God made it as a means for the Muslims to know who were the true hypocrites among them. This chapter is named *At-Taubah* with reference to verses 102 - 104 which stated that God accepts the repentance of those who recognize their faults, seek forgiveness and make amends for their mistakes. It is also called *surah* or chapter *Al-Bara'ah* which means Declaration of Disavowal with reference to the first word of the chapter which directs the Prophet and the Muslims to renounce and cancel the treaties and agreements with the disbelievers in view of their repeated breach of agreements, and lays down rules for dealing with them. This chapter is unique in the way that it is written as well as recited without the initial mention of *basmalah* (i.e. the proclamation of "*In the name of God*") at the beginning of the chapter unlike all other chapters because the Prophet did not direct its writing.

Declaration of Disavowal

¹ This is a declaration of disavowal by God and His Messenger to the idolaters with whom you have made a treaty. ² (Announce to these infidels,) "Go then, travel freely throughout the land for the next four months but know that you can never escape God's reach; and verily, God will disgrace all those who refuse to accept the truth (and persist in their hostility)."

³ This is a public proclamation from God and His Messenger to all mankind on the day of the Great Pilgrimage that God and His Messenger hereby disavow the idolaters. Hence, if you repent, it will be for your own good. But if you turn away, then know that you can never escape God's reach. So, give good news to those who persist in opposing the truth that a grievous punishment awaits them. ⁴ But for those idolaters who have not failed you in anything and have not supported anyone against you, fulfill your treaty with them until their term expires. Indeed, God loves those who are always mindful of Him and strive to keep their duty to Him diligently.

⁵ Then, when the sacred months have passed, kill the (hostile) idolaters (who refuse to make peace) wherever you find them; or capture, surround or wait for them at every conceivable place of ambush. But if they repent and establish their prayer and render the purifying dues, let them go their way.

Indeed, God is Most Forgiving, Most Compassionate. ⁶ And if any of the idolaters seek your protection, grant him protection so that he may hear God's words from you. Then escort him to his place of safety. That is because these people are still ignorant of the truth.

Reasons for the Disavowal

⁷ How could there be a binding treaty with God and His Messenger for such (hostile) idolaters? But as for those with whom you have already made a treaty at the Sacred Mosque, be true to them so long as they remain true to you. Indeed, God loves those who are always mindful of Him (and do not exceed their bounds). ⁸ How (can you trust those who are hostile towards you)? If they prevail against you, they will respect neither the ties of kinship with you nor the treaty (that you have established with them). They flatter you with their mouths while their hearts remain adamantly hostile. Indeed, most of them are defiantly disobedient.

⁹ They trade away God's revelations for a trifling worldly gain and hinder others from His path. Evil indeed is what they have done (and will continue to do). ¹⁰ They neither honor the ties of kinship with the believers nor observe the obligations of treaties. They are the ones who (constantly) transgress (the bounds of what is right). ¹¹ But if they repent, establish prayer and render the purifying dues, then they are your brothers in religion. This is how We spell out Our revealed signs clearly to people with knowledge (for them to ponder).

¹² But if they violate the treaty after they have sworn to keep it and defame your religion, then fight the leaders of those infidels who have no regard for their own pledges so that they will desist (from aggression). ¹³ (O believers!) Will you not fight against those people who have broken their solemn pledges, determined to expel the Messenger, and were the first to attack you? Do you fear them? (Nay!) It is God Who is more deserving of your fear, if you are true believers. ¹⁴ So fight them! Verily, God will punish them by your hands and bring disgrace upon them. He will ultimately grant you victory over them and soothe the hearts of those who believe; ¹⁵ and remove the rage from their hearts. Verily, God accepts repentance from whomsoever He wills. He is indeed All-Knowing, All-Wise.

¹⁶ O you who believe! Do you think that you will be left alone while God has not yet tested who among you have striven hard in His cause and taken none as friends and protectors except God, His Messenger and those who believe in Him? Indeed, God is fully aware of everything that you do.

Idolaters' Service of the Sacred Mosque

[17] It is unbecoming for the idolaters to maintain God's houses of worship while they bear witness against their own souls that they are the deniers of truth. Verily, their deeds are worthless and they will remain in the Hellfire forever. [18] God's houses of worship are only to be maintained by those who believe in God and the Last Day, those who are steadfast in their prayer, those who spend in charity and stand in awe of none except God alone. It is they who are entitled to true guidance.

[19] Do you regard the mere giving of water to pilgrims and the maintenance of the Sacred Mosque as being equal to the deeds of those who believe in God and the Last Day and strive hard in God's cause (to uphold justice)? Verily, they are not equal in the sight of God. And God does not guide those who are unjust and wicked. [a] [20] Those who believe, then emigrated (from their homes to forsake evil), and strive hard in God's cause with their possessions and their lives - they have the highest rank in the sight of God. It is they who will triumph in the end. [21] Their Lord gives them good news of His grace and pleasure, and of the gardens that await them, full of eternal bliss; [22] they will remain in there forever. Indeed, with God lies a great reward.

The True Implication of Faith

[23] O you who believe! Do not take your fathers and your brothers as allies if they prefer disbelief over belief. And whoever among you takes them as allies, then such people are wrongdoers. [24] Say, "If your fathers, your sons, your brothers, your spouses, your relatives, the wealth which you have acquired, the trade you fear will decline and the homes in which you take pleasure and cherish - are more beloved to you than God and His Messenger and striving in His cause, then wait until God manifests His (stern) decision.[b] (Verily,) God does not guide those who are defiantly disobedient."

---

[a] In chapter 107, the Qu'ran presents us with a scenario where the merits that are supposed to be gained from performing obligatory prayer and other ritual acts will be nullified if they are followed with ill treatment on others. And in this verse, we are told that noble hospitality has no value in the sight of God if injustice is being committed at the same time. What other service can be nobler than ensuring the comfort of pilgrims and upkeeping the Sacred Mosque? But even this was rejected by God. In other words, we are being sternly reminded to never take for granted that our generosity and good deeds will always gain us merit and God's pleasure especially when we become a party to injustice, either directly or indirectly. See also verse 11:113 and its footnote.
[b] His wrath.

Success Does Not Depend on Numerical Strength

[25] Verily, God granted you His support on many battlefields but not in the Battle of Hunayn when you took pride in your numerical strength, for it availed you nothing. For all its vastness, the earth seemed too narrow for you (on that day), and you turned back fleeing. [26] Then (finally), God sent down His tranquility upon His Messenger and upon those who are steadfast in their faith in Him. And (as an act of His grace), He sent down forces that you could not see, to punish those who opposed the truth (so that you could vanquish them). Such is the requital of those who reject the truth. [27] Yet after all this, God still turns in mercy to whomsoever He wills (among the believers) after they (realized their error and) repented, for God is Most Forgiving, Most Compassionate.

Relations with Other Religions

[28] O you who believe! Indeed, (the faith and spiritual state of) those who associate partners with God is impure (and corrupt). After this year, do not let them go near the Sacred Mosque. And if you fear poverty (as a result of your dissociation with them, have faith that) God will enrich you out of His bounty if He so wills. Surely God is All-Knowing, All-Wise. [29] (For repeatedly violating their peace treaties and continuously acting in hostility towards you, you are hereby commanded to) fight those who do not believe in God nor the Last Day, nor hold as forbidden what God and His Messenger have declared as forbidden, nor acknowledge the religion of truth, even if they are people of earlier revelation); until they agree to pay the submission tax [a] with a willing hand, and are utterly subdued.

[30] The Jews say, "Ezra [b] is the son of God!" And the Christians say, "Messiah is the son of God!" These are merely verbal assertions in imitation of the sayings of those disbelievers who preceded them. May God ruin them. How deluded are they! [31] They have taken their rabbis and their monks and the Messiah - son of Mary as Lords besides God, whereas they were commanded

---

[a] Jizyah.

[b] Uzayr in Arabic. The vociferous claim that Ezra is the son of God was made by some Jews and not by all Jews. This is in reference to their over-reverence of him as an exceptionally righteous person which does not carry the literal meaning that he is really the son of God much like how the Christians regard Jesus because Jews are generally monotheistic. However, it is possible that some Jews of the past might regard Ezra as the son of God in a literal sense due to sheer ignorance of their own religion. Incidentally, the term "son of God" is used in the Hebrew Bible as a way of referring to those who the Jews believe have close and special relationship with God.

to worship none except the One True God. (Behold!) There is no god except Him alone. Glorified and exalted is He from what they associate Him with (and all other imperfections). ³² They seek to extinguish God's light with their mouths, but God will not allow this to pass except that He will perfect His light, however hateful this may be to those who are bent on opposing the truth. ³³ It is He Who has sent His Messenger with guidance and the religion of truth making it prevail over all others, however hateful this may be to the idolaters.

The Evils of Hoarding Wealth

³⁴ O you who believe! Indeed, many of the rabbis and the monks wrongfully devour the possessions of others and turn people away from God's path. To those who hoard gold and silver and do not spend it in the cause of God, announce to them the news of a grievous punishment; ³⁵ on the Day when the possessions that they hoard will be heated in the Fire of Hell and their foreheads, flanks and backs will be seared with it; and they will be told, "This is what you hoarded for yourselves before. So taste now (the pain of) what you hoarded!"

The Observance of Sacred Months

³⁶ Indeed, the number of months with God is twelve as set by His decree on the day when He created the heavens and the earth. Of these, four are sacred, according to the ever-true law of God. Therefore, do not sin yourselves by violating them. And fight against the idolaters altogether as they fight against you altogether, and know that God is with those who are mindful of Him. ³⁷ Indeed, the postponement (of sacred months) is adding to disbelief which causes the infidels to be led (further) astray. They declare it permissible one year and forbidden another year so that they may make up the number of months which God has declared as sacred, thus making lawful what God has forbidden. The evil of their deeds is made fair-seeming (and alluring) to them; but God does not guide those who disbelieve.

The Tabuk Expedition

³⁸ O you who believe! What is amiss with you that when it is said to you, "Go forth to fight in God's cause!", you cling heavily to earth? Are you content with the comforts of this world in preference over the life to come? Paltry indeed are the enjoyments of life in this world when compared with those to come. ³⁹ If you do not go forth to fight in God's cause, He will punish you severely and bring other people in your place. (Know that) your (defiance) will not harm God in any way, for He has absolute power over all things.

⁴⁰ If you do not help the Prophet, certainly God will, as He had helped him at the time when the infidels drove him out of Makkah while he was together only with his other companion.*ᵃ* When these two were alone in the cave, he said to his companion, "Do not grieve (and fear), for God is with us." Thereupon, God bestowed on him the gift of tranquility and sent to his aid forces that you could not see. He brought the word of the infidels utterly low, while the word of God remained supreme. (Verily,) God is Almighty, All-Wise.

⁴¹ March forth then, whether you be lightly or heavily armed, and strive in God's cause with your possessions and your lives. This will be best for you if only you knew.

Manifestations of Hypocrisy

⁴² Had there been a prospect of an immediate gain and a short journey, the hypocrites would have certainly followed you; but the distance was too far for them. Yet they will swear by God, "Had we been able, we would surely have joined you." With this lie, they bring nothing upon themselves except ruin and doom. Verily, God knows that they are indeed liars.

⁴³ God has forgiven you (for your oversight O Prophet)! Why did you grant them permission to stay behind before it became clear to you who were speaking the truth and who were the liars? ⁴⁴ Those who believe in God and the Last Day will never ask your permission to be excused from fighting in the cause of God with their belongings and their lives. (Verily,) God knows well who are mindful of Him (and strive to keep their duty to Him diligently). ⁴⁵ Only those who do not truly believe in God and the Last Day will ask you for exemption. Their hearts are filled with doubt and they waver in their faith. ⁴⁶ Had they truly intended to march forth to fight, they would have certainly made some preparation for it. But God was averse to their going forth, so He caused them to hold back, and they were told, "Stay with those who stay behind."

⁴⁷ Had they set out with you, they would have added nothing but trouble, and they would be scurrying to and fro in your midst actively seeking chances to sow discord among you. There are also some among you who would be eager to lend them an ear (and this would only encourage them further. Indeed,) God has full knowledge of the wrongdoers. ⁴⁸ Even in the past, they tried to sow discord and also devised evil plots against your affairs until truth came and God's decree prevailed, much to their disgust.

ᵃ Abu Bakr.

⁴⁹ And among them is he who says, "Grant me permission to stay behind, and do not put me through a hard test!" Verily, by making such a request, they had already failed in their test and succumbed (to evil's temptation). Behold! Hell will most certainly engulf the disbelievers! ⁵⁰ If you are blessed with good fortune, it distresses them. But if a trouble befalls you, they say, "Verily, we are lucky to have taken our precautions earlier (and not followed Muhammad to the battlefield)." And they turn away rejoicing (in their false belief).

⁵¹ (Say to them), "Nothing will ever befall us except what God has decreed for us. He is our Guardian. And in God alone let the believers place their trust." ⁵² Tell them, "What you await to befall upon us is nothing but one of the two best things! *ᵃ* And what we await for you is that God afflicts you with punishment either directly from Himself or by our hands. So continue to wait. We too shall wait with you."

⁵³ Tell them, "Whether you spend willingly or unwillingly, it will not find acceptance with God, for you are indeed a people who are truly disobedient." ⁵⁴ Their disbelief in God and His Messenger prevents their spending from being accepted. Moreover, they do not come to prayer except in laziness (and reluctance) nor do they donate anything for a righteous cause without being resentful. ⁵⁵ So do not let their riches and children to impress (and dazzle) you. Verily, God intends to punish them through these pleasures in this worldly life and then cause their souls to depart in a state of disbelief.

⁵⁶ They swear by God that they are part of you whereas they are not. They are merely cowards who are overwhelmed by fear. ⁵⁷ If they could find a place of refuge, or caves, or a place to crawl into, surely they would turn around and rush headlong into it. ⁵⁸ Among them are those who speak ill of you concerning (the distribution of) alms. If they are given a share of it, they are pleased; but if not, then they are enraged. ⁵⁹ (It would have been much better for them) had they contented themselves with what God and His Messenger gave them, and said, "Sufficient is God for us. He will give us out of His bounty, and so will His Messenger too. To God alone do we turn in hope."

⁶⁰ Alms are only for the poor and destitute, and those who work in the administration of such affairs, and those whose hearts are to be won over, and for the freeing of people in bondage and debtors, and to further God's cause, and for the traveler (in distress). This is a duty ordained by God (upon the believers), and God is All-Knowing, All-Wise.

⁶¹ And among them are those who insult the Prophet by saying, "He (is gullible and) will listen to anything." Tell them, "He listens only for your

---

ᵃ Either martyrdom or victory.

good. He believes in God, trusts the believers, and he is (a manifestation of God's) mercy for those of you who truly believe (in the truth)." Indeed, a painful punishment awaits those who insult God's Messenger. ⁶² They swear to you by God in order to please you, (O believers). Yet it is God and His Messenger that they should strive to please, if indeed they are true believers. ⁶³ Do they not know that anyone who opposes God and His Messenger will be (thrown) in the Hellfire and remain in there forever? That is the ultimate disgrace.

⁶⁴ The hypocrites are afraid that a chapter be revealed about them, informing the believers of what is in their hearts. Say (to them), "Continue mocking as you wish. Indeed, God will bring forth what you fear." ⁶⁵ And if you ask them, they will surely say, "We were merely jesting and being playful." Say, "Were you making jokes about God, His divine signs and His Messenger?"

⁶⁶ Make no excuses. Indeed, you disbelieved after you professed your faith. Though We may pardon some of you (who turn to Us in repentance), We shall punish the others who continue to be in their sinful ways.

⁶⁷ The hypocrites, be they men or women, are all alike. They encourage what is evil, forbid what is good, and withhold their hands (from spending in God's way). They (ignore and) forget God, so He (ignores and) forgets them (too). Verily, the hypocrites - it is they who are the disobedient ones. ⁶⁸ God has promised the hypocrites - both men and women - and the infidels, the Fire of Hell where they will remain in it forever. This will be sufficient for them. God has rejected them and they will suffer an everlasting torment.

⁶⁹ (Say to these hypocrites, "You are just) like those who lived before your time. (In fact,) they were mightier than you in power with more wealth and children. They enjoyed their portion of worldly pleasures as you are enjoying yours now and you are also indulging in lies and idle talk now just as they did before. Their deeds have come to nothing in this world and in the life to come. They are indeed the (biggest) losers.

⁷⁰ Have they not heard the news of their predecessors - the peoples of Noah, 'Aād, Tsamud, Abraham, the dwellers of Madyan, and the overturned cities (of Lot)? Their Messengers came to them with clear evidence of the truth (but they rejected it. So,) it was not God who was unjust to them. Instead, it was they who were unjust to their own souls.

⁷¹ Believing men and women are protectors of one another. They (encourage and) order what is right and forbid what is wrong; they are steadfast in their prayer, and render their purifying dues, and obey God and

His Messenger. It is upon such people that God will bestow His grace. Indeed, God is Almighty, All-Wise. [72] God has promised believing men and women gardens that rivers flow beneath them where they will remain in there (forever), and blessed mansions in gardens of everlasting bliss. [a] But the greatest bliss of all is God's acceptance and His good pleasure. That is truly the ultimate success!

Stern Warning to the Hypocrites Who Shirked Jihad

[73] O Prophet! Strive against the infidels and the hypocrites and be stern with them. Their home is Hell - an evil destination! [74] These hypocrites swear by God that they said nothing but they had certainly uttered the word of blasphemy and became infidels after they professed their submission to God. And they sought to do what they could not accomplish, (that is, to undermine and destroy you). Verily, the only reason they are not openly resentful (to *Islam*) is because God and His Messenger have enriched them through His bounty. If they repent, it will be better for them. But if they turn away, God will punish them with grievous suffering both in this world and in the life to come. There is no one on earth to protect or help them (when God unleashes His wrath).

[75] Some of them have pledged to God, "If God gives us (wealth) out of His bounty, we shall certainly spend in charity and surely be among the righteous!" [76] But when He did bestow them (what they asked for) out of His bounty, they became stingy and turned away in aversion (of their pledges). [77] So He caused hypocrisy to take root in their hearts and to remain in there until the Day they meet Him because they reneged on their promise with God and because they kept lying (again and again).

[78] Do they not realize that God knows their secret thoughts and what they talk about in private, and that God has full knowledge of all things that are hidden and unseen? [79] These hypocrites who scoff at the believers who donate generously to charity and deride those who have nothing to give except what they earn through their hard effort will be derided by God. They will suffer grievous punishment.

[80] (O Prophet! It is all the same) whether or not you pray for their forgiveness. Even if you were to pray seventy times for their forgiveness, God will not forgive them because they have rejected God and His Messenger. Indeed, God does not guide those who are defiantly disobedient.

---

[a] The garden of Eden.

[81] Those who did not follow (the Tabuk expedition) were happy to stay behind after the departure of God's Messenger because they hated to strive with their wealth and their lives in God's cause. They said to one another, "Do not go to war in this heat!" Say (to them), "The Fire of Hell is far hotter!" If only they could understand this! [82] So let them laugh a little now because they will certainly weep much in the end in return for what they have earned.

[83] (O Prophet!) If God brings you back to a group of them (after your battle expedition) and they ask your permission to follow (in your next battle), tell them, "Never will you follow me nor fight alongside me against any enemy. You were happy to stay behind the first time, so continue to remain with those who stayed behind." [84] Do not ever hold prayers for any of them if they die nor stand by their graves; for they disbelieved in God and His Messenger, and died while they were in the state of defiance. [85] Do not let their wealth and children to impress (and dazzle) you. Verily, God intends to punish them through these in this life and cause their souls to depart in a state of disbelief.

[86] And when a chapter is revealed commanding them to believe in God and strive and fight along with His Messenger, the affluent among them would ask you to excuse them, by saying, "Allow us to stay with those who remain behind." [87] (Indeed,) they were satisfied to be with those who stayed behind. So a seal was set upon their hearts and they were unable to understand the truth. [88] But the Messenger and those who believed in him strived hard in God's cause with their wealth and their lives. It is they whom the most excellent rewards await (in the life to come) and it is they who are the successful ones. [89] God has prepared for them gardens which rivers flow from right beneath them where they will remain in there forever. That is indeed the supreme triumph!

[90] Some from among the Bedouins also came with their excuses asking to be granted exemption so that they can stay behind, while those hypocrites who lied to God and His Messenger merely sat quietly. Soon, grievous punishment will befall all those who disbelieved among them. [91] There is no blame on the disabled, the sick, and those lacking the means to stay behind, so long as they are sincere to God and His Messenger, for there is surely no reason to blame those who strive to do good beyond their means. And God is Most Forgiving, Most Compassionate.

[92] Likewise, there is no blame too against those who, when they came to you requesting that you give them mounts (to go to the battlefront), you said, "I can find nothing for you to ride on"; and then they turned away with their eyes streaming with tears of sorrow because they could not find anything to contribute (in God's cause). [93] Verily, blame is only on those who have the

means to follow you but asked to be excused because they are contented to stay behind (with the helpless). So God sealed their hearts, making them oblivious (to the punishment that will befall them). [94] (O believers!) They will offer excuses to you when you return (from the battlefield,). But say (to them), "Do not give excuses, for we shall never believe you. Verily, God has enlightened us about you. God and His Messenger will keep a watch over your conduct. Then you will be brought back to the One Who knows all that is hidden and manifest. Thereupon, He will apprise you about everything that you have done. (There is no way for you to escape from Him)."

[95] Upon your return, they will (surely) swear to you in God's name (by repeating their excuses) so that you will (forgive them and) leave them alone. Let them be. They are indeed filthy (and loathsome), and their final place of return is Hell - a fitting requital for the evil that they have earned. [96] They will also swear to you in order to please you. But even if you become pleased with them and accept their excuses, God will still not be pleased with those who are defiantly disobedient.

[97] The desert Bedouin Arabs are far more stubborn in their refusal to acknowledge the truth and in their hypocrisy, and are more likely to be ignorant of the limits that God has revealed to His Messenger. Indeed, God is All-Knowing, All-Wise. [98] And among the Bedouins are some who consider what they spend (in God's cause) as a loss and they await for your turn of misfortune (because of their apprehension towards you). May ill fortune befall them! (Indeed), God hears all, knows all. [99] But among the Bedouins are also some who believe in God and the Last Day, and consider what they spend as a means of bringing them nearer to God and the blessings of His Messenger. Behold! This is certainly a means of drawing near to God and He will admit them to His grace. Indeed, God is Most Forgiving, Most Compassionate.

[100] And of those who led the way - the first and foremost among the emigrants *a* and the helpers, *b* and those who followed them with excellence - God is well-pleased with them and they are well-pleased with Him. He has prepared for them gardens which rivers flow beneath them where they will remain in there forever. That is the greatest success! [101] And among the Bedouins who dwell around you, some are hypocrites; and so are some of the people of Madinah too, for they have become accustomed to hypocrisy. You do not know them, but We do. (Verily,) We shall punish them twice (in this world), and then they will be returned to a mighty (dreadful) punishment (in the life to come).

---

a Muhaajirun
b Ansar.

¹⁰² And (there are also) others who confessed their wrongdoings after mixing righteous and evil deeds together. (If they repent and stop doing this,) it is likely that God will accept their repentance, for God is indeed Most Forgiving, Most Compassionate. ¹⁰³ (Hence O Prophet,) accept a portion of their wealth that is offered (for God's sake) as charity so that they may be cleansed and grow in purity. And pray for their blessings too, for this will be a source of comfort for them. Verily, God hears all and knows all.

¹⁰⁴ Do they not know that it is God Himself who accepts repentance from His servants (without any intercessor) and receives what they offer in charity for His sake? He is indeed the Acceptor of Repentance, the Most Compassionate. ¹⁰⁵ Say (to them O Prophet), "Do as you will! Indeed, God, His Messenger and the believers will be witnesses to your actions. In the end, you will be brought back to Him Who knows all that is hidden and manifest. Then He will apprise you about everything that you have done." ¹⁰⁶ And there are still others (who stayed behind and did not fight alongside you) whom God has deferred His decree. He may either punish or pardon them, for God is indeed All-Knowing, All-Wise.

A Mosque Without Value

¹⁰⁷ And there are those who built a mosque (out of evil motives) to cause harm, disbelief and disunity among the believers, and also as a station for those who fought God and His Messenger before. Yet they will surely swear, "We have only the best of intentions." But God bears witness that they are indeed liars. ¹⁰⁸ Do not ever set your foot there! Only a house of worship that is founded on true devotion to God from its first day is worthy for you to pray in. There you will find men who love to purify themselves, and God loves those who purify (and reform) themselves.

¹⁰⁹ Now, who is better? Is it he who laid the foundation of his building on consciousness of God and (desire for) His good pleasure, or he who laid the foundation of his building on the edge of a cliff that is about to collapse which then tumbles with him into the Fire of Hell? (Verily,) God does not guide wrongdoers. ¹¹⁰ The building they built will never cease from fueling suspicion (and hypocrisy) in their hearts until their hearts are torn into pieces. And God is All-Knowing, All-Wise.

Supreme Triumph

¹¹¹ Indeed, God has purchased from the believers their lives and their wealth in exchange for Paradise. They fight in the cause of God, and they either kill or are killed. This is a true promise that He has made binding upon

Himself in the Torah, Gospel and the Qur'an. Who could be more faithful to his promise than God? So rejoice in the transaction that you have contracted with Him. That is indeed the supreme triumph! [112] (The believers are) those who turn (to God) in repentance (whenever they have sinned. They are those) who worship and praise (Him in adoration), who fast, who bow down and prostrate themselves (before Him), who encourage what is right and forbid what is wrong, and who keep within the bounds set by God. (They are the successful ones!) So give good news (of God's promise) to such believers.

Do Not Pray for God to Forgive the Idolaters

[113] It is not appropriate for the Prophet and the believers to pray for the forgiveness of those who associate partners with God even though they may be their close relatives after it has become clear that they will be the inmates of the Blazing Fire. [114] As for Abraham, his asking of forgiveness for his father was because of a promise which he made to him earlier. But when it became clear to Abraham that his father was an enemy of God, he dissociated from his father. Indeed, Abraham was compassionate and forbearing.

[115] And God would not consider those He has guided to faith for being deviant until He makes it entirely clear to them what they should avoid and guard themselves against. Verily, God has perfect knowledge of all things. [116] Indeed, to God belongs the dominion of the heavens and the earth, He gives life and causes death. And you do not have any protector or helper besides God.

God's Compassion Towards Those Who Repent

[117] Verily, God relented towards the Prophet, the emigrants, and the helpers who stood by him in the hour of hardship when the hearts of some of them had almost deviated from the right path. (But when they maintained their course,) He turned towards them (in mercy and accepted their repentance). Indeed, He is Most Tender and Most Compassionate to them. [118] And (He also turned in mercy) to the three who stayed behind. Their guilt troubled them so much to such a degree that the earth seemed too narrow despite its vastness and their souls had become too constricted until they were certain that there was no refuge from God except by returning to Him. Then He turned to them in mercy for them to repent. Indeed, God is the Acceptor of Repentance, the Most Compassionate.

The Command to Fight in God's Cause

[119] O you who believe! Be ever mindful to God and be among those who

are true to their word. [120] It is not fitting for the people of Madinah and the Bedoiuns around them to abandon God's Messenger in his battle expedition and cared about themselves more than him. That is because whenever they suffer from thirst, exhaustion or hunger in God's cause, and whenever they take any step which angers the infidels, or receive any injury from the enemy, all this is recorded in their favor as a righteous deed. Verily, God does not fail to reward those who (strive to) excel in good deeds. [121] And whenever they spend anything for the sake of God - be it little or much - or cross a valley in support of God's cause, all this is recorded in their favor so that God can reward them in accordance with the best of their deeds.

[122] And not all the believers should go forth to battle together. A group of them should stay behind and devote themselves to acquire (deeper) knowledge (of the religion) so that they can teach and warn their homecoming fellow-brothers to beware (and guard themselves against evil).

[123] O you who believe! Fight the infidels who come near you and let them find out for themselves how strong (and fierce you are against the enemy). Know that God is together with those who are always mindful of Him.

[124] And whenever a new chapter (of this Qur'an) is revealed, some of the hypocrites ask the believers (in jest), "Which of you has had his faith increased by this?" As for those who believed, it has increased them in faith and they rejoice over this.[125] But those whose hearts are afflicted with the disease of hypocrisy, (every new chapter) only adds wickedness to their existing wickedness, and so they die as disbelievers. [126] Do they not see that they are tried once or twice every year? Yet they do not turn in repentance nor do they pay heed. [127] Whenever a chapter is revealed, they look at one another asking, "Is anyone watching?" Then they silently slip away. Indeed, it is God Who turned their hearts away from guidance because they are a people devoid of understanding

[128] There certainly has come to you a Messenger from among yourselves who is distressed by your suffering, concerned of your well-being and kind and compassionate to the believers. [129] But if they turn away from you (O Prophet), then say to them, "Sufficient is God for me. There is no god except Him. In Him alone do I put my trust. And He is the Lord of the Mighty Throne."

10. Yūnus
[Jonah : 109 verses]

This is a Makkan chapter which deals with the fundamentals of faith, namely the belief in God as the Sole Creator, Nourisher and Sustainer of all beings, and worshipping Him alone to the exclusion of all imaginary deities. It draws to the fact that God has sent His Prophets and Messengers with Books of guidance to different peoples at different times, and that His final Messenger - Prophet Muhammad, was given the final Book of guidance replacing and overriding previous Scriptures. Further to this, the chapter also stresses the fact of resurrection after death followed by judgment and the requital of deeds. These matters are illustrated with reference to the stories of some Prophets like Noah, Moses and Jonah (i.e. Yunus), and how their respective people responded to them. Reference is also made to the attitude of the Makkans towards Prophet Muhammad wherein a challenge was thrown out to them and to all disbelievers of all times to produce a text that could rival the Qur'an's linguistic beauty and supremacy along with the facts of truth that it carries. The chapter is named after Prophet Yunus whose people were forgiven and saved from punishment as they ultimately believed in the message that was delivered to them after initially rejecting it.

In the name of God, the Most Gracious, the Most Compassionate.

A Book Full of Wisdom

¹ *Alif Lām Rā.* These are verses of the Divine Book that is full of wisdom.
² (O Muhammad!) Do (your) people find it strange that We have inspired a man from their own midst to warn (them and all) mankind (of their erroneous belief) and to also give good news to those who believe (in Our message) that they will have an honorable status with their Lord? *ᵃ* Yet those deniers of truth say, "Behold! This man is obviously a skilled sorcerer (with spellbinding eloquence)!"

³ Verily, your Lord is God (the Almighty) Who created the heavens and the

---

ᵃ It is clear that the essence of the Prophet's mission was to invite people to submit to God Almighty and concurrently establish justice, affirm what is right and eradicate evil. The Muslim community he was to establish would be a fair and virtuous one whose members acknowledge God, call on others to embrace Him, follow His path, and look forward in meeting Him in the Hereafter. Such a community had stood tall during his time and during the early generations after his death by opposing tyranny and oppression, and was also incorruptible by wealth and power. See also verse 3:110 and its footnote.

earth in six phases, and He is firmly established on His (Supreme) Throne, regulating and governing all that exists. There is none who may intercede with Him except by His permission. That is God your Lord, so worship Him alone. Will you not take heed of this message then? **⁴** It is Him you will all return to and that is God's true promise. Indeed, He is the One Who originates the process of creation and will repeat it (on the Day of Resurrection) so that He may justly reward those who truly believe and do good deeds. But those who deny and reject Him will have a scalding drink and a grievous punishment for their disbelief.

⁵ It is He Who made the sun a shining glory and the moon a (reflected) light *ᵃ* and determined for it phases so that you may know the number of years and the count of time. God has not created this except (to fulfill a purpose that is) in accordance with the truth (which He has decreed). He makes His revealed signs clear to people of knowledge. **⁶** Verily, in the alternation of night and day and in what God has created in the heavens and the earth are signs for people who are ever mindful of Him (and strive to diligently fulfill their duty to their Lord).

⁷ Indeed, those who do not expect the meeting with Us and are content and satisfied with the life of this world, and those who are heedless of Our signs and revelations; **⁸** will have the Fire for their home because of the evil that they have (committed and) earned. **⁹** But those who believe and do good deeds will be guided by their Lord through their (unwavering) faith. Rivers will flow from right beneath them in the Gardens of Bliss. **¹⁰** And in that state of happiness, their prayer will be, "Glory be to You, O God (Who are free from all imperfections)!"; and they will be answered with the greeting, "Peace (be upon you)!"; and the closing of their prayer will be, "All praise is due to

---

ᵃ This is another one of the many scientific miracles put forward by the Qur'an to the bewilderment of those who are sincerely seeking for the truth. The Arabic word for sun in the Qur'an, is *shams*. It is referred to as *diya* which means "shining glory", or *siraaj*, which means a "radiant lamp" or as *wahhaaj* which means "a blazing splendor". All three descriptions are appropriate for the sun, because it generates intense heat and light by its internal combustion. On the other hand, the Arabic word for moon is *qamar* and it is described in the Qur'an as *muneer* (i.e. bright) or *nur* (i.e. light) where its shine is not self produced. This is explicitly described in this verse where the sun is described as *diya'* while the moon as *nur* which reflects the light from the sun instead of producing its own. For thousands of years, earlier civilizations believed that the moon emanates its own light. But modern scientific discovery tells us that the light of the moon is reflected light just as it is stated in the Qur'an that was revealed 1,450 years ago. Not once in the Qur'an is the moon mentioned as *siraaj, wahhaaj* or *diya*, and the sun as *nur* or *muneer*. See verses 25:61, 71:16 and 78:13.

God alone, the Lord of all the worlds."

[11] And if God were to hasten upon people (the consequences of) evil in the way He hastens for them the good (that they invoke), surely their term (on earth) would have long expired. But We leave those who have no hope of meeting Us lost in their error (and overweening arrogance), blindly wandering (to and fro). [12] And when affliction touches man, he cries out to Us, whether lying on his side, or sitting, or standing. But when We remove the affliction from him, he goes on as if he had never invoked Us to remove the affliction that befell him earlier. This is how the misdeeds of those who commit excesses (and squander their own souls) are made fair-seeming (and alluring) to them. [a]

[13] Verily, We destroyed many generations before you (which had risen to heights of glory) when they persisted to indulge in injustice and wrongdoings. Their Messengers came with clear proofs (from Us to warn them of their transgressions) but they refuse to believe (and ignored the reminders). That is how We requite those who were lost in sin. [14] Then, We appointed you as their successors on earth to see how you would fare. [b]

[15] And when Our revealed verses are recited to them as clear evidence (of God's Oneness and the existence of Hereafter), those who do not hope for the meeting with Us say, "Bring us a different discourse or make changes to this." Say, "It is not for me to change anything as I please. I only follow (and recite) what is revealed to me. Indeed, if I were to disobey my Lord, I fear the punishment of a mighty (dreadful) Day (that awaits all who defy Him)." [16] Tell them (further), "Had God willed (otherwise), I would not have recited this

---

[a] Humans are vulnerable and weak. When faced with hardship, they can easily feel completely helpless, despondent and exposed. Crises can overwhelm and subdue them. It is at such moments that many people seek God and plead for His help. But as soon as the difficulty is overcome and the ordeal is over, their faith dwindle and their yearning towards God fade away. See also verses 22-23.
[b] The Muslim *ummah* of today has miserably failed to take heed of this warning by allowing injustice and corruption to reign just like the cursed nations of the past that the Qur'an narrates. This has weakened Muslim communities and nations to the point where we do not have the ability and might to defend our dignity. When brutal murders and atrocities are committed upon our brethren by those who hate Islam and also by wayward Muslims, we could only sit and helplessly watch all these on TV and social media. This humiliation is the price that we are paying for infecting ourselves with the disease of *Al-Wahn* (see see verses 102:4, 3:112, 6:123 and 28:77). The plight of the Palestinians, Yemenis, Syrians, Bosnians, the Rohingyas in Myanmar, the Uyghurs in China, and scores of other suffering Muslim communities all over the world are left to themselves to endure without any effective intervention from other Muslim nations to put a stop to all this misery and establish peace.

Qur'an to you, nor would He have made it known to you. Indeed, I have spent a lifetime among you before it was revealed to me. Can you not (see its truth) through reason (and trust me like you used to)?" ¹⁷ Who is more (wicked and) unjust than someone who attributes his lying inventions to God or denies His (divine) revelations? Surely the sinners will not be successful.

¹⁸ And they worship other than God things that can neither harm nor benefit them, and they say, "These are our intercessors with God." Say to them, "Do you want to teach God about things in the heavens and the earth that (you foolishly think) He does not know?" Limitless is He in His glory and exalted is He above what they associate Him with (and all the imperfections that they attribute to Him).

¹⁹ Humanity was once a community of a common faith but they differed (and followed different ways because of selfish rivalry and jealousy among one another). Had it not been for the word proclaimed by your Lord (to give respite to everyone before He gathers them all to Him), their differences would have surely been settled (by an instant retribution). ²⁰ And they (still) ask, "Why has not a miracle been sent down to Muhammad by his Lord?" Say (to them), "The knowledge of what is hidden and unknown is only with God alone. So wait! Indeed, I too shall wait with you."

²¹ When We let people taste some mercy after hardship, they suddenly turned around and plotted against Our revelations. Tell them, "God is even swifter in planning." Indeed, Our (heavenly) Messengers ^{*a*} write down everything that you plot (in your book of deeds).

²² He is the One who enables you to travel over land and sea. When you sail in ships with a favorable breeze, you rejoice. But when a storm arrives and the waves dash against them from all sides, suddenly they realize that they have been caught in it. Then (at that moment), they would call upon God, professing sincere devotion to Him alone, "Verily, if You save us from this calamity, we shall certainly be most grateful (for Your mercy and shall worship You alone)." ²³ But as soon as He rescued them, they rebelled in the land unjustly. O people! Do you not know that your outrageous deeds are harming your own souls? (You care only for the short-lived) enjoyment in the life of this world, (and forget that) you will finally return to Us in the end. Then, We shall inform you about everything that you have done (and make you fully accountable for them).

²⁴ The parable of the life of this world is like the rain that We send down from the sky to water the crops on earth that men and animals eat. But when

---

^{*a*} The Angels.

the earth is adorned with its finest appearance and the people to whom it belongs begin to feel that the crops are under their full control, Our command suddenly descends at night or in the day, and the crops were mowed down to stubble as if they had not flourished yesterday. This is how We expound the signs for people who reflect.

Addressing the Human Mind

²⁵ And (know that) God invites (man) to the home of peace. He guides whom He wills (that accepts His guidance) to the straight path. ²⁶ Hence, those who do good will have the best reward and even more. Neither gloom nor shame will cover their faces. Such are the residents of Paradise who will remain in it forever. ²⁷ As for those who committed evil deeds, they will be requited with its equivalent. They will be covered with humiliation and have no one to defend (and protect) them from God's (wrath). Their faces will look as if they are covered with patches of the night's darkness. Such are the inmates of the Fire who will remain in it forever.

²⁸ And on the Day when We gather them altogether, We shall say to those who associated partners with God, "Stand where you are - you and those whom you have associated as partners to God!" Then, We shall separate them, and those who they regarded as God's partners will say, "It was not us that you worshipped. (Instead, you were worshipping your own lusts). ²⁹ Sufficient is God as witness between us. We were certainly unaware that you were worshipping us." ³⁰ Thereupon, every soul will be put to trial for what it did in the past and they will all be returned to God, their true Lord. Then all their invented falsehoods will be not be able to help them.

³¹ Ask them, "Who provides you with sustenance out of the heaven and the earth? Who controls hearing and sight? Who brings forth the living from the dead and the dead from the living? Who governs everything?" They will surely say, "God!" So ask them, "Then, why do you not fear Him (and take heed of His reminders)?" ³² That is God, your true Lord. What else can be beyond truth except error? How could you lose sight and be dissuaded from the truth? ³³ (Verily,) this is how your Lord's word about those who defiantly disobeyed Him is proved true. But these infidels will not (come to their senses and) believe (in the truth)!

³⁴ Ask (them O Prophet), "Is there any among those whom you regard as God's partners has the ability to originate creation and then bring it back to life (after it dies)?" Ask (them), "Is it not God alone Who can do this? How then can you become so deluded (and deny Him)?" ³⁵ Ask (them further), "Is there any among those whom you regard as God's partners can guide to the truth?"

Say (to them), "It is God alone Who guides to the truth. So who is more worthy to be followed - He that guides to the truth, or he who cannot find the right way unless he is guided? What is amiss with you (that you are unable to even sort this)? How do you judge?" [36] (Indeed,) most of them follow nothing except conjecture and surely these have no value at all against the truth. Verily, God has full knowledge of everything that they do.

[37] This Qur'an could not have been (possibly) produced by anyone other than God. It is a confirmation of what was revealed before - a clearer (and fuller) explanation of the previous Scriptures. Let there be no doubt that it is certainly from the Lord of all the worlds.

[38] Or are they saying that the Messenger has invented the Qur'an himself? Say (to them), "If that is the case, then bring forth just one chapter like it and seek help from whoever you can besides God to assist you, if what you claim is true." [39] In fact, they deny everything that they cannot comprehend even before its explanation reached them, just like how those before them did. So see what happened in the end to those wrongdoers. [40] Among them are some who (will finally come to their senses and) believe in the truth, and some who will persist in disbelief. Your Lord knows best those who corrupt the truth

[41] And if they reject you as false, tell them, "My deeds are for myself and your deeds are for yourselves. You are not responsible for what I do, nor am I responsible for what you do." [42] Yet some of them (pretend to) listen to you (with the evil intention to deride you). But can you make the deaf hear if they do not bother to use common sense and think? [43] And some of them (pretend to) look at you. But can you show the way to the blind who are bereft of sight?

[44] Indeed, God is never unjust to anyone but it is people who are unjust to themselves. [45] On the Day when He will gather them altogether, it will seem to them as if they had stayed in this world for only an hour of a day (with barely enough time) to get acquainted with one another. Ruined indeed are those who disbelieved in the meeting with God. They are not the guided ones. [46] And whether We show you (O Prophet), some of the retribution that We promised them, or We cause you to die before you can witness this, it is to Us they will all be finally returned. Indeed, God is a witness to everything that they do.

[47] For every community is a Messenger and only after their Messenger has appeared (and delivered God's message) is judgment passed on them in fairness. None will ever be wronged. [48] They ask you (mockingly), "When will this promise (of God's retribution be fulfilled) if what you say is true?" [49] Answer them, "I have no control over any harm or benefit to myself, except what God wills. A specified term has been appointed for every community. When their time arrives, they can neither delay it by a single moment, nor

hasten it."

⁵⁰ Say, "Have you ever considered what you will do if His retribution were to (suddenly) befall you at night or in the day? (Would you be able to avert it?)" So why are the sinners seeking to hasten its coming? ⁵¹ Will you believe in it only after it happens (on the Day when you will be asked) - "Do you believe in it now after (you had arrogantly kept) calling for its speedy advent?"

⁵² Then the evildoers will be told, "Taste now the everlasting punishment (that you used to deride)! How else can you be rewarded except according to what you have done?" ⁵³ And they will ask you (O Prophet), "Is all this true?" Answer them, "Yes, by my Lord! It is most certainly true and you will never be able to escape from it."

⁵⁴ And if every soul that wronged itself possessed all that is on the earth, it would surely offer it as ransom (to buy its way out on the Day of Judgment. When they finally see the suffering that awaits them), they will not be able to express their (deep regret and) remorse (for denying the truth earlier). But they will be judged with justice and will not be wronged. ⁵⁵ Without a doubt! Indeed, all that is in the heavens and the earth belongs to God. Verily, God's promise will surely be fulfilled. But most people do not know (and understand this). ⁵⁶ It is He Who gives life and causes death, and to Him will you be (finally) returned (for judgment).

⁵⁷ O mankind! Verily, counsel and enlightenment has come to you from your Lord. It presents a healing for what is in your hearts, and guidance and mercy for every believer. ⁵⁸ So tell (them O Prophet), "Let them rejoice in God's bounty and grace (which We have sent down through this Book)." It is better than all (the wealth and riches) that they could ever amass.

⁵⁹ Say (to them further), "Are you aware that out of the sustenance which God has bestowed upon you, you have taken it upon yourselves to make some things lawful and others unlawful?" Ask them, "Did God permit you to do so, or are you inventing lies against Him?" ⁶⁰ What will be in the thoughts of those who invent lies against God when the Day of Judgment finally arrives? (Do they expect to be forgiven and spared from the Hellfire? Nay, far from it!) Indeed, God's bounties for mankind are truly infinite but most people are ungrateful (because they willfully choose to reject God's grace by denying His signs and revelations).

⁶¹ O mankind! There is never a situation that you are in, whether reciting from the Qur'an or doing something else, except that We are always watching you everything that you do. And not even an atom's weight on earth or in

heaven escapes your Lord's knowledge; and neither is there anything smaller or greater than that except it is written in a clear record. ⁶² Without a doubt! Surely those who are close to God have nothing to fear nor grieve.

⁶³ Those who believe in God and are ever mindful of Him; ⁶⁴ for them is good news in the life of this world and in the life to come, and there will never be any change in what God has promised. That is the supreme triumph! ⁶⁵ Do not let their (offensive) speech grieve you (O Prophet)! Indeed, all honor and glory belongs to God alone. He alone hears all and knows all. ⁶⁶ Without a doubt! Indeed, to God alone belongs everything that is in the heavens and the earth. Those who invoke others besides God follow nothing but conjecture and they utter nothing but falsehood. ⁶⁷ It is He who has made the night for you so that you may rest in it, and the day (bright) so that you can see. Verily, in this are sure signs for those who listen (to His message and ponder).

⁶⁸ They say, "God has taken a son." Most Pure is He (from all the falsehood that they accuse Him of)! He is All-Sufficient, and to Him belongs whatever is in the heavens and the earth. You have no authority and proof for this (claim). Why are you saying about God what you do not know? ⁶⁹ Say, "Indeed, those who invent a lie against God will never succeed." ⁷⁰ (Know that) life in this (fleeting) world is nothing except a short-lived amusement. In the end, they will all return to Us (for judgment). Then, We shall make them taste severe punishment for (persistently) denying the truth.

Unheeded Warnings

⁷¹ Now narrate to them the story of Noah when he said to his people, "O My people! If my presence among you and my reminders to you of God's (divine) revelations offend you, then know that I put all my trust in God. So decide your plot, gather your associates and make your plan known. Then do whatever you intend against me without delay." ⁷² "But if you turn away, remember that I have never asked for any reward from you (to deliver God's message). My reward rests with God alone and I have been commanded to be among those who completely submit to Him." ⁷³ But they rejected Noah (and called him a liar). So We saved him and those who were with him in the ark, and made them inherit the earth after We drowned those who denied Our signs (of truth). So reflect on the fate of those who did not take heed of Our warning.

⁷⁴ Then after him, We sent forth other Messengers to their people who brought to them clear evidence of the truth. But they too would not believe in what they had rejected earlier. That is how We seal the hearts of the wrongdoers. ⁷⁵ Then after them, We sent forth Moses and Aaron to Pharaoh and the chieftains of his people with Our signs (of truth). But they persisted in

their arrogance. Verily, they were a people who were lost in sins.

⁷⁶ When the truth came to them from Us, they said, "Indeed, this is clearly an outright sorcery!" ⁷⁷ Moses replied, "Is this what you say about the truth when it has come to you - 'Can this be sorcery?' But sorcerers will never be successful!" ⁷⁸ They said, "Have you come to turn us away from the faith of our forefathers so that both of you will gain supremacy in this land? Nay! We shall never believe you." ⁷⁹ Then Pharaoh said, "Bring to me every skilled sorcerer (in this land)!" ⁸⁰ So when the sorcerers came, Moses said to them, "Throw down what you wish to throw!" ⁸¹ Then when they did, Moses said, "What you have brought is sheer sorcery which God will surely destroy. Verily, God does not approve the acts of those who go around corrupting the truth; ⁸² and God will make the truth prevail with His words no matter how hateful it is to those who are lost in sin."

⁸³ But no one believed Moses, (even his own people), except some youths, while others held back for fear of Pharaoh and their chieftains, lest they would be persecuted. Pharaoh was certainly a cruel tyrant in the land who transgressed all bounds." ⁸⁴ Moses said, "O My people! If you (truly) believe in God and have truly submitted to Him, then place your full trust in Him." ⁸⁵ They answered, "We have placed our trust in God. O Lord, do not make us a target of persecution by these tyrants; ⁸⁶ and save us, by Your grace, from the people who oppose You." ⁸⁷ And so We revealed to Moses and his brother, "Set aside for your people some houses in Egypt and turn these houses into places of worship, be constant in your prayer, and give good news (of God's help) to the believers."

⁸⁸ And Moses said, "O Lord! The splendor and wealth that You bestowed on Pharaoh and his chieftains in the life of this world have allowed them to mislead people from Your path. So destroy their wealth O Lord, and harden their hearts so that they will not believe (in the truth) until they face the grievous punishment (that You have prepared for evildoers)." ⁸⁹ God said, "Verily, your prayer has been answered. So be steadfast on the straight path and do not follow the path of those who have no knowledge (of the truth)."

⁹⁰ And so We took the children of Israel across the sea. But Pharaoh and his army followed them in outrage and enmity until he was at the point of drowning when he finally said, "I believe that there is no god except He in Whom the children of Israel believe and I submit myself to Him (now)." ⁹¹ And God replied, "Only now? ᵃ Were you not adamant in your rebellion (against Us) and were aggressively causing disorder and corruption (in the

---

ᵃ God does not accept eleventh-hour repentance and proclamation of faith. See verses 4:18 and 4:48.

land before this)? ⁹² So today, We shall save only your corpse so that it will serve as a sign (of truth in God's revelation) to those who will come after you.ᵃ Indeed, most people are heedless of Our signs and revelations."

⁹³ Then, We settled the children of Israel in an honorable settlement and We provided them with sustenance out of the good things. It was not until knowledge of the truth was given to them (through their Prophets) that they began to dispute among themselves (when the evil among them manipulated it to suit their evil desires). Verily, your Lord will judge their dispute on the Day of Judgment.

⁹⁴ And so (O Prophet), if you ever are in doubt about the stories that We have revealed to you (regarding the children of Israel), ask those who have been reading the Scriptures (that were revealed) before you. The truth has indeed come to you from your Lord (which affirms the message of His monotheism that was clearly revealed in all the earlier Scriptures). So do not be among those who are in doubt; ⁹⁵ nor among those who are bent on denying (the truth in) God's signs and revelations, or you will surely be among the (greatest) losers.

⁹⁶ Indeed, those whom your Lord's decree (of punishment) is justified will not believe it; ⁹⁷ until they come face to face with the woeful punishment (in the life to come), even if every divine sign is brought to them now. ⁹⁸ Had they believed, their community would have surely profited from its faith as in the case of the people of Jonah when We removed the affliction of shame in the life of this world from them and granted enjoyment until an appointed time after they became believers. ᵇ

ᵃ It was not until the late 19th century when mummies were first discovered by archaeologists. When the Qur'an was revealed 1,200 years earlier in the 7th century, the tombs of the Egyptian kings lay buried deep under layer upon layer of desert sand. Little was known of the science of mummification to the people of that age, certainly not to the Arabs. No books or tradition, religious or otherwise, had ever hinted at the rescue of Pharaoh's body let alone mention its subsequent preservation. Yet, this is what the Qur'an claims. No man could have dreamt of making such a statement without any historical evidence at the time of the revelation of the Qur'an. But the illiterate Prophet Muhammad did so. Today, the preserved corpses of two of the greatest Pharaohs who lived during the time of Moses i.e. King Ramses II and his son Merneptah (who drowned in the Red Sea while pursuing Moses and the children of Israel), lay as exhibits in the Museum of Egypt in Cairo for all to see, fulfilling the prophecy of this Qur'anic verse.
ᵇ See verses 21:87-88, 37:139-148 and 68:48-50.

⁹⁹ And if your Lord had so willed, everyone on earth would have surely become believers (without a choice). So do you want to compel people to believe (against their will) then? ¹⁰⁰ No soul can truly believe (in God) except by His grace (which He bestows on those who sincerely turn to Him in search for the truth. On the other hand,) He brings disgrace on those who do not use (His gift of) reason (to ponder over His signs of truth). ¹⁰¹ Tell them, "Observe carefully all that is in the heavens and the earth (to appreciate God's greatness)." But neither signs nor warnings will mean anything to those who refuse to (ponder and) accept the truth.

¹⁰² They are not waiting for anything except like what had befallen those (who rejected the truth) before them. So tell them, "Wait then, and I too shall wait with you." ¹⁰³ (And when the calamity finally arrives), We shall only save Our Messengers and those who believe, for it is Our obligation to save those who truly believe.

Clarification of Issues

¹⁰⁴ Say (to them O Prophet), "O mankind! If you doubt my faith, then know that I do not worship what you worship besides God. I worship the One and Only God alone Who (gave you life and will) cause you to die. I have been commanded to be a believer; ¹⁰⁵ and (I have also been commanded) to tell you to set your face towards the religion that is upright and not to be one of those who associate partners with God; ¹⁰⁶ and not to invoke anything else other than God alone who can neither benefit nor harm you. If you do, then you will surely be among those who are truly unjust." ¹⁰⁷ And if God afflicts you with adversity, there is no one who can remove it from you except Him; and if He intends good for you, there is no one who can repel His bounty. He grants His bounty on whomsoever He wills among His servants, and He is the Most Forgiving, the Most Compassionate.

¹⁰⁸ Say (to them further O Prophet), "O mankind! Verily, the truth has come to you from your Lord. So whoever (chooses to) follow the right path, does so for his own good. And whoever (chooses to) go astray, does so at his own peril. ᵃ I am not a guardian over you."

¹⁰⁹ So follow what is revealed to you (O Muhammad) and be patient until God brings forth His judgment. And He is surely the Best of all Judges.

ᵃ See verses 2:256 and 18:29.

11. Hūd
[Hūd : 123 verses]

This is a late Makkan chapter revealed after the death of the Prophet's first wife - Khadijah, and uncle - Abu Talib. Like all Makkan chapters, it concentrates on the fundamentals of faith namely monotheism, Messegership of Prophet Muhammad, the truth of the Qur'an as a Book of divine revelation, resurrection, Day of Judgment, reward and punishment. The Islamic mission and the Muslims had been passing through a difficult phase at that time due to the opposition and persecution of the disbelieving Makkan leaders. The chapter therefore consoles and encourages the believers by drawing attention to the fact that all the previous Prophets had to face similar opposition and enmity of the disbelieving leaders and their followers, and that God had always helped and rescued His Prophets and the believers who followed them. In this context, the story of Prophet Noah is related in some detail. This is followed by the story of Prophet Hūd who was sent to the people of 'Aād and whose name is taken as the title of this chapter. In addition, references are also made to the missions and struggles of Prophets Saleh, Lot, Shu'aib [i.e. Jethro], Moses and his brother Aaron with the underlying emphasis that all the previous Prophets had delivered the same message of monotheism and Islam.

In the name of God, the Most Gracious, the Most Compassionate.

The Message Spelled Out

[1] *Alif Lām Rā.* This is a Book which its verses have been perfected and its message distinctly spelled out, (bestowed on you O Muhammad) from the One Who is All-Wise, All-Aware.

[2] (So proclaim,) "Worship none except God alone. Indeed, I come to you from Him as a warner and bearer of good news; [3] (to tell you) that you should seek your Lord's forgiveness and turn to Him in repentance. He will grant you a blessed provision for an appointed term (in this world) and bestow His grace on those who have earned His pleasure. But if you turn away, then indeed I fear the (dreadful) punishment of a big Day that awaits you. [4] (Know that) to God will you all finally return and He has power over all things."

[5] Behold! Those who deny His message, (try to) enshroud what is in their hearts to hide it from Him. But even if they cover themselves up completely with their garments, He still knows what they conceal and what they reveal. Indeed, He knows all that is in (the deepest recesses of) their hearts.

[6] There is not a living creature that moves on earth except that its

sustenance depends on God; and He knows where it lives and its (final) resting place. All this is written in a clear record. ⁷ It is He who created the heavens and the earth in six phases, and His Supreme Throne (of dominion) extends over water, ^{*a*} (the source of life for every living thing. Thus God reminds you of your dependence on Him) to test who among you are the best in their deeds and conduct. Yet if you say (to them), "You will be resurrected after death!", those who persist in their disbelief will reply, "This (Qur'an) is nothing but plain sorcery (that is intended to bewitch us)." ⁸ If We defer their punishment until a certain time, they are sure to say, "What is preventing it (from coming now)?" Without a doubt! On the day when it finally arrives, they will not be able to escape from it. And what they used to deride will completely encircle them.

⁹ If We allow man to taste (some of) Our mercy and then withdraw it from him, he becomes utterly hopeless and ungrateful (to the favors that We have allowed him to taste earlier). ¹⁰ And if We let him taste Our favors after adversity has touched him, he says, "Misfortune has left me!", and becomes jubilant and boastful; ¹¹ except those who are patient in adversity and do good deeds. They will have forgiveness and a great reward.

¹² So (O Prophet), will you omit some of what is revealed to you (because those who reject the truth dislike it) and you feel distressed at their saying, "Why has not a treasure been sent down to him, or why has not an Angel come with him?" Behold! (They fail to understand that) you are merely a warner, whereas it is God Who is the absolute Guardian and has control over everything. ¹³ Or (are you distressed by) their accusation that, "He has invented the Qur'an?" Tell them, "Then invent and bring ten chapters of similar merit and call anyone other than God to assist you if you think you are right." ¹⁴ If they do not answer you, then know that the Qur'an has been revealed out of God's knowledge (alone) and there is no other god except Him. So ask them, "Will you submit yourself to God now?"

¹⁵ To those who desire the life of this world and its glitter, We shall pay them in full for everything that they have done in this life and will not withhold anything. ¹⁶ Yet these are the people for whom there is nothing but Fire in the life to come. Vain and worthless are all that they have accomplished in this world, and useless are all their deeds.

¹⁷ Can he, (who cares for no more than the life of this world be compared to the one) who has clear evidence ^{*b*} from his Lord that is being revealed as a guide and mercy (to all mankind) - which was preceded by the Book of

---

^{*a*} Refer to verse 21:30 and its corresponding footnote.

^{*b*} The Qur'an.

Moses - and then recites it (clearly for all to take heed) while his Lord stands as his witness? (Are they both the same?) Indeed, those who believe in this message (understand it well), whereas those who grouped together in sects (with a common hostility against the message contained in this Book) will have the Fire as their appointed place (of return in the life to come). So do not be in doubt about it (O Prophet). Indeed, it is the truth from your Lord, but most people refuse to believe so.

¹⁸ Now, who could be more wicked than the one who invents lies against God? Such men will be brought to their Lord, and witnesses will testify, "These are the ones who lied against their Lord." Beware! God's curse is on those evil wrongdoers. ¹⁹ (They are) the ones who obstruct others from God's path and seek to make it crooked; and they also refuse to acknowledge the truth about (the existence of) the life to come. ²⁰ Such people cannot escape (from God) on earth (even if they remain unscathed) and they will not be able to find any protector besides Him too. (In fact), their punishment (in the life to come) will be multiplied because they failed to hear and see the truth (during their short stay on earth).

²¹ These are the ones who have squandered their own souls, and all the fancies that they invented will forsake them. ²² Without a doubt, they will be the greatest losers in the life to come. ²³ Indeed, those who believe and do good deeds and humble themselves before their Lord, they are the residents of Paradise and will remain in there forever. ²⁴ The comparison between these two groups is that of a man who is deaf and blind, and another who can hear and see. Can they be equal? Why then do you not take heed and reflect (on this logically)?

A Historical Perspective

²⁵ Verily, We sent Noah to his people (with the same message). And so he said, "Indeed, I bring a clear warning to you; ²⁶ that you should worship nothing except God (alone). Indeed, I fear the punishment of a grievous day for you." ²⁷ But the leaders of his people who refused to acknowledge the truth said, "We do not see you except only as a human being like us, and we do not see you being followed except by the most abject among us - those who are undiscerning and rash. And we do not see that you are better than us. In fact, we think you are liars. *ᵃ*

²⁸ Said Noah, "O my people, think! If I have a clear proof from my Lord and He has blessed me with His grace (of Prophethood) which you fail to see,

---

ᵃ See verses 26:106-116.

can we then compel you to accept it against your will? ²⁹ O my people! I do not demand any wealth from you in return. My reward is with God. And I shall not drive those who believe away from me. Indeed, they (know that they) are destined to meet their Lord, whereas in you I see a people who are ignorant of what is right and wrong. ³⁰ And O my people! Who would shield me against God's (wrath) if I drove them away? Will you not then take heed (of this message that I convey to you)? ³¹ "I do not say that I hold God's treasures or have any knowledge of what is unseen and hidden. I do not claim to be an Angel, nor can I say that God will not grant any good on those who are despised in your eyes; for only God knows best what is in their souls. And if I claim all these, I shall surely be unjust."

³² They replied, "O Noah! You have argued with us and disputed at length. Bring down the punishment that you threaten us with if you speak the truth!" ³³ Noah said, "Verily, only God will bring it down on you whenever He wills, and you cannot escape from it. ³⁴ Even if I wish to advise you aright, my counsel will not benefit you if God intends that you go astray (because of your defiance), for He is your Lord and it is to Him Whom you will be returned."

³⁵ Or (perhaps O Prophet, you may be distressed by) those who say, "(Muhammad) has invented this story!" Tell them, "If I have invented it, then upon me is (the consequence of) my crime, but I am (surely) innocent of what (crimes) you commit."

³⁶ (Before you came,) this was revealed to Noah : "None of your people will believe (in the truth that you convey) except those who are truly sincere in faith. So do not be distressed by what they do. ³⁷ Now build an ark under Our observation and according to Our inspiration. Do not plead with Me for those who have wronged. They will be drowned." ³⁸ So he began to build the ark. And every time the leaders of his people passed by, they would ridicule him. He said (in return), "If you laugh at us, then know that we shall laugh back at you (some day) just as you laugh at us (today). ³⁹ Soon you will know who will be seized by a humiliating punishment and a lasting torment."

⁴⁰ And when Our command was issued, (water gushed forth from the source and) the earth's lowlands began to overflow. We said, "Take into the ark a pair of every kind (of creature), members of your family, and those who have believed, except those against whom (Our) sentence (of doom) has been passed." But only a few believed with him. ⁴¹ And Noah said, "Embark in it! In the name of God it will sail and anchor. Indeed, my Lord is Most Forgiving, Most Compassionate."

⁴² And it sailed with them on waves (towering) like mountains, and (at that moment) Noah called out to his son who was separated from him, "O my son!

Come aboard with us. Do not be with those who disbelieve." ⁴³ Replied his son, "I shall go up a mountain that will keep me safe from the water." Said Noah, "There is no getting away from the decree of God today, except for those on whom His has granted mercy." Then the waves came between them and he was among those who drowned.

⁴⁴ Then it was said, "O earth, swallow up your water! And O sky, withhold!" And so the water subsided and the decree was fulfilled. The ark came to rest on Mount Judi and it was said, "Gone are those (cursed) wrongdoers!" ⁴⁵ And Noah called upon his Lord and said, "O my Lord! My son was indeed of my family and Your promise always comes true. Verily, You are the Most Just of all Judges."

⁴⁶ God answered, "O Noah! Truly, he is not from your family. His conduct was not righteous, so do not ask Me about what you have no knowledge. Verily, I warn you not to become one of those who are ignorant (of what is right)." ⁴⁷ Replied Noah, "O my Lord! Indeed, I seek refuge in You from asking what I have no knowledge about. And unless You forgive me and have mercy on me, I shall certainly be among the losers."

⁴⁸ And it was said, "O Noah! Get down (from the ark) with peace from Us, and blessings on you and the righteous descendants of those who are with you. As for the others, We shall allow them to enjoy life for a little while before a grievous punishment from Us befall them."

⁴⁹ These are some news of the unseen that We reveal to you (O Prophet), which neither you nor your people knew about before. So endure (adversity) with patience. Indeed, the future belongs to those who are ever mindful of God (and lead a righteous life)."

The Promise That Never Fails

⁵⁰ And to the people of 'Aād, We sent their brother Hūd who said, "O my people! Worship God. You have no god other than Him. As it is, you do nothing except invent lies and falsehood (about Him)! ⁵¹ No reward do I ask from you in return for this reminder. My reward rests with Him who created me. Will you not then use common sense (and think)? ⁵² And O my people! Seek your Lord's forgiveness and turn to Him in repentance. He will send down for you rain in abundance from the sky and grant you extra strength. So do not turn away (from this message) as people who are lost in sin."

⁵³ They replied, "O Hūd! You have brought us no clear evidence (that you are a Prophet). We shall not forsake our gods on your mere words, nor will we

believe in you. ⁵⁴ We think that perhaps some of our gods may have seized you with something evil (and turned you crazy)!" Replied Hūd, "I call upon God to witness, and you too bear witness, that I am free from the sin of ascribing divinity to anything else; ⁵⁵ besides Him. So plot against me all of you and give me no respite. ⁵⁶ Indeed, I place my trust in God alone who is my Lord and your Lord. (Know that) there is no creature that moves on the earth which He does not control. Verily, the path of my Lord is straight. ⁵⁷ So if you turn away, then remember that I have delivered to you the message I was sent with. (Soon,) my Lord will put other people in your place and you will never be able to harm Him. It is my Lord Who is the Guardian over everything."

⁵⁸ And when Our command was issued, We rescued Hūd by Our grace together with those who believed; and saved them from a severe punishment. ⁵⁹ These were the people of 'Aād who denied the signs of their Lord and rebelled against His Messengers, and they followed the command of every stubborn (and cruel) tyrant. ⁶⁰ So they were accursed in the world and (they will be damned) on the Day of Resurrection. Indeed, (the people of) 'Aād turned away from their Lord. So, away with 'Aād - the people of Hūd!

⁶¹ And to the people of Tsamud, We sent their brother Saleh. He said, "O my people! Worship God. You have no other god than Him. He is the One Who brought you into existence out from the earth *a* and settled you on it (until an appointed time). So seek His forgiveness and then turn to Him in repentance. Indeed, my Lord is ever near and responsive." ⁶² They said, "O Saleh! We placed great hopes in you before this (as someone we could trust) but you forbid us from worshipping what our fathers have been worshipping (for so long). Indeed, we are suspicious and doubtful about what you invite us to." ⁶³ He said, "O my people! Have you considered that if I have a clear proof from my Lord and He has blessed me with His grace (of Prophethood), who will save me from God if I disobeyed Him? (Your rejection of the message I deliver and your desire for me to follow your evil faith) will do nothing for me except increase my ruin."

⁶⁴ "And, O my people! Here is God's she-camel, a clear sign (of His trial) for you. Leave her to graze at will on God's earth and do not harm her, otherwise a swift punishment will befall you." ⁶⁵ Yet, they cruelly slaughtered her. Then Saleh said, "Enjoy life in your homes for three more days. This is not a false promise." ⁶⁶ So when Our command arrived, We saved Saleh by Our grace together with those who believed from the disgrace of that day. Indeed, your Lord is Powerful, Almighty.

⁶⁷ And so the wicked ones were seized by a thunderous blast. And when

---

a See verse 71:71 and its corresponding footnote.

morning came, they lay lifeless on the ground in their very homes; [68] as though they had never lived there before. Beware! The people of Tsamud had turned away from their Lord. So, away with them!

Abraham's Special Guests

[69] Indeed, Our (heavenly) Messengers [a] came to Abraham with good news and said, "Peace (be upon you)." Abraham answered, "Peace (be upon you too)." Then he hastened to bring them a roasted calf. [70] But when they did not stretch their hands towards it, he felt strange and became suspicious and fearful of them. They said, "Do not be afraid! Indeed we are being sent by God to the people of Lot (and we are dropping by to deliver good news to you)."

[71] And his wife who was standing (nearby), smiled. Then We gave her the good news of (a son to come whose name will be) Isaac; and after him, (a grandson) Jacob. [72] She said, "Woe to me! Shall I bear a child while I am already an old woman and my husband here is an old man? Indeed, this is something really astounding!" [73] They said, "Are you astounded at God's decree? May God's grace and blessings be upon you, O members of this household. Indeed, He is All-Praiseworthy, All-Glorious."

[74] When Abraham's fear was dispelled after the good news reached him, he pleaded with Us for the people of Lot. [75] Indeed, Abraham was certainly most clement, tender-hearted and devout. [76] "O Abraham, desist from pleading!", they said. "Your Lord's command has already been issued, and a punishment that cannot be averted is bound to fall on them."

[77] So when Our Messengers came to Lot, he was uneasy with their presence and his chest felt constricted (with worry of how his people would behave towards his guests). He exclaimed, "This is indeed a woeful day!" [78] And his people who have been immersed with abominable acts, came rushing to him (as soon as they heard of his good-looking guests). And Lot said to them, "O my people! Here are my daughters, they are purer and lawful for you; (so marry them and repent from your immoral acts). Have fear in God and do not disgrace me in the presence of my guests. Is there not among you a right minded man (who can see the truth)?"

[79] They said, "Verily you know that we have no desire and interest in your daughters. And indeed, you know very well what we want." [80] He said, "If only I have power over you or I could take refuge in a strong support, (I would

---

[a] The Angels.

surely stop you from indulging further in your despicable sin)."

⁸¹ Then the Angels said, "O Lot! Indeed, we are Messengers from your Lord, and your people will never be able to harm you. So travel with your family - except your (defiant) wife - during a part of the night, and let not anyone among you look back. Indeed, the punishment that will strike them will also strike her, and their appointed time is in the morning. Is not the morning near?" ⁸² So when Our command arrived, We turned the (sinful) city upside down and rained upon its inhabitants with stones of baked clay in quick succession; ⁸³ marked (with a sign) from your Lord. Such punishment is never far from other evildoers.

Social Perspective

⁸⁴ And to the people of Madyan, We sent their brother Shu'aib. He said, "O my people! Worship God. You have no other god except Him. And do not cheat anything in measure and weight. Indeed, you look prosperous but I fear the doom of an Overwhelming Day for you (if you continue to cheat). ⁸⁵ And O my people! Give full measure and weight in justice and do not deprive others from what is due to them. Do not act wickedly in the earth, spread corruption (and cause disorder). ⁸⁶ The (little) remains left to you by God are better (than whatever you sinfully squander from others) if you are true believers. And I am not a guardian over you."

⁸⁷ They said mockingly, "O Shu'aib! Do your prayers compel you to demand us to renounce what our forefathers have been worshipping (for ages) and that we must refrain from doing what we please with our wealth? Indeed, you are (surely) the only clement and righteous man (left in this land)!" ⁸⁸ Shu'aib replied, "O my people, think (and ponder)! If I stand upon a clear proof from my Lord and He has provided me with goodly provision from Himself, (should I corrupt it by mixing with unlawfully earned wealth)? Verily, I do not wish for myself what I forbid you from. Instead, I only wish to set things right (and bring you back to the right path) as best as I can. And I am not able to perform my duty except by God's will. In Him I have placed my trust, and to Him do I always turn (for help)."

⁸⁹ "And O my people! Let not your mistake in opposing me bring upon you a fate similar to what had befallen the people of Noah, Hūd or Saleh. In fact, the people of Lot were not far away from you (and surely you must know of what happened to them)." ⁹⁰ "So pray to your Lord for forgiveness and turn to Him in repentance. Indeed, my Lord is Most Compassionate, Most Loving."

⁹¹ They said, "O Shu'aib! Much of what you say is meaningless to us. And

indeed, we consider you weak among us. And if not for your family, surely we would have stoned you, for indeed you have no power against us." ⁹² Shu'aib answered, "O my people! Is my family mightier to you than God? Indeed, you have placed Him behind your backs (with contempt). Verily, know that my Lord encompasses all that you do (with His knowledge and might)."

⁹³ "Hence, do (to me) what you wish within your power O my people, while I (continue to) labor (in God's way). Soon you will come to know who will be visited by a humiliating punishment and who is the liar (between us). Watch then (for what is coming); and I too shall watch with you." ⁹⁴ So when Our command arrived, We saved Shu'aib by Our grace, together with those who believed. But the wicked ones were seized by a thunderous blast; and (when morning came,) they lay lifeless on the ground in their very homes; ⁹⁵ as though they had never lived there before. Condemned were the people of Madyan just as those of Tsamud before them!

⁹⁶ And certainly We sent Moses with Our revealed signs and a clear authority; ⁹⁷ to Pharaoh and the chieftains of his people, but they followed the command of Pharaoh even though his command was misguided. ⁹⁸ On the Day of Resurrection, Pharaoh will be ahead of his people leading them into the Fire (just as he led them astray on earth). And wretched is the place towards which they are led. ⁹⁹ And they were followed by a curse in this life right until the Day of Resurrection. Wretched is the gift that they will receive on that Day!

Single Message, Different People

¹⁰⁰ These are a few accounts of ancient settlements that (you did not witness O Muhammad, but) We narrate to you (as proof of truth in Our revelation, and also as a lesson for mankind to take heed). Verily, some of these cities still survive, and some have been mowed down to utter destruction. ¹⁰¹ No wrong did We do to them, but it was they who wronged themselves. All the false gods that they invoked besides God were of no help when your Lord's command came. In fact, they only increased their ruin. ¹⁰² Such is the punishment of your Lord when He seizes communities while they are in the midst of their evil acts. His punishment is indeed grievous and severe.

¹⁰³ In this is surely a sign for those who fear the torment in the life to come. That is the Day when mankind will be assembled altogether, and that is the Day when everything will be made evident (for all to see). ¹⁰⁴ And not is that Day delayed, except that it is deferred until a time that We have ordained. ¹⁰⁵ And when the Day arrives, no soul will dare say a word except by His permission. Some will be doomed and some will be blessed with happiness.

[106] And those who are doomed will be (hurled) in the Hellfire. (There will be nothing) in there for them (except) sighing and wailing. [107] They will remain in there for as long as the heavens and the earth endure, unless your Lord wills otherwise. Verily, your Lord does and accomplishes whatever He wants. [108] And as for those who are blessed with happiness, they will remain in Paradise for as long as the heavens and the earth endure, as a gift (that will last eternally) without interruption, unless your Lord wills otherwise. [109] So do not be in doubt about what these people worship, for they are only worshipping what their forefathers had worshipped before them. And indeed, We shall certainly pay them their share (of punishment) in full without any reduction.

[110] Indeed, We gave the Scriptures to Moses, and there was disagreement among his people over what We revealed. Had it not been for a decree that had been set by your Lord (to defer the coming of the Last Hour until an appointed time), judgment would indeed have been (instantly) passed on them. Yet, they are in grave doubt and full of suspicion about this.

[111] Your Lord will surely requite everyone in full for all their deeds, (both good and bad). Verily, He is completely aware of everything that they do. [112] So stand firm as you are commanded together with those who turn in repentance with you, and do not transgress (the bounds that have been set for you). Indeed, God sees all that you do. [113] Do not incline towards those who are unjust (and cruel) or you will be caught by the flames of the Hellfire. *ᵃ* There is no one other than God who can protect you (from the severe punishment that awaits those who condone and commit injustice). And you will not be able to find any help (if God does not help you).

ᵃ The following *hadith* underscores the gravity of this verse : Abu Dharr reported that the Messenger of God (peace be upon him) said, "God Almighty said: 'O My servants! I have forbidden injustice for Myself and among you. So do not be unjust and cruel.'" [Sahih Muslim, no. 2577]. It is clear that God abhors injustice and has forbidden it to ever be associated with Him and prohibits His servants from playing any part in it. In fact, His stern threat of punishment even includes anyone who is inclined to be associated with the perpetrators of injustice, let alone commit it. No Muslim can regard himself as a true Muslim if he is a party to injustice, regardless whether his involvement in this evil act is either direct or indirect. By merely associating with those who are unjust alone is enough to incur God's wrath and will be caught by the flames of the Hellfire. One of the clearest examples of this that we are witnessing today is the muted response and stance taken by Muslim leaders towards the atrocities and oppression perpetrated by the Zionist Jews against the people of Palestine, and also those who support corrupt leaders that practice double standard in the implementation of law, steal from their people and cause their countries to become poor and beholden to evil powers that provide aid to these impoverished countries and people with ulterior motives.

¹¹⁴ And establish the prayer at the two ends of the day and at the approach of the night. ^{*a*} Verily, good deeds will (cleanse and) remove evil deeds. This is a word of reminder to those who are mindful of God. ¹¹⁵ And be patient in adversity; for indeed, God does not let the reward of those who (are upright and always strive to) excel in good deeds to go waste.

¹¹⁶ (Alas!) If only there had been (many) righteous people with a remnant of good sense among the (destroyed) generations before you, who forbade others from causing corruption on earth as did the few whom We saved. (Regrettably, most) were wicked and pursued the vain pleasures of life and became lost in sin. ¹¹⁷ (Know that) your Lord would not destroy a community unjustly while its people sincerely strive to reform themselves (by following the true teachings of the Messengers that God sent to them).

¹¹⁸ And if your Lord had willed, He could have easily made the entire humanity a single community (of the same race and religion). But this would still not prevent them from fights and disputes (where most would end up following erroneous ways); ¹¹⁹ except whom your Lord has bestowed upon them His grace (for their willingness to accept the truth and be steadfast in His cause). And it is for this (gift of freedom of choice) that He has created mankind (in various tribes and nations ^{*b*} to test who among them would choose truth over falsehood and do good deeds. For those who choose to reject the truth and become wrongdoers), then that word of your Lord which says, "Most certainly shall I fill Hell with Jinn and men altogether!" will certainly hold true for them.

¹²⁰ (O Muhammad!) The histories of earlier Messengers that We narrate to you are meant to strengthen your heart. Through these accounts has the truth come to you, as well as lessons and reminders for all believers. ¹²¹ To those who refuse to believe (in Our words), say to them, "Do as you wish (to your full extent) while we (continue to) labor (and strive in God's cause). ¹²² And wait (for what is coming), for indeed, we too are waiting."

¹²³ And to God belong the secrets of the heavens and the earth, and to Him will everything be returned. So worship Him (alone) and put your (full) trust in Him. Your Lord is never once unaware of what you do.

---

^{*a*} See verse 20:130 and its corresponding footnote.
^{*b*} See verses 49:13 and 17:70.

12. Yūsuf
[Joseph : 111 verses]

This is a late Makkan chapter revealed during the time when Prophet Muhammad and his followers were experiencing a difficult period brought upon by the Quraysh pagans who were becoming more hostile. The chapter is named after Prophet Joseph (i.e. Yusuf) whose story is narrated in it, highlighting the trials and difficulties he had to face because of the deep jealousy of his own brothers, the intrigue of some others in his new domicile in Egypt and his imprisonment there, emphasizing that God saved him from all the trials and difficulties, and ultimately gave him success and honor. Just like the accounts of the other Prophets in the Qur'an, the story of Joseph is also aimed at consoling and encouraging Prophet Muhammad in his struggle and mission. The Qur'an characterizes the story of Joseph as the best accounts. While the accounts of other Prophets in the Qur'an are usually given in parts over several chapters, the account of Joseph is given only in this particular chapter which makes it special than the rest.

In the name of God, the Most Gracious, the Most Compassionate.

A Favorite Child is Lost

¹ *Alif Lām Rā.* These are the verses of the Book that make things clear.
² Indeed, We have sent it down as a discourse in Arabic so that you (O people), will use reason (to understand it well). ³ Through the revelation of this Qur'an, We relate to you (O Muhammad), the best of narratives that you had no previous knowledge.

⁴ Behold! (This is the narrative of that time when) Joseph said to his father, *ᵃ* "O my father! Indeed, I saw (in my dream that) eleven stars, as well as the sun and the moon all prostrating before me." ⁵ His father replied, "O my son! Do not relate your dream to your brothers lest they may devise an evil plot against you (at the instigation of Satan). Indeed, Satan is a clear enemy to man. ⁶ As such, your Lord will choose you and teach you to interpret (dreams and) events. He will perfect His blessing on you and on the family of Jacob, as He has perfected it to your forefathers - Abraham and Isaac. Your Lord is certainly All-Knowing, All-Wise." ⁷ Surely there are signs (and lessons to learn from) in the story of Joseph and his brothers for those who seek to know (the truth).

⁸ (And so O Muhammad, narrate to them the story of Joseph) when his

---

ᵃ Jacob or Yaqub in Arabic.

brothers spoke to one another, "Indeed, Joseph and his brother *a* are more beloved to our father than us, even though there are many of us. Indeed, our father is clearly mistaken." ⁹ (Said one of them,) "Let's kill Joseph or cast him to some distant land so that you will receive your father's attention. After this is done, you can (repent and) live righteously." ¹⁰ But said another, "If you really must do something to Joseph, do not kill him but throw him in the depths of a well. A passing caravan might find him (and take him far away from us)."

¹¹ Thereupon, they (approached their father and) said, "O father! Why do you not trust us with Joseph while we really mean well for him? ¹² Let him go out with us tomorrow so that he may enjoy himself and play. We shall take good care of him." ¹³ Said Jacob, "Indeed, it really worries me that you want to take him with you. I fear that a wolf might eat him while you are not paying attention." ¹⁴ They replied, "If a wolf were to eat him while there are many of us, then we would all be really unworthy and hopeless." ¹⁵ And when they took Joseph away, they resolved to cast him into the depths of a well. But We inspired him, "You will tell them about this (evil) act at a time when they (do not recognize you and) do not expect (the meeting to ever take place)."

¹⁶ And so at nightfall, they returned to their father weeping (in false pretense). ¹⁷ They said, "O father! Indeed, we went racing with one another leaving Joseph behind to guard our belongings when a wolf (pounced and) ate him. But (surely) you will not believe us even though we are telling the truth." ¹⁸ And they brought Joseph's shirt with false blood on it. Said their father, "Nay! Your souls have led you to (commit an evil) act. Patience (is indeed a virtue and it) is most fitting (for me). It is to God alone Who I turn for help in this misfortune that you have described."

¹⁹ Then a caravan passed by the well and a water-drawer was sent to fetch some water. He let down his bucket into the well and suddenly saw Joseph as he pulled up the bucket. He exclaimed, "What a lucky find. Here is a boy!" They hid him like a piece of merchandise but God was certainly well aware of what they did (and had in mind). ²⁰ And they sold him for a very low price, just for a few *dirhams*, *b* because they were not interested in him (and wanted

---

a Benjamin or Bunyamin in Arabic.

b Some Christian textual critics point out that the Qur'an made an error by using the word *dirham* here because this currency did not exist at the time Joseph was sold as a slave in Egypt around 1600 BC. While it is true that the *dirham* did not exist yet at that time, the usage of its term in this verse generally represents any form of precious metal such as gold, silver or copper that was used as currency. This was the currency that the Arabs were familiar with because it had been in use for a long time during the Byzantine Empire. Syrian merchants from Byzantine were known to have been actively

to quickly have him disposed).

Facing Up to Trial

²¹ An Egyptian who bought Joseph (took him home and) said to his wife, "Make his stay in our home comfortable. Perhaps he may be of benefit to us or we could even adopt him as a son." This is how We established Joseph in the land and taught him the knowledge to interpret dreams and events. (Verily,) God has full control over His affairs but most people do not realize this. ²² And when he reached maturity, We gave him wisdom and knowledge. This is how We reward those who excel in good deeds.

²³ (To Joseph's surprise,) the lady of the house sought to seduce him. She shut the doors and said, "Come on to me!" But Joseph replied, "I seek refuge in God (from you evil intention). Indeed, your husband is my master who has taken good care of me (and I shall not betray him). Those who indulge in wrongdoings will never succeed." ²⁴ And indeed she desired him, and he would have desired her too had he not seen his Lord's proof. *ᵃ* This is how We kept evil and indecency away from him. He was truly one of Our most pure-hearted servants (whom We have chosen to be Our Prophet).

²⁵ Then they raced to the door and she tore his shirt from behind. Suddenly, they both found her husband at the door. So she asked (in false pretense), "What penalty does a man who intended evil against your wife deserve, other than to be imprisoned or inflicted with a painful punishment?"

²⁶ Joseph said, "(I am free from blame.) It was she who actually sought to seduce me!" Then a witness from her household suggested, "If his shirt is torn from the front, then she has spoken the truth and he is a liar. ²⁷ But if his shirt is torn from the back, then she is lying and he is telling the truth." ²⁸ So when her husband saw that Joseph's shirt was torn from the back, he said to his wife, "Surely this is a woman's ploy, and the ploys of women are great! ²⁹ Turn

---

engaged in trade with the Arabs during the pre and post Islamic times which caused *dirham's* wide circulation in Arabia long before Prophet Muhammad was born. Hence, regardless of what the actual name of currency that was actually being used in Egypt circa 1600 BC, the Qur'an's usage of *dirham* as the currency term in this verse served as a general monetary unit which the Arabs at the time could relate with, before it became the Islamic Empire's official currency together with *dinar*, after the Prophet's death.

ᵃ An inspiration from God which roused his conscience that it was sinful and not worthy for him to yield to the temptation lured by his master's wife.

away from this, O Joseph. and (as for you O woman,) seek forgiveness for your sin, for you are surely the one at fault!'"

³⁰ (Thereupon,) the womenfolk in the city started gossiping, "The minister's wife is trying to seduce her slave boy who has captured her heart. Indeed, we see her in such a clear error." ³¹ When she heard about their gossip, she sent for them and prepared a banquet. She gave each one of them a knife (for paring fruit) and then called out to Joseph, "Come out here and show yourself to them!" When they saw him, they were wonderstruck (by his looks) that they cut their hands (without realizing it), and exclaimed, "Truly perfect is God! This cannot be a mortal. He must be a noble Angel!" ³² (And so) she said, "This is the one you blamed me for. I sought to seduce him but he (preserved himself and) resisted. And if he does not do what I order, he will surely be put in prison and suffer disgrace."

³³ Joseph said, "O my Lord! Prison is dearer to me than what they invite me to. And if You do not avert from me the guile of these women, I might (in my youthful folly,) succumb to their attraction and lapse into ignorance." ³⁴ So his Lord responded to his prayer, and turned their (evil) plot away from him. Indeed, God hears all and knows all. ³⁵ And yet, in spite of having seen clear signs (and proof of Joseph's innocence), they found it better to imprison him for a while (to hide their shame).

From Prison to Palace

³⁶ And there were two young men imprisoned with him. Said one of them, "Indeed, I see myself (in a dream) pressing grapes for wine." And then the other one said, "I dreamt of carrying bread over my head from which birds were eating. Tell us the interpretation (of these dreams if you know O Joseph). Indeed, you seem like a virtuous (and knowledgeable) person." ³⁷ Joseph answered, "I shall give you its interpretation before the meal that you will be served arrives. This knowledge is one of the things my Lord has taught me. But behold! (You should first know that) I reject the ways of those who do not believe in God and also deny the existence of the Hereafter; ³⁸ and I follow the true faith of my forefathers - Abraham, Isaac and Jacob - and we are forbidden from associating anything with God. (Indeed,) this command is certainly an act of God's grace upon us and all mankind (for it is intended to save us from the torment of the Hellfire). But most people are not grateful (for this great favor)!"

³⁹ "O my two prison companions! Which is better? To believe in many different lords, or to believe in the One and Only God - the Most Supreme and Irresistible (Who holds absolute power over all that exists)? ⁴⁰ What you

worship besides Him are nothing but idle names that you and your forefathers have assigned without any authority from God. Whereas judgment (to what is right and wrong) rests solely with God and He has commanded that you worship none except Him alone. (Verily,) this is the ever-true upright faith, but most people (choose to be heedless and) ignorant about it."

⁴¹ "O my two prison companions! One of you will serve wine to your master, and the other will be crucified and the birds will eat from his head. The matter on which you both inquired has indeed been decided." ⁴² Then Joseph said to the one whom he considered would be saved, "Mention about me to your master (when you leave this place)." But Satan made him forget to do this (after he was released), and so Joseph remained in prison for several (more) years.

⁴³ Then one day, the King *ᵃ* said to his courtiers, "Indeed I saw in my dream seven fat cows being eaten by seven lean ones, and seven ears of grain that were green and (seven) others that were dry. O courtiers! Explain to me the significance of my dream if you can interpret them." ⁴⁴ (Answered the courtiers, "We think) they were only confused dreams. Moreover, we do not know how to interpret them." ⁴⁵ At that point, the man who had been released from prison suddenly remembered (Joseph) after so long. He said, "I shall tell you the interpretation (of this dream). But send me forth (to meet Joseph at the prison to find the answer)."

⁴⁶ (And so when he met Joseph, he said,) "O Joseph, man of truth!

ᵃ This is an amazing historical fact which proves the miraculous nature of the Qur'an and its divinity. During the time when Joseph was in Egypt, rulers of the land were not Egyptians. Instead, they were foreigners who were called The Hyksos. According to the World History Encyclopedia, The Hyksos invaded Egypt and occupied the northern part of the land for a little over than two centuries from 1782 to 1570 BC before the Egyptians drove them out to reclaim control over the land. Because they were not native Egyptians, the Qur'an specifically referred them as Kings (i.e. *Malik*) instead of Pharaohs. This is mentioned in five places in this chapter including this verse. The other four places are in verses 50, 54, 72 and 76. In contrast, other passages in the Qur'an that narrate stories about Moses use the term Pharaoh (i.e. *Fir'aun*) for the ruler of Egypt during that time since Pharaoh is the specific name that was given to Egyptian Kings and rulers of indigenous descent. The question is : How did Prophet Muhammad know about this histrorical fact which had taken place about 2,200 years before his coming with pin point accuracy? Even the Bible - in the Book of Genesis - which the Jews and Christians believe was written by Moses about 2,000 years before the revelation of the Qur'an, named the ruler during the time of Joseph as Pharaoh (see chapter 41 of Genesis), giving an impression that the ruler during that time was an Egyptian King of indigenous descent when in fact he was not.

Explain to us (the meaning of the King's dream) about seven fat cows being eaten by seven lean ones, and seven ears of grain that are green next to (seven) others that are dry, so that I may return to the people and inform them."

⁴⁷ Joseph answered, "You will sow (grain) for seven consecutive years as usual. Store all that you reap and leave them in the ears, except for the little which you may eat. ⁴⁸ Then there will come seven years of hardship which you will consume the grain you had saved, except a little from which you will store away." ⁴⁹ Then after that, will come a year when the people will be given abundant rain and they will press (grapes)."

⁵⁰ And (when) the King (heard this, he) said, "Bring this man to me." But when the King's messenger returned to Joseph, he was told, "Go back to your master and ask him to inquire about the women who (had accidentally) cut their hands (at a banquet many years ago). Indeed, My Lord has full knowledge of their plot."

⁵¹ So the King asked the women, "What is the story about your attempt to seduce Joseph (many years ago)?" They answered, "God forbid! We do not know of any evil about him." Then the wife of the minister confessed, "Now the truth has come to light. Actually, it was I who tried to seduce him but he is indeed a man of virtue."

⁵² (When Joseph learned what had happened, he said to the King's messenger, "I asked for this confession) so that my former master will really believe that I never betrayed him in secrecy. Indeed, God will surely not allow (the schemes of) those who betray to ever succeed."

⁵³ Joseph continued, "And I do not pretend to be blameless, for the soul is prone to evil unless my Lord bestows His mercy (and guidance). Indeed, my Lord is Most Forgiving and Most Compassionate (to those who turn to Him in repentance and devotion)." ⁵⁴ When Joseph's words were relayed to the King, he said, "Bring him to me! I shall appoint him exclusively for myself." Then when he spoke to Joseph, he said, "Indeed, today you are firmly established in a rank of trust with us." ⁵⁵ Joseph said, "Appoint me over the treasuries of the land. Indeed, I shall guard over them with knowledge (and wisdom)."

⁵⁶ This is how We gave Joseph authority in the land. (He was also) free to live wherever he wished. (Verily,) We bestow Our grace on whomsoever We please and We do not let the reward of those who (are virtuous and) excel in good deeds to go waste. ⁵⁷ Surely, in the life to come, a better reward awaits those who believe in God, are ever mindful of Him (and refrain themselves from evil).

Brothers' Reunion

⁵⁸ And (some years later,) Joseph's brothers came (to Egypt) and presented themselves to him (to transact a trade). He immediately recognized them but they did not know him. ⁵⁹ And when he had furnished them with their provisions, he said, "(When you come here again,) bring along your brother from your father's side (whom you mentioned about to me earlier). Do you not see that I have given full measure and have also been a very good host to you? ⁶⁰ If you do not bring him to me, you will never again receive a single measure (of grain) from me nor will you (be allowed to) come near me." ⁶¹ They said, "We shall try to get permission from his father to let him follow us (next time), and we shall indeed do it." ⁶² Then Joseph ordered his servants, "(Quietly) put back their traded merchandise into their saddle-bags so that they will (unexpectedly) find it there when they return home and (be more eager to) come back here."

⁶³ When they returned to their father, they pleaded, "O our father! Further measure of grain is (to be) withheld from us (unless we bring Benjamin to Egypt). So send our brother with us so that we shall be given another measure. We (promise to) surely guard him well." ⁶⁴ Jacob replied, "Should I to entrust him to you now like I once did to his brother before? *ª* (Nay!) God is the best Guardian and He is the Most Compassionate of all those who show compassion."

⁶⁵ And when they opened their bags, they discovered that their merchandise was returned to them. They exclaimed, "O our father, (look at this)! What more could we desire? Even our merchandise has been returned to us. We must go back there again with our brother to get more provision for our family, and we should be able to get an increase in measure of a camel's load. That is indeed an easy measurement (to accomplish. Indeed, we promise to take good care of our brother if you let him go with us)." ⁶⁶ Their father replied, "Never will I let him go with you until you give me a promise by God that you will bring him back to me (safely) unless you are surrounded by enemies (or overtaken by misfortune)." And when they gave him their promise, he said, "God is indeed the (witness and) guardian over what we say."

⁶⁷ And he added, "O my sons! (Take heed of my advise that all of you) should not enter the city from a single gate, but (spread out and) do so from different gates (to avoid any untoward incident from befalling all of you at once). But (be mindful that) I cannot avail you against what God may have

---

ª In reference to Joseph.

willed (and decreed), for all decisions belong to God alone and it is in Him do I rely (and place my full trust). So let everyone rely (and put their full trust) in Him too."

⁶⁸ And when they entered (the city) following the way their father had ordered, it was not meant to avail them against God's will and decree. Instead, it was only to fulfill Jacob's heartfelt desire (and intention for his children to take the necessary precautions to protect themselves). Indeed, he was endowed with (revealed) knowledge (concerning the virtues of caution and faith) *ᵃ* which We had taught him. But most people do not know (and understand) this.

⁶⁹ And when they came to Joseph, he drew his brother (Benjamin) to himself and said, "Indeed, I am actually your (lost) brother. Do not be sad over what they did (to me) before." ⁷⁰ So when he had furnished them with their supplies, he slipped the King's drinking cup in his brother's saddle-bag. Then suddenly, a herald announced, "O people of the caravan! Indeed, you are thieves."

⁷¹ They turned to the herald (in surprise) and asked, "What is it that you have lost?" ⁷² (The herald said,) "We have lost the King's drinking cup! Whoever brings it will have a camel-load (of grain as reward). I pledge my word for it." ⁷³ They said, "We swear by God (that we have nothing to do with this). You must know we did not come to commit any crime in this land, nor are we thieves." ⁷⁴ (Then the herald said, "In that case,) what will be the punishment of this crime if we find that you are lying?" ⁷⁵ They replied, "The punishment for the person in whose bag the cup is found (is enslavement). That is how we punish wrongdoers."

⁷⁶ Thereupon, Joseph began to search their bags (first) before (looking into) his brother (Benjamin's) bag where he found the drinking-cup and took it out. This was how We devised a plan for Joseph (to achieve what his heart desired). Had We not willed it to be this way, he would not be able to simply detain his brother (to keep with him), for he had no right to do so under the King's law. (Verily,) We exalt in knowledge whomsoever We will; but above everyone who is endowed with knowledge, there is (always) The One Who knows all.

⁷⁷ (Seeing this, one of his brothers) said, "If he has stolen, then verily one

---

ᵃ This refers to the concept of *Tawakkul* in Islam. It is about placing full faith and trust in God's will and ultimate plan to deliver the final and best outcome of all affairs, whether favorable or not to man, after all necessary efforts and precautions have been undertaken first to the best of man's ability towards accomplishing a certain objective that he has in mind. Man proposes, God disposes.

of his brothers had stolen before too." Hearing this, Joseph felt disdain and secretly kept this to himself without revealing it to them. Then he said to himself, "You are in a far worse position, and God knows best about the truth that you speak." [78] (And then) they said further, "O Minister! Indeed, he has a very old father, so take anyone of us as his replacement. Verily, we see that you are a (virtuous and) magnanimous man." [79] Joseph replied, "God forbid that we should detain anyone other than the person on whom we found our stolen property, or we would surely be among those who are committing (cruel) injustice."

A Child's Dream Comes True

[80] So when they despaired from persuading Joseph to release their brother, they secluded themselves in private consultation. The eldest of them said, "Do you not recall that your father took a pledge in God's name from you, and before that you failed in your duty with regard to Joseph? I shall not leave this land until my father gives me permission or God passes judgment in my favor. He is certainly the Best of all Judges. [81] (As for the rest of you,) return to your father and say, 'O our father! Indeed, your son has committed theft. We bear witness to only what we know. (Although we gave you our pledge earlier), we are unable to guard against something unforeseen (like this). [82] You may ask the people of the town where we were and the people of the caravan who we traveled with (to verify our story). Indeed, we are certainly telling the truth."

[83] (And when they returned to their father and told him what had happened,) he exclaimed, "Nay! Your souls have enticed you to make up this story. As for me, (I shall console myself to face this trial with) patience - it is indeed (a virtue that is) most fitting. Perhaps God may bring them all back to me (some day). Indeed, He is All-Knowing, All-Wise."

[84] Then he turned away from them and cried, "Alas for Joseph!" His eyes turned white with grief, and he was suppressed (with sorrow). [85] They said, "By God! You will not cease to remember Joseph until you ruin your health or die." [86] He replied, "I only complain of my suffering and my grief to God (alone), and I know from God what you do not know." [87] "O my sons! Go in search of Joseph and his brother and do not despair from the grace of God. Indeed, no one should despair from God's grace except those who are devoid of faith."

[88] When they returned to Joseph, they said, "O minister! Calamity has befallen us and our people. We have come with goods of only little value but seek your kindness to pay us full measure; so please (show mercy and) be charitable to us. Indeed, God rewards those who are (merciful and) charitable."

⁸⁹ (Suddenly) he replied, "Do you remember what you did to Joseph and his brother (a long time ago) when you were ignorant?" ⁹⁰ They asked in surprise, "Are you really Joseph?" He answered, "Yes, I am Joseph, and this here is my brother - (Benjamin). God has indeed been gracious to us. Verily, if one remains conscious of Him and is patient (in adversity), God will not fail to reward those who are (pure-hearted and) excel in their deeds." ⁹¹ They said, "By God! Certainly God has preferred you over us and we have indeed been guilty of sin." ⁹² (But Joseph said,) "No penalty will be inflicted on you today. May God forgive you, for He is the Most Compassionate of all who are compassionate." ⁹³ "Go with this shirt of mine and lay it over the face of my father; he will regain sight. Then come back here together with all your family."

⁹⁴ And when the caravan departed (from Egypt), Jacob (who was in Palestine) said (to the people around him), "You may think that I am senile but I can certainly smell Joseph's scent." ⁹⁵ They said, "By God! You are still lost in your old delusion."

⁹⁶ Then as the bearer of good news arrived and laid Joseph's shirt over the face of his father, his eyesight was restored. Jacob said, "Did I not tell you that indeed, I know from God what you know not?" ⁹⁷ Said the sons, "O our father! Pray for us that our sins be forgiven, for we have indeed sinned." ⁹⁸ He said, "In time, I shall ask forgiveness for you from my Lord. Indeed, He is the Most Forgiving, the Most Compassionate."

⁹⁹ And when they all arrived in Egypt and presented themselves before Joseph, he drew his parents to himself, saying, "Enter Egypt (in peace)! If God so wills, you will be secure (from all evil with me here)." ¹⁰⁰ And he raised his parents upon the throne (to honor them); and all his brothers fell down before him, prostrating themselves (in homage). Thereupon Joseph said, "O my father! This is the meaning of that dream I had long ago, which my Lord has made it come true (today). ^a Indeed He was gracious to free me from prison, and brought you out of the desert to me after Satan had sown discord between me and my brothers. Verily, my Lord is Most Subtle in (the way He brings about) whatever He wills. Indeed, He alone is All-Knowing, truly wise!

¹⁰¹ "O my Lord! You have indeed bestowed upon me dominion, and taught me how to interpret dreams and events. O Originator of the heavens and the earth! You alone are my protector in this world and in the life to come; so let me die in true devotion to You, and count me among the righteous."

---

^a This is the fulfillment of the dream which Joseph had when he was a young boy where he had a vision that eleven stars together with the sun and the moon prostrated to him as mentioned in verse 4 of this chapter.

One Message to Mankind

¹⁰² This is news of the unseen which We reveal to you (O Muhammad) even though you were not with Joseph's brothers when they devised their evil scheme against him. ¹⁰³ Yet, however strongly you desire for people to attain faith (and become believers), most will still refuse (to accept the truth); ¹⁰⁴ even though you do not ask any reward from them for conveying Our message. Verily, this is certainly a reminder to all mankind.

¹⁰⁵ And how many signs (of God's greatness) in the heavens and the earth do they pass by every day but continue to ignore? ¹⁰⁶ Not only do they not believe in God, but they (dare to) also ascribe divine powers to others besides Him. ¹⁰⁷ Do they really feel safe from the fear of an overwhelming terror of God's punishment? Or (do they not fear) the Last Hour that might suddenly come upon them suddenly when they least expected it?

¹⁰⁸ Say (to them O Prophet), "This is my way. Both I and all those who follow me hereby call upon all mankind to God on the basis of clear evidence. Glorified and exalted is God (from any imperfection that they attribute to Him) and I am surely not among those who associate partners with Him."

¹⁰⁹ (Even before your time, all) the Messengers whom We gave Our revelations to were mortals. We chose them from among people of their own community. Have those who deny you then not traveled across the land and seen what was the end of those who lived before them? And surely, the home in the life to come is the best for those who are ever mindful of God (and strive to fulfill their duty to Him diligently). Will you not then use reason (to see the truth in this message O people)?

¹¹⁰ (All the earlier Messengers were tested with suffering and persecution for a long time) until they despaired and thought that they were being denied (of Our help). Then when Our help finally came, We saved whomsoever We willed (for their patience in holding firm to Our message and in enduring adversity. Behold!) Never can Our mighty punishment be averted from the sinners (who rejected Our signs of the truth and continued to glory in their arrogance).

¹¹¹ Verily, in the stories of these men is a lesson for those who are endowed with insight and wisdom. This is (indeed a revelation from God and) not an invented tale. It is a confirmation of previous revelation, a detailed explanation of all things as well as guidance and grace for those who truly have faith in God.

13. Ar-Ra'd
[The Thunder : 43 verses]

This is a Madinan chapter. It draws attention to the existence of God and His wonderful creation of the heavens and the earth, the sun and the moon, the stars and everything in them of living and non-living beings. It also speaks about the inevitability of death and God's absolute power over life and death. Distinction between truth and falsehood is also emphasized through appropriate examples. The chapter is named *Ar-Ra'd* with reference to verses 12-13 where mention is made of lightning and thunder as illustration of God's power and wondrous creation.

In the name of God, the Most Gracious, the Most Compassionate.

A Glance at Wide Horizons

¹ *Alif Lām Mīm Rā.* These are the verses of the (Divine) Book. Whatever that has been revealed to you from your Lord is the truth (O Prophet), yet most people refuse to believe. *ᵃ* ² God is the One Who raised the heavens that you could see without pillars and then firmly established Himself on the (Supreme)

ᵃ Those who choose to disbelieve and reject the truth actually have no reasonable argument to support their stand. Even if no revelation had been sent from God to humanity, there is ample evidence in the universe around us to prove God's existence and sovereignty. Reflection and intelligent observation of the physical and cosmological phenomena of the universe would reveal that denial of God is neither a rational nor a reasonable position to take. It is simply illogical to think that this whole universe and all the creatures that it contains came into existence without a Supreme Power and Ultimate Creator behind them Who set the laws of nature in the first place and then regulate it in perfect harmony. All this cannot happen by chance. Even those who believe in the Theory of Evolution and all other theories that reject the existence of God, need to ask themselves : Who set the law of evolution and then made it possible for creatures to intelligently undergo the process perfectly? See also verses 27:60-64, 45:5-6 and their footnotes. In fact, it would also lead to the conclusion that submission to or worship of other man-made gods is a nonsensical and absurd practice. And if we can finally come to the rational belief that God does exist, the next logical question would be : Who is this God that is The Ultimate Creator of everything, and how do we learn about Him and "communicate" with Him? Shouldn't we be looking for factual evidence to satisfy this question? After all, every living being will surely face death one day. Are we not curious to find out what will happen to us after we die? Where can we find this information if not from God's proven divine revelation.

Throne. And it is He Who has made the sun and the moon subservient (to His laws), each running in its own course until an appointed term. He governs the entire order (of all the worlds perfectly) and makes clear the signs (of His greatness) so that you will be certain of the meeting with your Lord. ³ And He is the One Who spreads the earth wide and set therein firm mountains and flowing rivers.ᵃ And of every fruit, He made them in pairs of two kinds, (some sweet and some not), and He is the One Who causes the night to overlap the day. Surely in these are clear signs (of the Ultimate Creator) for those who (reflect and) ponder.

⁴ And on the earth are many tracts of land neighboring each another (with their differing type of soil and fertility). On them are vineyards, crops, and date-palms - some are clustered and some standing alone, all irrigated with (the same) water from a single source. And yet, We make some taste better than others. Verily in all these, there are sure signs for people who care to use reason (and common sense to ponder deeply). ⁵ And if you are astonished at the marvels of God's creation, then more astonishing indeed is those who ask, "What? (Did you say that) after we have become soil (and dust in the ground), we shall be restored to life in a new act of creation?" They are the ones who are adamant in denying their Lord, and such people will wear shackles around their necks (on the Day of Judgment). They are the ones who will be the inmates of the Fire where they will remain in it forever.

⁶ (And because of their arrogance in denying the truth O Prophet,) they challenge you to hasten the coming of evil upon them instead of hoping for good even when there have been clear examples of God's retribution before them. But despite their wrongdoings, your Lord is still full of forgiveness for mankind (by affording them ample chances to mend their ways). But behold, your Lord is also truly severe in retribution (if they continue to reject and defy Him)! ⁷ And those who refuse to acknowledge the truth (mock and deride you by) saying, "Why has not a (miraculous) sign been sent down to Muhammad from his Lord (as proof of his Prophethood)?" (They forget that) you are only a warner and a guide for all people, (not their guardian).

⁸ (Verily,) God knows what every female carries in her womb and by how much the wombs may fall short (in gestation), or by how much they may exceed (from the average period). And everything with Him is in due measurement (and proportion). ⁹ (He is the) Knower of all that is unseen and manifest. He is the Greatest, the One far above everything (there is and could ever be)! ¹⁰ It is all the same to Him whether any of you conceals his thoughts or brings them into the open, and whether he seeks to hide (his evil deeds) under the cover of night or walks freely in the light of day.

ᵃ See verse 15:19 and its corresponding footnote.

¹¹ For everyone are Angels who take turn guarding in front and behind him by the command of God. Indeed, God will not change the condition of a people until they change what is within themselves first. And when God wills people to suffer evil (as the consequences of their evil deeds), it can never be averted because they cannot find a protecter other than Him.

¹² He is the One Who displays before you the lightning (and thunder) to give rise to both fear and hope, and He is the One Who raises thick (and heavy) clouds (high above you). ¹³ Indeed, even the thunder glorifies His perfection with (unceasing) praises and so do the Angels, out of their (awe and) fear of Him. He sends the thunderbolts and strikes whomsoever He wills with them. Yet, they still (stubbornly) dispute about Him (even though His signs of existence are clear). His punishment is very severe.

¹⁴ All supplications are truly due to Him (alone, because) those (other beings or powers) that people invoke besides Him cannot respond to them in any way. As such, he who does that is like the one who stretches his hands towards water (hoping) that it would reach his mouth, but it does not. And not is the prayer and supplication of the disbelievers except straying in grievous error. ¹⁵ And to God prostrates all that is in the heavens and the earth - either willingly or unwillingly - and so do their shadows in the mornings and in the afternoons.

¹⁶ Ask them, "Who is the Lord of the heavens and the earth?" They will surely answer, "God (the Almighty)!" Then ask them, "(If so,) why do you take other than Him as protectors who have no power over their own gain or loss?" Ask them (further), "Are the blind equal to those who can see? Or is darkness equal to light? Or do they really believe that there are other divine powers besides God that have created the like of what He creates and their creations appear similar to His? Say, "God is the Creator of all things; and He is the One Who holds absolute power over everything that exists."

¹⁷ It is He Who sends down rain from the sky so that riverbeds flow according to their measure. The current then carries a swelling foam just like the foam that appears when metal is heated in the fire to make ornaments or utensils. In this way does God illustrate (the difference between) truth and falsehood. As the foam casts away as scum, what benefits people stay behind to remain on earth. This is how God sets forth parables (for people to ponder). ¹⁸ For those who respond to their Lord (in obedience), a rich reward awaits them. But for those who ignore Him, they will surely (try to) offer all their possessions - even if it is the earth with all its content and twice over - as their ransom (when they finally see the suffering that awaits them in the Hereafter). Theirs will be an awful reckoning and Hell will be their permanent home. What an evil resting place!

Nature of Faith and Prophethood

[19] Then, is he who knows what has been revealed to you from your Lord is the truth, the same as the one who is blind? Verily, only those who are endowed with insight and wisdom pay heed (to His message). [20] They are the ones who fulfill the covenant of God and do not break their pledge; [21] and those who keep together what God has commanded to be held together, and stand in awe of their Lord and fear the harshness of the reckoning; [22] and those who remain patient (in adversity) seeking the (pleasure and) countenance of their Lord and are steadfast in their prayer; and those who spend on others out of what We have provided them, either secretly or openly; and those who repel evil with good. For them is the ultimate home; [23] which is the Gardens of Perpetual Bliss that they will enter together with the righteous among their parents, spouses and offspring. And the Angels will also enter upon them from every gate; [24] (greeting,) "Peace be upon you for what you have patiently endured." Excellent indeed is your final place of return!

[25] As for those who break their covenant with God after establishing it and cut asunder what God has commanded to be held together, and they go about spreading corruption (and disorder) on earth, such people will be cursed and they will finally return to an (everlasting) evil home. [26] (Verily,) God extends abundant provision to whomsoever He wills and restricts it to whomsoever He wills (according to His wisdom as a means to test one's faith. And almost always, those who are given abundance) would rejoice in the life of this world (in excess of their bounds). But not is this world except a (place of brief pleasure and) enjoyment compared to the next life to come (which is eternal).

[27] And those who are bent on denying the truth say, "Why has a (miraculous) sign not been sent down to (Muhammad) from his Lord?" Tell them (O Prophet), "Indeed, God lets go astray whomsoever He wills (that denies His message) and guides to Himself whomsoever that turns to Him (in obedience and true sincerity)." [28] These are the believers whose hearts find peace and comfort in the remembrance of God. Truly, it is in the remembrance of God do hearts find peace and comfort. [29] They are the ones who believe (in Him wholeheartedly) and (and follow-up their faith by) doing good deeds. They will be blessed and rewarded with happiness (in the life of this world) and an excellent place of return (in the life to come).

[30] And so (O Prophet), We have sent you to a community - like We did with other communities in the past (that have incurred Our wrath because of their defiance) - so that you may recite to them what We have revealed to you

(for them to take heed). ^a Yet, they reject the Most Gracious (Lord, just like those before them did). Say (to them), "He is my Lord and there is no god except Him. In Him alone do I place my trust, and to Him alone is my return."

³¹ And even if (they listen to) this Qur'an by which mountains could be moved, or the earth cleft asunder, or the dead made to speak; (those who are bent on opposing the truth would still refuse to accept it as Our divine revelation). Indeed, with God alone lies the power to decide (their final outcome). Do those who believe still not know that God could have guided all of humanity aright if He so willed? (But He gave them reason and intellect to discern between right and wrong, and sent His Messengers to teach them His message so that they could choose truth over falsehood out of their own volition. But because of their persistence in committing misdeeds), calamity will not cease to befall (directly on) those who reject the truth or fall close to their homes (thus making their lives in this world miserable) until God's promise (of resurrection) comes to pass (where their end will be far worse). Indeed, God never fails to fulfill His promise.

³² And surely, the Messengers before you were mocked, but I granted respite to those who refused to accept the truth (and persisted to ignore My warnings) before I seized them (with a sudden blow). How (dreadful) was My retribution! ³³ Then, can He Who continuously watches over every soul for whatever it has earned and acquired, (be deemed equal to anything else)? And yet they dare to associate partners with God! So say (to them), "Give your false gods any name (you like). And do you (really think that you could) teach God about anything on earth that He does not know? Or are you merely making (the foolishness of) your empty words apparent (for all to see)?" The truth is, the evil schemes of those who refuse to accept the truth have been made fair-seeming (and alluring by *Iblis*) to them. As a result, they are hindered from the right path. And whoever God lets go astray (because of his own defiance), he can never find any guide. ³⁴ For them, there is punishment in the life of this world, and surely the punishment in the life to come is more severe. And they will have no one to defend them against God (when He

---

^a As mentioned here and in verses 27:91-92, 29:45 and in several others too, the Prophet was commanded in many instances to recite the Qur'an to his people. But the meaning of recitation of the Qur'an here is more than just a simple reading of Qur'anic passages. Instead, it includes the study, interpretation, and understanding of the principles, ideas and concepts that the Qur'an is putting forward. It also means the translation of those ideas into actions, relationships, programs, and practical systems that can help uplift the human situation and improve the quality of life. In addition, the recitation of the Qur'an especially when committed to memory, protects it against tampering and distortion.

unleashes His wrath).

³⁵ The parable of Paradise promised to those who are mindful of God (is like a garden) where rivers will flow from right beneath it. (But unlike an earthly garden,) its fruits will be everlasting and (so will) its shade too. This is the ultimate destiny of those who are ever mindful of God, while the end for those who reject the truth is the Fire (of Hell).

³⁶ And (among) those to whom We gave earlier revelations, (some) rejoice at what has been revealed to you; but among them are also groups that deny a part of it. Say (to them), "I have been commanded to worship God alone and not associate partners with Him. Therefore, to Him alone do I call upon, and to Him will be my (ultimate) return." ³⁷ And so (O Prophet), We have sent down this Qur'an to you as a code of judgment in the Arabic tongue (that clearly sets apart the truth from falsehood). But if you follow their desires after you have been given all the knowledge, then (know that) you will have no one to protect and shield you (against God's wrath).

³⁸ And certainly, We sent Messengers before you and We assigned to them mates and offspring. And it was not for a Messenger to produce a miracle except by God's permission. Verily, for every period, an ordinance is prescribed (to the people of that time to regulate their affairs). ³⁹ And God abrogates or retains whatsoever He wills (of the ordinances that He has prescribed earlier, by way of new revelations that He sends down to His Messengers from time to time); and with Him alone is the Mother of the Book.ᵃ ⁴⁰ And whether We let you see the fulfillment of what We have promised them in your lifetime or whether We cause you to die before its execution, your duty is no more than to deliver the message; while the reckoning is Ours.

⁴¹ Do they not see how We visit the earth (with Our punishment), gradually depriving it of all that is best therein? Verily, when God decides, there is no power that can overrule His decision, and He is indeed swift in reckoning. ⁴² And certainly, those who lived before these sinners (with you now) had also devised many evil plots. But to God belongs the entire plot and He knows what each soul deserves. (In time to come,) those who reject the truth will know who will ultimately have the most excellent home (to return to). ⁴³ And those who refuse to accept the truth say, "(Surely) you are not a Messenger (of God)!" Say to them (O Prophet), "Sufficient is God and whoever that has knowledge of this divine Book as witness between me and you (of your refusal to accept the truth)."

ᵃ The source of all revelations.

14. Ibrāhīm
[Abraham : 52 verses]

L ike the other Makkan chapters, this chapter also deals with the fundamentals of faith, namely belief in God, the Messengership of Prophet Muhammad, resurrection, judgment, reward and punishment with particular emphasis on the fact that all the Prophets were tasked with the duty to deliver the same message - calling men to the worship of God alone and showing them the way to come out from the darkness of disbelieve and paganism to the light of the faith and right path. It emphasizes the fact that all the Prophets were normal humans but specially chosen by God to convey His message to the people of different nations in their respective language, and that the miracles that they performed happened only by God's permission. In this connection, reference is made to the mission of Prophet Moses and how he endeavored to bring his people to the right path and how they had disbelieved and opposed him fiercely. The chapter is named after Prophet Abraham whose act of settling a branch of his family - Hagar and Ishmael at Makkah for the practice and propagation of monotheism and whose prayer to God for blessings is specifically mentioned

In the name of God, the Most Gracious, the Most Compassionate.

One Message for All Mankind

¹ *Alif Lām Rā.* This is a Book which We have revealed to you (O Muhammad) so that you may lead mankind out of the depths of darkness into light, by their Lord's permission, onto the path that leads to the Almighty, the One to Whom all praise is due. ² He is God, the One to Whom belongs all that is in the heavens and the earth. And woe to the rejecters of truth who will be afflicted with a severe punishment; ³ (that awaits) those who choose the life of this world (as the sole object of their love, preferring it) over the life to come; and (those who also) turn others away from God's path and seek to make it crooked. Such people have indeed gone far astray.

⁴ And never have We sent forth any Messenger except he would speak in the language of his people so that he could make Our message clear to them. Then God lets go astray whomsoever He wills (that rejects the truth) and guides whomsoever He wills (that accepts the truth and submits to Him in true devotion). He is indeed the Almighty, the All-Wise.

⁵ And verily, We sent Moses with Our signs (of truth), saying, "Lead your people out from the depths of darkness into light and remind them of the Days of God (when everyone will be resurrected and judged for all their deeds)."

Indeed, in this are sure signs (of God's greatness) for all who are patient (in adversity) and grateful (to Him).

⁶ And (so O Prophet! Tell the people of earlier revelation to call to mind) when Moses said to his people, "Do you not remember God's favor upon you when He rescued you from the people of Pharaoh who had afflicted you with evil torment, slaughtered your sons and spared your women? And in that was a great trial from your Lord!"

⁷ And (remember) when your Lord proclaimed, "If you are grateful (of My blessings and strive to fulfill your duty to Me diligently), I shall surely increase My favors to you; but if you are ungrateful, My punishment is indeed severe." ⁸ And (remember too when) Moses said, "If you and everyone else on earth were to deny God, know that God (is never in need of anything from anyone, for He) is indeed All-Sufficient, Immensely Praiseworthy."

⁹ Have you not heard about the fate that befell those who lived before you - the people of Noah, 'Aād, and Tsamud, and those who came after them? No one knows about them (now) except God. Their Messengers came to them with clear evidence of the truth, but they put their hands over their mouths and said, "We disbelieve in what you (claim to) have been sent with, and we are in grave doubt and suspicion about what you invite us to."

¹⁰ Said the Messengers who were sent to them, "Can there be any doubt about God, the Originator of the heavens and the earth? He invites you to His path so that He may forgive you of your sins and grant you respite for an appointed term (to repent before He takes your life away)." They replied, "You are nothing except mortals like us who wish to turn us away from what our forefathers used to worship. Bring to us then, a clear proof of authority (if you speak the truth)!" ¹¹ Replied their Messengers, "We are only humans like you, but God bestows His grace on whomsoever He wills of His servants. And it is not within our power to bring you any proof of authority except by God's permission. It is in God that all believers must place their trust. ¹² And why should we not place our trust in God when He has shown us the (right) path to follow? Hence, we shall certainly bear with patience whatever harm and injustice that you do to us. In God alone let all those who trust in Him, rely upon."

¹³ And those who denied the truth said to their Messengers, "We shall most certainly drive you out of our land unless you return to our ways." Thereupon, their Lord revealed to them, "We shall surely destroy those wicked wrongdoers; ¹⁴ and establish you in their place after they are gone. This (promise is) to all who dread standing before Me, and fear My warnings."

¹⁵ And they prayed for God's help and victory for the truth so that every (cruel and) obstinate tyrant who opposes the truth will be destroyed. ¹⁶ Trailing behind him is Hell where he will be made to drink pus; ¹⁷ sipping it little by little, hardly able to swallow it. Death will overwhelm him from every side, yet he will not die. And more severe suffering still trails him from behind.

¹⁸ The parable of those who are bent on denying their Lord is that their deeds are like ashes on which the wind blows furiously on a stormy day. They have no control over anything that they have earned. Verily, rejecting God's message is indeed (the worst one can do and) the farthest limit of going astray. ¹⁹ Do you not see that God has created the heavens and the earth (to fulfill a purpose that is) in accordance with the truth (which He has decreed)? If He so wills, He can remove you and bring into existence a new creation (in your place). ²⁰ And that is not something difficult for God (to do).

²¹ And all (mankind) will come forth before God for judgment. Then the weak will say to those who were arrogant, "Indeed, we were your followers. Can you help us with anything against God's punishment (today)?" They will say, "If God had guided us, surely we would have guided you too. It is the same for all of us now whether we rage or endure (His torment) with patience. There is indeed no escape for us."

²² And when (the reckoning is over and) everything has been decided, Satan will say, "God has made you a true promise. And I made promises to you too, except that I did not keep them. The truth is, I had no power over you at all. All I did was to call you, and you gladly responded. Hence, do not blame me for the predicament that you are in now, but blame yourselves. (Verily,) I cannot be your helper, nor can you be my helper. Indeed, I hereby deny your association of me with God earlier." Verily, grievous suffering awaits every evil wrongdoer. ²³ (On the other hand,) those who believe and do righteous deeds will be admitted into gardens which rivers flow from right beneath them. They will remain in there forever with their Lord's permission. Greetings among themselves therein will be, "Peace (be upon you)."

²⁴ Do you not see how God compares a good word (or a noble deed) with a healthy tree? Its roots are firm and its branches reach high to the sky. ²⁵ It yields fruits in all seasons by the grace of its Lord. This is how God sets forth parables for people so that they will reflect. ²⁶ And the parable of an evil word is like a rotten tree without a stable base that can be easily uprooted from the surface of earth. ²⁷ This is how God grants firmness (in faith) to those who believe in the word that is unshakably true in this world and also in the next one to come but let's go astray those who are unjust (and commit evil deeds). Verily, God does whatever He wills (in His infinite wisdom).

Grace and Gratitude

²⁸ Have you not seen those who sold away the blessings of God in exchange for defiance and led their own people to doom? ²⁹ That is Hell! In it they will burn forever. What a wretched place as final settlement! ³⁰ And they set up equal partners to God to mislead people away from His path. Say to them, "Enjoy yourselves in this life (for a while); for verily, the Fire will be your final destination."

³¹ (O Prophet!) Tell My servants who have embraced true faith that they should attend to their prayer regularly and spend in My cause - either secretly or openly - out of the sustenance that We have granted them. Do this before there comes a day when there will neither be any ransom nor friendship (to save them from God's severe retribution). ³² It is God Who has created the heavens and the earth. It is God too Who sends down rain from the sky with which He brings forth fruits for your sustenance. He has placed under your service, ships that sail through the seas by His command, and made the rivers subservient (for your benefit).

³³ He has subjected for you the sun and the moon that constantly pursue their fixed courses (to help you keep count of time). And He also made the (alternation of) night and the day subservient (to His laws) for your benefit too. ³⁴ And He gives you of what you ask from Him. If you try to count God's blessings, you will never be able to enumerate them. Yet man is always unjust (to himself by ascribing divinity to others besides his Creator) and is ungrateful (for everything that he has been blessed with).

³⁵ And (call to mind) when Abraham said, "My Lord! Make this a city of peace,ᵃ and keep me and my children away from ever worshipping idols. ³⁶ My Lord! Indeed, these false objects of worship have certainly led many people astray. So whoever follows me in worshipping You alone, then indeed he is with me. And whoever disobeys me, then indeed, You are Most Forgiving, Most Compassionate. ³⁷ Our Lord! I have settled some of my offspring in a barren valley near Your Sacred House with the hope that they may be steadfast in their devotion to You. So fill the hearts of people with love towards them and provide them with sustenance so that they will always be grateful (to You)."

³⁸ "Our Lord! You certainly know what we conceal and what we bring into the open; for nothing whatsoever that is on the earth or in the heaven can be hidden from God. ³⁹ All praise is due to God alone, the One Who has

---

ᵃ Makkah.

granted me Ishmael and Isaac in my old age. Indeed, my Lord hears all prayers. [40] My Lord! Make me and my descendants steadfast in performing our prayer (and in our devotion to You). O My Lord! Accept my supplication. [41] Our Lord! Forgive me, my parents, and the believers on the Day of Reckoning."

[42] And do not think that God is unaware of what the wrongdoers do. In fact, He has allowed them (a little) respite until the Day when their eyes will stare (in horror); [43] and they will be dashing around (in confusion) with their heads lifted upwards, their gaze unable to turn away from what they see, and their hearts utterly void.

[44] (Hence O Prophet!) Warn mankind of the Day when suffering will befall them; and when those who were wicked (and unjust during their lifetime) will say, "Our Lord! Grant us respite for a short while so that we can (return to earthly life and) respond to Your call and follow Your Messengers." (But it will be said to them,) "Why (are you pleading now)? Did you not (arrogantly) swear in the past that you will never perish? [a] [45] And did you not live in the places of those who had sinned against their own souls before your time, while it was made obvious to you how We had dealt with them? Did We not put forth many examples for you (to take heed)?"

[46] And indeed they devised their plots, but all their plots were within God's grasp even if these (evil) plots could move mountains. [47] So do not think that God will fail to keep His promise to His Messengers. Indeed, God is Almighty, He is the Lord of Retribution.

[48] (Hence, warn them of) the Day when the earth and the heavens will be (destroyed and) replaced, and everyone will be brought together (to assemble) before God - the One Who holds absolute dominance (and power) over all that exists. [49] And on that Day, you will see all those who are lost in sin, bound together in chains; [50] clothed in garments of tar that are black pitch, and their faces (will look as if they were) covered with flames. [51] (Everyone will be judged fairly on that Day) and God will requite each soul according to what it has earned (during its lifetime). Indeed, God is swift in reckoning.

[52] This is a (clear) message to warn all mankind beforehand that He is indeed the One and Only Almighty God (Whom everyone will finally return to). Let those who are endowed with wisdom and insight take heed (of this news and be well prepared to face it).

---

[a] See also verse 23:99-100 and its footnote.

15. Al-Ḥijr
[The Rocky Tract : 99 verses]

This is also a Makkan chapter which deals with the fundamentals of faith - monotheism, the truth of Prophet Muhammad's messengership, resurrection, reward and punishment. It draws attention to the destruction of disbelieving and sinful nations of the past, particularly the people of Tsamud whom Prophet Saleh was sent to. They lived in *Al-Hijr*, a region in North Arabia between Madinah and Syria, where their ruins are still visible. This chapter is named after it and account is given in the context of the theme that all the previous Prophets and Messengers of God were opposed and ridiculed by the disbelievers of their respective people. The chapter also speaks about the creation of Adam and the disobedience of *Iblis* who vowed to mislead all of Adam's progeny. It concludes by consoling Prophet Muhammad by reminding him of God's great favor in sending down the Qur'an to him, asking him to bear the opposition and enmity of the disbelievers of his own community with patience and giving him the good news of God's help and victory in the near future.

In the name of God, the Most Gracious, the Most Compassionate.

Preserving the Qur'an

¹ *Alif Lām Rā.* These are verses of the (Divine) Book that set things clear (for everyone). ² There will come a time when those who are bent on opposing the truth will wish that they had submitted themselves to God. ³ So leave them alone (for now). Let them eat and enjoy themselves while the false hope (of victory) beguile them. Soon they will know (the truth). ⁴ Never have We destroyed any city (for the wrongdoings of its people) until its appointed time arrives. ⁵ No community can ever hasten (the end of) its term nor delay it.

⁶ And they say (to you O Prophet), "O you who claim this reminder has been sent down to! Indeed, you are mad. ⁷ If you are really a man of truth, why do you not bring Angels to us (to support your claim)?" ⁸ (Behold!) We do not send down Angels (to the disbelievers) except to enforce (justice and) the truth. No more respite will be given to them after that.

⁹ Indeed, It is We who have sent down this reminder and it is We who shall guard (and preserve it eternally from any corruption). ᵃ ¹⁰ And certainly

---

ᵃ Muhammad Asad commented that this prophecy has been strikingly confirmed by the fact that the text of the Qur'an has remained free from all alterations, additions or deletions ever since it was enunciated by the Prophet in the 7th century, and there is no other instance of any book, of whatever description, which has been similarly

(O Muhammad,) We sent Messengers before you to people of earlier communities; [11] but no Messenger ever came to them without being ridiculed. [12] This is how We let such act of disbelief to enter into the hearts of those who are lost in sin. [13] Verily, they are the ones who refuse to believe in Our message despite (clear examples of) what had befallen the people of earlier times. [14] And even if We opened to them a gateway to heaven and allowed them to continuously ascend through it (in broad daylight); [15] they would still say, "Indeed, our eyes have been dazzled. We have surely been bewitched!"

Great Universal Expanse

[16] We have indeed set up constellations in the heavens and beautified them for all to see; [17] and We have protected them from every accursed Satan. [18] Anyone who tries to eavesdrop will surely be pursued by a clear burning flame. [19] We have also spread out the earth,*ᵃ* placed firm mountains on it, and made everything grow there in a well-measured and balanced manner. [20] And We have placed various means of livelihood on it for you, as well as for those other creatures that you do not have to provide for. [21] And there is not a thing that exists except its (inexhaustible) treasures are with Us, and We do not (randomly) send this down except in precise measure.

[22] And We let loose the winds to fertilize (plants) and We send down water from the sky for you to drink. And it is not you who are the keepers of its stores. [23] And indeed it is We Who grant life and cause death, and We shall be the sole inheritor (of everything). [24] And verily, We know those who lived before you and also those who will come after you. [25] And surely your Lord will gather them altogether one day. He is indeed All-Wise, All-Knowing.

Man and His Sworn Enemy

[26] Indeed, We have created man out of dry clay from black mud, molded into shape; [27] whereas the Jinn We created before him from scorching fire.

---

preserved over such a length of time. The early-noted variants in the reading of certain words of the Qur'an represent no more than differences in respect of diacritical marks or of vocalization, and do not affect the meaning of the passage in question. (See also verse 85:22 and its corresponding note that explains the expression *Lawh Mahfuz*.)
ᵃ See also verses 13:3, 51:48, 55:10, 79:30, 71:19-20, 88:20 and 91:6. The phrase which says that the "earth is being spread out" in all these verses does not mean that the earth is literally flat. Instead it is a metaphor of the earth's wide expanse that enables people and other creatures to travel on it extensively. The actual shape of the earth is spherical. Its clue was given by the Qur'an 1,450 years ago in verse 39:5.

²⁸ (Behold!) When Your Lord said to the Angels, "Indeed, I am going to create a human being out of dry clay from black mud that will be molded (into shape); ²⁹ and when I have fashioned him and breathed My spirit into him, fall down (all of you) in prostration before him (as a mark of respect to My perfect creation)!" ³⁰ Thereupon, the all Angels prostrated together; ³¹ except *Iblis* who refused to prostrate like the others.

³² God said, "O *Iblis*! Why do you refuse to prostrate like the rest (as I commanded)?" ³³ *Iblis* replied, "I shall not prostrate to a human whom You created out of dry clay that is molded from black mud." ³⁴ God said, "Then get out of here, for indeed you are accursed!" ³⁵ "And indeed, upon you will be the curse until the Day of Judgment." ³⁶ Replied *Iblis*, "O my Lord! In that case, give me respite until the Day when everyone will be resurrected." ³⁷ God said, "Then indeed, you are granted respite; ³⁸ until the Day of the appointed time."

³⁹ *Iblis* said, "My Lord! Because You have denounced me astray, I shall make (evil to appear) fair-seeming (and alluring) to everyone on earth and I shall most certainly mislead them all (into grievous error); *ᵃ* ⁴⁰ except those who are Your truly sincere and devoted servants."

⁴¹ God said, "This is the way *ᵇ* which will lead straight to Me. ⁴² Indeed, You will have no power over My servants, except those who (choose to) follow you and are lost in error. ⁴³ And indeed, Hell is the promised destiny for all of them; ⁴⁴ which has seven gates leading into it, and each gate will receive its assigned sinners." ⁴⁵ But the God-fearing will dwell amidst gardens and water springs. ⁴⁶ (They will be greeted,) "Enter here in peace and security!"; ⁴⁷ and We shall remove whatever bitterness from their hearts. (They will rest in there) like brothers, facing one another (in happiness) on elevated couches. ⁴⁸ No fatigue will touch them nor will they ever be asked to leave. ⁴⁹ Tell My servants that I am the Most Forgiving, the Most Compassionate; ⁵⁰ but the punishment that I shall inflict (on those who defy Me) is surely most grievous.

Lessons of History

⁵¹ And tell them about the guests of Abraham; ⁵² when they visited him and said, "Peace (be upon you)!" But Abraham replied, "Indeed, we are afraid of you (because you do nor look familiar)." ⁵³ They replied, "Do not be afraid. We bring good news to you about the birth of a son who will be endowed with knowledge." ⁵⁴ He said, "Are you giving me this good news now when I have already been overtaken by old age? What (strange) news is this?" ⁵⁵ They said,

---

ᵃ See footnote for verse 2:36
ᵇ In reference to *Taqwa* or God-consciousness. See footnote for verse 2:183.

"We give you good news about something that will surely come true. So do not be among those who despair." ⁵⁶ Abraham replied, "No one should ever lose hope of his Lord's grace except those who are misguided and have utterly lost their way."

⁵⁷ (Then) he asked, "So what is your mission, O Messengers of God?" ⁵⁸ They replied, "We have indeed been sent to (destroy) a community that is immersed in sin; ⁵⁹ except the family of Lot. Indeed, we shall surely save them; ⁶⁰ except his (stubborn) wife, (of whom God says,) 'We have decreed that she will remain with those who stay behind (to receive Our retribution).'"

⁶¹ And when the Messengers of God came to Lot and his family; ⁶² he said to them, "Verily, you do not look familiar." ⁶³ They answered, "Yes indeed! We (are Messengers of God who) have come to you with (a torment) that those (who are immersed in evil) do not believe (would happen); ⁶⁴ and we are bringing to you the certainty of its fulfillment (from God). Behold, we are speaking the truth. ⁶⁵ So depart with your family in the darkness of the night and follow closely behind them. Proceed to where you are commanded and no one should look back." ⁶⁶ And We made known to him (the decree) that the last remnants of those (sinners) will be destroyed by early morning.

⁶⁷ In the meantime, the people of the city came to Lot rejoicing (at the news of his good-looking visitors). ⁶⁸ Lot said, "Indeed, these are my guests. Do not put me to shame. ⁶⁹ Fear God and do not bring disgrace to me." ⁷⁰ They said, "Did we not forbid you from meddling into other people's affairs?" ⁷¹ Lot replied (in exasperation), "These are my daughters for you to take them in marriage if you wish so."

⁷² By your life (O Muhammad)! Indeed, they were blindly wandering in their intoxication (of lust). ⁷³ So the awful blast of punishment seized them at sunrise; ⁷⁴ and We turned the city upside down and rained upon them stones of baked clay. ⁷⁵ Surely in this are signs for those who (care to ponder and) discern. ⁷⁶ And indeed, the place (where this occurred) lies along an established route. ⁷⁷ Verily, there is a sign in this for true believers (to reflect and take lesson from).

⁷⁸ And the dwellers of Al-'Aikah (in Madyan) were wrongdoers too. ⁷⁹ So We took retribution from them. Indeed the desolate locations of both these sinful communities lie along a clear highway (and is plain to see until this day).

⁸⁰ Likewise, the people of Al-Ḥijr also denied the Messengers of God (who were sent to them). ⁸¹ We gave them Our signs, but they turned their backs on those signs. ⁸² Out of the mountains, they carved their homes and

lived in them securely. [83] But the awful blast of punishment seized them early in the morning; [84] and all (the wealth) that they had earned (and amassed) was of no use to them.

[85] And We have not created the heavens and the earth and whatever is between them except (to fulfill a purpose) that is in accordance with the truth (that We have decreed). Indeed, the appointed Hour will certainly come. Hence, forgive (men's failings) with gracious forbearance (O Prophet). [86] Indeed your Lord, He is the Creator of everything, the All-Knowing.

Keeping to the Path of Truth

[87] And indeed, We have bestowed upon you seven of the most repeated (verses) and (have laid open before you) this Glorious Qur'an. [a] [88] (So) do not extend your eyes (covetously) to the good things that We have granted to some among those (who deny the truth), nor grieve over the state of error that they are in. But (spread and) lower your wings (of graciousness) to the believers instead; [89] and say, "Indeed, I am being sent with a clear warning"; [90] (a warning) just like what We sent to those who divided (and fragmented the earlier Scriptures); [91] (and) who are doing the same to the Qur'an too, breaking them into fragments, (believing in some and rejecting others as they please). [b] [92] So by your Lord! We shall surely question them all; [93] for everything that they have done.

[94] Proclaim what you are commanded and turn away from those who associate partners with God. [95] Indeed, sufficient are We for you against all who deride (Our reminders); [96] those who claim that there are other gods besides the One and Only God. But soon they will surely come to know (the truth). [97] Verily, We know how distressed is your heart by the (blasphemous) things they say. [98] So glorify the perfection of your Lord by praising Him (abundantly) and be among those who prostrate (to Him in true devotion). [99] And (be steadfast in) worshipping your Lord until the certainty (of death) comes to you.

---

[a] In reference to the first chapter of the Qur'an, *Al-Fatihah.*

[b] Not only did the Jews and Christians in the ancient past not accept the entirety of their revealed Scriptures (i.e. Torah and Injeel), those who lived during the time of Prophet Muhammad did the same to the Qur'an too. Unfortunately, many Muslims fall into the same trap after the demise of the Prophet until today due to their own ego and lusts. There are a plethora of factions among Muslims with each rejoicing in their distorted faith and erroneous practices that have never been taught by the Prophet. See verses 21:93, 23:53 and 42:13.

16. An-Naḥl
[The Bee : 128 verses]

This is another Makkan chapter and just like all other Makkan chapters, it concentrates on the fundamentals of monotheism and faith, revelation, Prophet Muhammad's messengership, resurrection and judgment. In bringing home these themes, it draws attention to God's wondrous creations - the heavens, the sun and the moon, the stars, the earth, the mountains, the seas, the rivers, the trees and plants, the beasts and animals, all of which point unmistakably to the Creator and His caring and consoling hand behind them. It also emphasizes that all these creations pay obeisance to God, and have all been subjected to perfectly designed laws that make them serviceable to man. With all these favors bestowed upon man, it is only natural for man to express gratitude by only worshipping God alone. None of these objects and natural phenomena, however gigantic and stupendous they may seem to be, deserves any worship. The chapter is named *An-Nahl* which means The Bee. It is mentioned in verses 68 - 69 as one of God's wonderful creations which offers plenty of amazing benefits to mankind.

In the name of God, the Most Gracious, the Most Compassionate.

God, The Creator of All

¹ God's judgment is sure to come; so do not seek to hasten it impatiently. Glorified and exalted is He above what they associate Him with (and from all other imperfections). ² He sends down the Angels with this (divine) inspiration *a* by His command upon whomsoever He wills of His servants, saying, "Warn mankind that there is no god except Me alone. So be ever mindful of Me (and strive to fulfill your duty to Me diligently)."

³ He is the One Who created the heavens and the earth (to fulfill a purpose) that is in accordance with the truth (which He has decreed). Exalted is He above what they associate (Him with). ⁴ He creates man out of a mere clot of semen, then behold! This same man grows up to be a clear adversary (and challenges God openly).

---

a Divine inspiration or revelation is another meaning for *Ruh* in Arabic which literally means "the Spirit". See also verse 42:52. It is this spirit of the Qur'an which inspired the Arabs and transformed them from a nation of marauding tribes with a marginal place in history into a dynamic and vigorous social force that went on to lead the world.

⁵ And He also created cattle; from them you derive warmth and other benefits. And from them too you obtain food. ⁶ There is beauty (and joy) as you bring them home (in the evening) and as you take them out (in the morning to graze). ⁷ And they carry your loads to distant lands that you could not have otherwise reached without much hardship. Your Lord is certainly Most Kind, Most Compassionate.

⁸ He created horses, mules and donkeys for you to ride and for splendor. And He (also) created (many) other things that you have no knowledge about. ⁹ It is God alone who points and guides to the right path. Yet many swerve (and deviate) from it (because of their own arrogance). Had He so willed, surely He would have guided everyone, (but He grants you free will for you to make your own choices that you will be called to account for someday).

¹⁰ He is the One Who sends down water from the sky for you. From it you drink and from it grows vegetation that you feed to your cattle. ¹¹ And with it too, He causes crops, olive trees, date-palms, grapes, and fruits of every kind to grow for you. Surely there is a sign in this for people who ponder. ¹² (And for your benefit,) He has subjected the night and day, the sun and moon, and the stars (by making them) all subservient to His command. Indeed, there are signs in this for people who (care to) use reason (and common sense). ¹³ He has also produced and multiplied all kinds of things on earth with varying colors. Surely there is a sign in this for those who take heed.

¹⁴ And He is the One Who has subjected the sea for you to eat fresh meat from it and bring forth ornaments to wear. And you see ships ploughing their way through (the waves) so that you may be able to seek His bounty and be grateful (for the favors that He has blessed you with). ¹⁵ It is He Who also placed firm mountains on earth (as pegs and anchors) lest it shakes with you (as it rotates around its axis), ᵃ and (together with) rivers and pathways for you to find your way; ¹⁶ as well as (other) landmarks and stars to guide people.

ᵃ Here is another scientific miracle presented by the Qur'an. In verse 78:7, it is stated that mountains are placed on earth as pegs and anchors. Take note that the roots of mountains are normally extended underground as far as 5-6 times their actual height on the surface of the earth. And in verse 15 of this current chapter, it states that the reason for this is to prevent the earth from shaking. Why does the earth shake and vibrate? Now consider the movement of the earth's surface with respect to the planet's axis. With a circumference of roughly 40,075 kilometers, the earth rotates once every 24 hours. Thus, the surface of the earth at the equator moves at a speed of roughly 1,670 km/hour as it rotates around its axis. Therefore, the mountains' roots that go deep underground act as anchors and stabilizers to hold the earth's fractured surface and the tectonic plates underneath them from moving and shaking violently as the earth rotates around its axis at such high speed.

¹⁷ Then, is He Who creates, equal as the one who does not? Can you not think? ¹⁸ And if you try to count God's blessings, you will never be able to enumerate them. Indeed, God is Most Forgiving, Most Compassionate. ¹⁹ God knows all that you keep secret and all that you bring into the open. ²⁰ And those whom some people invoke besides God cannot create anything. Instead, they themselves are created. ²¹ They are dead, not alive, and they do not (even) know when they will be raised (from the dead).

Divergent Outlooks and Attitudes

²² (Verily,) your God is only One God. Those who reject the Hereafter have hearts that are in denial. They are arrogant. ²³ There is no doubt that God knows what they conceal and what they reveal. He certainly does not love those who are arrogant.

²⁴ When they are asked, "What has your Lord sent down?" they answer (mockingly, "Just) fables of ancient times!" ²⁵ On the Day of Resurrection they will bear the full weight of their burdens, as well as the burdens of those whom they have misled without true knowledge. Evil indeed is the burden they will bear! ᵃ ²⁶ Those who lived before them schemed (evil plots too). But God uprooted the whole structure of their plot from its foundation and its roof fell on top of them. Punishment came upon them from directions they did not expect.

²⁷ Then, on the Day of Resurrection, He will bring them all to disgrace. He will ask, "Where are those alleged partners of Mine whom you had wholeheartedly defended while opposing Me?" Thereupon, those who are

---

ᵃ In everyday society, this kind of rebuttal against the truth normally comes from the ignorant elites or the leaders and opinion-shapers who have the capacity to influence the masses and mislead them. The Prophet is reported to have said: "Whoever influences people to error will carry the burden of its sin like those who committed it without their sins being diminished even a bit." [Sahih Muslim, no. 2674]. On the other hand, people should also think critically and be ever vigilant and discerning with regard to the principles and ideas they choose to accept and believe in. They should not allow themselves to be easily misled because their hearing, sight, and intention in the heart will all be called to account on the Day of Judgment. See verse 17:36 and its footnote. However, what is mentioned here should not be confused with verses 17:15 and 53:38 that read, "No soul will be made to bear the burden of another.." which essentially means no one can expect to absolve his sins, or to have his sins atoned by transferring them to others. Sins cannot be absolved or atoned this way. Instead, their burden will be equally shared in full with those who were responsible in influencing and misleading others to follow their wrongdoings.

endowed with knowledge will say, "Indeed on this Day, humiliation and misery will fall upon those who have been denying the truth!" [28] They are the ones whose souls are taken by the Angels while in the midst of their sinful acts. And only then would these disbelievers offer their full submission and plead, "We never (meant to) engage in any evil." And the Angels will answer them, "Nay! Verily, God has full knowledge of everything you did! [29] Now enter the gates of Hell where you will remain in it forever!" Evil indeed is the (permanent) home of those who are arrogant.

[30] And when the righteous are asked, "What has your Lord revealed?" They will answer, "Something excellent!" Indeed, there is goodness in this world for those who do good, but their home in the life to come is far better. How excellent is the (permanent) home of the righteous! [31] They will be welcomed into the Gardens of Perpetual Bliss with rivers flowing from right beneath them. They will have everything they wish in there. This is how God rewards those who keep their duty to Him diligently. [32] They are those whose souls are taken by the Angels in the state of purity with the greeting, "Peace be upon you! Welcome to Paradise that has been prepared as a reward for your (noble) deeds."

[33] Are these infidels waiting for the Angels to appear in front of their eyes or for your Lord's command to seize them (before they would want to accept Our message)? Verily, those who were before them did the same too (but look at how was their end). Verily, God was never unjust to them, but it was they who were unjust to themselves. [34] (In the end), all the evil consequences of their misdeeds fell back upon them. Indeed, they were overwhelmed by the very thing they used to deride.

[35] Those who worshipped others besides God say, "Had God willed, neither we nor our forefathers would have worshipped anything other than Him, nor would we have declared anything forbidden without His command." Those before them gave the same excuse too. Are Our Messengers bound to do anything other than deliver the message that We entrust to them clearly?

[36] We had certainly sent a Messenger to every community who said, "Worship Almighy God alone and shun false gods." Among them were some whom God guided (when they accepted the truth) while others strayed because of their own error (and defiance). So travel throughout the earth and see what was the end for those who denied the truth.

[37] (O Prophet) However eager you desire to show them the right way, (know that) God does not give guidance to those whom He wills to let go astray (because of their own defiance). And they will not have anyone to help them too.

38 And they swear by God with their strongest oaths that God will not resurrect the dead. Nay! (On the contrary,) this is a promise that is incumbent upon Him (to fulfill) but most people do not know (and care about) this. 39 (On the Day of Resurrection,) He will make clear to them about what they used to dispute so that those who disbelieved (will be told that God knows) they had been lying. 40 (Resurrecting the dead is easy for Us.) Whenever We will anything, We only need to say, "Be!" and it is.

41 As for those who emigrated for the sake of God after suffering injustice, We shall certainly bless them with a good home in this life. But the reward in the life to come is far better. If only they knew! 42 (Such reward is granted to) those who persevere in patience, and place their reliance and trust in their Lord.

43 And even before your time (O Muhammad), the Messengers whom We sent were none other than mere mortals to whom We revealed (Our message). If you do not know, then ask those who have knowledge (about this from the people of earlier revelation); 44 (and they will tell you that their Prophets too were mortals whom We had endowed them) with clear evidence of the truth and Scriptures (of divine wisdom). And upon you too do We send this reminder for you to make clear to people about what has been sent down to them so that they will (reflect and) ponder.

45 Then, do those who devise evil schemes feel safe from God that He will not cause them to sink into the earth, or (guarantee that they will be completely free from) any torment that might befall them when they least expected it? 46 Or He might suddenly seize them as they freely move about and cannot escape from? 47 Or (are they sure) that He would not seize them through gradual loss (of wealth, or other form of misfortunes)? But indeed, your Lord is surely Full of Kindness, Most Compassionate. (Hence, he grants them respite so that they might repent.)

48 Have they not considered that whatsoever God has created casts its shadow to the right and to the left, prostrating to God while in a state of complete submission to His will? 49 And (indeed,) to God prostrates everything in the heavens and earth, every creature that moves, even the Angels too - who are free from arrogance. 50 They fear their Lord Who is high above them and they do whatever they are commanded.

The One and Only God

51 And God said, "Do not take two (or more) gods for worship, for He is truly the One and Only God. Hence, stand in awe of Me alone!" 52 To Him

belongs whatever that is in the heavens and the earth, and to Him (alone) worship (and obedience) is due. Does it then make sense that you should revere and serve anything other than the One and Only God?

⁵³ Whatever good pleasure you enjoy is from God. And whenever hardship afflicts you, it is to Him alone you should cry out for help. ⁵⁴ Yet when He removes the hardship from you, behold! Some of you (foolishly continue to) associate partners with their Lord. ⁵⁵ So let them show their (ingratitude and) denial for (the favors and bounties) that We have granted them. (Say to them,) "Enjoy then (the brief time you have on earth, O disbelievers)! Soon you will know (the truth)."

⁵⁶ And they assign a portion (of the provision) that We give them to things which they know nothing about.ᵃ By God! You will certainly be called to account for your false inventions. ⁵⁷ And they also assign daughters to God. Whereas for themselves they choose whatever they desire. Glorified and exalted is God above what they associate Him with (and also from all other imperfections)!

⁵⁸ And when the news of a female child's birth is brought to one of them, his face darkens as he suppresses his grief. ⁵⁹ He tries to avoid his people because of the bad news that he has been given, debating within himself whether should he keep the child despite the shame he feels, or should he bury her in the ground? Evil indeed is their judgment. ⁶⁰ Those who do not believe in the life to come deserve to be characterized with evil attributes, whereas to God applies the highest attributes. He alone is Almighty, All-Wise!

⁶¹ And if God were to (instantaneously) punish mankind for their wrong-doings, He would not have left any living creature on earth. But He delays them for an appointed term (that is known only to Him). Then when their time arrives, they will not be able to delay it even for a moment, nor can they hasten it. ⁶² (How ironic it is that) they assign to God what they hate for themselves while their own tongues assert the lie that the best belongs to them. Without doubt, for them is the (home of) Fire and they will be abandoned in there.

⁶³ By God (O Muhammad)! We have certainly sent Messengers to various communities before you, but Satan made their evil deeds seem fair and alluring to them. He is the patron of the disbelievers today (as he was to those who were immersed in sin before). Hence, grievous punishment awaits (all of) them. ⁶⁴ We have sent down this Book to you for no other reason than for you to make clear to them what they dispute about, and to serve as guidance and grace to those who believe (in the truth).

ᵃ In reference to the false gods that they worship.

⁶⁵ And God sends down rain from the sky and revives the earth with it after the earth has been dead. Indeed, in that is a sign for people who listen. ⁶⁶ And indeed in cattle too, you have a (worthy) lesson. We give you pure milk from what is in their bellies - produced alongside excretions and blood - pleasant to those who drink it. ⁶⁷ And from the fruits of date-palms and grapes, you derive intoxicants and also good wholesome food. Surely there is a sign in this for people who care to use reason (and common sense to ponder).

⁶⁸ And your Lord has also inspired the (female) bee, *ᵃ* "Take up homes in hills, on trees and in structures that people have built; ⁶⁹ then eat from all the fruits and follow the paths your Lord has made smooth for you." Comes forth from its bellies *ᵇ* a drink of varying colors, in which is a healing for people. Indeed, in that is a sign for people who (think and) reflect.

⁷⁰ It is God Who has created you and in time will cause you to die. Some of you are sent back to the most feeble stage of life, so that they no longer know what they previously knew. God is indeed All-Knowing, infinite in His power.

⁷¹ God has favored some of you with more provision than others. But those who have been given more are unwilling to share their provision with their slaves and make them as their equals.ᶜ How could they (continue to still believe in falsehood and) deny God's favors and blessings?

⁷² And God has given you spouses of your own kind. Through them, He gives you children and descendants, and provides you with sustenance out of the good things in life. Then, will they still continue to believe in falsehood and deny God's blessings? ⁷³ So instead of God, they worship something that cannot provide them with any provision from the heavens or the earth. (In fact,) these (false gods) are incapable of anything. ⁷⁴ So do not compare God with anything. Indeed, God knows everything whereas you do not, (except only what He lets you know).

ᵃ It was only known recently that the worker bees which gather pollen and make honey are female bees, not male bees. But the Qur'an has mentioned this 1,450 years ago. This is established in verse 69 where the command in Arabic for the bee to *"eat from all the fruits and follow the paths"* was specifically directed to the female gender.
ᵇ The other amazing fact is that the word *"its bellies"* means that there is more than one stomach in each bee because it was expressed in a plural form. It was also not until recently when it was discovered that female bees actually have two stomachs - one for its digestive system and the other one for it to store the honey that it makes.
ᶜ If the Arab pagans were not prepared to share equal status with their slaves, how could they bring themselselves to assign equal partners to God in divinity?

⁷⁵ God presents the parable of a man who is enslaved with no power over anything, and another on whom We have bestowed with good provision, from which he (freely) spends secretly and openly. Can these two be equal? (Verily,) all praise is due to God alone! But most people do not (even) understand (this simple fact). ⁷⁶ God presents another example of two men, one dumb and unable to do a thing. He is a burden to his master. Wherever he is sent, he accomplishes nothing good. Can he be considered equal to the one who commands justice and follows the right path?

Denying the Undeniable

⁷⁷ To God alone belongs the hidden secrets of the heavens and the earth. The coming of the Last Hour will be accomplished in a blink of an eye, or even quicker. Indeed, God has power over all things. ⁷⁸ And God brought you forth to this world from the wombs of your mothers when you knew nothing, and then endowed you with hearing, sight and conscience (to discern truth from falsehood) so that you may be grateful. ⁷⁹ Do those (who persistently deny God's message) never considered the birds and how they are enabled to fly in the sky? None but God holds them aloft. ᵃ Indeed, in these parables are signs for people who believe (in God and stand in awe of His greatness).

⁸⁰ And it is God Who has given you (the ability to build) houses as your resting place, and has endowed you with (the skills to make) homes out of the skins of animals that you find easy to handle when you travel and set up camp; and to make furnishings and comfort for a while from their wool, fur, and hair. ⁸¹ And out of the many things God has created, He has also made shade (for your protection), places of shelter in the mountains and has endowed you with (the ability to make) garments to protect you from heat (and cold), as well as coats (of mail) to protect you from your mutual violence (of wars). In such ways does He perfect some of His favors upon you so that you may submit yourselves to Him (in devotion).

⁸² So if they turn away from you (O Muhammad), remember that your duty is only to convey Our message clearly. ⁸³ They are certainly aware of God's favors, yet they simply refuse to acknowledge them because most people are (ungrateful) disbelievers. ⁸⁴ (They are heedless of) the Day when We shall resurrect a witness from every community (to testify against their defiance). On that Day, those who rejected the truth (during their lifetime) will not be allowed to plead (ignorance), nor will they be allowed to make amends. ⁸⁵ And when these evil wrongdoers finally see the suffering that awaits them, it will in no way be lightened for them, nor will they be granted respite.

ᵃ See verse 67:19 and its footnote.

⁸⁶ And when those who associated partners with God see these alleged partners on that Day, they will say, "Our Lord! These are the beings whom we used to invoke instead of You." But those beings will throw their word back at them, saying, "Indeed, you are liars!" ⁸⁷ On that Day, they will (try to) offer their submission to God because all (the false gods) that they invented will forsake them.

⁸⁸ Upon those who were bent on opposing the truth and hindered others from God's path, We shall add further punishment to their suffering because of all the corruption they did and spread (on earth). ⁸⁹ And on that Day, We shall resurrect a witness among themselves from every community (to testify against their transgression); and We shall also bring you (O Muhammad,) to be a witness against your people (who have transgressed). We sent down the Book to you to explain everything clearly and to provide guidance, grace and good news to those who fully submit themselves to God.

Absolute Justice

⁹⁰ Verily, God commands that justice, kindness and generosity towards relatives (and fellow-men to always be upheld); and He forbids immorality, impropriety and oppression. He warns you about this (repeatedly) so that you will take heed. ⁹¹ So fulfill the covenant with God whenever you make a pledge. Do not break your oaths after you have sworn them and made God as your (witness and) surety. God certainly knows everything that you do.

⁹² Do not use your oaths as a means to deceive one another - like a woman who unravels the yarn that she has tightly spun - simply because one party may be more numerous (and looks greater) than the other. By this, God puts you to a test. Surely on the Day of Resurrection, He will make clear to you regarding every matter that you are disputing (now).

⁹³ Had God so willed, He would have surely made all of you as one single community. But He lets go astray whomsoever He wills (that is bent on denying the truth) and guides aright whomsoever He wills (that strives to seek the truth). And you will certainly be called to account for all that you have done (during your lifetime).

⁹⁴ And do not use your oaths as a means of deceiving (and betraying) one another, lest your foot slips after it has been firmly planted. As a result, you will taste the evil consequences of hindering others from God's path (in this world) with (an even) greater punishment that awaits you in the life to come.

⁹⁵ Do not trade away your covenant with God for a trifling price. Surely,

what is with God is far better for you (than anything else), if only you knew! [96] Whatever you have is certain to come to an end, but what is with God will remain. And We shall certainly reward those who remain steadfast according to the best of their deeds. [97] Whoever does righteous deeds, whether man or woman, and is a believer, We shall most certainly let them live a good life. And We shall indeed reward them according to the best of their deeds.

[98] So when you recite the Qur'an, seek refuge in God from Satan, the accursed. [99] Indeed, he certainly has no power over those who have truly attained to faith and (firmly) place their trust in their Lord. [100] Verily, Satan's power is only over those who take him as their patron and those who associate partners with God.

[101] And now that We replace a (revealed) sign for another (O Muhammad) - and only God knows best what He reveals - those (who deny the truth) accuse you by saying, "Indeed, you are making this up!" But the fact is, most of them do not know (the truth). [102] Tell them, "It is the Holy Spirit *a* who has brought it down from your Lord, setting forth the truth to strengthen (the faith of) the believers; serving as guidance (to the right way) and as good news to those who submit themselves (in true devotion only to their Creator alone)."

[103] We know full well that they (accuse you by) saying, "Surely he is being taught by another man!" But the man to whom they so maliciously allude speaks a foreign tongue whereas this (revelation) is in eloquent Arabic - pure and clear. *b* [104] Indeed, those who do not believe in God's revelations will not be guided by God, and a grievous suffering awaits them. [105] (Verily,) only those who invent falsehood are the ones who do not believe in God's revelations. Indeed, it is they who are liars.

---

a The Angel of revelation - Gabriel.

b This is in relation to a slander perpetrated by the Arab pagans against the integrity of the Prophet during the early stages of his mission. They used to say that he had been taught the Qur'an by Jewish and Christian elders, or someone well-versed in the knowledge of earlier Scriptures. The implication was that these mysterious mentors were non-Arab. Ironically however, they had not explained why none of them had come forward to claim credit for their alleged contribution. The Qur'an immediately points out the absurdity of the accusation and the fallacy of the argument, for how could a non-Arab, no matter how skilled and versed in the knowledge of earlier Scriptures, be able to compose a religious text of such utter beauty, perfection, and purity as to be considered by all literary experts as a unique masterpiece of Arabic prose unmatched to this day, without speaking a word, or very little, of the language itself? Moreover, if such a mentor did happen to exist, why on earth would the Arabs keep his identity a secret? Surely, the obvious action would have been to confront Muhammad with him in order to discredit his mission and expose him as an impostor.

¹⁰⁶ Whoever rejects God after believing in Him, and then willfully opens his heart to disbelief - except the one who is forced to renounce his religion under duress while his heart remains firmly convinced of the true faith - then upon such people is God's wrath and a mighty punishment lies in store for them. ¹⁰⁷ That is because their love for the life of this world takes preference over the next life to come. Hence, God does not bestow His guidance on those who reject the truth. ¹⁰⁸ They are the ones whose hearts, ears and eyes are sealed by God; such are the heedless. ¹⁰⁹ Without doubt, they will surely be the losers in the life to come.

¹¹⁰ But for those who emigrated after enduring trials and persecution, then strived hard in God's cause and remained patient, you will surely find that your Lord is certainly the Most Forgiving, Most Compassionate. ¹¹¹ (So be conscious and fearful O mankind, of) the Day when every soul will come pleading for itself. On that Day, every soul will be paid in full for everything that it did, and no one will be wronged.

¹¹² (Verily,) God sets forth (for you) the parable of a city which once enjoyed peace and contentment, with provision coming to it abundantly from everywhere. But its people denied God's favors (and were ungrateful to the blessings that He showered upon them). So God afflicted them with a miserable taste of hunger and fear (as punishment) for their misdeeds. ¹¹³ And indeed a Messenger from among them came (to warn about their errors), but they denied him. So they were seized by punishment while they were committing injustice.

Forbidden for Consumption

¹¹⁴ Eat then from all the lawful and good things that God has provided for you, and be grateful to God for His favors, if it is Him alone that you (must) truly worship. ¹¹⁵ He has only forbidden to you carrion, blood, the flesh of swine, and what is slaughtered in any name other than God. But if you are compelled by absolute necessity (to consume them) - neither coveting it nor exceeding (your immediate need) - then indeed, God is Most Forgiving, Most Compassionate. ¹¹⁶ And do not (utter falsehoods by) letting your tongues (arbitrarily) declare, "This is lawful!" and "That is forbidden!", thus fabricating lies against God. Surely, those who fabricate lies against God will never succeed. ¹¹⁷ Their enjoyment (in this world) is brief and an (everlasting) painful torment awaits them (in the life to come).

¹¹⁸ (O Prophet,) We forbade the Jews what We have mentioned to you

before.^a We did not wrong them, but it was they who persistently wronged themselves. ¹¹⁹ But indeed your Lord (grants forgiveness) to those who commit evil out of ignorance, and then repent and mend their ways. Thereafter, your Lord is certainly Most Forgiving, Most Compassionate.

Advocacy by Example

¹²⁰ Indeed, Abraham was a model of excellence who was devoutly obedient to God alone. He was an upright monotheist who did not ascribe divinity to anything other than God. ¹²¹ He was always grateful for the blessings bestowed by God Who had chosen him and guided him to a straight path. ¹²² And so, We graced him with all goodness in this world, and in the life to come he will surely be among the righteous.

¹²³ Thereupon, We inspired you with this message (O Muhammad), "Follow the creed of Abraham, who was an upright monotheist, and who was not one of those who associated partners with God." ¹²⁴ As for the observance of Sabbath, it was decreed only upon those who held divergent views about Abraham's (ethnicity and religion).^b Certainly, your Lord will judge between them on the Day of Resurrection regarding their dispute.

¹²⁵ So call people to the path of your Lord with wisdom and words of good advice, and reason with them in the best manner. ^c Your Lord knows best who strays from His path and who are rightly guided. ¹²⁶ If you should retaliate (to their aggression), then do so in proportion to the wrong done to you. ^d But if you can bear their conduct with patience, that is indeed the best for those who are patient.

¹²⁷ So be patient (O Prophet, and be mindful that) your patience comes only from God. And do not grieve over those (who oppose you), nor be distressed by their evil plots (against you). ¹²⁸ Indeed, God is with those who are ever mindful of Him and excel in good deeds.

---

^a See verse 6:146.

^b This is in reference to the claim by the Jews that Abraham was a Jew whereas he was not. See verse 3:67 and its corresponding footnote..

^c Overcome Islamophobia by reasoning with the disbelievers in the best manner and never through violence just as how the Prophet (peace be upon him) and his followers were commanded to do before.

^d God does not approve of extremism. See verses 2:190-193.

17. Al-Isrā'
[The Night Journey : 111 verses]

T
his is also another Makkan chapter that carries the same theme which deals with the fundamentals of faith - monotheism, the truth of Prophet Muhammad's messengership, resurrection, judgment, reward and punishment. But the distinguishing feature of the chapter is that it opens with a reference to one of the most important miracles that happened to Prophet Muhammad, namely his Night Journey (*Isra'*) from the Ka'bah in Makkah to *Bayt al-Maqdis* or Jerusalem in Palestine which took place by God's will. It formed the first stage of a longer and still more miraculous journey, which is his ascension to heaven, as indicated elsewhere in the Qur'an (53:13-18) and as described in detail in authentic traditions. The chapter is named after this memorable event. Within the context of the fundamentals of faith, the chapter speaks about the Children of Israel, particularly their disobedience towards God's commandments; and also about God's creation in general, which bears an eloquent testimony to the Creator and His Absolute Lordship over everything. It also contains a series of commandments for social and personal conduct (verses 23-29). Further, it points out the folly of the polytheists in setting partners with God by attributing sons and daughters to Him. It is also emphasized that the Qur'an is sent down by God that even if all men and Jinn came together and jointly attempted to produce the like of it, they would never be able to do so (verses 85-88). The chapter ends by once again stressing the doctrine of monotheism that God has no partner, nor does He take any son and need any assistant or helper.

In the name of God, the Most Gracious, the Most Compassionate.

God's Infinite Power

¹ Glory be to the Most Perfect One Who took His servant for a journey on a (blessed) night from *Masjidil Haraam* (in Makkah) to *Masjidil Aqsa* (in Jerusalem) *ᵃ* where its surrounding area We have blessed so that We may

---

ᵃ Linguistically, the word *Masjid* is derived from the root word *sajada* which means "to prostrate". Therefore, *Masjid* literally means "a place of prostration" without any religious distinction. This is reinforced in verse 7 of the current chapter where the word *Masjid* is also used in reference to the Temple of Jerusalem for the Jews. As such, the argument brought forth by some critics that this verse is erroneous by virtue of the fact that the physical building of *Masjidil Aqsa* mentioned herein was not yet built during the time of Prophet Muhammad is irrelevant. This is because the verse does not actually refer to the physical building of a mosque. Instead, it refers to a place where the Prophet prostrated in Jerusalem during his Night Journey which became the site where the Al-Aqsa Mosque was erected later. In fact, even the physical building of *Masjidil*

show him some of Our signs. Indeed He alone is the One who hears all and sees all.

² Verily, We gave Moses the Book *ᵃ* and made it a source of guidance for the children of Israel, commanding, "Do not take anyone else as protector besides Me." ³ (They were) descendants of those whom We carried in the ship with Noah. Indeed, he was a grateful servant. ⁴ And We forewarned the children of Israel in the Book, "You will surely cause corruption on the earth twice, and you will become extremely arrogant; (and each time, you will be severely punished)." ⁵ So when the first promise of the two warnings came true, We sent against you some of Our servants of great military prowess who ransacked your homes (throughout the land). Our promise was duly fulfilled. *ᵇ* ⁶ Then We gave you a return victory over them. And We reinforced you with wealth and offspring, and made you more numerous (than before). ⁷ And We said, "If you do good, you will do so for your own gain; but if you do evil, then you will do so for your own loss." And so, when the second promise of warning came true (after you dishonored your pledge to Us again), We (raised new enemies against you, and) allowed them to humiliate you utterly, and to enter the *Masjid* *ᶜ* just as their predecessors had entered it before, and to destroy all that they had conquered with total destruction. *ᵈ* ⁸ We said, "Your Lord may show mercy on you (if you repent). But if you revert (to your old ways), We shall return (with retribution). And We have (indeed) made Hell a prison for those who refuse to accept the truth."

⁹ Verily, this Qur'an guides to what is most straight and gives good news to the believers who do righteous deeds that they will have a great reward; ¹⁰ and (declares to) those who do not believe in the Hereafter that We have prepared a grievous suffering (for them). ¹¹ Yet man (often) prays for things that are bad as he prays for good, for man is prone to be hasty (and impatient).

Haraam in Makkah too was not in existence yet during the time this verse was revealed. What existed at that time was only the Ka'bah which was built by Prophet Abraham and his son Prophet Ishmael about 2,300 years before the birth of Prophet Muhammad.

ᵃ The Torah.

ᵇ A possible allusion to King Nebuchadnezzar of Babylon.

ᶜ The Temple of Solomon, also known as Temple of Jerusalem.

ᵈ An allusion to Rome's occupation which lasted for 400 years starting from 70 BC while the Romans were still pagans and then continued for another 300 years when they became Christians before Umar al-Khattab - the 2ⁿᵈ Caliph of the Islamic Empire - gained control of Jerusalem and Palestine circa 640 AD. Both invasions (i.e. Nebuchadnezzar and the Romans) involved the destruction of the Temple of Jerusalem. See also verses 5:20-22 and 7:137 together with their footnotes.

[12] We made the night and the day as two great signs (for man to ponder). We effaced the sign of night to make the sign of day bright and visible so that you may seek your Lord's bounty and know the number of years and the reckoning (of time). And We have spelled out everything in detail. [13] We have bound each man's ledger of deeds around his neck; and on the Day of Resurrection, We shall present it as a book spread open; [14] (and We shall tell him,) "Read your ledger (now)! Sufficient are you (alone) as your own reckoner today."

[15] Whoever chooses to follow guidance does so for his own good; and whoever goes astray will incur his own loss. (Verily, no one should ever expect his burden of sin to be borne by others, because) no soul will be made to bear the burden of another, nor would We inflict punishment (on any community) until We send a Messenger (to make truth distinct from falsehood first). [a] [16] And when We decide to destroy a community, We (will) issue Our command to its people who are corrupted by wealth (to mend their ways first). But if they (persist in their) disobedience, then Our sentence (of doom) on the community will take effect and We shall destroy it with complete destruction. [17] And how many generations have We destroyed since Noah's time! Sufficient is your Lord to note the sins of His servants, for He is well aware and fully observant (of the conduct of all His creations).

[18] Whoever desires the pleasures of this fleeting life (alone), We shall hasten (and readily grant) whatever We will from it to whomsoever We wish. But in the end, We shall consign him to (the torment of) Hell where he will burn in it, be condemned and abandoned! [19] But whoever desires (the best reward in) the life to come and strives for it accordingly as a true believer, his effort will surely be appreciated (by his Lord). [20] Yet on all - to these (who desire the best reward in the life to come) as well as to those (who only desire the brief pleasures of this fleeting life) - We extend some of your Lord's bounty (during their temporary stay on earth). No one is denied and restricted (from this favor. Instead, it is granted to everyone in a measure that He sees fit according to His great wisdom).

---

[a] Not everyone who did not submit to God according to the way He prescribed and as taught by His Messenger (i.e. Prophet Muhammad) will be punished in the Hereafter. After the Prophet's demise, it became incumbent upon every Muslim to continue his legacy in spreading Islam far and wide. Non-Muslims who did not receive God's message of truth and were genuinely ignorant of it will be spared from punishment, provided they were not unjust and cruel to others. Muslims around them who did not enlighten them about Islam may be faulted for this. But if they did receive sound knowledge about Islam and then knowingly chose to still reject the truth, then they will be deemed as disbelievers who will suffer dire consequences in the Hereafter.

²¹ Just see how We manifest this by positioning some above others (in this world). But in the life to come, (only those who deserve to be rewarded with His infinite bounty) will enjoy the greatest rank and favors. ²² (So) do not set up another (false) god besides Almighty God, or you will find yourself disgraced and forsaken (when the time finally comes).

A Code Based on Justice

²³ Your Lord has decreed that you should worship none but Him alone and to (always) be kind to your parents. If one or both of them live to their old age in your lifetime, do not say to them a word of disrespect or chide them, but speak to them in a noble manner. ²⁴ And humbly spread over them the wings of your tenderness, and say, "My Lord! Bestow on them Your mercy just as they raised and cared for me (with love and kindness) ever since I was a child." ²⁵ (Indeed,) Your Lord knows best what is in your heart and mind. If you are righteous, (rest assured that) He is surely Most Forgiving to those who frequently turn to Him (in repentance, seeking His guidance and mercy).

²⁶ And render to the near of kin their due rights, to the destitute and to the traveler (in distress) too. Do not squander your wealth wastefully. ²⁷ Indeed, those who waste and squander are brothers of Satan, and Satan is most ungrateful to his Lord. ²⁸ And if you (must) turn away from the needy (because you are) seeking to obtain your Lord's grace which you are hoping for, then speak to them gently. ²⁹ Do not miserly let your hand remain shackled to your neck (in stinginess), nor stretch it out too generously, lest you find yourself blamed (by your dependents) or reduced to destitution. ³⁰ Verily, your Lord extends provision either in abundance or in scant measure to whomsoever He wills (according to His wisdom, as a means to test one's faith). He is indeed fully aware of all His servants, and sees them all.

³¹ And do not kill your children for fear of poverty. It is We who shall provide for them and for you. Indeed, their killing is a great sin. ³² And do not come anywhere near fornication. It is indeed an abomination and an evil path. ³³ And do not kill the soul which God has forbidden (and made it sacred), except in the case of legal retribution. ᵃ And whoever is killed wrongfully, We have given his heir the authority (to seek just retribution). But do not let his heir exceed the limits of retaliation. Indeed, he is aided (by God's law).

³⁴ And do not come near the property of an orphan before he reaches maturity, except with the best (and noble) intentions. Be true to all your promises, for you will be called to account for every promise that you have

---

ᵃ See verse 6:151, 5:32 and its corresponding footnote.

made. ³⁵ And give full measure whenever you are measuring, and weigh with accurate scales. That is fair and best (for everyone) in the end. ³⁶ And do not follow (anyone blindly in matters) of which you have no knowledge. Indeed, your hearing, sight, and (actual intention in the) heart will all be called to account (on the Day of Judgment).ª ³⁷ And do not walk upon the earth with pride and arrogance. You will never be able to crack the earth, nor can you rival the mountains in height. ³⁸ All these are evil and hateful in the sight of your Lord.ᵇ ³⁹ (O Prophet!) This is part of the wisdom your Lord has revealed to you. (So) do not set up any (false) god besides Almighty God, lest you will be cast into Hell - rebuked, abandoned (and deprived of every good).

God, The One and Most Glorious

⁴⁰ (O disbelievers! Does it make sense) that your Lord has chosen sons for you and taken daughters for Himself in the guise of Angels? Certainly, you are uttering a monstrous lie! ⁴¹ And verily, We have expounded the truth (in diverse ways) in this Qur'an so that those who are ignorant of the truth might take heed. But all this only aggravates their aversion (and drives them farther away).

⁴² Say (to them O Prophet), "Had there been (other) gods besides Him as they claim, then (even) these (false gods) would have to strive to find a way to the Lord of the (Supreme) Throne." ⁴³ Glorified is He from all imperfections (and everything that they associate Him with). He is high above all (the falsehood) that they say! (He is truly) Exalted and Great (beyond measure)! ⁴⁴ The seven heavens, the earth, and all that is within them proclaim and glorify His perfection. There is nothing that does not extol His sanctity with (unceasing) praise. But you (O men), do not understand their hymns of praise. Verily, He is Most Forbearing, Exceedingly Forgiving.

⁴⁵ And when you recite the Qur'an, We place a hidden veil between you and those who do not believe in the life to come. ⁴⁶ We cast a veil over their

---

ª Everyone will be made accountable for the faith that he chooses to believe in and the deeds that he does. There is no compulsion in religion, for truth is clearly distinct from falsehood (verse 2:256) and man is given the freedom to choose whatever he wants to believe which comes with its own consequences (verse 18:29). Therefore, it is incumbent upon everyone to seek true knowledge about the purpose of life in order to submit to the true God Who is the Creator and sole Owner of the entire universe, and correctly practice the religion that He has prescribed for all mankind. Indeed, those who stand in awe of His greatness and fear His wrath are those with true knowledge (verse 35:28).
ᵇ See verse 76:1 and its corresponding footnote.

hearts which makes them unable to grasp its meaning, and their ears We make deaf. And so, when you mention your Lord in the Qur'an as the One and only (God), they turn their backs in aversion. [47] We know best what is in their hearts when they listen to you (reciting the Qur'an). When they are secluded among themselves, these evildoers would say to one another, "The man you follow is certainly bewitched (and deluded)."

[48] Just look at how they describe you (O Muhammad)! They have indeed strayed far and are unable to find the right way. [49] They ask (you mockingly), "When we are reduced to bones and crumbled particles, shall we truly be raised up again as a new creation (like what you claim)?" [50] Tell them, "(Yes! You will most certainly be brought back to life,) even if you were (as hard as) stones or iron; [51] or even some other form of creation which may seem to you most difficult (to create)." Then they will ask, "Who is it that will bring us back to life?" Tell them, "The One Who created you the first time." Thereupon they will shake their heads in disbelief at you and ask, "So when will this be?" Say, "It may very well be near at hand. [52] It will be on the Day when He will call you and you will answer with praises to Him, and feel that you have stayed (on earth) for only a short while."

[53] Tell my servants that they should speak in the best (manner to others regardless of their beliefs). Verily, Satan is always ready to stir up discord between them; for indeed, Satan is man's clear enemy! [54] Your Lord knows you best. If He so wills, he will bestow His grace upon you (if you follow His path); and if He so wills, He will punish you (for rejecting His message). Hence, We have not sent you to them to be their guardian (O Prophet). [55] And again, Your Lord is the One Who knows best about all those who are in the heavens and in the earth. Verily, We have favored some (mortals as) Prophets above others. Thus We gave David, (who was a mere shepherd, a great kingdom and) the Book of Psalms.

[56] Say to those idolaters, "Call on those whom you claim (to be gods) besides Him and you will find that they have neither the power to remove any misfortune from you, nor shift it elsewhere." [57] Verily, those (saintly beings) who are being invoked are themselves seeking a way to their Lord - each trying to be nearer to Him - hoping for His mercy and dreading His punishment; for indeed, your Lord's punishment is something to be truly feared.

Honor Granted to Mankind

[58] There is no community that (will be allowed to) persist in its defiance against Us, except that We shall destroy or inflict severe punishment upon it

before the Day of Resurrection. All this is laid down in Our decree. [59] And We refrain from sending the (miraculous) signs (that they ask for) because the people of former generations (had too often) rejected them as lies. We gave the she-camel to the (people of) Tsamud as a clear sign, but they treated her wrongfully. (Verily,) We did not send those signs for any other purpose than to convey a warning (and put the fear of God in their hearts so that they will stop their sinful deeds).

[60] And (recall) when We told you (O Prophet), "Indeed, your Lord's dominion encompasses all mankind." And We did not make the wondrous vision which We showed you [a] you except as a trial for mankind, as was the accursed tree [b] (in Hell which We) mentioned in the Qur'an. We keep warning them (but the warnings) would only increase the defiance (of those who are bent on opposing the truth).

[61] And (O mankind! Take heed of the occasion) when We said to the Angels, "Prostrate to Adam!", all of them prostrated except *Iblis* who said, "Should I bow down to the one whom You created from clay?" [62] And he added, "Tell me - is this the one whom You have honored above me? Indeed, if You allow me respite until the Day of Resurrection, I shall most certainly cause his descendants to blindly obey me and lead them to destruction, except for a few (who are Your truly sincere and devoted servants). [c] [63] God answered, "Go (the way you have chosen)! As for those who follow you, behold! Hell will be the requital for all of you - a requital that is (most fitting and) ample indeed. [64] "Entice (and mislead) whoever you can among them with your voice (and whisperings), and assault them with your cavalry and infantry. And be their partner in all sins relating to their wealth and children, and promise them every desire." Yet Satan promises those who follow him nothing but delusion (and deceit). [65] "But as for My (sincere and devoted) servants (O *Iblis*), you will have no power over them. Sufficient is your Lord as their guardian."

[66] (O people!) Your Lord is the One Who causes ships to cruise smoothly through the sea for you to seek His bounty. He is indeed Most Compassionate to you. [67] When a calamity befalls you at sea, all those whom you invoke will forsake you, except God. But when He delivers you safely to the shore, you turn away (from Him). Man is indeed most ungrateful.

[68] Can you feel so sure that He will not let a tract of the earth to cave in and swallow you (when you are back on land), or let loose a deadly sandstorm

---

[a] *Mi'raj* or the Ascension to heaven.
[b] The tree of *Zaqqum*. See verses 37:62-63, 44:43 and 56:52.
[c] See verse 15:40

against you, whereupon you would find no one as your protector? ⁶⁹ Or can you feel so sure that He will not let you go back to sea again, and then let loose against you a violent hurricane of wind to drown you for your defiance, whereupon you would not be able to find anyone to help you (avenge) against Us?

⁷⁰ And We have certainly honored the children of Adam and carried them over land and sea. We provided for them sustenance out of the good things in life, and favored them far above many of Our creatures. *a* ⁷¹ But beware of the day when We shall summon every community together with their leaders. Whoever is given his record of deeds in his right hand, then such people will read their record (with joy and happiness). They will not be wronged even as much as a hair's breadth. ⁷² But whoever is blind (to the truth) in this world will be blind in the Hereafter, even further from the (true) path.

No Compromise In Matters of Faith

⁷³ (Behold O Prophet!) They strived to tempt you away from the truth that We have revealed to you, hoping that you would invent something else (in Our name), in which case they would have made you as their trusted friend (and ally). ⁷⁴ And if We had not made you firm, you might have inclined to them a little. ⁷⁵ And (if you had succumbed to their deceit,) We would surely make you taste double (the punishment) in life and in death, and you would not find any helper against Us. ⁷⁶ And (since they cannot persuade you,) they resorted to scare you off from the land of your birth. But they will not remain (in it) for more than a little while after you. ⁷⁷ Such has been Our way with the Messengers We sent before you. And you will find no change in Our ways.

⁷⁸ So perform your regular prayers at the decline of the sun until the darkness of night, and recite (the Qur'an) at dawn. Indeed, the recitation at dawn is witnessed (by Angels). ⁷⁹ And rise from your sleep and pray (with the recitation of the Qur'an) during part of the night, as additional offering for your (own soul); *b* It may be that your Lord will raise you to a praiseworthy

---

a Only the human race is bestowed with the gift of intellect, the ability to reason, the powerful creativity of the mind and the physical perfection to produce, improvise and innovate all kinds of things. These are the special attributes of the only creature that God has shaped and formed far above the others to be His emissary on earth (see verses 2:30 and 95:4). With this, the human race has the unique ability to continuously bring progress and life of good quality to mankind, and care for God's other creatures too. How could man then have the audacity to be arrogant and reject his Creator or take false gods as his object of worship instead? See also verses 2:30-33.
b This command is also mentioned in verse 73:20.

station (in the life to come).

⁸⁰ And say in your prayer, "O my Lord! Let me enter (upon all my affairs) in a true (and sincere) manner, and let me exit from it in a true (and sincere) manner too; and grant me from Your grace the strength that would help me (to always be steadfast in Your path)." ⁸¹ And proclaim (to the disbelievers), "Truth has come and falsehood has vanished. Indeed, all falsehood is bound to vanish."

The Qur'an is God's Grace for Mankind

⁸² And so (step by step), We send down the Qur'an that heals (and cherishes the soul) and as mercy to those who have faith, while it adds nothing to the wrongdoers except loss and ruin. ⁸³ Yet whenever We bestow favors upon man, he arrogantly turns away and distances himself (instead of coming to Us). But whenever evil touches him, he falls into despair. ⁸⁴ Say, "Everyone acts in his own way. But your Lord (is fully aware and) knows well who has chosen the best-guided way."

⁸⁵ And they ask you about (the nature of) divine inspiration *ᵃ* (O Prophet). Say (to them), "This inspiration comes at the behest of my Lord; and you (cannot understand its nature O men, since) you have not been given any knowledge about it, except a little." ⁸⁶ And if We so willed, We could take away what We have revealed to you (through this inspiration, and leave you without guidance. If We did this,) you would certainly not be able to find any helper (to recover it) from Us. ⁸⁷ (Whatever you have received is nothing) except grace from your Lord. Indeed, His favor upon you is ever great!

⁸⁸ Say to them, "Indeed, if all mankind and Jinn were to assemble together to produce something like this Qur'an, they would not be able to do so however much they helped each other." ⁸⁹ In this Qur'an, We have indeed expounded all kinds of parables to people. Yet most refuse to (take heed and) believe. ⁹⁰ They say, "We shall never believe you until you cause a spring to gush out of the ground for us; ⁹¹ or you have a garden of date-palms and grapes, and cause rivers to flow abundantly in their midst; ⁹² or you cause the sky to fall upon us in pieces as you have threatened, or you bring God and the

---

ᵃ The Arabic word that is used here is *Ruh* which literally means soul. While most commentators are of the opinion that the meaning of *Ruh* here is the "soul of man", others opined that it refers to "the revelation of the Qur'an". This is based on the context of the preceding and subsequent verses that relate explicitly to the Qur'an, hence to the phenomenon of divine revelation. See verses 16:2 and 42:52 where the word *Ruh* is also used to refer to divine revelation instead of the soul of man.

Angels to us, face to face; [93] or you have a house that is made of ornaments, or you ascend into the sky. Even then, never will we believe in your ascension until you bring down for us a book to read." Say (to them), "Glorified is my Lord (above all imperfections)! I am only a mortal (without any supernatural power, appointed by God) as His Messenger."

Justice of Retribution

[94] Yet whenever guidance came, nothing ever prevented people from believing, except that they would say, "Did God send a mortal (to us) as His Messenger?" [95] Say to them, "If the earth is (the natural abode) for Angels to walk about freely, then surely We would send down an Angel from heaven as Our Messenger."

[96] So say, "Sufficient is God as a witness between me and you. Indeed, He is fully aware of His servants, and He sees all things." [97] Whomsoever God guides (because of his willingness to accept guidance), then he would be rightly guided. But those whom God lets go astray (because of their defiance), never can you find anyone to protect them from Him. And We shall gather them on the Day of Resurrection (fallen) on their faces - blind, dumb and deaf, with Hell as their final home. And every time the Fire subsides, We shall increase its Blazing Flame for them.

[98] Such will be their requital for rejecting Our revealed signs and for (mocking them by) saying, "Shall we be really raised from the dead again as a new creation after we become bones and crumbled particles?" [99] Have they not considered that God, Who has created the heavens and the earth (all by Himself) certainly has the power to create them anew in their own likeness again? There is no doubt that He could easily fix a term for their resurrection (anytime He wills). And yet the evildoers refuse to accept anything other than to persist in their disbelief. [100] Say (to them), "If you were to own the treasures of my Lord's grace, then surely you would withhold them for fear of spending. Indeed, man has always been stingy (whereas God is Most Generous)."

Pharoah's Fatal Error

[101] And indeed, We gave Moses nine clear signs [a] (as evidence of his Prophethood). Ask then, the children of Israel (to tell you what happened, O

---

[a] Refer to verses 7:107, 108, 130, 133 and 28:35 that mention his staff which turned into a serpent, his hand shone brightly, years of drought and shortage of crops, flood, locusts, lices, frogs, water that turned into blood, and Pharaoh rendered powerless to harm him.

Muhammad). Indeed, when he came to Pharaoh and his people (inviting them to God's path), Pharaoh said to him, "Verily O Moses, I think you have been bewitched (and deluded)!" [102] Moses said, "You know full well that none other than the Lord of the heavens and the earth has revealed these (eye-opening signs as proof of my Prophethood). Indeed O Pharaoh, I really think you will be doomed (for arrogantly rejecting God and my Prophethood)!"

[103] And so, Pharaoh was determined to uproot and annihilate Moses and the children of Israel from the face of earth, but We drowned him together with everyone with him; [104] and thereafter We said to the children of Israel, "Dwell now on earth (as a people who are free from slavery). Then when the promise of the Hereafter arrives, We shall bring you forth (from your graves) all mixed together in a huge assembly of people." *a*

The Qur'an is Revealed in Truth

[105] We have revealed the Qur'an in truth, and it is with the truth that it has descended. And We have not sent you (O Muhammad), except as a bearer of good news and warner (to mankind). [106] We have divided the Qur'an in parts so that you could recite it to people at intervals; and for this reason too did We (gradually) send it down in stages (to address particular occasions).

[107] Say to them (O Prophet, "Whether you want to) believe in the Qur'an or not, (the choice is yours)." Verily, those who have been given (true) knowledge (of the Scriptures) before the revelation of this Qur'an, (they believe in your Lord's promise). Whenever the Qur'an is recited to them, they fall down upon their faces in prostration; [108] and they say, "Glory be to our Lord (Who is free from all imperfections)! Indeed, the promise of our Lord (to send down His final revelation to His final Messenger) has been fulfilled!" [109] And they fall down upon their faces weeping; and it increases their humility.

[110] Say, "Call upon God or call upon the Most Gracious (Lord). By whichever name you call, it is to Him Whom the Most Beautiful Names (and Attributes) belong to. Do not raise your voice too loud in prayer, nor too soft. Rather, seek a way of moderation in between." [111] And say, "All praise is due to God alone Who has never begotten a son; nor any partner in His dominion; nor does He need anyone - out of weakness - to protect Him." So magnify Him with limitless greatness!

---

a The idea that the children of Israel are a "chosen people" with special privileges is clearly refuted here. On the Day of Judgment, all mankind will be resurrected and mixed together in a huge assembly without special treatment and previliges.

18. Al-Kahf
[The Cave : 110 verses]

This is also a Makkan chapter which deals with monotheism and faith. These themes are illustrated by three stories, namely the Companions of the Cave, Prophet Moses's encounter with a righteous servant of God, and about a great conqueror whose name is Dzul-Qarnayn. The Companions of the Cave were a group of young men who were believers that fled for the sake of their faith and took shelter in a cave seeking God's protection from their disbelieving and inimical people. God made them sleep therein for 309 years. When they woke up, they thought they had slept only for a little while but found that the things and people around them had changed very much. The story illustrates God's power and the inevitability of resurrection. It also indicates the continuity of the monotheistic faith and its faithful adherents throughout the ages. The chapter is named after this incident. The second story is about the encounter of Moses with a righteous servant of God who Moses accompanied for a period of time with a mission to acquire knowledge. The story illustrates the principle of modesty in the seeking of knowledge and the fact that God may give knowledge of some unseen matters to whomsoever He wills. Some such unseen and unusual matters of which knowledge was given by God to his righteous servant over which Moses could hardly remain patient are mentioned in the course of this story. The third story is that of a powerful monarch by the name of Dzul-Qarnayn whom God gave a vast kingdom along with wisdom, righteousness and justice and who accomplished a number of good deeds including the construction of a gigantic barrier against the incursions of two ferocious tribes known as Gog and Magog (i.e. Ya'juj and Ma'juj). Along with these stories are also other parables and facts that are mentioned to emphasize that truth and faith are not interlinked with worldly affluence and power.

In the name of God, the Most Gracious, the Most Compassionate.

A Distinctive System of Values

¹ Praise be to God Who has revealed to His servant this Book that is free from all crookedness; ² (and perfectly) straight, to warn people of a severe punishment from Himself; and to give good news to those who believe (in this Book) and do righteous deeds that for them is a good reward (that awaits them in Paradise); ³ where they will remain in it forever.

⁴ And also to (fiercely) warn those who say, "God has begotten a son!" ⁵ (Verily,) they do not have any knowledge about this, nor did their forefathers. Mighty dreadful indeed is the word that comes out from their mouths, for they say nothing except lies. ⁶ (And so O Prophet), would you then torment yourself to death with grief over them if they are not willing to believe

in the message that you bring? (Don't be!)

⁷ Indeed, We have made all that is on earth as adornment so that We may put people to a test to make evident who among them are the best in their deeds (and conduct);*ᵃ* ⁸ and in time, We shall indeed reduce all that is on the ground to barren dust.

⁹ (O Prophet!) Do you consider (the story of) the Companions of the Cave and the (Tablet with) inscriptions (of their names on it) so wondrous among all Our other signs?

¹⁰ Verily, when those youths took refuge in the cave, they prayed, "Our Lord! Bestow on us Your grace, ease our affairs and guide us aright." ¹¹ So We cast a veil over their ears (and lulled them to sleep) in that cave for a number of years; ¹² and then We woke them up to test which of the two groups (among them) could best account for the period they had remained in that state.

¹³ (And now,) We shall narrate to you their story in truth. Verily, they were young believing men who truly had faith in their Lord, so We increased them in guidance; ¹⁴ and strengthened their hearts when they stood up and proclaimed, "Our Lord is the Lord of the heavens and the earth. We shall never call upon and worship any other god besides Him. If we ever do, we shall be uttering an outrageous lie!"

¹⁵ (They said to one another,) "These men who are our own people, have taken (other) gods besides the Almighty God. Why do they not bring any clear evidence (to prove that what they worship are indeed real gods)? Who can be more (wicked and) unjust than the one who invents lies against God? ¹⁶ And since you have withdrawn from them and all that they worship besides God, it is better to take refuge in the cave. God will well spread His grace over you and ease your affairs."

¹⁷ Had any of you witnessed, you would have seen that as the sun rose, its inclined away from their cave towards the right; and as it set, it declined away from them towards the left, while they were asleep in a spacious chamber

---

ᵃ Those who are zealous in performing all sorts of ritual practices that have been infused in the traditions and culture that are inherited from their forefathers without taking into consideration whether they were authentically taught and practiced by the Prophet (may peace be upon him) should carefully re-examine their practices. Emphasis should be on the quality of our deeds, not on quantity. The best deeds are those that are precedented and taught by our Prophet. These can be found in books written by early scholars who compiled the Prophet's authentic sayings (i.e. *hadith*) and practices (i.e. *sunnah*). See also verse 67:2.

inside the cave. This is one of God's (wondrous) signs! (Verily,) whomsoever God guides (because of his willingness to accept guidance), then he will be rightly guided; and whomsoever God lets go astray (because of his refusal to accept the truth), you will find no protector nor guide (to show him the way).

¹⁸ Moreover, you would have thought that they were awake whereas they were actually asleep. And We turned them over repeatedly to their right and left sides, with their dog stretching out its forelegs at the cave's entrance. Had you come upon them, you would have certainly turned away from them in flight, filled with fear at the sight of them.

¹⁹ In time, We woke them up (in a miraculous way) and they began to question one another. One of them asked, "How long did you remain in this state?" Some answered, "We remained so for a day or part of a day", but the others said, "Your Lord knows better how long we remained in this state. Now send one of you to the city with your silver coins to find who has the cleanest and best food, and bring some back. But be careful not to let anyone know about you." ²⁰ Indeed, if they come to know about you, they will stone you or force you back to their (erroneous) ways. Then, never will you succeed (to attain any good), ever."

²¹ In this way We caused them to be discovered, so that people may know that God's promise (of resurrection) is true and there is no doubt about (the coming of) the Last Hour. But there were people who argued among themselves regarding this matter (after the youths had passed away). Some said, "Build a wall around the cave (to seal off their remains and leave them alone), for their Lord knows best about them." But those who prevailed regarding this matter said, "We shall raise a house of worship over them."

²² (And in time to come,) some will say, "They were three, the fourth of them being their dog", while others will say, "Five, with their dog being the sixth of them", idly guessing the unknown. Yet others will say, "They were seven, the eighth of them being their dog." Say (to them O Prophet), "My Lord knows best how many they actually were. And only very few people have real knowledge about them. So do not argue about them except with sure knowledge and do not ask any of these people about them."

²³ (O Prophet!) When you intend to do something, do not just say, "Indeed, I shall do that tomorrow"; ²⁴ without adding, "If God so wills." But if you forget, then remember your Lord and say, "May my Lord guide me even closer to what is right."

²⁵ (Some say) the Companions of the Cave remained in their cave for

three hundred years, and add nine more.*ᵃ* ²⁶ Say (O Prophet), "Only God knows best how long they remained there, and He alone knows the secrets of the heavens and the earth. How perfectly does He see and hear! Indeed, those who argue with you do not have any protector besides Him, and He does not need to consult with anyone about His decision."

Faith Based on Free Will

²⁷ So continue to recite what has been revealed to you from your Lord's Book. There is nothing that can replace His words and you can find no refuge except with Him. ²⁸ And be patient (and persevere) with those who call upon their Lord in the morning and evening, seeking His (pleasure and) countenance. Do not let your eyes turn away from them, desiring the adornment (and splendors) of this worldly life. And do not obey (and follow) the one whose heart We have rendered oblivious from remembering Us because he follows only his own lust and exceeds all bounds (in his affairs).

²⁹ Say, "The truth has come from your Lord. So let those who wish to believe in it do so, and let those who wish to reject it do so." *ᵇ* Indeed, We have prepared for those who unjustly (reject the truth) a Fire whose walls will surround them from all sides. And if they call for relief, they will be given a drink which is like molten brass that will scald their faces. Wretched is the drink, and evil is their resting place!

ᵃ 300 solar years more or less equals 309 lunar years. 300 solar years has 109,500 days (365 days x 300 years) which is close to 109,386 days in 309 lunar years (354 days x 309 years). It would never be possible for Prophet Muhammad to calculate these numbers by himself for their mention and recitation here. These are very large numbers to compute and there was certainly no necessity at all for anyone to count these large numbers in the 7ᵗʰ century, more so if he was illiterate. Furthermore, how would he know anything about solar months and years when he spent all his life living in a society and environment that measured time and day using lunar months for over thousands of years?

ᵇ In this life, man is free to believe or not to believe in God, for there is no compulsion religion (see verse 2:256). A believer recognizes the existence of God and is conscious of this reality, dedicates his life to the pursuit of God's pleasure and the hope of meeting Him in the Hereafter. He is fully aware that death does not signal the end of existence but is simply the staging post for a journey into another life. In contrast, a non-believer is firmly rooted in this life and spends it entirely in pursuit of his personal pleasures, needs, and desires. He views the present and whatever remains of his life as the only reality and that his existence will end at death with no prospect of a next life to come. In essence, the believer strives for a beautiful death with a rewarding eternal afterlife, while the non-believer strives for a beautiful life in this temporal world without hope of an afterlife.

³⁰ As for those who believe and do righteous deeds, We shall certainly not let their reward to go waste. ³¹ Their place (of final return) will be the Gardens of Perpetual Bliss where rivers flow from right beneath them. There, they will be adorned with bracelets of gold and will wear green garments of silk and brocade, reclining on adorned couches. How excellent is their reward, and how magnificent is their resting-place!

³² Now set forth for them the parable of two men. We gave one of them two vineyards - each garden encircled with date-palms and a field of grain in between. ³³ Each of the two gardens yielded its produce and never failed to do so in any way. In their midst, We caused a stream to flow. ³⁴ And so he had fruit in abundance. Then he boasted to his companion while talking with him, "I am richer and I also have more manpower than you." ³⁵ And so he entered his garden while he was being unjust to himself, saying, "I do not think that what I have here will ever perish; ³⁶ nor do I think that the Last Hour will ever come. But even if it does and I am brought before my Lord, I shall surely find something even better there." *ᵃ*

³⁷ (Hearing this,) his companion replied while talking with him, "Do you not believe in the One Who created you from soil, then from a clot of semen, then fashioned you into a man? ³⁸ As for me, He is God, my Lord, and I do not associate anyone with my Lord."

³⁹ "When you entered your garden, why did you not say, 'It is by God's will (and grace that I have been granted this bounty); for indeed, there is neither any power nor ability to achieve anything without God's help.' Even though you may see me inferior in wealth and children than you; ⁴⁰ it is possible that my Lord may give me a garden which is better than yours (if He so wills), and He may send a thunder bolt from the sky upon your garden and turn it into a barren plain (in the morning); ⁴¹ or its water may sink deep into the ground that you will never be able to find it."

⁴² (And so it was, that) all his produce was surrounded (by ruin) and he began to wring his hands (in sorrow at the loss) of what he had spent on. And on seeing it fallen down upon its trellises, he said, "How I wish I had not (been arrogant and) associated anyone with my Lord (in worship!)" ⁴³ And he had none to help him other than God, nor was he able to help himself. ⁴⁴ There (and then did he realize that) all power of protection rests with God alone, the True One. And He is the best in granting rewards and the best in deciding every final outcome.

⁴⁵ Hence, give them a parable of this worldly life : It is like the rain that

---

ᵃ See verses 96:6-7.

We send down from the sky which mingles with the plants on earth (and grow lush). Soon they turn into dry stubble and then get scattered by the winds. Indeed, it is God alone Who holds invincible power over all things. ⁴⁶ (So bear in mind that) wealth and children are (nothing but) mere adornment of this worldly life, whereas good deeds will endure and they are of far greater merit in the sight of your Lord, and a far better source of hope (for salvation).

Heedless of Divine Warnings

⁴⁷ (O mankind! Be mindful of) the Day when We shall set the mountains in motion and you will find the earth void and bare. On that Day, We shall assemble all men together, leaving none behind. ⁴⁸ And they will be presented before your Lord in rows and He will say, "Indeed, you have come to Us just as We created you the first time. In fact, (some of) you had audaciously claimed that We would not fulfill this promise!"

⁴⁹ The Record of Deeds will be laid open on that Day, and you will see the sinners filled with dread of what their records contain. They will cry, "Woe to us! What record is this? It leaves out nothing small or great but takes everything into account." And they will find that everything they have done is being presented before them. ^a And your Lord is not unjust to anyone.

⁵⁰ Now (take heed of the occasion) when We said to the Angels, "Prostrate yourselves before Adam", they all did so except *Iblis* who was of the Jinn and he (defiantly) disobeyed his Lord's command. (O mankind!) Will you then, take *Iblis* and his progeny for your masters instead of Me even though they are your clear enemies? Wretched indeed is what the wrongdoers have exchanged for! ⁵¹ Verily, I did not call them to witness the creation of the heavens and the earth, nor are they witnesses of their own creation too. And I do not seek for anyone's aid, especially from those who lead people astray, to help Me in anything.

⁵² On the Day of Resurrection, God will say to them, "Now call upon all those whom you claimed (to be My partners)." Thereupon, they will invoke

---

^a Most people are negligent and forgetful. Conveniently, the present moment in their lives overshadows and obliterates the past and ignores the future. But this only makes facing God a more frightening and traumatic experience. The Day of Judgment is indeed a day of shocks and surprises. It is only then that the transgressors and wrongdoers will realize the extent of their folly and their despair. But until this moment arrives, man will continue to be complacent and indifferent to God's warnings and will only see the truth when it is too late.

those beings but their call will not be responded, and We shall make for them a common pit of doom. [53] And those who were lost in sin will see the Fire (on that Day) and know that they are all bound to fall into it. They will find no escape from this.

[54] And surely, We have explained (the truth) in this Qur'an using every kind of parable for people (to ponder). But man (chooses to ignore Our message and continues to be) contentious in most affairs (regarding faith without knowledge).

[55] What is keeping back people from believing (in Our message) and from seeking forgiveness from their Lord when guidance has been brought to them? Are they waiting for the fate of the sinful people from past generations to also befall them, or for the suffering to be brought in front of their eyes first (before they would accept the truth)? [56] And (know that) We did not send the Messengers except as bearers of good news and warners. For those who disbelieve, they would continue to dispute Our Messengers with falsehood and persist in ridiculing My revelations and warnings.

[57] Who could be more (wicked and) unjust than the one who - when reminded of his Lord's revelations - turns away from them and forgets what his own hands have done? We have cast veils over their hearts that prevent them from grasping the truth, and deafness into their ears. So even if you call them to this (heavenly) guidance, they will never be guided.

[58] And (be reminded that) Your Lord is Most Forgiving and limitless in His grace. If He were to seize those (who deny Him) for the wrongs they have done, surely He would have hastened for them their doom. But He has fixed for them an appointed time from which they will never find an escape; [59] (just like) the other (earlier) communities that We destroyed when they persisted in their wicked acts. We had certainly appointed an (appropriate) time for their destruction.

A Special Lesson for Moses

[60] (O people of earlier revelation! Call to mind of the incident) when Moses said to his servant, "I shall not cease my journey until I reach the junction of the two seas, or (I shall) keep walking for a long time." [61] But when they reached the junction between the two seas, they forgot about their fish, and it made its way back into the sea by burrowing a tunnel. [62] Then after continuing their journey for a while, he said to his servant, "Bring us our mid-day meal. We have really suffered much tiredness from this traveling." [63] The servant said, "Do you know what happened when we took a rest at the rock

(earlier)? Indeed, I forgot about our fish and it was Satan that caused my attention to be distracted from it. So the fish made its way back into the sea in such an amazing way."

⁶⁴ And so Moses said, "That is the place we are seeking!" So they turned back, retracing their footsteps; ⁶⁵ and found one of Our servants - a man to whom We had bestowed Our grace upon and whom We had taught a certain knowledge of Our own. ⁶⁶ Moses said to him, "May I follow you on the understanding that you will teach me something about the right guidance (and wisdom) that you have been taught?" ⁶⁷ He answered, "You will surely not have the patience to bear with me; ⁶⁸ for how can you be patient with something which you cannot fully comprehend?" ⁶⁹ Moses replied, "You will find me patient, if God so wills; and I shall not disobey you in anything." ⁷⁰ He said, "If you follow me, then do not ask me anything I do until I mention to you about it myself."

⁷¹ And so the two went on their way until they embarked on a boat which he (damaged it by) making a hole in it. Moses exclaimed, "Did you make a hole in the boat to drown its passengers? You have certainly done something terrible!" ⁷² He replied, "Did I not say that you would never be able to bear with me patiently?" ⁷³ Moses pleaded, "Do not take me to task for forgetting my promise, and do not be hard on me if I am causing you any difficulty."

⁷⁴ Then they both set out until they met a boy whom he killed. Moses exclaimed, "Did you kill an innocent soul who has never taken another man's life? You have really done something (terribly) evil!" ⁷⁵ He replied, "Did I not make it clear to you that you will never be able to have patience with me?" ⁷⁶ Moses said, "If ever I question you again, do not keep me in your company; for then you would have had enough excuses from me."

⁷⁷ And so they both continued their journey until they came to a town where they asked its people for food, but they were refused all hospitality. There they found a wall which was about to collapse, so he rebuilt it to set it straight. Moses said, "Had you wished, you could have taken payment for what you did." ⁷⁸ He replied, "This is where we should part ways. I shall now explain the reason and meaning behind all those events that you were unable to bear with patience."

⁷⁹ As for the boat, it belonged to some poor people who were working in the sea for their livelihood. I damaged it slightly because I knew that there was a (cruel) King who was pursuing behind them to seize every (seaworthy) boat by force.

⁸⁰ And as for the boy, his parents were true believers. (Based on God's revealed knowledge), we feared that he would burden them with his rebellion and disbelief (when he grows up). ⁸¹ And so we intended their Lord to replace for them a far better son with greater purity (at heart) and closer (to them) in affection.

⁸² And as for the wall, it belonged to two orphan boys living in the town and beneath it was a buried treasure that belongs to them. Their father was a righteous man. So your Lord has willed that when they reach maturity, they will dig up their treasure by your Lord's grace. I did not do any of this on my own accord (except by God's instructions). Such is the real meaning of all those events that you were unable to bear with patience."

Accurate Historical Accounts

⁸³ And they ask you about Dzul-Qarnayn.ᵃ Say to them, "I shall narrate to you an account of him (that is worthy of remembrance)." ⁸⁴ Indeed, We established him with power on earth and gave him the means (to achieve everything he wanted). ⁸⁵ So he set out on an expedition; ⁸⁶ until he reached the place where the sun sets and saw it setting in the midst of a dark murky spring. Near it, he found a certain community. We said, "O Dzul-Qarnayn! You may either punish or treat them kindly."

⁸⁷ He said, "As for the one who is persistent in his wicked acts, we shall soon punish him. Then he will return to his Lord Who will punish him (even more) severely. ⁸⁸ But the one who believes and does righteous deeds will have an excellent reward (from his Lord), and we shall assign him with tasks that are easy to fulfill."

⁸⁹ Then he set out on another expedition; ⁹⁰ until he reached the place where the sun rises and he found it was rising on a people for whom We had provided no shelter from it. ⁹¹ (And so, Dzul-Qarnayn left them) as they were. Verily, We encompassed everything he knew. ⁹² Then he set out on another expedition; ⁹³ until he reached a place between two mountains where he found beside them a people who could barely understand him.

⁹⁴ They said, "O Dzul-Qarnayn! Indeed, Gog and Magog are spreading corruption (and causing disorder) in this land. Can we pay you a tribute to build a barrier between us and them?" ⁹⁵ He answered, "Whatever (power) my Lord has granted me is good enough and better (than any tribute you offer).

ᵃ Dzul-Qarnayn is believed to be Cyrus the Great of Persia. See the footnote for verse 7:137.

But assist me with your strength and I shall erect a (strong) barrier between you and them.

⁹⁶ "Now bring me sheets of iron." Then after he had leveled and filled up the gap between the two mountain-sides, he said, "(Light a fire and) blow it." And after he made the (iron glow like) fire, he said, "Bring me the molten metal to pour over it." ⁹⁷ And so (the barrier was erected and) their enemies were unable to scale it, nor could they dig their way through it. ⁹⁸ Said Dzul-Qarnayn, "This is grace from my Lord. But when my Lord's promise is fulfilled, He will raze this barrier to the ground; and my Lord's promise always comes true."

Final Reminder

⁹⁹ And on that Day, We shall (call forth all mankind and) leave those (who rejected Our message) to surge against one another (towards Us in confusion). The trumpet of judgment will then be blown, and We shall gather them altogether (in an assembly). ¹⁰⁰ And on that Day too, We shall present Hell - all spread out in a display - to those who had rejected (Our message of truth); ¹⁰¹ who turned a blind eye and a deaf ear to My warning.

¹⁰² Do those who refuse to accept the truth think they can take My servants as patrons alongside Me? Indeed, We have prepared Hell to welcome these rejecters of truth. ¹⁰³ Say (to them O Prophet), "Shall we tell you who stand to lose the most from their deeds? ¹⁰⁴ It is they whose efforts are misguided during their stay on earth while they think what they are doing is right." ¹⁰⁵ They are the ones who (have chosen to ignore and) disbelieve in their Lord's revelations and in the meeting with Him. Hence, their deeds are all in vain and We shall assign no weight to them on the Day of Resurrection. ¹⁰⁶ Hell will be their requital for rejecting faith and for making My revelations and My Messengers a target of their mockery.

¹⁰⁷ For those who believe (in their Lord and worship Him alone) and do righteous deeds, they will be given the Gardens of Paradise with (the best) everlasting hospitality; ¹⁰⁸ to remain in there forever, never wishing to leave.

¹⁰⁹ Say (to them O Prophet), "If the whole ocean were ink for writing the words of my Lord, it would surely run dry before the words of my Lord were exhausted, even if we were to add another ocean to it." ¹¹⁰ And tell them, "Verily, I am only a mortal like you to whom it has been revealed that your God is only the One Almighty God. So whoever hopes for the (best) meeting with his Lord (on the Day of Judgment), let him do righteous deeds and not associate anyone in the worship of his Lord."

19. Maryam
[Mary : 98 verses]

This is also a Makkan chapter which deals with monotheism - belief in the existence and Oneness of God together with belief in resurrection, judgment, reward and punishment. In the context of these themes, stories of some Prophets are mentioned. Reference is made first to Prophet Zachariah, whom God bestowed a son John [i.e. Yahya], at a very advanced age when Zachariah's wife - Elizabeth, was already barren. This fact is mentioned to illustrate God's power. It is followed by an even more miraculous power of God, namely the birth of Jesus to Mary without a father. This chapter is named after her. It also refers to some other Prophets, namely Isaac, Jacob, Moses, Aaron, Ishmael, Enoch [i.e. Idris] and Noah to bring home the fact that God's message of monotheism through all these Prophets has always been the same together with the call to abandon all shades of polytheism and idoltary. Attention is drawn also to the inevitability of resurrection and judgment, and the horrors accompanying those who defy God. In the end, the sin and enormity of ascribing a son to God is emphatically denounced.

In the name of God, the Most Gracious, the Most Compassionate.

God's Unbridled Will

¹ *Kāf Hā Yā 'Ayn Ṣād.* ² This is a mention of your Lord's grace towards His servant, Zachariah; ³ when he called out to his Lord in the secrecy (of his heart); ⁴ praying, "My Lord! My bones have become feeble and my head is covered with grey hair. But never has my prayer to You remain unanswered, my Lord. ⁵ Indeed, I fear what my kinsfolk will do after I am gone, for my wife is barren. So bestow then upon me, out of Your grace, a successor; ⁶ who will be my heir as well as an inheritor of the house of Jacob. And make him, O my Lord, one whom You are pleased with."

⁷ (Thereupon he was told by Angel Gabriel,) "O Zachariah! Indeed, We bring you good news of a son whose name will be John. *ᵃ* Never have We assigned this name to anyone before him." ⁸ Zachariah said, "My Lord! How can I have a son when my wife is barren and I am well advanced in years?" ⁹ Answered (Angel Gabriel), "This is what your Lord has said, 'It is easy for Me, for (it is beyond doubt that) I created you when you were nothing before.'"

¹⁰ Zachariah said, "My Lord! Grant me a sign." (Angel Gabriel) replied,

---

ᵃ Yahya in Arabic.

"Your sign will be that for three full nights and days you will not speak to people even though you are sound in health." [11] Then, he came out to his people from his prayer chamber and signaled them to glorify their Lord's perfection in the morning and evening.

[12] (And so, to his son We said,) "O John! Hold firm to the Scripture." We granted him wisdom while he was still a child; [13] as well as affection and purity, all by Our grace, and he was always righteous; [14] and dutiful to his parents, and never was he insolent and disobedient. [15] So peace was upon him on the day he was born, on the day of his death, and on the day when he will be raised to life again.

[16] Now, recite from the Book the story of Mary and how she withdrew from her family to a place in the east; [17] where she kept herself in seclusion from them. Then, We sent to her Our Angel (of revelation) *a* who appeared in the shape of a perfect man. [18] She exclaimed, "May the Most Gracious (Lord) protect me from you. (Do not come near me) if you fear God." [19] (Gabriel) answered, "Verily, I am only a Messenger from your Lord, and I have come to give you good news (that you will give birth to) a son endowed with purity." [20] She said, "How can I have a son when no man has ever touched me, nor have I ever been unchaste?" [21] (Gabriel) said, "So will it be! Your Lord says, 'It is easy for Me. We shall make him a sign (of Our greatness and truth) for mankind and an act of grace from Us. It is a matter that We have decreed.'"

[22] And so she conceived him and retired to a remote place. [23] Then, the throes of childbirth drove her to the trunk of a palm-tree. (In her anguish,) she cried, "O! How I wish I had died before this and had become someone totally forgotten." [24] Thereupon, (a voice) called out to her from below, "Do not give in to grief. Your Lord has provided a stream running under you; [25] and if you shake the trunk of the palm tree towards you, fresh ripe dates will fall near you. [26] So eat, drink and be consoled. And if you see anyone, say, 'Indeed, I have vowed to the Most Gracious (Lord) to abstain from speech. So I shall not speak to anyone today.'"

[27] Thereafter, she returned to her people carrying her newborn child. (When they saw this,) they exclaimed, "O Mary! You have indeed done something horrible (and unprecedented)." [28] They said further, "O Sister of Aaron! *b* Your father was not an evil man, nor was your mother unchaste. (So

---

a Gabriel.

b In ancient Semitic usage, a person's name was often linked with that of a renowned ancestor or founder of the tribal line. Since Mary belonged to the priestly caste that descended from Aaron, the brother of Moses, she was called a "sister of Aaron," in the same way as her cousin Elizabeth, the wife of Zachariah, is spoken of in Luke 1:5 as

how could you do something grave like this?)" [29] Then she pointed to her newborn and they exclaimed, "How can we speak to a child who is still in the cradle?"

[30] (And suddenly the child cried out, "My mother is certainly chaste and) I am indeed a servant of God. He has given me the Scripture and made me a Prophet; [a] [31] and He has made me blessed wherever I may be. He has commanded me to pray and give purifying dues as long as I live; [32] and (always be) dutiful to my mother. He has not made me insolent and bereft of grace. [33] Peace was upon me on the day I was born, on the day of my death and on the day when I shall be raised to life again." [34] That was Jesus - the son of Mary who delivered a statement of truth about which they were in dispute.

[35] It is not befitting for God to beget a son. Glory be to Him (Who is free from all imperfections and weaknesses)! When He decrees a matter, sufficient is for Him to only say, "Be!" and it is.

[36] Said Jesus, "And indeed, God is my Lord and your Lord, so worship Him alone. This is a straight path to follow." [b] [37] And yet, the sects (that

---

one of "the daughters of Aaron." In fact, Jesus too was called the "son of David" in Matthew 15:22. Therefore, there is no historical mistake in this verse. Instead, it is in perfect agreement with the Semitic ancient custom.

[a] This verse relates the extraordinary story of Jesus and his mother - Mary. What Jesus said to the Jews is sufficient proof for the innocence and integrity of his mother. The unusual manner of Jesus' conception and birth eventually gave rise to a new religion which was built on the mistaken premise that since Jesus had no human father, then his father must have been God, and that therefore like his father, he must also be divine. This logic led to the introduction of a third god - the Holy Spirit who blew into Mary's womb so that she could conceive. Thus emerged the so-called doctrine of the Holy Trinity as a fundamental Christian dogma. Such a doctrine was unprecedented in earlier religious belief and had never been introduced by any Messenger or Prophet of God. This begs the question : Do the words Father, Son and Holy Spirit denote one and the same entity or essence, or are they the titles of three separate and distinct entities? They are rather ambiguously said to identify three separate entities which are in fact one! But if the essence is one, how can a title assume another entity, become flesh, be crucified and raised to heaven while the Father just looks on? Or do the titles represent three different aspects of one whole essence? No satisfactory answer can be found and none of the foregoing hypotheses that try to explain the doctrine of Holy Trinity is logical and can satisfy reason. The simple truth is that God is One and Jesus was merely His mortal servant.

[b] Nowhere in the Bible can it be found that Jesus proclaimed himself as God and commanded people to worship him. It was Paul the Tarsus who invented this idea which gave birth to the new religion of Christianity. The fundamental doctrinal tenets

follow the Gospel) are in a big disagreement among themselves (about him). Woe then, to all who deny the truth when that mighty (dreadful) Day arrives! ³⁸ How clear will they hear and see (the truth) on the Day when they come to Us! But for today, the wrongdoers are clearly lost in error (because they choose to stubbornly deny the truth).

³⁹ Hence, warn them about (the coming of) the Day of Regret when everything will be decided (and irreversible) by then because they are heedless and refuse to believe (in it now). ⁴⁰ Ultimately, We alone shall inherit the earth and whoever that is on it. (Verily,) to Us will everything be finally returned.

A Long Line of Prophets

⁴¹ (O Muhammad!) Narrate from the Book the story about Abraham. Indeed, he was a man of truth (and unflinching faith). He was an (eminent) Prophet. ⁴² (Take heed of the occasion) when he said to his father, "O my father! Why do you worship something that could neither hear nor see and is of no benefit to you? ⁴³ O my father! A knowledge that has not reached you has indeed come to me. So follow me so that I will guide you to a straight path. ⁴⁴ O my father! Do not worship Satan, for Satan has indeed rebelled against God, the Most Gracious (Lord). ⁴⁵ O my father! I fear that a punishment from the Most Gracious (Lord) might strike you and you may end up as one of Satan's companions (in the Fire)."

⁴⁶ Answered his father, "Are you denouncing my gods, O Abraham? If you do not stop, I shall most certainly have you stoned. Now begone from me for good!" ⁴⁷ Abraham replied, "Peace be upon you (O father)! I shall pray to my Lord to forgive you, for He has always been gracious to me. ⁴⁸ I shall withdraw from you and all that you call upon besides God. I shall only call upon my Lord and I trust my prayer to Him will not go unanswered." ⁴⁹ Thereupon, Abraham withdrew himself from his people and the false gods they worshipped besides God (Almighty). Then We bestowed upon him Isaac, and then Jacob, and made both of them Prophets. ⁵⁰ We bestowed upon them Our grace and granted them high renown (and honorable reputation).

⁵¹ And narrate from the Book (O Muhammad) the story about Moses too. Indeed, he was (also) chosen as a Messenger and an (eminent) Prophet.

---

of Christianity, namely that Christ is God as man incarnate who was born in the flesh, that his sacrificial death on the cross atones for the sins of mankind, and that his resurrection from the dead guarantees eternal life to all who believe can be traced back to Paul, not to Jesus. This doctrine is called Pauline Christianity. See also verses 5:116-117.

[52] (Behold!) We called him from the right side of Mount (Sinai) and brought him near Us for a (secret) communion. [53] And We appointed for him out of Our grace, his brother Aaron as a Prophet (to assist him).

[54] And narrate from the Book too the story about Ishmael. Indeed, he was true to his promise and was a Messenger and a Prophet. [55] He commanded his household to be constant in prayer and spend in charity; and his Lord was well pleased with him.

[56] And narrate also from the Book the story about Enoch.[a] Indeed, he was a man of truth and a Prophet; [57] and We raised him to a high position.

[58] These are the Prophets upon whom God bestowed His favor from the seed of Adam, and (from the seed) of those whom We carried (in the ark) with Noah, and from the seed of Abraham and Israel, [b] and also from those whom We guided and chose (for an exalted position. These were the people that) whenever the verses of the Most Gracious (Lord) were recited to them, they would fall down in prostration, weeping.

[59] But they were succeeded by a people who neglected their prayer and pursued their lusts. Soon, those who refused to accept the truth will meet their doom; [60] except those who repented, believed (in God) and did good deeds. Such people will enter Paradise and will not be wronged (and unjustly treated) in any way. [61] (Theirs will be the) Gardens of Perpetual Bliss in a realm of unseen that the Most Compassionate Lord has promised His servants. Indeed, His promise will most certainly be fulfilled. [62] They will not hear any vain talk therein but only the greetings of peace. And they will have their provision therein, in the mornings and evenings. [63] Such is the Paradise which We shall give the righteous among Our servants to inherit.

Descent of Revelation

[64] (Said Angel Gabriel, "O Muhammad!) We do not descend (with revelation) except by the command of your Lord. To Him belongs everything that lies open in front of us, all that is hidden from us and all that is in between. Verily, your Lord never forgets (anything)." [65] He is the Lord of the heavens and the earth and all that is in between them. So worship Him alone and remain steadfast in your worship to Him. Do you know of anyone who is equal to Him?

---

[a]   Idris in Arabic.
[b]   Jacob or Yaqub in Arabic.

Two Interlinked Lives

⁶⁶ And man asks (in disbelief), "What! Will I be brought back to life again after I am dead?" ⁶⁷ Does he not remember that We created him when he was nothing before? ⁶⁸ By your Lord, We shall most certainly bring them forth together with the Satans, and then We shall surely gather them on their knees (around Hell). ⁶⁹ Thereupon, We shall drag out from every faction, those who had been the most intense in their rebellion against the Most Gracious (Lord). ⁷⁰ (Indeed,) We know best who deserves most to burn in it.

⁷¹ (Verily,) there is not one among you who will not pass over the Hellfire. This is a decree from your Lord that will certainly be fulfilled. ⁷² But We shall save the devout and leave the evil wrongdoers there (trembling) on their knees.

⁷³ (As it is,) when Our (divine) verses are recited to them with all clarity, those who reject the truth say to those who believe, "Which group between us is better in status and more excellent to be with?" ⁷⁴ (Do they not see) how many generations We have destroyed before their time that were more superior in material possessions and splendor?

⁷⁵ Say to them, "As for him who lives in error, may the Most Gracious (Lord) lengthen the span of his life!" (Let them say whatever they wish) until they finally see the (doom) that they have been forewarned, whether it be suffering (in this world) or the Hour (of Judgment in the next life). Then they will realize who is worse in position and weaker in forces. ⁷⁶ But God gives more guidance to those who (willingly) accept His guidance. Verily, lasting (merit from) acts of righteousness is better in the sight of your Lord for reward and yield far better returns.

⁷⁷ Have you ever given thought about what will ultimately happen to the one who denies Our revelations and boasts, "I shall surely be given wealth and children!"? ⁷⁸ Has he obtained any knowledge of the unseen future (about this certainty), or has he taken from the Most Gracious (Lord) a promise (regarding this matter?) ⁷⁹ By no means! We shall (certainly) record what he says and We shall greatly extend his suffering. ⁸⁰ Ultimately, We shall inherit everything that he boasts about and he will come to Us all alone.

⁸¹ They worship false deities instead of God hoping that they will be given power and glory. ⁸² By no means! (On that dreadful Day of Judgment,) these false deities will renounce their worship and turn against them as enemies instead.

⁸³ (O Prophet!) Are you not aware that We have sent Satans to incite disbelievers with fervor (to commit sin and oppose the truth)? ⁸⁴ So, do not be impatient (in seeking God's punishment) against them. We are indeed counting their days. ⁸⁵ The day will surely come when We gather the God-fearing before the Most Gracious (Lord) as honored guests; ⁸⁶ and drive those who are lost in sin to Hell like a thirsty herd. ⁸⁷ (On that Day,) none will have the benefit of intercession unless he entered into a bond *^a* with the Most Gracious (Lord, during his earthly life and honored it).

Blasphemous Accusation

⁸⁸ And they *^b* (blasphemously) say, "The Most Gracious (Lord) has taken a son for Himself!" ⁸⁹ Verily, you have put forward such a terrible falsehood. ⁹⁰ (It is such a monstrosity that) the heavens almost tear apart, the earth splits asunder, and the mountains collapse in utter ruin; ⁹¹ when they accuse the Most Gracious (Lord) of having a son. ⁹² It is not befitting (and inconceivable) that the Most Gracious (Lord) would take to Himself a son.

⁹³ Verily, no one in the heavens and the earth will come to the Most Gracious (Lord on the Day of Resurrection and be granted with mercy and compassion) except those who fully submit to Him. ⁹⁴ Indeed, He is fully aware of who they are and has counted them all accurately. ⁹⁵ On the Day of Resurrection, everyone will return to Him all alone (and be held fully accountable for everything that they have done). ⁹⁶ But for those who believe and do righteous deeds, the Most Gracious (Lord) will bless them with enduring love and affection (for one another).

⁹⁷ And to this end, We have indeed made the Qur'an easy (to understand) in your own tongue (O Muhammad), so that you may convey the good news (about Paradise) to the righteous and a fierce warning (of God's nearing judgment) to those who are contentious.

⁹⁸ (Are these people not aware of) how many generations that We have destroyed before them? Can you find any of them now or hear from them as much as a whisper?

---

^a This refers to those who firmly believe in God's Oneness, worship only Him alone, and follow the true teachings of His Prophet.
^b The Christians

20. *Ṭa Ha*
[135 verses]

This is also another Makkan chapter which, like all other Makkan chapters, concentrates on the fundamentals of the faith - monotheism, prophethood, resurrection and judgment. It starts with consoling the Prophet and the believers, that the Qur'an has not been sent down to cause distress to them. The chapter mentions in some detail about the story of Prophets Moses and Aaron with the Pharaoh and the Children of Israel. A quick reference is also made to the story of Adam to point out God's mercy on him and to remind how *Iblis* has ever since been man's enemy, trying to lead him astray in every possible way. Some account is given also of the scene and circumstances of resurrection and the Day of Judgment. Another important historical fact to remember in connection with this chapter is about 'Umar al Khattab who would later become one of Islam's most illustrious Caliphs, if not the most. He embraced Islam in the 7th year of the Prophet's mission after reading the first 8 verses of this chapter which he retrieved from his sister Fatimah and her husband Sa'id after making an unexpected detour to their house in rage and anger while he was on his way to kill the Prophet.

In the name of God, the Most Gracious, the Most Compassionate.

Divine Admonition

¹ *Ṭa Ha.* ² We did not send down the Qur'an to you to cause you distress (O Prophet); *ᵃ* ³ but only to serve as a reminder for those who stand in awe (of God).

⁴ It is a revelation from the One Who created the earth and the high heavens; ⁵ the Most Gracious (Lord) Who is firmly established on the Throne (of Supreme Authority). ⁶ To Him belongs all that is in the heavens and the

---

ᵃ The man to whom the Qur'an was revealed was well-known to his own people for his honesty, and trustworthiness and not even his fiercest enemies could deny him these qualities. Muhammad, who had never been known to lie to his people or deceive them, thought that as soon as he conveyed God's revelation to them, they would believe him without hesitation. He was sadly mistaken, since arrogance and bigotry drove some of them to reject the Qur'an and accuse him of lying and branded him a madman. Nothing is more hurtful to an honest man than to be falsely accused. In the case of the Prophet, it pained him deeply, prompting God Almighty to comfort him and raise his spirits by assuring him that he was only a Messenger conveying God's revelation to the people and he would always be in God's protection while undertaking this divine mission.

earth as well as all that is between them, and everything that is beneath the ground too. ⁷ And whether you say anything aloud (or whisper it, He hears all). Indeed, He (even) knows your secret (thoughts) and what is kept most hidden (in the deep recesses of your heart).

⁸ God, there is no other god except Him. To Him belong the Most Beautiful Names (and all attributes of perfection).

The Story of Moses

⁹ Has the story of Moses reached you (O Prophet)? ¹⁰ Behold! When he saw a fire (in the desert), he said to his family, "Stay here! Indeed, I saw a fire. Perhaps I can bring a lighted torch from there for you or find some guidance."

¹¹ But when he came close to it, a voice called out to him, "O Moses! ¹² Indeed, I am your Lord! Take off your sandals, for you are in the sacred valley of Thuwa. ¹³ Verily, I have chosen you as My Messenger, so listen to what will be revealed to you. ¹⁴ Indeed, I am God (and) there is no other god except Me. So, worship Me alone and establish prayer (regularly) to remember Me. ¹⁵ Indeed, the Last Hour will surely arrive. I have willed to keep the time of its coming hidden so that every soul will be requited in accordance with what it strived for. ¹⁶ "Hence, do not let anyone who does not believe in its coming and follows his lust turn you away from it, or you will perish."

¹⁷ "Now, what is that in your right hand, O Moses?" ¹⁸ Moses said, "It is my staff. I lean upon it, and with it I bring down leaves for my sheep, and also other uses that I may have for it." ¹⁹ God said, "Throw it down, O Moses!" ²⁰ So he threw it down, and behold! It turned into a serpent that moved swiftly. ²¹ God said, "Seize it and have no fear. We shall return it to its former state. ²² Now put your hand (in your garment) under your armpit. It will come out shining white, without blemish, as another sign (of your miracle); ²³ so that We may show you some of Our greatest signs. ²⁴ Now, go to Pharaoh (and convey to him My message). Indeed, he has transgressed all bounds (and needs to be reminded)."

²⁵ Said Moses, "O my Lord! Open up my heart (to Your light); ²⁶ and ease for me my task; ²⁷ and free my tongue from its impediment; ²⁸ so that people may understand what I say. ²⁹ And appoint for me a helper from my family; ³⁰ Aaron, my brother. ³¹ Reinforce my strength through him; ³² and let him share my task; ³³ so that we may glorify Your perfection abundantly; ³⁴ and remember You always. ³⁵ Indeed, You are always watching over us."

³⁶ God replied, "O Moses! Verily, your requests are hereby granted.

³⁷ And indeed, We have actually bestowed Our favor upon you before this;
³⁸ when We inspired your mother saying; ³⁹ 'Place your child in a chest and
float it in the river. The river will cast him ashore and he will be picked up by
someone who is an enemy of Mine and his.' Verily, I lavished My love on you
so that you will be brought up under My watchful eye."

⁴⁰ "Then your sister approached them and said, 'Shall I direct you to
someone who might take care of him?' Thereupon, We returned you to your
mother so that her heart will be at ease and not be sad anymore. (And when
you became an adult), you (accidentally) killed a man; but We saved you from
all grief and tested you through various trials. Then you stayed with the people
of Madyan for some years and came here as I decreed." ⁴¹ (O Moses! Indeed) I
have chosen you to serve Me. ⁴² Go forth with your brother (Aaron) and My
signs, and never slacken in remembering Me. ⁴³ Go forth both of you to
Pharaoh. Indeed, he has transgressed (all bounds and needs to be warned)!
⁴⁴ But speak to him gently so that he might take heed of your advice and
become fearful (of My warning)." ⁴⁵ They both said, "O Our Lord! We fear he
might behave insolently towards us or become violent."

⁴⁶ Answered God, "Have no fear. I shall (always) be with you. I hear and
see all. ⁴⁷ Go then both of you to him and say, 'Indeed, we are Messengers
from your Lord. Free the children of Israel to follow us and stop oppressing
them. Verily, we have come to you with a message from your Lord. Peace
(and salvation) will be for whoever follows the right guidance. ⁴⁸ It has been
revealed to us that suffering will befall those who deny the truth and turn away
from it.'"

⁴⁹ Pharaoh replied, "So who is your Lord, O Moses?" ⁵⁰ Moses said, "Our
Lord is the One Who gives everything its (unique) form and then guides it
(towards its fulfillment)." ⁵¹ Pharaoh asked, "And what about the former
generations?" ⁵² Moses said, "That knowledge is with my Lord, recorded in
the Book. My Lord does not err, nor does He forget."

⁵³ He is the One Who has made the earth your cradle and traced out for
you the ways (of livelihood) in it; and sends down rain from the sky with
which We bring forth pairs of plants ^{*a*} in variety. ⁵⁴ Eat then, and pasture
your cattle. In this are sure signs (of God's greatness) for those who are
endowed with intelligence. ⁵⁵ From the earth We created you, and into it We
shall return you, and out of it We shall raise you once again (for the reckoning
of your deeds).

---

^{*a*} It has been scientifically discovered that a great variety of plants, not all, come in
separate genders of male and female, hence the expression that they were created in
pairs which the Qur'an foretold in the 7th century.

⁵⁶ And indeed, We showed Pharaoh Our signs, but he denied them and refused to take heed. ⁵⁷ Pharaoh said, "Have you come to us to drive us out of our land with your sorcery, O Moses? ⁵⁸ In that case, we shall most certainly produce sorcery for you to match it. Set then for us an appointment at a suitable open place that neither we nor you will fail to keep." ⁵⁹ Moses answered, "Your appointment will be before noon on the day of festival when (many) people gather." ⁶⁰ Then Pharaoh went away, put together his plan and returned (with his group of sorcerers on the appointed day to challenge Moses).

⁶¹ At the time of the encounter, Moses said to them, "Woe to you! Do not invent falsehoods against God, lest He destroy you with a (great) punishment. Those who invent lies will surely fail (and become losers)." ⁶² Then, Pharaoh's sorcerers debated among themselves about what to do but they kept their counsel secret; ⁶³ saying, "Indeed, these two sorcerers *a* intend to drive you out of your land with their sorcery and put an end to your exemplary way of life (and honorable traditions). ⁶⁴ So put together a plan you intend to pursue and come forward (united) in a row. Indeed, whoever prevails today will triumph."

⁶⁵ And so Pharaoh's sorcerers said, "O Moses! Either you throw (what is in your hand) first, or we shall be the first to throw ours." ⁶⁶ Moses replied, "Nay, you throw first!" Then behold! (Because of their sorcery,) the ropes and staves that they threw down appeared to Moses as if they were moving (rapidly like snakes). ⁶⁷ Seeing this, Moses's heart was filled with fear. ⁶⁸ And so We said to him, "Have no fear; for it is you who is superior than them (and it is you who will prevail). ⁶⁹ Now throw down what is in your right hand and it will swallow everything that they made. Verily, they have produced nothing but a sorcerer's deceitful trick, and sorcerers can never bring any good no matter where they come from."

⁷⁰ So, down fell the sorcerers in prostration (when they witnessed how their sorcery was defeated by God's power), and they declared, "We hereby believe in the Lord of Aaron and Moses." ⁷¹ (Seeing this,) Pharaoh exclaimed, "How could you believe in Moses before I allowed you? Surely, he must be your master who has taught you witchcraft (behind me)! I shall most certainly cut-off your hands and feet on opposite sides, and crucify you on the trunks of palm trees. Then you will surely know who (has the power to) inflict a severe and lasting punishment!"

⁷² Answered the sorcerers, "Never shall we prefer you over the clear proofs that have come to us, nor over Him who has created and brought us into

---

a Moses and Aaron.

being! Decree whatever you wish, for your decree holds sway only in this brief worldly life. ⁷³ As for us, we have come to believe in our Lord. And we hope that He will forgive our faults and all that sorcery which you have forced us (to practice). God is certainly the Best and He is Everlasting."

⁷⁴ Verily, whoever comes to his Lord on the Day of Judgment laden with sin will be consigned to Hell where he will be in a state of neither dead nor alive (to suffer everlasting torment). ⁷⁵ But whoever comes to Him as a believer having done righteous deeds will be exalted to the highest ranks; ⁷⁶ (and admitted in the) Gardens of Perpetual Bliss where rivers flow from right beneath them to remain in there forever. Such will be the reward for whoever purifies himself (from corrupt faith and sins).

⁷⁷ And verily, We inspired Moses, "Proceed with My servants in the night and strike for them (using your staff) a dry passage in the sea (to walk across). Have no fear of being captured (by Fir'aun) nor be afraid (of drowning)." ⁷⁸ Then Pharaoh pursued them with his armies but they were fully overwhelmed by the sea which covered and drowned them; ⁷⁹ for Pharaoh had led his people astray instead of guiding them aright.

⁸⁰ O children of Israel! We rescued you from your enemy and then We made a covenant with you on the right side of Mount (Sinai). We sent down *Al-Manna* and quails for you (as food while you were wandering in the desert). ⁸¹ Eat of the wholesome things which We have provided for you and do not (transgress and) overstep the limits, lest My wrath will descend on you. Anyone whom My wrath descends on has indeed thrown himself into utter ruin. ⁸² But indeed, I am Most Forgiving to whoever repents, believes (in Me) and does righteous deeds, and thereafter keeps to the right path.

The Israelites Relapse into Transgression

⁸³ And God said, "O Moses! What has caused you to leave your people behind in such haste?" ⁸⁴ He answered, "They are treading in my footsteps behind me while I have hastened to You, my Lord, so that You might be pleased with me." ⁸⁵ Said God, "(Then know that) We have indeed put your people to a test in your absence, and Samiri has led them astray."

⁸⁶ And so, (after his communion with God,) Moses returned to his people, angry and aggrieved. He said, "O my people! Did your Lord not make a goodly promise to you? And did the fulfillment of this promise seem too long in coming (that you doubted its truth)? Or did you dishonor your promise (of obedience) to me because you wish to see your Lord's condemnation fall upon you?"

⁸⁷ They answered, "We did not deliberately break our promise to you. We did so because we were burdened with the weight of our people's gold ornaments (that we carried out from Egypt). Then we decided to throw them into the fire, and so did Samiri." ⁸⁸ Then (from the molten gold,) he produced a statue of a calf which had a lowing sound and thereupon they said (to one another), "This is your god and the god of Moses whom he forgot (and neglected to inform us about)." ⁸⁹ Did they not see that the statue could not return a word to them and had no power to either harm or bring them any benefit?

⁹⁰ And indeed, Aaron had said to them earlier, "O my people! Verily, you are being tempted to evil by this statue. Verily, your only Lord is (He Who is) the Most Gracious! So follow me and do as I command you." ⁹¹ But they replied, "By no means shall we stop from worshipping this statue until Moses returns."

⁹² (And so, after rebuking his people upon his return,) Moses (turned to Aaron and) said, "O Aaron! What prevented you (from correcting them) when you saw them going astray; ⁹³ from my way? Did you (deliberately) disobey my command?" ⁹⁴ Aaron replied, "O son of my mother! Do not seize me by my beard, nor by my head. Indeed I was afraid that you would say (to me), 'You have caused a split among the children of Israel because you did not pay heed to my words.'"

⁹⁵ (After listening to Aaron's explanation,) Moses (turned towards Samiri and) said, "What is your reason (for this evil act) O Samiri?" ⁹⁶ He answered, "(I believe) I have gained insight into something (spectacular) which they could not see. So I took a handful of dust from the trail (that I think belongs to) the (heavenly) Messenger ^{*a*} and flung it (into the fire). That was how my soul prompted and enticed me." ⁹⁷ Moses said, "Begone then! And indeed, (you will be an outcast for the rest of your life) and (cursed to say, 'Do not touch me!' (to those who wish to harm you in this life). But (in the Hereafter), you will surely face a destiny where there is no escape from. Now look at your god whom you are so devoted to. We shall burn and scatter its remains (far and wide) in the sea." ⁹⁸ Verily, your true god is none other than Almighty God and there is no other god except Him. His knowledge encompasses (and extends over) all things."

Man's Sojourn on Earth

⁹⁹ This is how We relate to you some news that happened in the past

---

^{*a*} Angel Gabriel.

(which you did not witness O Prophet). And We have certainly given you Our reminder (to convey to mankind). [100] Whoever turns away from it, then indeed he will bear a (heavy) burden on the Day of Resurrection. [101] They will remain in the Fire forever because of the evil burden that they carry with them on the Day of Resurrection.

[102] And when the trumpet is blown on that Day, We shall gather all the sinners together. Their face will turn blue (with terror). [103] They will whisper among themselves, "You stayed (on earth) for only ten days." [104] But We know best what they will say when the most upright among them will say, "Nay! Your actual stay (on earth) was not more than a day (and you have unwisely spent it in vain)!"

No Escape

[105] They ask you about the mountains (O Prophet), "Where will they go (if your promise of doom is true)?" Say, "My Lord will blast (and crush) them to fine dust (and then scatter them away). [106] Then He will leave the earth flat and desolate; [107] where you will not see any valley or peak (on it anymore)." [108] On that Day, the (sinners) will follow the Caller's shout. None of them will be able to deviate and escape from (where they are told to assemble). Then, all voices will be hushed in the presence of the Most Gracious (Lord). You will hear nothing except a faint murmur. [109] Intercession will be of no benefit to anyone On that Day, except to whom the Most Gracious (Lord) has granted permission and whose words He approves.

[110] He knows all that is ahead and behind them, whereas their knowledge does not encompass this. [111] All faces will be humbled before the Ever-Living, the Self-Subsisting Lord; and those who carry (with them the sins of their) evil deeds will despair. [112] But the one who does righteous deeds while believing in God will neither fear injustice nor deprivation (on that Day).

[113] And so, We have sent down this Qur'an (to you) in Arabic (O Muhammad) and expounded its warnings (in diverse ways) so that those (who listen to you) should become mindful of God (and shun evil), or cause them to remember Him more. [114] Exalted is God, the Sovereign, the Truth. Be not in haste to recite the Qur'an before its revelation to you is complete, but always pray, "My Lord! Increase me in knowledge (and guide me aright)."

Man's Long-Drawn Battle

[115] And indeed, We made a covenant with Adam earlier. But he forgot, and We found him lacking in steadfastness. [116] And recall when We said to the

Angels, "Prostrate yourselves before Adam!" All of them did, except *Iblis* who (rebelled and) refused. [117] Then We said, "O Adam! He is indeed an enemy to you and your wife. Do not let him drive both of you out of Paradise and make you miserable. [118] Verily, you will not be hungry and naked in Paradise; [119] nor become thirsty and suffer from the heat of the sun." [120] But Satan (deceivingly) whispered to him, saying, "O Adam! Shall I lead you to the tree of eternal life and to a kingdom that will never decay?" [121] And so both Adam and his wife ate (the fruit) from that (forbidden) tree. Then their nakedness became exposed to them and they began to cover themselves with leaves from the Garden. Adam had disobeyed his Lord and strayed into error. [122] Thereafter, his Lord chose him (for His grace). Then He turned to him (in forgiveness) and gave him guidance. [123] (And so God commanded,) "Get down all of you from this place! (Verily, take heed and learn from this lesson that) some of your descendants will always be enemies (and inflict injustice) upon one another (as a consequence of succumbing to evil temptations). So when guidance comes to you from Me, whoever follows it will neither go astray nor suffer misery.

[124] But whoever turns away from My remembrance (and ignores My warning) will have a wretched life. And on the Day of Resurrection, We shall raise him blind"; [125] whereupon he will say, "O My Lord! Why have You raised me blind today whereas I had sight (before)?" *a* [126] God will answer, "That is because you ignored our signs (and revelations) when they were brought to you. So today, We shall ignore you (in return)." [127] That is how We requite the one who commits excesses (in arrogance) and does not believe in the signs (and revelations) of his Lord. Indeed the punishment in the life to come is far more severe and lasting.

[128] Did they not find any guidance and lesson from the many generations that We destroyed before them whose dwellings they freely walk about now? Verily, there are sure signs in these ruins for those endowed with intelligence and wisdom (to learn from). [129] (O Prophet!) If it were not for a preordained respite from your Lord, punishment would have surely befell (the Arab pagans

---

a This warning revolves around the dangers implicit in forgetting one's obligations to God or forsaking His guidance. Involuntary casual forgetfulness is normal and harmless because one usually remembers afterwards and quickly acts to redress the situation. The real danger however, is greater when lack of God consciousness becomes the norm in one's life, making him blind to the truth and an easy prey to the influences of temptation and deviation. Paradise is therefore reserved for those who are alert and conscious of God and who are resolute in their resistance against temptation. God, in His grace and mercy, has provided room for redress and correction against this weakness. Those who remember will always be offered the chance to make good their mistakes, but those who persist in their heedlessness "will have a wretched life. And on the Day of Resurrection, We shall raise him blind..."

like the fate of the disbelievers that were destroyed in the past). But God has fixed their time.

Persevere in Faith

¹³⁰ So be patient over what they say, and glorify the perfections of Your Lord by praising Him before the rising of the sun and before its setting. Then (continue to) glorify Him during the hours of the night and at the extremes of the day too, *ᵃ* so that you may find peace and contentment.

¹³¹ And do not extend your eyes (covetously) towards the enjoyment that We have given to some among them (who do not believe in Us). Indeed, these are the temporary splendors of worldly life by which We test them with, whereas your Lord's provision (in the next life) is far better and more lasting. ¹³² So command your family to pray and be steadfast in it. We do not ask you for provision. Instead, it is We Who provide for you; and the best outcome (in the Hereafter) is only for those who are God-conscious (and strive to keep their faith pure).

¹³³ They ask, "Why does Muhammad not bring us a sign from his Lord (to prove that he is indeed a God's Messenger)?" Is not this (Qur'an) which contains all the teachings of the former Scriptures that is being brought to them now a clear evidence (of Our sign)?

¹³⁴ Had We destroyed them with a (severe) punishment before his coming, (surely) they would have said, "O Our Lord! Why did You not send to us a Messenger earlier so that we could follow Your revelations and not be humiliated and disgraced today?" *ᵇ* ¹³⁵ Tell them (O Prophet), "Everyone is waiting (for his end), so wait (for yours too). Soon you will know who are the people of the right path that are rightly guided."

ᵃ This verse explains the requirement for Muslims to perform their five times a day obligatory prayers. (1) Before the rising of the sun is called *Fajr*. (2) Before its setting is called *Asr*. (3) During the hours of the night is *Isha*. (4) There are three extremes of the day : (a) When the sun is about to rise is *Fajr*. (b) When the sun starts to decline is *Zuhr*. (c) When the sun sets is *Maghrib*.
ᵇ The Day of Resurrection and Judgment.

21. Al-Anbiyā'
[The Prophets : 112 verses]

Like the other Makkan chapters, this chapter also deals with the fundamentals of faith, namely monotheism, resurrection and the Day of Judgment. It starts with the mention of man's indifference to the inevitability of resurrection, judgment and the life in the Hereafter. Reference is then made to the evidence in the many wondrous creations, pointing to the Creator and His power to sustain the entire universe and all that exists without help from anyone. Mention is made also about the disbelievers' attitude, particularly their ridiculing and disbelieving the Prophet, and about the destruction of the sinful communities by way of God's punishment. These themes are brought home by the short accounts of some Prophets, namely Isaac, Jacob, Lot, Noah, David, Job, Ishmael, Enoch, Ezekiel, Jonah, Zachariah and Jesus – illustrating the fact that all the Prophets delivered the same message of monotheism and had to face the sarcasm, opposition and enmity of their disbelieving people. The chapter is named *Al-Anbiyā'* or The Prophets, after them.

In the name of God, the Most Gracious, the Most Compassionate.

Clear Solid Evidence

¹ The time of reckoning for mankind has drawn near, yet they turn away in heedlessness (and disbelief from the warning). ² There is not a new (and fresh) reminder that comes to them from their Lord except that they would listen to it in amusement (and ridicule); ³ with their hearts (preoccupied with worldly affairs and) distracted (from the remembrance of God). And those who do wrong, secretly whisper to one another, "Is Muhammad not a mortal just like you? Are you going to allow yourself to be tricked by his spellbinding eloquence with your eyes wide open?" ⁴ Say (to them O Prophet), "My Lord knows every word that is spoken in the heaven and the earth (whether secretly or openly). He is the One who hears all, knows all."

⁵ Yet they say, "These (revelations that he claims to receive) are nothing but confused dreams. In fact, surely he must have invented these words. Of course, he is only a poet! (If he is indeed a Messenger of God as he claims,) then let him bring to us a (miraculous) sign just like the Messengers of the past (had brought to their people)."

⁶ Not a (single) community which We destroyed before them believed (in Our revelation). So, do you expect your people to (readily) believe you (now, O Prophet)? ⁷ Even before you, never did We ever send any message except through men whom We inspired. (So tell those who are doubtful of Our

message,) "If you do not know this, then ask the (true) followers of the earlier revelation (about it)."

[8] Verily, We did not endow the Messengers with bodies that would need no food, nor were they immortals. [9] In the end, We made good to them Our promise. We saved them and all whom We willed to save, and We destroyed those who transgressed (the limits that We have set). [10] O mankind! Indeed, We have sent down to you a Book as a reminder of everything that you should know. Will you not use reason (and common sense to ponder over its content)?

[11] And how many communities that were unjust (and persisted in their evildoings) have We utterly demolished (before this), and then raised a new group of people (to replace them)? [12] And as soon as they sensed that Our torment was near, behold! They fled. [13] (But they were told,) "Do no run away. Instead, return to your comforts and to your homes so that you will be called to account (for everything that you have done)." [14] They said, "Alas! Woe to us, for we have indeed brought injustice upon ourselves!" [15] And their cry did not cease until We reduced them to stubble - still and silent.

[16] Verily, We did not create the heaven and the earth and what is between them in mere idle play (without purpose). [17] Had We willed to indulge in a pastime, We would have indeed found one near at hand; if at all We were inclined to do so. [18] Nay! We hurl the truth against falsehood and it crushes the latter; and behold! It withers away. And woe to you for all the false claims that you ascribe (against God). [19] To Him belongs all that is in the heavens and the earth. The Angels who are in His presence are never too proud to worship Him, nor do they ever become weary. [20] They (unceasingly) glorify His perfection night and day, tirelessly.

[21] Now, have those disbelievers chosen any gods from the earth that have the power to give life to the dead? [22] (Can they not think that) had there been other gods besides God, surely both (the heavens and the earth) would have gone to ruins. Glory be to God, the Lord of the (Supreme) Throne, Who is far above all their false allegations!

[23] None can question Him about what He does. Instead, they are the ones who will be questioned; [24] and yet the disbelievers still take some (false) gods for worship besides Him. Say (to them O Prophet), "Bring forth your proof (to justify your act)! Here now (is a Book with) a reminder for those of my time, and there were also Scriptures with similar reminder for people before me." But most people do not know the truth and (stubbornly) turn away (from it).

[25] And We have not sent any Messenger before you except We revealed to him that, "There is no god except Me, so worship only Me (alone)." [26] But

those (misguided followers of Jesus) say, "The Most Gracious (Lord) has begotten a son." Glorified is He (Who is free from all the lies and imperfections that they have invented about Him)! In fact, those (whom they so designate as His children) are actually His honored servants; [27] who do not precede Him in speech and will only act by His command.

[28] He knows all that lies ahead of them and all that is hidden behind them, hence they cannot intercede for anyone except those whom He is pleased with. Verily, they themselves tremble in awe before His greatness. [29] And if any of them dare claim, "Indeed, I am also a god besides Him", We shall surely requite him with Hell. This is how We punish those who deliberately do wrong (and act in defiance against Us).

[30] Are they who refuse to accept the truth unaware that the heavens and the earth were (once) fused before We parted them asunder; [a] and that We made every living thing from water? [b] Will they still not believe (in Our revelation)? [31] Verily, We set firm mountains on the earth (as pegs and anchors) lest it shakes with them [c] (as it rotates around its axis), And We provided broad passageways between these mountains so that men will be naturally guided (to find their way); [32] and We have set up the sky as a well-secured canopy (to shield the earth from harmful external effects). Yet they stubbornly turn away from (pondering about) all these (wondrous) signs. [33] And He is (also) the One Who created the night and the day, and the sun and the moon, each floating in its own orbit (in total submission to Him). [d]

---

[a] The unitary origin of the universe, described in the Qur'an as "the heavens and the earth that were onced fused", strikingly anticipates the view of majority modern astrophysicists that this universe originated from a single entity and was parted asunder by a great force. This theory, which is famously known as the Theory of The Big Bang is indeed one of the greatest scientific theories of all times. It was proposed by Georges Lemaître, a Belgian physicist, in 1927, which then served as a critical platform for an American astronomer - Edwin Hubble, to further discover in 1929, that the universe is not static but is instead steadily expanding (see verse 51:47). A large majority of cosmologists and theoretical physicists endorse this theory as the evidence supporting the idea is extensive and convincing. How could this be foretold by an illiterate man who lived in the desert of Arabia during the early 7th century?

[b] No life form can take place without living cells. The cytoplasm which is the basic substance of every living cell is made up of 80% water. Modern research has revealed that most organisms consist of 50% to 90% water. Water is the basic ingredient without which, no living organism or entity could originate, come into existence and survive. See also verse 71:17 and its corresponding footnote.

[c] Refer to footnote for verse 16:15 for a detailed explanation on this.

[d] See verse 36:38-40 and its footnote.

³⁴ Never did We ever grant immortality to any man before you (O Muhammad). So if you die, do they hope to live forever? ³⁵ Every soul will taste death, and We subject everyone to both hardship and ease by way of trial. (In the end,) it is to Us that you will all be returned. *^a* ³⁶ And whenever those disbelievers see you, they make you the target of their ridicule, saying to one another, "Is this the one who speaks (so contemptuously) against your gods?" Yet they are the ones who, at every mention of the Most Gracious (Lord), are quick to deny Him.

A Warning Not to be Ignored

³⁷ (Verily,) man is a creature of haste and impatience; and in time, I shall make obvious to you (the truth of) My messages. So do not impatiently urge Me to hasten it! ³⁸ But they keep asking (you), "Tell us when will the threat (of doom and punishment) befall us if you speak the truth?" ³⁹ If only these disbelievers knew (that there will come) a time when they will not be able to shield the (flames of) Fire neither from their faces nor from their backs; and they will not be able to find any help. ⁴⁰ Nay! It will suddenly overwhelm and stupefy them. (And when it arrives,) they will not be able to avert it, nor will they be granted respite. ⁴¹ (And indeed O Muhammad, even) other Messengers before you were also derided. But those who scoffed at the Messengers were afflicted by what they used to deride.

⁴² Ask them, "Who can protect you from the Most Gracious (Lord, if His punishment befalls you) in the night or the day?" Yet they (stubbornly) turn away from the remembrance of their Lord. ⁴³ Do they really think that they have gods that could shield them from Us? Those alleged deities are not even able to help themselves, let alone be protected from Us. ⁴⁴ Nay! We have allowed these sinners and their forefathers to enjoy good things in life for a long time. Do they not see how We visit the earth with punishment, gradually depriving it from all that is best therein? (Is it not amusing that) they still expect to prevail (against Us)?

⁴⁵ Tell them, "Behold! I warn you only with the revelation that I receive (from God about the coming of Judgment Day)!" But the deaf (of heart) do not hear this call, however often they are warned. ⁴⁶ And if as much as a whiff of your Lord's torment touches them (on that Day), surely they will say, "O woe to us! Indeed, we have been unjust (to ourselves for rejecting the truth)."

---

^a God will surely put all of us to test of faith in this world - sometimes with tribulations and sometimes with ease of life to see who among us are patient and who would lose hope as we undergo the trials; and also who are grateful with the favors we are blessed with and who are not. See also verses 2:156, 2:214 and 29:2-3.

⁴⁷ (Verily,) We shall set up the scales of justice on the Day of Judgment and not a single soul will be wronged in the least. Even if a deed is equal to the weight of a mustard seed, We shall bring it forth (for reckoning). Sufficient are We as a (meticulous) Reckoner.

One Community of Believers

⁴⁸ And verily, We gave Moses and Aaron the criterion that distinguishes right from wrong, a guiding light and a reminder for those who are mindful of God; ⁴⁸ who fear (the wrath of) the unseen Lord and tremble at the thought of the Last Hour. ⁵⁰ And (like those earlier revelations,) this Qur'an too is a blessed reminder that We have revealed. Will you still reject it then?

⁵¹ And indeed long before (the time of Moses), We bestowed upon Abraham guidance (and sound judgment). We knew him very well. ⁵² (Take heed of the occasion) when he said to his father and his people, "What are these statues that you are so devoted to?" ⁵³ They said, "(These are our gods that) we found our forefathers worshipping them." ⁵⁴ He said, "Indeed, you have clearly gone astray just like your forefathers." ⁵⁵ They replied, "Have you come to us with the truth or are you just playing around?" ⁵⁶ He said, "(I have come to let you know that) indeed, your (true) Lord is the Lord of the heavens and the earth - the One Who created them both; and I bear witness to this. ⁵⁷ By God! I shall most certainly bring about the downfall of your idols as soon as you turn your backs and walk away."

⁵⁸ Then he broke all the idols into pieces except the biggest one so that his people might turn to it (for explanation of what had happened). ⁵⁹ When they saw their idols in this state, they exclaimed, "Who did this to our gods? Surely he must be a wicked person!" ⁶⁰ Then, one of them said, "We have heard of a young man by the name of Abraham who speaks (bad) about our gods." ⁶¹ The others said, "Then bring him here for everyone to see so that they may witness (his trial)."

⁶² They asked, "O Abraham! Was it you who did this to our gods?" ⁶³ Abraham answered, "Nay! It was this biggest idol who (is still standing that) did it. Ask (the broken idols) yourselves if they can speak!" ⁶⁴ Thereupon, they turned to one another to search for their conscience (and blamed themselves) saying, "Behold! It is you who are wrong (for rashly suspecting Abraham)!" ⁶⁵ (Confounded,) they then relapsed into their old position and said to Abraham, "You know very well that these idols cannot speak!" ⁶⁶ Abraham retorted, "Then why are you worshipping something that can neither benefit nor harm you in any way, instead of God?" ⁶⁷ "Woe to you for what you worship instead of God. Do you not have any common sense at all?"

⁶⁸ Then they reacted by instructing their fellow-men, "Burn him and defend your gods if you are (true) men of action!" ⁶⁹ And so We said, "O fire! Be cool and safe for Abraham." ⁷⁰ Indeed, they wished to harm him with their evil plot but We made them become the greatest losers. ⁷¹ And so We saved him and (his brother's son) Lot and guided them to the land which We had blessed for all times to come. ⁷² And in addition, We gave him Isaac, and then Jacob as well; all of whom We made good righteous men. ⁷³ And We made them leaders who guide others by Our command, and We inspired them to do good deeds, to be constant in their prayer and to regularly spend in charity. And they worshipped none except Us alone.

⁷⁴ And to Lot, We gave sound judgment and knowledge. We saved him from a community that was immersed in shameless acts. They were indeed a people who were evil and defiantly disobedient. ⁷⁵ And We admitted him into Our grace, for he truly one of the righteous. ⁷⁶ And (long before that,) Noah called out to Us. So We responded to him and saved him with his household from a great calamity; ⁷⁷ and helped him against the people who denied Our divine signs and were lost in evil. We drowned them all.

⁷⁸ And remember David and Solomon when both gave judgment concerning the field which the sheep of some people had strayed into and grazed. We were witness to their judgment. ⁷⁹ We gave Solomon insight into the case, and sound judgment and knowledge to both of them. And We made the mountains and the birds to glorify Our perfection together with David. Indeed, it was We Who did all these things. ⁸⁰ And We also taught David how to make coats of armour to protect you from each other's violence. Why are you still not grateful?

⁸¹ And to Solomon, We subjected the wind, blowing forcefully by his command *a* to the land which We had blessed. It is We who have full knowledge of everything. ⁸² And of the devils (from the community of Jinn), were some who would dive for him into the sea and perform whatever tasks he commanded. But it was We who kept a watch over them.

⁸³ And (remember) Job,*b* when he called to his Lord, "Indeed, I am sorely afflicted by adversity and You are indeed the Most Compassionate of all." ⁸⁴ We heard his prayer and removed his affliction. We restored his family to him and gave new offspring as an act of grace from Us, and as a lesson and reminder to those who serve Us (obediently). ⁸⁵ And (remember) Ishmael, Enoch *c* and Ezekiel. *a* They were all men of fortitude; ⁸⁶ and We admitted

---

a See verses 34:12 and 38:36 and the footnotes.
b Ayyub in Arabic.
c Idris in Arabic.

them to Our grace, for they were among the righteous.

[87] And (remember) Dzan-Nun [b] who walked away in anger (from the people he was sent to when they disobeyed God's message that he was conveying) and thought We would never decree anything upon him (after he impatiently aborted his mission). So (We made a fish swallow him and) he regretfully cried out in the deep darkness (of the fish's belly, "O God!) There is no god except You. Glory be to You (Who are completely free from all imperfections)! Indeed, it is I who have actually been unjust to myself (and deserve all blame)." [88] So We responded to his prayer and saved him from his distress. That is how We save those who truly believe in Us.

[89] And (remember) Zachariah when he cried out to his Lord, "My Lord! Do not leave me alone (without any heir), indeed You are the Best of Inheritors." [c]   [90] We heard his prayer and gave him John, and cured his wife (from barrenness). These were people who hastened to do good deeds and prayed to Us in hope and awe, and were always humble before Us. [91] And (remember) Mary too who guarded her chastity, whereupon We breathed into her from Our spirit and caused her, together with her son, to become a symbol (of Our grace) for all the worlds.

[92] (O believers! Verily,) this community of yours is a single (and united) community (of the same faith), with Me as your One and Only Lord. So worship Me alone (and nothing else). [93] (But people allow themselves to be taken over by their ego, selfish rivalries and lusts.) Hence, they tear asunder their unity (and divide themselves into factions of misguided faiths and practices). Yet to Us will everyone be (ultimately) returned for reckoning. [94] And so, whoever does righteous deeds and is a true believer (in God and the Hereafter), his efforts will not be rejected (and go to waste); for behold, We shall record them (in his favor). [95] And as for those (who were immersed in evil deeds) whose towns and cities We destroyed, they will not be able to return (to earthly life again and make amends).

A Reminder of the Last Hour

[96] And so, when Gog and Magog are unleashed (upon the world), they will swarm down from every elevated corner (of the earth, bringing terror and pain to whoever they come across). [97] (Verily, such event will mark) the near

---

[a] Dzulkifl in Arabic.
[b] Prophet Jonah or Yunus bin Matta in Arabic. See verses 10:98, 37:139-148 and 68:48-50. He was believed to be sent to Niveneh which is Mosul in Iraq today.
[c] Meaning : "You will still be there in eternity after everything else is gone."

approach of the Last Hour, hence the fulfillment of Our true promise. (And when the Last Hour finally arrives,) behold! The eyes of those who disbelieve will stare (in horror while they say), "Oh, woe to us! Verily, we were heedless of the signs (that we have been forewarned). Indeed, we have been unjust (to ourselves)!"

⁹⁸ Verily, you and what you worship besides God will be the firewood of Hell. And Hell is where you will all enter! ⁹⁹ If those objects of your worship had truly been divine (as you claim), then surely they would not be cast into Hell (with you). Yet, this is where you will all stay forever. ¹⁰⁰ There, they will be groaning (in great anguish but their false gods) will not hear anything, (let alone help them).

¹⁰¹ Behold! As for those whom We have decreed the best reward, they will be kept far away from the (Hellfire). ¹⁰² They will not hear even the slightest sound of it and will live forever in the midst of what their souls desire. ¹⁰³ The greatest terror (of the Day of Resurrection) will not affect them at all, and the Angels will receive them by greeting, "This is your Day (of Triumph, the Day) which you have been promised!"

¹⁰⁴ On that Day, We shall roll up the heavens like a scroll of parchment. *ᵃ*

ᵃ For a very long time, the idea of the world and universe meeting its end was something unimaginable, even from the scientific standpoint. It was not until the early 20ᵗʰ century when the theory of the Big Bang and consequently the state of the expanding universe was convincingly proposed and accepted by most space scientists (see verses 51:47 and 21:30, and their corresponding footnotes). And now, scientists are debating on several theories about how the universe will come to its end one day. Bear in mind that these are just theories that are being discussed and debated today. Nothing is conclusive yet. But the Qur'an has already given a clue to the answer more than 14 centuries ago by saying that one of the hotly debated theories which scientists call the Big Crunch - a phenomenon that is opposite to the Big Bang, will occur. Under this scenario, the universe will finally lose its mysterious energy, which is being termed as "Dark Energy" that works in the opposite direction of gravity and propels all cosmic objects to move away from its point of origin as the universe keeps expanding. And once this happens, the force of gravity will bring the universe's expansion to a halt and then reverses. Stars and galaxies would start rushing towards each other, and as they collide and clump together, their gravitational pull would get even stronger. Space would get tighter and temperatures would soar. The size of the universe would contract until everything would crunch together and compress into such a small space. The result would be an incredibly dense, hot, and compact universe - a lot like the state that preceded the Big Bang. The Qur'an graphically describes this scenario by saying that the heavens will be rolled-up like a scroll of parchment. See also verses 39:67 and 81:1. This analogy is used to make the scenario quite imaginable to the people who

And just as We originated the first creation, so shall We repeat it. That is a promise (which We have made binding) upon Ourselves. Behold, We are able to do (anything We will).

A Mercy to All the Worlds

[105] And verily, We have laid it down in the Psalms after the reminder (in the Torah earlier) that the righteous among My servants will (in the end) inherit and rule the earth. [106] Indeed, there is an (important) message in this for people who worship God.

[107] And We have not sent you (O Muhammad), except as (a manifestation of) Our grace (and mercy) to all the worlds. [a] [108] Say, "It has been divinely revealed to me that your God is the One and only God. Will you submit to Him?" [109] If they turn away, then say, "Verily, I have proclaimed (the message) to all of you fairly (without hiding anything). And I do not know whether the judgment that you have been promised (by God) is near or far in time.

[110] Indeed, He knows what you say aloud and what you hide in your hearts. [111] I have no knowledge (of the unseen except what God reveals to me). So, it could be (that this delay in judgment is) a test for you (in the form of respite) to continue enjoying (the fleeting pleasures of the world) a little while longer."

[112] And so the Prophet pleaded, "My Lord! Judge (between us) in truth. (Indeed,) our Lord is the Most Gracious, the One Whose help is sought against all the blasphemies that (the disbelievers) ascribe (to Him)."

---

lived in the plain desert of Arabia in the 7th century who do not have the slightest clue about science and also about what is happening in the heavens above them and how the world will inevitably end one day. Its truth will never be factually proven because everyone will be dead when the apocalyptic end of the world finally arrives and no one will survive to be able to tell its story. But for discussion purposes, it is only a matter of time before this theory may be accepted like all the other facts that the Qur'an presented long before they were finally proven scientifically.

[a] Grace and mercy to all the worlds are antithesis to violence and terrorism. Abu Huraira reported that the Messenger of God said, "I was sent to perfect good character." [Adab al Mufrad by Imam al Bukhari, no. 273]. Surely, excellent character, manners and conduct must be manifested in demonstrating compassion and fairness to all, and firm intolerance towards injustice and oppression. See also verses 33:21 and 3:31.

22. Al-Hajj
[The Pilgrimage : 78 verses]

This is a Madinan chapter. It deals with both the fundamentals of faith as well as some rules of *shari'ah* (i.e. Islamic law). It starts with drawing attention to the inevitability of resurrection and the Day of Judgment. These themes are brought home by drawing attention to God's creation of man through different stages of in the mother's womb which presents a great scientific miracle of the Qur'an considering the fact that this very detailed process of embryonic development was accurately recited by an illiterate man who lived in the plain desert of Arabia during the 7th century when no scientific knowledge was available at that time. It points out that if God can create man in the first instance, surely He is more than capable of recreating and resurrecting him later. It also refers to the judgment, reward and punishment in the Hereafter. It further emphasizes that everything in the heavens and the earth submits to God. Along with these, the chapter contains permission for fighting back those who wage war against the Muslims and to carry out *jihad* in God's way. It also commands the duty to perform pilgrimage to the Sacred Ka'bah and lays down rules for it and for making sacrifices on the occasion. The chapter is named after this specific duty and pillar of Islam.

In the name of God, the Most Gracious, the Most Compassionate.

The Last Hour and Resurrection

¹ O mankind! (Always) be mindful of your Lord (and fear His wrath)! Indeed, the convulsion of the Last Hour is (truly violent and) dreadful. ² On that Day, you will see every nursing mother abandoning her infant, and every pregnant woman delivering her burden before her time, and you will see people reeling like drunkards even though they are not drunk - all because the punishment of God is very severe indeed. ³ And yet, among people there are some who argue and dispute about God without knowledge, and follow every rebellious Satan; ⁴ (even though) it has been (clearly) decreed that whosoever takes Satan as a friend will surely be led astray into error and be guided towards the torment of the Blazing Fire.

⁵ O mankind! If you are in doubt about resurrection, remember that We have created you from soil, then from a clot of semen, ᵃ then from a (leech-

---

ᵃ *Nutfah* in Arabic. This is sperm in the form of a gel-like seminal fluid ejaculated inside the female reproductive tract that helps the sperm swim to the female egg cell.

like) clinging zygote,*a* then from a (chewed-like) embryonic lump *b* (with cells that are) formed and unformed *c* so that We might clearly manifest (Our power) to you. And We cause to rest what We will in the wombs for an appointed term, and then We bring you forth as an infant, (then We nourish you) so that you may reach your age of full strength. Some of you We cause to die young, and some We allow to live on to their abject old age until they do not remember what they once knew. (Now) look at the soil when it is dry and barren. As soon as We send down rain upon it, it begins to stir and swell, bringing forth radiant and blooming plants of every kind. *d* **6** That is because God alone is the ultimate truth. It is He Who gives life to the dead and it is He Who has the power over everything. **7** (So, be mindful) that the Last Hour will surely come, beyond any doubt; and God will certainly resurrect all who are in their graves (to reckon their deeds).

The Danger of Basing Faith on Conjecture

8 And yet, among people there are some who argue and dispute about God without knowledge, without true guidance, and without (the help of a divine) Book to enlighten them. **9** They turn away in arrogance to lead others astray from God's path. Humiliation is in store for them in this world. And on the Day of Resurrection, We shall make them taste the suffering of the Burning Fire. **10** They will be told, "This is the outcome of your own doing. Verily, God is never unjust to His servants."

11 And among mankind is he who serves God half-heartedly and remains on the fringe of true faith. If good befalls him, he is content with it. But if an ordeal afflicts him, he turns his face away (and reverts to disbelief) thus losing

---

a *Alaqah* in Arabic. This is a zygote which is the union of the sperm cell and the female egg cell. Also known as a fertilized ovum. After 6 to 10 days of its fertilization, the *Alaqah* or zygote takes shape like a leech and starts clinging to the wall of the uterus. The fact that the zygote was foretold in the Qur'an that it clings to the uterus is by itself truly astounding.

b *Mudghah* in Arabic. This is the 2 weeks old zygote that has already taken shape like a lump of flesh called an embryo which looks a bit like a chewed gum. The embryo would later become bigger and be termed as fetus beginning the 11th week of pregnancy.

c *Mukhallaqah wa ghairi mukhallaqah* in Arabic literally means something that is "formed and unformed". In this context, it is a possible reference to the "specialized and unspecialized cells (or stem cells)" in the embryo when they were being initially created and divided rapidly during 2 weeks of its zygote stage.

Note : See also verse 23:14 and its corresponding footnote.

d See verse 71:17 and its corresponding footnote.

his place in this world and in the life to come. Indeed, this is clearly a loss (beyond comparison). [12] He invokes instead of God, something that can neither harm nor benefit him. This is the worst for one to go astray. [13] Indeed, he invokes one that is far more likely to cause harm than benefit. Evil indeed is such a master and evil indeed is such a companion! [14] And as for those who believe and do righteous deeds, God will certainly admit them into gardens which rivers flow from right beneath them. Indeed, God does whatever He wills.

[15] (O Muhammad!) If any (of your enemies) think that God will never be able to help (His Messenger) in this world and in the life to come, ask him to extend a rope to the sky (and climb it). Then tell him to cut it off (so that he will fall to his death). Let's see whether this scheme will be able to remove what enrages (and distresses) him so much. [16] Thus, (it is with lucid examples that) We sent down clear verses (of this Quran to mankind as guidance). Verily, God guides whomsoever He wishes (that turns to Him for guidance). [17] Indeed, the believers, the Jews, the Sabians, the Christians, the Magians, and the idolaters will all be judged by God on the Day of Judgment (as to who among them are of the true faith). God is surely a Witness over everything.

[18] (O Prophet!) Are you not aware that to God prostrates whosoever is in the heavens and the earth; and so too the sun, the moon, the stars, the mountains, the trees, the beasts, and many among mankind? Yet there are also many who deserve their punishment (in the life to come because of their defiance towards God). And whosoever God humiliates (on the Day of Resurrection) will have none to raise him up in honor. God certainly does what He so wills.

Different Fates

[19] These two adversaries (of believers and disbelievers) have become engrossed in dispute about their Lord. As for the disbelievers, garments of fire will be tailored for them; and scalding water will be poured over their heads; [20] melting all that is in their bellies as well as their skins; [21] and there will also be hooked rods of iron to lash them. [22] Whenever they try to escape from their agonizing torture, they will be forced back therein and will be told, "Taste the torment of Fire (that you used to mock in disbelief before)!"

[23] Indeed, God will admit those who believe and do righteous deeds into gardens which rivers flow from right beneath them. They will be adorned with bracelets of gold and pearls, and their garments will be of silk; [24] for they were guided to the best speech and also to the path of the One Who is worthy of all praise.

The Sacred House and Pilgrimage

[25] Behold! As for those who disbelieve and hinder others from God's path and from the Sacred Mosque - which We have set up (as a place of worship) for all people, residents and visitors alike - and whosoever seeks to profane it with wrongdoing, We shall make him taste grievous suffering.

[26] (Take heed that) when We assigned the site of the Sacred House to Abraham, (We said,) "Do not associate anything with Me. Purify My House for those who will circumambulate it and those who will stand (before it in reverence), and those who will bow down and prostrate themselves (in worship)." [27] Hence (O Prophet)! Proclaim to mankind the (duty of) pilgrimage, (and you will see that) they will come to you on foot and riding along distant (roads and) mountain highways on lean and slender beasts. [28] And in doing so, they might witness and experience some of the benefits (that God has allotted for them in this life). Hence, extol God's name on the appointed days (during the course of pilgrimage) and also over the sacrificed cattle that He has provided. Eat then, of such pure sacrificed cattle and feed the unfortunate and the poor.

[29] Thereafter, let them complete their prescribed duties, let them fulfill their vows, and let them circumambulate the (sacred) Ancient House. [a] [30] All this is ordained (by God). And whoever honors God's sacred commandments, that would be best for him in the sight of his Lord. Verily, all kinds of cattle have been made lawful to you (for sacrifice and food) except what is mentioned to you (as forbidden). Shun then the filthy (belief and practice of) idol worship, and shun every word that is untrue.

[31] Now turn uprightly to God, ascribing divinity to none other than Him alone. And whosoever associates partners with God, it is as though he had fallen from the sky and then snatched by birds (of prey), or as though the wind had blown him to a far God-forsaken place. [32] That is how it is! Those who observe and revere the rituals that God has commanded them, their actions indeed reflect the piety that is in their hearts. [33] (Know that) in these (cattle) are benefits for you until an appointed term. In the end, their place for sacrifice is near the Ancient House.

[34] For every community We have appointed sacrifice as an act of worship so that they will pronounce God's name over the cattle that He has provided when you slaughter them. Indeed, your God is the One and Only God. Hence, submit yourselves to Him alone and give good news to those who humble

---

[a] The Ka'bah.

themselves to Him; [35] those whose hearts tremble with awe whenever God's name is mentioned, and those who endure whatever befalls them with patience, attend regularly to their prayer and spend in charity out of what We provide them.

[36] We have included sacrificial camels among the symbols of (devotion to) God (during pilgrimage). There is much good for you in them. So invoke God's name when you slaughter them while they are standing. And after they have fallen lifeless on their sides to the ground, eat of their flesh and feed the needy who (is contented with his lot and) does not beg, as well as he who is forced to beg. We subjected these animals to your needs in this way so that you will be grateful (to God). [37] Verily, neither their meat nor their blood reaches God; instead it is your (God-consciousness and) piety that reaches Him. He has subjected these animals to you so that you will magnify Him for having guided you. So, give good news to those who excel in good deeds. [38] God will certainly defend (and ward off evil from) those who believe. Surely God does not love anyone who betrays his trust and is ungrateful.

Permission to Fight

[39] Permission (to fight) is granted to those whom war is being wrongfully waged against. Most certainly, God has the power to grant them victory (if they stay firm in His path and do not take Satan as their patron). [40] These are the ones who have been unjustly driven from their homelands only because they proclaim, "Our Lord is God (the Almighty)!" [a] If God does not allow and enable people to defend themselves against (the transgressions of) others, then monasteries, churches, synagogues and the mosques wherein God's name is often mentioned will surely be destroyed. God will most certainly help those who help His cause. Verily, God is certainly Most Powerful, Almighty. [41] They are those who, if We firmly establish them on earth, would be steadfast in prayer, give out charity, command what is right and forbid what is wrong. Then, with God rests the final outcome of all affairs.

---

[a] This verse is relevant to the plight of the people of Palestine today who have been bullied by the Zionists of Israel with inhumane acts of atrocities since 1948 as they blatantly rob the Palestinians of their land and cruelly drive them out of their homes with impunity. Sadly, the Palestinians are being left alone in their weak condition to retaliate and fight this oppression against the powerful Zionist military force that is aided by America and many other western countries. The Muslim *ummah* is powerless to stop this cruelty because selfish, corrupt and disunited Muslim leaders have become complicit in injustice for the sake of worldly gains. They have sold their souls to evil powers, taken Satan as their patron and made their lust and vain desires as god. See verses 10:13-14, 25:43, 45:23, 102:1-2 and 11:113 together with their footnotes.

Blind Hearts

⁴² And if they deny you (O Muhammad), remember that before them, the people of Noah, 'Aād and Tsamud had also denied their Prophets; ⁴³ as did the people of Abraham and the people of Lot; ⁴⁴ and so did the dwellers of Madyan. In fact, Moses too was branded a liar. In every case, I granted some respite to those who rejected the truth before I seized them. How dreadful was My punishment!

⁴⁵ How many towns have We destroyed (that lie in desolate ruin now) with their roofs caved in because their people had immersed themselves in wicked deeds? How many wells lie abandoned and how many towering palaces (in the past) lie empty (today)? ⁴⁶ Have these people (of Makkah) not journeyed through the lands, letting their hearts to understand and ears to hear? (But even if they did, they would surely not gain any lesson from this), for it is not their eyes that are blind but it is the hearts in their chests that are rendered blind.

⁴⁷ They challenge you to hasten the coming of God's punishment upon them; but God never fails to fulfill His promise. Indeed, a day in the sight of your Lord is like a thousand years in your reckoning. ⁴⁸ And to how many cities did I give respite while their people were immersed in wicked deeds? Then I seized them, and (only) to Me are all destined to return. ⁴⁹ So say (to them O Prophet), "O mankind! Verily, I am only a clear warner to you (of a Day when everyone will be resurrected from their graves for the reckoning of their deeds)." ⁵⁰ Those who accept the truth and do righteous deeds will be granted forgiveness and a noble provision; ⁵¹ whereas those who deliberately seek to deny and discredit Our revealed verses will be the inmates of the Blazing Fire. ⁵² Never did We send a Messenger or a Prophet before you (O Muhammad) except that whenever he wished (his warning would be heeded), Satan would interfere and cast aspersion on it. But God would remove Satan's insinuations and strengthen His message (for those whose faith is firm and earnestly strive in His cause). Verily, God is All-Knowing, All-Wise.

⁵³ As for those in whose hearts there is a disease (of selfishness and hypocrisy) and whose hearts have become hardened (with hatred towards you), God lets whatever aspersions Satan may cast become a trial for them. Indeed, the wrongdoers' persistent dissension has placed them in a position that is far astray (from the truth). ⁵⁴ But for those who are endowed with knowledge, they will know with certainty that this Qur'an is the truth from your Lord. They will believe in it and make their hearts humbly submit (to God). Verily, God will surely guide those who believe to a straight path.

⁵⁵ Yet those who are bent on denying the truth will not cease to be in doubt about Him until the Last Hour suddenly comes upon them, or until the greatest suffering befalls them on a Day that is devoid of all hope. ⁵⁶ On that Day, all dominion will belong to God and He will judge (everyone and make a distinction) between them. Those who believe and do righteous deeds will find themselves in Gardens of Bliss. ⁵⁷ But those who refused to accept the truth and denied Our revelations will be requited with a humiliating punishment.

The Faithful Will be Established

⁵⁸ As for those who emigrate (to forsake evil) and strive in God's cause and then are killed or die (in thir journey), God will most certainly grant them a generous provision, for God is indeed the Best of all Providers. ⁵⁹ He will most certainly admit them into a place where they will be well pleased, for God is surely All-Knowing, Most Forbearing.

⁶⁰ So will it be! And if one retaliates in proportion to the injury he has received, and then is wronged again, God will certainly help him (to claim his right). God is certainly the One who absolves sin, (for He is indeed) Most Forgiving. ⁶¹ That is because God is Almighty, and He is the One who makes the night to enter into the day, and the day to enter into the night. And indeed, God hears all, sees all. ⁶² And so will it be too because God alone is the Ultimate Truth, and everything else that they invoke besides Him is sheer falsehood. Verily, He is the Most High, the Most Great.

Why Deny God?

⁶³ Do you not see that God sends down rain from the sky and then causes the earth to become green? Indeed, God is Most Subtle, All-Aware. ⁶⁴ To Him belongs all that is in the heavens and the earth. And indeed, God is All-Sufficient, Immensely Praiseworthy. ⁶⁵ Do you also not see that God has made subservient to you all that is on earth including the ships that sail through the sea by His command? And it is He Who holds the sky so that it will not fall on the earth except if He allows it. Indeed, God is Full of Kindness and Most Compassionate to mankind.

⁶⁶ It is He who gave you life, then causes you to die and will bring you back to life again. But man is indeed bereft of gratitude. ⁶⁷ For every community, We have appointed the rites of worship they must follow. So, let them not dispute with you concerning your way of life (O Muhammad). Instead, invite them to Your Lord with wisdom, for you are surely guided on the right path. ⁶⁸ And if they argue with you, then say, "God knows best about everything that you do." ⁶⁹ God will judge between all of you on the Day of

Resurrection concerning your disputes (about His Messenger and His revelations). [70] Do you not know that God has complete knowledge of everything that occurs in the heavens and the earth? All these are noted and kept in a record (near Him). That is easy for God to do. [71] And yet they worship besides God what He did not send down any authority for people to do and what they have no knowledge about. Verily, the wrongdoers will surely have none to help them (against God's wrath when they are brought to Him on the Day of Judgment).

[72] And whenever Our verses are recited to them in all clarity, you can see denial (and disdain) on the faces of those who refuse to accept the truth. It is as if they are about to assault those who recite Our verses. Say (to them), "Shall I tell you of something worse than that (rage which is in you)? It is the Fire which God has promised to those who deny Him. How wretched is the destination!"

[73] O people! A parable is hereby set forth for you. So listen to it carefully. Indeed, those whom you invoke besides God will never be able to create a single fly even if they all gathered and combined their forces to do so. And if the fly were to snatch anything away from them, they would not be able to retrieve what it has taken. Weak indeed are those who invoke and those that are being invoked. [74] They have not appraised God with the true appraisal that He rightfully deserves. Indeed, God is All-Strong, Almighty.

[75] Verily, God chooses His Messengers from among Angels and human beings (to convey His message). Indeed, God hears all, sees all. [76] He knows all that lies open in front of them and hidden behind them. To God will all things (finally) return. [77] O you who believe! Bow down, prostrate yourselves and worship your Lord (alone without partners). And do good deeds so that you may attain success.

[78] (O believers!) Strive hard in God's cause in the right way that is due to Him (as exemplified by the Prophet). It is He who has chosen you (to serve Him) and has not laid upon you any hardship in the religion (that He has ordained for mankind). This is indeed the creed of your forefather, Abraham. It is God who has named you *Muslims* in the past and in this Book now (by virtue of the common belief in the One and Only God and your willful submission to Him). The Messenger will bear witness over you and you will bear witness over all mankind (regarding this matter). So establish and be steadfast in your prayer, be punctual in rendering your purifying dues,[a] and hold firmly to God's commands. Verily, He alone is your Guardian - the Best of all Guardians and the Best of all Helpers.

---

[a] *Zakah* : Alms or tithes.

23. Al-Mu'minūn
[The Faithful Believers : 118 verses]

This is a Makkan chapter. Its first eleven verses describe the characteristics of faithful believers and the reward that awaits them. The chapter is named after them - *Al-Mu'minūn* which means The Faithful Believers. Like other Makkan chapters, this chapter deals with the fundamentals of faith - monotheism, messengership, resurrection and judgment. In addition, the chapter also speaks about God's creation of the heaven and the earth, His sending down of the rain and growing of plants, trees and fruits, and His providing of domestic animals with various benefits for man, together with an emphasis on the fact that man will die and be raised-up on the Day of Resurrection. The theme of messengership is emphasized with reference to the accounts of some Prophets like Noah, Hūd, Moses and Jesus, pointing out that all these Prophets delivered the same message of monotheism, that all of them were rejected and opposed by their people and that all of them were helped and rescued by God. Reference is then made to the similar disbelief and opposition of the Makkan chieftains to the message delivered to them. The chapter ends by referring once again to the inevitability of resurrection and to the fact that man will not have a second chance to return to worldly life and make amends for his lapses and mistakes.

In the name of God, the Most Gracious, the Most Compassionate.

Man, Faith and the Universe

¹ (Blessed and) successful indeed are the believers; ² those who perform their prayer with utmost humility and submission (to their Lord); ³ who turn away from all that is vain and frivolous; ⁴ who are punctual in rendering their purifying dues; *ᵃ* ⁵ who strictly guard their private parts; ⁶ except from their spouses or from those whom they rightfully possess (through wedlock. With these,) then they are indeed free from blame. ⁷ But whoever seeks beyond this are transgressors.

⁸ (The believers are also) those who are faithful to their trusts and promises; ⁹ and who guard their prayer diligently. ¹⁰ Such are the heirs; ¹¹ who will inherit Paradise where they will remain in it forever.

¹² Indeed, We created man from the essence of clay; ¹³ then We made him from a clot of semen and lodged him a safe resting place (in an egg cell). ¹⁴ Then, We create the clot of semen into a (leech-like) clinging zygote, then We create the clinging zygote into a (chewed-like) embryonic lump, then We

---

ᵃ *Zakah* : Alms or tithes.

create the embryonic lump into bones before clothing them with flesh.*ᵃ* And then (finally) We made it develop and grow into another creation. Most Blessed is God, the Best of Creators. ¹⁵ Thereafter you are destined to die; ¹⁶ then indeed, you will be brought back to life on the Day of Resurrection.

¹⁷ And indeed, We have created above you seven paths (of heavens) and We do not neglect any aspect of Our creation. ¹⁸ And We send down rain from the sky in due measure, then We cause it to settle in the earth. And (if We will,) We are most certainly able to take it all away (in any manner We please). ¹⁹ And with this water We bring forth for you gardens of date-palms and grapevines, yielding abundant fruit, and from which you may eat; ²⁰ as well as the (olive) tree that grow out from (the lands adjoining) Mount Sinai, yielding oil and condiments for all to eat.

²¹ And behold! In the cattle too there is indeed a lesson for you. We provide you with drink out of what they have in their bellies, and there are also other benefits that you derive from them. And of their (meat), you eat; ²² and on them and also on ships you are carried (as transport).

One Message for All Mankind

²³ And verily, We sent Noah to his people. He said, "O my people! Worship God alone. You have no god other than Him. Will you not be mindful (and heed) Him?" ²⁴ But the leaders of his people who refused to accept the truth said, "This man is nothing but a mortal like yourselves who wants to make himself superior over you! Verily, if God had willed to convey a message to us, He would have surely sent down Angels. Moreover, we have never heard of anything like this from our forefathers. ²⁵ He is nothing but a madman; so bear with him for a while."

ᵃ This verse should be read in conjunction with verse 22:5 and its corresponding footnotes. In this verse, an additional stage of the embryonic and fetus development process regarding the formation of bones that takes place before flesh is revealed. It presents another accurate scientific fact that is impossible for anyone who lived in the 7ᵗʰ century to have any idea of this very intricate process. Other than this, the phrase "grow into another creation" mentioned after that refers to the final and miraculous result of the birth of a living human that originated from a *Nutfah* or a "clot of gel-like semen with sperm" (see verse 75:37). The pin-point accuracy of this entire embryonic development process was revealed more than a thousand years before any camera or scientific device ever existed to see what was actually taking place in the womb during this intricate process. Only the Creator of mankind can reveal this information accurately, which without a doubt presents one of the greatest undisputed miracles of the Qur'an and proof of its divinity.

²⁶ And so Noah said, "My Lord! Help me because they have denied me."
²⁷ So We inspired him, "(Now) build an ark (that will save you and those who follow you) under Our watchful eye and according to Our instruction. And when Our command was issued, waters gushed forth (from the source) and the earth's lowlands began to overflow. We said, "Take into the ark a pair of every kind (of creature) together with members of your family (who believe), except those against whom the sentence (to drown) has been passed. Do not plead with Me on behalf of those who have wronged. Indeed, they will surely be drowned."

²⁸ And when you and those accompanying you have boarded the ark, (be grateful to God and) say, "All praise is due to God alone who has saved us from those wicked people." ²⁹ And also say, "My Lord! Let my landing be blessed. Verily, You are the Best for us to rely upon for safe landing."
³⁰ Behold! There are indeed important signs (and lessons in this story for those who care to think); for verily, We always put people to test.

³¹ Then after these people, We raised a new generation. ³² And We sent forth to them a Messenger from among themselves, (saying), "O my people! Worship God alone, for you have no god other than Him. Will you not be mindful (and heed) Him?"

³³ But the leaders of his people who refused to acknowledge the truth and denied the meeting with God in the life to come - because they had become corrupted by the ease and comfort in this worldly life that We had endowed upon them - said, "This man is nothing but a mortal like yourselves who eats what you eat and drinks what you drink. ³⁴ And if you obey a mortal who is just like yourselves, you will surely end up as losers."

³⁵ "Does he promise you that when you are dead and reduced to soil and bones, you will be brought back to life again? ³⁶ How preposterous and utterly far-fetched is what you are promised! ³⁷ Indeed, there is no life other than the life of this world. (Surely) we shall die (someday) but we shall not be raised from the dead (like he said because we only live once). ³⁸ He is nothing but a man who has invented lies against God. We should not believe him."

³⁹ And so the Messenger prayed, "My Lord! Help me because they have denied me." ⁴⁰ God replied, "Leave them alone. Soon, they will be filled with regret." ⁴¹ And then the awful blast of Our punishment actually seized them and We made them become like rubbish of dead leaves. And so, away with those wicked people! ⁴² Then We raised new generations after them. ⁴³ (Verily,) no community can ever hasten (the end of) its term, nor can they delay it.

⁴⁴ Then We sent forth Our Messengers one after another (to convey Our message of truth). Every time a Messenger came to his community, they denied him (and accused him of falsehood). So, We caused those who rejected the truth to follow one another into ruin and reduced them to bygone tales. And so, away with those who would not believe!

⁴⁵ And then, We sent forth Moses and his brother Aaron together with Our signs and clear authority; ⁴⁶ to Pharaoh and the leaders of his people but they behaved arrogantly. They were really a conceited lot. ⁴⁷ They said, "Should we believe in two men who are mere mortals like us while their people are our slaves?" ⁴⁸ So they denied both Moses and Aaron and earned their place among those who were doomed.

⁴⁹ And verily, We gave Moses the Book ᵃ so that his people may be guided. ⁵⁰ (Just like how We honored Moses,) We also did the same to the son of Maryam and his mother by making them a sign (of Our grace for mankind. And when Maryam was about to give birth,) We gave them shelter on a (nice) lofty ground of meadow with a fresh water spring.

Higher Values of Life

⁵¹ O Messengers! Eat of the good things and do righteous deeds. Indeed, I am well aware and have full knowledge of all your actions. ⁵² Verily, these are the people of your community, a single and united community of the same faith; with Me as your One and Only Lord. Hence, (always) be mindful of Me (and keep your duty to Me diligently).

⁵³ But people (allow themselves to be taken over by ego, selfish rivalries and lusts, hence they) tear asunder the unity of faith and divide themselves into factions with each rejoicing (in their own misguided faith and practices). ⁵⁴ So leave them alone in their confusion until a certain time (when they return to God for judgment). ⁵⁵ Do they think that by giving them wealth and children; ⁵⁶ We favor them (from others) and are hastening good for them? By no means! In fact, they do not realize (that they are actually being led further astray because they are being distracted from their remembrance of God).

⁵⁷ Verily, those who become cautious (of their thoughts and actions) because they stand in fear (and awe) of their Lord; ⁵⁸ and those who believe in the signs and revelations of their Lord; ⁵⁹ and those who do not associate any partner with their Lord; ⁶⁰ and those who give and spend in charity with their hearts trembling at the thought that they are destined to return to their Lord

---

ᵃ The Torah.

some day; [61] it is they who vie with one another in good deeds and it is they who are the forerunners (in attaining God's pleasure).

[62] And We do not burden any soul with more than it can bear. Verily, with Us is a record that speaks the truth (about what everyone has done). Indeed, none will be treated unfairly. [63] Nay! (As for those who have torn asunder the unity of faith,) their hearts are lost in confusion from recognizing the truth (because they have been led far away from it by their own evil lusts). And apart from that (breach of unity), they immerse themselves in committing a wide range of misdeeds (as they become lost in the pursuit of worldly pleasures); [64] until We seize the affluent ones among them with punishment, then they cry out for help (in belated supplication).

[65] (But they will be told,) "Do not cry for help today. You will surely not receive any help from Us! [66] Verily, (time and again) My verses have been recited to you, but (each time) you would turn back on your heels; [67] reveling in your arrogance, (mocking and) speaking evil about what was recited to you until late into the night."

[68] Do they not reflect carefully over the Qur'an? Or is it because what has come to them now was unknown to their forefathers? [69] Or do they deny their Messenger because they do not know him well? [70] Or do they think he is possessed with madness? Nay! He has surely come to them with the truth, but most of them hate the truth.

[71] Had the truth been tailored to suit their fancies (and low desires); then verily the heavens, the earth and all that dwell in them would have surely been corrupted (and ruined). Nay! We have brought a reminder to save them (from the torment of the Hellfire and at the same time bring glory to their worldly life), yet they turn away from it.

[72] Or are you asking any reward from them (for conveying Our message)? Indeed, your Lord's reward is the best (and unrivaled) since He is the Best of Providers. [73] Verily, your duty is only to call them to a straight path (O Prophet); [74] and indeed, those who do not believe in the life to come will surely turn away and deviate from the path (that you call to).

[75] And even if We were to show them mercy and remove whatever hardship and distress that might afflict them (in this life), they would still persist in their overweening arrogance, blindly stumbling to and fro. [76] And verily, We tested them with suffering, but they neither submitted to their Lord nor supplicated humbly to Him (for help). [77] (So leave them alone) until the time when We shall send a torrent of severe punishment upon them and plunge them into utter despair.

Man's Insolence

⁷⁸ Verily, He is the One Who has endowed you with hearing, sight, and conscience (so that you may be able to learn and discern truth from falsehood). Yet, how seldom do you give thanks. ⁷⁹ And He is the One Who multiplied you on earth; and to Him will you be ultimately gathered. ⁸⁰ And He is the One Who also grants life and causes death; and in His control is the alternation of the night and the day. Will you not use common sense (to realize that only He alone is worthy of worship)?

⁸¹ Nay! Instead, they say what the people of olden times used to say. ⁸² They say, "What! After we have died and become soil and bones, shall we really be raised to life again? ⁸³ Indeed, this promise to us is the same as what was promised to our forefathers a long time ago. It is nothing but fables of ancient times!"

⁸⁴ So ask (them O Prophet), "Who controls the earth and all it contains, and to Whom does it all belong? Tell me (the answer) if you know." ⁸⁵ They will say, "To God!" So say (to them), "Why will you not take heed then?" ⁸⁶ (Ask them), "Who is the Lord of the seven heavens and the Mighty Throne?" ⁸⁷ They will answer, "God!" Say (to them), "Will you not fear Him then?" ⁸⁸ Ask (them further), "Tell me if you really know : Who has the dominion over all things in His hand and gives protection to all, while none can be protected against His (wrath)?" ⁸⁹ They will answer, "God!" Then (ask them), "How is it that you can be so confused and deluded (about the truth when you already know it)?" ⁹⁰ Nay! We have brought the truth to them and yet they are intent on lying (to themselves).

⁹¹ Never has God begotten a son, nor is there any other god besides Him. If there were, then each god would have certainly taken away with him his own creation and they would have surely sought to overpower one another (to become the Supreme God). Glory be to Almighty God alone Who is far above (the lies and imperfections) that they attribute to Him! ⁹² Only He knows what is hidden and what is manifest. Sublimely exalted is He above what they associate Him with.

⁹³ Say, "O My Lord! If it is Your will to show me what they are warned against; ⁹⁴ then, do not place me among those wicked wrongdoers, my Lord." ⁹⁵ (So pray for Our mercy and protection,) for indeed, We are surely able to let you witness the fulfillment of what We promised them! ⁹⁶ (But whatever they may say or do,) repel the evil that they commit with something that is better. We are fully aware of what they falsely ascribe (against Us). ⁹⁷ And say, "O my Lord! I seek refuge with You from the instigations and promptings of the

devils (and my own evil impulses); [98] and I seek refuge only with You my Lord, so that they will not come near me."

Justice and Grace

[99] (As for those who do not believe in the life to come, they go on lying to themselves) until when death approaches any of them, he (suddenly acquires faith and) prays, "O my Lord! Let me return to life; [100] so that I can act righteously in whatever I have failed previously." [a] Nay! Never will this ever take place! Indeed, it is nothing but a (meaningless) word that he utters; for behind those (who leave the world) there is a barrier (of death that stands) until the Day they are ressurected. [b] [101] Then, when the trumpet (of resurrection) is blown, no ties of kinship will prevail among them on that Day, nor will they (have the time to) inquire about one another.

[102] As for those whose weight (of good deeds) is heavy on the scale, it is they who will be victorious! [103] But for those whose weight (of merit) is light

---

[a] This passage points out that man's life in this world is short and that he must always seek the truth and fight temptation and misleading beliefs before it is too late. It reminds man of death and how he might react when it approaches him. Elsewhere, the Qur'an also depicts the scene where those who died in the state of disbelief will plead to be returned to the world and be given a second chance to mend their ways. See verses 6:27, 14:44, 25:27, 26:97-101, 32:12, 35:55 and 63:10. For those who believe that man's fate in the Hereafter is predetermined and that his pleading will have no influence on it, verse 115 of this chapter might shed some light on this gross misunderstanding : "Do you think We created you for nothing and you will not be returned to Us?" Know that God Almighty is fair towards everyone. He has equally blessed all human beings with the gift of life, and gave them senses and perception together with the faculties of intellect and reason to distinguish between good and bad, right and wrong. He has given some people good health and inflicted others with ailments, and also made life a mixture of happiness and suffering - all these in order to enrich the human experience and make people recognize the reality and value of God. People can choose either to be vigilant and prepare for their encounter with Him, hence invest for life in the Hereafter; or they can choose to reject God and dismiss any accountability to Him. But when it is too late, excuses will avail no one.

[b] This verse confirms that spirits of those who have died will never be able to come back to this world nor can they communicate with those who are still alive. Their spirits dwell in a different realm and dimension, awaiting for the Day of Resurrection to arrive. There is a barrier that stands between their realm and the world where those who are alive live in.

on the scale, it is they who will lose their souls. They will (enter) Hell and remain it it forever. ¹⁰⁴ Verily, the Fire will scorch their faces and they will frown in despair in there.

¹⁰⁵ (They will be asked,) "Were My verses not recited to you (before this) and did you not deny them?" ¹⁰⁶ Their reply will be, "Our Lord! (We did not intend to defy You on purpose. Instead,) misfortune had overwhelmed us so much that (we did not realize) it caused us to go astray. ¹⁰⁷ So bring us out of this suffering O our Lord, (and send us back to earth so that we can make amends). And if we still return (to our bad ways), then surely we (deserve to be deemed as) evildoers." ¹⁰⁸ God will say, "Remain despised (in the Fire) and do not ever speak to Me!"

¹⁰⁹ And among My servants, there were also those who (always) said, "Our Lord! We believe in You. Forgive us and have mercy on us; for You are the best of those who show mercy." ¹¹⁰ But you made these humble servants of Mine the target of your mockery to the point where it made you forget all remembrance of Me; and you went on (mocking and) laughing at them. ¹¹¹ Verily, I have rewarded them today because they persevered in their patience. Indeed, it is they who have achieved triumph.

¹¹² And then He will ask (the doomed), "How many years do you think you had lived on earth?" ¹¹³ They will reply, "A day, or possibly less. But ask those who kept count." ¹¹⁴ He will say, "You stayed there only for a moment, if only you knew this! *ᵃ* ¹¹⁵ Do you think We created you without purpose and will not return you back to Us?"

¹¹⁶ Sublimely exalted is God, the Ultimate Sovereign, the Ultimate Truth. There is no god other than Him, the Lord of the Glorious Throne. ¹¹⁷ Whoever invokes (and worships) any other deity besides Almighty God whose existence he has no evidence to show, he will be brought to account before his Lord (Who created him). *ᵇ* Most certainly, those who rejected the truth will never attain any success. ¹¹⁸ Hence O believer, say, "O my Lord! Grant me forgiveness and bestow Your mercy upon me; for You are the best of those who show mercy!"

ᵃ This is to give us an impression of how short life on earth is compared to the eternal nature of the Hereafter. See also verse 79:46.

ᵇ The value and role of enlightened faith which is the result of authentic religious belief is not built on mythology, folklore, and superstition. True religion respects rational thought and accords the human mind its rightful place in understanding the world and shaping it. And because humans are gifted with the power of thought and free will, all of us will be made accountable for our actions.

24. An-Nūr
[The Light : 64 verses]

This is a Madinan chapter. It is named *An-Nūr* or The Light after verse 35 where God's light is contrasted to the darkness in which the disbelievers find themselves engulfed, and also because it contains the light of guidance in building and preserving character and integrity of the individual, the family and the society. More specifically, the chapter clarifies several regulations for the Muslim community, mainly to do with marriage, modesty, obedience to the Prophet, and appropriate behavior in the household. The initial context is the false rumor against A'isha, the Prophet's wife, who was accidentally left behind by her traveling companions after wandering away in search of a necklace that she had accidentally dropped. She was escorted back to Madinah by Safwan Ibn Mu'attal who arrived at the scene later and found her there. A slanderous rumor then quickly took place which accused A'isha of committing an extra marital affair with Safwan that caused so much pain and anguish to her. A'isha's innocence was finally proclaimed by God in verse 26.

In the name of God, the Most Gracious, the Most Compassionate.

The Punishment for Adultery

¹ (O believers!) This is a chapter that We have sent down and made obligatory (for you to follow). We have revealed clear verses in it so that you will take heed.

² The woman and the man guilty of fornication, flog each one of them with a hundred lashes. *ᵃ* And let not your compassion for them keep you from carrying out this law that is prescribed by God in His religion if you truly believe in God and in the Last Day. And let a number of believers witness the punishment inflicted on them.

³ (It is unbecoming for a believer to commit fornication, for it is the way of those who are devoid of faith and practice idol worship. Hence,) those who fornicate are only fit to marry their kind. Such behavior is indeed forbidden to those who have truly placed their faith (in God and His Messenger).

⁴ As for those who accuse chaste women (of fornication) and cannot produce four witnesses, flog them with eighty lashes. Do not accept their testimony ever after, for such people are defiantly disobedient; ⁵ except those

---

ᵃ This is the "way out" that God gave from the earlier punishment of "lifetime house arrest" as mentioned in verse 4:15.

who repent thereafter and make amends to reform themselves. Then indeed, God is Most Forgiving, Most Compassionate.

⁶ And as for those who accuse their own wives of adultery but have no witnesses except themselves, let each of them swear four times in the name of God that he is indeed telling the truth; ⁷ and swear a fifth time that God's curse be upon him if he is telling a lie. ⁸ However, punishment is averted from the wife if she would also testify by calling upon God's name four times that her husband is indeed telling a lie; ⁹ and swear a fifth time that God's wrath (and curse) be upon her if he is telling the truth. ¹⁰ Were it not for God's favor and grace upon you, (surely you would not have been given a way to redeem yourselves from this grave accusation). Verily, God is the only Acceptor of Repentance, He is All-Wise.

¹¹ Verily, those who falsely accuse others (of being unchaste) are actually from a group among you. (For those who are victims of slander,) do not regard this as something (entirely) bad for you. Nay! (In fact) it is something good for you (if you exercise patience and place your trust in God because He will surely reward you well). As for the slanderers, each one of them will be accounted for the sin that he has earned. (On top of this,) a great suffering awaits the one who took the lead among them (in spreading the slander). *ᵃ*

¹² Whenever such a rumor is heard, why do the believing men and women not think the best of one another and say, "This is obviously an (outrageous) lie!"; ¹³ and why did they not (demand the accusers to) produce four witnesses (to prove their allegation)? Indeed, since the accusers have failed to produce witnesses, then they are certainly regarded as liars in the sight of God.

¹⁴ (O people!) Were it not for God's favor and grace upon you in this world and in the life to come, a great punishment would have surely been afflicted upon you (instantly) for the calumny that you indulged in; ¹⁵ when you took it up with your tongues and uttered with your mouths something of which you have no knowledge, thinking it is a light matter, whereas it is indeed a grave sin in God's sight.

ᵃ Verses 11-20 of this chapter relates to an incident which occurred on the Prophet's return from the campaign against the tribe of Mustaliq in the year 5H. The Prophet's wife 'A'isha, who had accompanied him on that expedition, was accidentally left behind when the Muslims struck camp before dawn. After having spent several hours alone, she was found by one of the Prophet's companions by the name of Safwan ibn Mu'attal, who led her to the next halting-place of the army. This incident gave rise to malicious insinuations of misconduct on the part of 'A'isha; but these rumors were short-lived and her innocence was established beyond all doubt.

¹⁶ When you heard it, why did you not say, "It is not right for us to speak of this. Glory be to You O God! This is indeed a great slander!" ¹⁷ God warns you from ever repeating the same mistake if you are to remain as believers. ¹⁸ And God makes plain and clear to you His revelations, for God is All-Knowing, All-Wise.

¹⁹ Indeed, those who love (and are happy) to see (rumors and) indecency spread among the believers will receive stern and grievous punishment in this life and in the next one to come, for God knows the (full) truth whereas you do not. ²⁰ Were it not for God's favor and grace upon you, (surely you would not have been given respite to redeem yourselves from this grave sin). Verily, God is Full of Kindness, and He is Most Compassionate.

²¹ O you who believe! Do not follow Satan's footsteps. He will only urge those who follow him to indecency and evil. If God had not bestowed His favor and grace upon you, none of you would have been able to ever cleanse yourselves from the sins that you have committed. It is God Who purifies whomsoever He wills (that sincerely turns to Him in repentance). Indeed, God hears all, knows all.

²² Hence, those among you who have been graced with God's favor and ease of life should never swear to cease helping the ones (who made unintentional mistakes) among their near of kin, and the needy, and those who have emigrated from their homes for the sake of God. Instead, (it is better and more virtuous to) pardon and forbear (from punishing them). Do you not love (and desire) God to forgive you of your sins too? (Be ever mindful that) God is (certainly) Most Forgiving, Most Compassionate.

²³ Verily, those who (falsely) defame chaste women who may have been unthinkingly careless but have remained true to their faith will be cursed in this world and in the life to come. They will endure a great punishment; ²⁴ on the Day when their own tongues, hands and feet will testify to what they did. ²⁵ On that Day, God will requite them in full for whatever they rightfully deserve, and they will come to know that God alone is the Ultimate Truth, Who makes the truth manifest.

²⁶ (Verily,) bad women deserve bad men, and bad men deserve bad women; whereas good women are for good men, and good men are for good women. Those who are innocent of what they are being wrongly accused of, there is forgiveness and a noble provision for them. ^{*a*}

---

^{*a*} This is God's declaration of Aisha's innocence from the evil slander that was made against her.

Measures to Preserve Decency

²⁷ O you who believe! Do not enter houses other than your own unless you have obtained permission and greeted their occupants (with proper salutation). This is enjoined upon you for your own good so that you will be mindful (of your mutual rights). ²⁸ If you find no one in the house, do not enter until you are given permission. And if you are told, "Go back!", then do so as this would be (most proper and) purer for you. Remember that God has full knowledge of everything that you do. ²⁹ (On the other hand,) you will incur no sin if you freely enter uninhabited houses that serve a useful purpose to you. And always remember that God knows everything that you do, either openly or discreetly.

³⁰ Tell the believing men to lower their gaze and to guard their chastity. That will be purer for them. Verily, God is certainly aware of everything that they do. ³¹ And tell the believing women to (also) lower their gaze and guard their chastity, and not display their beauty (and adornment in public) beyond what is (ordinarily) apparent thereof. They should draw their head-coverings ᵃ over their bosoms and not display their beauty except to their husbands, or their fathers, or their husbands' fathers, or their sons, or their husbands' sons, or their brothers, or their brothers' sons, or their sisters' sons, or among their womenfolk, or those whom they rightfully possess, or such male attendants who are beyond all sexual desire, or children that are not yet aware of the private aspects of women. They should also not stomp their legs while walking to draw attention to their hidden adornment (just like most women of disrepute normally do). And always turn to God in repentance all of you O you believers, so that you will attain success!

³² And marry off the single from among you as well as the righteous among your male and female slaves (who are fit for marriage). If they, whom you intend to marry are poor, (let this not deter you; for) God will grant them sufficiency out of His bounty. Verily, He is All-Encompassing, All-Knowing.

³³ And as for those who do not have the means for marriage, let them preserve their chastity until God grants them sufficiency out of His bounty. And if any of those whom you rightfully possess desire to obtain a deed of freedom, write it out for them if you are aware of any good in them; and give them something from the wealth that God has given you. And do not - in order to gain some of the fleeting pleasures of this worldly life - coerce your slave

---

ᵃ *Khumur* : plural. *Khimar* : singular. It refers to the head-covering customarily worn by Arabian women before and after the advent of Islam. Muslim women are obliged to maintain this and let it down loosely over their bosoms. See also verse 33:59 and its corresponding footnote.

maidens into prostitution while they hold dearly to their chastity. And if they are coerced into it, God (will surely forgive them) after such coercion, for God is Most-Forgiving, Most Compassionate. ³⁴ We have sent down to you clear revelations showing the right path together with examples of those who have gone before you, and a lesson to those who are mindful of God (and strive to keep their duty to Him diligently).

³⁵ God is the Light of the heavens and the earth. The parable of His light is like a niche containing a lamp; the lamp within a glass, the glass is like a radiant star lit from a blessed tree - an olive tree that is neither of the east nor west, whose oil would almost glow even though untouched by fire. Light upon light! God guides to His light whomsoever He wills (that submits to Him in true devotion). And God sets forth parables for all people to learn from. Verily, God alone has full knowledge of all things.

³⁶ (Indeed, God's light is found) in houses of worship which He has ordered to be raised, where His name is remembered (and mentioned) in them with (praises of limitless) glory in the mornings and evenings; ³⁷ by men who neither commerce nor (worldly) gain can divert them from the remembrance of God, and from being constant in their prayer, and from regularly giving out charity. They are men who fear (the thought) of the Day when hearts and eyes will flutter (with trepidation); ³⁸ and who only hope that God may reward them in accordance with the best that they ever did and lavish His bounty upon them. Verily, God gives (His bounty) to whomsoever He wills without measure.

³⁹ But as for those who reject the truth, their good deeds are like a mirage in a lowland (or a desert), which the thirsty thinks it is water, until when he approaches it he finds nothing. Instead, he finds that God has always been present with him and that his account will be paid by God in full. Indeed, God is swift in reckoning. ⁴⁰ Or, (the state of the deniers of truth is also) like utter darkness in a deep sea which is covered by waves, on which is another wave, above which is a (dark) cloud. Darkness upon darkness! When one puts out his hand, he can hardly see it. Whomsoever God withholds light from, will find no light at all.

⁴¹ Do you not see that all that is in the heavens and the earth (unceasingly proclaim and) glorify God's perfection, even the birds too as they spread their wings in the air? Each of His creatures certainly knows how to submit itself in prayer to Him and also how to glorify His perfection. God has full knowledge of everything that they do. ⁴² Verily, only to God belongs the (absolute) dominion of the heavens and the earth, and to Him will all things return (in the end).

⁴³ Can you not see that it is God who gently drives the clouds, gathers them together, then piles them up in masses until you see rain comes forth from their midst? He is the One Who sends down hail stones from the sky-charged mountains of clouds, striking with it and also averting from it whomsoever He wills. And the flash of His lightning almost deprives people of their sight. ⁴⁴ It is God who causes night and day to alternate. In this too there is surely a lesson for all who have eyes to see. ⁴⁵ God has created every moving creature from water. *ª* Among them are some that creep on their bellies, some that walk on two legs, and others that walk on four. God creates what He wills and indeed, He has power over all things.

Guidance to the Straight Path

⁴⁶ Verily, We have sent down clear revelations (showing the right path), and God guides whomsoever He wills to this path (when they sincerely turn to Him for guidance). ⁴⁷ They say, "We believe in God and the Messenger, and we obey." But some of them immediately turn their backs after that. Surely these are not believers.*ᵇ* ⁴⁸ And when they are called to God and His Messenger to judge between them, some of them turn away; ⁴⁹ but if the truth is on their side, they come to him promptly and obediently. ⁵⁰ Is there sickness in their hearts? Or are they full of doubt? Or do they fear that God and His Messenger will be unjust to them? Nay! It is they who are unjust (to themselves and yet they do not realize this).

⁵¹ But for the believers, their answer when summoned to God and His Messenger for him to judge between them, is none other than, "We hear and we obey." It is they who will ultimately be successful. ⁵² Verily, whoever obeys God and His Messenger, fears God's (wrath) and is ever mindful of Him, such people are the ones who will certainly triumph in the end.

⁵³ And (as for those who waver in their faith), they swear by God with their strongest oaths that if you should ever order them to go forth for battle, they would most certainly march forth. Say to them (O Prophet), "Do not swear. Proving your obedience (through action) is better. Indeed, God is certainly well aware of all that you do."

⁵⁴ Say (to them), "Obey God and obey the Messenger! But if you turn away from the Messenger, then know that he is only responsible for the duty

---

ª See verse 21:30 and its corresponding footnote.
ᵇ Muslims who typically refuse to accept God's teachings and the leadership examples of the Prophet in political, legal, and economic matters are usually non-practicing Muslims who do not observe their basic Islamic obligations. See also verses 70:22-35.

placed on him (which is to convey God's message clearly to mankind), and upon you is the duty placed on you (which is to obey him and submit to God). So if you obey him, then surely you will be (rightly) guided. Verily, (know that) the Messenger is not bound to do more than to clearly deliver the message (that has been) entrusted to him."

⁵⁵ God has promised those of you who believe and do good deeds that He will make them successors in the land as He did to those before them. He will firmly establish the faith He has chosen for them and replace their fear with security. So let them worship Me alone and no one else besides Me. As for those who still choose to reject the truth after (having understood) this, then such people are indeed defiantly disobedient (and they will end up as losers). ⁵⁶ So, attend to your prayer regularly and render the purifying dues (punctually), and obey the Messenger, so that you will be bestowed with God's grace. ⁵⁷ Never think that those who persistently deny the truth can escape (from their final reckoning even if they remain unscathed) on earth. In the end, the Fire of Hell will be their final home. What a wretched destination!

Perfect Manners

⁵⁸ O you who believe! Let those whom you rightfully possess (that serve you in your home) and those who have not reached puberty among you ask your permission before entering your private chamber on three occasions of the day - before the dawn prayer, at noon when you put aside your garments (to have your rest), and after the night prayer. These are three occasions of privacy for you (which you may happen to be undressed). Beyond these occasions, it is not wrong for you or them to move about freely, attending to one another. This is how God makes clear to you His revelations. Indeed, God is All-Knowing, All-Wise. ⁵⁹And when the children among you reach puberty, let them ask permission to enter (your private chamber) at all times just like those who have reached maturity before them do. This is how God makes His revelations clear to you. God is indeed All-Knowing, All-Wise.

⁶⁰ Tthere is no sin for women who are advanced in age and no longer feel any sexual desire to discard their outer garments, provided they do not intend to flaunt their charms (and attract attention). But if they refrain from this out of modesty, that would be better for them. Verily, God hears all, knows all.

⁶¹ (O believers! You are all brothers to one another.) Hence, there is no restriction on the blind, nor on the lame, nor on the sick (to accept charity and food from the hale), and neither is there any restriction on you to eat with them

in your houses. *ᵃ* You are also permitted to eat in the houses of your fathers, or the houses of your mothers, or the houses of your brothers, or the houses of your sisters, or the houses of your paternal uncles, or the houses of your paternal aunts, or the houses of your maternal uncles, or the houses of your maternal aunts, or in the houses whose keys you possess, or in the house of a friend. There is no blame on you whether you eat together with them or separately. *ᵇ* But when you enter their houses, greet each other with a greeting from God, blessed and good. This is how God makes clear for you His revelations so that you may use reason (to understand them).

⁶² True believers are those who believe in God and His Messenger, and when they are engaged with him upon a matter of importance (to the community) that requires collective action, they do not depart until they obtain his permission first. Those who ask for your permission are indeed the ones who truly believe in God and His Messenger. Hence, when they ask your permission to attend to their affairs (with a valid reason), grant permission to the deserving ones among them and pray to God to forgive them. Indeed, God is Most Forgiving, Most Compassionate.

⁶³ (O people!) Do not address God's Messenger in the manner you address one another. Verily, God knows those of you who secretly sneak away under the guise of some excuses. So let those who act in violation of His command be fearfully aware that a trial may afflict them or grievous suffering may befall them.

⁶⁴ Without a doubt! Indeed to God belongs all that is in the heavens and the earth, and He knows very well whatever state you are in. And on the Day when all who have ever lived will be brought back to Him, He will apprise them about everything that they have done (and justly requite them for all their deeds), for God has full knowledge of everything.

ᵃ The society as a whole owes the sick, the lame, the blind and the handicap the privilege to have their meal anywhere and at any house to satisfy their hunger.

ᵇ Sayyid Abul Ala Maududi explained this verse as follows : The moral teachings of the Qur'an had so thoroughly changed the Arab mind that they had become highly sensitive with regard to the distinction between the lawful and the unlawful. According to Ibn `Abbas, when God commanded them "Do not devour one another's wealth unjustly." (4:29), the people became unduly cautious and would not eat freely at each other's house; so much so that unless a formal invitation was extended, they considered it unlawful even to dine in the house of a relative or a friend. This verse puts things back in the right perspective.

25. Al-Furqān
[The Criterion : 77 verses]

This is a Makkan chapter and like other Makkan chapters, it focuses on the fundamentals of the faith, especially the truth of the Qur'an and the Prophethood of Muhammad, resurrection, reward and punishment on the Day of Judgment. It refers to the doubts and objections raised by the disbelievers against these matters such as the Qur'an being "ancient tales", and that it was fabricated by the Prophet with the assistance of others. They also questioned why did God not send an angel instead of man as His Messenger. And if at all a man was chosen as God's Messenger, then he should have been among the rich and highly influential people of the community. On top of all these, they audaciously demanded the Prophet to bring God in person to them to prove his claim. The chapter gives proper replies to such objections and demands of the disbelievers. In doing so, it also refers to some of the previous Prophets and Messengers and how their respective communities such as the people of Noah, 'Aād, Tsamud, al-Rass, and Lot had rejected them and were then punished. The chapter is named *Al-Furqān* or The Criterion which is mentioned in the first verse. This is another name for the Qur'an that serves to clearly distinguish between truth and falsehood, belief and disbelief, light and darkness, and guidance and error.

In the name of God, the Most Gracious, the Most Compassionate.

Distinguishing Right from False

¹ Blessed is He Who sent down to His servant the criterion to discern truth from falsehood, so that he may be a warner to all the worlds. ² It is He to Whom the dominion over the heavens and the earth belongs, and Who begets no offspring, and has no partner in His dominion. It is He who created everything and determined its exact measure. ³ Yet, they have taken false gods besides Him that create nothing while they themselves are being created; and they do not possess for themselves the power to cause any harm or bring any benefit, nor can they control death, life or resurrection.

⁴ Those who refuse to accept the truth say, "This (discourse) is nothing but a lie which has been devised by Muhammad with the help of others." Verily, it is they who have actually perpetrated injustice and a lie. ⁵ And they assert (further), "These are indeed fables of ancient times which Muhammad had them written down, and then dictated to him in the morning and evening (to help him memorize)."

⁶ Say (to them O Muhammad), "Verily, this Qur'an is sent down by the

One Who knows the secrets of the heavens and the earth. Indeed, He is Most Forgiving, Most Compassionate, (so repent and submit yourselves to Him before it is too late)."

⁷ But they refuted, "How is it that this man who calls himself a Messenger of God eats and walks about in the markets (just like any ordinary person)? Why has not an Angel been sent down to act as a warner with him? ⁸ Or (why has not) a treasure been granted to him by God, or a bountiful garden (at least), so that he could eat from it (with ease)?" And then these evildoers say (to one another), "If you were to follow Muhammad, then surely you will be following someone who is bewitched (and deluded)!"

⁹ Look at their ghastly allegations toward you by calling you all sorts of names (O Muhammad)! They have certainly gone so far astray and have completely lost their way back (to the true path). ¹⁰ Blessed is He Who - if He wills - can give you better than that. He can certainly give you gardens with rivers that flow from right beneath them and He can give you palaces too. (This is easy for God to do).

¹¹ Nay! It is the Last Hour that they actually deny! And for those who deny this, We have prepared a Blazing Fire for them. ¹² When it sees them from a distance, they will hear its fury and roaring rage. ¹³ And when they are thrown into a tight space in there - bound in chains - they will cry out for their total destruction (and extinction there and then, for the suffering is far too much for them to bear). ¹⁴ But they will be told, "Do not ask for a single destruction today but pray for many times over (because your suffering will never end!)"

¹⁵ Now ask (the infidels who have been preoccupied with mocking you), "Which is better, do you think? (That scene in Hell which God has described to you,) or the Garden of Eternity which is promised to those who are always mindful of Him? (Indeed,) this will be the reward and ultimate home (for those who pay heed to God's reminders and live a righteous life)." ¹⁶ They will remain in it forever and have everything they wish for. It is a promise honored by your Lord in fulfillment to what they (have always) prayed for.

¹⁷ (For those who rejected the truth), He will gather them on that Day together with everything that they worshipped besides God, and He will ask (those false gods), "Was it you who led My servants astray, or did they willfully choose to stray from the right path themselves?" ¹⁸ They will answer, "Glory be to You (O God, Who are free from all imperfections)! It was inconceivable for us to take anyone as our protector (and patron) except You. But (as for them), You allowed them and their forefathers to enjoy (the comforts of life) until they forgot all remembrance (of You). They became

people devoid of any good and led themselves to ruin." ¹⁹ (Thereupon, God will say to them,) "Verily, your false gods have clearly refuted all your claims and assertions (of ascribing divinity to them) and you can neither avert your doom nor receive help from anyone. We shall make those who are unjust (and wicked) taste a great punishment (today)."

²⁰ (Even before you O Muhammad,) We never sent Messengers other than mortal men who surely ate food and went about in the markets (like ordinary people). Indeed (O men), We have made some of you as a means to test others (so that those who are just and unjust among you will be made evident). Will you not then be patient (to endure Our trials?) Verily, your Lord is All-Seeing (and is completely aware of everything).

Mentality that is Lower than Cattle

²¹ Those who do not believe that they are destined to meet Us, say, "Why are Angels not sent down to us, or why can we not see our Lord?" Indeed, they have become too proud and arrogant of themselves and have gone too far in their insolence. ²² On the day when they see the Angels, there will be no good news for the sinners (as they had hoped for). Instead, the Angels will say to them, "(Go away!) You are (barred from God's favor and) forbidden from crossing the barrier (to go back to earthly life to correct your mistakes)." *a* ²³ And We shall turn to whatever (supposedly good) deeds they have done and reduce them to scattered dust. ²⁴ (Whereas) the residents of Paradise will be graced with the best home and (final) resting place (to return to).

²⁵ And on that Day, the heavens together with the clouds will burst asunder, and the Angels will be sent down, streaming with a grand descending. ²⁶ True dominion on that Day will belong to the Most Gracious (Lord) alone. And it will be a day of great distress for those who rejected the truth (during their sojourn on earth). ²⁷ It will be a Day on which the wrongdoer will bite his hands (in despair) crying, "Oh, how I wish had followed the path shown to me by the Messenger! *b* ²⁸ O woe to me! I wish I had not taken so-and-so as my friend. ²⁹ Indeed, he led me astray from the remembrance of God after it came to me!" (Behold! Have We not repeatedly forewarned you that) Satan will always betray man? ³⁰ And the Messenger will say, "O my Lord! My people have indeed treated this Qur'an like a thing to be discarded and forsaken." ³¹ This is how enemies from those who are engulfed in sin are made for every Prophet. But sufficient is your Lord as a guide and helper.

---

a See verse 23:100 that mentions about the barrier.
b See also verse 23:99-100 and its footnote.

³² And those who deny the truth also say, "Why was the Qur'an not revealed to him (in a single revelation) all at once?" (O Prophet!) We (gradually revealed and) recited this Qur'an to you in a proper and deliberate pace (over a period of time) so that your heart may be strengthened with it. ³³ And whenever the deniers of truth come to you with a parable (to argue against the Qur'an), We bring to you the truth and the best explanation (to counter it). ³⁴ (Tell them that on the Day of Resurrection,) those who (are bent on opposing the truth) will be gathered and driven to Hell upon their faces, (and it is they who) will be in the worst position and the farthest astray from the right path!

A Lesson in the Fate of Former People

³⁵ Verily, We gave the Scripture to Moses and appointed his brother Aaron to assist him (in delivering Our message). ³⁶ Then We said, "Go both of you to the people who have denied Our signs and revelations." Then We destroyed those deniers of truth with complete destruction (after they stubbornly rejected Our message).

³⁷ And as for the people of Noah, We drowned them when they denied the Messengers, ᵃ and made their end as a sign for mankind (to take heed and reflect). Indeed, We have prepared a grievous punishment for wicked wrongdoers. ³⁸ And (take heed too of how We punished the people of) 'Aād, the people of Tsamud, and the dwellers of Ar-Rass, and many (generations of sinners) in between. ³⁹ We (warned) each one of them by citing the examples (of those who were destroyed before them). And then (when they ignored Our warnings,) We annihilated all of them completely.

⁴⁰ And they (who now deny Our message) must have surely come across that town which was showered upon by a rain of evil .ᵇ Do they not see it (as they pass by its ruins during their journeys)? Nay! (How could they see and take any lesson from this if) they are too steeped in arrogance and refuse to believe in resurrection?

⁴¹ When they see you (O Prophet), they sneer at you in ridicule and say, "Is this the one whom God has sent as His Messenger? ⁴² Indeed, had we not held firm to our gods, he would have surely turned us away from them!" But in time, they will realize who is actually more misled from the right path when they finally see the suffering (that awaits them with their naked eyes).

ᵃ Refer to footnote verse 4:164.
ᵇ The city of Sodom.

⁴³ (O Prophet) Have you seen the one who takes his lusts and vain desires as god? *ᵃ* (Is he the same as those who fear God's promise of resurrection? Nay!) You are not his guardian (and how could you be held responsible for his actions)? ⁴⁴ Do you think that most of them can hear or understand (the truth that is being conveyed to them? Nay!) In fact, they are no better than the cattle (that are bereft of reason). In fact, they are (even worse and) farther astray from the right path.

Pondering Over God's Signs

⁴⁵ Do you not see how your Lord causes the shadow to extend (in the bright hours of the morning)? Had He so willed, He could have indeed made it stand still. But We made the sun as a guide (and indicator to tell time). ⁴⁶ (As the sun climbs up), We gradually draw the shadow back to Us (until it sits right under your feet. Then it gets extended again towards the night until it vanishes before it reappears in the morning of a new day).

⁴⁷ And He is the One Who makes the night as garment (for your comfort), your sleep a rest, and every new day like a resurrection. ⁴⁸ And He is the One Who sends forth the winds as good news in advance of His coming grace; and then We send down pure water from the sky; ⁴⁹ so that We can revive a dead land with it, and as drink to (quench the thirst of) many animals and people We have created. ⁵⁰ And indeed, it is We Who distribute rain and water among them so that they may be mindful (and thankful of Our grace). But most people persist in their disbelief (and ingratitude).

⁵¹ And had We so willed, We could have (continued to) raise a warner in every single city and community (just like We did in the past, but We have indeed chosen you O Muhammad as Our last and final Messenger to all mankind, and have entrusted the Qur'an upon you to convey its message to all). ⁵² Hence, do not relent and .obey the likes and dislikes of those who deny the truth. Instead, (be steadfast in faith and) strive hard against them with this Qur'an (with utmost striving).

⁵³ He is the One Who has brought the two bodies of flowing water to meet; one palatable and sweet, and the other salty and bitter. And He has placed a barrier between them, a partition that is forbidden (for these water to pass).*ᵇ*

ᵃ See verses 45:23 and 79:38.

ᵇ Modern science has discovered that in estuaries, where fresh and salt water meet, the situation is somewhat different from what is found in places where two seas meet (see 55:20). It has been discovered that what distinguishes fresh water from salt water in estuaries is a "pycnocline zone" with a marked density discontinuity separating the

⁵⁴ And He is the One Who created man from water *ᵃ* and established for him bonds of lineage and marriage. And your Lord is indeed All-Powerful. ⁵⁵ Yet people worship, instead of God, things that can neither benefit nor harm them. Indeed, these deniers of truth are surely helpers (of one another in evil) against their Lord.

⁵⁶ And (verily), We have not sent you (O Muhammad), except as a bearer of good news and a warner (to all mankind). ⁵⁷ Say then (to those stubborn rejecters of truth), "No reward do I ask from you for what I have been tasked to do. All I ask is that he (who hears my call to) take the right way leading to his Lord."

⁵⁸ Hence, place your trust in the Ever Living Lord, the One Who does not die; and glorify His perfection by praising Him (abundantly). Sufficient is He Who is well aware of all the sins committed by His servants (whether openly or discreetly). ⁵⁹ He is the One Who created the heavens and the earth and all that is between them in six phases, and He is firmly established on His (Supreme) Throne. He is indeed the Most Gracious (Lord). Ask then about Him (O men), to those who are well informed.

⁶⁰ Yet when (those arrogant disbelievers are) told, "Prostrate to the Most Gracious (Lord)," they retorted, "What is this Most Gracious (Lord that you tell us to worship)? Should we prostrate to whatever you order us (when we do not believe that there is only One God)?" And they grow more rebellious.

⁶¹ Blessed is He Who has set up in the heavens great constellations and has placed therein a radiant lamp and a bright moon. *ᵇ* ⁶² And He is the One Who causes the night and the day to (smoothly) succeed one another (as a clear sign) for whoever that cares to reflect and be grateful (for His limitless blessings and grace).

The True Servants of God

⁶³ Verily, true servants of the Most Gracious (Lord) are those who walk on

---

two layers. This partition or zone of separation has a different salinity from the fresh water and from the salt water and its information has been discovered only recently, using advanced equipment to measure temperature, salinity, density, oxygen dissolubility, etc. The human eye cannot see the division of water in estuaries into the three kinds: fresh water, salt water and the partition (i.e. pycnocline zone of separation).

ᵃ See the footnote for verse 71:17
ᵇ See the footnote for verse 10:5.

the earth in humility. And when the ignorant ones behave insolently towards them, they respond with (words of) peace; [64] and they are also the ones who spend the night prostrating and standing in praise of their Lord; [65] and who say, "Our Lord! Keep away from us the punishment of Hell." Its suffering is indeed unbearable; [66] (and) it is certainly an evil home and (a wretched) resting place (for those who refuse to submit to their Creator).

[67] (The true and wise servants of the Most Gracious Lord are) those who are neither extravagant nor stingy whenever they spend, but always maintain a just balance between the two (extremes). [68] And they (also) do not invoke any other god besides Almighty God, nor take a life which God has forbidden except in the pursuit of justice, [a] nor do they fornicate. And whoever commits any of them will meet the penalty; [69] that will be compounded for him on the Day of Resurrection, and he will remain in it forever in humiliation; [70] except those who repent and become believers and do righteous deeds. It is they whom God will turn their (previous) bad deeds into good ones. Indeed, God is Most Forgiving, Most Compassionate. [71] (And so,) whoever repents and follows-up with righteous deeds, he is deemed to have truly turned to God through his act of repentance.

[72] And (know that the true servants of God are) those who do not give false testimony, and they shun profanity with dignity and grace; [73] and (also) those who, whenever they are reminded of their Lord's revelations, attend with open ears and eyes; [74] and who pray, "Our Lord! Grant us spouses and offspring who will give joy and comfort to our eyes, and make us as an exemplary model for those who are righteous." [75] These (are the true believers who) will be rewarded with the loftiest places (in Paradise) for their patience (and fortitude), and they will be met therein with greetings of (welcome and) peace. [76] That is the best place for final settlement and rest, and they will remain in there forever.

[77] So say (to those who are bent on denying the truth O Muhammad), "You have no value in the sight of My Lord if you do not worship Him. If you continue to deny His message (and do not repent before death comes to you), you will never be able to avert the inevitable punishment (that awaits you on the Day when everyone will be resurrected from their graves to face judgment)."

---

[a] This is in reference to legal retribution.

26. Ash-Shu'arā'
[The Poets : 227 verses]

This is also a Makkan chapter that deals with the fundamentals of faith, more specifically with monotheism, the Messengership of Prophet Muhammad, and resurrection. It opens with a reference to the Qur'an and the attitude of the disbelievers who turned away from it despite of it being a clear guidance to the truth. Reference is then made by way of illustrating the attitude of the disbelievers of all times and the theme of monotheism, to some of the previous Messengers and how they were treated by their disbelieving people. In this context, the accounts of Moses and Aaron in relation to their mission to Pharaoh and his people, of Abraham and his efforts to bring his people to worship God alone, and the mission and efforts of Noah, Hūd, Saleh, Lot and Shu'aib are given one by one, pointing out the way how God dealt with them. Further, the respective fates of the God-fearing and the sinful on the Day of Judgment are also mentioned. Towards the end, the chapter replies the disbelievers' accusations that the Qur'an was a work of Satans or a composition of the Prophet. It also emphatically warns the believers not to fall into the trap of believing false stories that are being told by poets who wander in every valley to create confusion. The chapter is named *Ash-Shu'arā'* or The Poets in reference to this.

In the name of God, the Most Gracious, the Most Compassionate.

A Statement Made Clear

¹ *Ṭa Sīn Mīm.* ² These are the (revealed) verses of the clear Book. ³ Would you torment yourself to death with grief because they refuse to become believers (O Muhammad)? ⁴ Had We so willed, We could have sent down to them a sign from the heaven so that their necks would be forced to bow down in humility. (But We are sending down this Qur'an instead for them to discern truth from falsehood and then submit to Us out of their own free will). ⁵ Yet whenever any fresh reminder comes to them from the Most Gracious (Lord), they would turn away from it (in their overweening arrogance). ⁶ They have indeed denied (and rejected Our message). Soon they will come to know the truth of what they used to mock.

⁷ Do they not look at the earth and observe how We grow all kinds of noble things on it (in abundance)? ⁸ Indeed, there is a sure sign of (Our greatness) in this, yet most of them would still not believe (in the truth that is

being conveyed to them)." ⁹ And indeed your Lord; He is the Almighty, the Most Compassionate.

The Story of Moses: A Debate With Pharaoh

¹⁰ (Now take heed of the occasion) when your Lord summoned Moses and said, "Go to those wicked people; ¹¹ the people of Pharaoh. Do they not fear Me?" ¹² Said Moses, "My Lord! Indeed, I fear that they will deny me; ¹³ and then my chest will be tight and my tongue will not express well; so send Aaron (to assist me). ¹⁴ Moreover, they have a charge of crime against me, so I fear that they will kill me."

¹⁵ God replied, "By no means (will that happen without My permission! Now), go forth both of you with Our signs. We are with you, listening (and observing everything). ¹⁶ So go, both of you to Pharaoh and say, 'Indeed, we are Messengers from the Lord of all the worlds. ¹⁷ Let the (enslaved) children of Israel be free to go with us.'"

¹⁸ (And when Moses approached Pharaoh,) he was taunted, "Did we not raise you (with love and care) in our home when you were a child, and you had lived with us (under good protection) for many years of your life?" ¹⁹ "Yet you committed that (heinous) act of yours (by murdering one of us). What an ungrateful person you are."

²⁰ Moses answered, "I did it when I was (ignorant and) misguided. ²¹ So I fled from you because I feared your retaliation. Then my Lord gave me authority (and wisdom) and made me one of His Messengers. ²² And do you consider enslaving the children of Israel a favor that you have done for me (and wish to remind me about it so that I would be foolishly indebted to you

---

" Verses 2-8 : In His infinite wisdom, God chose the Qur'an as the sign that Prophet Muhammad will present to the world - a book to be recited and handed down from one generation to the next, which would appeal to man's mind and above all else, address his intelligence. Muslims must remember that the Prophet's mission was a universal and eternal one; and they are now the custodians of the Qur'an which represents the definitive and conclusive message that God has conveyed to humanity designed to govern and organize life on this earth. During the Prophet's time, the Makkans however, were stubbornly demanding miracles, stunning indications or signs that would convince them that he was telling them the truth. The irony was that such signs were in existence all around them, both in the realms of place and also of time, and they could readily observe them any time of the day or night. In fact, even if the Prophet produced a stunning miracle for them, they would still refuse to believe him (see verse 54:3) and insisted that he was a skilled sorcerer instead (verse 10.2).

and feel obliged to condone your evil transgressions)?"

²³ (Dumbfounded with the argument that Moses presented,) Pharaoh (changed the subject and) asked, "So what is this Lord of the worlds (that you claim and wish to speak about to me now)?" ²⁴ Moses said, "(He is the) Lord of the heavens and the earth and whatever is between them if you really care to (ponder about and) believe."

²⁵ (Hearing this,) Pharaoh (sneered and) said to those around him, "Did you hear what he just said?" ²⁶ Moses continued, "Verily, He is your Lord as well as the Lord of your forefathers." ²⁷ Said Pharaoh (to his people), "Indeed, this self-proclaimed Messenger who has been sent to you is surely a madman!" ²⁸ And Moses continued further, "He is indeed the Lord of the east and the west and all that is in between them, if only you would use common sense (and ponder)."

²⁹ Pharaoh exclaimed, "(How dare you!) If you take any other god than me, I shall most certainly throw you in prison!" ³⁰ Moses replied, "Even if I bring a clear proof (of my claim) to you?" ³¹ Pharaoh answered, "Then bring it to me if you really speak the truth." ³² So Moses threw down his staff and behold! It became a serpent, clear for all to see. ³³ And then he drew out his hand (from his shirt), and behold! It was shining white for everyone to see.

³⁴ Seeing this, Pharaoh said to the leaders of his people around him, "Indeed, he is a very skilled sorcerer; ³⁵ who wants to (scare and) drive you out of your land with his sorcery. What then do you advise (me to do)?" ³⁶ They said, "Let him and his brother wait while we send heralds to every corner of all the cities; ³⁷ to (find and) bring very skillful sorcerers to you."

³⁸ And so the sorcerers were brought together at a time that was set on an appointed day; ³⁹ and the people were asked, "Will you all come to the gathering?" ⁴⁰ (They replied, "Yes we shall,) so that we may follow (in the footsteps of) the sorcerers if they win." ⁴¹ When the sorcerers came forth (for the encounter with Moses), they asked Pharaoh, "Will there be a handsome reward for us if we win?" ⁴² Pharaoh answered, "Yes indeed! And you will surely be among those who are closest to me too."

⁴³ And so (when they met), Moses said to them, "Throw down what you want to throw." ⁴⁴ So they threw down their ropes and their staves and said, "By the might of Pharaoh, we shall surely be victorious!" ⁴⁵ Then Moses threw his staff, and behold! It swallowed all their deceptions; ⁴⁶ and all the sorcerers fell down in prostration. ⁴⁷ They said, "(Moses certainly did not practice magic. Instead, he brought signs of the truth). We believe in the Lord of all the worlds (now); ⁴⁸ the Lord of Moses and Aaron." ⁴⁹ Pharaoh retorted, "How

could you believe in Him before I allowed you to? Surely, Moses must have been your master who (secretly) taught you witchcraft (and conspired against me). But in time, you will come to know (how powerful I am). I shall surely have your hands and feet cut off on opposite sides, and I shall certainly impale all of you." ⁵⁰ They said, "No harm (can you do to us if God wills to protect us). Verily, it is to our Lord Whom we will all be finally returned (in the end). ⁵¹ We certainly hope that our Lord will forgive our sins, since we are the foremost to profess our belief in Him (today as a result of this incident)."

⁵² And so We inspired Moses, "Travel by night with My servants. Indeed, you will be pursued (by Pharaoh with vengeance)." ⁵³ Then Pharaoh sent heralds to every corner of all the cities to gather his army; ⁵⁴ and he said to them, "Verily, these (children of Israel) are only a small band; ⁵⁵ but they are really enraging us; ⁵⁶ and indeed, we are great in number and fully prepared (against any danger)."

⁵⁷ And so We drove Pharaoh and his people (in rage) out of their gardens and springs; ⁵⁸ and from their treasures and honorable positions. ⁵⁹ So it was! And (in time), We gave the children of Israel these favors too.

⁶⁰ Finally, Pharaoh and his people caught up with them at sunrise. ⁶¹ When the two hosts came in sight of each other, the followers of Moses said, "(There is no way for us to escape from this). We shall certainly be overtaken and caught." ⁶² Moses said, "Nay! Indeed, my Lord is with me and He will guide me (to rescue us all)." ⁶³ And so We inspired Moses, "Strike the sea with your staff." Then the sea parted and each side became like a lofty mountain. ⁶⁴ Then We brought Pharaoh and his army near it; ⁶⁵ and We saved Moses and all who were with him; ⁶⁶ while We caused the rest to drown. ⁶⁷ Behold! In this (story) is indeed a sign (and lesson for people to ponder) but most of them would not believe (and even care to consider). ⁶⁸ And indeed your Lord, He is the Almighty, the Most Compassionate.

The Story of Abraham: God's Unceasing Blessings

⁶⁹ Now, narrate to them the story of Abraham; ⁷⁰ when he said to his father and his people, "What is that you worship?" ⁷¹ They answered, "We worship idols, and we shall remain devoted to them." ⁷² Asked Abraham, "Do they hear you when you call them? ⁷³ And can they bring any benefit or cause any harm to you?" ⁷⁴ They said, "Nay! But this is what we found our forefathers did."

⁷⁵ Asked Abraham further, "Have you ever considered what is it that you have been worshipping (all this while); ⁷⁶ you and your forefathers? ⁷⁷ Indeed, these (lifeless idols) are my enemies, except the Lord of all the worlds; ⁷⁸ the

One Who created me and gave me guidance. [79] He is the One Who provides me with food and drink. [80] And when I fall ill, He is the One who restores me to health; [81] and He is also the One Who will cause me to die and then bring me back to life; [82] and the One Who I hope will forgive me for my faults on the Day of Judgment."

[83] (Then Abraham prayed,) "My Lord! Grant me wisdom (to discern between right and wrong), and include me among the righteous; [84] and grant me an honorable mention among later generations; [85] and make me among those who will inherit the Gardens of Delight; [86] and forgive my father; for he is indeed among the ones who have gone astray. [87] And let me not suffer disgrace on the Day when everyone is raised from the dead." [88] That is the Day when neither wealth nor children will be of any benefit; [89] except he who returns to God with a (sound and) serene heart.

[90] And verily, Paradise will be brought near to the righteous; [91] and the Hellfire will be made manifest to those who were lost in grievous error. [92] And it will be said to them, "Where is now all that you used to worship; [93] besides God? Can they help you or help themselves (today)?"

[94] (Behold!) These false gods will be hurled into Hell together with those who were lost in grievous error; [95] and the troops of *Iblis* altogether. [96] In it, they will say in their mutual bickering and dispute; [97] "By God! We were certainly in clear error before; [98] when we equated you with the Lord of all the worlds. [99] And not have we been misguided except by the sinners. [100] So now we have no one to intercede for us; [101] nor a close friend (to help us). [102] And if we could only be given a chance to return to the world now, we shall certainly become believers!" *ᵃ*

[103] Behold! Indeed there is a sign (for people to ponder in this story) but most of them (do not care because they) refuse to believe. [104] And indeed your Lord, He is the Almighty, the Most Compassionate.

The Story of Noah: Judgment that Belongs to God

[105] The people of Noah denied their Messengers too. *ᵇ* [106] Behold! Their brother Noah said to them, "Will you not be mindful of God? [107] Indeed, I have been sent to you as a trusted Messenger. [108] So, be mindful of God and obey me. [109] No reward do I ask from you (for conveying this message). Indeed, my reward is only from the Lord of all the worlds; [110] So, be mindful

---

ᵃ See verse 23:99-100 and its footnote.
ᵇ Refer to footnote for verse 4:164.

of God and obey me."

¹¹¹ But they answered, "Why should we place our faith in you when you are only being followed by outcasts?" *ᵃ* ¹¹² Noah replied, "What knowledge do I have as to what they used to do (before they came to me)? ¹¹³ Verily, their reckoning rests with my Lord, if only you realize (and understand) this. ¹¹⁴ Hence, I shall not drive away any of those who profess to be believers. ¹¹⁵ Indeed, I am only a clear warner." ¹¹⁶ Said his people, "If you do not desist O Noah, you will surely be stoned (to death)."

¹¹⁷ And so Noah prayed, "My Lord! Indeed, my people have denied me. ¹¹⁸ So, lay wide open the truth between me and them, and save me together with the believers who are with me." ¹¹⁹ So We saved him and those with him in the fully laden ark; ¹²⁰ and We drowned the rest. ¹²¹ Behold! Indeed there is a sign (for people to ponder in this story) but most of them (do not care because they) refuse to believe. ¹²² And indeed your Lord, He is the Almighty, the Most Compassionate.

The Story of Hūd: How the Mighty Fall

¹²³ The people of ʿAād denied (God's) Messengers too. *ᵇ* ¹²⁴ (Behold,) when their brother Hūd said to them, "Will you not be mindful of God? ¹²⁵ Indeed, I have been sent to you as a trusted Messenger. ¹²⁶ So, be mindful of God and obey me. ¹²⁷ No reward do I ask from you (for conveying this message). Indeed, my reward is only from the Lord of all the worlds.

¹²⁸ Do you build (idolatrous) altars on every height just to amuse yourselves; ¹²⁹ and make fortresses for yourselves (hoping) that (death will never come near you so that) you can live forever? ¹³⁰ And why do you always

---

ᵃ A feature of contemporary civilization is that it marginalizes God and drives people away from Him into the arms of materialism and agnosticism. This lesson can be learned from this passage where the rich and strong among the people of Noah inflicted degrading and demeaning treatment on the poor and weak who they regard as the society's outcasts. See also verse 54:24. They also harshly rebuked Noah for accepting these folks as his followers by issuing a violent threat against him as mentioned in verse 116. It is obvious that discrimination and class distinction in society have been practiced since the dawn of human history. It is not surprising therefore, to find that it is the poor, the under-privileged, and the weak who are the first social groups that came out to support the Prophets and Messengers who gave them hope through the true teachings that were being conveyed. What they seek is justice and equality and the restoration of their dignity and self-pride. The same took place in Makkah during the time of Prophet Muhammad too. See verses 6:52-53.
ᵇ Refer to footnote for verse 4:164.

exercise your power (excessively) like cruel tyrants? [131] (You should) be mindful of God and obey me. [132] Be ever mindful of the One Who has given you knowledge (and taught you what you did not know before). [133] Indeed, He has (so amply) provided you with cattle and children; [134] and gardens and springs. [135] Verily, I fear for you the (dreadful) punishment of a mighty Day (if you continue to reject Him)."

[136] They answered, "It is all the same to us whether you try to advise us or not. (We shall still not believe you.) [137] What we practice is inherited from our forefathers; [138] and we should not be punished (for adhering to our tradition). [139] So they denied him, and We destroyed them subsequently. Behold! Indeed there is a sign (for people to ponder in this story) but most of them (do not care because they) refuse to believe. [140] And indeed your Lord, He is the Almighty, the Most Compassionate.

The Story of Saleh: A Blatant Challenge to God

[141] The people of Tsamud denied their Messengers too. [a] [142] (Behold,) when their brother Saleh said to them, [142] "Will you not be mindful of God? [143] Indeed, I have been sent to you as a trusted Messenger. [144] So, be mindful and obey me. [145] No reward do I ask from you (for conveying this message). Indeed, my reward is only from the Lord of all the worlds. [146] Do you think you will (always) be left secure here (to enjoy the pleasures of this world); [147] amidst these gardens and springs; [148] and fields, and these palm-trees with slender spathes; [149] and that you could (continue to) carve dwellings from the mountains with great skill? [150] (You should always) be mindful of God and obey me. [151] And do not obey the command of those who transgressed (God's limits). [152] They are the ones who spread corruption (and cause disorder) on earth instead of setting things right."

[153] They answered, "You are certainly one of those who are bewitched (and deluded). [154] Indeed, you are just an ordinary mortal like us. So bring to us a sign (of your Prophethood) if you speak the truth." [155] Saleh replied, "Here is a she-camel. She will have her drinking share, and you too will have your drinking share, each on an appointed day. [156] And do not touch her with the intention to harm, otherwise suffering will befall you on a mighty (dreadful) Day." [157] But they killed her and regretted what they did. [158] And then, punishment befell them afterwards. Behold! Indeed there is a sign (for people to ponder in this story) but most of them (do not care because they) refuse to believe. [159] And indeed your Lord, He is the Almighty, the Most Compassionate.

---

[a] Refer to footnote verse 4:164.

The Story of Lot: Perversion Leading to Ruin

[160] The people of Lot denied their Messengers too. *a* [161] (Behold,) when their brother Lot said to them; [161] "Will you not be mindful of God? [162] Indeed, I have been sent to you as a trusted Messenger. [163] So, be mindful of God and obey me. [164] No reward do I ask from you (for conveying this message). Indeed, my reward is only from the Lord of all the worlds. [165] Of all people, must you (lustfully) approach men; [166] and shun the wives that your Lord has created for you? You are indeed a people who have transgressed all bounds (of what is right)!"

[167] They answered, "O Lot! If you do not desist in trying to stop us, you will surely be driven out of here!" [168] Said Lot, "Indeed, I am utterly disgusted with your (despicable) behavior. [169] My Lord! Save me and my family from what they do." [170] So We saved him and his family; [171] except an old woman who was with those who remained behind. [172] Then We destroyed them all; [173] and rained down upon them a (devastating) shower (of stones). Evil indeed was the rain that fell upon those who were forewarned (but paid no heed). [174] Behold! Indeed there is a sign (for people to ponder in this story) but most of them (do not care because they) refuse to believe. [175] And indeed your Lord, He is the Almighty, the Most Compassionate.

The Story of Shu'aib: Fair Dealings for All

[176] The dwellers of Al-'Aikah denied their Messengers *b* too. [177] (Behold,) when their brother Shu'aib said to them, "Will you not be mindful of God? [178] Indeed, I have been sent to you as a trusted Messenger. [179] So, be mindful of God and obey me. [180] No reward do I ask from you (for conveying this message). Indeed, my reward is only from the Lord of all the worlds. [181] Always give full measure, and do not be among those who (unjustly) cause loss to others. [182] Weigh (truthfully) with scales that are upright (in all your dealings); [183] and do not deprive people of what is rightfully theirs nor act wickedly on earth by spreading corruption (and disorder); [184] and fear Him who has created you as well as the (countless) generations before you."

[185] They answered, "You are certainly one of those who are bewitched (and deluded). [186] And you are just an ordinary mortal like us (without any special power). In fact we think you must surely be a liar. [187] Make the fragments of the sky to fall down on us (now) if you speak the truth! [188] Answered Shu'aib, "My Lord knows fully well everything that you do (and

---

a Refer to footnote verse 4:164.
b Refer to footnote verse 4:164.

will requite you accordingly)." [189] But they denied him. And so they were seized with a terrible punishment on the day (the clouds came with deadly) dark shadows. It was really a torment of a mighty (dreadful) Day. [190] Behold! Indeed there is a sign (for people to ponder in this story) but most of them (do not care because they) refuse to believe. [191] And indeed your Lord, He is the Almighty, the Most Compassionate.

The Truth is Veiled from Those Immersed in Sin

[192] Most certainly, this Qur'an is a sign and revelation from the Lord of all the worlds; [193] brought down by the trustworthy Spirit; *a* [194] into your heart (O Muhammad) so that you may give warning; [195] in clear Arabic tongue. [196] The same message was indeed foretold in the revealed Scriptures of the former people. [197] Is it not enough proof for the Arab pagans that some learned men from the children of Israel recognized (the Qur'an's) truth (and accepted Muhammad's Prophethood and then fully submitted themselves to God)? *b*

[198] Had We revealed it to a non-Arab; [199] and he recited it to them, surely they would not believe in it at all. [200] This is how We caused this message to pass (unheeded) through the hearts of those who are lost in sin. [201] (As such,) they will not believe in Our message until they see the grievous punishment; [202] that will come upon them in a sudden when they least expected it. [203] And then they will plead, "Can we be given respite?" [204] So, do they still wish (to challenge) Us to hasten Our punishment?

[205] But have you considered that if We let them enjoy this life for some (extra) years; [206] and then the promised punishment suddenly falls upon them; [207] how will this (short lived) enjoyment benefit them?

---

a Angel Gabriel.
b Notable learned Jews of Medina in the lifetime of the Prophet who became Muslims are 'Abdullah ibn Salam and Ka'b ibn Malik. During the reign of 'Umar al-Khattab as the 2nd Caliph, Ka'b al-Ahbar the Yemenite was another learned Jew who became Muslim along with a number of his compatriots. In addition, there have been countless other Jews throughout the world who embraced Islam in the course of centuries. According to Muhammad Asad (i.e. a renowned Jewish Muslim exegete of the Qur'an) the reason why only learned Jews and not learned Christians are spoken of in this context lies in the fact that contrary to the Torah, which still exists albeit in a corrupted form, the original revelation granted to Jesus (i.e. the *Injeel*) has been lost and therefore cannot be cited in evidence of the basic identity of his teachings with those of the Qur'an.

Punishment Will Never Be Afflicted Before Warning

²⁰⁸ Never have We destroyed any community until we sent warners to them first; ²⁰⁹ to remind (what awaits them in the next life to come if they persist in their transgression), for We are never unjust (to anyone). ²¹⁰ (This divine revelation is such a reminder now) and Satan certainly plays no part in bringing it down; ²¹¹ for, neither does it suit their purpose, nor is it in their power (to impart it to man). ²¹² Indeed, they are even prevented from overhearing it!

²¹³ Hence, do not invoke any other god besides Almighty God or you find yourself among those who will suffer grievous punishment. ²¹⁴ And warn your closest kinsfolk (of this impending torment); ²¹⁵ and spread the wings (of your tenderness) over all the believers who follow you.

²¹⁶ But if they disobey you, then say, "I am not responsible for what you do". ²¹⁷ And (continue to) place your trust in the Almighty, the Most Compassionate; ²¹⁸ the One Who sees you when you rise (for prayer); ²¹⁹ and also sees your movements among your fellow worshippers. ²²⁰ Indeed, it is He alone who hears all, knows all.

The Companions of Satan

²²¹ (O people!) Shall I tell you upon whom does Satan and his evil troops descend? ²²² They descend upon every slandering (and lying) sinner; ²²³ who (readily lend their ears to falsehood and then freely) spread what they hear (without restraint). Indeed, most of them are (evil) liars!

²²⁴ And as for the poets, ^{*a*} only those who are misguided follow them. ²²⁵ Do you not see how they wander (aimlessly) in every valley; ²²⁶ claiming to do what they did not? ²²⁷ (Verily, most people are typically like this) except those who truly believe (in their Lord), do righteous deeds, always remember God, and (are not afraid to) defend themselves when they are wronged. And soon those wicked evildoers will know the (wretched) destiny that awaits them.

---

^{*a*} The Arab pagans regarded the Qur'an as as product of the Prophet's supposedly poetic mind because they refused to accept it as God's divine revelation. See verses 69:40-43.

27. An-Naml
[The Ants : 93 verses]

This is a Makkan chapter and is closely related to the one preceding it and the one following it in respect of themes and the period of revelation. In fact these three chapters - *Ash-Shu'arā', An-Naml* and *Al-Qasas* - were revealed consecutively during the mid-Makkan period just as how they are arranged in the Qur'an. Like the other Makkan chapters, this one also deals with monotheism, the Messengership of Muhammad, the truth of the Qu'ran as a scripture that was sent down by God; and of resurrection, judgment, reward and punishment. These themes are brought home by drawing attention to the various aspects of the wonderful creations of God and by a reference to some of the previous Prophets who all conveyed the same message, pointing out how God's retribution befell their disbelieving and disobedient peoples. In this context, the accounts of Prophets Moses, Saleh and Lot are briefly mentioned while those of Prophets David and Solomon are given in some detail. These two Prophets were special in the sense they were also kings at the same time who were graced by God with special favors and capabilities, such as being able to communicate with birds and other animals. Notwithstanding their high standing as kings, these two Prophets had faithfully delivered the message of truth to their people and also to their contemporary rulers and kings, especially so in the case of Solomon whose call to the truth to the Queen of Sheba had resulted in her humble submission to God. The chapter is named *An-Naml* or The Ants with reference to the incident of the warning given to a community of ants by its leader to quickly save themselves from being crushed by Prophet Solomon and his army that were approaching the valley where the ants lived, as mentioned in verse 18..

In the name of God, the Most Gracious, the Most Compassionate.

The Qur'an: A Definitive Description

¹ *Ṭa Sīn.* These are the (revealed) verses of the Qur'an, a Book that makes everything clear; ² (that gives) guidance and good news to those who truly believe (in the One and Only God); ³ those who are steadfast in prayer and regularly spend in charity, and those who believe in the Hereafter with utmost certainty.

⁴ As for those who do not believe in the Hereafter, We make their (sinful) deeds fair-seeming (and alluring). And so they wander blindly to and fro (thinking that they are on the right path). ⁵ Those are the ones who will have an evil punishment, and who in the next life to come will be the greatest losers. ⁶ And indeed you (O Muhammad), are surely receiving this Qur'an from the One who is All-Wise, the All-Knowing.

Dialogue Between God and Moses

⁷ (Now narrate to them the story of) Moses when he said to his family (while they were traveling in the desert at night), "I see a fire far away. I shall approach it to bring some news to you (so that we will be guided in our journey), or perhaps I could bring a burning torch for you to warm yourselves." ⁸ But when he reached it, a voice called out, "Blessed are all who are within (reach of) this fire and who are near it. And glory be to God (Who is free from all imperfections. He is indeed the) Lord of all the worlds."

⁹ "O Moses! Indeed, I Am God, the Almighty, the All-Wise." ¹⁰ (Then Moses was commanded), "Throw down your staff!" Then when he (threw it down, he) saw it moving like a serpent and fled with no thought of turning back. And God said, "O Moses! Do not fear. Indeed, My Messengers have nothing to fear in My presence"; ¹¹ nor should anyone who has done wrong, (repent) and strive to replace the wrong with good. Verily, I Am Most Forgiving, Most Compassionate."

¹² "Now place your hand (inside your shirt) over your bosom and it will come out shining white without blemish. These are among the nine signs that you will show Pharaoh and his people (as proof of your Prophethood). Indeed, they are a people who are defiantly disobedient."

¹³ And so, when Our enlightening signs were shown to them, they said, "This is clear sorcery!" ¹⁴ They knew within their souls that these signs were true. But in their wickedness and arrogance, they rejected the signs. So see what happened in the end to those who spread corruption (and disorder on earth).

Solomon and the Queen of Sheba

¹⁵ And verily, We gave David and Solomon knowledge (and insight), and both of them said, "All praise is due to God who has favored us above many of His believing servants." ¹⁶ (Subsequently,) Solomon succeeded David. And he said, "O people! We have been taught the language of birds and we have been given (a share) of everything. Indeed, this is a clear favor (and great privilege from God)."

¹⁷ (And so one day,) Solomon's subjects were assembled before him. They were among the Jinn, men, and birds; and they were led forth in orderly ranks. ¹⁸ And when they marched to a valley full of ants, one of them exclaimed, "O ants! Get into your homes quickly or you will be unknowingly crushed by Solomon and his troops (who are coming your way)!"

¹⁹ Thereupon Solomon who was amused at her words, smiled and prayed, "O my Lord! Inspire me, and grant me the power (and ability) to always be grateful for Your favors which You have bestowed on me and on my parents so that I shall (continue to) do righteous deeds that are pleasing to You. And include me, by Your grace, among Your righteous servants."

²⁰ And then he looked in vain for a particular kind of bird (among his subjects, who was missing from the assembly,) and said, "Why is it that I do not see the Hoopoe? Is he absent? ²¹ I shall surely punish him severely or even slaughter him unless he brings me a convincing excuse!" ²² But the Hoopoe was not long in coming. (And when he finally arrived,) he said, "I have just learnt something that is unknown to you, for I have come to you from (the land of) Sheba with news that is certain."

²³ "Verily, I found a woman there ruling the land, and God has favored her and her nation with all good things (in life). Indeed, she has a magnificent throne. ²⁴ But I found she and her people prostrating to the sun instead of God. Indeed, Satan has made their deeds fair-seeming (and attractive), thus turning them away from God's path. Hence, they receive no guidance. ²⁵ (Verily, Satan has misguided them) away from (worshipping and) prostrating to God - the One Who brings forth all that is hidden in the heavens and the earth, and knows everything that you conceal and reveal." ²⁶ God, there is no god except Him - the Lord of the Mighty Throne.

²⁷ And so Solomon said, "We shall see whether you speak the truth or you are a liar. ²⁸ Go with my letter and deliver it to them. Then turn away from them and see what is their response."

²⁹ When the Queen read Solomon's letter, she said, "O you nobles! A truly distinguished letter has been delivered to me. ³⁰ Behold! It is from Solomon, and it says, 'In the name of God, the Most Gracious, the Most Compassionate.' ³¹ 'Do not exalt yourselves against me. Instead, come to me in willing submission to the One and Only God.'"

³² She added, "O you nobles! Give me your opinion on this matter. Indeed, I would not decide upon such an important matter without your counsel." ³³ They replied, "We are indeed endowed with great strength and mighty prowess in war (and therefore can defend ourselves against Solomon); but the decision is yours. Consider then, what you wish to command (and we shall abide by it)."

³⁴ She replied, "Verily, whenever Kings invade a country, they (will surely) ruin it and turn the most honorable of its people into the most abject. Is this not what they will do? ³⁵ Hence, I shall send a gift to these people (to

subdue them) and then see what is the answer that our envoys will bring back from them."

³⁶ And so when the Queen's envoy came to Solomon (with the gifts), he said, "Is it wealth that you are offering me? Verily, what God has given me is much better than all that He has given you. Yet you rejoice in the little wealth that He has given you (and try to tempt me with this gift of yours). ³⁷ Go back to your people and (be well informed that) we shall certainly come to them with forces that they will not be able to match and resist. Indeed, we shall certainly oust them from the land in disgrace, and they will be utterly humbled (if they persist in being ungrateful to God)."

³⁸ Then Solomon turned to his people and said, "Which of you nobles can bring her throne here before they come to me in submission?" ³⁹ Said a strong one among the Jinn, "I shall bring it to you before you rise from your position. I am powerful enough to do it and worthy of trust (to perform the task)."

⁴⁰ But suddenly, someone (from among the men) with knowledge of the Scripture said, "Nay! I can bring her throne to you even before your eyes blink!" And when Solomon saw her throne appeared in front of him, he exclaimed, "This is truly an outcome of my Lord's favor to test me whether I am grateful or not. Verily, whoever is grateful, then it is for his own good. And whoever is ungrateful, then he should know that my Lord is indeed All-Sufficient, Most Noble." ⁴¹ And he continued, "Alter (the appearance of) her throne. Let us see whether or not she can recognize it."

⁴² And so, as soon as she arrived, she was asked, "Is your throne like this?" She answered, "It looks almost the same, (for it resembles mine in every aspect!" Thereupon, Solomon said to his nobles, "All praise is due to God) for giving us (divine) knowledge and faith which caused us to submit to Him long before she (witnessed this miraculous feat and became inclined to the truth). ⁴³ What she has been worshipping other than The One and Only Almighty God (since birth) has kept her away from the right path, for she comes from a nation of disbelieving people (who do not worship the true God and this has naturally shaped her erroneous belief)."

⁴⁴ After that, she was told, "Enter the palace." And as soon as she saw its court, she thought that she was entering into a pool of water; so she quickly bared (her legs up to) her shins. But Solomon said, "Behold! This is just a palace court that is smoothly paved with glass." Upon realizing this, she said, "O my Lord! I have indeed been unjust to my soul all this while (for not being able to discern the truth from falsehood even though Your signs have been made clear to everyone). Verily, I hereby submit myself to God, the Lord of all the worlds, with Solomon (as my witness)."

Plotting to Kill a Prophet

⁴⁵ And We had indeed sent to (the people of) Tsamud their brother Saleh, who said, "Worship God alone!" And suddenly, they broke into two quarrelling factions. ⁴⁶ He said, "O my people! Why do you seek to hasten evil instead of hoping for good? Why do you not seek God's forgiveness so that you may be graced (with His mercy)?"

⁴⁷ They answered, "(O Saleh!) Indeed, we augur bad omen and evil from you and your followers." But Saleh answered, "The evil you augur can come only from God (as a result of your own wicked deeds). You are a people who are actually being tested."

⁴⁸ And there were nine ring-leaders in the city who spread disorder in the land and never cared to rectify (their wicked deeds). ⁴⁹ They said, "Let us swear a mutual oath by God that We shall attack Saleh and his family at night. Then We shall say to his heir, 'We did not witness the destruction of his family, and we are indeed telling the truth.'" ⁵⁰ So they devised an evil scheme; and We too devised a plan while they were unaware.

⁵¹ Behold! See what happened to their scheme. Instead, it was We Who utterly destroyed them together with their people. ⁵² Their dwellings now lie (empty and) ruined because of the injustice that they committed. Indeed, there is truly a sign (and lesson) in this for people of knowledge. ⁵³ And We saved those who believed and kept their duty to Us diligently.

Perversion Leading to Ruin

⁵⁴ And (We saved) Lot too, after he said to his people, "How could you commit this (perverted) immoral act while you know (for a fact that it is against the law of nature)? ⁵⁵ Why do you approach men with lust instead of women? Nay! You are indeed a people who are grossly foolish (and have been misled far away from the truth because you deliberately chose lust as the object of your worship)."

⁵⁶ But the answer of his people was, "Expel Lot and his followers from your town! Indeed, they think they are so pure (and holy)." ⁵⁷ So We saved him and his family, except his (defiant) wife whom We made her stay behind. ⁵⁸ And then We rained down on them a shower (of devastating stones). Evil indeed is such rain which fell on those who have been forewarned (but remained stubbornly defiant). ⁵⁹ Say, "All praise is due to God, and peace be upon His servants whom He has chosen. Is God not far better than all those that they associate Him with?"

Of God's Own Making

[60] Who can create the heavens and the earth and send down (life-giving) water for you from the sky (other than God)? Indeed, this is how We make gardens of beauty and delight to grow, whereas it is not in your power to cause even a single tree to grow (without Our permission). Could there be any divine power other than Almighty God (Who single-handedly set the entire universe's law of nature in harmony)? Nay! They (who think so) are people who have surely swerved (from the truth).

[61] Or who made the earth a stable settlement for living things and caused rivers to flow in its midst? Who set firm mountains on it and made a barrier between the two flowing bodies of seas? Could there be any divine power other than Almighty God? Nay! Most of them (who think so) do not know (what they are saying).

[62] Or who hears the cry of a distressed soul when it calls out to Him? Who relieves the affliction (that caused the distress)? And who makes you inherit the earth (as a place to live during your temporary stay on it)? Could there be any divine power other than Almighty God? How little do you take notice and reflect!

[63] Or who guides you in the midst of the deep darkness of land and sea? And who sends forth the winds as good news in advance of His coming grace (to send down rain)? Could there be any divine power other than Almighty God? Sublimely exalted is God above all those that they associate with Him!

[64] Or who originates the creation (of all life) and then repeats it? And who is it that provides you (with sustenance for your livelihood on earth) from the heavens and the earth? Could there be any divine power other than Almighty God? Say (to them), "Bring forth your proof if you speak the truth!" [a]

---

[a] The disbelievers mock God's promise of resurrection and outrightly deny His existence. The rebuttal to this is presented in verses 60-64 and the Prophet was instructed to use this argument to bring his people face to face with the reality of the Hereafter. In the modern era, the denial of God can be considered as a by-product of arrogance and fanciful theorization which cannot be accredited with any logic or intellectual respectability. In essence, its denial is a syndrome that is not based on sound philosophy or accurate science. Instead, it is a rehash of corrupt ancient pagan beliefs that take form in scientific materialism today which does not know how to deal with the realm of the unseen. Its danger lies in the fact that it has come to be considered as true science based on seeming evidence and tangible proof whereas it is not. On the contrary, it is nothing but a bunch of glamorous theories that sound sophisticated but keep going around in circles in trying to figure out how the entire

⁶⁵ Say (further), "No one in the heavens and the earth has any knowledge of the unseen except God. And those who disbelieve do not have any clue when they will be resurrected." ⁶⁶ In fact, (the total sum of) their knowledge stops short of comprehending the Hereafter. Verily, that is because they are in doubt of it and they are indeed blind (to the truth).

⁶⁷ And those who reject the truth say, "What! Are you saying that when we and our forefathers have become soil (and dust), We shall be brought back to life again?" ⁶⁸ "Indeed, the same was promised to us and our forefathers before, (but nothing has happened yet so far). Surely this is nothing but empty tales of ancient times!" ⁶⁹ Say to them, "Travel through the land and see how (terrible) was the end of the sinners." ⁷⁰ So do not be in distress and grieve over them because of what they plot (against you, O Prophet).

⁷¹ They ask (you mockingly), "When will this promise be fulfilled if what you say is true?" ⁷² Answer (them), "Perhaps what you so hastily demand has already drawn close to you." ⁷³ Your Lord is indeed most bountiful to people but most of them are (simply) ungrateful. ⁷⁴ And indeed, your Lord surely knows what they conceal in their hearts and what they declare openly. ⁷⁵ There is nothing hidden in the heavens and the earth except it is recorded in a clear book (with Him).

⁷⁶ Behold! This Qur'an (also) explains to the children of Israel about the many things that they are in disagreement among themselves. ⁷⁷ And indeed, the Qur'an is truly a guidance and grace (from God) for those who (want to) believe (in the truth). ⁷⁸ Verily, your Lord will judge between them in His

---

universe and life came into existence by stubbornly refusing to acknowledge the role of God, the Ultimate Creator of all things. This thinking is the underlying cause behind today's global malaise which is leading humanity to disaster. See verse 13:1, 45:5-6 and their footnotes. Rightfully, all researches, especially the scientific ones, must be based on the concept of acknowledging God's existence first, as the Ultimate Creator of all things (verses 96:1-5) Who has decreed a perfect set of universal laws in place to govern the operations of the entire universe that He has created together with all that it contains with utmost precision. Science can always explain how things work but it cannot always explain why things exist. Only the Ultimate Creator has the answer for this. Sufficient is for us to believe in full conviction that they are all brought into existence for a purpose (verse 3:191) that is known to Him alone if scientific answers and explanations could still not be found yet. We should be mindful that the Prophet's mission was to give the world a civilization that is propelled by the power of science with a strong faith in God that is built on authentic revelation instead of conjectures, where the behavior of societies are shaped by the belief in the Hereafter and its peoples are taught and prepared to face accountability in the next life. See also verse 28:77.

wisdom; for He alone is Almighty, All-Knowing. ⁷⁹ So, place your trust in God (O Prophet)! Indeed, you are upon (the path of) clear truth.

⁸⁰ Verily, you cannot make the dead hear (and take heed of your advice), nor can you make the deaf hear your call when they turn their backs away from you in retreat; ⁸¹ nor can you also guide the blind away from their error (if they refuse guidance). Instead, only those who believe in Our signs and revelations will listen (to the message that you deliver); and they are the ones who willfully submit themselves to Us (in obedience). ⁸² And when the word of truth is fulfilled ^{*a*} against those who choose to be deaf and blind, We shall bring forth for them a creature out of the earth to speak to them ^{*b*} (in a language of pain and suffering) because (by that time, most) people would not believe and have faith in Our signs and revelations (anymore).

The Day of Gathering

⁸³ And then, on the Day (of Judgment), We shall gather from every community a large group of people who denied Our revelations, and they will be grouped (according to the gravity of their sins); ⁸⁴ until when they have all arrived, their Lord will ask, "Did you deny (and ignore) My messages without making proper attempt to understand them? So what have you been doing then?" ⁸⁵ And the promise of torment will be fulfilled against them in the face of all the injustice that they had committed, and they will not be able to utter a single word of excuse.

⁸⁶ Are they not aware that it is We Who made the night for them to rest in it and the day bright (for them to go about the earth seeking Our provision)? Indeed there are sure signs in this for those who (want to) believe (in the truth).

⁸⁷ And (beware of) the Day when the trumpet (of resurrection) will be

---

^{*a*} An allusion to the approach of the Last Hour.
^{*b*} Abdullah Yusuf Ali and Muhammad Asad interpret "the creature that is brought forth from the earth" as a metaphor of gross materialism. It is man's outlook on life which promotes a hegemony of gross materialism that dominates a misguided and rapidly degenerating world. Beneath the material achievement and modernity that would evidently prevail in almost all societies, mankind on the other hand would be experiencing a grievous spiritual suffering that is void of clear purpose and direction. Hence, the emergence of this "creature" is a clear sign of the world coming close to its Last Hour, intensifying the self-inflicted spiritual torment that man has no escape from. All these serve as a clear precursor to his imminent destruction, both in this life and in the life to come, brought about by his misguided or lack of belief and faith in God.

sounded. Everyone in the heavens and the earth will be stricken with terror, except those whom God wills (to exempt). Everyone will (be raised from their graves and) come to Him in utter humility.

⁸⁸ You see the mountains, thinking they are firmly fixed. But they are actually in motion just like the clouds *ᵃ* (and will all crumble to dust on that mighty dreadful Day). Such is (the artistry of) God Who perfected all things (and has also fixed the time for their end). Indeed, (be mindful that) He is fully aware of all that you do (because His infinite knowledge encompasses everything).

⁸⁹ (And so,) whoever comes to Him with good deeds, his reward will be far better than the value of the deeds he brings forth. Such people will be safe from the terror of that (final) Day; ⁹⁰ whereas those who come with evil deeds will have their faces thrust into the Fire (and be told), "Are you not being (fairly) requited now for what you have done (in your life)?"

⁹¹ (Tell them O Prophet,) "Verily, I am commanded only to worship the Lord of this city *ᵇ* Who has made it sacred. To Him belongs everything (in the heavens and the earth). And I am commanded to be of those who fully submit to God; ⁹² and to also recite the Qur'an (and convey its message to you clearly)." So whoever chooses to follow the right path, does so for his own benefit. And whoever chooses to go astray, then tell him, "I am only a plain warner."

⁹³ And say, "All praise is due to God (alone)! In time, He will make you see (the truth of) His signs and revelations, and you will know them (for what they really are)." And your Lord is never once unaware of everything that you do.

ᵃ In the 1950s, geologists discovered that the lateral relative movements of tectonic plates where mountains sit on are actually in motion even though we see them as firmly planted in the ground. Their movements typically vary from 0 to 100mm annually. The usage of the expression "they are actually in motion just as the clouds" in the passage here is not to be understood literally, but rather metaphorically, to stress on the fact that even though the foundation of the mountains are absolutely firm, they are in reality not static as in the case of some very big clouds that may sometimes seem static to our eyes but are actually in motion, albeit very slowly. Who could have ever known about this scientific fact in the 7ᵗʰ century?
ᵇ Makkah.

28. Al-Qaṣaṣ
[The Stories : 88 verses]

This is also a Makkan chapter which belongs to the group of the two previous chapters in respect of both the period of revelation and themes dealing mainly with monotheism, the Messengership of Prophet Muhammad, and resurrection. In fact, this chapter supplements and complements the two previous chapters. It is called *Al-Qasas* or The Stories with main reference to Prophet Moses and his encounter with Pharaoh which is narrated in greater detail in this chapter compared to its mention in other chapters.

In the name of God, the Most Gracious, the Most Compassionate.

The Story of Moses

¹ *Ṭa Sīn Mīm.* ² These are the (revealed) verses of the clear Book. ³ We shall narrate to you the story of Moses and Pharaoh to set out the truth for those who believe (in Almighty God and in the next life to come).

⁴ Indeed, Pharaoh elevated himself (high and mighty) in the land (of Egypt) and divided its people into groups. One of the groups he deemed its people utterly low as outcasts and set out to oppress (and impoverish them). So he killed their sons and kept their women alive. He was truly one of those who spread corruption (and disorder on earth). ⁵ But it was Our will to bestow Our favor upon those who were oppressed in the land and to make them as forerunners (in faith), and to also make them heirs (to Pharaoh's glory); ⁶ and to establish them securely on earth. Through them, We willed to show Pharaoh, Haman, ᵃ and their soldiers (the fulfillment of) what they feared most. ᵇ

⁷ And (so when Moses was born,) We inspired his mother, "Suckle him (for a while); and if you are afraid for his life, then cast him in the river and do not fear nor grieve (for his safety). We shall restore him to you and make him one of Our Messengers." ⁸ (And then,) some members of Pharaoh's household (found and) picked him up; completely unaware that he would one day become their enemy and a cause for grief. Indeed, Pharaoh, Haman and their soldiers were (great) sinners (and We have brought Moses to them as their

---

ᵃ Haman was Pharaoh's chief architect during the during the time of Moses.
ᵇ The fuldillment of Pharaoh's dream that his power and rule would come to an end at the hands of a boy from the children of Israel.

trial). ⁹ And so, Pharaoh's wife said, "This child is a joy and comfort to my eyes and yours! Do not kill him, for he may be of use to us, or we may adopt him as a son." Verily, they had no inkling (of what would happen in future).

¹⁰ In the meantime, the heart of Moses' mother was empty (and sorely distressed for the loss of her son). Had We not endowed her heart with enough strength to keep alive her faith (in Our promise), she would have disclosed all about him (to Pharaoh's household in her attempt to get him back). ¹¹ So she said to his sister, "Follow (and keep an eye on) him"; and the girl watched him from a distance, while they who had taken him were not aware of it.

¹² Right from the very beginning, We caused him to refuse being suckled by (the Egyptian) wet-nurses. (And when his sister came to know of this,) she offered them, "Shall I direct you to a family who might raise him up for you and take good care of him?" ¹³ Thus We restored him to his mother so that her eyes would be comforted and not grieve anymore, and realize that the promise of God is always true - even though most people do not know. ¹⁴ And when he reached maturity and attained full strength, We bestowed upon him wisdom and knowledge. This is how We reward those who excel in good deeds

¹⁵ And (so one day,) he entered the city at a time when its people were unaware (of his presence). He found there two men fighting, one from his own people *ᵃ* and the other of his enemy. And the one from his own people cried out to him for help against the one from his enemy, whereupon Moses struck him down with his fist and (accidentally) killed him. He exclaimed, "This is of Satan's doing! Indeed, he is an open foe clearly seeking to lead man astray." ¹⁶ He said, "My Lord! Indeed, I have wronged my soul, so forgive me." Then God forgave him. Indeed, He is the Most Forgiving, the Most Compassionate. ¹⁷ He said, "My Lord! By the favors (and good things) that You have blessed me with, (protect me) from ever being a helper to those who sin (and disobey You)."

¹⁸ Then when he was walking in the city again next morning, being fearful and vigilant, behold! The one who sought his help the previous day cried out to him again for help. Moses said to him, "Indeed you are surely someone who is clearly misguided!" ¹⁹ And so when he was about to strike the one who was their (common) enemy, the latter exclaimed, "O Moses! Do you want to kill me just like you killed a man yesterday? Indeed, you seem set to become a tyrant on earth instead of someone who wants to set things right."

²⁰ Then a man came running from the farthest end of the city and said, "O Moses! (I hear that) the chieftains are discussing to kill you (for the crime you

---

ᵃ An Israelite.

committed yesterday). So leave (this city quickly if you wish to be safe). Indeed, I am giving you a sincere advice." [21] So he left the city in fear and with vigilance. He prayed, "My Lord! Save me from these wicked people."

[22] As he made his way towards Madyan, he said, "Hopefully my Lord will guide me to the right path." [23] When he arrived at the wells of Madyan, he found there a group of people drawing water (for their herds and flocks), and at some distance from them he found two women who were holding back (their flock). He asked them, "What is the matter with both of you?" They said, "We cannot water our animals until the herdsmen drive away their flock (because it is improper for us to be in their company). Our father is a very old man (who is too weak to carry out this task)." [24] So he watered (their flock) for them and then he went back into the shade and prayed, "My Lord! Indeed, I am in dire need of whatever good You may send down to me."

[25] (Not long after that,) one of the two women came to him, walking shyly. She said, "Indeed, my father invites you to (come over) so that he may reward you for having watered (our flock) for us." So when Moses came to him and told him his story (of why he fled Egypt), the old man said, "Have no fear. You are now safe from those unjust (and wicked) people." [26] Then one of the women said, "O my father! Hire him (to work for us). Indeed, the best person that you could hire is one who is strong and trustworthy." [27] The father replied, "I shall give you one of these two daughters of mine in marriage on condition and understanding that you will remain in my service for (at least) eight years. But if you complete ten, it will be of your own choice. I do not wish to impose any hardship on you and God willing, you will find me a righteous man (who will not dishonor my word)." [28] Moses answered, "This is agreed between me and you. Whichever of the two terms I fulfill, I trust I shall not be wronged. Verily, God is witness over what we say."

[29] And so, Moses fulfilled the term. And then when he was traveling with his family (in the desert one night on his return to Egypt), he saw a fire on the slope of Mount (Sinai). He said to his family, "Stay here! Indeed, I see a fire. Perhaps I might be able to bring for you some information or a burning wood from the fire so that you may warm yourselves." [30] But when he came close to it, a call was sounded from the right-side of the valley's edge out of the tree (that was burning) on its blessed ground, "O Moses! Verily, I am God - the Lord of all the worlds!"

[31] (And Moses was told,) "Throw down your staff!" Then when he threw it down and saw it moving like a serpent, he turned around and fled (in fear), with no thought of turning back. (Then God spoke to him again,) "O Moses! Come back and have no fear. Indeed, you are of those who are safe (and unharmed). [32] Now place your hand (inside your shirt) that covers your bosom,

and it will come out shining white without blemish. Then draw your arm close to your side to allay your fear. Behold! These are two proofs from your Lord (for you to bring) to Pharaoh and his chieftains. They are indeed a group of people who are defiantly disobedient (and need to be warned)."

³³ Said Moses, "My Lord! Indeed, I have killed one of their men (before this). I fear that they will (retaliate and) kill me now. ³⁴ (Verily,) my brother Aaron is more eloquent than me. So send him with me as a helper so that he (can assist me to convey Your message) and verify the truth of my speech, for I fear that they will accuse me of lying." ³⁵ Said God, "Indeed, We shall strengthen you with your brother's help (just as you have asked for), and We shall grant you both with (power and) authority so that they will not be able to harm you. By virtue of the (miraculous) signs that We send you with, you and those who follow you will prevail."

³⁶ But as soon as Moses came to them with Our clear signs, they said, "All this is nothing but sorcery devised by man! Never have we heard of anything like this during our forefathers' time." ³⁷ Moses replied, "My Lord knows best who comes with guidance from Him and will inherit the ultimate home (of everlasting delight in the Hereafter). Those who are cruel and commit injustice will not be successful." ³⁸ And Pharaoh said, "O leaders of my people! I do not know if there is any god for you other than me. Now kindle me a fire (for baking bricks of clay) O Haman, then build me a lofty tower so that I can (climb to) look for the God of Moses. I think he must surely be a (great) liar!"

³⁹ Verily, Pharaoh and his people behaved arrogantly on earth without any right, thinking that they will never return to Us. ⁴⁰ And so We seized him and his armies and cast them all in the sea. Just look at what happened in the end to those wicked evildoers! ⁴¹ (Verily,) We set them up as (evil) leaders inviting others to the Fire (of Hell. Behold!) They will not receive any help on the Day of Resurrection. ⁴² And We have also caused a curse to follow them in this world. On the Day of Resurrection, they will be among those who are truly despised.

A Prophet Like Moses

⁴³ And so, after We had destroyed those earlier generations, We gave Moses the Book [a] providing insight for mankind as guidance and grace, so that they will reflect and remember (how grateful they should be to God for the favors that He has bestowed upon them).

---

[a] The Torah.

44 (O Prophet!) You were certainly not present on the western side (of the mountain) when We decreed the commandments to Moses, nor were you among those who (witnessed the events). **45** But (between them and you,) We brought into being many generations and prolonged their span of life. And neither did you dwell among the people of Madyan to convey Our messages to them. The fact is, We have always been sending Our Messengers (to mankind so that they will be rightly guided to Our path). **46** And neither were you present on the slope of Mount (Sinai) when We called out (to Moses. And now, you too have been sent) as an act of your Lord's grace to warn people to whom no warner has come before you, so that they would think (and reflect about their Lord and the true purpose of their creation and existence on earth). **47** Otherwise, if some calamity were to befall them because of their own misdeeds (and injustice), surely they would say, "Our Lord! Why did you not send a Messenger to us so that we could (be guided to follow Your revelations and) become believers?"

48 But when the truth has come to them from Us (now), they say, "Why is Muhammad not given (miracles) like those given to Moses (earlier)?" Do they not (realize that they are also) rejecting the truth that was given to Moses? They say (of the Torah and the Qur'an now, "These are just) two examples of delusion, seemingly in support of each other." And they add, "Behold! We refuse to accept any of them as true!" **49** Say to them (O Prophet), "If this is what you say, then bring another divine Book from God which offers better guidance than either of these two (and I shall follow it) if what you say is true!"

50 But if they do not respond to you, then know that they are only following their (misguided conjectures and) lusts. Who could be more astray than the one who follows his own lust without guidance from God? Indeed, God does not guide those who are unjust. **51** Verily, We have conveyed Our word to them (over and over again) for them to take heed (but they refused).

The Truth Clear for All

52 (And there are some among) those to whom the Scriptures were given before this, (recognize the truth and) believe in this Qur'an. **53** And when it is recited to them, they say, "We believe in it and know it is the truth from our Lord. Indeed, even before this, we have submitted ourselves to Him." *ᵃ*

54 These are the ones who will be given their reward twice for being patient in adversity, for repelling evil with good, and for spending in charity

---

ᵃ See verse 26:197 and its footnote.

out of what We have provided for them. ⁵⁵ And when they hear vain talk, they turn away from it and say, "For us are our deeds and for you are your deeds. Peace be upon you! We do not seek (and desire the way of) the ignorant."

⁵⁶ (O Prophet!) Indeed, you cannot (force nor) grant guidance to whomsoever you love to the truth.^{*a*} Instead, it is God Who guides whomsoever He wills (that opens his heart to Him). And only He knows best who will come to guidance. ⁵⁷ Those who do not wish to be guided say, "(We are afraid that) if we go along with you and accept your guidance, We shall be driven out from our land." But have We not established a safe sanctuary (in Makkah) for them, where all kinds of fruits are brought as provision from Us? But most of them are ignorant (of this).

⁵⁸ And how many towns that once flourished in their wealth and means of livelihood have We destroyed? Just see their dwellings today. Only a few of which they left behind are being inhabited. In the end, it is We alone Who shall inherit everything. ⁵⁹ Verily, your Lord would never destroy a community without first sending a Messenger to its main city who would recite and convey Our verses (of truth) to its people. And never would We destroy a community unless its people persisted in committing injustice (and wrongdoings despite Our stern warnings). ⁶⁰ And (remember that) whatever you are given now is only the embellishment for the passing enjoyment of life in this fleeting world, whereas what is with God (in the next life) is far better and everlasting. Will you not use common sense (and ponder about this)?

⁶¹ Then, is he to whom We have given a goodly promise which he will see fulfilled (on the Day when he is resurrected), same as the one whom We have provided all the enjoyments of this worldly life but will find himself among those brought to Us on the Day of Resurrection (in full of fear)?

⁶² On that Day, He will call the ones (who stubbornly rejected the truth) and ask, "Where are now those whom you claim to be My partners?" ⁶³ And when the (leaders among the evildoers whom the) verdict will be passed

---

^{*a*} According to several well-authenticated traditions, this verse relates to the Prophet's inability to persuade his dying uncle - Abu Talib, whom he loved dearly and who had loved and protected him throughout his life, to renounce the pagan beliefs of his ancestors and to profess faith in God's oneness. Influenced by some Makkan chieftains at his deathbed, Abu Talib died professing, in his own words, "the creed of Abdul Muttalib" (Sahih Bukhari, No. 1360). However, the Qur'anic statement "you cannot guide whoever you love to the truth" has undoubtedly a timeless message as well. It stresses the inadequacy of all human endeavors to "convert" any other person, however loving and loved, to Islam, or to prevent him from going astray and falling into error, unless that person wills to be guided by God's grace.

against them are brought to God, they will say, "Our Lord! we had (unintentionally) led these people to error just as we were in error. We plead innocence before You (of all blame because we had never forced them to follow us). Moreover, it was not us that they worshipped. (Instead, it was their own lusts that they worshipped.)" ⁶⁴ (And then) they will be told, "Call on all those whom you used to associate with Me (to help you in this predicament now!)" They will call out to their false gods but will not receive any response. Instead, they will see the suffering that awaits them and wish that they had accepted their Messengers guidance (when they had the chance earlier).

⁶⁵ On that Day, He will call upon them and ask, "What did you answer My Messengers (when they conveyed My message to you)?" ⁶⁶ They will be so confounded and not be able to think of any reply, nor will they ask one another (for help). ⁶⁷ As for him who (turned to God and) repented in this life, became a believer and did righteous deeds, then he may hope to be among those who will (be graced with God's mercy and) attain victory on that Day.

⁶⁸ Your Lord creates whatever He wills and chooses (for His tasks whomsoever He wills). It is not for anyone else to make the choice (and decision in this matter). Glory be to God (Who is free from all imperfections) and exalted is He above all that they associate with Him as partners. ⁶⁹ Your Lord (certainly) knows everything their hearts conceal and bring out in the open. ⁷⁰ And He is God; there is no (other) god but He. To Him alone is due all praise from the beginning until the end (of time), and with Him rests all judgment. And only to Him will you all be (finally) returned.

⁷¹ Say (to them O Prophet), "Have you considered that if God were to make the night endless over you without a break until the Day of Resurrection, is there any god other than Almighty God that could bring you light? Will you not then listen (to the truth that is being conveyed to you)?" ⁷² Say (further), "Have you (also) considered if God were to make the day endless over you without a break until the Day of Resurrection, is there any god other than Almighty God that could bring you night for you to rest? Will you not then see (the truth in the divine signs that God has presented for people to ponder)?"

⁷³ It is out of His grace that He has made for you the night and the day so that you may rest during the night and seek (your livelihood from) His bounty during the day. Why are you not grateful (to Him then)? ⁷⁴ And indeed on the Day of Resurrection, He will call those (who defied Him) and ask, "Where now are those whom you alleged to be My partners?" ⁷⁵ And then We shall call a witness from every community and say to them, "Produce the evidence (for your claim)!" At that time, all their false inventions will abandon them and they will finally know that truth belongs to God alone.

The Story of Korah, the Ingrate

⁷⁶ Indeed, Korah *ᵃ* was from the people of Moses but he (arrogantly exalted himself above his people and) treated them unjustly. We granted him such treasures that even the keys (to his treasure-chests) alone would burden a group of strong men (to carry. When his people saw his arrogance,) they advised him, "You should not gloat (O Korah)! Verily, God does not like those who gloat (in arrogance). ⁷⁷ Rather, seek the good of the life to come by means of what God has granted you without forgetting your rightful share in this world. *ᵇ* Do good (and be generous) to others as God has been good (and generous) to you. Do not spread corruption (and cause disorder) on earth. God does not love those who are (wicked and) corrupt."

⁷⁸ But Korah retorted, "Verily, I have been given this wealth only because of the knowledge that I possess (and my cleverness." *ᶜ* But if this was indeed true, then why) did he not know that many generations before him that were mightier in strength and greater in their accumulation (of wealth) were

---

ᵃ *Qarun* in Arabic.
ᵇ Islam's fundamental paradigm of life is its emphasis on the inescapable death and the ensuing afterlife that is eternal in nature, not on the world's temporal nature that is deceiving. No one gets to live in this world forever. Hence, man is constantly reminded to make the necessary preparation to face this inevitable certainty by striving hard to purify his *fitrah* (verse 91:9) and attain *Taqwa* (verse 2:183) through establishing an excellent relationship with his Creator and also with fellow humans concurrently (verse 3:112). By no means does Islam forbid people from working hard to become wealthy. Otherwise, the *ummah* will be weak and there will be no one to ease the hardship of the poor and destitute. Be wealthy and use wealth as a means to seek God's pleasure instead of incurring His displeasure. The evil is when one goes overboard with excessive love for this world that will corrupt and infect his soul with the *Al-Wahn* disease (verses 102:1-2) leading him to commit evil and injustice out of his insatiable greed, and then causing corruption and disorder to prevail on earth. The following *hadith* complements the message of this verse : Ibn Umar reported that the Messenger of God (peace be upon him) said, "Be in this world as if you were a stranger or a traveler along a path." [Sahih Bukhari, no. 6416]. A traveler should only take what is sufficient for him to sustain during his journey rather than greedily amass and hoard the things his lust desires that he sees along the journey. Unfortunately, most people behave as if they will live in this world forever and become obsessed with amassing wealth as if this will secure them immortality (verses 104:2-3). They end up being oblivious to the reckoning that they will face on Judgment Day. The ultimate goal should be to attain *Taqwa*. Only those who can successfully restrain themselves from indulging in their vain desires and lusts will be able to attain *Taqwa* and emerge victorious (verse 79:40-41).
ᶜ See verses 96:6-7

completely destroyed by God? Verily, such sinners (like Korah) will not be immediately called to account for their sins. (Instead, they are given respite until an appointed time).

⁷⁹ And so he went forth to his people in all his pomp and grandeur. Those who cared only for the life of this world said in envy, "Oh, if only we could also have like what Korah has been given! He is certainly a man of great fortune!" ⁸⁰ But those who were endowed with true knowledge (and insight) said, "Woe to you! Verily, God's reward is far better for whoever that believes (in Him) and does righteous deeds. But none can ever achieve this blessing except those who endure (His trials) with patience."

⁸¹ In the end, We caused the earth to swallow Korah together with his home. There was no one to help him other than God, nor was he able to save himself. ⁸² And so the same people who envied him for his position the day before, began to (realize and) say, "Alas! (We forgot that) it is indeed God Who extends the provision to whomsoever He wills and restricts it from whomsoever He wills among His servants. Had God not been gracious to us, He could have caused the earth to swallow us too. Alas! (We forgot that) those who refuse to accept the truth will never attain true success."

The Ultimate Return

⁸³ As for the excellent home in the next life, We reserve it for those who seek neither superiority, nor go about spreading corruption on earth. Indeed, the ultimate good is only for those who are ever mindful of God. ⁸⁴ Whoever comes to Him with a good deed will be given a far better reward; and whoever comes with an evil deed will be requited only to the extent of his misdeeds.

⁸⁵ (O Prophet!) Verily, He Who has ordained upon you this Qur'an (to be conveyed to mankind) will surely bring you back to the (best) place of return (in the Hereafter). So say (to the disbelievers), "My Lord knows best who is rightly guided and who is obviously lost in error." ⁸⁶ You had never expected that this Book would be sent to you. Yet it is revealed to you by the grace of your Lord. Hence, do not take side and be a helper to those who reject the truth. ⁸⁷ Let no one turn you away from God's revelations that have been sent down to you. Invite people to your Lord (with knowledge, wisdom and patience), and be not of those who associate partners with God.

⁸⁸ So, invoke no other (false) god besides God (the Almighty), for there is no god except Him alone. Everything, except (Him and) His countenance, will perish (in the end). To Him alone rests all judgment and only to Him will you all be (finally) returned.

29. Al-'Ankabūt
[The Spider : 69 verses]

This is another mid-Makkan period chapter that deals with the themes of monotheism, resurrection, judgment, reward and punishment. The main emphasis of this chapter is in reiterating that all God's Prophets brought the same message of monotheism and complete submission to God and that faith entailed the undergoing of tests and trials, especially in an environment of disbelief and polytheism. All the previous Prophets and their followers had to undergo such tests and trials and suffered opposition, enmity, oppression and persecution for the sake of faith. Such was also the case with Prophet Muhammad and his followers, especially during the Makkan period. Belief or faith is not just a matter of assertion, but very much proven by conduct and practice as emphatically stated in verse 2 which reads : "Do people think that just by their mere saying, "We are believers", they will be left alone without being put to test?" In this context, reference is made also to the conduct of the opponents of truth such as the peoples of 'Aād and Tsamud, and individuals like Korah and Haman who are specifically mentoned in this chapter, and how they were dealt with by God. It is then emphasized in verses 47-49 that the Qur'an, which was conveyed by Prophet Muhammad to his people, was clearly sent down by God and is impossible for it to have been composed by the Prophet himself because he could neither read nor write. The chapter is named *Al-'Ankabūt* or The Spider with reference to the comparison made in verse 41 that the idolaters' taking of false gods for worship and invocation is as futile and frail as the spider taking its house in the form of a web which is the weakest structure for protection.

In the name of God, the Most Gracious, the Most Compassionate.

The Inevitable Test

1 *Alif Lām Mīm.* ² Do people think that just by their mere saying, "We are believers", they will be left alone without being put to test? ³ Indeed, We (shall surely test them just as We) have tested those who lived before them. Most certainly, God will make evident those who are truthful and those who are liars. ⁴ Or do those who do evil deeds think they can escape Us? Bad indeed is their judgment!

⁵ Whoever looks forward to the meeting with God (on the Day of Resurrection, then let him be ready for it. Verily,) the end that God has set (for everyone) is sure to come. Indeed, He alone hears all, knows all. ⁶ Hence, whoever strives (hard in God's cause) do so for the benefit of his own soul. Indeed, God is (completely) free of any need from all His creations. ⁷ As for those who believe and do righteous deeds, We shall most certainly erase and

remove (the sins of their) bad deeds and reward them for their best actions.

⁸ And (among the best of righteous deeds that) We have commanded man is to be good and kind to his parents. But if they strive to make you associate Me with something which you have no firm knowledge of, then do not obey them (but decline them politely instead). Verily, it is to Me that you will all be returned. Then, I shall let you know (and hold you accountable for) everything that you have done. ⁹ For all those who believe (in God) and do righteous deeds, We shall most certainly count them among the righteous (in this world and in the life to come).

¹⁰ (Verily,) among people there are those who say, "We believe in God," yet when they are made to suffer in God's cause, they consider the persecution at the hands of man as (if it were) God's punishment (and so they shift their obedience from God to man instead). But if help comes (in the form of victory) from your Lord, (they want a share of this and would shamelessly) say, "(O Muhammad!) Indeed, we have always been on your side. (So share with us what you gained from the victory)." Have they forgotten that God is fully aware of what is in the heart of every creature? ¹¹ And God will surely make evident those who truly believe in Him and those who are hypocrites.

¹² Those who are devoid of faith say to the believers, "Follow our way, and we shall bear (the burden of) your sins." But never will they be able to do this (because no one can ever have their sins absolved by others except only by God alone). They are liars indeed. ¹³ And most certainly will they have to bear the burden of their own sins together with the sins of those who they have misled in addition to their own sins. And on the Day of Resurrection, they will surely be called to account for all the lies that they have fabricated.

Noah, Abraham and Lot

¹⁴ And verily, We sent Noah to his people and he lived among them for a thousand years less fifty. And then the flood seized the wrongdoers (who were lost in their sins). ¹⁵ But We saved him together with all who were in the ark which We set as a sign of Our grace for all mankind (to take lesson from).

¹⁶ And Abraham too was inspired by Us when he said to his people, "Worship God alone and be mindful of Him. This is the best for you, if only you knew. ¹⁷ (As it is,) you worship lifeless idols in place of God and fabricate lies! Behold, those things and beings that you worship instead of God do not possess any power to determine your provision (and sustenance). Seek then, all your provision from Almighty God. Worship Him alone and be grateful to Him. Indeed, it is to Him that you will all be ultimately returned." ¹⁸ (He

continued,) "If you persist in denial, know that other communities before you did the same too. And a Messenger's duty is nothing more than to clearly convey (the message that has been entrusted to him) clearly."

¹⁹ Do they not consider how God originates creation and then repeats its process? This is indeed easy for God. ²⁰ Say (to the disbelievers), "Travel all over the earth to observe and ponder how He originated creation (in the first instance). And (then you will certainly realize that) God indeed has the power to recreate life in a new form later (in the Hereafter). Verily, God has the power to do anything He wills."

²¹ He punishes whomsoever He wills (that defy Him) and He is merciful to whomsoever He wills (that obeys Him). In the end, it is to Him Whom you will finally return (for requital). ²² And never can you elude Him - not on earth nor in the heavens. There is no one who can ever protect or help you besides God. ²³ And those who reject God's signs (and revelations) and their meeting with Him have given-up all hope of My grace and mercy. And it is they who grievous punishment and suffering awaits (in the life to come).

²⁴ As for Abraham's people (who were dumbstruck with the argument that he put forth), their only answer was, "Kill him or burn him!" But God saved him from the fire (that his people had prepared for him. Behold!) Indeed, there are surely signs (and lessons) in this story for those who believe (in God). ²⁵ And Abraham said, "You have chosen to worship idols instead of God for no other reason than to have a bond of love in this worldly life between yourselves (and your ancestors). But on the Day of Resurrection, you will disown and curse one another (when you finally realize how terribly wrong you have been). Verily, your home will be the Fire and there is no one who can ever help you."

²⁶ Thereupon, (his brother's son), Lot, believed in him and said, "Verily, I too shall emigrate (with you away from evil) to my Lord. Indeed, He alone is Almighty, the All-Wise." ²⁷ And so for Abraham, We bestowed upon him Isaac and Jacob, and made Prophethood (and revelation) to continue among his offspring. And We granted him his reward in this world. Verily in the life to come, he will certainly be counted among the righteous.

²⁸ And Lot (too, was also inspired by Us) when he said to his people, "Verily, you are committing filthy acts that no one in the world before you has ever done! ²⁹ Must you (go against the order of nature by) approaching men (lustfully), thus cutting off the way (of procreation) and (blatantly) commit these evil (and despicable acts) in your gatherings?" But his people's only answer was, "(Leave us to do as we please.) Bring down God's punishment on us if you are a man of truth!" ³⁰ He prayed, "My Lord! Help me against these

evil corrupters (who are causing disorder on earth)."

Opposition to Truth Ever a Failure

[31] And so, when Our (heavenly) Messengers came to Abraham with the good news (of Isaac's birth), they also said, "Behold! We are about to destroy the people of that town, for its people are truly evil wrongdoers (who have transgressed the bounds of what is right)." [32] Upon hearing this, Abraham exclaimed, "But Lot lives there!" They answered, "We know very well who lives there. Most certainly we shall save Lot and his family (together with his followers), except his wife (who refuses to accept the truth). She will be among those who remain behind (and perish)."

[33] Then, when Our (heavenly) Messengers came to Lot, he was distressed and worried as he was unable to protect them (from his wicked people). But they said, "Do not fear and grieve! Behold, We shall save you and your family (together with your followers) except your wife (who continue to stubbornly reject Our message of truth). She will be among those who remain behind (and be doomed). [34] Most certainly, we shall bring down on the people of this town a punishment from the sky for their defiant disobedience." [35] And verily, We left a clear sign in this incident for people who will use reason (to ponder and take lesson from).

[36] And to the people of Madyan, (We sent) their brother Shu'aib who said, "O my people! Worship God and be prepared to face the Last Day. Do not act wickedly by spreading corruption (and causing disorder) on earth." [37] But they denounced him as a liar. Thereupon, an earthquake seized them and they sprawled lifeless on the ground in their homes.

[38] And (We destroyed the people of) 'Aad and Tsamud too. Indeed (their destruction) is clearly apparent to you from their ruined dwellings. (They perished) because (they followed) Satan who made their (evil) deeds fair-seeming (and alluring) which distracted them from the right path even though they were endowed with insight (to perceive the truth). [39] And (We also destroyed) Korah, Pharaoh and Haman. And certainly, Moses came to them with clear evidence (of truth) but they (rejected him and) behaved arrogantly on earth. They could not escape Us.

[40] We took each of those people (that We mentioned) to task for their sins. Upon some We let loose a deadly storm of wind, some We seized with an awful blast, some We caused to be swallowed by the earth, and some We made them drown (in the sea). It was not God Who was unjust to them. Instead, it was they who brought injustice upon themselves.

Like a Spider's Web

⁴¹ The parable of those who take other than God as their patrons (and protectors) is like the spider who builds its own house. Indeed, the spider's house is the weakest of all houses. If only people could understand this (message clearly)! ⁴² Indeed, God knows whatever they invoke besides Him. And He is certainly the Almighty, the All-Wise.

⁴³ And so, We present these parables to man but none can grasp their meaning except those with knowledge (and insight). ⁴⁴ (Verily,) God created the heavens and the earth (to fulfill a purpose that is) in accordance with the truth (which He has decreed). Indeed, in this is a clear message for people who (want to) believe (in the truth and strive to find it). ⁴⁵ So recite (and convey) to others what has been revealed to you from the Book (O Prophet) and attend to prayer regularly, for prayer prevents indecency and evil. *ᵃ* And surely, remembering God (constantly and submitting one's self to Him wholeheartedly in humility) is the greatest (form of worship that brings peace and comfort to the heart, and yields the best outcome). Hence, (be mindful that) God knows everything that you do.

Confused Concepts

⁴⁶ And do not argue with the people of earlier revelation unless in the best (and fairest) manner, except with those among them who are unjust (and intent on wrongdoing). Say (to them), "We believe in what has been revealed to us and to you. Our God and your God is One (and the same), and it is Him alone Who we have truly submitted ourselves to."

⁴⁷ And so, We have sent down and revealed to you this Book (O Prophet)! And to those (you are acquainted with) whom We have already given the (earlier) Scripture, some believe (in what We are revealing to you now. Likewise,) there are also some among the (Arab pagans) who believe in it too. And none reject Our revelations except those who are bent on denying the

---

ᵃ If we still indulge in indecent and evil acts despite performing the prayer, then We shall need to seriously examine the level of our faith in God and in the promise of Judgment Day. See verses 107:4-7 and the corresponding footnote. At the same time, God acknowledges that it is not easy to attain this state unless if we are truly humble in spirit (verse 2:45) and have attained the state of *Taqwa* by constantly striving to purify our soul as enjoined in verse 91:10. Striving to live up to the teachings of the Qur'an and the Prophet's practices (i.e. the *sunnah*), voluntary fasting outside of Ramadhan on a regular basis (footnote of verse 2:183), generously giving out charity and helping the poor are among the means that would help us reach this goal.

(obvious) truth.

⁴⁸ Never have you ever recited any heavenly Scripture before this, nor transcribed one with your hand. Otherwise, those who cling to falsehood would have had (a greater) cause to doubt (the message that you are conveying to them now). ⁴⁹ In fact, in the hearts (and minds) of those who are endowed with knowledge, these are indeed clear signs (of the truth). None would (willfully) deny Our signs and revelations except those who are unjust (to themselves and persist in their rejection of the truth).

⁵⁰ They ask, "Why is it that no (miraculous) signs have been sent down to him by his Lord?" Say to them, "Such signs are in the power of God alone; while I on the other hand, am only a plain warner." ⁵¹ Is it not enough for them that We have revealed to you this Book which is being read out to them (clearly)? Indeed it is a grace and reminder only for people who (want to) believe. ⁵² Say, "Sufficient is God as a witness between me and you! He knows all that is in the heavens and the earth. Those who believe in falsehood and refuse to believe in God are the real losers."

Warning and Consolation

⁵³ They challenge you to hasten their punishment. Indeed, had not a term been set for it (by your Lord), the punishment that they ask for would have already befallen them. (Verily,) it will most certainly come upon them in a sudden while they least expected it. ⁵⁴ (And) they (continue to still) challenge you to hasten their punishment. Without doubt, Hell will surely encompass these disbelievers from all sides; ⁵⁵ on the Day when suffering will overwhelm them from above and also from under their feet. God will then say, "Taste now the consequence of your own doings!"

⁵⁶ O My servants who believe! Indeed, My earth is vast, so worship Me and Me alone (and do not be afraid to emigrate for the sake of safeguarding your faith). ⁵⁷ Every soul will taste death (no matter where you are). Then to Us will you be (ultimately) returned (for judgment).

⁵⁸ As for those who believe and do righteous deeds, We shall surely give them lofty mansions in Paradise with rivers that flow beneath them. They will remain in there forever. How excellent is the reward of those who act (upon their faith); ⁵⁹ who are steadfast (in their labor) and place full trust in their Lord.

⁶⁰ And how many creatures are there on earth that do not carry (nor give any thought of) their own provision? Is it (not) God Who provides for them

and for you? Verily, He hears all, knows all. (So, do not fear for your livelihood when you strive and persevere in God's path.)

⁶¹ And (so it is with most people) if you ask them, "Who created the heavens and the earth, and keep the sun and the moon subservient (to His laws)?" They would surely say, "God!" So how could they be deluded (at the same time)? ⁶² It is God Who grants provision in abundance, or gives it in small measure to whomsoever He wills of His servants (according to His wisdom, as a means to test their faith). Indeed, God has full knowledge of everything.

⁶³ (And) if you were to ask them (further), "Who is it that sends rain from the sky which gives life to the earth after it had been lifeless?", they will surely answer, "God!" So say to them, "(Then you ought to know that) all praise (and worship) is due to God alone." Yet most of them fail to use common sense (to understand this simple truth). ⁶⁴ (For if they did, then they would surely know that the) life of this world is nothing but a passing delight and mere play, whereas the next life to come is truly where the (real and everlasting) life is. If only they knew (and understood) this!

⁶⁵ And when they embark on a ship and encounter danger, they call upon God alone in sincere devotion of their faith and worship. But as soon as He delivers them safely to the land, behold! They (forget their promise and) begin to associate partners with Him (again); ⁶⁶ denying the rescue that We have given them and instead enjoy in the pleasures (of the this world in a state of disbelief). But soon they will surely face the truth (that they choose to stubbornly ignore now).

⁶⁷ Do they not see (and realize) that We have given them a safe sanctuary (in Makkah) whereas people around them are being snatched away (in fear and despair)? Will they still continue to believe in falsehood and (ungratefully) deny God's favors? ⁶⁸ And who is more unjust (and wicked) than the one who invents a lie against God or denies the truth when it has (clearly) come to him? Is Hell then not the (suitable) place of return for those who (choose to willfully) disbelieve (and reject the truth)?

⁶⁹ (Verily,) We shall certainly guide to Our ways those who strive hard for Our cause. And indeed, God is surely with those who excel in good deeds.

30. Ar-Rūm
[The Romans : 60 verses]

his is a Makkan chapter. And like other Makkan chapters, it deals with the
themes of monotheism, Prophethood of Muhammad, resurrection, judgment,
reward and punishment, and brings home these themes by various arguments
and proofs. The chapter was revealed around seven years before the *Hijra* or migration
to Medina. It starts with a reference to a devastating defeat of the Romans by the
Persian pagans at that time, and foretells that in less than ten years, the Persians
would be defeated by the Romans. It also foretells that on that day, the Muslims would
rejoice at the victory given to them by God. The prophecy was fulfilled in the second
year of Hijra when the Muslims were given a significant victory by God at the Battle of
Badr and by which time the Persians were also defeated by the Romans. This
prophecy of the Qur'an is a manifest miracle which attests its truth. The chapter is
named *Ar-Rūm* or The Romans with reference to this important fact mentioned in its
first six verses.

In the name of God, the Most Gracious,
the Most Compassionate.

Signs to Reflect Upon

¹ *Alif Lām Mīm.* ² The Romans have been defeated; ³ in the neighboring
land. But after this defeat, they will gain victory; ⁴ within three to nine years. *ᵃ*
(Verily,) with God rest (the fate and destiny of) all affairs in the past and in the
future. And on that day (of victory), the believers (too) will have a
(significant) cause to rejoice;*ᵇ* ⁵ in God's help. Indeed, He gives help to
whomsoever He Wills. He is the Almighty, the Most Compassionate. ⁶ This is
indeed God's promise. God never fails to fulfill His promise but most people
do not know. ⁷ They only know (and care about) what is apparent in this
worldly life but are (ignorant and) oblivious of the realities in the next life.

ᵃ Emperor Heraclius of the Eastern Roman Empire, which is better known as the
Byzantine Empire, launched a campaign against Persia in 624CE and marked a
significant victory by destroying Adur Gushnasp, the famous Zoroastrian fire Temple at
Takht-i-Suleiman in West Azerbaijan, which took place 9 years after this verse was
revealed. This accurately fulfilled the Qur'an's prophecy that the Romans will rise to
triumph over the Persians within three to nine years from their earlier devastating
defeat when no one had expected that the Romans could ever rise again.
ᵇ The Muslims were also given a significant victory by God at Battle of Badr in the
same year of 624CE (i.e. 2 Hijra). This was the first battle that the Muslims fought, and
they were greatly outnumbered by the army of the disbelievers i.e. 313 Muslims
against a force of around 1,000 Arab pagans.

⁸ Do they not ponder (and reflect) about themselves? Verily, God did not create the heavens and the earth and whatever between them except (to fulfill a purpose) that is in accordance with the truth (which He has decreed) for an appointed term. But many people refuse to believe in the Almighty Lord and their meeting with Him (in the next life where all their deeds will be reckoned).

⁹ Have they not traveled throughout the earth to observe the fate of those who lived before them? They were far superior in might, and they tilled the land and built on it more than (the Arab pagans) who are denying you now have ever accomplished (O Prophet). Their Messengers also came to them with all evidence of the truth. Yet, it was not God who was unjust to them, but it was they who brought injustice upon themselves (by rejecting the teachings of the Messengers that were conveyed to them). ¹⁰ And so, wretched was the end of those (corrupt) evildoers because they denied God's signs and revelations and made a mockery of them.

¹¹ Indeed, it is God Who originates the creation (of man). Then He will repeat this (in the afterlife). It is to Him Whom you will be finally returned (for the reckoning of your deeds and judgment). ¹² And on the Day when the Final Hour takes place, those who are lost in sin will be in utter despair. ¹³ Those who they used to allege as (God's) partners will not rescue and intercede for them (as expected). In fact, they will reject these alleged partners (of God when they finally see the suffering that awaits them). ¹⁴ And on the Day when the Final Hour takes place, everyone will be separated (according to their creed and deeds). ¹⁵ Those who believed (in Our message) and performed righteous deeds will rejoice in a Garden; ¹⁶ while those who rejected it, denied Our signs and (disbelieved in) the meeting (with God) in the life to come will be brought forth to face their punishment.

¹⁷ Extol then, the limitless glory of God (Who is free from all imperfections) in the evening and (also when you rise) in the morning. ¹⁸ To Him (alone) is due all praise in the heavens and the earth, as well as in the afternoon and when the sun begins to decline. ¹⁹ He is the One Who brings the living out from the dead and the dead out from the living, and He gives life to the earth after it had been lifeless (by sending down rain). Likewise will you be (resurrected and) brought forth (from the grave).

²⁰ And among His signs is that He created you from soil, then behold! You become human beings that multiply (and are scattered throughout the earth).

²¹ And among His signs is that He created for you spouses from out of your own kind so that you will find tranquility in them, and He placed love

and compassion between both of you. Indeed there are clear signs in this for those who (care to reflect and) ponder.

²² And among His signs is the creation of the heavens and the earth, and the diversity of your languages and colors (of skin). Indeed there are clear signs in this for those who are endowed with knowledge (and insight).

²³ And among His signs is your sleep (and rest) at night and your seeking of (livelihood from) His bounty during the day. Indeed there are clear signs in this for those who listen (and take heed of His message).

²⁴ And among His signs is the display of lightning to you, giving rise to both fear and hope. And then He sends down rain from the skies, giving life to earth after it was lifeless. Indeed, there are clear signs in this for those who use reason (and common sense to ponder).

²⁵ And among His signs is that the heavens and the earth stand firm by His command. Then in the end, when He summons you from the earth with a single call, you will be brought forth (from your graves). ²⁶ To Him belongs every being that is in the heavens and the earth. All obey His will (except those who are heedless of His message and willfully defy Him). ²⁷ He is the One Who originates creation and then (easily) repeats it. To Him belongs the highest attributes in the heavens and the earth, and He alone is the Almighty, Truly Wise.

²⁸ He puts forward to you this parable, drawn from your own lives : Would you make your slaves equal partners in the wealth that We have given you? And do you fear them as you fear those of your own kind? This is how We spell out Our messages for those who use common sense. ²⁹ Nay! Those who are unjust (and wicked) follow nothing except their own lusts because they are devoid of knowledge (and reason). And who could guide those whom God lets go astray (because of their own arrogance)? Indeed, they will have none to help them (when the final moment arrives).

³⁰ So (be steadfast in) setting your face towards the ever-true and upright religion which is (in harmony with) your *fitrah* ᵃ that God has created (and instilled in) every human being. There will not be any change to (this pure religion) that God has created (and bestowed His full measure of blessings

---

ᵃ *Fitrah* is natural disposition. It refers to man's pure state of inborn intuition that allows him to discern between right and wrong, truth and falsehood, thus having the inherent ability to naturally sense God's existence and Oneness (*tawhid*), and fully submit to Him in humility. See also verses 7:172, 17:70, 54:5, 91:7-10 and 95:4 together with their corresponding footnotes.

upon it). *a* This is (indeed) the (one and only) ever-true religion (for everyone to follow) but most people do not know (and do not care). [31] So turn in repentance to Him and be ever mindful of Him (if you believe in resurrection). Be constant in prayer and do not be of those who associate partners with Him (in divinity); [32] or among those who split and divide the unity of their faith into different factions with each group rejoicing in its (false) belief.

Bringing Life Out of the Dead

[33] And when hardship touches people, they call upon their Lord's (help) and turn to Him in repentance. Then when He gives them a taste of His mercy (by removing that hardship), behold! A group of them would associate partners with their Lord; [34] in defiance of the favors that We have granted them. So enjoy yourselves for a little while but soon you will know what awaits you.

[35] Or did We ever send down to them any authority (that justifies) their act in associating others with God (in His divinity)? [36] And when We give people a taste of Our grace, they rejoice. But if an evil afflicts them for what they did with their own hands, they fall into despair. [37] (What is amiss with them?) Do they not see that God extends provision and also restricts it to whomsoever He wills (according to His wisdom, as a means to test their faith)? Indeed in all this, surely there are (clear) signs for those who believe.

[38] So give the near of kin his right, and also to the poor and the traveler (in distress) too. That is best for those who desire God's (pleasure and) countenance. It is they who will (attain felicity and) ultimately become victorious. [39] What you lend with usury to increase your wealth will bring you no benefit in the sight of God. Whereas what you give out in charity for the sake of God's (pleasure and) countenance, then those who do so will be blessed with multiple rewards.

[40] (So remember that) it is God Who created you. Then He provides you sustenance and will eventually cause you to die. And then He will bring you back to life (to reckon your deeds). Can any of your partners (whom you regard divine) do any of these? Glorified is God from all imperfections and exalted is He above everything that the disbelievers associate Him with!

[41] Corruption and chaos have appeared and become rife on land and sea

---

a See verse 5:3.

because of what people have done with their own hands. *ᵃ* Hence, God lets them taste the consequences of some of their wrongdoings (as a stern reminder) so that they will (realize their errors and) turn back (to the right path before their term on earth expires). *⁴²* Say (to these deniers of truth), "Travel through the land and see how was the end of those (sinners) who lived before you. Most of them were those who associated partners with God (in his divinity)." *⁴³* So stand firm in your devotion to the upright religion before the arrival of the Day where there is no chance of escaping from God. On that Day, people will be divided (according to their creed and deeds). *⁴⁴* Whoever rejects God, then the burden of that rejection will act against himself. But those who (believe in God and) do righteous deeds will make good provision for themselves. *⁴⁵* God will reward from His bounty, those who are firm in their belief and do righteous deeds. Verily, He does not like those who reject the truth.

⁴⁶ And among His signs is He sends forth the winds bearing good news before He gives you a taste of His grace (through life-giving rain) and also by making ships sail (with the aid of the winds) at His command, hence enabling you to seek from His bounty so that you may be grateful.

⁴⁷ Verily, long before you (O Muhammad), We sent Messengers (as bearers of good news and stern warnings) with clear proofs to their own people. For those who (ignored Our message and) persisted in committing

---

ᵃ Serious global warming effects due to greenhouse gas emissions and massive deforestation that cause ozone layer depletion and the melting of glaciers at an accelerated rate are all resulting in an unprecedented abrupt climate change that give rise to severe droughts and deadly floods that gravely affect the lives of billions of people around the globe. As if this is not enough, the world is currently experiencing the merciless onslaught of Covid-19 pandemic since December 2019 that has registered around 500 million cases of infection and killing close to 6.2 million lives at the time of this writing (refer to the Coronavirus Worldometer website). It has also rendered this modern and sophisticated world helpless, placing it literally on standstill with an unimaginable catastrophic economic impact on almost every nation on this planet and its people. The virus could have been manufactured in laboratories by scientists, or a product of a natural consequence when humans with strange appetite for exotic wild animals (i.e. which is believed to be bats in this case) deliberately disturbed their natural habitat. This resulted in the animals' stress level to heighten which in turn caused the virus that they naturally carry inside them to mutate, become more robust and then crossed to humans who indulged in these animals. Regardless of how the virus actually came into existence, the final result is a colossal global pandemic when human to human transmission became possible and grew widespread exponentially. Either way, make no mistake that it is man who is the primary cause of all these self-inflicted calamities as clearly foretold by God in this verse.

sins, We inflicted Our retribution upon them. But for those who believed (and accepted Our message), it became Our duty to help them.

⁴⁸ It is God Who sends the winds to stir and raise the clouds. He spreads them in the sky as He pleases and makes them into fragments so that you can see rain coming forth from their midst. Then He causes it to fall upon whom He wills of His servants. And behold! They rejoice at it. ⁴⁹ And certainly they were indeed in despair before it was sent down upon them. ⁵⁰ So observe the effects of God's grace - see how He gives life to the earth after it has been lifeless. Indeed, that is how easy it is for Him to revive the dead, for He has power over everything. ⁵¹ But if We send a wind (that scorches their land) and they see (their crops) turn yellow, they will surely continue in their disbelief after that.

⁵² So (do not be sad for them O Prophet). Indeed you cannot make those (whose hearts are) dead hear, nor can you also make the deaf hear your call when they turn their backs on you and walk away (defiantly); ⁵³ nor can you guide those who are blind (to the truth) out from their error. Verily, there is none who you can make to hear your call except those who (want to) believe in Our signs and (willingly) submit themselves to Us. ⁵⁴ (Remember that) it is God Who created you in an initial state of weakness (and helplessness). Then after that weakness, He gave you strength. Then after that strength, He made you (become old and) weak again with gray hair. (Verily,) He creates what He wills and He is All-Knowing, All-Powerful.

⁵⁵ On the Day when the Hour will come to pass, the wicked wrongdoers will swear that they had only stayed in the world for not more than an hour. That is how they were deceived (by the fleeting life of the world). ⁵⁶ But those who were endowed with knowledge and faith will say to them, "Indeed, your length of stay on earth was according to God's decree (and you have chosen to wait) until the Day of Resurrection (before deciding to believe in Him). Now, this is the Day of Resurrection which you denied any knowledge about, (despite the reminders that were conveyed to you)." ⁵⁷ And so on that Day, excuses will be of no avail to those who committed evil deeds, nor will they be allowed to make amends.

⁵⁸ And verily, We have explained everything that everyone should know in this Qur'an using many parables. But no matter what sign you bring to them (O Prophet), those who are bent on denying the truth will still say, "You are only making false claims!" ⁵⁹ As such, God seals the hearts of those who refuse to know (and follow the truth). ⁶⁰ So remain patient (and persevere O Prophet)! Indeed, God's promise (of resurrection) is true. Let not those who lack certainty in faith cause you to waver.

31. Luqmān
[34 verses]

Just like the other Makkan chapters, this chapter too deals with the fundamentals of faith namely monotheism, messengership, resurrection and judgment. It starts with drawing attention to the Wise Book - The Qur'an, which has been given by God as guidance and mercy for the righteous and then points out God's creation of the heavens and the earth for the benefit of man. The chapter is named *Luqmān* in reference to the story about a sage who was given wisdom by God and how he advised his son about monotheism, the sin of *shirk* (i.e. associating partners with God), the duty to be obedient to parents, to pray regularly and not to be proud and self-conceited (verses 12 - 19).

In the name of God, the Most Gracious, the Most Compassionate.

A Sage's Admonition

¹ *Alif Lām Mīm.* ² These are verses of the Wise Book; ³ a guidance and mercy for those who (strive to) excel in good deeds; ⁴ those who attend to their prayer constantly and spend in charity (regularly), for it is they who firmly believe in the life to come. ⁵ It is they who are being rightly guided by their Lord to become victorious (and enjoy everlasting happiness).

⁶ And among men is he who purchases vain talks (and stories) to mislead people from the path of God in ignorance, and turns God's signs and revelations into ridicule. *ᵃ* For such people, a humiliating punishment awaits them. ⁷And when Our verses are recited to him, he turns away arrogantly as if he did not hear them, as though there was deafness in his ears. So give him news of a grievous punishment (that is in store for him).

⁸ Indeed, those who believe and do righteous deeds, for them are Gardens of Delight; ⁹ where they will remain in there forever. This is God's promise, and God's promise is always true. Verily, He is the Almighty, the All-Wise.

¹⁰ He is the One Who created the heavens that you see without pillars and placed firm mountains on the earth (as pegs and anchors) lest it shakes with

---

ᵃ Al-Wahidi mentioned in his *Asbab ul-Nuzul* that this verse was revealed about Nadr ibn al-Harith who used to travel to Persia for trade. He bought some ancient Persian stories to distract the Arab pagans of Makkah from listening to the Qur'an.

you ^{*a*} (as it rotates around its axis), and then He dispersed all kinds of creatures through out the earth. And We send down rain from the sky and cause to grow on it all kinds of fine plants. ¹¹ Such is the creation of Almighty God. Now show Me what those (false deities) besides Him (that you worship) have created. Nay! The wrongdoers are obviously lost in error.

¹² And verily, We gave wisdom to Luqmān ^{*b*} (and said), "Be grateful to God." Whoever is grateful (to God) will indeed be grateful for (the benefit that he will earn for) himself. Whoever is ungrateful, then (he will suffer his own loss). Indeed, God is All-Sufficient, Immensely Praiseworthy.

¹³ And (mention O Prophet) when Luqmān said to his son while he was advising him, "O my son! Do not associate partners with God. Indeed, associating partners with Him is surely an act of great injustice."

¹⁴ And (in addition), We have commanded man to be dutiful to his parents. His mother carried him (for nine months) in weakness upon weakness and his weaning is in two years. And so We said, "Be grateful to Me and to your parents. Verily, with Me is where all journeys' end." ¹⁵ (So, revere your parents,) but if they force you to associate with Me anything that you have no knowledge about, then do not obey them. But continue to treat them with kindness in this world and follow the path of those who (sincerely) turn to Me (in humility). In the end, it is to Me Who your final return will be and I shall apprise you about everything that you have done (during your lifetime).

¹⁶ (Luqmān said to his son,) "O my son! Verily, even if your deed is like the weight of a grain of a mustard seed and it is (hidden) in a rock or (anywhere) in the heavens or the earth, God will (still account for it and) bring it forth for reckoning. Indeed, God is All-Subtle, All-Aware."

¹⁷ "O my son! Be constant in prayer and command what is right and forbid what is wrong, and be patient over whatever befalls you. Indeed, these are

---

^{*a*} Refer to footnote of 16:15 for a detailed explanation on this.
^{*b*} According to Muhammad Asad, Luqmān is a legendary figure firmly established in ancient Arabian tradition as a sage who disdains worldly honors or benefits and strives for inner perfection. Celebrated in a poem by Ziyad ibn Mu'awiyah (better known under his pen-name Nibighah adh-Dhubyani) who lived in the sixth century of the Common Era, the person of Luqmān had become a focal point of innumerable legends, stories and parables expressive of wisdom and spiritual maturity long before the advent of Islam; and it is for this reason that the Qur'an uses this mysterious figure, as it uses the equally mysterious figure of Al-Khidr in chapter 18, as a vehicle for some of its admonitions bearing upon the manner in which man ought to behave.

among God's foremost commandments (that require firm faith and determination to act upon)." ¹⁸ And do not turn your cheek (in pride) from men, nor walk on earth arrogantly. Indeed, God does not like self-conceited boasters. ¹⁹ And be moderate in your pace and lower your voice (when you speak); for indeed, the most disgusting of all voices is surely the braying of donkeys."

God's Absolute Knowledge

²⁰ Do you not see that God has made subservient to you all that is in the heavens and the earth, and has lavished upon you His bounties that are both apparent and hidden? Yet some people argue about God without knowledge, without guidance, and without any enlightening revelation (from Him). ²¹ And when it is said to them, "Follow what God has revealed!", they reply, "Nay! We shall follow the traditions of our forefathers." (Will they follow) even if it is Satan who is calling them to the punishment of the Blazing Fire?

²² And whoever submits himself to God and excels in good deeds, then he has indeed grasped the most trustworthy handhold. And with God rests the final outcome of all matters. ²³ And whoever chooses to turn away from the truth, do not let his disbelief grieve you (O Prophet). To Us will ultimately be their return, and then We shall surely apprise them about everything that they have done (during their lifetime and make them accountable for all their deeds). Indeed, God knows all that is in (everyone's) hearts. ²⁴ (So for now,) We shall let them enjoy themselves for a little while. In the end, We shall force them to endure a severe punishment (because of their defiance to the truth).

²⁵ And (so it is with most people that) if you ask them, "Who created the heavens and the earth?", they will surely answer, "God!" So say (to them, "Then you should know that) all praise is due to God alone." Yet most of them do not understand (what it implies, and continue to ignore Our reminders). ²⁶ (Verily,) to God belongs whatever is in the heavens and the earth. Indeed, God is All-Sufficient, Immensely Praiseworthy.

²⁷ And if all the trees on the earth were pens and the oceans (were ink), the words of God would never be exhausted even if seven (more) oceans were added to it. Indeed, God is Almighty, All-Wise.

²⁸ (Verily,) for God to create and resurrect all of you (at once) is just like creating and resurrecting a single soul. Indeed, God sees all, hears all. ²⁹ Do you not see that God causes the night to enter into the day and the day to enter into the night? He also subjected the sun and the moon to orbit around their

own specific courses until an appointed term. God is very well aware of what you do. ³⁰ That is because God alone is the Ultimate Truth, and all that which they call upon besides Him is false. Indeed God is the Most Exalted, Truly Great.

An Inescapable Doom for the Ingrates

³¹ Do you not see how the ships sail (calmly) through the seas by the grace of God (delighting those who are onboard? Ponder deeply) so that (you may appreciate some of) the signs that God makes it clear for you to see. Indeed, there are lessons in these signs for everyone who is steadfast (in his faith) and grateful (for the blessings that he enjoys). ³² And when the waves (suddenly) engulf them like canopies, they would surely turn to God and pray, (pleading for safety), being sincere in their faith in Him alone. But as soon as He rescues them and brings them safely to land, some among them who would waver between doubt and belief. But none would (dare) deny and reject Our signs (and revelations) except those who are utterly deceitful and ungrateful.

³³ O mankind! Fear (the wrath of) your Lord, and fear the Day when no father can avail anything for his son, nor a son can avail anything for his father. ª Verily, God's promise (of resurrection) is true, so let not the life of this world deceive you, nor (your own) deceptive thoughts about God delude you.

³⁴ Indeed with God alone rests the knowledge of when will the Last Hour arrive. It is He Who sends down rain and He knows what the wombs (of pregnant mothers) contain whereas no one knows what they will earn tomorrow and in which land they will die. Indeed, God is All-Knowing, All-Aware.

ª Every man is responsible for his own destiny. If he is saved, it will be because of the true faith that he has followed and the good deeds that he has managed to do with God's permission. Otherwise, his corrupt faith and evil deeds will cost him an irredeemable loss that even all the wealth in the world that he may have amassed during his lifetime will not be of any use to save him. See verse 5:36

32. As-Sajdah
[The Prostration : 30 verses]

This is a Makkan chapter. And like the other Makkan chapters, the chapter deals with the fundamentals of faith. It starts with stressing that the Qur'an has been sent down by God and gives a reply with cogent arguments to the allegations of the disbelievers that it was fabricated by the Prophet. It also draws attention to the wonderful creation of God - the universe, and dispels the doubts of the disbelievers regarding resurrection, judgment, reward and punishment. The chapter is called As-Sajdah or The Prostration with reference to the response of the believers who would prostrate when they hear verses of the Qur'an that mention this (verse 15).

In the name of God, the Most Gracious, the Most Compassionate.

The Main Issues of Faith

¹ *Alif Lām Mīm.* ² It is without a doubt that this Book is (revealed and) sent down from the Lord of all the worlds. ³ And yet they (defiantly) assert, "It is Muhammad who invented it!" Nay! It is indeed the truth from your Lord (bestowed upon you O Prophet) to warn a people to whom no warner has come before you so that they will be guided.

⁴ (Behold!) God is the One Who created the heavens and the earth and all that is between them in six phases, and He is firmly established on His (Supreme) Throne. You neither have any protector nor intercessor other than Him. Will you then not take heed (and reflect upon His signs)? ⁵ It is He Who regulates and governs (all that exists) from the heavens to the earth. Each affair ascends to Him in a day (or period) whose measure is a thousand years according to your normal count.

⁶ Such is He Who knows all that is hidden as well as all that can be witnessed (by His creatures). He is (indeed) the Almighty, the Most Compassionate; ⁷ the One Who perfected everything He created. Verily, it is He Who originated the creation of man from clay; ⁸ then He made for man his progeny out of the essence of an unworthy (humble) fluid; ⁹ and then He formed him in accordance with what he is meant to be and breathed into him from His Spirit. Then He endowed you with hearing, sight, and conscience (so that you may be able to learn and discern truth from falsehood). Yet how little thanks do you give!

¹⁰ (Instead,) they say, "What! After we have (been dead and) disappeared into the earth, shall we really be restored to life in a new act of creation?" Nay!

By saying this, they deny the truth that they are destined to meet their Lord. [11] Say (to them, "Indeed,) the Angel of death who is in charge of you will (most certainly) take your soul away (at the appointed time), and then you will be returned to your Lord."

Believers and Disbelievers: A Comparison

[12] If only you could see (the Day) when the sinners will stoop their heads (in shame) in front of their Lord, (they will say), "Our Lord! We can now see and hear (that what You promised is indeed true). So please send us back (to earth) so that we can make amends and do righteous deeds. Indeed, we truly believe (in You now)." [a] [13] (But they will be told,) "If We had so willed, We could have surely given guidance to every soul, (but We gave you reason for you to discern between truth and falsehood so that you may turn to Us in true devotion out of your own free will). And the word from Me which says "I shall surely fill Hell with (evil) men and Jinn together" is an inevitable truth that is now fulfilled (because you have misused My gift of reason and free will by denying Me instead)." [14] Taste then the punishment for choosing to be oblivious of Our meeting today; for verily, We are now oblivious of you too. So taste this eternal punishment as the requital for your evil deeds!"

[15] Verily, whenever people are given good counsel and reminded (with Our verses), only those who (truly) believe in Our signs and revelations would fall down to prostrate (in humility) and glorify the perfection of their Lord with (abundant) praises, and they are not arrogant. [16] Their bodies forsake their beds at night as they (wake up to perform their prayer in deep devotion. They) call upon their Lord, fearing (His displeasure) and in hope (of His mercy). And they spend (generously in Our cause) out of the provision that We have granted them. [17] No soul can imagine the comfort and delights that are being kept hidden from their eyes now as reward for their noble deeds (that await in the next life to come). [b]

[18] Then, is one who is a true believer the same as another who disobeys (his Lord) defiantly? Surely they cannot be equal! [19] And so, for those who believe and do righteous deeds, for them are gardens of refuge (from their Lord) as reward for their (noble) deeds.

---

[a] See also verse 23:99-100 and its footnote.
[b] The impossibility of man imagining the true pleasures of Paradise was summed up by the Prophet in the following *hadith* : "God says, 'I have prepared for My righteous servants what no eye has ever seen, and no ear has ever heard, and no heart of man has ever conceived.'" (Narrated by Bukhari No. 4780 and Muslim No. 2824).

²⁰ But for those who are defiantly disobedient, their refuge will be the Hellfire. Every time they wish to come out from it, they will be hurled back and told, "Taste the torment of the (Blazing) Fire which you used to deny (before this)!" ²¹ And surely, We shall let them taste a suffering that is closer at hand (in the form of disasters and calamities of the world) before they experience the greater suffering (in the next life), so that they will repent (and stop their transgressions). ²² And who is more unjust than the one who still turns away (arrogantly) after being reminded of his Lord's (words of) revelation? Indeed, We shall inflict Our retribution on those who are (clearly) lost in sin (because of their defiance in rejecting the truth).

Faith Attained at the Wrong Time is Useless

²³ And indeed (O Muhammad), We gave the Torah to Moses (before you). So do not be in doubt about receiving the same message (that you will find in the Qur'an which We are revealing to you now). And We made the Torah a guidance for the children of Israel. ²⁴ When they persevered with patience and firmly believed in Our revelations, We raised leaders among them and gave guidance with Our command.

²⁵ Indeed, it is your Lord alone Who will judge among people on the Day of Resurrection about what they used to differ (and dispute). ²⁶ Do those (who deny the truth) still not learn any lesson from the many nations and generations that We have destroyed before them amidst whose dwellings they move about now? Surely there are many signs in this (to learn from). Are they not able to hear (and take heed of Our warnings that are being conveyed to them)? ²⁷ Do they also not realize that it is We who drive rain to a barren land and bring forth crops with it for them and their cattle to eat? Can they not see (the signs of Our grace and at the same time be mindful of Our severe retribution)?

²⁸ But they question (you in arrogance instead), "If you are really speaking the truth (O Muhammad), then tell us when will the Day of Decision (that you threaten us with), come?" ²⁹ (Tell them,) "On the Day of the Final Decision, it will be utterly useless for those who in their lifetime were deniers of the truth to suddenly profess faith. They will be granted no respite (to make amends)."

³⁰ So leave them alone, and wait (for the truth to unfold). Indeed, they too are waiting (for their imminent doom).

33. Al-Aḥzāb
[The Confederate Tribes : 73 verses]

This is a Madinan chapter that was revealed between 5 and 7 Hijra. It refers to the famous Battle of Khandaq or the Battle of the Confederate Tribes. The disbelievers of Makkah had formed an alliance with the Jewish tribe of Bani An-Nadir that had already been expelled from Madinah, and another Jewish tribe of Bani Qurayzah that was still in Madinah, together with the hypocrites and some other Bedouin tribes that boasted a combined and well equipped army of 10,000 strong. This confederation of army laid siege to Madinah in the month of Shawal of 5 Hijra with the aim to completely root out the Muslims and Islam. Under the Prophet's guidance and on the suggestion of a companion by the name of Salman al-Farisi – a convert from Persia, the Muslims dug a deep trench (*khandaq*) around the exposed parts of Madinah in preparation of the attack. The siege lasted about three weeks during which the Jewish tribe of Bani Qurayzah and the hypocrites that were in Madinah had secretly attempted to help the enemy. Ultimately, all their attempts were foiled and the confederate army was obliged to withdraw in utter disarray and confusion. The conquest and expulsion of Bani Qurayzah followed shortly. Besides these events, the chapter also lays down the rule that adopted sons are not to be regarded as sons anymore which is the normal practice of the Arabs, but they are to be strictly ascribed to their biological fathers. Other than this, the pre-Islamic custom of *zihar* which is to compare the wife's back with the back of the husband's mother should no longer constitute a proper divorce. Finally, believers are also commanded to take note that the family of the Prophet are to be duly respected and his wives are to be regarded as Mothers of the Believers.

In the name of God, the Most Gracious,
the Most Compassionate.

False Relations Abolished

¹ O Prophet! Fear God and do not obey those who openly refuse to accept the truth and also the hypocrites (who constantly waver between truth and falsehood). Indeed, God is All-Knowing, All-Wise. ² (Instead,) follow what is inspired to you from your Lord. Indeed, God is very well aware of what you do. ³ And place your trust in God. Sufficient is God alone as your Guardian.

⁴ (O believers!) God did not place two hearts inside the body of a man; nor did He make the wives (you reject) equal as your mother when you compare their backs; *ᵃ* nor did He make those whom you adopt as sons to be

---

ᵃ In the pre-Islamic Arabian custom, it often happened that during a family quarrel, the husband in the heat of the moment would say to his wife: "*Anti alayyaka zahri ammi*"

regarded as your own. These are only (misguided) words from your mouths, while God proclaims the truth and directs people to the right path. ⁵ (Verily,) you are commanded to call your adopted sons after their true fathers, for that is more equitable and proper in the sight of God. But if you do not know their true fathers, then regard them as your brothers in faith and as protégés (who are entrusted to you). No blame upon you for your unintentional mistake, except only for what your hearts deliberately intend. Verily, God is Most Forgiving, Most Compassionate.

⁶ The Prophet has greater concern for the good of the believers than they have for their own souls, while his wives are regarded as their mothers. God has decreed that blood-relatives have greater claim (to inheritance) over other believers (from Madinah) and emigrants (from Makkah), though you may still bestow gifts on your protégés as an act of kindness. This is inscribed in God's Book.

⁷ And (be mindful O Muhammad,) when We took a solemn pledge from all the Prophets, and from you, as well as from Noah and Abraham, Moses, and Jesus the son of Mary. We took an inviolable solemn pledge from all of them; ⁸ so that (on the Day of Judgment,) He will ask these truthful servants about the truth (that they were being commanded to deliver). Verily, He has prepared a grievous punishment for those who rejected His message.

Rallying All Hostile Forces

⁹ O you who believe! Remember God's favor to you when the armies (of your enemies combined their forces and) came to (attack) you (in Madinah), whereupon We let loose a violent wind together with invisible (heavenly) forces against them. God sees everything that you do. ¹⁰ (Remember what you felt) when your enemies approached you from (a plain that is) above you and (also from another position) below you. Your eyes were stupefied with horror

---

which literally means: "You are to me like the back of my mother." But its real implied meaning is: "To have sexual relations with you would be like having sexual relations with my mother." This is called *zihar* and was looked upon as tantamount to the pronouncement of divorce, even of greater effect than that, for they took it to mean that the husband was not only severing his marital relations with his wife but was also declaring her to be permanently unlawful for himself like his mother. On this very basis, the Arabs thought reunion could be possible after a divorce but it was impossible after *zihar*. As evident from the first four verses of chapter 58 - which was revealed somewhat earlier than the present chapter - this cruel pagan custom had already been abolished by the time this verse was revealed.

and your hearts leapt to your throats, and you began to entertain conflicting thoughts about God. ¹¹ It was there where the believers were truly tested and shaken with a severe shock.

¹² And (call to mind how it was) when the hypocrites and all those with disease in their hearts said (to one another when they saw the size of the enemies' joint forces), "Indeed, God and His Messenger have promised us nothing but delusion." ¹³ And (call to mind too) when a party of them said, "O People of Yathrib! ^a This is certainly not a place for you to withstand (the enemy). So go back (home)." Then, a group of them asked permission from the Prophet to leave, saying, "Indeed, our houses are exposed to the enemy," but in fact it was not. Their intention was only to flee (from the battle-front). ¹⁴ And if the enemy were to enter upon them from all its sides and these hypocrites had been asked (by the enemy) to commit treachery, surely they would have done so without hesitation; ¹⁵ although they had indeed promised God earlier that they would not turn their backs (and flee). And surely God will question them about this promise.

¹⁶ So say (to them O Prophet), "Running away will not benefit you. Even if you manage to escape from death or killing, you will still not be able to enjoy (the pleasures of life) except for a little while." ¹⁷ Say (further), "Who can protect you from God if He intends harm to fall upon you, and who can prevent Him from granting mercy to you if He intends so?" And surely they will not be able to find for themselves any other protector (or helper) other than God.

¹⁸ Verily, God knows well those among you who hinder others from fighting in His cause, as well as those who (coyly) say to their brothers, "Come to us (and let's prepare for battle)" while they themselves do not come out to battle, except for a few. ¹⁹ They are misers who are unwilling to offer any help to you. But when danger comes, you see them looking at you (hoping to be protected) with their eyes rolling as though they were on the verge of fainting at the approach of death. But when danger departs, they smite you with their sharp scissor-like tongues and do not extend any kindness and assistance. They (are selfish and) never truly believe in God, and so God has caused their deeds to become worthless. That is indeed easy for God (to do).

²⁰ They think the joint forces have not withdrawn. And if the joint forces were to mount another assault, they would prefer to be in the desert with the Bedouins, asking about your news from afar. And even if they remain among you, they would not fight, except for only a few of them.

---

^a The ancient name of Madinah before The Prophet's emigration.

²¹ Certainly, there is an excellent example in the Messenger of God (to emulate and follow) for the one who puts his hope in God and the Last Day, and remembers Him much. *ᵃ* ²² As for the true believers, when they saw the invading joint forces, they cried out, "This is what God and His Messenger have promised us, and God and His Messenger have spoken the truth." And it only served to increase their faith and submission (to God).

²³ Among the believers, there are men who honored their pledge to God. Some have already fulfilled it (through death), and some are still waiting. Their (determination) has not changed a bit. ²⁴ (Such trials are ordained) so that God may reward the faithful for being true to their word, and punish the hypocrites if He so wills or accepts their repentance. Verily, God is Most Forgiving, Most Compassionate.

²⁵ (In the end), God (spared the believers the need to fight and) repulsed the infidels back (to Makkah empty handed) with their hearts seething in rage; no benefit did they gain (from this failed expedition). *ᵇ* Verily, sufficient is God to protect the believers in battle. Indeed, God is Most Powerful, Almighty.

²⁶ As for the Jewish traitors who had supported the invading joint forces, He brought them down from their fortresses, casting terror in their hearts. Some you killed, and some you took captive. ²⁷ And then He made you inherit

---

ᵃ This verse should be read in conjunction with verse 3:31, "Say (to them O Prophet), "If you love God, then follow me, for God will love you and forgive your sins." These two verses are sufficient to quash the belief of those who claim that the Qur'an alone is sufficient as guidance for Muslims without having to follow the teachings and practices of Prophet Muhammad (may peace and blessings be upon him) which is called the *sunnah*. The Qur'an actually serves as the overall policy or guideline of Islam while the Prophet's *sunnah* shows how the Qur'an should be practiced and applied. These two go hand-in-hand together just as the Muslims' *shahada* or proclamation of faith does, which bears witness that there is only One Almighty God who deserves all worship and Muhammad is His final Messenger. Islam is incomplete without one of the other. Furthermore, his speech and actions are guided by God. See verses 53:3-4.
ᵇ The siege lasted several weeks but all attempts by the confederates to cross the trench were repulsed with heavy losses even though the trench was manned by a smaller number and less well-armed Muslims. On top of this, dissensions - based on mutual distrust - gradually undermined the alliance between the Jewish and the pagan Arab tribes. Their frustration became complete when a bitterly-cold storm-wind raged for several days, making life unbearable even for hardened warriors. And so, finally, the siege was raised and the confederates dispersed, thus ending the last attempt of the pagans to destroy the Prophet and his nascent community.

their land, their homes, their properties, and a land where you had never set foot yet (in Khaybar). Verily God has power over all things.

Unlike All Women

²⁸ O Prophet! Say to your wives, "If you seek the world and its embellishments, then come! I shall make some provision for you and release you in an honorable way. ²⁹ But if you desire God and His Messenger and the (excellent) life in the Hereafter, then indeed, God has prepared a great reward for those of you who excel in good deeds (and remain steadfast)." *ᵃ*

³⁰ O wives of the Prophet! If any of you commit a clear immorality, her punishment will be double (of other sinners). And it is (indeed) easy for God (to have this executed). ³¹ And whoever among you is obedient to God and His Messenger and does good deeds, We shall double her reward (in the life to come), and We have prepared for her a generous provision.

³² O wives of the Prophet! Your (status) is unlike other women. If you are truly mindful of God (and do not want to incur His displeasure), then do not be too soft in speech to men, lest he - in whose heart might have a disease - might be moved with desire and covet you. Instead, speak in an appropriate and firm manner. ³³ Stay in your homes and do not show-off yourselves like (how the womenfolk) during the former time of ignorance used to do. Be constant in prayer, render the purifying dues (punctually), and obey God and His Messenger. O members of the Prophet's household! Verily, God intends to remove impurity from you and to purify you completely. ³⁴ Be ever mindful of what is recited in your homes from God's verses and the (tradition of prophetic) wisdom. Indeed, God is All-Subtle, All-Aware.

³⁵ For all men and women who have submitted themselves to God, all men and women who are believers, all men and women who are truly devout, all

---

ᵃ By the time this verse was revealed, the Muslims had conquered the rich agricultural region of Khaybar, and the community had grown more prosperous. But while life was becoming easier for most of its members, this ease was not reflected in the household of the Prophet who, as before, allowed himself and his family only the absolute minimum necessary for the most simple living. In view of the changed circumstances, it was no more than natural that his wives were longing for a share in the comparative luxuries which other Muslim women could now enjoy. But an acquiescence by the Prophet to their demands would have conflicted with the principle observed by him throughout his life, that the standard of living of God's Messenger and his family should not be higher than that of the poorest of the believers. See also verses 66:5-6.

men and women who are true to their word, all men and women who are patient in adversity, all men and women who humble themselves to God, all men and women who spend in charity, all men and women who fast, all men and women who are mindful of their chastity, and all men and women who always keep God in their remembrance; verily, God has prepared forgiveness and a great reward for all of them. [36] (Therefore,) it is not befitting for a believing man or woman to seek other options when a matter has been decided by God and His Messenger. Whoever disobeys God and His Messenger has clearly strayed into error.

God's Will Shall Always Prevail

[37] (O Prophet! Call to mind) when you said to the person who had received God's grace and your favor, "Hold on to your wife and be mindful of God," while you were concealing within yourself what God was about to reveal for fear of what people (might think of you), whereas it is God alone Whom you should fear more. So when Zayd formally ended his claim on her (through divorce), We gave her to you in marriage so that there would be no restriction on the believers after this concerning the wives of their adopted sons when the latter have ended their claim of marriage on their spouse (through divorce). And the command of God must be carried out. *a*

---

a Several years before Muhammad's call to Prophethood, his wife Khadijah gave him a present of a young slave - Zayd ibn Harithah, a descendant of the North-Arabian tribe of Banu Kalb, who had been taken captive as a child in the course of one of the many tribal wars and then sold into slavery at Makkah. As soon as he became the boy's owner, the Prophet freed him, and shortly afterwards adopted him as his son; and Zayd in his turn, was among the first to embrace Islam. Years later, impelled by the desire to break down the ancient Arabian prejudice against a slave's or even a freedman's marriage to a "free-born" woman, the Prophet persuaded Zayd to marry his (i.e. the Prophet's) own cousin, Zaynab binti Jahsh. Hence, she consented to the proposed marriage with great reluctance, only in obedience to the Qur'anic injunction of verse 33:36. Since Zayd too, was not at all keen on this alliance (being already happily married to another freed slave - Umm Ayman), it was not surprising that the marriage did not bring happiness to either Zaynab or Zayd. On several occasions the latter was about to divorce his new wife who, on her part, did not make any secret of her dislike of Zayd; but each time they were persuaded by the Prophet to persevere in patience and not to separate. In the end, however, the marriage proved untenable, and Zayd divorced Zaynab in the year 5H. Shortly afterwards, the Prophet was commanded by God to marry Zaynab to fulfill His decree that was designed to remove the society's customary restriction and taboo regarding marriage between a guardian and his or her adopted child or their former spouses, which was deemed as incestuous because they regarded adopted sons the same as a biological son. Against such negative "public

³⁸ There can be no blame upon the Prophet concerning what God has ordained for him. Such is the way of God that has prevailed with (all the Prophets) in the past (and will always continue to prevail). And the command of God is a destiny decreed. ³⁹ Those who (have been chosen to) convey God's messages fear and stand in awe of Him alone and no one else. Sufficient is God as the Reckoner of all things.

⁴⁰ (O believers! Verily,) Muhammad is not the father of any of your men, but he is the Messenger of God and the seal of Prophethood. Verily, God has full knowledge of everything.

⁴¹ O you who believe! Remember God with much remembrance; ⁴² and glorify His (perfection) in the morning and evening. ⁴³ It is He Who blesses you while His Angels (pray for you) so that He may lead you out of the depth of darkness into light. Indeed, He is Most Compassionate to the believers. ⁴⁴ Their greetings on the Day when they meet Him will be "Peace!" And He has prepared a noble (and generous) reward for them.

⁴⁵ O Prophet! Indeed, We have sent you as a witness, and a bearer of good news and a warner; ⁴⁶ and as one who invites people to God by His grace, like a beacon of light (showing the way to all). ⁴⁷ So give good news to the believers that God has a great bounty (in store for them). ⁴⁸ Do not obey those who openly refuse to accept the truth and the hypocrites. Disregard their hurtful remarks and put your trust (only) in God. Sufficient is God as the Guardian (Whom you entrust your affairs to).

---

opinion", it was natural for the Prophet to feel quite uncomfortable about what he was tasked to do. To compound the problem, the hypocrites quickly took advantage of the situation to launch a slanderous attack on the Prophet in an attempt to divide the Muslim community. However, this baseless taboo was objected by the Qur'an and the marriage was justified through the revelation of verse 4 of this chapter which mentioned that treating adopted sons as real sons was forbidden, and that there should now be a complete break with past beliefs that hold no ground with divine decrees. For further clarity, the Qur'an then spelled out in 4:22-26, the types of marriages that are forbidden in Islam on the basis of blood relationships. Hence, any union between a man and woman that is not mentioned in this list, such as the marriage between someone to the former wife of his adopted son as in this case in question now, is clearly permissible in Islam. As such, the marriage between the Prophet and Zaynab was no less than a duty imposed upon him by God that must be fulfilled to serve its divine purpose, and at the same time become a living example and reference of Islam's ruling over the society.

Detailed Legal Provision

⁴⁹ O you who believe! When you marry believing women and divorce them before you have touched them, then there is no waiting period on their part that you should reckon. Hence, make provision for them (at once) and release them in an honorable manner.

⁵⁰ O Prophet! We have made lawful for you your wives whose bridal dues you have paid, as well as those slave-girls in your possession whom God has given you (from the captives of war), and the daughters of your paternal uncles and aunts, and the daughters of your maternal uncles and aunts who have migrated with you (to Madinah), and any believing woman who offers herself to the Prophet whom he might be willing to marry. Verily, this privilege is yours alone to the exclusion of other believers whom We have made known the rulings that We imposed upon them concerning their wives and slave-girls they rightfully possess so that you will not be at fault (if you exercise your privilege). Verily, God is Most Forgiving, Most Compassionate.

⁵¹ (O Prophet!) It is permissible for you to defer or receive whoever your please among your wives. There is no blame on you if you desire (and invite) anyone whose turn you had previously set aside. This is most proper so that their eyes may be gladdened (whenever they see you) and not grieve (by the thought of being overlooked), and will find contentment in whatever you give them. (Therefore O wives of the Prophet, be mindful that) God knows all that is in your hearts; for God is All-Knowing, Most Forbearing.

⁵² (O Prophet!) From this point onwards, no other women will be lawful for you (to marry), nor are you (allowed) to replace any of them with new wives even though their beauty may be pleasing to you. ᵃ However, those slave-girls whom you rightfully possess are an exception ᵇ (if you wish to marry them. Remember that) God keeps watch over all things.

ᵃ This verse deals with the prohibition that was imposed on the Prophet from marrying anymore than those whom he was already married to. Most early commentators believe this verse was revealed in 7H after the Battle of Khaybar which saw the Prophet's marriage to Safiyya bint Huyayy who is of Jewish descent, whose father and husband were killed in that battle. This marriage is believed to be his last before this verse was revealed.

ᵇ This exception to the marriage prohibition mentioned in the preceding passage refers to the Prophet's marriage to his handmaiden - Mary the Copt, a slave-girl who was sent as a present by the Christian Muqawqis of Egypt to the Prophet. She became the mother of the Prophet's only son - Ibrahim, who died in his infancy.

⁵³ O you who believe! Do not enter the Prophet's houses without permission except when invited for a meal. But do not come too early to wait for its preparation. Enter only when you are invited and disperse when you have eaten without lingering around in idle talk. Such behavior troubles the Prophet and he feels shy (and awkward) in asking you to leave. But God does not feel shy in telling the truth. And if you have to ask (his wives) for anything, speak to them from behind a partition. This is purer for both your hearts and theirs. It is not proper for you to annoy the Messenger of God, nor to ever marry his wives after him. This would be a grievous offence in the sight of God. ⁵⁴ Indeed, God has full knowledge of all things whether you reveal them or not.

⁵⁵ There is no blame upon the wives of the Prophet to appear freely before their fathers, their sons, their brothers, their brothers' sons, their sisters' sons, their womenfolk, or (such slaves) whom they rightfully possess. Therefore (O wives of the Prophet!) Be ever mindful of God, for God is a witness over everything.

⁵⁶ Verily, God and His Angels shower their blessings on the Prophet. Hence, O believers! Invoke (divine) blessings on him too, and greet him with a (respectable) salutation of peace. ⁵⁷ Verily, God has laid His curse in this world and in the life to come upon those who insult Him and His Messenger, and has prepared a humiliating punishment for them. ⁵⁸ And those who hurt (the feelings) believing men and women for no fault of theirs will bear the guilt of slander and a flagrant sin.

⁵⁹ O Prophet! Tell your wives and daughters, and all believing women to draw their outer garments over themselves (loosely). *ᵃ* This will make it more likely for them to be recognized (as decent women) and avoid from being (harassed and) harmed. And God is Most Forgiving, Most Compassionate.

⁶⁰ If the hypocrites, those with sickness in their hearts, and those who spread lies in the city do not desist (from vile acts that include harassing women), We shall rouse you against them and make their days as your neighbors numbered. ⁶¹ Accursed, they will be seized and put to death mercilessly wherever found. ⁶² Such is God's way with those before you. You will never find any change in God's way.

ᵃ As clearly spelled-out here, the wives and daughters of the Prophet, and all other Muslim women were being commanded to loosely cover their body with outer garments that should conceal its shape and also not expose their necks and bosoms in the presence of those who were not included in the list of people mentioned in verse 55 of this chapter and also in 24:31

Too Heavy for Mountains

⁶³ (O Prophet! When) people ask you about the (Last) Hour, say, "Its knowledge is only with God. But who knows - perhaps the Hour may be close at hand!" ⁶⁴ Indeed, God curses those who reject the truth and has prepared for them a Blazing Fire; ⁶⁵ (where they will) remain in it forever and they will not find any protector or helper. ⁶⁶ On that Day when their faces are being tossed about in the Fire, they will say, "O how we wish we had obeyed God and His Messenger (before)!" ⁶⁷ And they will say, "Our Lord! Indeed, we (have wrongly) obeyed our leaders and our great men, and they misled us from the right way. ⁶⁸ O our Lord! Give them double punishment and curse them with a great curse."

⁶⁹ O you who believe! Do not distress (your Prophet) just like how the children of Israel used to do to Moses (with their antics). But God cleared him of all the (frivolous demands and) allegations that they made against him and he was highly honored in the sight of God. *ᵃ*

⁷⁰ O you who believe! (Always) be mindful of God and speak the truth. ⁷¹ He will rectify your deeds and forgive your sins. And whoever obeys God and His Messenger has certainly achieved a great triumph.

⁷² Indeed, We offered the trust (of reason and volition) to the heavens, the earth, and the mountains but they refrained from bearing the burden, for fear (of the great responsibility that comes with it). But man took this task upon himself for he is indeed unjust and ignorant (of the consequence). ⁷³ As such, God will punish men and women who are hypocrites, as well as men and women who associate partners with Him (as the consequence of their betrayal of this mighty trust). But He will turn in His mercy to believing men and women (who repent from their mistakes and mend their ways), for He is indeed Most Forgiving, Most Compassionate.

ᵃ This is an allusion to the aspersions occasionally cast upon Moses by some of his followers and mentioned in the Old Testament (e.g. Exodus 17:1-7), as well as to the blasphemous demands that the Qur'an mentions about, for example : "O Moses! We shall never believe you (and will not follow what you have instructed us) until we clearly see God with our own eyes." (2:55), or "So go forth and fight both of you, just you and your Lord!" (5:24). These instances are paralleled here with the frequently cited accusations by the disbelievers that Muhammad had invented the Qur'an and then falsely attributed it to God, that he was a madman, and so forth; as well as with frivolous demands to prove his Prophethood by bringing about miracles or by predicting the date of the Last Hour as stated in verse 63 of this chapter.

34. Saba'
[The Nation of Sheba : 54 verses]

T his is an early Makkan chapter that emphasizes on the fundamentals of faith namely monotheism, the Prophethood of Muhammad, resurrection and judgment. These themes are brought home by various arguments. Reference is made to Prophets David and Solomon on whom God had bestowed special favors. Reference is also made to the people of *Saba'* (i.e. the nation of Sheba in Yemen) to whom God had blessed with peace and prosperity together with a thriving agriculture but they turned ungrateful. Hence their prosperity was destroyed by the bursting of the Ma'arib Dam. This chapter is named after this incident.

In the name of God, the Most Gracious, the Most Compassionate.

Infinite and Accurate Knowledge

¹ Praise be to God to Whom belongs all that is in the heavens and the earth, and praise be to Him in the Hereafter too. He is truly All-Wise, All-Aware. ² He knows all that goes into the earth and all that comes out of it, and all that comes down from the heaven and all that ascends to it. And He is the Most Compassionate, the Most Forgiving.

³ But those who reject the truth say, "The (Last) Hour will not come to us." Say (to them), "Nay! By my Lord, it will surely come to you. He is the Knower of the unseen." Nothing escapes Him, not even an atom's weight in the heavens or earth; nor anything smaller or bigger than that. It is all written in a clear record; ⁴ so that He may reward those who believe and do righteous deeds. They will have forgiveness and a noble provision. ⁵ But for those who strive against Our signs and revelations seeking to undermine them, a severe and grievous punishment (awaits them).

⁶ (O Prophet!) Those who are endowed with knowledge are well aware that what has been revealed to you by your Lord is indeed the truth, and that it guides to the way that leads to the Almighty, to Whom all praise is due. ⁷ But those who refuse to accept the truth (deride you and) say, "Shall we show you a man who claims that when you have completely disintegrated (in the soil), you will be raised (to life again) in a new creation?" ⁸ (They add further,) "Is he telling lies about God, or is he mad?" Nay! Indeed, those who do not believe in the life to come are doomed and have gone hopelessly astray. ⁹ Do they not consider how little of the heavens and the earth lies open before them, and how much is actually hidden from them? If We so willed, We could cause the earth to swallow them, or cause fragments of the sky to fall upon them

(because of their stubbornness). Indeed, there is truly a sign in this for every servant of God who turns to Him (for guidance).

Contrasting Attitudes

¹⁰ And verily, We bestowed Our bounty upon David. We commanded, "O mountains! Echo his songs of praise to God. And you birds too!" We also made iron soft and pliant for him; ¹¹ saying, "(O David!) Make coats of armour and measure their links accurately (so that they will fit perfectly). Work righteously (and do good); for indeed, I am watching over everything that you do."

¹² And to Solomon, (We subdued) the wind - its morning course covered the distance of a month's journey and its evening course also a month's journey.ᵃ We gave him a stream flowing with molten copper, and (We

---

ᵃ This verse should be read in conjunction with verses 21:81 and 38:36. Some classical commentators alluded the story of Solomon and the wind that God made subservient to him in a literal sense where he could travel to far places on a flying carpet. The story originated from a particular Jewish exegesis called the *Midrash* and is also mentioned in the Jewish Encyclopedia. Another possible interpretation of this verse looks at it from a more rational perspective. It is a historical fact that the kingdom of Solomon (i.e. Palestine today) rose to unrivaled prominence and enjoyed peace and prosperity due to his great rule and astute diplomacy with neighboring and distant kingdoms. At the same time, he was also known to have a large naval fleet under his command. In a book titled "On The Shores of The Great Sea" written by M.B. Synge that was published in 1909, the following passage is found in pages 45-48 under the chapter called King Solomon's Fleet: "Guided by Phœnician pilots and manned by Phœnician sailors, the Phœnicians and Israelites sailed forth together on their mysterious voyages, into the southern seas. They sailed to India, to Arabia and Somaliland, and they returned with their ships laden with gold and silver, with ivory and precious stones, with apes and peacocks. The amount of gold brought to Solomon by his navy was enormous. Silver was so abundant, as to be thought nothing of in those days, and all the king's drinking-cups and vessels were of wrought gold, and every three years his fleet returned with yet more and more gold and silver." It is without doubt that the movement of ships during that time depended very much on the power of wind to sail (see verse 42:33). In view of this, a more plausible explanation of this verse is to view it as a metaphor of God gifting Solomon with the knowledge to effectively harness the natural power of wind to direct his large fleet of ships to faraway lands to actively conduct trade that consequently brought riches and great prosperity to his kingdom. With regard to the phrase "*its morning course covered the distance of a month's journey and its evening course also a month's journey*" mentioned in this verse, this could metaphorically mean that the voyages performed by these ships were surely many times speedier than traveling across land on foot.

subdued for him) some of the Jinn, who by his Lord's permission, worked (under his control) in front of him. And whoever among them deviated from Our command, We made them taste the punishment of the Blazing Fire.

¹³ (And so) they made for Solomon what he desired - elevated chambers, statues, bowls like reservoirs, and cauldrons fixed (in their places. Then We said,) "Keep working in gratitude to your Lord, O family of David; for indeed, only few of My servants are grateful."

¹⁴ And when We executed Our decree of death on Solomon, nothing indicated to the Jinn that he was dead except termites eating away his staff. Then when he fell down, it became clear to the Jinn that if they had really known the (secrets of the) unseen, (surely) they would not have remained in their humiliating servitude.

¹⁵ Indeed, in (the luxuriant beauty of) their homeland, the people of Sheba enjoyed a sign (of God's grace). They were given two (vast expanses of) gardens, one to the right and the other one to the left. (And they were told,) "Eat from what your Lord has provided you and be grateful to Him. Your land is good and your Lord is Most Forgiving." ¹⁶ But they turned away (from their Lord in defiance); so We let loose upon them a (devastating) flood from the dam (of Ma'rib) and replaced their gardens with others that produced bitter fruits, tamarisk bushes and a few Lote trees. ¹⁷ This was how We punished them for their ingratitude (and arrogance). And none do We punish (in this manner) except those who are ungrateful.

¹⁸ (Before their downfall), We placed other prominent towns with well-measured stages of journey between them and the towns that We had blessed (so that they would find ease in their travel. Then We said,) "Travel safely in this land by night and day." ¹⁹ But they pleaded, "Our Lord! Lengthen the distance between our journey stages (so that we could expand our trade)." And (because of their greed,) they wronged themselves (when they became oblivious of God as the consequence of being too indulged in their worldly affairs). So We reduced them to bygone tales and dispersed them (throughout the land) in scattered fragments. Indeed, in this (story) are sure signs (and important lessons to draw from) for those who are steadfast and grateful.

²⁰ And *Iblis* had certainly found his notion (and expectation) of men proven true. ª Indeed, most followed him, except a group of devoted believers. ²¹ Yet he had no power over them but We (allowed him to have his way for Us

---

ª The notion that man will not be grateful to God for all the favors that he has been blessed with (see verse 7:16-17) and choose to disobey and act in defiance against God.

to) make evident between the one who believes in the life to come, and the one who is in doubt about it. And your Lord is a Guardian over all things.

Distinct Ways, Different Ends

²² (O Prophet!) Say (to those who deny you), "Call upon those whom you worship besides God (if you will). They do not even hold an atom's weight of authority in the heavens or earth, nor do they have any share of partnership in (creating and governing) them, nor are they even helpers to God."

²³ God does not entertain any (plea for) intercession except to those whom He permits (to intercede and those whom He permits to receive. So on the Day of Judgment, those who expect to be granted   intercession will wait in hope and suspense) until terror is lifted from their hearts and then they will ask (those who are permitted to intercede for them), "What did your Lord say?" They will reply, "The truth (as He promised! Intercession is only granted to those who are permitted to give and receive).   Verily, He alone is the Most Exalted, the Most Great."

²⁴ Ask (those disbelievers O Prophet), "Who provides you sustenance from the heavens and the earth? Is it not God? Surely only one of us can be rightly guided, while the other is clearly astray." ²⁵ Tell them, "You will not be called to account for our sins, nor will we be called to account for what you did." ²⁶ Say, "Our Lord will gather us together, then He will judge between us in truth (and justice), for He alone is the One Who is the Ultimate Decider of the Truth, the All-Knowing." ²⁷ Say, "Show me those whom you have joined with Him as partners (in worship). By no means (can they ever be God)! In fact, He alone is God, the Almighty, the All-Wise."

Futile Argument

²⁸ (O Prophet!) We have not sent you except as a bearer of good news and a warner for all mankind. But most people do not know (and care about this). ²⁹ They ask you, "When will this promise of resurrection be fulfilled if you speak the truth?" ³⁰ Say (to them), "Your day has been fixed and you can neither delay nor advance it even by a moment."

³¹ Those who are bent on opposing the truth (among the idolaters) say, "We shall never believe in this Qur'an, nor in any Scripture before it." If you could only see when these wrongdoers are arraigned before their Lord (on the Day of Resurrection), they will hurl charges against the others. The weak (followers) will say to their arrogant (leaders), "Had it not been for you, we would have surely become believers. (It was you who misled us)!" ³² But the

arrogant (leaders) will reply to their weak (followers), "Did we force you away from (God's) guidance after it came to you? Surely not! Instead, you became sinners (out of your own volition and are now guilty of your own doing)."

³³ Then the weak (followers) will say to their arrogant (leaders), "By no means! We are in this predicament now because of your scheming - night and day - ordering us to not believe in God and to set up others as His equals." And (when they see the suffering that awaits them,) all of them will not be able to express (the full depth of) their remorse while We place shackles on the necks of these rejecters of truth. They will not be requited except for what they have done (and earned from their evil deeds).

³⁴ We did not send a warner to any city except its wealthy (and influential) ones would say, "Behold! We refuse to believe in the message that you (claim to) have been sent with." ³⁵ And they added, "We have more wealth and children than you, and surely nothing can harm us." ³⁶ Say (to them), "Indeed, my Lord extends and restricts provision to whomsoever He wills (according to His wisdom), but most people do not know (that this is a test of faith from Him)."

³⁷ And it is not your wealth nor your children that will bring you nearer to Us. Instead, whoever believes (in God, the Day of resurrection) and does righteous deeds, then for them will be a two-fold reward for what they have done and they will live peacefully in the mansions of Paradise; ³⁸ whereas those who strive against Our signs (and revelations) seeking to defeat their purpose will be brought to punishment. ³⁹ Say, "Indeed, my Lord extends and restricts the provision for whomsoever He wills among His servants (according to His wisdom, as a means to test their faith). And whatever you spend in His cause from the provision that He has granted you, He will replace it (generously). He is indeed the Best of Providers.

⁴⁰ And on that Day, He will gather them altogether and then say to the Angels, "Was it you that these people used to worship?" ⁴¹ The Angels will reply, "Glory be to You (O God Who are the Most Perfect)! You are our Protector, not them. But they used to worship the Jinn in whom most of these (misguided) people believed." ⁴² So on that Day, none of you will have any power to benefit or harm one another. And to the evil wrongdoers, We shall say, "Taste now the punishment of the (Blazing) Fire which you had (persistently) denied (in arrogance)!"

Final Warning

⁴³ And whenever Our messages are clearly conveyed to those (idolaters), they say, "This (Muhammad) is nothing but a man who wants to turn you

away from what your forefathers have been worshipping (for ages)." And they say, "This (Qur'an) is nothing but a lie invented (by Muhammad)." And when the truth came to those who refuse to believe it, they declared, "This is nothing but a clear evil spell (meant to bewitch us)!" [44] Yet, never have We given them any Scripture to study, nor have We sent them any warner before you (O Prophet). [45] (This was how) their forefathers denounced the truth too. Verily, those who deny you now have not even received a tenth of (the wealth, skill and power) that We had granted to their predecessors. (Do they not see) how dreadful was My rejection (to those who denied My Messengers in the past)?

[46] Say (to them O Prophet), "Verily, Let me give you a piece of advice : Whether you are in the company of others or you are alone, stand up for God's sake and then ponder (about Muhammad whom you know very well). Indeed, there is no madness in this fellow-man of yours. Instead, he is only a warner who is being sent to you before the coming of a severe punishment (that will fall upon those who stubbornly defy God's revelations)." [47] Say to them, "No reward have I ever asked you out of anything that is yours. (Keep it for yourself.) My reward is from God alone. Verily, He is a witness over all things." [48] Say, "Indeed, my Lord sends down the truth (and makes it evident from all that is false)." Verily, only He has full knowledge of all that is hidden and unseen.

[49] Announce to them, "The truth has arrived. All the falsehood (that you worship) can neither bring forth anything new, nor bring back (what has passed)." [50] Say (further), "If I am astray, that is my loss. But if I am rightly-guided, then it is because of what my Lord has revealed to me. Verily, He is All-Hearing, Ever Near." [51] And if only you could see how terrified the disbelievers will be (on the Day of Resurrection)! They will have no escape and will be seized from a place near (the Hellfire before they are hurled into it). [52] And then they will say, "We believe (in Your revelation) now!" But how can they hope to attain salvation at a place that is so far away (from where they had spent their earthly life earlier)?

[53] And certainly, they had rejected the truth before and cast slanders about the unseen [a] from a place far away (from the Hereafter). [54] And so (on that Day), a barrier will be placed between them and what they desperately wish for, [b] just like the fate of those of their kind that came before. Indeed, this is the consequence of their suspicious doubts (and rejection of Our revelation).

---

[a] The Day of Resurrection.
[b] A chance to return to the world and repent.

35. Fāṭir
[The Originator of Creation : 45 verses]

This is another Makkan chapter that deals with the same theme of faith as in the other Makkan chapters. It opens with emphasizing that all praise is due to God alone Who is the Originator and Creator of the entire universe and all beings - both animate and inanimate. It is He alone Who sustains and manages all creations and provides for every being without the help of any partner. The chapter is named after this attribute of God which is mentioned in its first verse.

In the name of God, the Most Gracious, the Most Compassionate.

Giving All Grace

¹ All praise is due to God, the Originator of the heavens and the earth, Who made the Angels as His message bearers, having two, three, or four wings. He adds to His creation whatever He wills. Verily, God has power over everything. ² Whatever grace God opens for people, none can withhold it. And whatever He withholds, none can release it. And He alone is the Almighty, Truly Wise.

³ O mankind! Remember God's favor upon you. Is there any creator other than God who can provide sustenance for you from the heaven and the earth? Indeed, there is no god but He (alone). How then are you being deluded from this truth? ⁴ If they deny you (and call you a liar O Muhammad), other Messengers before you were certainly treated the same way too. (So do not despair, because) everything will be brought back to God (for judgment in the end).

The Lurking Enemy

⁵ O mankind! Verily, God's promise (of resurrection) is true, so let not the life of this world deceive you, nor let (Satan and your) deceptive thoughts about God delude you.

⁶ Behold! Satan is an enemy to you, so treat him as an enemy. Verily, he invites his followers (to his way) so that they will all be among the inmates of the Blazing Fire (with him). ⁷ For those who disbelieve in God (and the Day of Resurrection), there is severe punishment in store for them; whereas for those who believe and do righteous deeds, forgiveness and a great reward awaits them.

⁸ How (awful) is (the straying of) the person for whom his evil deeds have been embellished and made attractive to him (by Satan)? Indeed, God lets go astray whomsoever He wills (that refuses to accept guidance) and guides aright whomsoever He wills (that turns to Him in repentance and devotion. So) do not waste your soul with sorrow for them (O Prophet). Verily, God is All-Aware of everything that they do.

⁹ And God is the One Who sends the winds so that they stir and raise the clouds. Then We drive them to a dead land and revive it (with rain) after it was lifeless. That is how the dead will be resurrected (one day). ¹⁰ (Therefore,) those who seek honor and glory should know that all honor and glory belongs to God alone. (Verily,) all good words ascend to Him, and all righteous deeds are lifted up by Him. But as for those who cunningly plot evil deeds, severe punishment awaits them; and all their plotting will only come to waste.

Fashioning All Creations

¹¹ And (remember, that it is) God Who created you from soil, then from a clot of semen, then He made you into pairs (of male and female). There is not a female who conceives, nor delivers a child except with His knowledge. No one is given a long life nor is his life shortened except it is (already decreed and written) in a register. That is certainly easy for God.

¹² And not alike are the two bodies of water. One is fresh, sweet, and pleasant to drink; and the other is salty and bitter. And from both you eat fresh meat and extract ornaments that you wear. You also see ships ploughing through it so that you may seek His bounty and be grateful to Him.

¹³ He causes the night to enter into the day and causes the day to enter into the night, and He has subjected the sun and the moon, each running in its specific course for an appointed term. That is God, your Lord; to Him belongs the dominion of all the worlds. And those whom you invoke besides Him do not possess even the membrane of a date-seed. ¹⁴ If you invoke them, they do not hear your call. And even if they could hear, they would not (be able to) respond to you. And on the Day of Resurrection, they will deny that you have associated them with God. And none can inform you of the truth like Him Who is All-Aware.

Individual Responsibility

¹⁵ O mankind! It is you who stand in need of God. As for God, He is All-Sufficient, Immensely Praiseworthy. ¹⁶ If He so wills, He can obliterate you and replace you with a new creation. ¹⁷ And that is not difficult for God (at all). ¹⁸ (Verily,) no soul will be made to bear the burden of another. Even if a

heavily laden soul cries for help, none of its load will be carried by anyone, not even by his near of kin. Hence, you can only warn those who stand in awe of their unseen Lord (to not disobey Him) and attend regularly to their prayer. Whoever purifies himself does so for (the benefit of) his own soul. And to God is the final return (of all things).

[19] (Verily,) the blind and the seeing are not alike; [20] nor darkness and light; [21] nor shade and heat; [22] nor are the living and the dead. Behold (O Prophet)! God can make whomsoever He wills hear (His message); whereas you certainly cannot make those who are in their graves, hear. [23] Verily, you are only a warner. [24] Indeed, We have sent you with the truth as a bearer of good news and a warner. And there is not a community (before you) except a warner has been sent to (convey Our message of truth to) them. [25] And if your people reject you, so did those before them to whom came their Messengers with clear signs, Scriptures and the Book, all giving light (for guidance). [26] Then (in the end), I seized those who rejected (My Messengers). How (dreadful) was My rejection (of them)!

Reciters of God's Revelations

[27] Do you not see how God sends down rain from the sky, then We produce fruits of various colors with it? And in the mountains are tracts with streaks of varying shades of white, red and other colors including pitch-black. [28] Likewise people, moving creatures and cattle are of various colors too. Verily, only those among His servants with knowledge are the ones who (truly stand in awe of Him and) are fearful of His (wrath if they defy Him). [a] Indeed,

---

[a] Those who care to study, observe and ponder with pure sincerity in the name of The Ultimate Creator about the existence of this universe and what it contains including the existence of life will be truly amazed and awed by the sheer power and greatness of this Supreme Being whom we call God. Nothing He has created is in vain and serves no purpose (verse 3:191). Everything is created with a reason that is known to Him alone. Our limited knowledge and brain power will never make it possible for us to understand the purpose of the zillion things that He has created. As the ultimate source of knowledge, He teaches and reveals to us only what He wills and whatever He conceals and withholds from us will never be known (verse 2:255). Nevertheless, man is being commanded to earnestly seek as much knowledge as he can about these creations (96:1-5) as the means to appreciate His greatness and be truly humbled by His mightiness and awesome power. These magnificent and wondrous creations and signs are imprinted all over the universe and also within ourselves too for us to explore (verse 41:53) so that mankind can benefit from the knowledge gained. By exploring them too, we should come to the realization of how weak humans really are and how dependent we are on our Creator's mercy, for we are not in control of many things that are around us and also within us. Even our own internal body functions are beyond our

God is Almighty, Most Forgiving.

²⁹ Verily, those who recite the Book of God and are constant in their prayer and spend (in His cause) either secretly or openly out of what We have provided them, it is they who hope for a trade that will never suffer loss; ³⁰ for He will grant them their full reward and may give them more out of His (infinite) bounty. Indeed, He is Most Forgiving, Most Appreciative of His devotees. ³¹ (O Prophet!) What We have revealed to you of the Qur'an is the truth, confirming the Scriptures and Books that came before it. Verily, God is well aware of His servants; He sees and observes everything.

³² And so, We chose some of Our servants to inherit the Book. Some of them were unjust to their own souls; some were half-way (between right and wrong); and some, by God's grace, were foremost in good deeds - and that indeed is of the greatest merit! ³³ They will enter the Gardens of Eternity, adorned with bracelets of gold and pearls, and (wearing) garments of silk. ³⁴ And they will say, "All praise is due to God, Who has removed all sorrow from us. Indeed, our Lord is surely Most Forgiving, Most Appreciative; ³⁵ the One Who, out of His Bounty, has settled us in this everlasting home where no fatigue or weariness will ever touch us."

³⁶ (As for those who (persistently) reject the truth, the Fire of Hell awaits them. There, they will not be silenced and die, nor will their torment be lightened. That is how We requite every ungrateful disbeliever. ³⁷ And they will cry, "Our Lord! Take us out (from here and return us to the world!) We shall (believe and) do righteous deeds, unlike what we used to do." ª And they will be told, "Did We not give you a life long enough for anyone to take heed (if he wanted to)? Besides, did a warner not come to (convey Our message of truth to) you? So taste now (the torment for your obstinance). Indeed, there

---

control and we take this all for granted and are seldom grateful for the blessings that we receive. Rightfully, we must be mindful of how we should lead our lives during our brief transit and sojourn on His earth to be in accordance with what He - our Landlord and The Ultimate Creator of all - has prescribed in order to earn His pleasure and avoid His wrath. In the end, no matter how strong and powerful we think we are, We shall inevitably grow old and become feeble (verse 16:70) before we return to Him for the reckoning of our deeds. No one can ever escape this. Only those who truly have faith in the One and Only Almighty God are always mindful of Him, and fear this; and hope that they will be graced with His mercy and compassion on the day when everyone is made to stand before Him to account and be requited for all their deeds. Indeed, only those with knowledge of the truth are the ones who are truly in awe of Him and will wholly submit themselves to Him, knowing in full conviction that only He alone deserves all worship.

ª See verse 23:99-100 and its footnote.

will be none to help the (evil) wrongdoers."

The Fate of Evil Design

[38] Verily, (only) God knows the unseen (secrets of the) the heavens and the earth. Indeed, He fully knows what is contained in everyone's heart. [39] He is the One Who made you His emissaries on earth. Those who deny the truth will bear the consequences. Their denial adds nothing except the wrath of their Lord against them and an increase to their own loss.

[40] Ask (them O Prophet), "Have you ever seen those (patrons and) partners whom you invoke besides God? Show me what part of the earth have they created, or what share of the heavens do they have?" Have We given these disbelievers a Book with a clear proof in it (that allows them to associate others with God in His divinity)?" Nay! The evil wrongdoers promise each other nothing but delusion. [41] Behold! It is God (alone) Who holds the heavens and the earth from (falling apart and) vanish. And if they ever (fall apart and) vanish, there is no one else who can hold them back besides Him. Indeed, He is Most Forbearing, Most Forgiving.

[42] And they swore by God their most solemn oaths that if a warner ever came to them, surely they would be better guided than any other community. Yet when a warner did come to them, his coming only increased their aversion to the truth. [43] They also became more arrogant in the land and (intensified their) plotting of evil. Yet their evil plot will harm no one except its own plotters. So can they expect for anything better than what had befallen those of earlier times (who had also rejected the truth? Surely,) you will never find any change in the way God (handles those who oppose His religion).

[44] Have they not traveled throughout the land and observed how was the end of those (who were mightier than them in) earlier times? There is nothing in the heavens and the earth that is beyond the power of God and can escape Him. Indeed, He is All-Knowing, All-Powerful.

[45] And if God were to instantly punish people for their misdeeds, not a single creature would be left alive on the surface of the earth. But He grants them respite until an appointed term. And when their term comes (to an end), then (they will finally realize that) God has always been watching over all His servants and knows everything that they do.

36. Ya Sīn
[83 verses]

This is a Makkan chapter which deals with the fundamentals of faith namely monotheism, the truth of revelation and the Prophethood of Muhammad, resurrection, judgment, reward and punishment. It starts with an oath by God that Prophet Muhammad is indeed His Messenger and that the Qur'an is truly a revelation sent down by the Lord Who is Almighty, All-Wise. It then refers to the disbelief and opposition of the Makkan pagans and in this context, mention is made of the inhabitants of a township (*qaryah*) who disbelieved the Messengers that were sent to them. Attention is then drawn to God's creation of the universe and the various aspects of nature such as the sky, the stars, the sun, the fortnightly course of the moon, the night and day each succeeding and merging into the other and the sailing of ships of the seas all point to the unrivaled power of God and His absolute Oneness. Emphasis is then laid on the truth of resurrection, judgment, punishment and reward. The chapter is named *Ya Sīn* after the disjointed letters which represents one of the linguistic miracles of the Qur'an. This chapter is also regarded as the heart of the Qur'an by the Prophet.

In the name of God, the Most Gracious, the Most Compassionate.

Appeal to Reason

¹ *Ya Sīn.* ² By the Qur'an that is full of wisdom. ³ Indeed, you (O Muhammad) are surely one of Our Messengers; ⁴ upon a straight path; ⁵ (with a divine revelation) that is sent down from the Almighty, the Most Compassionate; ⁶ so that you may warn a (nation of) people whose forefathers had never been warned and who are therefore heedless (of the truth). ⁷ Certainly, the word of God's condemnation is bound to come true against most of them, but they do not believe (in Our warnings).

⁸ Indeed, We have placed iron shackles around their necks reaching up their chins to force their heads up. *ᵃ* ⁹ And We have made a barrier in front of them and behind them, *ᵇ* and placed a veil over them so that they cannot see

---

ᵃ Their "heads are forced-up" can be taken to mean that they are being led further astray because of their arrogance, thus they are unable to see the right path.
ᵇ God placed this barrier so that they can neither advance nor go back. It is a metaphor of utter spiritual stagnation as a result of rejecting the teachings of the Prophet and for siding with injustice which renders people to become insensitive and unresponsive to the truth.

(the truth that they hate so much). ¹⁰ And so, it is the same whether you warn them or not, they will still refuse to believe.

¹¹ Verily, you can only warn whoever is willing to take the reminder (to heart), and who stands in awe of the Most Gracious (Lord) although He is unseen. So give him the good news of his Lord's) forgiveness and a noble reward (that awaits him). ¹² Indeed, it is We Who give life to the dead (when we originate their first creation) and record every deed that they send ahead ª and every trace that they leave behind (during their temporary stay on earth). ᵇ Verily, We keep an account of all things in a clear register.

¹³ Now, narrate to them a parable, the story of (how) the people of a city (responded) when Our Messengers came to them. ¹⁴ Verily, We sent to them two (Messengers) but the people of that city denied them both. So We strengthened them with a third (Messenger), and they said, "Indeed, we are Messengers who have been sent to you (by God to convey His message)." ¹⁵ Said the people, "(All of) you are nothing except mere mortals like us (who do not have special abilities and powers). And We do not know who you are because the Most Gracious (Lord) did not reveal anything to us about you. You must surely be lying (to gain attention)." ¹⁶ The Messengers replied, "Our Lord knows that we have indeed been sent to you; ¹⁷ and our duty is only to convey His message clearly." ¹⁸ The people retorted, "Indeed, we see you as an evil omen for us. Desist, or we shall stone you and make sure that you receive a painful punishment from us!" ¹⁹ Said the Messengers in return, "The evil omen is within yourselves (for straying from God's path)! Are you saying this because you are being asked to take heed (of God's reminder that you vehemently oppose)? In fact, you are a people who have transgressed."

²⁰ Then a man came running from the farthest end of the city and said, "O my people! Follow the Messengers. ²¹ Follow those who do not ask for any reward from you, for indeed they are rightly guided. ²² And as for me, what excuse do I have to not worship the One Who has created me and to Whom you will all be finally returned? ²³ And why should I take other gods besides Him whose intercession will not help me, nor can they save me if the Most Gracious (Lord) intends harm to befall me? ²⁴ (If I do,) then surely I would be clearly misguided!" ²⁵ Verily, I only believe in your Supreme Lord, (the One and Only God Who holds dominion over all the worlds); so listen to my advice."

²⁶ (Instead, those wicked people killed him because he proclaimed the

---
ª Good and evil deeds that they did for themselves.
ᵇ Good and evil deeds that have impacted others.

truth. And upon his death,) the Angel said to him, "Enter Paradise!", whereupon He exclaimed, "Oh! If only my people knew; [27] how my Lord has forgiven me and placed me among the honored ones (for my unwavering faith in Him)." [28] And after him, We did not send down any army from heaven to reprimand his people, nor was it needful for Us to do so. [29] Nothing was needed except a single deafening blast. Then behold! They were extinguished. [30] What a pity for My (stubborn) servants! No Messenger ever came to them except that they would deride him. [31] Do they not see how many communities and generations that We have destroyed before them? And those who were destroyed will never be able to return (to warn the living). [32] In the end, every soul will surely be brought (back) to Us (for judgment).

Signs Galore

[33] And a sign for the disbelievers to ponder is the lifeless earth. We give life to it and We bring forth from it grain for them to eat. [34] And We also placed on it gardens of date-palms and grapevines and caused springs of water to gush out from it; [35] so that they may eat its fruits. And indeed, it was not their hands that made these fruits, (but it is We Who made all these as provision for them to enjoy). Will they then not be grateful (for Our favors)? [36] Glory be to the One Who (is the Most Perfect and has) created everything in pairs - all of which that grows from the earth, the gender of their offspring and (the countless) other things that they do not know.

[37] And the night is another sign for them. We strip the day from it, then behold! They are plunged in darkness. [38] And the sun runs in an (orbital) course of its own which has been determined and decreed by the Almighty, the All-Knowing. [39] And the moon, We have set for it several phases until it returns (to appear) like the old (dried and curved) date stalk. [40] Not is the sun permitted to overtake the moon, nor can night outstrip the day. They float in their (own separately appointed) orbit. *ᵃ*

ᵃ The message in verses 38-40 here is generally the same as verses 21:33, 35:13 and 39:5 that mention the sun and the moon running or floating in their respective orbits. The moon orbits around the earth at a velocity of 3,683 km/hour to complete a full rotation in 27.3 days while the sun runs in an orbit of its own around the Milky Way at a velocity of 828,000 km/hr which takes about 230 million years to complete. How did Prophet Muhammad who lived in the 7th century know that the moon and the sun are actually running in their own separate orbits when it was widely believed for many centuries before and after his time that they were both orbiting around the earth together? It was not until 1610 when Galileo Galilei, an Italian natural philosopher, astronomer and mathematician discovered through direct observation from a telescope which he built by himself that the sun did not orbit together with the moon around a fixed earth but is separately orbiting around the Milky Way instead. For announcing this

⁴¹ And yet another sign for them is We carried the descendants (of their early forefathers) in a laden ark; *ᵃ* ⁴² and We also created things of similar kind for their (offspring) to ride in (later). ⁴³ And if We wished, We could drown them (all) with none to respond (to their cries for help), nor would they be rescued; ⁴⁴ except by an act of mercy from Us to let them enjoy the pleasures of life a little longer.

⁴⁵ And yet when they are told, "Be mindful of what is ahead of you *ᵇ* and what has gone before you *ᶜ* so that you may be shown mercy; ⁴⁶ they ignore every sign that comes to them from their Lord. ⁴⁷ And when they are told, "Spend (in the cause of God) from what He has provided you (by feeding the needy)", those who oppose the truth say to those who believe, "Why should we (trouble ourselves to) feed people whom God could feed them Himself if He wanted to?" Say to them, "You have clearly gone (very far) astray!"

⁴⁸ And they ask you (O Prophet), "When will this promise (of doom) take place if you speak the truth?" ⁴⁹ (The truth is) they are waiting for nothing except a mighty blast that will seize them while they are busy arguing (with each other about worldly matters). ⁵⁰ (So sudden will their end be that) they do not have any chance to settle their affairs, nor return to their households. *ᵈ*

---

discovery and standing firm by it, Galileo was placed under house arrest by the Catholic church until his death in 1642 because it contradicted the church's position which believed that the earth was the centre of the universe while the sun and all other celestial objects were orbiting around it based on what Psalm 93:1, Psalm 96:10 and 1 Chronicles 16:30 mentioned in the Bible. Galileo was fortunate to be spared from torture by the church's inquisition because his powerful friends intervened on his behalf. It was unfortunate that he was not introduced to the Qur'an at that time. Otherwise, who knows that maybe he might have embraced Islam if he had found out that his scientific discovery was actually foretold in the Qur'an 1,000 years earlier. The church finally admitted to this mistake 359 years later in 1992 when it officially announced that Galileo's scientific discovery was right after all. Why did the Holy Spirit not protect the Pope and the church from this grave error when they accused Galileo of being a heretic and nearly killed him?

ᵃ This is in reference to the people of Noah who were saved from the great flood.

ᵇ The Day of Judgment.

ᶜ The doom that befell some earlier communities.

ᵈ Two of the most fundamental religious principles of Islam is resurrection and judgment. Modern society ignores these two vital tenets and looks upon them with disdain. Modern culture teaches that a person's life, just like that of an animal, ends here in this world. There is no resurrection, judgment and accountability. But the truth is - just like death - the arrival of doom is not possible to predict and will take people by complete surprise. The verse brings to our knowledge and attention that when the Hour

⁵¹ And when the trumpet of resurrection is blown, behold! They will come out of their graves rushing to their Lord; ⁵² nervously exclaiming, "O woe to us! Who woke us from our sleep?" whereupon they will be told, "This is what the Most Gracious (Lord) promised, and the Messengers have indeed spoken the truth." ⁵³ Then there will be a single deafening shout and every soul will be brought to Us. ⁵⁴ On that Day, no soul will be (unjustly treated and) wronged in the least because you will only be (fairly) requited for your own deeds.

⁵⁵ Indeed, the residents of Paradise will be busy enjoying themselves on that Day. ⁵⁶ Together with their spouses, they will be in cool shades, reclining on couches. ⁵⁷ In there, they will have (all kinds of) fruits and whatever their hearts desire. ⁵⁸ "Peace (be upon you)!" will be the greeting from their Most Compassionate Lord. ⁵⁹ (Whereas the guilty ones will be told,) "Stand apart (from the believers) today, O sinners! ⁶⁰ O children of Adam! Did I not command you not to (serve and) worship Satan who is your clear enemy; ⁶¹ and that you should only worship Me alone? Indeed, this is the straight path (which I have chosen for you, but you rejected it in sheer arrogance). ⁶² Behold! Satan has led astray a great many of you, (and yet you are still blind to see this). Why do you not use common sense and (reason to think)?" ⁶³ "(Now) this is the Hell which you have been promised. ⁶⁴ Burn in it today because you refused to believe (and continued to ignore all Our warnings)!" ⁶⁵ On that Day, We shall seal their mouths. Their hands will speak to Us and their feet will bear witness to everything that they have done.

⁶⁶ Had it been Our will, We could have (easily) obliterated their sight and let them struggle to find their way. If this was the case, how could they see (the truth)? ⁶⁷ And had it also been Our will (to not give them the freedom to choose between right and wrong), We would have surely given them a different nature (by making them creatures) that are firmly rooted in their places and are unable to move forward nor turn back. ⁶⁸ (And let them also remember that) whoever We grant long life, We could easily reverse him in creation (by causing him to become feeble and senile as he grows older). Why do they not use common sense (and reason to ponder about the purpose of their creation)?

What Prevents Resurrection?

⁶⁹ We have not taught (Muhammad) poetry, nor is it befitting for him (to recite poetry). Verily, not is this (Qur'an a made-up poetry) except a reminder and a divine discourse that gives clear explanation; ⁷⁰ to warn those whose hearts are alive that (in time, God's) promise will be proven true against those

---

of Truth arrives, it will happen while people are going about with their normal activities. It will be swift, decisive and catch people unprepared.

who refuse to believe (and submit themselves Him).

⁷¹ Among the things that Our hands have fashioned, can they not see that it is We Who have created the cattle for them to own; ⁷² and made this animal subservient to them so that some they could ride and some they would eat; ⁷³ and also derive other benefits from, including its milk to drink? Will they then not be grateful (for such favors that they have been granted to enjoy)? ⁷⁴ Yet they have taken other (false) deities besides God (for worship), hoping that they will be (given a blessed life and) helped (when they are afflicted with misfortune). ⁷⁵ But these (false deities) will never be able to help them. Instead, they will be brought (to Us on Judgment Day) as the disbelievers' helpless hosts. ⁷⁶ So let not the speech of those who are devoid of faith grieve you (O Prophet). Indeed, We know what they conceal and what they reveal.

⁷⁷ Does man not realize that We created him from a mere clot of semen? Then behold! He grows up and becomes a clearly (arrogant and rebellious) opponent; ⁷⁸ and sets for Us a parable (to argue about resurrection), forgetting the origins of his own creation by asking, "Who can give life back to bones after they have (decayed and) crumbled?" ⁷⁹ Tell him, "He Who gave them life and brought them into existence the first time will give them life (once again)! Indeed, it is He alone Who has full knowledge of every creation. ⁸⁰ He is also the One Who makes green trees produce fire, *ᵃ* so that you can kindle (your own fire) with it. ⁸¹ (So think!) Is the One Who (single handedly) created the heavens and the earth unable to recreate (and restore the lives of) those (who have died) like (how He originated) them (the first time)? Of course (He can)! He is indeed the Supreme Creator Who has full knowledge of everything."

⁸² (Verily,) whenever He intends anything, suffice for Him to only command the word, "Be!" and it is. ⁸³ Glory be to the One in Whose hand is the dominion of all things. It is to Him Whom you will all be returned.

ᵃ The mention of green trees and its relationship with fire is an allusion to the metamorphosis of green plants into fuel through desiccation or man-made carbonization (i.e. charcoal), or by a natural subterranean process of decomposition into oil or coal over thousands of years that all serve as the main sources of energy used by man from the beginning of time. See also verse 56:72. In addition, the emphasis on green trees also relates to the existence of chlorophyll - a key component in the process of photosynthesis which sustains plant life and produces oxygen for the entire planet. Fire cannot be kindled without oxygen.

37. *Aṣ-Ṣāffāt*

[Those Standing in Rows : 182 verses]

This is an early Makkan chapter, and like other Makkan chapters, it deals with the themes of monotheism, Prophethood of Muhammad, resurrection, judgment, reward and punishment. It starts with God's swearing of His Angels who stood in rows (*Aṣ-Ṣāffāt*) to receive His commands by which the chapter is named after. Reference is next made to the rebellious Satan and the disbelievers' doubts about resurrection and their persistence in polytheism. Mention is then made of the punishment and despicable life of the disbelievers in the Hereafter and in contrast, the reward and honorable life of the believers. Emphasis is then made on the fact that God has sent Messengers from time to time to guide mankind to the truth and to worship of God alone. Mention is also made in this connection of Prophets Noah, Abraham and his sacrificing son Ishmael in obedience to God's command, Isaac, Moses, Aaron, Elijah, Lot and Jonah. It ends with an emphasis again on monotheism and the polytheists' persistence in associating partners with God and their mistaken notion of the Jinn being God's daughters.

In the name of God, the Most Gracious, the Most Compassionate.

An Admonition Never to be Ignored

¹ By the (Angels) who stand arrayed in rows; ² who drive away (evil forces) forcefully; ³ and (unceasingly) recite the remembrance (of God). ⁴ Indeed, your Lord is surely One; ⁵ Lord of the heavens and the earth and all that lies between them, and Lord of each point of sunrise.

⁶ Behold! We have decorated the nearest heaven with an adornment of (twinkling) stars; ⁷ to protect it against every rebellious Satan. ⁸ They are prevented from eavesdropping the (secrets of the) Exalted Assembly, and are being pelted from all sides; ⁹ to repel them away. And a lasting suffering awaits them (in the life to come). ¹⁰ And if any of them succeeds in snatching a glimpse of such knowledge, he will be pursued by a piercing flame.

¹¹ So ask those who deny the truth: Which is more complex in creation - is it they, or the many other (marvels of the worlds) that We have created? Behold! We created them only from sticky clay. ¹² Yet, while you are humbled and filled with awe (of God's greatness), they on the other hand, deride. ¹³ And when they are reminded (of the truth), they ignore and pay no heed. ¹⁴ And when they see a sign (from Us that you bring to them O Prophet), they ridicule it; ¹⁵ and say, "This is nothing but pure sorcery."

¹⁶ (Then they ask mockingly), "Is it true that when we are dead and have become soil and bones, We shall be brought back to life again; ¹⁷ together with our forefathers?" ¹⁸ Answer (them), "Yes indeed, and you will be humiliated too!" ¹⁹ It will only be a single deafening blast, then behold! They will see (the promise that awaits them comes true). ²⁰ And only then will they (finally realize and) utter (in bewilderment), "O woe to us! Is this really the Day of Judgment?" ²¹ They will be told, "(Yes indeed!) This is the Day of Distinction (between truth and falsehood) which you have been denying all along."

The Judgment

²² (And it will be said to the Angels,) "Gather those who were unjust and all those like them together with what they used to worship; ²³ besides Almighty God, and lead them to the path of the Blazing Fire; ²⁴ and detain them (there). Indeed, they will be questioned (for everything that they have done during their lifetime)."

²⁵ (There, they will be asked by the Angels,) "What is the matter with you? Why do you (seem lost and) not helping one another now (as you used to boast about before)?" ²⁶ Nay! On that Day, they will surrender themselves whole-heartedly (to God). ²⁷ (But it will be too late and) they will turn upon one another, questioning (and demanding from) each other (to relieve them from the burden of their past sins).

²⁸ (Some among them) will say, "Indeed, you used to come to us (deceptively) from the right." ²⁹ To which their companions will reply, "Nay! You yourselves had no faith, ³⁰ nor had we any authority over you. Indeed, you rebelled (against the truth. So do not blame us for your own mistake). ³¹ The word of our Lord has proven to be true against us. Indeed, We shall all taste (the punishment together and there seems to be no escape for us). ³² Even if it is true that we led you astray, it was only because we were lost ourselves." ³³ And verily on that Day, they will all be partners in punishment.

³⁴ Indeed, that is how We deal with those who were lost in sin. ³⁵ They were the ones who when it was said to them, "There is no god except the One and Only Almighty God", they behaved arrogantly; ³⁶ and said, "Should we abandon our gods for the sake of a crazy poet (who claims to receive direct revelations from God)?"

³⁷ In fact, he has come with the truth and confirms the message of the Messengers (before him). ³⁸ Indeed, you will surely taste grievous punishment (for rejecting the message that he brings); ³⁹ but you will be requited no more than the (wicked) deeds that you have done.

⁴⁰ But not so for the true servants of God who are sincere and devoted (in their worship to Him). ⁴¹ For such people, an (excellent) provision has been prepared for them; ⁴² as fruits (of their labor) and they will be honored (and raised in ranks); ⁴³ in Gardens of Delight; ⁴⁴ sitting on couches facing each other (in joy and excitement); ⁴⁵ with cups filled with a drink from a flowing spring, being passed around; ⁴⁶ (crystal) clear and a delight to those who drink it; ⁴⁷ neither dulling the senses nor intoxicating.

⁴⁸ And they will be accompanied by companions of modest gaze with lustrous eyes; ⁴⁹ like sheltered eggs (in a nest). ⁵⁰ Then they will approach one another, asking (about their past lives). ⁵¹ One of them will say, "Indeed, I once had a close friend (on earth); ⁵² who asked me: 'Are you indeed of those who believe, ⁵³ that after we die and become soil and bones, We shall be brought back to life to face judgment? (I for one, do not believe this!)'"

⁵⁴ Then he would say (to his companions in Paradise), "Will you (follow me to) look for him?" ⁵⁵ And then he looks around and finds that friend in the midst of the Hellfire; ⁵⁶ and says, "By God! Verily, you almost ruined me (with your allurements)! ⁵⁷ Had it not been for my Lord's grace (that helped to keep me steadfast in his path), I would have certainly been among those brought along (to Hell today)."

⁵⁸ (Then he turned to his companions in Paradise and asked), "Is it really true that We shall not die again (here); ⁵⁹ beyond the death that we have just experienced, nor shall we ever be made to suffer? ⁶⁰ (If it is,) then this is truly a great triumph!" ⁶¹ To attain a triumph like this, strive all you can, O those who wish to strive!

⁶² (Now ponder!) Which gives better welcome - is it this, or the tree of *Zaqqum*? ⁶³ Indeed, We have made the *Zaqqum* as a trial for the wrongdoers. ⁶⁴ Verily, it is a tree that springs out from the pit of Hellfire. ⁶⁵ The shoots of its fruit-stalks are (as repulsive) as Satans' heads. ⁶⁶ And indeed, the evil wrongdoers will eat from it and fill their bellies with it. ⁶⁷ Then on top of that, they will be given a (horrible) mixture of scalding water. ⁶⁸ Behold, the Blazing Fire will be their final return!

⁶⁹ Verily, they found their forefathers on the wrong path; ⁷⁰ yet they hasten to blindly follow in their footsteps. ⁷¹ And (before them,) many of the earlier people had gone astray. ⁷² Indeed, We sent warners from among them (to guide them aright, but they stubbornly rejected these warners). ⁷³ So see how was the end of those who were warned (but paid no heed). ⁷⁴ (Verily,) except for the (true) servants of God who are sincere and devoted in their worship to Him, (others are inclined to go astray).

Noah and Abraham

⁷⁵ And indeed, (it was for this reason that) Noah called upon Us. And how excellent was Our response! ⁷⁶ We saved him and his family from a great calamity. ⁷⁷ We made his descendants survive (and inherit the land); ⁷⁸ and We left him for (honorable mention) among later generations. ⁷⁹ "Peace be upon Noah throughout the worlds." ⁸⁰ Verily, that is how We reward those who excel in good deeds. ⁸¹ Indeed, he was among Our (truly) faithful servants ⁸² (So We saved him and those who followed him), while We drowned the others.

⁸³ Verily, among those who followed his way was Abraham; ⁸⁴ who turned to his Lord with a sound and serene heart; ⁸⁵ and asked his father and his people, "What are you worshipping?" ⁸⁶ "Why do you desire (and choose) false gods instead of the One and Only True God? ⁸⁷ What are your thoughts about the Lord of all the worlds?"

⁸⁸ Then he cast a glance at the stars (and reflected deeply); ⁸⁹ and said (to his people), "Indeed, I feel sick (today and will not be able to join you)." ⁹⁰ So they left him and went away.

⁹¹ Then he turned to their gods and said, "Why do you not eat (any of the offerings that have been placed in front of you)? ⁹² What is the matter with you that you do not speak?" ⁹³ Then he began striking down the idols with his right hand; ⁹⁴ and his people hurried towards him (to question what had happened). ⁹⁵ So he asked them, "Why do you worship something that you carved (and produced) by yourselves; ⁹⁶ when it is actually God Who created you and (made it possible for you to produce) all your handiwork?" ⁹⁷ They retorted (angrily), "Build a structure (with furnace) for him and throw him into the blazing fire (for denouncing our gods)!" ⁹⁸ So they plotted against him but We (failed it and) humiliated them.

⁹⁹ And Abraham said, "Verily, I shall (leave this land and) go wherever my Lord guides me!" ¹⁰⁰ And he prayed, "O Lord, grant me (a son who will be) among the righteous ones." ¹⁰¹ So We gave him the good news of a gentle and forbearing child (named Ishmael).

¹⁰² Then when his son grew old enough to work alongside him, he said, "O my son! Indeed, I saw a vision in my dream that I should offer you as a sacrifice. So consider (what I have been inspired) and tell me what you think." His son replied, "O my father! Do as you are commanded. If God wills, you will find me among those who are patient (to endure His trials)."

[103] Then after both of them had submitted (to God's will) and as Abraham was placing his son down prostrating upon his forehead (to be sacrificed); [104] We called out to him, "O Abraham! [105] Verily, you have fulfilled the (purpose of the) dream-vision." Indeed, this is how We reward those who excel in good deeds. [106] Behold, this was truly a clear trial (to prove their true faith and characters). [107] Then We ransomed (his son) with a great sacrifice; [108] and We left him for (honorable mention) among later generations. [109] "Peace be upon Abraham." [110] This is how We reward those who excel in good deeds. [111] Indeed, he was among Our (truly) faithful servants.

[112] And (in time), We gave him the good news of (another son named) Isaac, (who would be) a Prophet too from among the righteous. [113] And We blessed him and Isaac. But among their descendants are some who would excel in good deeds and some who would (commit evil, hence) bringing clear injustice upon themselves.

Moses, Aaron, Elijah, Lot and Jonah

[114] And verily, We graciously conferred Our favor upon Moses and Aaron. [115] We saved them and their people from the great distress (inflicted by Pharaoh); [116] and We helped them to become victorious (in the end); [117] and then We gave them the clear Book; *[a]* [118] and We guided them to the straight path; [119] and We left them for (honorable mention) among later generations. [120] "Peace be upon Moses and Aaron." [121] Indeed, this is how We reward those who excel in good deeds. [122] Verily, they were among Our Our (truly) faithfu servants.

[123] And indeed, Elijah *[b]* too was one of the Messengers. [124] (Behold,) when he said to his people, "Have you no fear of God? [125] Why do you call upon *Ba'l* and forsake the Best of Creators; [126] God - your Lord and the Lord of your forefathers?" [127] But they denied him, therefore they will most surely be arraigned (before God); [128] except the (true) servants of God who are sincere and devoted in their worship to Him. [129] And We left him for (honorable mention) among later generations. [130] "Peace be upon Elijah." [131] Indeed, this is how We reward those who excel in good deeds. [132] Verily, he was among Our (truly) faithful servants

[133] And indeed, Lot was also among Our Messengers. [134] (Call to mind) when We saved him and all of his family; [135] except a (stubborn) old woman who was among those who remained behind. [136] Then We destroyed the

---

[a] The Torah.
[b] Ilyas in Arabic.

others. ¹³⁷ And indeed, you pass by their ruins in the morning; ¹³⁸ and at night (during your journeys). Will you then not use reason (to draw any lesson from what you see of the ruins)?

¹³⁹ And indeed, Jonah *ᵃ* was among Our Messengers too. ¹⁴⁰ (Call to mind) when he ran away to the laden ship (after he aborted his mission); ¹⁴¹ then he drew lots and became the loser. ¹⁴² And so (he was cast in the sea and) the fish swallowed him while he was blameworthy. ¹⁴³ Had he not been among those who would (constantly) glorify God's (perfection while in the deep darkness of distress with great regret and begged for forgiveness); ¹⁴⁴ he would have surely remained in its belly until the Day everyone is resurrected. *ᵇ*

¹⁴⁵ And so, We cast him forth on the barren shore, sick as he was; ¹⁴⁶ and We caused to grow over him a creeping plant of the gourd kind (out of the barren soil); ¹⁴⁷ and We sent him to a hundred thousand (people) or more (to guide them to the truth once again); ¹⁴⁸ and they finally believed (in the divine message he conveyed). So We allowed them to enjoy the good things of life until an appointed time.

The Infidels' Absurdity

¹⁴⁹ Now, ask those deniers of truth (about their belief, O Muhammad). Does (it make sense for) their Lord (to) have daughters while they have sons? ¹⁵⁰ Or did they witness We created the Angels as females (which gave rise to their blasphemous claim)? ¹⁵¹ Without a doubt, it is out of their (audacious inclination to) falsehood that they dare say; ¹⁵² "God has begotten!" Indeed, they are (despicable) liars! ¹⁵³ Has He chosen daughters (for Himself) in preference over sons? ¹⁵⁴ What is the matter with you? How did you come to such (an absurd) conclusion? ¹⁵⁵ Why will you not (use common sense to) reflect (upon this erroneous belief)? ¹⁵⁶ Or do you have any clear authority (to stand firm by it)? ¹⁵⁷ Bring your Book (to prove your claim) if you are saying the truth.

¹⁵⁸ They assigned (a blasphemous relationship) between Him and the Jinn

---

ᵃ Yunus bin Matta in Arabic. He was a Prophet from the Children of Israel who lived in the northern region of Palestine about 800 years before Jesus. He was commanded by God to go to Nineveh (which is Mosul in Iraq today about 1,000 km from north Palestine) to convey God's divine message and guide its people out of their wickedness to the truth. But he aborted his mission when they rejected him and fled to Joppa (which is Jaffa near Tel Aviv today) to take passage in a ship that carried him away. The rest of the story is narrated in verses 140-148. See also verses 10:87-88.
ᵇ See verses 68:48-50.

(that produced) a lineage. But the Jinn knew (that this is false and) they will surely be brought (to Him for Judgment). [159] Glory be to God Who is far above (all the lies and imperfections) that they attribute (to Him)!

[160] Not as such is (the behavior of) God's true servants. (Indeed, they do not indulge in any blasphemy) and they are truly sincere and devoted in their worship to Him. [161] (O you who deny the truth)! Indeed you and all the objects of your worship; [162] cannot tempt (anyone) away from God; [163] except the one who will enter the Blazing Fire (because he allowed himself to be misled).

[164] (The Angels say,) "There is not one of us who does not have his appointed place (of worship assigned by God); [165] and we are truly of those who stand in rows (before Him in worship); [166] and we (constantly proclaim and) glorify Him (Who is free and Most Pure from all imperfections)."

[167] And indeed those who deny the truth (have been accustomed to) say; [168] "Had we receive a reminder from the people before us; [169] we would have surely been loyal and sincere servants of God." [170] And yet, (even when this divine Book is brought to them now,) they refuse to believe in its truth. In time to come, they will surely know (their terrible fate).

[171] Verily, We have already given Our promise to Our Messengers; [172] that they will surely become victorious (in the end). [173] And indeed, those who support (Our cause) will certainly triumph. [174] So, turn away from those (defiant infidels) for a time; [175] and just watch them. Soon they will see (what they refuse to believe now).

[176] Do they really want Us to hasten Our punishment? [177] When it descends near them, how evil will that morning be for those who had been forewarned! [178] So turn away from them for a time; [179] and just watch. Soon they will see (what they have been denying all along).

[180] Glory be to your Lord, the Lord of Honor, Who is far above (all the lies and imperfections) that they ascribe (to Him)!; [181] and peace be upon the Messengers. [182] And all praise is indeed due to God alone, the Lord of all the worlds.

38. Ṣād
[88 verses]

This is also an early Makkan chapter which deals with the fundamentals of faith that include monotheism, Prophethood of Muhammad, resurrection, judgment, reward and punishment. It starts by emphasizing that the Qur'an is truly a Book sent down by God and then refers to the amazement of the disbelievers of Makkah at the coming of a Messenger of God from among them and at the concept of the Oneness of God instead of a multiplicity of deities to which they had been used to. It then makes mention, by way of warning the disbelievers, of what befell the previously disbelieving nations of God's retribution. In this context, it mentions the stories of some earlier Messengers of God such as Prophets David, Solomon, Job, Isaac, Jacob, Ishmael and Ezekiel and the trials and tribulations they had to undergo, by way of consoling the Prophet. Along with these, the chapter points to some of the wonderful aspects of this universe in bringing home the theme of God's Absolute Oneness. The chapter is named *Ṣād* after the disjointed letter with which it starts which represents one of the Qur'an's linguistic miracles.

In the name of God, the Most Gracious, the Most Compassionate.

Unjustifiable Reaction

¹ *Ṣād.* By the Quran that is full of reminder (for those who truly believe in God). ² But those who are bent on denying the truth are steeped in pride and defiance. ³ How many generations before them have We destroyed. They cried out to Us (in regret) when it was already too late for escape.

⁴ And they deem it strange that a warner has come to them from their own people. So these deniers of truth (accuse him by) saying, "He is indeed a sorcerer who is full of lies! ⁵ Has he turned all the gods into only One? This is indeed a strange thing!"

⁶ Then their leaders stepped forward and said, "Continue to be steadfast in worshipping the gods (of our ancestors). Indeed, this is the right thing to do. ⁷ We have never heard a claim like this in (our ancestors') faith. This must be a new invention (to challenge us). ⁸ How could God reveal His message to Muhammad (alone) instead of to the nobles among us?" Nay! They are actually in doubt of My message (that you convey O Prophet, but conveniently find fault in you). Indeed, they have not tasted My punishment yet!

⁹ Or do they own the treasures of your Lord's grace - the Almighty, the Bestower (of all bounties)? ¹⁰ Or do they have dominion over the heavens and

the earth and whatever is between them? (If so,) let them ascend (to heaven) by every conceivable way (if they can). ¹¹ (Know that) whatever forces there are and (however strong they are) leagued together as an alliance, they will surely suffer defeat (if they refuse to accept the truth).

¹² And before them, the people of Noah, 'Aād, and Pharaoh who is the Lord of the Stakes, denied (Our message) too. ¹³ And (so did) the people of Tsamud and Lot, and the dwellers of Al-'Aikah. All of them were allies (in falsehood). ¹⁴ They denied the Messengers (who were sent to them), so My retribution to them was justified. ¹⁵ Those who reject the truth now are waiting for nothing except a single shout which will not be delayed (when its time arrives). ¹⁶ Yet, they still (have the audacity to mock Us by) saying, "O Our Lord! Hasten for us our share of punishment before the Day of Reckoning."

¹⁷ So be patient over what they say (to deride you O Prophet). Remember Our servant David who was endowed with strength. Indeed, he always turned to Us (in repentance). ¹⁸ Verily, We subjected the mountains to join him in (proclaiming and) glorifying God's perfection in the evening and at sunrise. ¹⁹ And all the birds in their flocks too would turn with him (to God in praising His glory). ²⁰ And We strengthened his kingdom, gave him wisdom and decisiveness (in delivering sound and fair judgment).

Tests for Prophets

²¹ Has the story of the litigants who climbed over the wall of David's chamber, reached you (O Prophet)? ²² As they entered David's chamber, he was alarmed, but they said, "Do not fear. We are only two litigants who have come to seek your counsel. One of us has wronged the other. So judge between us in truth and do not be unjust. Guide us to the right path. ²³ Now here is my brother. He has ninety-nine ewes while I have only one; and yet he said, 'Let me take charge of her!' and prevailed over me with his argument."

²⁴ David said, "He has surely wronged you by demanding to add your ewe to his flock. Indeed, many partners tend to wrong one another. Those who believe (in God) and do righteous deeds do not do this, but how few are they (in this world)!" Then it suddenly occurred to David that We were actually testing him (with this incident so that he would rule his kingdom fairly). So he prayed for his Lord's forgiveness, fell down in prostration and turned to God in repentance. ²⁵ We forgave him for that (temporary lapse). And indeed, He has surely earned a high rank with Us and an excellent place of final return.

²⁶ "O David! Indeed, We have made you a (Prophet and Our) emissary on earth. So judge (fairly and) truthfully between people and do not follow your

whims and desires as it will lead you astray from God's path. Indeed, those who stray from His path will be punished with a severe torment because they ignored (and disbelieved in) the Day of Reckoning."

²⁷ We did not create the heaven and the earth and whatever is between them without meaning and purpose. Only those who deny Us assume so. Woe to those disbelievers (who will suffer) in the Fire! ²⁸ (Is it fair that) We treat those who believe and do righteous deeds in the same manner as those who spread corruption (and cause disorder) on earth? Or (is it fair that) We treat the pious like the wicked? ²⁹ This is a blessed Book which We have revealed to you (O Prophet) so that people may ponder over its verses, and those who are endowed with insight and wisdom may be reminded (about Our message and draw important lessons from it).

³⁰ And We bestowed to David (a son whose name was) Solomon. How excellent (did he grow up) as Our servant! Indeed, he regularly turned to Us (in repentance). ³¹ (Behold!) When they brought and displayed nobly bred swift horses to him in one evening; ³² he said, "Verily, my love of good things is part of my remembrance of my Lord!" (And as he continued to glorify God, the horses raced away) until they were hidden by the veil (of distance); ³³ whereupon he commanded, "Return them to me!" And (when they were brought to him), he stroked their shanks and necks (affectionately, in appreciation of the beauty of God's magnificent creation).

³⁴ And certainly We had tested Solomon (before this) by letting (him inherit kingship from his father at a very young age. ᵃ His parable was like) a (lifeless) body on the throne (at that time, who was still lacking in maturity and wisdom). So he (constantly) turned to Us in repentance; ³⁵ praying, "O my Lord! Forgive me (for my errors and shortcomings) and grant me the gift of a (great) kingdom that will not be surpassed by anyone after me. Indeed, You are surely the Bestower (of all that is good)."

³⁶ Thereupon, We (endowed him with power and wisdom, and) made the wind subservient to him so that it would flow steadily by his command wherever he wished; ᵇ ³⁷ and the devils too - builders and divers of every kind; ³⁸ together with many others that were bound in chains (whom We subjugated them all under his command). ³⁹ (And We told him,) "This is Our gift, so spend or withhold as you please without account." ⁴⁰ And indeed, (Solomon grew to be a rightly guided and wise King, and) he certainly earned a high

---

ᵃ The book of 1 Kings, passage 3:7 from the Bible mentions that Solomon was a child when he ascended the throne. According to The Bible Exposition Commentary by Warren W. Wiersbe, Solomon became King at the age of 15.

ᵇ See verses 21:81 and 34:12 and their footnotes.

rank with Us and an excellent place of final return.

⁴¹ And remember Our servant Job *ᵃ* who cried to his Lord, "Indeed, Satan has afflicted me with distress and suffering." ⁴² And thereupon he was told, "Stomp the ground with your foot. This is a spring of cool water to (bathe and) wash yourself with, and also to drink." ⁴³ Eventually, We restored his family to him and doubled their number as an act of Our grace, and as a (lesson and) reminder to those who are endowed with insight and wisdom. ⁴⁴ (And then we told him,) "Take a bunch of grass in your hand and strike (your wife gently) with it so that you would not break your oath." Indeed, We found him patient in adversity and an excellent servant who always turned to Us.

⁴⁵ And remember Our (other) servants too - Abraham, Isaac and Jacob; (all of them) whom We endowed with strength and insight. ⁴⁶ Verily, We purified them with a sterling quality through their sincere (and constant) remembrance of the (final) home. ⁴⁷ In Our sight, they were truly among the chosen and excellent ones. ⁴⁸ And remember Ishmael, Elisha *ᵇ* and Ezekiel *ᶜ* too. All of them were truly among the best.

Contrasting Ends

⁴⁹ Let (all) this be a reminder (to those who believe in God). Surely for those who take heed, we have prepared an excellent place of return; ⁵⁰ Gardens of Eternity with gates that are open wide to them; ⁵¹ reclining in there, they may (freely) call for fruits and drink that are in abundance; ⁵² with chaste companions of modest gaze, equal in age, by their side. ⁵³ This is what you are promised for on the Day of Reckoning. ⁵⁴ Indeed, this is Our provision for which there is no depletion. ⁵⁵ This is so (for the virtuous)! But for the wrongdoers, an evil place of return awaits them; ⁵⁶ the Hellfire, in which they will burn. And wretched indeed is their resting place. ⁵⁷ This is so (for the deniers of truth)! Then let them taste it - boiling fluid and pus; ⁵⁸ and further suffering of similar nature.

⁵⁹ (Observing the disbelievers advancing to Hell, the gate-keepers of Hell will say to the leaders of these people,) "There is a crowd of people rushing to join you." And they will reply, "There is no need to welcome them. They will burn in the Fire just like us." ⁶⁰ And their followers will reply, "Nay! There is no welcome for you either. It is you who brought this (evil fate) upon us. What a wretched settlement it is!" ⁶¹ And they will plead, "Our Lord! Whoever

---

ᵃ Ayyub in Arabic.
ᵇ Ilyasa' in Arabic.
ᶜ Dzulkifl in Arabic.

brought this upon us, double the punishment for him in the Fire (of Hell)!" ⁶² They will also say to one another, "Why do we not see those whom we considered to be bad; ⁶³ and whom we made the target of our ridicule (before)? Or did our eyes miss them?" ⁶⁴ Indeed, that is the truth. This is how the inmates of the Fire will quarrel among themselves.

Man's First Creation

⁶⁵ (O Prophet!) Tell those who refuse to accept the truth, "Verily, I am only a warner to remind you that there is no other god except Almighty God, the One and Only, the Supreme; ⁶⁶ Lord of the heavens and the earth and all that is between them, the Almighty, the Most Forgiving." ⁶⁷ Say to them, "It is a magnificent news; ⁶⁸ yet you (ignore and) turn away from it. ⁶⁹ "Indeed, I have no knowledge of what was deliberated (and hidden from me concerning the creation of man) in the Exalted Assembly." ⁷⁰ Instead, I only know of matters that are being revealed to me because I am nothing more than just a clear warner (to mankind)."

⁷¹ (Behold,) when your Lord said to the Angels, "Indeed, I am going to create a human being from clay. ⁷² After I have shaped him and breathed into him from My (life-giving) spirit, fall down in prostration to him (as a mark of your respect to My perfect creation)." ⁷³ So the Angels prostrated, all of them together; ⁷⁴ except *Iblis*; he was arrogant and became one of those who rebelled and defied God's command. ⁷⁵ And so God asked, "O *Iblis*! What prevented you from prostrating to the man I have created with My (own) hands? Are you arrogant, or do you deem yourself superior?" ⁷⁶ Replied *Iblis*, "I am better than him! You created me from fire whereas him from clay. (So, why should I prostrate to him?") ⁷⁷ And so God said, "Get out of here! For indeed, you are accursed; ⁷⁸ and indeed, My curse will remain upon you until the Day of Judgment." ⁷⁹ *Iblis* answered, "My Lord! Then give me respite until the Day when they will be resurrected." ⁸⁰ God said, "Then indeed, you are of those given respite; ⁸¹ until the Day which the hour has been appointed." ⁸² *Iblis* said, "Then I swear by Your Might and Glory, I shall surely strive to mislead them all; ⁸³ except Your servants who are sincerely devoted (in their worship to You)." ⁸⁴ God said, "Then, this is the truth! And only the truth do I state. ⁸⁵ Most certainly, I shall fill Hell with you and all those who follow you!"

⁸⁶ So say (to those who refuse to accept the truth O Prophet), "I do not ask any reward from you for conveying (God's) message and I am not someone who pretends (to be His Messenger to impress you). ⁸⁷ This (Qur'an) is indeed a reminder for all mankind; ⁸⁸ and you will surely know its truth in time to come."

39. Az-Zumar
[The Throngs : 75 verses]

This is a Makkan chapter which like other Makkan chapters, deals with the themes of monotheism, Prophethood of Muhammad, resurrection, judgment, reward and punishment. It starts with an emphasis that the Qur'an is indeed a divine revelation from God and He is entitled to exclusive worship and devotion. Attention is then drawn to His creation of the heavens and the earth, the subjection of the sun and moon to order, the making of the night and day, and above all the creation and development of man in the mother's womb and the provision of his sustenance, all of which point to God's Absolute Lordship and exclusive entitlement to worship. The chapter ends by pointing out how the disbelievers will be led in throngs (*zumar*) to hell and how the believers will also be led in throngs to paradise and welcomed there. The chapter is named *Az-Zumar* or The Throngs after these concluding verses.

In the name of God, the Most Gracious, the Most Compassionate.

The Diversity of God's Creation

¹ This Book is sent down from God, the Almighty, the All-Wise. ² Indeed, We have sent down this Book to you with profound truth (O Prophet). So worship God, sincere in your faith and religion in Him alone.

³ Without doubt, only God deserves all worship and pure devotion. And yet, those who take other patrons (and protectors) besides Him say, "We do not actually worship them. (Instead, we believe) they can (intercede on our behalf and) bring us closer to God." Verily, God will judge between them regarding their differences. And God surely does not guide whoever persists in lying and refuses to accept the truth. ⁴ Had God intended to take a son (for Himself), He could have chosen from any of His creation that He likes. Glory be to Him (Who is far above all the lies that they fabricate against Him). He is the One and only God, the Omnipotent (Who deserves all worship).

⁵ (Verily,) He created the heavens and the earth with profound truth (and precision). He wraps the day around the night, and wraps the night around the day.ᵃ He has made the sun and moon subservient (to His laws), each running

---

ᵃ The Arabic term used here is *yukawwiru* which literally means "to wrap or roll around something". Therefore, the shape of the earth has to be spherical for it to be seamlessly wrapped around by the alternation of day and night. In essence, the phenomenon of day and night is the result of a spherical shaped earth that is constantly rotating on its axis from left to right. As such, the earth continuously takes

(according to its appointed course) for a specified term. *a* Is He is not the Almighty, the Most Forgiving?

⁶ It is He Who created you from a single soul. Then from this, He made your mate (of the opposite sex). And He sent down to you (His grace by creating) eight livestock in four pairs each (of sheep, goat, cow and camel to be reproduced and used for your benefit). He creates you in the wombs of your mothers, stage by stage, within three layers of darkness. *b* Such is God, your Lord. To Him alone belongs all dominion. There is no god except Him alone, so how can you (be so deluded and) turn away (from the truth)?

⁷ If you are ungrateful, (know that) God is not in need of you. Nonetheless, He does not approve of ingratitude in His servants. Whereas if you show gratitude (through unwavering faith and kindness to others), He is pleased (to see) this in you. (Know that) no soul will be made to bear the burden of another; (hence, no one should ever expect to pass his burden of sin to others). In time, it is your Lord Whom you will all return to and He will apprise you about everything that you have done (during your lifetime and justly requite you for all your deeds). Indeed, He is well aware of everything that lies hidden in your hearts.

As Comfort Replaces Affliction

⁸ And when adversity afflicts man, he cries out to his Lord, turning to Him (for help). But as soon as God blesses him with His favors, he forgets what he cried and prayed for earlier, sets up equals to God and misleads others away from His path. Say (to them O Prophet), "Enjoy yourself in your (foolish) disbelief for a while. Indeed, you are among the Fire's inmates!"

⁹ (Now ponder over this) : Is the one who devoutly worships God during the hours of the night, prostrating or standing in prayer in fear of the next life

---

turn to expose one of its sides to the sun's brightness and hide the other in darkness as it makes a full rotation every 24 hours which causes the sun to appear rising in the east and setting in the west. The term *yukawwiru* would not be used here if the earth's shape is flat.

a See verses 36:38-40 and its footnote.

b "..within three layers of darkness" mentioned in this verse may well refer to: (1) the anterior abdominal wall; (2) the uterine wall; and (3) the amniochorionic membrane in the womb. This was only discovered in the 20th century through scientific and technological advancements that brought forth the invention and application of sophisticated equipment in the field of medical science but was foretold in the Qur'an in the 7th century when science was literally unknown.

to come and hoping for his Lord's mercy, (same as the one who is indifferent towards Him)? Ask them, "Can those with knowledge (of the truth) and those who ignore it be deemed equal?" Verily, only those who are endowed with insight and wisdom (and constantly strive in God's cause) will take heed (of His words).

The Losers

[10] Tell (them O Prophet, "This is what God said) : O My servants who believe! Be ever mindful of your Lord (and keep your duty to Him diligently). Indeed, a good end awaits those who do good in this world. God's earth is wide and spacious, (so worship Him freely therein). Verily, those who (strive in My path with) patience will be given their reward without measure." [11] Tell them, "Indeed, I am commanded to worship God, sincerely dedicating my entire faith to Him alone; [12] and I am commanded to be foremost [a] among those who submit themselves (to Him)."

[13] Say, "Indeed, I fear the punishment of a mighty (dreadful) Day if I disobey my Lord." [14] Say (to them further), "It is God alone Who I worship, sincerely dedicating my entire faith to Him. [15] And (it is up to you to) worship whatever you wish besides Him, (O sinners)!" Say, "Indeed, the (real) losers are those who will lose their own souls and their families on the Day of Resurrection (when they will all be hurled into the Fire for worshipping falsehood during their lifetime). Behold, that is indeed the (worst and) most obvious loss!" [16] (In Hell,) they will be covered by layers of fire above and below them. This is God's (stern) warning to His servants. "So be (truly) conscious of Me (and fear My retribution) O My servants!"

[17] But for those who shun the worship of false gods and turn to God (Almighty), there is glood news for them. Give then, this good news to those servants of Mine; [18] who listen closely to all that is said and follow what is best. They are the ones whom God has graced with His guidance and endowed with insight and wisdom. [19] Then, can he against whom God's sentence of punishment has been decreed be rescued by anyone? Do you think you can save anyone who is (hurled) into the Fire (O Prophet)?

---

[a] This verse should not be confused with the same proclamation made by Prophet Abraham in verse 6:163. The proclamation in this verse should be understood in the context of the lapse of time from Prophet Abraham and his son Ishmael (who was the progenitor of the Arabs) to the time when Prophet Muhammad came about 2,300 years later. No Messenger was believed to have been sent to the Arabs during this long lapse of period. As such, Prophet Muhammad was the first among the Arabs to have been directly commanded by God to submit to Him after the long lapse of time.

²⁰ But those who fear (displeasing) their Lord (and perform noble deeds for His sake), there will be lofty mansions built for them one above the other with rivers flowing beneath them (in Paradise). This is a promise from God and He does not fail to keep His promise.

²¹ Do you not see how God sends down rain from the sky and guides its flow to become springs in the earth; then with it He brings forth crops of different colors, and (in the end) they wither and you see them turn yellow? Then finally, He causes them to crumble to dust. Indeed, in that is a reminder for those endowed with insight and wisdom.

²² What about the one who God has opened his heart to accept *Islam* and then follows a path that is illumined by a light from his Lord? (Is he the same as the one who learns no lesson from what he observes?) Woe then to those whose hearts are hardened against all remembrance of God, (their true Lord). They have clearly gone astray!

The Best of All Discourses

²³ (Verily,) God has sent down the best of all teachings (to mankind) in the form of a Book (where many of) its verses are similar to one another and often repeated (in different ways for people to take lessons from). It causes the skins of those who stand in awe of their Lord to quiver. But their skins and hearts would turn soft at the remembrance of God's (grace). Such is God's guidance. He guides with it whomsoever He wills (that turns to Him in devotion), whereas the one who God lets go astray (because of his defiance) can never find any guide.

²⁴ Is he who will have to shield his bare face against the horrible punishment on the Day of Resurrection (same as the one who is at peace)? On that Day, the evil wrongdoers will be told, "Taste now what you have earned (from your stay on earth)!" ²⁵ Verily, those before them had denied (God too). So, they were made to suffer punishment that came upon them from where they did not expect. ²⁶ And so God made them taste the disgrace in the life of the world, and certainly the suffering that awaits them in the life to come is greater, if only they knew.

²⁷ Indeed We have presented mankind with many parables in this Qur'an for them to ponder. ²⁸ (And We have revealed it as) a clear discourse in the Arabic tongue, free of all crookedness, so that they may (draw lessons from it and) be ever mindful of God. ²⁹ (To illustrate,) God puts forward this parable : (Consider) a man who is owned by several quarreling partners and another who is owned exclusively by one person. Are they equal in comparison?

(Nay!) All praise is due to God alone! Yet, most of them (are ignorant and) do not know (the truth about monotheism and continue to worship false gods). [30] (O Prophet!) You will (ultimately) die (one day) and so will those (who oppose you). [31] Then on the Day of Resurrection (when the Hellfire is shown to everyone), they will all blame one another in the presence of their Lord (for rejecting His words during their short stay on earth).

Rejecters will be Abased

[32] Now, who can be more unjust (and wicked) than the one who lies about God and denies the truth when it has clearly come to him? Do these disbelievers not deserve Hell as their home (and final place of return)? [33] But the one who brings the truth and those who accept it (whole-heartedly), such are the people who are truly mindful of God. [34] They will have whatever they wish from their Lord (when they are admitted in His grace on the Day of Reckoning). Such is the reward for those who excel in good deeds. [35] Hence, God will erase and remove from their record the worst that they ever did and reward them for the best that they have done. [36] Is God not sufficient for His servant (whom He has appointed to convey His message) ? Yet they threaten you with those (helpless false gods that they worship) besides Him. Whomsoever God lets go astray (because of his own defiance), there is no guide for him. [37] And whomsoever God guides aright (because of his acceptance of the truth), none can lead him astray. Is not God the Almighty, the Lord of Retribution?

[38] And if you ask them who created the heavens and the earth, surely they will answer, "(It must be) God!" So ask them (further), "Then, why are you invoking something else besides God? Can they prevent any harm from striking me if God wills that it will fall upon me? Or can they withhold His grace if He intends a favor for me?" Say, "God is sufficient for me. Indeed, in Him alone should all who trust Him, place their trust."

[39] Say (to them O Prophet), "O my people! Go ahead to do the best you can (to undermine God), while I continue to labor and strive (in His way). In time, you will know; [40] who will suffer humiliation (in this life) and an everlasting torment (in the next)." [41] Indeed, We sent down the Book to you with the truth for all mankind (to take heed of). So whoever follows its guidance does so for the benefit of his own soul, and whoever strays from it does so at his own peril. (We did) not (appoint) you to be a guardian over them.

Punishment Cannot be Averted

⁴² (Verily,) God takes away the souls (of those who die) at the time of their death and also those who are alive during their sleep. He withholds the souls of those ordained for death and sends back the others until their appointed term. Indeed, surely there are signs in this for people who (relect and) ponder. ⁴³ Or have they taken intercessors besides God? Ask them, "(Do you do this) even though (it is obvious that) these false gods possess nothing, nor have any intelligence?" ⁴⁴ Say, "To God alone belongs (the sole right to grant) all intercession, and to Him belongs the dominion of the heavens and the earth. Then to Him will you be (ultimately) returned (in the end)."

⁴⁵ And whenever God alone is mentioned, the hearts of those who do not believe in the life to come are filled with resentment, and when those other than Him are mentioned, behold! They rejoice. ⁴⁶ Say, "O God, the Originator of the heavens and the earth, the Knower of the unseen and the manifest! You alone will judge between Your servants for the things they differed (and fought) about."

⁴⁷ And if those who commit injustice and evil were to possess the entire treasures of the earth twice over, they will surely offer all of it as ransom to free themselves from the terrible punishment (that will befall them) on the Day of Resurrection. (They will be shocked to see) all their sins (that they had never bothered to take into account during their sojourn on earth) be brought and shown to them by God (at that time) for reckoning. ⁴⁸ (On that Day,) the evil implications of their sinful deeds will become fully apparent to them and what they used to mock will overwhelm them.

⁴⁹ (Verily,) when adversity befalls man, he cries out to Us. But when We grant him a favor from Us, he says, "Indeed, I have been granted this because of my knowledge (and cleverness)." Nay! This (bestowal of) favor (to you) is only a test but most of them do not know. ⁵⁰ Indeed, those who lived before them said the same, but everything that they earned (and accomplished) could not help them (against God's punishment); ⁵¹ because the consequences of their evil deeds fell back upon them. The same will also happen to anyone who committed wicked deeds (and met their death before they repented). Indeed, all the evil deeds that they earned will eventually fall back upon them and they will not be able to escape from God.

⁵² Do they not know that God extends and restricts the provision for whomsoever He wills (according to His wisdom as a means to test one's faith)? Indeed, surely there are signs in this for people who believe.

Divine Mercy

⁵³ Say (to them O Prophet, "This is what God said) : O My servants! Those who have transgressed against their own souls (out of ignorance) should not despair of God's grace (and mercy). Indeed, God forgives all sins (whenever the sinner sincerely repents and turns to Him in full devotion). Verily, He is the Most Forgiving, the Most Compassionate." ⁵⁴ Hence, turn in repentance to your Lord (at once) and submit to Him (wholeheartedly) before His punishment arrives because you will not receive any help at that time.

⁵⁵ So follow the (Qur'an, which is the) best of what has been revealed to you from your Lord before punishment suddenly comes upon you at a time when you least expected it; ⁵⁶ lest a soul would cry on The Day of Judgment, "Woe to me for neglecting my duty towards God and for being among those who derided (the truth)!" ⁵⁷ Or it would say, "If only God had guided me, I would have surely been among the righteous!" ⁵⁸ Or plead when it finally sees the punishment, "If only I could have another chance, I would surely (not hesitate to) be among those who (strive to) excel in doing good deeds!"

⁵⁹ (But these unrepentant sinners will be told,) "Nay! Surely, My (clear) signs and revelations had indeed come to you (before this), but you (fiercely) denied them and became arrogant, and (had willfully) chosen to be among those who opposed the truth."

⁶⁰ On the Day of Resurrection, you will see that the faces of those who had lied against God turn dark. Is Hell not the home for those who are arrogant? ⁶¹ But for those who kept their duty to God diligently, He will deliver them to their place of salvation. No evil will touch them, nor will they grieve. ⁶² God is indeed the Creator of all things and He is (also) the Guardian over all of them. ⁶³ To Him belong the keys of the heavens and the earth. And those who reject the signs (and revelations) of God are the real losers.

The Final Judgment

⁶⁴ Say (to them O Prophet), "Are you ordering me to worship something other than God, O ignorant (and foolish) people? ⁶⁵ And verily, it has been revealed to you and to those before you that if you set partners (or associate anything) with God, your deeds will surely become worthless and you will certainly be among the losers. ⁶⁶ Behold! It is only God alone who deserves your worship, and be you among the thankful ones."

⁶⁷ Indeed, they did not appraise God with the true appraisal (that is rightfully due to him). On the Day of Resurrection, the entire earth will be in

His grip (and none will be able to escape). The heavens will be (rolled up) and folded *a* in His right hand (commanding absolute power and authority). Glory be to Him (Who is far above all the lies that they have falsely invented against Him)! Sublimely exalted is He above everything that they associate Him with.

⁶⁸ And when the trumpet is blown, whoever that is in the heavens and the earth will fall dead except those God wills (to exempt). Then it will be blown again for the second time, and behold! They will rise and be shown (the horror of what they used to deride before). ⁶⁹ And when the earth shines with its Lord's light, (everyone's) record of deeds will be laid bare and the Prophets and other witnesses will be brought in (to testify). Then, everyone will be judged (fairly) in truth and none will be wronged. ⁷⁰ Verily, every soul will be paid in full for what it has done; and God's knowledge encompasses everything that they do.

Driven in Throngs

⁷¹ And so, all those who denied the truth will be driven to Hell in throngs. When they arrive, its gates will be opened and its keepers will ask them, "Did there not come to you any Messenger from among you reciting the (divine) verses of your Lord and forewarning you of this Day?" They will answer, "Yes!" But (it will be too late for them to make amends at that time because) the sentence of punishment would have (already) fallen upon these rejecters of truth. ⁷² Then it will be said to them, "Enter the gates of Hell (and remain) in there forever. Wretched indeed is the (final place of return and permanent) home of the arrogant!"

⁷³ As for those who were (always) mindful of their Lord (and kept their duty to Him diligently), they will be ushered to Paradise in throngs. When they arrive, its gates will be opened and its keepers will greet them, "Peace be upon you! You have done well. Come in here to stay forever." ⁷⁴ And they will exclaim, "All praise is due to God Who has fulfilled His promise to us. It is He Who gave us the earth to inherit (so that we could do good deeds in order to earn our place in Paradise. And now,) we are free to dwell wherever we please in Paradise. How excellent is the reward for those who (strived and) labored (in God's way)!"

⁷⁵ And you (O Prophet), will see the Angels surrounding the Throne, glorifying their Lord's perfection by praising Him (unceasingly). Everyone will be judged in truth (and fairness on that Day), and it will be proclaimed, "All praise is due to God alone, the Lord of all the worlds!"

---

a See verses 21:104 and its footnote.

40. Ghāfir
[Forgiver : 85 verses]

This is a Makkan chapter. It deals with the fundamentals of faith, namely the truth of the Qur'an, monotheism, resurrection, judgment, reward and punishment. It starts with an emphasis that this Qur'an has been sent down by God the Almighty, the All-Knowing and the Forgiver of sins. It then points out that none but the disbelievers dispute about the truth sent down by God and that the previous nations similarly disbelieved the truth delivered by their respective Messengers. In this context, the story of Pharoah's rejection of the message delivered by Moses is conveyed with particular reference to a believer among Pharoah's people who tried to persuade them to accept the truth and consequently became the target of Pharoah's persecution. But God protected him and caused the destruction of Pharoah and his disbelieving followers. The chapter also refers to some of the scenes of the Day of Judgment, and concludes by drawing attention to God's making provision for His creation in various ways. The chapter is named *Ghāfir* or Forgiver by which God refers to Himself at its beginning. It is also called *Al-Mu'min* or The Believer with reference to the story of the believer among Pharoah's family which the chapter describes.

In the name of God, the Most Gracious, the Most Compassionate.

A Prayer by Angels

¹ *Ha Mīm.* ² This Book is sent down from God the Almighty, Whose knowledge encompasses everything. ³ He is The Forgiver of Sins, the Acceptor of Repentance, yet Stern and severe in Retribution, and He is the Owner of Infinite Bounty.ᵃ There is no god except Him and to Him will everything be ultimately returned. ⁴ There is none who dispute the revelations of God except those who are bent on rejecting the truth. Do not let their (affluence and) free movement in the land deceive you.

ᵃ This passage can be paraphrased as follows : "God forgives sins and accepts repentance. At the same time, His punishment is severe and His bounty is infinite." This is one of the characteristics of the Qur'an's unique style. When addressing mankind with teachings, it often combines promises of good news with stern warnings to inculcate the paired feeling of fear and hope - fear of God's wrath for disobeying Him and hope in His infinite grace when we live our lives according to the teachings of His Book as taught by His Prophet. This is intended to balance man's behavior and attitude in quelling over-confidence and arrogance in him while instilling a deep sense of humility. The Prophet was specifically sent by God as a bearer of good news and warner to mankind. See verses 4:165, 17:105, 46:12, and 48:8.

⁵ (Verily,) the people of Noah denied (the truth) before your people (O Muhammad) and so did those who formed (evil) alliances after them. Every community plotted against its Messenger and they strived to defeat truth with falsehood. But it was I Who seized them (in the end), and behold! How (terrible) was My retribution. ⁶ Such is the fulfillment of your Lord's word against those who opposed and defied the truth which decreed that they will be the inmates of the Fire.

⁷ The (Angels) who carry the Lord's Throne (of Supremacy) and the others around it (proclaim and) glorify their Lord's perfection by praising Him (unceasingly). They have faith in Him and plead forgiveness for those who believe, by praying, "Our Lord! (Indeed) You encompass everything with Your grace and knowledge. So forgive those who turn to You in repentance and follow Your path. Save them from the torment of the Hellfire. *ᵃ* ⁸ O Our Lord! Admit them into the Gardens of Eternity that You have promised together with the righteous among their forefathers, spouses and offspring. Indeed, You alone are Almighty, All-Wise. ⁹ And protect them from (the consequences of) evil. Whoever You protect from evil on that Day would surely be blessed with Your grace (and mercy). And that is indeed the greatest triumph."

Failure of Opponents

¹⁰ But for the disbelievers, they will be told, "Surely, God's contempt for you when you rejected His invitation to faith (before this) is far greater than your (regret and) self-disgust (that you feel today)." ¹¹ Then they will plead, "Our Lord, twice have You caused us to die and twice have You given us life.*ᵇ* We confess our sins (to You) now. Is there any way out (for us from this doom)?"

ᵃ Aggression and injustice are often supported by false arguments that are deliberately contrived. All Prophets, except for Solomon and his father David, suffered abuse and ill-treatment, and so did their followers. However, life is filled with trials and appraisals, and those who are sincere ought to persevere and face the challenges no matter how oppressive and demanding they may be. This passage reassures believers who are steadfast in their belief that God's Angels are watching over them and praying for their guidance and salvation.

ᵇ Verse 76:1 says that man was not even a mentionable thing initially (i.e. non-existent). Then he was given life in the womb of his mother and brought to the world. And then died at the end of his earthly life before being resurrected and given life for the second time to face judgment. Twice dead and twice alive. See also verse 2:28.

¹² (But they will be told, "The cause of your dreadful condition now) is because when God alone was invoked (and worshipped), you disbelieved (and turned away). But when some other things were associated with Him, you believed (in them). So (today), all judgment lies with God, the Most High, the Most Great (Whom you had arrogantly rejected before. Do you expect Him to listen to your plea for mercy now)?"

¹³ He is the One Who shows you His (wondrous) signs and sends down provision for you from the sky. Yet none takes heed except those who turn to Him (in repentance and devotion). ¹⁴ Therefore (O believers), call upon God with sincere faith and devotion, even if those who oppose the truth hate this (very much). ¹⁵ He is truly Exalted in Rank, for He is the Lord of the (Supreme) Throne. He sends down (divine) revelation by His command to whomsoever He wills of His servants to warn people about the Day of the Meeting (where everyone will be questioned and reckoned for their deeds).

¹⁶ That is the Day when they will come forth (from their graves) and nothing about them will be hidden from God. (On that Day, they will be asked,) "To whom belongs the entire dominion of this Day?" (God Himself will answer,) "To Almighty God, the One Who holds absolute power over everything!" ¹⁷ (It will then be said,) "On this day, every soul will be fully requited for its deeds and for what it has earned. No one will be wronged (and unfairly treated) today. Indeed, God is swift in reckoning."

¹⁸ So warn them of the (dreadful) Day that is drawing closer (O Prophet)! The Day when hearts (full of suppressed grief) will leap to their throats, choking (them in terror). No loyal friend can the wrongdoers depend on, nor will (the plea of mercy from any) intercessor be heeded. ¹⁹ (Verily,) God is even aware of the most stealthy glance and all the secrets that the hearts conceal; (for indeed, there is nothing that can ever escape Him). ²⁰ God judges in truth, whereas those who they invoke besides Him cannot judge at all. Indeed, God is the All-Hearing, All-Seeing.

²¹ Have they not traveled throughout the land and observed how was the end of those before them? They were superior in strength and left behind more splendid traces on the land. But God seized them for their sins, and they had no one to protect them from God's wrath (when His decree fell upon them). ²² That was because when their Messengers came to them with clear proofs, they (turned their backs and) refused to believe. And so God seized them. Indeed, He is All-Powerful, Stern in Retribution.

A Believer Among the People of Pharaoh

²³ Verily, We sent Moses with Our signs and a clear authority; ²⁴ to Pharaoh, Haman, and Korah but they called him a sorcerer and a liar. ²⁵ Then when he brought to them the truth from Us, they said, "Kill the sons of those who believe with him but spare their women." But the (evil) plotting of (wicked) disbelievers always ends in vain. ²⁶ Said Pharaoh, "Leave Moses for me to kill and let (me see) him call his Lord (to save him). Indeed, I fear that he will change your traditions or spread disorder in the land." ²⁷ Moses said, "Indeed, I seek refuge in my Lord and your Lord from every arrogant person who does not believe in the Day of Reckoning."

²⁸ And then behold! A believing man from the family of Pharaoh who (until then) had concealed his faith, (came forward and) said, "Will you kill a man just because he says, 'My Lord is God (the Almighty)!' and he has brought to you clear proofs from your Lord? If he is a liar, then upon him is his lie. But if he speaks the truth, (are you not afraind that) you might be struck by some of what he threatens you with?" Indeed, God does not guide anyone who deliberately exceeds His limits and lies (shamelessly).

²⁹ (Then he continued,) "O my people! Today the kingdom is yours and you reign supreme in the land. But who will save us against God's punishment if it befalls us? Pharaoh answered, "(O my people!) I do not show you other than what I see (is best for you) and I only guide you to the right way." ³⁰ Thereupon, the believer said, "O my people! Indeed, I fear for you a fate that is similar to (the dreadful) day of the (evil) alliances (in the past who opposed their Prophets); ³¹ like the plight of the peoples of Noah, 'Aād, Tsamud and those who came after them. God does not wish any injustice for His servants."

³² "O my people! Indeed I fear that you will encounter a Day when you will cry out (in vain to one another for help); ³³ and when you try to flee from God, there will be no one to protect you from Him. And whoever God lets go astray (because of his own stubbornness), there will be no one to guide him. ³⁴ "And indeed, Joseph came to you earlier with clear proofs (from God) but you continued to doubt the message he brought. After he died, you said, 'Never will God send a Messenger (to us) after him.'" This is how God lets astray anyone who transgresses His boundaries and is filled with doubt (about the truth).³⁵ (Verily,) those who dispute God's messages without any authority are doing something very despised by God and the believers. This is how God seals the heart of every arrogant tyrant.

³⁶ And so Pharaoh said, "O Haman! Build me a (lofty) tower so that I may

(climb to) reach; ³⁷ the heavens and look for this God of Moses even though I am convinced that he is a liar." This was how Pharaoh's evil deeds were embellished (and made fair-seeming to him that caused him to become arrogant) and be hindered from the right path. (Verily,) Pharaoh's scheming led only to his own ruin.

³⁸ And then, the person who believed said, "O my people! Follow me and I shall guide you to the right way. ³⁹ O my people! The life of this world is truly (deceiving. It is) nothing but a (short-lived) enjoyment and (a fleeting) delight, whereas the life in the Hereafter is indeed the everlasting home (to return to). ⁴⁰ Whoever does an evil deed will only be requited with its equivalent. But any man or woman who acts righteously and truly believes (in God and the Day of Judgment) will enter Paradise and be given (generous) provision without measure."

⁴¹ "And O my people! How strange it is for me to call you to salvation while you call me to the Fire! ⁴² You call me to disbelieve in God and to associate Him with what I have no knowledge of, whereas I call you to the Almighty, the Most Forgiving. ⁴³ There is no doubt that what you call me to worship is not worth to be called upon in this world and in the life to come. Certainly to God alone will be our return and those who (arrogantly) exceeded His limits will be the Fire's inmates. ⁴⁴ Soon you will remember what I am saying to you (now with great regret). I entrust my affairs only to God, for He is surely ever watchful over His servants."

⁴⁵ And so, God protected him from the evils that they plotted, whereas a dreadful torment encompassed the people of Pharaoh (when they all drowned). ⁴⁶ (Then in their graves), they will be exposed to the Fire (of Hell) in the morning and evening. And on the Day when the Last Hour arrives, (the keepers of Hell will be commanded by God), "Make the people of Pharaoh (and all those who rejected the truth) enter the most grievous punishment!" ⁴⁷ And they will then quarrel with one another in the Fire. The weak will say to those who were arrogant, "Indeed, we were your (loyal) followers (on earth). Can you (help to) avert a portion of the Fire from us?" ⁴⁸ The arrogant ones will reply, "(Can you not see that) we are all in this pit together? Indeed, God has already passed His judgment on all His servants (and there is absolutely nothing we can do to save ourselves now)."

⁴⁹ Then, all those in the Fire will plead to the keepers of Hell, "(Please) ask your Lord to lighten our punishment just for a day." ⁵⁰ The keepers of Hell will ask, "Did your Messengers not come to you with clear proofs (of the truth before this?) They will answer "Yes they did (but we foolishly denied and opposed them)." The keepers of Hell will reply, "Then call (upon the Lord yourselves to plead for your case)!" But the call of those disbelievers will only

be in vain.

⁵¹ Indeed, We shall surely help Our Messengers and those who believe during their stay in this world and also on the Day when witnesses will arise (to testify against the wrongdoers in the Hereafter). ⁵² (That is) the Day when excuses offered by the wrongdoers (on why they rejected the truth) will be of no value. They will have a (lasting) curse and a woeful home (to finally return to).

⁵³ And indeed We gave Moses (true) guidance and We made the children of Israel inherit the Book (of Torah that we sent down to him); ⁵⁴ as guidance and reminder to those endowed with insight and wisdom. ⁵⁵ So be patient (O Muhammad). Indeed, the promise of God is ever true. Seek forgiveness for your sins and shortcomings, and glorify your Lord's perfection by celebrating His praise in the evening and morning.

Always Responding to Prayers

⁵⁶ Indeed, for those who argue against God's signs without authority, there is nothing except vain pride that fills their hearts which they will never be able to satisfy. So seek refuge in God. Indeed, He hears all, sees all.

⁵⁷ Surely, the creation of the heavens and the earth is a greater act than the creation of man. But most people do not know (and do not care to ponder about this). ⁵⁸ Never can the blind and the seeing be equal; nor those who believe and act righteously be compared to those who do evil. How seldom do you think and reflect!

⁵⁹ Indeed, the Final Hour will surely arrive and there is no doubt about it. But most people (choose to neglect its signs and) do not believe (in the Hereafter). ⁶⁰ (So remember what) your Lord said, "Call upon Me, and I shall respond to your call! Those who are too (proud and) arrogant to worship Me will enter Hell in humiliation."

⁶¹ God is the One Who made the night for you to rest and the day visible (and bright for you to earn your livelihood). Indeed, God is limitless in His bounty to mankind, but most people are ungrateful. ⁶² Such is God, your Lord, the Creator of all things. There is no god except Him. How then are you so deluded (and misled from the truth)? ⁶³ This is how those who rejected and denied the signs of God became deluded (and were led astray).

⁶⁴ God is the One Who made the earth a dwelling place for you and made the sky a canopy; and then He shaped you and perfected your form, and gave

you good things (as sustenance). Such is God, your Lord. Blessed is God, the Lord of all the worlds. [65] He is the Ever-Living; there is no god except Him. So call upon Him in sincere faith (and devotion). All praise is due to God, the Lord of all the worlds. [66] Say (to them O Prophet), "Indeed, I have been forbidden to worship those whom you call upon (and worship) besides God after clear proofs have come to me from my Lord. And I am commanded to fully submit to God alone, the Lord of all the worlds."

[67] It is He Who created you from soil, then from a clot of semen, then from a (leech-like) clinging zygote; then He brings you out as an infant and lets you grow into full maturity and (gradually) become old (before you finally die). But some among you He may cause to die sooner. (It is God Who sets) your specific life term (on earth. Ponder deeply over this) so that you will understand (His absolute power and control over you and everything else). [68] He is (indeed) the One Who gives life and causes death. And when He decrees a matter (that He wills), He need only say, "Be!" and it is.

[69] (Are you not perplexed) seeing those who still dispute God's (obvious) signs? How is it that they are turned away (and confounded from the truth)? [a] [70] In time, those who deny this Book and the (earlier Books) that We sent with Our Messengers, will come to know the truth; [71] when (they are forced to carry) shackles around their necks and chains (on their legs), dragged; [72] into the boiling water and then burned in the Fire. [73] There they will be asked, "Where are those things that you used to associate; [74] with God (in worship)?" They will answer, "They have forsaken us; or rather, what we used to call upon (and worship) before, did not actually exist." This is how God lets the disbelievers go astray; [75] all because you used to rejoice (in falsehood) without justification and behaved insolently on earth. [76] So enter now into the gates of Hell (to remain) in there forever. How horrible is the home of the arrogant!"

[77] Hence, remain patient (against their rejection O Prophet), for God's promise is ever true. Whether We show you a part of (the woeful consequences) that We have promised them (while you are still in their midst), or We recall you from this world (before that retribution takes place), it is to Us that they will all be ultimately brought back (in the end).

---

[a] Islamophobes who detest Islam are grossly ignorant of the truth. They are actually the product of a materialistic civilization where its people are driven towards greed and immediate gratification, and belong to a society that is founded on a morality of permissiveness, injustice, hypocrisy, and the superiority of the white race over the rest of humankind. On the other hand, there is no denying that the Muslims have neglected their heritage and noble mission in this world but they should do better than to allow themselves to be led blindly into the abyss by this ungodly, heedless civilization.

When it is Too Late to Believe

⁷⁸ And indeed, We have sent forth (many) Messengers before you. Among them are some who We narrated (their stories) to you and many more We did not. *ᵃ* No Messenger can bring any sign except with God's permission. When God's command (of doom) comes, judgment will be passed in truth (and fairness), and the followers of falsehood will end up as the greatest losers.

⁷⁹ God is the One Who made cattle for you so that some you may ride and some you may eat. ⁸⁰ In them are also other benefits for you. Through them, you are able to fulfill your heartfelt need (to travel to many places). Upon them, just like upon ships, you are carried (and transported safely). ⁸¹ (Such is an example of) His wondrous sign for you (to ponder O mankind). So is there any of God's signs that you wish to deny?

⁸² Have they - who still doubt the truth - not traveled through the land and observed the (terrible) fate of those before them? Verily, those people of the past were more superior in number and strength, and they left behind more splendid traces in the land. Yet all that they achieved was of no benefit to them; ⁸³ because when their Messengers came to them with clear evidence (of the truth), they arrogantly reveled in whatever (worldly) knowledge they had (and rejected the truth that was presented to them. In the end,) they were (seized and) overwhelmed by the very thing which they used to (reject and) mock. *ᵇ*

⁸⁴ And when they saw Our punishment, they exclaimed, "We believe in God alone now and we reject everything that we used to associate with Him." ⁸⁴ But their (sudden attainment of) faith after they saw Our punishment could not benefit them at all. Such is God's way of dealing with all His servants. Right there and then, those who defied Him were in utter ruin.

ᵃ See verse 4:164.

ᵇ Verses 82-83 : Many misguided people persist in their errors and refuse to recognize their mistakes even when reminders are brought to them until they are struck with some calamity that finally brings the truth home to them. In most cases, it is too late for them to do anything to save themselves. Human history is full of examples and lessons of this and the Qur'an narrates many stories of mighty ancient nations that suffer this fate out of rejection and arrogance to the truth. In essence, it fulfills the adage - "What goes around comes around", and "We reap what we sow." See verses 3:137-139 and its footnote.

41. Fuṣṣilat
[Elucidated : 54 verses]

This is a Makkan chapter which deals with the fundamentals of faith. It starts with an emphasis that the Qur'an has been sent down by God and that its verses are elucidated and set out in detail. It then refers to the attitude of the disbelievers and draws attention to God's creation of the heavens and the earth by way of bringing home the theme of monotheism and to the fate of the peoples of Tsamud and 'Aād who despite their being the most powerful nations of the time, met with destruction and ruin because of their disbelief and rejection of the truth. It then points out that on the Day of Judgment, the eyes, ears and skins of the sinful will bear testimony against them because God will enable these to speak. This is followed by the indication of the fate that awaits the righteous and the believers. The chapter ends by pointing out that God will show men His signs in the universe and in themselves, and will prove that the Qur'an is the truth (verse 53). The chapter is named *Fuṣṣilat* or Elucidated after its third verse which states that the verses of the Qur'an have been clearly presented and set out in detail.

In the name of God, the Most Gracious, the Most Compassionate.

Testimony of One's Own Senses

¹ *Ha Mīm.* ² (This revelation is) sent down from the Most Gracious, the Most Compassionate (Lord). ³ It is a (divine) Book with (clear) messages that have been elucidated in Arabic as a discourse for people with knowledge; ⁴ bringing good news as well as a (fierce) warning. And yet, most (of the Arab pagans) turn away (from it), refusing to take heed. ⁵ They say, "Our hearts are securely wrapped and veiled against (the faith that) you invite us to embrace (O Muhammad). In our ears is deafness and there is a huge barrier between us. So do whatever you wish, and so shall we." *ᵃ*

ᵃ Syaikh Muhammad al-Ghazali, a renowned Islamic scholar from Egypt who died in 1996 in Saudi Arabia, aptly commented verses 1-5 as follows : Revelation originates from God as guidance to humankind and protection against the evil of their thoughts, desires, prejudices, and deeds. It is the source of all the goodness and justice in this world. Sensible discerning people appreciate the benefits and the love these words convey to the true believers, and the warning they make to the foolish who are oblivious of the truth, but who are often a majority in society. The Qur'an stresses this fact, saying: "And yet most of them turn away, refusing to take heed" in verse 4. One major feature of the Qur'anic revelation is that it was received in the Arabic language. Translations in other languages do not have the same status as the Arabic original, because God, in His infinite

⁶ Tell them (O Prophet), "Verily, I am only a mortal like you to whom it has been revealed that your God is One. So take a straight path to Him and seek His forgiveness." And woe to those who associate others with Him; ⁷ who do not spend in charity and are in denial of the Hereafter. ⁸ Indeed, those who believe and do righteous deeds, for them is a never-ending reward.

⁹ Say, "Do you deny the One Who created the earth in two phases and dare set up rivals against Him? Verily, He is the Lord of all the worlds!" ¹⁰ It is He Who (while perfecting the earth,) placed firm mountains on it that tower above its surface, bestowed (so many) blessings on it, and equitably apportioned its means of subsistence to all who would seek it, in (a total of) four phases. *ᵃ*

¹¹ Moreover, His (supremacy) is firmly established over the (vast) heaven. And while it was (still in the form of) smoke (earlier), *ᵇ* He gave command to

---

wisdom, chose the Arabic language to be the medium for Qur'anic revelation and honored the Arabs with the task of conveying it to the rest of the world. And it is also because translations to other languages only convey the meaning of the Qur'an which do not have the same impact as the Arabic version. In the early days of Islam, the Arabs were reluctant to embrace it, with some of them showing tremendous resistance. Prophet Muhammad had to work very hard to persuade them to identify with Islam and then defend it with their lives and wealth. He also successfully produced successors who overran some of the most powerful and tyrannical empires in history. Sadly, today's Arabs have inherited two of the vilest characteristics : (i) the traditions of their arrogant forefathers during the decline of Islamic civilization, and (ii) the habits and illusions of today's materialistic and pleasure-seeking Western culture. There is nothing worse than an agnostic Arab. They are the most irrational, bigoted and unjust people. The Qur'an could not be more accurate by quoting what their ancestors said in verse 5 : "Our hearts are securely wrapped and veiled against (the faith) you call us to (O Muhammad). In our ears is deafness and there is a huge barrier between us. Do then whatever you wish, while we shall continue with our ways." Nevertheless, God has chosen them and their language for the unique honor of conveying His message to the world. See verse 44 of this same chapter.

ᵃ The two phases of earth's creation mentioned in verse 9 are part of the four phases mentioned here in verse 10. In addition, the creation of the seven heavens which took two phases as mentioned in verse 12, was completed earlier when the universe was still in the form of smoke after The Big Bang. Therefore, the total phases involved in the creation of the heavens and the earth is six as mentioned in verses 7:54, 10:3, 11:7, and 25:59, not eight.

ᵇ In November 2011, space scientists and astronomers concluded for the first time ever that they have finally found pristine clouds of primordial gas made up of the lightest elements (mostly hydrogen and helium) that formed in the first few moments after the

it and to the earth, "Come both of you, (submit yourselves to Me), either willingly or unwillingly!" to which both responded, "We hereby come (to You) willingly (and in obedience, O Lord!)" [12] Thereafter, He completed them as seven heavens in two phases and assigned each heaven its own duty. And We adorned the nearest heaven with lamps and guarded it. Such is the decree of the Almighty (Lord), the All-Knowing. [13] But if your people (still) turn away (from you O Prophet), tell them, "I forewarn you against a sudden thunderbolt like the one which fell upon the people of 'Aād and Tsamud."

[14] When (one after another of) God's earlier Messengers came to their people (speaking about the truth that is laid open) in front of them and (the Hereafter which is) hidden from them, saying, "Worship none but God!" their people answered, "If our Lord had willed, surely He would have sent down Angels (to guide us instead of mortals like you). Indeed, we do not believe in the message that you claim to have been sent with."

[15] As for (the people of) 'Aād, they had no right to behave arrogantly throughout the land. They said, "Who could be more superior than us in might?" Did they not consider that God, Who created them is surely far superior than them in might? But they still continued to reject Our signs. [16] Thereupon, We sent a furious wind to them for several disastrous days to make them taste a humiliating punishment in this worldly life. Most certainly, the punishment in the next life is far more humiliating. And they will not be helped.

[17] And as for (the people of) Tsamud, We guided them but they preferred blindness. So a thunderbolt of humiliating punishment seized them for the sins that they earned (from their evil deeds). [18] And We saved (only) those who believed and were mindful of Us.

Big Bang. Before this, scientists have always detected metals (i.e. elements heavier than hydrogen and helium) wherever they looked in the universe. According to Dr. Michele Fumagalli who was one of the lead scientists of this research that was conducted in the University of California Santa Cruz, this is the first time pristine gas that is uncontaminated by heavier elements was observed in space and the evidence fully matches the composition of the primordial gas predicted by the Big Bang theory. More than a thousand years ago, the Qur'an refers to these pristine clouds of primordial gas as smoke or *dukhān* in Arabic in reference to how it looks like from afar, and that it came into existence during the very early stage of the creation of the universe after the heavens and the earth were parted asunder by a great force from their earlier state of being fused together (see verse 21:30). Scientifically, the discovery of this pristine clouds of primordial gas lends greater credence to the truth in the Big Bang theory.

¹⁹ (Hence, warn everyone of the terrible) Day when the enemies of God will be gathered and driven to the Fire, arraigned in rows. ²⁰ And when they arrive, their ears, eyes, and skins will testify against them for everything that they have done (during their lifetime). ²¹ They will ask their skins, "Why are you testifying against us?" and their skins will reply, "God gave us speech as He gave speech to everything else (today to speak the truth). He is the One Who created you for the first time (when He brought you to the world) and it is to Him that you have been returned (now for reckoning after He resurrected you from death)."

²² You did not try to hide your sins because you never imagined that your ears, eyes and skins would one day testify against you. You also thought that God does not know much of what you were doing. ²³ Indeed, your erroneous assumption about your Lord has certainly ruined you and caused you to become great losers.

²⁴ Even if they endure in patience, (thinking that their suffering is only temporary, they would surely be grossly mistaken because) the Fire has been decreed to be their permanent home. And if they plead for a favor (by asking to be returned to the world so that they can make amends), they will be ignored. ²⁵ (And because of their persistent rejection of Our message during their short stay on earth,) We assigned to them intimate evil companions who made their past and present (misdeeds) look attractive and fair-seeming. And so, the sentence (of doom) is justified against them today as it was justified against those from the previous generations of Jinn and men. Indeed, they were losers.

Believers Strengthened

²⁶ These are the people who, when the Qur'an is recited to them, they would say to one another, "Do not listen to the Qur'an. Make noise when it is being recited so that your (noise) will prevail (against it)." ²⁷ We shall surely make these evil opponents of truth taste grievous punishment, and We shall certainly requite them according to their worst deeds. ²⁸ The Hellfire is the requital for God's enemies where they will have their lasting home as punishment for denying and rejecting Our signs (of truth). ²⁹ (After realizing there is no escape for them,) these (doomed) disbelievers will say, "Our Lord! Show us those Jinn and humans who have led us astray. We shall trample them under our feet so that they will be among the utterly lowest (in Hell and suffer a worse fate than us)!"

³⁰ Behold! As for those who say, "God is our Lord!" and then remain steadfast in the right path, the Angels descend to them (saying), "Do not fear

nor grieve. But rejoice in the good news of Paradise which you have been promised. [31] We are your friends and supporters in this world and in the life to come. There you will have everything your souls desire and what you prayed for; [32] as a gift from the Most Forgiving, the Most Compassionate (Lord)."

[33] Who is better in speech than someone who invites others to (the path of) God, does righteous deeds and says, "Indeed, I am among those who have submitted to God!" [34] Good deeds and evil deeds are not equal. Repel evil with what is better, and your enemy might turn into a dear friend (as though he had been one for a long time). [35] But no one will be granted this (sterling quality) except those who exercise patience and self-restraint, and those who are endowed with a great share of goodness (from their Lord). [36] So if an evil urge or temptation is prompted to you by Satan, seek refuge in God. Indeed, He is the One Who is All-Hearing, All-Knowing.

No Concealment from God

[37] And among His (wondrous) signs are the night and the day, and the sun and the moon. Hence, do not prostrate yourselves to the sun, nor the moon; but prostrate yourselves (in devotion) to God alone Who created them, if it is Him alone Whom you truly worship. [38] But if they are too arrogant to take heed of this reminder (O Prophet), then (the loss is theirs as God is not in need of their worship). Know that all those who are near your Lord [a] (unceasingly) proclaim and glorify His perfection tirelessly, night and day.

[39] And among His (wondrous) signs too is that you see the earth barren and lifeless. But when We send down rain on it, it stirs and swells with life. Verily, He who brings life to earth can surely restore life to the dead (as well), for behold, He has power over everything! [40] Verily, those who distort the meaning of Our messages are not hidden from Us. (So ponder!) Which of the two will be in a better state : the one who will be cast in the Fire or the one who will come safe to Us on the Day of Resurrection? So, do as you wish. Indeed, He sees everything that you do (and will hold you accountable for all your deeds).

[41] Verily, those who refuse to believe in this Reminder [b] when it is brought to them (are surely the losers, for) this is certainly a mighty Book (that is sublimely divine). [42] No falsehood can ever approach it from the front or rear. It is (a revelation that has been) sent down from the Most Wise, the Immensely Praiseworthy. [43] (O Muhammad!) Nothing is being said to you

---

[a] In reference to His Angels.
[b] *Adz-Dzkir* or The Reminder is one of the names of the Qur'an.

now that was not said to all the Messengers before you. (So do not despair, for) your Lord is not only the Owner of forgiveness but He is also the Owner of the most grievous retribution.

 ⁴⁴ Had We revealed the Qur'an in a language other than Arabic, then those who are rejecting it now would surely (have a valid excuse to) say, "Why is its verses and messages not clearly presented (in a language that we can understand)? How could a message intended for an Arab audience be delivered in non-Arabic?" Tell them, "To all who believe, this divine Book is indeed a (source of unfailing) guidance and a healing (for them). But to those who are devoid of faith, in their ears is deafness. Hence, God's message of truth will always remain obscure to them (even when it is delivered in the language of their own native tongue). They are like people who are being called from a far away place (who hears only a faint voice but cannot understand anything)."

Gradual Spread of Truth

⁴⁵ (In the past, indeed) it was We Who gave the Book (of Torah) to Moses. But (those with disease in their hearts) deliberately raised disputes (to question the truth in the message that Moses brought). Had it not been for a decree that preceded from your Lord (to postpone His retribution until a specified time), surely they would have been immediately punished (for their defiance, and there would not be any more dispute left) between them. Despite the reprieve, they were still doubtful and suspicious about the truth (that Moses brought). ⁴⁶ (The fact is,) whoever does righteous deeds, does so for the benefit of his own soul. And whoever does evil, does so against himself (and will suffer its evil consequences). Your Lord is never unjust to His servants.

⁴⁷ Knowledge of the (Final) Hour rests with Him alone. Not a fruit comes out from its sheath, nor does any female conceive (in her womb) or gives birth without His knowledge. And so on that Day, when He calls everyone to judgment, He will ask, "Where are now those partners that you used to associate with Me?" They will answer, "We hereby declare to You that none of us can be a witness to that (because they have all forsaken us)." ⁴⁸ Those whom they used to invoke will vanish (and leave them in a lurch) and they will finally realize that there is no escape (from the suffering that is laid bare in front of them).

⁴⁹ Man does not get tired of praying for good. But if misfortune afflicts him, he gives up hope and (is lost in) despair. ⁵⁰ And if We let him taste Our grace after he was afflicted with adversity, he will surely say, "This is what I deserve and I do not believe that the Hour of Doom will ever come. And even

if I am returned to my Lord, I shall surely enjoy the best reward from Him."
(But on the Day of Judgment,) We shall surely tell these disbelievers
everything they did (and how terribly wrong their assumptions were). And
then, We shall certainly make them taste a severe punishment.

⁵¹ And when We bless man with favor, he turns away and distances
himself (from Us in an aloof manner). But as soon as misfortune touches him,
he makes endless prayers (to plead for divine help). ⁵² Ask them (O Prophet),
"Have you ever given thought (about what would be your fate) if this Qur'an
is truly (a revelation) from God while you continue to reject it? Who could be
more misguided than the one who opposes (the truth) and alienates himself
(from God)?"

⁵³ In time, We shall show them Our signs in every corner (of the universe)
and within themselves (too), ᵃ until it becomes clear to them that this
(revelation) is indeed the truth. (Ask them, "Are the signs that are evident
now) still not sufficient for you to believe that your Lord is a Witness over
everything?"

⁵⁴ Behold! They are really in doubt about the meeting with their Lord (on
Judgment Day) whereas He truly encompasses everything (and nothing can
ever escape Him).

ᵃ The Qur'an comes with many scientific proofs and evidence that can be found all over
the vast universe and also within our own body, from the largest right down to the
minutest to validate its veracity as God's literal words. Many of what the Qur'an
mentioned in the 7th century could not be understood and fully appreciated at that time
and also for more than a thousand years after that due to the absence of scientific
knowledge and discoveries throughout those years. It was only during the 20th century
when scientific researches were being actively pursued and conducted with the advent
of technology that we begin to see these predictions and divine prophecies proven
true. Some of them are briefly presented in this book. There are still many more
wondrous and amazing evidence that we have yet to discover which only time will
eventually unfold their truth. With all these in place confirming the Qur'an's divinity, is
there any more reason to doubt the ultimate message of truth that the Qur'an puts
forward to mankind, which is, there is no other god but the only One Almighty God Who
is The God of all the worlds that deserves sole worship, and that Muhammad bin
Abdullah of Makkah who recited the entire Qur'an that was revealed to him is God's
last and final Messenger who He has chosen to convey His divine message to
mankind? Only those with knowledge of the truth stand in awe of God - The Ultimate
Creator and Sustainer of all, and will fully submit themselves only to Him alone. See
verses 51:20 and 35:28 and its footnote.

42. Ash-Shūrā
[The Consultation : 53 verses]

T his is a Makkan chapter which deals with the fundamentals of faith, namely monotheism, Messengership of Prophet Muhammad, resurrection, judgment, reward and punishment. It starts with the emphasis that God had sent down revelations to the previous Prophets and that it is the same message of monotheism and Islam which was delivered through all the Prophets. It then draws attention to the Absolute Oneness and Uniqueness of God in verse 11 and that to Him belong the keys of the heavens and the earth. This theme of monotheism is further illustrated with reference to His favors and grace upon His creations where His irrefutable signs are visible throughout the universe. Hence, man is called upon to respond to God's message before the coming of the day when there will be neither defense against it or refuge from it. The chapter is called *Ash-Shūrā* or The Counsel with reference to verse 38 where Muslims are required to conduct their public affairs by way of mutual consultation.

In the name of God, the Most Gracious, the Most Compassionate.

A Message Revealed by God

¹ *Ha Mīm.* ² *'Ayn Sīn Qāf.* ³ This is how He reveals (His divine message) to you (O Muhammad) just like He did to His Messengers before you. Such is God, the Almighty, the All-Wise. ⁴ To Him belongs all that is in the heavens and the earth. He is (truly) the Most Exalted, the Most Great. ⁵ The heavens almost split asunder from above as the Angels glorify (the perfection of) their Lord by praising Him (unceasingly) and ask forgiveness for those on earth. Verily, God is indeed Most Forgiving, Most Compassionate.

⁶ As for those who take patrons (and protectors) besides Him, God is ever-watching them; and you (O Muhammad) are surely not responsible for what they do.

⁷ And so it is that We have revealed to you this Qur'an in Arabic for you to warn the Mother of Cities ᵃ and those who live nearby about the inevitable Day of Gathering where a group will be in Paradise and another in the Blazing Fire. ⁸ Had God willed, He could have made them all into a single community (of believers), but He admits into His grace only whom He wills (because of their acceptance of the truth and the good deeds that they do), while the wrongdoers will have no one to protect and help them (from His torment on

---

ᵃ Makkah

that terrible Day). ⁹ (Are they so foolish) to choose other protectors (besides Him) whereas it is God alone Who is the ultimate protector? It is He Who gives life to the dead and only He has absolute power over everything.

Judgment is Given

¹⁰ Whatever you differ about, its decision and judgment rests with God. (Say to them O Prophet,) "Such is God, my Lord. In Him (alone) do I put all my trust and only to Him do I turn (for help)." ¹¹ He is the Originator of the heavens and the earth. He made for you mates from among yourselves and among the animals too, so that (all of) you may multiply. There is nothing ever like Him, and He alone hears all, sees all. ¹² To Him belongs the ultimate control of the heavens and the earth. He extends and restricts provision for whomsoever He wills (according to His infinite wisdom as a means to test one's faith). Indeed, He has knowledge over everything.

¹³ (O Muhammad!) He has ordained for you the same faith and religion that He gave Noah; and (inspired you through) revelation what We commanded Abraham, Moses, and Jesus to do - which is to remain steadfast in upholding true faith and not divide it into factions. ^{*a*} What you have been commanded to invite is (difficult and) heavy upon those who worship false

---

^{*a*} Islam is an everlasting, universal and comprehensive message addressed to all mankind with a definite beginning in time and a birthplace in Makkah in Arabia, and the whole world as its domain. Prophet Muhammad (peace be upon him) and his generation fulfilled their obligations admirably that within less than fifty years, Islam had conquered two of the world's most powerful empires (Persia and Eastern Rome which is also known as Byzantine) and was challenging the supremacy of the oppressive powers in Asia and Africa. But as for the earlier bearers of God's revelation, the Jews had turned religion into an ethnocentric heritage to cherish and take pride in; while under the Christians, the true principles of religion were overtaken by the corrupt doctrines of the Trinity, salvation, and the endless arguments over Jesus as the son of God. Islam announced its close relationship to Moses and Jesus right from the outset; and in this verse, it affirms that its message was a revival and an endorsement of theirs. The truth of the matter is that God's religion is one universal message, the same ever since man set foot on this earth, and it will remain so until the end of time. The seven heavens, the earth, and all that is in them praise God's glory. God created the human race to become His emissary and trustee on earth, and bestowed upon them endless bounties. The best and noblest among men in His sight are those who worship and submit to Him with diligence and humility (see verse 49:13) and strive to uphold justice. These concepts are the essence of Prophet Muhammad's message and teachings, and they are clearly expounded throughout the Qur'an.

gods. Indeed, God chooses (for His service) whomsoever He wills and guides towards Himself those who turn to Him in repentance.

¹⁴ (In the beginning, humanity was a single-faith community.) They were not divided (in God's true religion) until (His revealed) knowledge came to them (from His appointed Messengers who were ridiculed and rejected by their own people) out of selfish rivalry (and envy). Had it not been for a decree that preceded from your Lord (to postpone His retribution until a specified time), surely they would have been instantly punished (for their defiance, and there would not be any more dispute left) between them. And indeed, those who inherited the Scripture after them are in unsettled doubt about the knowledge that they have inherited.

¹⁵ So call them to true faith and stay firm (on the straight path) as you have been commanded (O Prophet), and do not follow their whims (and vain desires). Say (to them), "I believe in all the revelations that God has sent down and I have been commanded to establish justice among you. Verily, God is our Lord as well as yours, and we are responsible and accountable for our deeds just as you are for yours. Let there be no contention between us, for we shall all be ultimately gathered together by God (for judgment). With Him is where all journeys end." ¹⁶ As for those who still argue and dispute about God (without clear evidence) after He has been acknowledged, all their arguments are useless (and their pledges become invalid) in the sight of their Lord. His wrath will fall upon them and a severe punishment awaits them.

¹⁷ Verily, God is the One Who sent down the Book in truth (to discern between right and wrong) together with Balance (and wisdom to act justly). What will make you realize that perhaps the (Last) Hour is already near (so that you will submit yourself to Him without delay)? ¹⁸ Those who do not believe in the Last Hour deride it and ask for it to be hastened, whereas the believers stand in awe of it and know that it is the truth. Without a doubt, those who (continue to) argue about the Last Hour have indeed strayed far astray.

¹⁹ God is subtle (and gentle) to His servants. (Because of His bountiful grace) He gives (worldly) provision to whomsoever He wills (regardless of their faith. Verily,) He is the Most Strong, the Almighty (and there is nothing that can prevent Him from doing whatever He wills). ²⁰ Whoever desires harvest in the life to come, We shall increase for him his harvest. And whoever desires only the harvest of this world, We shall give him a share of it but he will have no share of the blessings in the life to come.

God's Dealing is Just

²¹ Do they (who only care for this world) have partners that prescribed to them another religion without God's permission? (Know that) had it not been for a decree that preceded from your Lord (to postpone His retribution until a specified time), the matter would have been decided once and for all between them (and they would have been immediately annihilated from the face of earth). Indeed, a grievous punishment awaits the wrongdoers (in the life to come). ²² (On Judgment Day,) You will see these wrongdoers fearful of the evil that they have done because the consequences of their actions are about to befall them. But those who believe (in God and the Hereafter) and do good deeds, they will be in the flowering meadows of the gardens. They will have whatever they desire from their Lord. That is surely the greatest bounty!

²³ This is the good news that God gives to His servants who believe (in Him) and are consistent in their righteous deeds. Say (to them O Prophet), "I do not ask from you any reward for my work except that you show love (and compassion) towards your kinsfolk (and others too)." Whoever does a good deed, We shall increase its merit for him. Surely God is Most Forgiving, Most Appreciative.

²⁴ Or do those wrongdoers accuse you by saying, "He has invented a lie about God!"'? (If this was true,) God would seal your heart if He so willed (and you would no longer be able to receive any revelation. Instead, tell them that) it is God Who obliterates all falsehood and establishes the truth with the words that He reveals (to you O Prophet). Indeed, He has full knowledge of what is in everyone's heart. ²⁵ (Moreover,) He is the One Who accepts repentance from His servants and pardons bad deeds. He knows everything that you do.
²⁶ And He is also the One Who responds to (the prayers of) those who truly believe (in Him) and do righteous deeds. (In the life to come), He increases for them from His bounty (far more than what they actually deserve). Whereas for those who persistently deny the truth, a severe suffering (awaits them).

²⁷ And if God were to extend (excessive) provision to His servants, surely they would go around transgressing (and cause disorder) in the land. But He sends down whatever (provision) He wills in due measure (according to His wisdom). Verily, He is fully aware of all His servants' needs and is observant of everything. ²⁸ He is the One Who sends down rain (to revive dead land) after people have lost all hope, and spreads His grace (far and wide). He is indeed the (ultimate) Protector, the (immensely) Praiseworthy.

²⁹ And among His signs is the creation of the heavens and the earth and (all kinds of) creatures that He scattered all over the heavens and the earth.

And He has the power to gather them all whenever He wills.

The Consequence of Misdeeds

³⁰ Whatever misfortune befalls you (on the Day of Judgment), it is the consequence of what your own hands have committed although He forgives much. ³¹ Your (wrongdoings) on earth will not escape (and go unnoticed). And (in the life to come), you will not have any protector or helper other than God.

³² And among His (wondrous) signs are ships that sail like floating mountains in the sea. ³³ If He so wills, He can cause the winds to become still so that those ships will remain motionless on its surface. Indeed, surely there are signs in this for those who are steadfast (in their faith) and are deeply grateful (to God for His limitless favors). ³⁴ Or He could destroy the ships because of the misdeeds the people have comiitted but He forgives much (and grants them respite). ³⁵ So let those who dispute (and argue about) Our signs know that there is no escape for them (from God's judgment).

³⁶ Hence, remember that whatever (enjoyment) you are granted now is only a passing delight in this fleeting world, whereas what is with God is far better and everlasting. It will be given to those who guard their faith and place their trust in their Lord. ³⁷ They are those who avoid the greater sins and immoralities, and who readily forgive when they are moved to anger. ³⁸ (They are also) who obey their Lord and attend to their prayer regularly, who conduct their worldly affairs by mutual consultation, who spend (in God's cause) from what We have provided for them; ³⁹ and who when are struck by tyranny (and oppression), they defend themselves.

⁴⁰ The requital for harm and injury is the equal of what was done. But those who pardon and make reconciliation will be rewarded (handsomely) by God. Indeed, He does not like those who are unjust (to others). ⁴¹ Surely, there is no blame against anyone who defends himself after he has been wronged. ⁴² The cause for blame is only against those who oppress people and commit excesses on earth without justification. A grievous punishment awaits these (evil perpetrators). ⁴³ But whoever remains patient and forgives (even though the right for retribution may be his), indeed exhibits the best of conduct.

The Fate of the Losers

⁴⁴ Whoever God lets go astray will not be able to find any protector other than Him. And when you see the wicked wrongdoers on the Day of Judgment (O Prophet), you will hear them exclaim (in horror) as soon as they see the punishment (that awaits them), "Is there any way we can return (to our earthly

life to make amends)?"

⁴⁵ You will see them being exposed to the punishment, humbled by disgrace. And they will be looking around with a stealthy glance (in a state of utter loss and humiliation). The believers will say, "Indeed, the losers are those who have lost themselves and their families on the Day of Resurrection." Without a doubt! The wrongdoers will remain in an everlasting torment. ⁴⁶ They will have none to protect them besides God, and whoever God lets go astray (on earth because of his defiance of the truth) will find no way (to escape in the life to come).

⁴⁷ So respond to the command of your Lord (now) before there comes a Day from God that cannot be averted. You will have no place of refuge on that Day, nor will you be able to deny (the wrongdoings that you have committed). ⁴⁸ (O Prophet!) If they (continue to ignore your call and) turn away (from the truth), know that We did not send you to be their guardian. Your task is no more than only to convey Our message. Indeed, when We give man a taste of Our grace, he rejoices in it. But if any misfortune afflicts them because of their own doing, they (fall into despair and) become utterly ungrateful.

Revelation Guide Aright

⁴⁹ (Verily,) the dominion of the heavens and the earth belongs to God alone. He creates whatever He wants, and grants the gift of daughters and sons to whomsoever He wills. ⁵⁰ To some, He grants the gift of sons and daughters together, and for some He makes them barren. Verily, He is All-Knowing, All-Powerful.

⁵¹ And it is not for any human that God should speak to him directly except through revelation, or from behind a veil, or by sending a (heavenly) Messenger *ᵃ* to reveal (His message) by His permission whatever He wills (to reveal).*ᵇ* Indeed, He is Most Exalted, the Most Wise. ⁵² And so it is that We have revealed to you (O Muhammad), a (divine) inspiration *ᶜ* by Our command. You did not know anything about this Book and faith (before). But We have made it a light by which We guide whomsoever We will of Our servants. And indeed, (We have chosen) you to guide mankind to the straight path; ⁵³ the way that leads to God, the One to Whom belongs all that is in the heavens and the earth. Without a doubt! To God return all matters (for judgment).

ᵃ The Angel Gabriel.
ᵇ The only person whom God ever spoke directly to was Moses. See verse 4:164.
ᶜ This is another meaning of *Ruh*. See also verse 16:2.

43. Az-Zukhruf
[The Ornaments : 89 verses]

This is another Makkan chapter, and like the other Makkan chapter, it deals with the fundamentals of faith, such as monotheism, the truth of the Qur'an, Messengership of Prophet Muhammad, resurrection, judgment, reward and punishment. It starts with the emphasis that God has sent down the Qur'an which is preserved in the Mother of the Book (*al-Lawh al-mahfūz*). The chapter is named *Az-Zukhruf* or The Ornaments with reference to verse 35 which points out that the ornaments and grandeur of this worldly life is only temporary while the life of the Hereafter is permanent. The chapter also refutes the claim of the disbelievers that a true Prophet must be rich. In addition, the fact that the angels are not God's daughters but His obedient servants is emphasized again. Similarly, the idea that Jesus could be the son of God is clearly denied.

In the name of God, the Most Gracious, the Most Compassionate.

Ignorance Based on Superstition

¹ *Ha Mīm.* ² By this divine Book that makes all things clear. ³ Indeed, We have made it a discourse in the Arabic tongue so that you may use reason (to grasp its meaning well). ⁴ And verily, it is inscribed in the Mother of all Books *ᵃ* with Us that is highly exalted and full of wisdom.

⁵ (O you who deny the truth!) Should We then take this reminder away from you and ignore you altogether because you are a people who (refuse to take heed of Our reminder and) deliberately transgress (the bounds that We have set)?

⁶ And how many Prophets have We sent to the people of earlier times; ⁷ yet never once did a Prophet come to them except they would mock and ridicule him. ⁸ And so in the end, We destroyed them even though they were stronger and more powerful (than those who disbelieve and oppose you today O Muhammad), and We made their example a lesson (for everyone to learn from).

⁹ And if you were to ask them, "Who created the heavens and the earth?" surely they will answer, "(Certainly they were created by God) the Almighty, the All-Knowing!"

ᵃ The source of all revelations.

¹⁰ (He is) the One Who laid out the earth for you like a cradle *ᵃ* and placed (natural) pathways on it so that you may be guided (to find your way around). ¹¹ And (He is also) the One Who sends down rain from the sky in due measure and revives dead land with it. This is how you too will be brought forth (from your graves on the Day of Resurrection). ¹² And He is the One Who created all living things in pairs, and made for you ships and cattle to ride on; ¹³ so that when you are mounted upon them, you may remember the favors of your Lord and say, "Glory be to Him Who (is the Most Perfect and) has subjected these to us, for we could never have accomplished this (by ourselves). ¹⁴ And most certainly, we shall surely return to our Lord." ¹⁵ Yet they made some of His servants a part of Him (by claiming that they are His children). Indeed man is most evidently ungrateful.

Polytheism Condemned

¹⁶ Has God taken daughters for Himself out of those He created and honored you with sons instead? ¹⁷ Yet (how ironic it is that) when one of them is given the good news (of a newborn daughter) like what he assigns to the Most Gracious (Lord), his face turns dark with suppressed rage; ¹⁸ and he would exclaim, "(What! Am I to have a daughter who) is to be raised only for the sake of adornment (and cannot help in a fight)?" And so he finds himself (torn by) an indecisive inner conflict (whether to keep or bury her alive).

¹⁹ And they also set the Angels who are servants of the Most Gracious (Lord) as females. But did they ever witness the creation (of these Angels as females)? Verily, their blasphemous testimony will be recorded and they will surely be called to account for their lies (on the Day of Judgment). ²⁰ And yet they (have the audacity to) say, "If the Most Gracious (Lord) had willed, we would certainly not have worshipped these Angels." The fact is they do not have any knowledge. They do nothing except (guessing and) lying.

²¹ Or did We ever give them any book (or authority) before this (to affirm their blasphemous claim), hence giving them a reason to hold to it firmly? ²² Nay! And yet they (could proudly) assert, "Indeed, we found our forefathers (in this faith and) practicing this tradition. So we continue to walk in their footsteps and are guided (by what they do)."

²³ And so it is (O Muhammad)! We did not send any Messenger before you to warn a city or community, except those who were corrupted by wealth would also say (the same), "Indeed, we found our forefathers practicing this

---

ᵃ This is an allusion to the earth being made smooth and easy to travel upon, a home for human life and a place to earn a decent living.

tradition. So we continue to follow (and walk in) their footsteps."

²⁴ And the warner replied, "Will you still persist even if I show you something better than (the faith and practices that) you inherited from your forefathers?" They said, "Indeed, we (reject and) do not believe (the message) you claim to be sent with." ²⁵ So We took vengeance upon them. Just see how (devastating) the end was for those who denied Our message.

Blindness Out of Choice

²⁶ (Now, narrate the story) of Abraham when he said to his father and his people, "Indeed, I renounce (and free myself from) what you worship; ²⁷ except the One Who created me; and behold! It is He Who will guide me (to the right way)." ²⁸ This is the word that Abraham left as a legacy to his descendants so that they may (always) turn to God (and be rightly guided).

²⁹ Verily, (as for those who came after him,) I allowed them - as (I had allowed) their forefathers - to enjoy their lives freely until the truth came to them through a Messenger (who would make all things) clear. ³⁰ But when the truth came to them, they said, "This is nothing except an evil spell (that is meant to bewitch us), and we do not believe in it." ³¹ They asserted further, "Why was this Qur'an not sent down upon a man (of high social status) from (either one of) the two main cities?" ᵃ

³² (Who gave them the right to say this?) Are they the ones who distribute your Lord's grace? (Nay!) It is We Who distribute their share of livelihood in the life of this world and raise some above others in rank (and wealth) so that they may (be privileged to) take others for service. But (verily,) your Lord's grace is better than all (the treasures) that they (amass and) hoard.

³³ Were it not (for the danger) that all mankind might become a single (evil) community (driven by lust and greed for power and wealth), We would

---

ᵃ The two cities are Makkah and Ta'if. The statement by the Arab pagans here clearly demonstrated a society that was built on an entrenched caste system that could not perceive religious leadership as being separate from class and status. The same was also with the Israelites who objected to Saul when God made him their ruler. See verse 2:247. Communities are made up of individuals with different skills, professions and aptitudes that complement one another. Human societies require men of high caliber and moral integrity to lead them, establish freedom and equality, and lift the spirits and the living standards of their people. Overindulgent individuals who prefer a life of comfort and affluence would not normally make good candidates for such a demanding task.

have surely given (everyone, including) all those who disbelieve in the Most Gracious (Lord) silver roofs for their houses and stairways to ascend; [34] as well as (silver) gates to their houses and also couches to recline on; [35] and ornaments of gold (too). But (We extend and restrict provision to whomsoever We will as a means to test one's faith so that they might learn and understand that) all those (glitters) are nothing except a passing delight in the life of this fleeting world. Whereas (eternal prosperity can only be found in) the next life to come with Your Lord, (granted exclusively) to those who serve Him obediently (during their temporary stay on earth).

Opposition to Truth is Punished

[36] And so, whoever turns away from the remembrance of the Most Gracious (Lord), We assign Satan as his intimate companion (in addition to his own enduring evil impulse). [37] And indeed, these evil forces hinder people from the right path, making them think as if they are rightly guided; [38] until when he comes to Us on the Day of Judgment, he will say (to his evil companion in regret), "If only the distance between us before this was as far as the east and west. What an evil companion (you have been)!" [39] But nothing will avail you on that Day, for you have been unjust (during your stay on earth). So be partners all of you (now) in punishment.

[40] Can you then make the deaf hear, or direct the blind and those lost in manifest error (to the right way, O Prophet)? [41] We shall surely inflict retribution on them whether We take you away (from this world first); [42] or make you see the end that We have promised them. Indeed, We have full power over them.

[43] So hold firmly to what has been revealed to you; for indeed, you are on a straight path. [44] And the Qur'an is indeed a reminder for you and your people (to persevere in God's path). In time, you will all be questioned (for everything that you have done during you lifetime). [45] And ask (too) any of Our Messengers whom We sent forth before you if We have ever appointed other gods to be worshipped besides the Most Gracious (Lord).

[46] And verily, We sent Moses with Our signs to Pharaoh and his chieftains, saying, "Indeed, I am a Messenger from the Lord of all the worlds." [47] But when he presented Our signs to them, behold! They (ridiculed him and) laughed; [48] although each sign We showed was greater than the one before. And then We seized them with Our punishment so that they might (realize their error and) return to the right path.

⁴⁹ (And so, whenever they faced an affliction) they would say (to Moses), "O sorcerer! Pray to your Lord for us by virtue of His pledge to you. Indeed, (we promise that) we shall certainly accept His guidance." ⁵⁰ But every time after We removed the affliction from them, behold! They broke their promise.

⁵¹ And Pharaoh (arrogantly) proclaimed, "O my people! Is this (great) kingdom of Egypt and the rivers that flow beneath my feet not mine? Can you not see (that I am your Lord)? ⁵² Am I not better than this despicable man who can hardly express himself clearly? ⁵³ (If he is truly God-sent,) why are gold bracelets not placed on him and why are there no Angels sent to accompany him?"

⁵⁴ And so Pharaoh (derided Moses and) made fools out of his people, yet they still obeyed him. Indeed, they were truly a disobedient lot of people (who were defiant towards God). ⁵⁵ They incurred Our wrath and We inflicted retribution by drowning all of them; ⁵⁶ and We made them a precedent and an example for people of later generations (to take heed of).

Jesus as Prophet

⁵⁷ And when the son of Mary's is cited as an example (of God's obedient servant), your people laugh and sneer (O Muhammad); ⁵⁸ saying, "Who is better - our gods, or he?" They do this merely to provoke you. Nay! They are a contentious lot of people. ⁵⁹ Verily, Jesus was nothing more than a servant whom We bestowed Our favor upon and made an example (of Our great sign) to the children of Israel. ⁶⁰ And if We willed, We could have placed Angels instead of you *ᵃ* (as Our emissaries) on earth (to do away with your arrogance).

⁶¹ Indeed, this (Qur'an that is being revealed to you now) *ᵇ* surely gives

---

ᵃ This is in reference to the Arab pagans who were mocking the Prophet in relation to verse 21:98 which reads, "Verily, you and what you worship besides God will be the firewood of Hell!" Hearing this, the Arab pagans laughed and said that Jesus too will be the firewood of Hell because he is being worshipped by the Christians. Verses 59 and 65 gave the answer that cleared Jesus from this evil idea and accusation. See also verses 5:116-117.

ᵇ Scholars have different opinions about what is actually being referred to as the sign of the Last Hour in this verse. Some opined that it is the second coming of Jesus, while some say it is the Qur'an. I am inclined to believe that this is in reference to the Qur'an because the second coming of Jesus has not occurred yet and no one knows when it will. Whereas at the end of the same verse, God clearly commanded those who believe in the coming of the Last Hour to follow Him. And the only way to follow God is to abide by the teachings of the Qur'an which He has already revealed in full through His final

knowledge (and warning) about the (Last) Hour (that will certainly come). Hence, do not have any doubt about it and follow Me. This is the straight path (to ultimate success). [62] And do not allow Satan to hinder you (from My path) for he is indeed your clear (and sworn) enemy.

[63] And so, when Jesus came with clear proofs (to his people before this), he said, "Verily, I have brought you wisdom,[a] and I have come to clear up some of the things that you have been disputing (among yourselves). So be ever mindful of God and obey me. [64] Indeed, the Almighty God is my Lord and your Lord, so worship Him alone. This is the straight path."

When Friends Turn Enemies

[65] Yet, factions emerged among those (who came after Jesus) when they began to hold divergent views (about him). Woe then to these wrongdoers (and corrupters of faith)! They will surely suffer the punishment of a grievous Day. [66] Are they (who are lost in sin now) waiting for that (dreadful) Hour to suddenly come upon them when they least expected it (before they would be willing to submit to Almighty God)?

[67] (But at that very moment, former) friends will become enemies, (arguing and blaming one another to vindicate themselves when the horror of their place of return is displayed right before their very eyes) on that (dreadful) Day, except for the righteous; [68] (to whom God will say,) "O My servants! Today you have nothing to fear nor regret; [69] (for you are) those who have believed in Our revealed signs and (wholeheartedly) submitted to God. [70] So, enter Paradise (today), both you and your (righteous) spouses. You will be filled with happiness."

[71] There they will be served with golden plates and cups, and they will have whatever their souls desire and their eyes delight, (and it will be said to them,) "You will remain in here forever. [72] This is the Paradise that you are given to inherit because of the good deeds that you labored (with utmost sincerity during your time on earth). [73] In there are plenty of fruits (and whatever you desire) to eat."

[74] But the sinners will remain in the torment of Hell forever. [75] Their punishment will not be lightened and they will remain in utter despair. [76] We have not been unfair to them. But it is they who brought injustice upon

---

Messenger 1,450 years ago as guidance for all mankind which still remains relevant today and will continue to be so until the arrival of the Last Hour.
[a] Divine revelation i.e. the *Injeel* or authentic Gospel revealed in Aramaic Hebrew.

themselves (by being persistently defiant towards God and His Messenger).

⁷⁷ And they will cry, "O Malik (the gate-keeper of Hell)! Please call upon your Lord to finish us off (now. We cannot bear this suffering anymore)." But Malik's reply will be, "Nay! You will remain in here forever, (alive and fully conscious to experience the everlasting torment)!" ⁷⁸ Verily, We have brought the truth to you but most of you hated and rejected it. (So suffer the consequences of your defiance now)!

⁷⁹ Or have those disbelievers resolved their intention (to ruin you O Prophet)? Then indeed We too are firmly resolved (to destroy them). ⁸⁰ Or do they think We cannot hear their hidden thoughts and private talks? Certainly (We can! Furthermore,) Our (heavenly) Messengers *ᵃ* are (always) with them, transcribing (all their actions in their book of deeds).

Intercession Rejected

⁸¹ Say (to them O Prophet), "If the Most Gracious (Lord truly) had a son, then I would (surely) be the first to worship him." ⁸² Glory be to the Lord of the heavens and the earth, the Lord of the (Supreme) Throne (Who is free from all imperfections and) far above (the lies that) they ascribe (to Him). ⁸³ Leave them alone to indulge in their lies, vanities and play until they face the (dreadful) Day which has been promised to them.

⁸⁴ (Without doubt,) He is the only God to be worshipped in the heaven and the earth. And He is the All-Wise, the All-Knowing. ⁸⁵ Blessed is He to Whom belongs the dominion of the heavens and the earth and whatever is between them. With Him alone is the knowledge of the Last Hour and it is to Him will you be ultimately returned.

⁸⁶ And (on the Day of Judgment), those whom the idolaters used to invoke besides Him have no power to intercede on their behalf, except those who testify to the truth with true knowledge. ⁸⁷ And if you ask those idolaters Who actually created them, they will surely say, "God!" Is it not strange then how they could be deluded (from the truth and oppose their own Creator instead)?

⁸⁸ (God has heard the Prophet's cry,) "O my Lord! Indeed, these are the people who would not believe (in the message that You have asked me to convey)." ⁸⁹ So turn away from them O Prophet, and wish them, "Peace." Soon they will come to know (the truth when they finally see their permanent home in the Fire that they have been denying all this while).

ᵃ The Angels.

44. *Ad-Dukhān*
[The Smoke : 59 verses]

This is another Makkan chapter which deals with the fundamentals of faith in Islam. It starts with the proclamation that God sent down the Qur'an on a Blessed Night of *Laylatul Qadr* or the Night of Decree, and that there is none worthy of worship except Him alone. See chapter 97 for its explanation. Then it refers to the rejection of the polytheists and disbelievers toward the Qur'an and its message. In this context, the story of Pharaoh and his people's opposition toward the truth that was delivered to them and their ultimate punishment by God is mentioned. Reference is then made to the Makkan disbelievers' attitude toward resurrection and the Hereafter too. The name *Ad-Dukhān* or The Smoke that is given to this chapter is taken from verse 10.

In the name of God, the Most Gracious, the Most Compassionate.

Smoke that Ushers Clarity

¹ *Ha Mīm.* ² By this divine Book that makes all things clear. ³ Behold! We sent it down on a blessed night, for indeed, We have always been warning (mankind about the Day when everyone will be raised from their graves for the reckoning of their deeds).

⁴ On that (blessed) night, the distinction (between good and bad) in all matters was made clear and in full wisdom; ⁵ by Our (divine) command. Verily, We have always been sending (Our message of truth and guidance); ⁶ as grace from your Lord (to all mankind so that you will turn to Him in total devotion and obedience). Indeed, He hears all, and knows all.

⁷ (Behold!) It is He Who is the Lord of the heavens and the earth, and everything that is between them. If only you are (among) those who could grasp this fact with true certainty (and realize what it implies)! ⁸ Verily, there is no god but Him. He is the One Who gives life and causes death. He is your Lord and the Lord of your forefathers. ⁹ Yet they (who lack certainty in faith) play around with their doubts. ¹⁰ Wait then, for the Day when the sky will bring forth a pall of smoke that will make (the arrival of the Last Hour) obvious; ¹¹ engulfing all mankind. Behold! Here comes the grievous punishment (that they have been denying all along).

¹² And so they will say, "Our Lord! Remove this punishment from us (and send us back to earthly life so that we can make amends). Indeed, we are believers now." ¹³ But how can this (sudden) remembrance (at the Last Hour

benefit them) when a Messenger had already come to them (earlier) with a clear message (and warning)? [14] Yet they turned away from him and said, "This is surely a well-tutored madman!"

[15] Indeed, even if We remove just a little bit of punishment (and send you back to earthly life), surely you will revert (to your old ways. But this will never happen.) [16] (Instead,) We shall seize (every sinner) with a mighty onslaught on that Day and inflict Our full retribution (on you).

A Confrontation With Pharaoh

[17] And certainly, long before their time, We tested Pharaoh's people by sending a noble Messenger to them. [18] He said, "Deliver to me the servants of God. [a] Indeed, I am a trustworthy Messenger who is being sent to you. [19] And do not (be arrogant and) exalt yourselves above God. Behold! I have come to you with clear authority (from Him). [20] And indeed, I seek refuge with my Lord and your Lord should you intend to stone me (to death). [21] If you do not believe me, then leave me alone."

[22] Then he called upon his Lord, saying, "(O Lord!) These people are truly lost in sin." [23] And so God answered, "Set out with My servants by night, and be mindful that you will surely be pursued. [24] And (after you have crossed the sea,) leave it parted (behind you). Indeed, they are an army (destined) to be drowned."

[25] Behold! How many (lushful) gardens and (flowing) springs have these (unjust and wicked) people left behind; [26] and sown fields and noble places; [27] and the comforts of life wherein they used to take delight (and enjoy)? [28] And so it was. We made what they left behind for another people to inherit. [29] The heaven and the earth did not shed tears for them, nor were they granted respite.

[30] And certainly, We saved the children of Israel from the humiliating punishment; [31] (that was inflicted upon them) by Pharaoh. Verily, he was the most arrogant among those who transgressed (the bounds set by God). [32] Indeed, We knowingly chose (the children of Israel) above all mankind (at that time as Our favor to them); [33] and We showed them signs in which there was a clear test for them (so that they would ponder and be firm in their faith).

---

[a] The children of Israel

Good and Evil Justly Requited

[34] Now behold! (As for the Arab pagans on the other hand,) this is what they say (with utmost conviction); [35] "There is nothing beyond our first death and surely We shall not be raised again (for judgment)! [36] If you are truthful (in your claim O Muhammad), then bring our forefathers back to life (now, so that they can tell us if there is indeed life in the Hereafter)!"

[37] Do these people think they are better than the people of Tubba' and those before them whom We destroyed because they were immersed in (the same) sin and transgression? [38] (Behold!) We did not create the heavens and the earth and whatever is between them in mere idle play. [39] And We have not created them except (to fulfill a purpose that is) in accordance with the truth (that We have decreed), but most people do not know.

[40] Indeed, the Day of Decision is an appointed time for everyone. [41] (That is) the Day when a friend will be of no use to his friend at all, nor will they receive help (from anyone); [42] except for those to whom God will bestow His grace and mercy. Verily, He is truly the Almighty, the Most Compassionate.

[43] Indeed, the (fruit from the) tree of *Zaqqum*; [44] will be the food of the sinners; [45] (hot) like molten brass that will boil in the bellies; [46] like the boiling of scalding water. [47] (On that dreadful Day,) a (thundering) voice will be heard, commanding, "Seize him and drag him into the depths of the Hellfire; [48] then pour the scalding water over his head as punishment! [49] Now taste this (you infidels)! Indeed, you used to consider yourselves mighty and noble, (and insolently rejected God's message of truth when it was brought to you). [50] Verily, this is the punishment which you used to doubt (and mock)."

[51] And as for the righteous, (they will be) in a safe place - well secured; [52] amidst gardens and springs; [53] dressed in fine silk and rich brocade, sitting face to face. [54] Such will be their place! And We shall wed them to damsels with beautiful (lustrous) eyes. [55] There, in full peace (and contentment), they will call for all kinds of fruit (to feast on); [56] And in it too, they will not taste death again after their first earthly death. And they will be kept safe from the torment of Hellfire; [57] as a favor from your (Most Compassionate) Lord. That indeed, is the greatest triumph!

[58] (O Muhammad!) We have indeed made this (Qur'an) easy (by revealing it) in your own tongue for people to take heed (and ponder). [59] So wait (for what the future will bring). Indeed, those who refuse to accept the truth are waiting too!

45. Al-Jātsiyah
[The Kneeling One : 37 verses]

This is a Makkan chapter that deals mainly with the belief in God and His Absolute Oneness together with the themes of the Qur'an's truth, the Messengership of Prophet Muhammad, resurrection, judgment, reward and punishment. It starts with the emphasis that the sending down or bestowal of the Qur'an is from God; and that the heavens, the earth, the creation of man and all other living and moving beings, the alternation of day and night, the sending down of rain which gives life to the earth, the movement of the winds all point to the power of their Creator and Lord. It then refers to the attitude of the disbelievers toward the Qur'an, its message and the Messenger, particularly about their disbelief in resurrection and the next life. The name of the chapter is taken after verse 28 which reads as follows : "On that Day, you will see every group of people kneeling down [i.e. *Jātsiyah*] in humility. Everyone will be summoned to face their record and they will be told, "Today you will be (justly) requited for all your deeds."

In the name of God, the Most Gracious, the Most Compassionate.

A Clear Way of Religion

¹ *Ha Mīm.* ² This Book is sent down from God the Almighty, the Most Wise. ³ Behold! Surely (in the creation of) the heavens and the earth are signs (of His greatness) for those who believe.

⁴ And in the creation of yourselves and all the creatures that He scatters throughout the earth, there are signs (of His creative might) for those who are firm in faith. ⁵ And (likewise) in the alternation of the night and day, in the provision that God sends down from the sky which gives life to the earth after it had been lifeless, and in directing the change of winds, there are (clear) signs (of His greatness) for people with common sense (to ponder). ⁶ These are indeed God's signs and revelations that We recite to you (O Prophet) to show the truth. Hence, in what other statement, if not in God's revelations, do those disbelievers want to accept and believe? *ᵃ*

ᵃ The discourse presented by the Qur'an in verses 1-6 and continued further in verses 12-13 is intended to establish a rational basis for religious faith so that it can be built on clear and logical principles. Contemplation and theoretical study are not by themselves sufficient to bring about happiness and prosperity for mankind. The powers and energies of the physical world have to be harnessed and deployed for the good of mankind. Not only does control over the physical world enhances man's material life in

[7] Woe then to every lying sinner; [8] who hears the verses of God that are being recited to him, yet arrogantly persists (in his erroneous ways) as though he has never heard them. Announce to him then, of a grievous punishment (that awaits him). [9] And whenever something about Our revealed verses come to his knowledge (and attention), he ridicules them. For such people, a humiliating punishment is in store for them. [10] Indeed, close on their heels is the Hellfire, and all that they have gained in this world will be of no benefit to them (on the Day of Reckoning). And neither will any of those (false gods) which they regard as their patrons (and protectors) instead of God, (be of any help to them). A great punishment has been prepared for them.

[11] This (Qur'an) is (indeed the true) guidance. For those who (continue to) deny their Lord's (divine) signs and revelations, a grievous punishment of foul nature will be inflicted upon them (in due time).

[12] (Verily,) God is the One Who subjugated the sea for you so that ships may sail on it by His command and for you to seek His bounty in it and be grateful to Him. [13] And He has also subjugated for you whatever is in the heavens and the earth, all (as a gift of grace) from Him. Surely there are clear signs (of His infinite grace and greatness) in these for those who care to think (and ponder).

---

this world, it also enables him to reinforce and preserve his faith in God. The Qur'an guides mankind with its principles and teachings while the physical world provides the tangible evidence for God's existence and power. In many instances however, this has not been the case. The study of physical sciences has not always been put to good use. Even though humans are now conquering space and can also see creation in action - as in the case of conception and the growth of human fetuses and embryos - many continue to still deny God and insist that there is no Creator. This is a salient feature of modern civilization. See also verses 13:1 and 27:60-64. Regrettably, the anomaly that we see in the field of empirical sciences is also found among many people of religious sciences. Being fossilized, they have lost their appeal and ability to positively influence human thought and world events. Most of the regression that we witness in the world can be blamed on institutionalized religion that are led by narrow-minded religious officials and preachers who promote their senseless interpretation of Islam to others, foolishly dismissing science together with its empirical evidence to give preference to baseless narratives oftentimes taken and exaggerated from false Prophetic sayings (i.e. *hadith*). This causes Islam to be seen as out of touch with reality, hence driving people away to atheism and agnosticism out of confusion. It cannot be denied that part of the blame for people's misconception and rejection of Islam can be largely attributed to the misrepresentation of the religion's truth by these half-baked preachers. See also verses 62:5 and 110:2 and their footnotes.

¹⁴ (O Prophet!) Tell the believers that they should forgive those who do not look forward to the coming Days of God. ᵃ (Leave this to God since) it is He alone Who will requite everyone for everything that they have done. ¹⁵ Whoever does a righteous deed, then it is for (the benefit of) his own soul; and whoever commits an evil deed, then he does so at his own peril. In the end, you will all be returned to your Lord (for judgment and requital).

¹⁶ Indeed, We gave the children of Israel the Book (of Torah), wisdom, and Prophethood, and provided them with good things as sustenance. We even preferred them over all mankind (of their time as Our favor to them). ¹⁷ We also gave them clear proofs in matters (of religion). But it was only after all this knowledge had come to them that they began to fall into disagreements, due to envy and jealousy among themselves. Behold! Your Lord will judge between them on the Day of Resurrection regarding their dispute.

¹⁸ And now, We have set you on a way that We have ordained regarding all matters (of faith and religion, O Prophet). So follow the way (that We gave) and do not yield to the desires of those who do not know (the truth); ¹⁹ for behold, they can never protect you against God's (wrath if you defy Him). The wrongdoers are indeed patrons (and protectors) of one another; whereas God is the protector of all who are mindful of Him (and strive to keep their duty to Him diligently).

²⁰ This Quran is (indeed the source of) enlightenment for mankind - a guidance and grace to those who are firm in their faith. ²¹ As for those who commit evil deeds, do they think that We shall hold them equal, in both their life and death, with those who believe and do righteous deeds? Bad indeed is their judgment! ²² And (know that) God has created the heavens and the earth (to fulfill a purpose) in accordance with the truth (which He has decreed). And (He has therefore ordained) every soul to be (fairly) requited for what it has earned. No one will ever be wronged.

²³ Have you seen the one who worships his lusts and vain desires? God lets such person go astray, sealed his hearing and heart, and drew a veil over his sight (because he chose to reject guidance). Who can guide him after God (abandons him)? Will you not take heed and learn any lesson from this? ᵇ

²⁴ And yet they say, "There is nothing beyond our life in this world! We die (once) and we live (once), and nothing but time destroys us." They have no knowledge about this at all and they do nothing but guess. ²⁵ And so, whenever

---

ᵃ The Day of Judgment.
ᵇ See verses 25:43, 7:172, 7:179, 91:7-10 and 18:29 with their corresponding footnotes.

Our messages are conveyed to them in all clarity, their only (foolish) argument is, "If what you say is true, then bring back our forefathers (from the dead) as witnesses (to support your claim)!" ²⁶ Tell (them O Prophet), "It is God Who gives you life and then causes you to die, and in the end He will gather you altogether on the Day of Resurrection, a Day of which there is no doubt (of its coming)." Yet, most people do not know (that God's promise is ever true).

To Whom Supremacy Belongs

²⁷ And to God belongs the dominion of the heavens and the earth. On the Day when the Last Hour finally arrives, the followers of falsehood will be doomed to loss. ²⁸ On that Day, you will see every group of people kneeling down in humility. Everyone will be summoned to face their record and they will be told, "Today you will be (judged and) requited for all your deeds. ²⁹ This is Our Record which bears witness about you in truth. We have indeed transcribed everything you did (during your stay on earth. Nothing is left out)."

³⁰ For those who held firmly to their faith and did righteous deeds, their Lord will admit them into His grace. That will be a clear and glorious triumph! ³¹ But for those who rejected the truth, they will be asked, "Were My messages not conveyed to you (earlier?" Of course they were,) but you gloried in your arrogance and became immersed in sin; ³² because when you were told, "Behold! God's promise always comes true and there can be no doubt about the coming of the Last Hour" - your reply was, "We do not care and wish to know anything about the Last Hour! We think it is no more than just empty talk and we are by no means convinced (that it will ever come)."

³³ And so, the evil of their deeds will be made clear to them (on that dreadful Day), and what they used to mock and ridicule will encircle them. ³⁴ They will be told, "Today, We shall forget (and abandon) you just like how you (have chosen to) forget and ignore your meeting of this Day. The Hellfire will now be your (permanent) home and there will be no one to help you. ³⁵ This is because you took the revelations of God in ridicule and allowed the (superficial trappings and pleasures of) worldly life to beguile (and deceive) you." Hence on that Day, neither will these people be taken out of the Fire, nor will they be given any chance to make amends.

³⁶ And so, all praise is certainly due to God alone Who is the Lord of the heavens and the earth, and the Lord of all the worlds. ³⁷ And to Him belongs all greatness (and grandeur) in the heavens and the earth, and He alone is the Almighty, the All-Wise.

46. Al-Aḥqāf
[The Sand Dunes : 35 verses]

This is a Makkan chapter that deals with the fundamentals of faith just like the other Makkan chapters. It starts by reiterating that the Qur'an is sent down by God and it denounces the worship of false and imaginary gods instead of God. It then points out the attitude of the disbelievers towards the Qur'an and the Messenger of God, and gives appropriate replies to their false allegations. Along with these, mention is also made about the two types of man - one who is righteous and obedient to his parents, and the other one who is the opposite of this. The consequence of disbelief and rejection of the truth is then pointed by a mention of the inescapable punishment that awaits the disbelievers in the Hereafter and also of the punishment that was inflicted on the disbelieving people of 'Aād who Prophet Hūd was sent to. The chapter's name - *Al-Aḥqāf*, refers to the sand dunes mentioned in verse 21 where these people used to live. It is the winding sandy tracts of the eastern region of Yemen.

In the name of God, the Most Gracious, the Most Compassionate.

One Universe, One Creator

¹ *Ha Mīm.* ² This Book is sent down from God the Almighty, the All-Wise. ³ We have not created the heavens and the earth and everything between them except (to fulfill a purpose that is) in accordance with the truth (which We have decreed) for an appointed term. But those who refuse to accept the truth (in God's revelation) paid no attention to His waning (about the Day of Judgment).

⁴ Ask (those pagans O Prophet), "Have you given serious thought about those whom you call upon besides God? Show me what they have created (anywhere) on earth, or do they have a share in the (creation of) the heavens? Bring me any divine Book (that has come to you) before this, or any remnant of knowledge (that supports your belief) if you are telling the truth." *ᵃ* ⁵ Who

---

ᵃ The passages from verse 4 to 12 present a debate between Prophet Muhammad and the Arab pagans over their beliefs and behavior. This begins with a reference to their deities and their failure to create anything, followed by their accusation that the Qur'an is the work of the Prophet. Refer to verse 16:103 for the answer to this accusation. Logically speaking, the Prophet should not be castigated for preaching the Qur'an and calling people to submit to God, to devote their lives to His service, and to seek His pleasure. Furthermore, Prophet Muhammad was a living example of such submission and devotion. No other revealed book could be compared to the Qur'an in its emphasis on the glorification of God and submission to His will

could be more misguided and lost than he who calls upon those besides God that cannot answer their prayers until the Day of Resurrection and are not even aware that they are being called upon? **⁶** And when mankind is gathered (for Judgment on that Day), those (who were taken as false gods) will be enemies to those (who worshipped them) and will deny their worship.

⁷ When Our clear verses are being recited, those who refuse to believe say about the truth that is brought to them, "This is obviously a clear sorcery (aimed to bewitch us)!" **⁸** Or, do they accuse the Prophet of fabricating the verses himself? So tell (them O Muhammad), "If I fabricated it, then (surely God's wrath will be upon me and) there is nothing you can do to protect me from it. Indeed, He knows fully well about the lies that you have been spreading. Sufficient is He as a witness between me and you. Verily, He is Most Forgiving, Most Compassionate."

⁹ Tell them, "I am not the first Messenger (ever sent by God), nor do I know what will happen to me or to you. I only follow what is revealed to me and I am no more than just a clear warner." **¹⁰** Say further, "Have you considered (the consequences that would befall you) if this reminder (that I convey to you now) *ᵃ* is indeed from God and you still reject its truth? Even a witness from the children of Israel has testified to a similar (reminder in the past) *ᵇ* and accepted it while you continue to glory in your arrogance (and disregard the same message that I am bringing to you now). Verily, God will not guide those who are unjust (to themselves for rejecting the truth)."

¹¹ Those who reject the truth say about those who believe, "Had there been any good in it, surely it would have been revealed to us first. Muhammad

---

and power. How could the Prophet be censured for advocating any of that? When the Prophet embarked on his mission he could not have known that it would lead to confrontation with his people or what the outcome would be. Nevertheless, he placed his trust in God and persisted with the task until he prevailed. Despite the suffering and the tribulation, he remained devout and loyal to God to the last breath of his life. He did no more than to call upon people to believe in God and hold fast to the straight path, and he was there to lead them along that path. Could this possibly have been the manner of an impostor? There are many people who reject the Prophethood of Muhammad today, many of whom do not believe in God anyway. This will never change until they can recognize God as the supreme Creator first.

ᵃ The Qur'an.

ᵇ The witness from the children of Israel referred here is Moses and the similar message and reminder that he conveyed to his people in the past was just like what is in the Qur'an too, which is the command to fully submit to the One and Only Almighty God.

and his followers would not have preceded us in believing it." Since they refuse to take guidance from it, they (conveniently) say, "This is nothing but a stale ancient lie!" ¹² Yet before this, the Book of Moses *ᵃ* was revealed as a guide and grace (from your Lord); and here is this Qur'an (now, presented) in (lucid) Arabic tongue, confirming (the same message that is in all earlier Scriptures). It is to also forewarn the wrongdoers and give good news (of what is in store) to those who excel in good deeds.

¹³ Indeed, those who say, "Our Lord is God (the Almighty)!" and then remain firm in their belief, they will have no fear nor will they grieve. ¹⁴ They are the residents of Paradise and will remain in it forever as a reward for their (good) deeds.

Two Types of Offspring

¹⁵ And (verily,) We have commanded man to treat his parents with kindness. His mother carried him in her womb with hardship and with much pain did she give birth to him. His bearing and weaning took thirty months. When he reaches the age of full strength and becomes forty years old, he says, "My Lord! Guide me to be grateful to You for the favors which You have bestowed on me and on my parents. (Guide me) to do good deeds that will please You and grant me righteous offspring. Indeed, to You alone do I turn in repentance, and I am indeed among those who have (wholeheartedly) submitted themselves to You."

¹⁶ Such are the people from whom We shall accept the best of their deeds and overlook their misdeeds. They will be among the residents of Paradise - a promise that they have been assured.

¹⁷ (And of people,) there is also such person who would say to his parents (whenever they try to advise him with faith in God), "Ahh.. to both of you! Are you warning me with resurrection when generations before me have already gone (and never came back)?" And so, both parents cry for God's help and say, "Woe to you! (Why do you not want to) believe? Indeed, the promise of God is true." But he replies, "This is nothing but fables of ancient times!"

¹⁸ It is against such people that God's sentence (of doom) has been passed along with (other sinful) communities of humans and Jinn that preceded them. Indeed they will all be losers. ¹⁹ (In the life to come,) everyone will be ranked according to their deeds, and He will fully requite them for what they have done. And no one will ever be wronged (and treated unfairly).

ᵃ The Torah

²⁰ And on the Day when those who deny the truth are brought to the Fire, they will be told, "You squandered your share of good things in the life of this world and sought comfort in them (without any remembrance of the life to come). So today, you will be requited with a humiliating punishment for having gloried in your arrogance on earth without right, and for being defiantly disobedient (to God)." *ᵃ*

When Prophets are Challenged

²¹ And remind them the story of (Hūd) a brother from the people of 'Aād who were the dwellers of the sand dunes when he was sent to forewarn them (of God's impending judgment). Verily, there were also other warners before and after him. (All of them) said, "Worship none but God! Indeed, I fear for you the torment of a mighty (dreadful) Day." ²² But they retorted, "Have you come to turn us away from our gods (and well estabilished traditions)? If what you say is true, then bring upon us what you are threatening us with!"

²³ (Hūd) replied, "Verily, the knowledge of when that moment will come is with God alone. I am only conveying the message which I have been sent with. But I see that you are a people who are ignorant (and incapable of distinguishing between right and wrong)."

²⁴ Then, when they saw (the torment in the form of) a cloud coming towards their valleys, they said, "This cloud will bring us rain." Nay! It is what you (had asked for and) wanted it to be hastened - a fierce wind bringing you a woeful punishment; ²⁵ destroying everything by the command of its Lord. And so (in the morning), there was nothing to be seen except (the ruins of) their dwellings. That was how We requited the sinners.

²⁶ And truly, We had established them (in power and prosperity) not in the same way how we have established you now (O people of Makkah). We endowed them with hearing, sight and conscience (so that they can learn and discern truth from falsehood). Yet none of these was of any use to them because they (still) went on to reject God's revealed signs. And in the end, they were overwhelmed by what they used to ridicule.

ᵃ It is not unusual for those who do not believe in the existence of God and also Muslims whose faith in God and the Day of Judgment is weak, to spend their whole lives indulging themselves and seeking to satisfy their carnal pleasures and desires. See also verses 25:43 and 45:23.

²⁷ And certainly, We have also destroyed other communities living in towns that once flourished around you, but not before We repeatedly gave Our message and warnings to them (in many different ways) so that they might (take heed and) return (to Our path). ²⁸ Why then did those (beings) whom they had taken as gods beside the Almighty God to get closer (to Him) not come to their aid (when We afflicted them with Our torment)? Nay! (These false gods) had in fact forsaken them (when We seized them). They were nothing but lies (and false beliefs) invented (by evil people).

Jinn Listening to the Qur'an

²⁹ Behold (O Prophet)! Remember when We turned a group of Jinn towards you to listen to the Qur'an. And when they attended (its recitation), they said to one another, "Listen in silence!" And when it was over, they returned to their people as forewarners (of Judgment Day). ³⁰ They said, "O our people! Indeed, we have heard a (heavenly) Book revealed after Moses, confirming all that was before it, guiding to the truth and to a straight path (of salvation)."

³¹ "O our people! Respond to the one who invites you to God and believe in him so that God will forgive your sins and protect you against a grievous torment. ³² And whoever that does not respond to the one who calls to God, will neither escape from Him on earth, nor have any protector besides Him (in the life to come). Such people are clearly astray."

³³ Are they - (who stubbornly refuse to accept the truth) - then not aware that God, Who created the heavens and the earth and never felt tired in creating them, has the power to bring the dead back to life? Yes indeed! He has power over everything. ³⁴ And so, on the Day when those who oppose the truth are brought within sight of the Fire, (they will be asked,) "Is this not the truth (which you had adamantly rejected before)?" They will (have no choice but to) admit, "Yes, by Our Lord, (this is the truth)!" Then God will say, "Now, suffer the (everlasting) punishment for having denied the truth."

³⁵ So persevere (O Muhammad), just as the Messengers who were endowed with determination before you did, and do not seek to hasten (a doom) for those who deny the truth. Verily, on the Day when they finally see what they had been warned against, they will feel as though they had stayed in the world for no longer than an hour of an (earthly) day. Indeed, the truth has been conveyed. Hence, none will be destroyed except those who persist in their defiance and disobedience (against their Lord).

47. Muḥammad
[38 verses]

This is an early Madinan chapter that deals with issues of war in relation to fighting in defense of Islam. In this connection, the chapter lays down the rules regarding *jihad* or fighting in God's cause, war captives and spoils. It also speaks about the character and conduct of the hypocrites who attempted to sabotage the nascent Muslim community and state. In addition, Muslims are urged to obey God in all matters, lest their good deeds become worthless on the Day of Judgment like those of the disbelievers and hypocrites. The chapter takes its name from the mention of Prophet Muhammad's name in verse 2.

In the name of God, the Most Gracious, the Most Compassionate.

Captives of War

¹ God will make the deeds of those who reject the truth and obstruct (others) from His path become worthless. ² But those who believe (in Him), do righteous deeds, and believe in what is being revealed to Muhammad - which is the truth from their Lord - will have their misdeeds erased by Him and their condition improved.

³ This is because those who reject the truth are followers of falsehood, while those who believe (in the Prophet's teachings) are followers of the truth that comes from their Lord. In this way does God set forth parables to show people (their true state of faith).

⁴ So when you meet those infidels in the battlefield, strike their necks (with a lethal blow) until you have thoroughly subdued them and take those who are alive as captives. Thereafter, you may set them free either by an act of grace or against ransom until the burden of war is lifted. Such is (God's decree upon you). Had God willed, He could have surely punished them (Himself), but (He wills you to struggle) to test some of you by means of others (who are hostile towards you because of your faith). And those who are killed in God's cause, He will never let their deeds be in vain and go wasted. ⁵ (In fact,) He will guide them aright and improve their condition; ⁶ and admit them into Paradise which He has promised.

⁷ O you who believe! If you strive to help God's cause, He will help you (in return) and make your steps firm. ⁸ But for those who disbelieve, ill fortune awaits them because He will make all their deeds go to waste. ⁹ That is because they hate what God revealed. So He made all their deeds worthless.

¹⁰ Have they not traveled throughout the land and seen how was the end of those before them? God destroyed them utterly and a similar fate awaits all who deny the truth. ¹¹ That is because God is the protector of the believers, whereas those who deny the truth have no one to protect them. ¹² Indeed, God will admit those who believe and do righteous deeds into gardens which rivers flow from right beneath them, but those who disbelieve enjoy themselves only in this life. They eat (and live) as cattle do. But in the life to come, the Fire will be their home.

¹³ And how many cities (and communities) that were stronger than the one that drove you out (O Muhammad)? Indeed, We destroyed them all and there was none to save them (from Our wrath). *ᵃ* ¹⁴ Can he who is leading a life based on clear proof from his Lord be compared to the one whose evil deeds are made attractive and (fair-seeming) to him and follow his own lusts?

¹⁵ Here is a parable of the Paradise that is promised to those who are always mindful of God (and strive to diligently keep their duty to Him) : In it will be rivers which time does not corrupt, rivers of milk which its taste never changes, rivers of (non-intoxicating) wine delightful to those who drink it, and also rivers of honey that is pure and clear. In it too they will find fruits of every kind (to enjoy) as well as forgiveness from their Lord. Can the fate of such people be compared to those who will remain in the Hellfire forever and be given scalding water to drink that will rip their bowels apart?

Fate that Awaits Those Whose Hearts are Sealed

¹⁶ And among those who (oppose you are some hypocrites who pretend to) listen to you (as you teach the believers, O Prophet). But as soon as they depart from you, they speak (with scorn) to those who have been given knowledge, saying, "What did he say just now?" Such are the men upon whose hearts God has set a seal because they follow nothing except their own (evil) lusts. ¹⁷ But for those who are willing to be guided, He increases their ability to follow His guidance and makes their awareness of Him (grow).

¹⁸ Then, are those (whose hearts are sealed) waiting for the Hour of Doom to overtake them by surprise (before they will pay heed to God's message)? Do they not realize that its signs have already come? And how is it possible that they could benefit from this reminder when (the Hour of Doom) arrives (while they ignore and pay no attention to it now)?

¹⁹ Therefore (O people), know that verily, there is no other god except the

---

ᵃ See verses 3:137-139 and the corresponding footnote regarding *sunatullah*.

One and Only Almighty God (who deserves all worship). Hence, seek forgiveness for your sins and for the sins of all other believing men and women. Indeed, God knows everything about (you, including all) your movements (during the day) and even your resting place (at night).

20 And the believers (used to) say, "Why is a chapter (allowing us to fight not) revealed yet?" But when a chapter with decisive revelation about fighting is (finally) ordained upon them, you see those in whose hearts is a disease (of hypocrisy) looking at you with a look of one who is about to faint for fear of death. It would have been better for them; **21** (to show) obedience (to God's call) and say good words (that would earn His pleasure). And it would have surely been better for them to prove to God their true faith (by living up to their words) now that the command to fight has been (finally) decreed. *ᵃ* **22** (And if you turn away from God's command and revert to your old ways,) would it not be reasonable to expect that you will corrupt the land and cut asunder your ties of kinship if you were being granted power and authority?

23 These are the ones whom God has rejected and cursed, whose ears He made deaf (to the voice of truth) and whose eyes He made blind (to guidance)! **24** Will they then not (use reason and) ponder over this Qur'an (to grasp its message), or are there locks set upon their hearts (that prevent them from accepting the truth)?

25 Indeed, those who turn back to disbelief after clear guidance has come, do so because Satan has embellished their fancies and filled (their hearts) with prolonged false hopes. **26** And because of this, the hypocrites say to those who openly hate what God has sent down, "We shall obey you in some matters (that benefit us)." Indeed, God is ever aware of their secret (plots). **27** Hence, how will they fare when the Angels strike their faces and backs while taking their souls at death?

28 That will happen because they follow the way that incurs the wrath of God and detest (whatever that would earn you) His pleasure. And so, He made all their deeds worthless. **29** Or do those in whose hearts is a disease (of hypocrisy) think that God will never bring their malice to light? **30** And if We wanted, We could surely show them to you (O Prophet), so that you will know them by their marks and appearance. But you will still know them from the way they twist their words. Indeed, God knows (everything that) you do (O

ᵃ Great missions cannot be executed by mere lip-service. Cowards and feeble-minded people have no leadership role to play in it. Falsehood is usually supported by audacious self-serving individuals, and can only be defeated by strong self-sacrificing believers who give all they have for the sake of upholding the truth and establishing the divine world order on this earth.

people).

³¹ (And at the same time,) We shall put you all to test (O believers) until We make evident the truly valiant and steadfast among you (who profess to fight in God's cause), and We shall also put to test all your assertions (to reveal your true intention to set you apart from the hypocrites). ³² Verily, (remember that) those who reject the truth, obstruct others from the way of God and oppose the Messenger after guidance has become clear to them, they will not be able to harm God in any way. Instead, it is God Who will make all their deeds become worthless.

Invitation to Sacrifice

³³ O you who believe! Obey God and obey the Messenger, and do not let your deeds become worthless. ³⁴ Indeed, those who reject the truth and obstruct others from God's way and die while they are in this state will never be forgiven by God. ³⁵ Therefore, when you fight for a just cause, do not be fainthearted and call for peace (for as long as your enemies are bent on opposing the truth and destroying you). Know that you have a higher standing than them in the sight of God (and you will triumph in the end). Verily, God is on your side and He will never deprive you (the reward) of your (noble) deeds.

³⁶ Indeed, the life of this world is nothing but amusement and a passing delight. But if you believe in God and are always mindful of Him, He will grant you your rewards and not ask (you to sacrifice all) your possessions (in His cause). ³⁷ Verily, if He were to demand (you to sacrifice everything) that you possess and urge you upon it, you will surely be stingy (and cling to them dearly); and this will certainly bring your (moral) failings to light.

³⁸ (And so O believers!) It is you who are called upon to spend (generously) in the cause of God, but among you are some who are stingy (because you have succumbed to the trap laid by Satan. Remember that) whoever is stingy is in fact stingy to himself; for God is indeed All-Sufficient whereas it is you who are in need of Him. So if you turn away (from Him, it is you who will be the loser. In due time), He will replace you with others who are not like you.

48. Al-Faṭḥ
[The Victory : 29 verses]

This is a Madinan chapter which was revealed shortly after the conclusion of the Treaty of Hudaibiyah in the year 6 Hijra between the Prophet and the Makkan leaders when he and 1,400 of his companions were being prevented from entering Makkah to perform their *'Umrah* (i.e. minor pilgrimage). The treaty is called "The Clear Victory" (*al-Fath al-Mubin*) because it was the precursor to the conquest of Makkah that took place two years later and the acceptance of Islam by all the inhabitants of Makkah who had previously opposed Islam very fiercely. The chapter is named in reference to the victory that ensued from this treaty. The chapter also speaks about the hypocrites of Madinah and the Bedouin tribes who gave lame excuses to not participate in the Prophet's march to perform the *'Umrah* in Makkah which only exposed their true character.

In the name of God, the Most Gracious, the Most Compassionate.

A Victory in the Making

¹ (O Prophet!) Indeed, We have granted you a clear victory (in the Treaty of Hudaibiyah); ² and it is through this that God may forgive your past as well as your future sins, and complete His full measure of His blessings upon you, and keep you on the straight path; ³ and help you with a mighty help.

⁴ He is the One Who sent down tranquility into the hearts of the believers so that their faith may increase further. And (know that) to God belong the forces of the heavens and the earth. Verily, God is All-Knowing, All-Wise. ⁵ (He does this) so that He may admit the true believers - both men and women - into gardens which rivers flow from right beneath them to remain in there forever, and so that He may also erase and remove (the sins of) their past misdeeds. That is indeed the greatest success in the sight of God! *ᵃ*

⁶ And (God has willed) to punish the hypocrites and those who associate

---

ᵃ Verses 4-6 were revealed while the Muslims were on their way back to Madinah from Hudaibiyah to reassure them and put their minds at rest. It also exposed those who chose to stay behind in Madinah in the first place and indicated how they should be dealt with. When the Muslims decided to perform the *'Umrah* at Makkah, the hypocrites of Madinah were certain that the Quraysh of Makkah would annihilate them if a armed confrontation broke out since the Muslims were smaller in number. So when the Muslims changed their plan and deferred their *'Umrah* for another year and returned safely to Madinah, the hypocrites were shocked and enraged.

others in His divinity - both men and women - who harbor (and entertain) evil thoughts about God. It is they who will be encircled by evil, for God's wrath (and curse) is upon them. He has rejected them (from His grace) and prepared Hell for them (as their permanent home). How terrible will their end be! [7] And to God belong the forces of the heavens and the earth. God is indeed Almighty, Truly Wise.

[8] (O Muhammad!) Indeed, We have sent you as a witness (to the truth), and as a bearer of good news and warner (to all mankind); [9] so that you (O believers), may have faith in God and His Messenger, honor and respect him, and glorify God's perfection in the morning and evening. [10] Verily, those who pledge allegiance to you are in fact pledging allegiance to God, for God's hand is over theirs. Hence, whoever breaks his pledge does so at his own peril; and whoever fulfills his pledge to God will be greatly rewarded by Him.

The Defaulters

[11] But the Bedouins who lagged behind will say to you, "Our properties and families have kept us occupied (and we are prevented from following you). So please ask forgiveness for us from God." They say with their tongues what is not in their hearts. Say to them, "Who then has the power to intervene with God on your behalf if He intends any harm or benefit for you? Nay! (Surely there is none. Hence, be mindful that you can never escape from whatever God wills upon you, and know that you cannot deceive Him, for) God is certainly well aware of everything that you do." [12] In fact, (the truth is) you had thought (and expected) that the Messenger and the believers would never return to their families; and this notion was embellished in your hearts because you harbored evil thoughts (about them. Indeed,) you are a people destined for ruin.

[13] (Behold!) Those who refuse to believe in God and His Messenger should bear in mind that We have prepared a Blazing Fire for such deniers of truth. [14] And (verily), to God belongs the dominion of the heavens and the earth. He forgives whomsoever He wills (that accepts the truth and strives in His cause), and punishes whomsoever He wills (that stubbornly opposes the truth). And God is indeed Most Forgiving, Most Compassionate.

[15] And as soon as you are about to set forth on a war that promises spoils, those who stayed behind (before this) will say, "Allow us to follow you." Indeed, they wish to change God's decision (that does not permit them to follow you). Tell them, "You will not come with us. God has already decreed before this to whom will all spoils belong." Thereupon, they will answer, "Nay! You are envious of us (and are trying to deprive us from our share)."

Verily, how little fo they understand!

¹⁶ Say to the Bedouins who stayed behind, "You will soon be called upon to fight against a people who possess great military might; and you will fight them (either until you die), or until they surrender (and stop harassing you). Then if you heed (that call), God will grant you a good reward, but if you turn away as you did before, He will inflict grievous punishment upon you."

¹⁷ (Behold!) There is no blame on the blind, the lame, and the sick (if they stay away from fighting in God's cause. Verily,) whoever heeds (the call) of God and His Messenger (wholeheartedly, either in deeds or even in the heart if he is not in the position to offer anything), God will admit him into gardens which rivers flow from right beneath them. But whoever turns away, then he will surely suffer grievous punishment.

Pledges and God's Promises

¹⁸ Certainly, God was pleased with the believers when they pledged allegiance to you under that tree (at Hudaibiyah O Prophet), for He knew what was in their hearts. And so, He sent down tranquility upon them and rewarded them with (the good news of) a near victory; ¹⁹ and of abundant gains that they will acquire. Indeed, God is Almighty, All-Wise.

²⁰ (O you who believe!) God has promised you many gains that you will acquire, and He has hastened this victory for you and withheld the enemies' hands from you so that it may serve as a sign (of His grace) to the believers, and so that He may guide you to the straight path; ²¹ and also over other (victories) that are not yet within your reach but which God has already encompassed them (for you). Verily, God has power over everything.

²² And even if the infidels fight against you (now), they would certainly turn their backs and retreat, and they would not be able to find any protector or helper (to support them). ²³ Such is the way of God that has indeed prevailed among those people who lived before you, and you will never find any change in the way (how) God (disposes and regulates all affairs).

²⁴ And He is indeed the One Who withheld their hands from you and your hands from them in (the valley of) Makkah after (you captured their forces and) He made you triumph over them. And God sees everything that you do. ²⁵ They are the ones who rejected the truth and hindered you from the Sacred Mosque and prevented your sacrificial offerings from reaching their destination. Had there not been believing men and women who were unknown to you in Makkah, (God would have certainly allowed you to fight your way

into the city). And this might cause them to be trampled under your feet, thus making you incur unwitting guilt on their account. (But He held back your hands), so that (in time) He may admit whomsoever He wills (among those disbelievers to embrace truth and) into His grace. Had they (who deserve Our mercy) stood apart (from the infidels and been clearly distinguishable to you), We would have certainly punished those infidels with grievous punishment (at your hands).

²⁶ And while those infidels who are bent on opposing the truth harbored a stubborn disdain in their hearts - the (type of) disdain that is born out of arrogant ignorance - God sent down His (gift of) tranquility upon His Messenger and the believers, and made them adhere to the word of piety, for they were more deserving and worthy of it. (Indeed,) God has full knowledge of everything.

The Victory

²⁷ God has certainly showed His Messenger the vision of truth. (Then He said, "O Muhammad!) If God so wills, you will certainly enter the Sacred Mosque (together with those who follow you); fearless and secure - some having their heads shaved and others having their hair shortened - for He always knows what you do not know; and He also granted you an imminent victory even before (the fulfillment of that vision)." ²⁸ (Verily,) He is the One Who sent His Messenger with (the task of spreading) guidance and the religion of truth so that He will make it prevail over all other religions (that are false). Sufficient is God as witness to the truth.

²⁹ Muhammad is indeed the Messenger of God, and those with him are firm against the opponents of truth and show compassion among themselves. You see them bowing and prostrating, seeking grace from God and His pleasure. Their mark is on their faces from the trace of prostration. That is their parable in the Torah. And their parable in the Gospel is like a seed which sends forth its shoot, then strengthens it, then it becomes thick and it stands firm upon its stem, delighting the sowers. (In this way too does God cause the believers to grow in strength) so that through them, He may enrage (and frustrate) the infidels. But to those who have chosen faith and do good deeds, God has promised forgiveness and a great reward.

49. Al-Ḥujurāt
[The Chambers : 18 verses]

This is a Madinan chapter. It is a short chapter but is full of important rules on manners and etiquette. It starts by directing that no decision should be made nor any opinion on any matter be expressed in advance of God's and His Messenger's. Then it directs Muslims not to engage in conversations with raised voices in the presence of the Messenger of God, and should address him with due respect and courtesy. Next it deals with a very important matter of social harmony and peace, namely not to lend ear to gossips and rumors and to ascertain the truth before jumping to any conclusion on information given by a person of doubtful integrity. It then directs the Muslims to settle their differences and quarrels mutually and reminds that they are brethren. Another equally important lesson given in the chapter is that no group of people should ridicule another group of people - males or females - nor defame one another. Further, it is advised not to spy on or backbite anyone. It also emphasizes that races, tribes and nations are created by God so that they may get to know one another and that real honor and merit lie in righteousness and fear of God, not in birth, race or color. The chapter ends by indicating the qualities of a true believer and by stressing that the act of believing is for one's own benefit, instead of a favor done to God and His Messenger. The chapter is called *Al-Ḥujurāt* or The Chambers with reference to verse 5 where Muslims were advised not to shout to the Messenger of God from behind his private chambers but to wait until he came out to them.

In the name of God, the Most Gracious, the Most Compassionate.

Respect for the Prophet

¹ O you who believe! Do not precede (in whatever that have not been decreed yet by) God and His Messenger. Be ever mindful of God, for God is indeed All-Hearing, All-Knowing.

² O you who believe! Do not raise your voices above the voice of the Prophet, nor speak loudly to him in the same way you speak loudly to others, lest your deeds become worthless while you might not even be aware of it. ³ Verily, those who lower their voices in the presence of God's Messenger are those whose hearts God has tested (and opened) for piety. For them is forgiveness and a great reward.

⁴ (O Prophet!) Indeed most of them who shout to you from outside your private chambers (are rude and inconsiderate because they) do not use reason (and lack common sense). ⁵ And if they were patient until you came out to them, that would certainly be better for them. Still, God is Most Forgiving,

Most Compassionate.

⁶ O you who believe! If a habitual sinner comes to you with an information, investigate first to ascertain the truth (instead of acting in haste) so that you will not wrong others unwittingly and then be filled with regret for (the mistake) you have done. ⁷ Keep in mind that the Messenger of God is in your midst (to guide and keep you in the right path). In many cases, you would have surely fallen into misfortune if he had accommodated your wishes. But God (protected you by) endearing this faith to you and made it pleasing in your hearts (to be obedient to His Messenger). He also made disbelief, defiance, and disobedience hateful to you. Those (who are blessed with this quality) are the ones who are rightly guided. ⁸ (This is a) bounty and favor from God. And God is All-Knowing, All-Wise.

⁹ And if two parties among the believers fall into fight, make peace between them. But if one of them (continues to) oppress the other, then fight the oppressor until he (submits and) complies with God's command. And if he complies, make peace between them with justice and deal (with them) equitably. Indeed, God loves those who are fair and just. ¹⁰ (Verily,) those who believe (in God and His Messenger) are brothers (to one another). Hence (whenever they are at odds), make reconciliation between your brothers and be ever mindful of God so that you may be graced with His mercy.

Respect for the Muslim Brotherhood

¹¹ O you who believe! Let not a people deride others, for it may well be that those whom they deride are better than them. And no woman will deride other women, for it may also well be that those whom they deride are better than them. And neither will you defame nor insult one another with (offensive) nicknames. Wretched it is to be called by a name connoting (evil and) disobedience after one becomes a believer. Verily, those who do not repent (from such acts) are evildoers.

¹² O you who believe! (You should also) avoid from being excessively suspicious (of one another) as some of this is (in itself) a sin. And do not spy upon nor speak ill of one another behind their backs. Would any of you like to eat the flesh of his dead brother? Surely, you would detest it! So be mindful of God and fear Him. Indeed, God is the Acceptor of Repentance, the Most Compassionate.

¹³ O mankind! We created you from a single pair of a male and female, and made you into nations and tribes so that you will get to know one another (with kindness and treat each other fairly, and to also glorify God's greatness).

Indeed, the (best and) noblest among you in the sight of God are those who are always mindful of Him (and strive hard to keep their duty to Him diligently in full submission). *ª* Verily, God is All-Knowing, All-Aware (of everything).

¹⁴ The Bedouins say, "We are (true) believers now!" Tell them, "You have not (truly) believed yet. Rather, you should say, 'We have (only begun to) submit', because true faith has not found its way and settled in your hearts yet. And if you (prove your faith by) obeying God and His Messenger, He will surely not deny you the reward of your deeds. Indeed, God is Most Forgiving, Most Compassionate." ¹⁵ Verily, the believers are those who have true faith in God and His Messenger and they do not have any doubt about this. They (gladly) strive with their wealth and their lives in the cause of God. Indeed, such are the truthful ones. ¹⁶ Say (further to those who profess themselves as true believers), "Are you trying to convince God of your faith (in His religion by mere words alone) whereas He knows all that is in the heavens and the earth? Verily, He has full knowledge of everything (including what is hidden in the deep recesses of your hearts)."

¹⁷ Indeed, they (have the audacity to) consider it a favor to you (by proclaiming) that they have submitted (to God). Tell them, "Do not consider your submission as a favor to me. In fact, it is God Who has conferred His favor to you by showing you the way to faith, if you are indeed men of truth (who can reason well). ¹⁸ God surely knows all the secrets in the heavens and the earth, and He is watching everything that you do."

ª The Prophet (peace be upon him) said in his Farewell Sermon, "O people! Verily your Lord is One and your father is one (i.e. Adam). An Arab has no superiority over a non-Arab, nor a non-Arab has any superiority over an Arab. And a white too has no superiority over a black, nor a black has any superiority over a white except by piety and good deeds.." [Musnad Ahmad, no. 22978]. Islam is a truly universal religion for all mankind which transcends race and ethnicity. Everyone will be solely judged by their faith and piety towards God and the good deeds that they do. Muslims are commanded to be fair to everyone regardless of race and religion (verses 5:8, 57:25 and 60:8), and to never condone injustice and oppression, let alone commit them. Those who have so much enmity and hatred in them towards others and are inclined to treat them unfairly are threatened with the punishment of the Hellfire (see verse 11:113). No other Scripture is known to literally mention this universal message of justice and racial equality except the Qur'an, as recorded in this particular verse.

50. Qāf

[45 verses]

This is a Makkan chapter that deals mainly with the belief in God and His Absolute Oneness together with the themes of the Qur'an's truth, the Messengership of Prophet Muhammad, resurrection, judgment, reward and punishment. The main emphasis of the chapter is however, on resurrection and the attitude of the disbelievers towards it. It brings home this theme by referring to God's creation of the heavens and the earth and all that exists and also His providing for the creatures in various ways. In this connection, reference is also made to what happened to the disbelieving nations of the past. It ends by mentioning some circumstances of death, resurrection and the Day of Judgment. The chapter is named after the disjointed letter with which it starts.

In the name of God, the Most Gracious, the Most Compassionate.

The Resurrection

¹ *Qāf.* By this Glorious Quran. ² Nay! They deem it strange that a warner has come to them from their own midst. And so these (confounded) disbelievers say, "This is something very strange! ³ What! (Are you saying that) when we die and have become soil and dust (We shall be brought back to life again)? Such return is far-fetched and is certainly impossible."

⁴ Surely We know how the earth consumes and diminishes their bodies. But as for their deeds, We preserve them all in a Book which records everything that they ever did. ⁵ Indeed, they denied the truth (about resurrection) when it was conveyed to them. As such, they (will arise from their graves) in a confused state. *ᵃ*

ᵃ Verses 2-5 : The Qur'an bases faith on sound rational argument and expresses it in the most powerful and lucid language. See also verses 45:5-6 and the footnote. In our daily life, we come across many miracles which, although we can understand, we may not able to explain. We know that the food we eat turns partly to energy and partly to bones and living body tissue. We also know that these bones and tissue carry genes which pass on traits and characteristics from generation to generation. At the same time, surplus or unwanted food is discarded and goes back into the soil where crops and plants grow in an amazing and wonderful cycle to feed living creatures and perpetuate life. In fact, life and death even occur inside every living body every second, through a process called cellular metabolism which releases free radicals that cause millions of old cells to naturally die and be replaced by new ones. Why is it then that people consider it far-fetched for humans

⁶ Have they not looked at the heaven above them and think how We structured and adorned it, and made it free from any flaw? ⁷ And the earth, We have spread it out and cast mountains on it that are firmly set (as anchors and pegs), and We also made every kind of beautiful vegetation to grow on it; ⁸ offering an insight and reminder to every servant who turns to God (in devotion).

⁹ And We send down blessed rain from the sky and grew gardens and grains for harvest; ¹⁰ and tall palm-trees (laden with clusters of dates), arranged layer by layer; ¹¹ as provision apportioned to men; and with this (rain too) do We give life to dead land. Indeed, this is (a parable of) how (the dead) will emerge (from their graves on the Day of Resurrection).

¹² (Long) before those (who now deny your Prophethood O Muhammad), the people of Noah too had denied it, and so did the dwellers of Ar-Raas and (the people of) Tsamud; ¹³ and the people of 'Aād and Pharaoh, and the brethren of Lot; ¹⁴ and the dwellers of Al-'Aikah *ᵃ* and the people of Tubba - who all denied and rejected the Messengers that were sent to them. And so, My threat (upon these deniers of truth) was duly fulfilled.

¹⁵ Were We ever tired with the first creation? Nay! But those who deny the truth are indeed lost in doubt about their second creation. ¹⁶ And verily, it is We Who have created man, and (certainly) We know everything that his soul whispers to him; for We are indeed nearer to him than the vein in his neck. ¹⁷ So remember that whenever the two (heavenly) scribes who are seated on the right and left sides (of him) record everything; ¹⁸ not a word that he utters will escape except that it will be recorded by the vigilant observer who is always ready. *ᵇ*

¹⁹ And when the agony of death finally comes before his eyes bringing the moment of truth (that has been promised, he will be told), "This is what you have been trying to avoid (all your life)!" ²⁰ And in the end, the trumpet of Resurrection will be blown. That will be the Day of a warning (fulfilled).

²¹ (On that Day,) every soul will come along with an Angel to drive him

---

who have died to be resurrected and brought back to life for judgment by their Creator? This passage denounces those skeptics who dispute this fact.

ᵃ Al-'Aikah is another name for Madyan.

ᵇ Verses 17 and 18 of this chapter should be read in conjunction with 10:61, 17:13-14, 34:3-5, 43:80, 82:10-12 and 99:6-8. Essentially, no one should ever expect any of his deeds to escape God's knowledge even if it is as small and light as an atom's weight. Everything is clearly recorded in his own ledger of deeds and will be openly presented for reckoning on Judgment Day.

and another Angel to bear witness (of his deeds); ²² and he will be told, "Certainly you were heedless of this Day (and have been lost in your fanciful false beliefs)! *ᵃ* We have removed your veil (today) making your sight sharp (to see what you have been promised)." *ᵇ*

²³ And his vigilant companion will say, "Here is (his record) that I have ready with me!" ²⁴ And then God will say, "Throw into Hell every stubborn infidel; ²⁵ who is an opponent of what is good (and right), a transgressor, and a doubter (of the truth); ²⁶ who had (defiantly) set up other gods besides Almighty God (despite the warnings that have been conveyed to him). Now throw him into the severe punishment!"

²⁷ And then his (evil) companion will plead, "Our Lord, I did not make him transgress, but he was himself in extreme error." ²⁸ God will reply, "Do not dispute with each other in My presence (today)! Did I not give you (ample) warning beforehand (about the imminent arrival of this day)? ²⁹ My judgment will not be changed and I am not unjust to My servants." ³⁰ Then We shall ask Hell on that Day, "Are you full?" and it will reply, "Are there more to come?"

³¹ (On that Day too,) Paradise will be brought close to those who are always mindful of God (and strive to keep their duty to Him diligently). No longer will it be a distant thing. ³² (They will be told,) "This is what you have been promised! It is for everyone who (always) turns to God and keeps (Him in mind); ³³ for everyone who stood in awe of the Most Gracious (Lord) Who is unseen, and for everyone who has come with a devoted heart (longing for His grace)." ³⁴ (And so they will be greeted), "Enter (Paradise) in peace!" (Indeed,) that will be the Day of Eternal Life. ³⁵ Therein, they will have whatever they desire, yet there is even more with Us to give.

Lessons to be Drawn from Past Generations

³⁶ And how many earlier generations that were far stronger in might have We destroyed before those who oppose you now (O Muhammad? When Our punishment befell them), they wandered all over the land (seeking a place for

---

ᵃ See verse 59:19 and its footnote.

ᵇ There is a huge difference between a life based on skepticism and one based on sound, unshakeable belief in the resurrection, accountability to God, and final judgment. Many religious systems and beliefs have failed to invigorate man's conscience and instill a fear of God within it. Most people today regard death as the end and the conclusion of all life on this earth, but this passage points out that these people will be taken aback with a rude awakening when they face the reality of afterlife. See verses 36:51-52

refuge). But did they find any? ^{37} Surely there is a lesson and reminder in this for every person who has a heart (that is wide awake), and always lends his ear with a conscious mind to bear witness (to the truth in God's messages).

^{38} Verily, (know that) We created the heavens and the earth and whatever is between them in six phases, and no fatigue ever touched Us. (Hence, inflicting Our retribution upon those who are bent on denying the truth is even easier. But We grant them respite so that they will add more to their sins.) ^{a} ^{39} Therefore (O Prophet), bear with what they say in patience and keep glorifying your Lord's perfection by celebrating His praise before sunrise and before sunset. ^{40} And glorify His perfection during a part of the night too and also at the end of every prayer.

^{41} And (always) listen for the Day when He Who issues the call (of death) will call (you) from a nearby place.^{b} ^{42} (And be reminded too of) the Day when everyone will hear the mighty blast in truth. That will be the Day when (the dead) will come forth (from their graves)! ^{43} Verily, it is We who grant life and cause death, and to Us is the final return (of all things). ^{44} On that Day, the earth will split asunder and everyone will rush out (of their graves like locusts ^{c} towards God for His judgment). Indeed, gathering the entire mankind is easy for Us.

^{45} (O Muhammad! Indeed) We are very well aware of what those (who deny resurrection) say and you can by no means force them (to believe in it). But nonetheless, (continue to) warn all those who may fear My warning with this Qur'an.

---

^{a} God remains in total control of the world and all its affairs and He is the source of life and livelihood for the vast multitudes of creatures that have lived in it for over millions of years. God sustains the movement of the galaxies and the planets and the stars of this vast universe without experiencing any fatigue. Were He to cease for even a single moment, the whole cosmic order would collapse! To accuse God of weakness is in fact a folly many senseless people have committed, and here we find the Qur'an strongly refuting this absurd concept and reaffirming God's absolute power and glory over all things. The Qur'an uses reason and rational argument in addressing the human mind and appeals to man's natural and instinctive inclination to reject such nonsense. See verse 45.

^{b} The "call from a nearby place" mentioned here is the call of death, for which man should always be prepared for.

^{c} See verse 54:7 and 101:4 together with its corresponding footnote.

51. Adz-Dzāriyāt
[The Dust-Scattering Wind : 60 verses]

This is an early Makkan chapter that emphasizes on the fundamentals of faith namely monotheism, the Prophethood of Muhammad, resurrection and judgment. It starts by emphasizing the inevitability of resurrection and the Day of Judgment. Next it refers to the disbelievers who reject the Qur'an and do not believe in resurrection, and the suffering that awaits them in the Hereafter which is in contrast to the condition of the believers and the righteous who will be in the state of everlasting happiness. It then refers to the heavens and the earth and all that exist as signs of God's power of creation and His Lordship over all things. In this context, reference is made to some of the Messengers whom God had sent with the message of monotheism and worship of God alone and how the previous nations had been destroyed because of their disbelief and persistent disobedience to God.

In the name of God, the Most Gracious,
the Most Compassionate.

Falsehood is Doomed

¹ By the dust scattering winds that disperses; ² and the heavy laden clouds (that hold Our grace); ³ and the ships that sail with ease. ⁴ Then, (by the heavenly Angels) who manage and distribute all affairs (by God's command)! ⁵ Verily, what you are promised is surely true. ⁶ And verily, (final) Judgment will most certainly take place.

⁷ By the heaven (that is interwoven) with its (cosmic) web! *ᵃ* ⁸ Verily (O

ᵃ This is one of the greatest discoveries of recent modern science. For a very long time, the word *al-Hubuk* in Arabic which literally means "the web" that is specifically mentioned in this verse, has been interpreted as "pathways or orbits". This is because no one could previously relate the word "web" with the heaven or sky due to the absence of any information about it. As such, this verse has been typically and commonly translated in English as "By the heaven and its pathways.. or orbits". It was not until the late 1980s when space scientists and astrophysicists discovered that the largest probable object in space is an endless network of super clusters of galaxies that are linked and tied together by filaments of a spider web-like structure. However, this structure is surrounded by dark matter which is an invisible and mysterious form of matter that accounts for 85% of the universe's mass. Dark matter cannot be seen, and the massive web structure that it veils would only became "theoretically visible" after employing highly complex numerical and computer simulations during the initial stages of the research on cosmic web. According to Prof. Michele Fumagalli, an astrophysicist at the Durham University in UK whom I have had the privilege to be in contact with

men), you are surely in dispute (regarding the truth and) in what you say.
 ⁹ Deluded in his views is the one who deceives himself (about the truth).

¹⁰ Cursed are the liars! ¹¹ (They are) those who are steeped in heedlessness
and are oblivious (of the Hereafter); ¹² those who (mockingly) ask, "When is
the Day of Judgment?" ¹³ (Tell them that) it is a Day when they will be tried
over the Fire; ¹⁴ (and will be told,) "Now taste the ordeal that you were so
impatiently asking for!"

¹⁵ (But) behold! Those who diligently keep their duty to God will be in
gardens and (flowing) springs; ¹⁶ (joyfully) receiving what their Lord will give
them. Indeed, their deeds in the past were truly excellent. ¹⁷ They would sleep
for only a little part of the night; ¹⁸ and ask for forgiveness in the early hours
before dawn; ¹⁹ and (would assign) a rightful share of their wealth for those
who asked and also for the (poor and) destitute.

²⁰ (Indeed), there are (many wondrous) signs on earth (that show God's
power and greatness to ponder) for those who are firm in faith; ²¹ just as there
are within yourselves too. *ᵃ* Do you not see them? ²² And in heaven is where
your provision and whatever you are promised (decreed). ²³ Then, by the Lord
of the heaven and the earth! Verily, what is being promised to you is surely the
truth, as true as the fact that you have been endowed with the ability to speak.

The Fate of Previous Nations

²⁴ (O Muhammad!) Has the story of Abraham's honored guests reached
you? ²⁵ (Now, take heed of the occasion) when they came to him and said,
"Peace (be upon you)!" to which he replied, "Peace be upon you too, O
unknown guests!" ²⁶ Then he went quietly to his family and brought a fat

---

regarding this matter, it was only very recently in the year 2019 that he and a group of
other scientists finally got the chance to directly observe the cosmic web for the first
time in its real live condition by using the powerful 10 meter wide Hubble Space
Telescope (HST) and spectrographs through a technique called Absorption
Spectroscopy. This discovery proved that the Qur'an has accurately mentioned about
the nature of celestial objects in the vast heaven as being interwoven and linked by a
web-like structure that scientists named it The Cosmic Web. It is simply impossible for
an illiterate man who lived in the desert of Arabia more than 1,450 years ago to author
the Qur'an and mention about the existence of this super-massive interwoven web
structure in space. Only divine revelation by the One Who created the entire universe
can foretell this phenomenon before any scientific knowledge known to man had ever
existed.
ᵃ See verse 41:53 and its corresponding footnote.

(roasted) calf. [27] He placed it near them, saying, "Will you not eat?"

[28] (And when they did not eat, he felt something amiss and) became afraid of them. Then they said, "Do not be afraid (of us O Abraham)!"; and gave him good news of (the birth of) a son who will be endowed with knowledge (and wisdom). [29] Hearing this, his wife came forward clasping her face (in astonishment), exclaiming, "(A son to) a barren old woman (like me)?" [30] Replied the guests, "This is what your Lord said. Indeed, He is All-Wise, All-Knowing."

[31] Asked Abraham, "So what is your mission, O (heavenly) Messengers?" [32] They replied, "Indeed, we have been sent to a people who are immersed in sin; [33] to bring down upon them stones of clay; [34] that have been marked by your Lord for those who have transgressed their limits (and squandered their souls)."[a]

[35] (And when Our heavenly Messengers arrived at that city,) We evacuated every believer there; [36] but We did not find anyone other than a single family (that belonged to Lot) who had submitted themselves to Us, (except his wife). [37] And so We left a sign there for those who (came later so that they would) fear the grievous punishment (that awaits anyone who rejects Our message).

[38] And in (the story of) Moses too (was another lesson) when We sent him with a clear (proof and) authority to (advise) Pharaoh. [39] But Pharaoh turned away with his supporters and accused Moses, saying, "He is either a sorcerer or a madman!" [40] So We seized him and his army, and cast them into the sea, for he was worthy of blame.

[41] And (you also have the same lesson) in (what happened to the people of) 'Aād when We let loose upon them a fatal wind; [42] which spared nothing that it came upon except reducing it to rubble. [43] And in (the story of the people of) Tsamud too (the same lesson was made evident), when they were told, "Enjoy yourselves for a little while." [44] But they rebelled against the command of their Lord. And so, a thunderbolt seized them while they were helplessly looking on; [45] for they were unable to even stand up or protect themselves. [46] And the people of Noah (were destroyed) earlier too. Indeed, they were a people who defiantly disobeyed Us.

[47] It is We Who built the heaven with (Our own) power and it is We Who are indeed steadily expanding it. [b] [48] And the earth, We spread it wide. How

---

[a] In reference to the people of Lot.
[b] Refer to footnote for verse 21:30.

excellent is the One Who spread it! *ᵃ* ⁴⁹ And We also created everything in pairs (and in opposites to one another) so that you will take heed (of God's immense power and submit yourselves to Him in awe).

⁵⁰ (So, say to them O Muhammad,) "Flee to God from all that is false and evil. Indeed, I am a clear warner to you from Him; ⁵¹ and do not set up any (false) god besides Almighty God. Indeed, I am a clear warner to you from Him."

⁵² That was how it has been in the past. No Messenger ever came to their own people except to be accused as a sorcerer or a madman. ⁵³ Did they hand down this (same way of thinking as a legacy to their successors)? Indeed, they are a people who have arrogantly transgressed (their limits).

⁵⁴ So turn away from them (O Muhammad), for you are not to be blamed (for their stubborn defiance). ⁵⁵ But (nonetheless), keep reminding; for indeed, such reminder may benefit those who (might come to their senses one day and) believe (in Our message of truth). ⁵⁶ And (let it be known that certainly,) I have not created Jinn and mankind except for them to serve and worship Me alone. *ᵇ* ⁵⁷ (Verily,) I do not ever need any provision from them, nor do I need them to feed Me. ⁵⁸ Indeed, God is the Bestower of all provision. (He is) the All-Powerful Lord, the Most Firm.

⁵⁹ And verily, the wrongdoers will have their share of punishment like what We have inflicted upon their (like-minded) predecessors. Therefore, they should not ask Me to hasten (their doom). ⁶⁰ Woe then to those who refuse to believe when they face their promised Day!

ᵃ See verse 15:19 and its footnote.

ᵇ These are the only two creatures that God has granted free will for them to make their own choice of faith that they will be accountable for. They were created with the natural disposition to worship only the Almighty God alone (see verse 7:172 and its footnote). By worshipping false gods, including his own lusts (verses 25:43 and 45:23), or to reject God's existence, man can no longer play the role as God's emissary on earth which he has been assigned to in the first place (see verses 2:30 and 2:36) because he would be rejecting the purpose of his creation. There is no compulsion in religion, but the choice that man makes out of his own free will shall determine his fate in the Hereafter, for truth is clearly distinct from falsehood (see verses verse 2:256 and 18:29).

52. Aṭ-Ṭūr
[The Mountain : 49 verses]

This is a Makkan chapter, and like other Makkan chapters, it deals with the themes of monotheism, Prophethood of Muhammad, resurrection, judgment, reward and punishment, and brings home these themes by presenting various arguments and proofs. It starts with a proclamation on the inevitability of the Last Hour, the Day of Resurrection, and the contrasting fate of the disbelievers and believers. Next it speaks about the Messengership of Muhammad and gives appropriate replies to the allegations of the disbelievers who rejected him. The chapter ends by denouncing the polytheists' worship of false gods, their stubborness in accepting the truth and the severity of their punishment in the Hereafter. The chapter is named *Aṭ-Ṭūr* or The Mountain, by which the chapter starts, in reference to Mount Sinai where Prophet Moses received the revelation of Torah from God.

In the name of God, the Most Gracious, the Most Compassionate.

Success of the Faithful

¹ By Mount (Sinai)! ² And by the Book inscribed; ³ in wide-opened scrolls. ⁴ By the much frequented (sacred) House. *ᵃ* ⁵ By the roof (of heaven) that has been raised high. ⁶ And by the boiling sea (when the day of doom arrives). *ᵇ*

ᵃ An allusion to either The Ka'bah that is much frequented by the pilgrims, or a sanctuary in the Heaven that is much frequented by the Angels.

ᵇ Syaikh Muhammad al-Ghazali commented the passage from verse 1 to 6 as follows : The link between Qur'anic revelation and previously revealed Scriptures is obvious. Moses received the Torah at Mount Sinai while Muhammad received the Qur'an near the Ka'bah, both of which conveyed a message of pure *tawhid* (i.e. the indivisible oneness concept of monotheism in Islam) and came with a religious faith based on tangible facts and laws rather than myths and mysteries. The chapter seems to point to the scrolls of Moses, while the reference to the sea appears to be a reference to the Red Sea where Pharaoh, with his false godhood, was drowned. It is important to point out here that the Torah was a book of religion as well as a book of law and statecraft. The same applies to the Qur'an. The Gospel of Jesus however, was supplementary to the Torah and an extension to it, introducing a limited number of concessionary rules. The Qur'an however, represents the final and complete version of divine religion and law. It is the revealed divine message for all time to come, and remains today as the sole authentic Scripture ever received by a human being.

[7] Indeed, your Lord's punishment is surely inevitable; [8] and no one will be able to prevent it; [9] on the Day when the heaven will shake with a great convulsion; [10] and the mountains will move with a (violent) movement.

[11] So woe on that Day to the deniers (of truth); [12] who amuse themselves in vain discourses. [13] On that Day, they will be pushed into the Fire of Hell with a violent thrust. [14] It will be said to them, "This is the Fire which you used to deny! [15] So is this magic? Or do you still not see it? [16] Burn in it (now)! Whether you are patient or not (to endure it), it would make no difference. For indeed, you are only being requited for what you have done."

[17] Verily, (on that Day,) those who are mindful of God (and strive hard to keep their duty to Him diligently) will find themselves in gardens and full of bliss; [18] rejoicing in their Lord's gifts, for He has saved them from the torment of the Blazing Fire. [19] And they will be told, "Eat and drink in satisfaction as a reward for your deeds." [20] And they will be (happily) reclining on couches that are arranged in rows and We shall wed them to maidens with lustrous eyes. [21] We shall unite the believers with their offspring who followed them in (pure) faith and not deny them any reward for their good deeds. (Indeed,) everyone is (responsible and) tied to what he has done.

[22] We shall also provide them with whatever fruit and meat they desire. [23] And they will pass on to one another a drink that will not give rise to idle-talk and sin. [24] They will also be waited upon and served by immortal youths who are like pearls that are protected (in their shells).

[25] Then they will turn to one another inquiring (about their past); [26] saying, "Indeed, when we were among our families before, we were fearful (to incur God's displeasure). [27] And so (today), God has graced us with His blessing and protected us from the punishment of the Scorching Fire. [28] Verily, we only invoked and called upon Him (alone) before, and now He has shown us that He is truly the Most Benign, and the Most Compassionate."

Opponents of Truth are Doomed

[29] So remind (those who deny the truth of the Day when they will all be resurrected, O Muhammad). By the grace of your Lord, you are neither a soothsayer nor a madman. [30] Or do they say, "He is a poet for whom we (eagerly) await a misfortune that will surely befall him soon."? [31] Tell them, "Wait then! For indeed, I too am waiting with you." [32] Do their minds really command them to say such things, or are they simply a people (who are so deeply) immersed in transgression (and have lost the ability to think)?

³³ Or do they say (to you), "He has fabricated (this Qur'an) by himself?" Nay! (The truth is,) they refuse to believe (in the message that you bring). ³⁴ (If they deem the Qur'an as the work of a mere mortal,) then let them produce another discourse like it to prove their claim. ³⁵ Or (do they think) they were created out of nothing? Or were they the creators (of their own existence)? ³⁶ Or did they create the heavens and the earth? Nay! (The truth is) they are devoid of faith.

³⁷ Or do they hold the treasures of your Lord and have absolute control (over them)? ³⁸ Or do they have a ladder to climb on and attempt to listen to what is transpiring in the Higher Realm? Then, let any of them who has listened to it produce a proof with clear authority. ³⁹ Or (do they believe that) God has (chosen) daughters for Himself and gave you sons? ⁴⁰ Or did you (O Muhammad,) ask them for any reward (for your preaching which they cannot afford, and fear) they would be overburdened with debt because of it?

⁴¹ Or do they have knowledge of the unseen (and are able to predict the future?) Can they write this down (for everyone to see)? ⁴² Or do they intend to trap you (with their evil plot)? But it is those who disbelieve that are actually trapped (with falsehood). ⁴³ Or do they have a god other than the One and Only Almighty God? Glory be to God (Who is free from all imperfections, and utterly remote is He) from whatever they associate Him with. ⁴⁴ (So stubborn are they that) even if they were to see some fragments of the sky falling down, they will say, "(This is only a) mass of heaped-up cloud!" *ª*

⁴⁵ So, leave them alone until they face the Day when they will be stricken with terror. ⁴⁶ That is the Day when all their plotting will not benefit them at all, nor will they be helped (by anyone). ⁴⁷ Verily, there are other punishments in store for these wrongdoers even before the coming of that Day, but most of them do not know.

⁴⁸ So be patient for the command of your Lord (O Muhammad)! Indeed you are (always) in Our sight. Glorify your Lord's perfection by celebrating His praise when you arise (in the morning); ⁴⁹ and at night too, and also when the stars retreat (during the early hours of dawn).

ª After the hard-hitting probing questions from verse 29 to 43, the Qur'an indicates that the disbelievers are so stubborn and arrogant that they would not even recognize their punishment when it falls upon them as mentioned in verse 44.

53. An-Najm
[The Star : 62 verses]

This is a Makkan chapter which starts with an emphasis on the truth of Prophet Muhammad's Messengership and that what he spoke was not from his own desire and imagination but revelation that was communicated to him by the Angel Gabriel. It is further emphasized that the Prophet once saw Gabriel in his actual form appearing in the horizon and again during the *Mi'raj* (i.e. the Prophet's night journey and ascension to heaven) near *Sidrat al-muntaha* which is the farthest point in the heaven up to which anything can reach. Next, the chapter refers to the mistake and folly of worshipping the false and imaginary gods and the notion of God having daughters or sons. It is stressed that God is the Creator of everything and His Lordship is over the heavens, the earth and all that exists. Mention is then made of the resurrection and judgment and that each person will be individually responsible and accountable for his deeds. The chapter is named *An-Najm* or The Star with reference to its first verse.

In the name of God, the Most Gracious, the Most Compassionate.

Eminence to be Attained by the Prophet

[1] By the star when it declines! [2] Your companion *a* is neither astray, nor is he deluded; [3] and he does not speak from his own whim and desire. [4] What he conveys to you is indeed a (divine) revelation inspired to him (by your Lord); [5] that is imparted to him by something mighty and powerful; *b* [6] who is endowed with immense wisdom. (Verily,) he came forth and stood poised; [7] at the highest part of the horizon; [8] and then he approached and came close; [9] until he was at a distance of two bows-length or even nearer; [10] and revealed to God's servant what He revealed. *c*

---

a Prophet Muhammad.

b Angel Gabriel.

c Verses 2-10 : This passage indicates how Prophet Muhammad received revelation. Knowledge received through revelation is real and absolute but it is only imparted to those with special personal gifts and traits that qualify them for such honor and privilege. Muhammad was a preeminent individual among this select group of human beings. Moses received his calling at Mount Sinai by the Red Sea where he was charged with carrying the banner of revelation for the Children of Israel, while Muhammad received his after several years of retirement and solitary meditation at a cave on Mount Hira' near Makkah. His task was to advance the word of God and establish His order on earth.

[11] (Verily,) the (Prophet's) heart did not give lie to what his eyes had seen. [12] Will you argue with him about what he saw? [13] And indeed he saw (Gabriel again) in another descent; [14] near the Lote Tree of the utmost boundary; [15] close to the Garden of Abode; [16] while the Lote Tree was veiled (with great splendor).

[17] (Verily,) the (Prophet's) sight did not deceive him, nor did it swerve. [18] Truly did he see some of the most greatest (and profound) signs of his Lord. [19] Can anything as such be considered true of Al-Lat, Al-'Uzza; [20] as well as Manaat - the third and the last of this triad (of idols)?

[21] Why is it (that you choose only) male offspring for yourselves whereas to God (you assign) females? [22] That indeed, is certainly an unfair assignment! [23] These (alleged divine beings) are nothing but empty names invented by yourselves and your forefathers, for which God has not sent down any authority (for you to do so). They (who worship these false gods) follow nothing but conjecture and what their souls fancy, even though guidance has already come to them from their Lord. [24] Does man think that he could have whatever he wishes for; [25] (despite the fact that everything) that is in the life to come and this present one belongs to God alone?

Nothing Avails Against Truth

[26] And how many Angels are there in the heavens whose intercession will not benefit anyone except after God has given permission to whom He wills and approves? [27] Indeed, those who do not believe in the life to come assign the Angels with female names. [28] And since they have no knowledge about what they assert, they follow nothing but conjecture. Yet, conjecture is no substitute for truth. [a]

---

[a] Throughout the ages, religion has been subjected to much abuse, distortion, and corruption. Myths and superstitions have crept into many religious beliefs, bringing religion into direct conflict with science, whereas they are both in fact fully compatible with one another and serve as legitimate means for seeking the ultimate truth. Human manipulations have distorted the original and pristine divine message and Islam has not been spared from this too. Distortion and tampering have crept into some Islamic doctrines, literature, and thought, where claims were made that Prophet Muhammad had once praised the Makkan idols and approved of their veneration. Fortunately, such claims have been completely disproved by rigorous and meticulous study. Religious knowledge is absolute knowledge, upheld and protected by divine revelation, based on rational argument and common sense. Any religious proposition or argument that does not stand up to rational and intellectual examination is not worthy of consideration.

²⁹ So turn away from those who turn away from Our reminder, for they do not desire anything except the (temporary enjoyments in the fleeting) life of this world. ³⁰ The extent of their knowledge does not go beyond this. Indeed, only your Lord knows who strays from His path and who is rightly guided. ³¹ And to God belongs all that is in the heavens and the earth. He will requite the evildoers for their misdeeds and reward those who do good with the best.

³² As for those who avoid grave sins and shameful indecencies even though they may sometimes stumble (and commit lesser ones), behold! Your Lord is vast in forgiveness. ᵃ He knows everything about you from the time He brought you into being out of the earth, and when you were still (hidden as) fetuses in your mothers' bellies. So do not claim yourselves to be pure (and be infatuated by your self-importance). He knows best who is truly conscious of Him (and earnestly strives to improve themselves).

Man is Only Entitled to What He Strives For

³³ (O Prophet!) Did you not see the one who turned away (from God's path); ³⁴ and spent very little (in God's cause out of the bounty he was graced with) and then withheld (stingily until his heart becomes hardened)? ³⁵ Does he have knowledge of the unseen and can see (the unknown)? ᵇ ³⁶ Was he not told about what is in the Scriptures of Moses; ³⁷ and of Abraham who fulfilled (his duty)?

³⁸ (Verily,) no soul will be made to bear the burden of another; (hence, no one should ever expect his burden of sin to be borne by others). ³⁹ (Behold!) Man will have nothing except what he strives for. ᶜ ⁴⁰ And in time, (the fruit of) his labor will soon come in sight; ⁴¹ whereupon he will be fully requited for it. ⁴² (Therefore O men! Be mindful) that it is with your Lord where all journeys will finally end.

ᵃ This passage confirms man's weakness and vulnerability to fall victim to his desires and prejudices. Sensible believers should always be on their guard and look to God's guidance and grace to save them from falling by the wayside. They should also be ever ready to respond to God's call and seek His pleasure out of a desire to elevate and purify their souls and liberate themselves from greed and caprice.

ᵇ These characteristic features are typical of those who reject faith in God. They arrogantly refuse to acknowledge God, look down upon others and display a sense of selfishness and self-regard.

ᶜ Personal accountability is a fundamental Islamic principle. No one can absolve his sins by transferring them to others. Hence, the idea of God sacrificing his only son - Jesus, to be killed on the cross to atone for the sins of humanity and that only those who believe in this can enter Paradise is categorically rejected by Islam.

⁴³ (Verily,) He is the One Who makes one laugh and weep; ⁴⁴ and He is the One Who causes death and grants life; ⁴⁵ and He is the One Who has created pairs of male and female; ⁴⁶ from a clot of semen when it is ejaculated. *ᵃ* ⁴⁷ And upon Him is the power to bring forth life for the second time; ⁴⁸ and it is He Who enriches and suffices; ⁴⁹ and it is He too Who is the Lord of Sirius. *ᵇ*

Submit to God Before it is Too Late

⁵⁰ And it is He Who destroyed the ancient tribes of 'Aād. ⁵¹ And of the people of Tsamud, He spared none; ⁵² as well as the people of Noah before them. Indeed, they were unjust and rebellious. ⁵³ And He completely destroyed the cities that He overturned; *ᶜ* ⁵⁴ and then covered them from sight forever. ⁵⁵ So which of your Lord's powers will you doubt?

⁵⁶ (Hence,) this (Messenger who is being sent to you now) is indeed a warner just like the warners of earlier times; ⁵⁷ (to caution men that) the Imminent Hour is drawing nearer; ⁵⁸ (and) there is none except God Who can unveil (when its arrival will be).

⁵⁹ Do you then, find this statement strange; ⁶⁰ and still laugh instead of weep; ⁶¹ and continue to keep yourselves in meaningless amusement? ⁶² (Nay! It is time that you should) prostrate yourselves before God and (devote your) worship to Him (alone).

ᵃ It was not until 1905 when an American geneticist by the name of Nettie Stevens discovered the chromosomal XY sex-determination system (i.e. the fact that males have XY sex chromosomes and females have XX sex chromosomes). Primarily, sex determination occurs at fertilization and depends upon the type of sex chromosome in the sperm that fertilizes an ovum. If it is an 'X' bearing sperm that fertilizes the ovum, the fetus is a female and if it is a 'Y' bearing sperm then the fetus is a male. The Qur'an points out clearly in this verse that sex of a fetus is determined by the nature of the sperm and not of the ovum i.e. *"from the clot of semen when it is ejaculated"*. This accurate pronouncement was made in the 7ᵗʰ century without the support of any scientific data that was of course unavailable at that time. This cannot be possible unless the pronouncement was made by the Creator of man Himself.
ᵇ The Qur'an calls this *Ash-Shi'ra*. Ibn Kathir in his commentary said "it is the bright star, named *Mirzam Al-Jawza'* (Sirius), which some Arab pagans used to worship."
ᶜ Sodom and Gomorrah.

54. Al-Qamar
[The Moon : 55 verses]

This is a Makkan chapter, which deals with the fundamentals of faith, such as resurrection, judgment, reward and punishment. It starts with a reference to the splitting of the moon that will occur before the coming of the Last Hour. The name of this chapter is taken from here. Mention is also made about the many nations of the past that rejected the message of guidance that was delivered to them and how God's wrath and punishment befell them. Finally the treatment of the disbelievers on the Day of Judgment is contrasted to the everlasting bliss the believers will enjoy.

In the name of God, the Most Gracious, the Most Compassionate.

Ignore Those Who Deny the Truth

¹ The Last Hour has drawn near and the moon split asunder.

² Yet whenever the disbelievers see any (miraculous) sign, they turn away and say, "Same old magic!" ³ They denied it and continued to follow their whims and vain desires. But everything has its time (and truth will surely trounce falsehood).

⁴ Indeed, stories (of doomed nations in the past) that should deter them (from transgression) have been conveyed (clearly); ⁵ with far-reaching wisdom. But such warnings (and reminders) mean nothing to them. *ᵃ* ⁶ So turn away from them (O Prophet. Verily,) on that (dreadful) Day (when everyone is resurrected), a Caller will summon them to a most horrifying event. ⁷ With eyes downcast, they will come forth from their graves like swarming locusts; ⁸ rushing (in panic and horror) towards the Caller, crying, "This is (truly) a woeful Day (for us)!"

The Fate of The Past Deniers of Truth

⁹ Before (your people O Prophet), the people of Noah also denied (the

---

ᵃ For anyone to respond to God's call, his conscience must be alive and his heart must be pure. This is what the Qur'an terms as *fitrah*. Without this, man will not be able to discern between right and wrong, truth and falsehood. He could either be directly perpetrating injustice or become an indirect supporter of injustice without realizing it. Either way, he is devoid from any feeling of sorry and remorse by being a party to transgression and oppression. He may even be someone who appears religious from the outside but is ignorantly violating God's prohibitions at the same time.

truth). They rejected Our servant, called him a madman and drove him out (from his community). [10] Thereupon he called out to his Lord, "Verily I am vanquished. Help me." [11] So We opened the gates of heaven with water pouring down (in torrents); [12] and We caused the earth to burst forth with springs, so both waters (from above them and under their feet) met to fulfill a predestined end. [13] And We carried him on an ark made of planks and nails; [14] which floated under Our supervision, a reward for him who was denied (by his own people who rejected the truth).

[15] And We have certainly left the ark as a sign (for people to take lesson from). But why won't anyone take heed (of it)? [16] How (dreadful) was My punishment when My warnings (were disregarded)! [17] We have certainly made the Qur'an easy to (take to heart and) remember. But why won't anyone take heed (of it)?

[18] Likewise, the people of 'Aād denied (the truth too). How (dreadful) was My punishment when My warnings (were disregarded)! [19] Indeed, We sent upon them a furious wind on a day of continuous calamity; [20] it swept the people away as though they were stumps of uprooted date-palms. [21] How (dreadful) was My punishment when My warnings (were disregarded)! [22] We have certainly made the Qur'an easy to (take to heart and) remember. But why won't anyone take heed (of it)?

[23] The people of Tsamud denied the warnings too. [24] They asked, "Why should we follow a mortal who stands alone among us? *a* That would surely be a gross error and madness! [25] Why would the (divine) reminder be sent to him alone out of all of us? Nay! He is nothing but a presumptuous and boastful liar (who is only trying to gain our attention)!" [26] (So We told Our Messenger - Saleh,) "Tomorrow they will know who the boastful liar is. [27] Behold, We are sending a she-camel as a trial for them. So watch them in patience. [28] And inform them that the water is to be shared between them (and the she-camel) with each taking turns to drink (every other day)."

[29] But they summoned the (boldest) companion among them and he cruelly killed (the she-camel) [30] How (dreadful) was My punishment when My warnings (were disregarded)! [31] Verily, We sent upon them a single thunderous blast and they became like fragments of dry twigs that are used by a fence maker. [32] We have certainly made the Qur'an easy to (take to heart and) remember. But why won't anyone take heed (of it)?

---

a See verse 64:6. It is in the nature of most people to look down upon those who are regarded as average members of the society that do not have authority, wealth and high social status. The same was also with the Israelites who objected to Saul when God made him their ruler. See verse 2:247.

[33] Likewise, the people of Lot denied the warnings too. [34] Verily, We sent upon them a hailstorm which spared no one except Lot's household, whom We saved by early dawn; [35] as a blessing from Us. That is how We reward the grateful. [36] Lot had warned them of Our seizure but they doubted the warnings; [37] and even demanded that he gave up his guests to them. Hence, We deprived them of their sight and said, Now taste My punishment from the warnings (I gave earlier)!" [38] So, the punishment that We decreed upon them came early in the morning. [39] (They were told again), "Now taste My punishment from the warnings (I gave earlier)!" [40] We have certainly made the Qur'an easy to (take to heart and) remember. But why won't anyone take heed (of it)?

[41] And certainly the warnings came to the people of Pharaoh too. [42] They denied all Our signs, so We seized them with a (dreadful) seizure of the Almighty, the Most Powerful.

[43] Are your disbelievers better than those (whom We have narrated here) or did the Scriptures promise you any special immunity (from Our punishment)? [44] Or do they say, "We are a united front that will protect one another (and will surely prevail!)"? [45] Soon, their united front will be defeated and they will turn their backs (in flight). [46] Nay! The Last Hour is indeed their promised time and it will be most grievous and bitter.

[47] Verily, those who are lost in sin (will know at that time that it is they who were sunk) in error and madness (instead of those who they used to mock and deride). [48] On the Day when they will be dragged into the Fire on their faces, they will be told, "Taste (now) the touch of Hell (which you used to ridicule before)!"

[49] Verily, We created everything in exact measure (and proportion). [50] And not is Our command except in a single word, executed in the blink of an eye.

[51] (O you who deny the truth!) We have indeed destroyed many like you (in the past). Why won't anyone take heed (of this warning)? [52] Everything they have done is inscribed in their records; [53] every action, small and big, is (accurately) noted.

[54] Indeed, the righteous will dwell in the midst of gardens and running streams; [55] seated in a place of true honor in the presence of The Most Powerful Sovereign.

55. Ar-Raḥmān
[The Most Gracious : 78 verses]

This is a Makkan chapter which deals with the fundamentals of faith, especially the Qur'an's revelation, God's innumerable favors upon man and all His creatures, the Hereafter, judgment, reward and punishment. It starts with the emphasis that God has sent down and taught the Qur'an, which is His most perfect favor, to man. It then draws attention to His creation and many other favors, interspersed with the challenge : "So which of the blessings of your Lord do you both wish to deny (O Jinn and men)?" that is repeated 31 times in this chapter. It is named *Ar-Raḥmān* after the first verse which is God's most distinguished attribute and the chapter's main theme.

In the name of God, the Most Gracious, the Most Compassionate.

Divine Beneficence

¹ The Most Gracious (Lord); ² taught the Qur'an; ³ created man; ⁴ and taught him speech. *ᵃ* ⁵ (At His command,) the sun and the moon follow their precisely calculated courses; ⁶ and the stars and the trees both prostrate *ᵇ* (to Him alone in full submission).

ᵃ One of God's most gracious blessings to mankind is to provide the guidance on how to live in this world. The Qur'an encompasses all previous revelations received by earlier Prophets and Messengers. Its supreme teachings, principles, and ideas help mankind to lead a fulfilled life for all time to come. This knowledge and guidance come in the form of divine revelation to His final Messenger, Muhammad bin Abdullah expressed at the end of verse 4:113 as follows: "And it is God Who has bestowed upon you (O Muhammad) His divine revelation and wisdom, and He taught you what you knew not." In addition, the Qur'an is also a blessing to all who study and teach it to others. Prophet Muhammad was reported to have said, "The best among you is he who learns the Qur'an and teaches it." [Sahih Bukhari, no. 5027] The noble act of learning and teaching the Qur'an is a continuation of the excellent tradition of God's Messengers and a commendable contribution to the enlightenment and education of individuals and communities. Incidentally, the gift of language is another divine blessing and unique feature to man that enables him to present ideas and concepts articulately, and communicate with one another effectively.

ᵇ This of course does not refer to the act of prostration in its literal sense. Rather, it metaphorically refers to how all creations obediently submit themselves in their own respective ways to the Almighty God Who created them.

[7] He raised the heaven high and set a (perfect) balance (for everything); [8] No one should corrupt the balance (He has set). [9] So weigh everything accurately (in your trade) and do not cheat the scale.

[10] And He spread out the earth for all living things; [11] in it are fruits and palm trees with dates in sheaths; [12] and fragrant grains with husks [13] So which of the blessings of your Lord do you both wish to deny (O Jinn and men)?

[14] He created man from dry clay like pottery; [15] and Jinn from the smokeless flame of fire. [16] So which of the blessings of your Lord do you both wish to deny (O Jinn and men)?

[17] He is the Lord of the two (farthest points of) sunrise, and the Lord of the two (farthest points of) sunset (in summer and winter). [18] So which of the blessings of your Lord do you both wish to deny (O Jinn and men)?

[19] It is He Who let loose the two seas so that they would meet and mix with each other; [20] yet between them is a barrier that prevents them from crossing over. [a] [21] So which of the blessings of your Lord do you both wish to deny (O Jinn and men)? [22] Pearls and corals come forth from both of them. [23] So which of the blessings of your Lord do you both wish to deny (O Jinn and men)? [24] And to Him belong the ships elevated in the sea like floating mountains. [25] So which of the blessings of your Lord do you both wish to deny (O Jinn and men)?

Judgment of the Guilty

[26] (Verily,) all that is on earth will perish; [27] but your Lord Himself - the

---

[a] In addition to the miraculous revelation regarding the existence of a barrier that separates fresh water from sea water (see 25:53), the Qur'an also mentions about another scientific miracle in this verse and also in 27:61 about the existence of a barrier in the ocean where the Mediterranean sea and the Atlantic ocean meet. Modern science has confirmed that this barrier divides these two seas to preserve the temperature, salinity, and density of each sea. The Mediterranean sea water is warm, saline, and less dense, compared to Atlantic ocean water. When the Mediterranean sea enters the Atlantic over the Gibraltar Sill, it moves several hundred kilometers into the Atlantic at a depth of about 1000 meters with its own warm, saline, and less dense characteristics. The Mediterranean water stabilizes at this depth. Although there are large waves, strong currents, and tides in these seas, they do not mix or pass this barrier. How could an illiterate man who lived in the desert of Arabia 15 centuries ago who has never seen, let alone been to any ocean, speak about this miraculous scientific fact at a place so far away from him if he was not divinely inspired?

absolute Owner of Majesty and Glory - will remain (forever). ²⁸ So which of
the blessings of your Lord do you both wish to deny (O Jinn and men)?
²⁹ Every creature in the heavens and the earth is dependent on Him; and He is
constantly governing and regulating all their affairs every moment. ³⁰ So
which of the blessings of your Lord do you both wish to deny (O Jinn and
men)?

³¹ (In time,) We shall take you to task (and hold you accountable for
everything that you have done), O you two (sin laden) creatures. ³² So which
of the blessings of your Lord do you both wish to deny (O Jinn and men)?

³³ O assembly of Jinn and men! If you are able to penetrate beyond the
regions of the heavens and the earth, then do so. But you will (most certainly)
not be able to penetrate beyond them without (your Lord's) authority (and
permission). ³⁴ So which of the blessings of your Lord do you both wish to
deny (O Jinn and men)?

³⁵ The flames of fire and smoke will be let loose upon you (on the Day of
Judgment), and you will not be able to defend yourselves. ³⁶ So which of the
blessings of your Lord do you both wish to deny (O Jinn and men)? ³⁷ And
when the heaven is split asunder (on that Day), it will become reddish like
murky oil. ³⁸ So which of the blessings of your Lord do you both wish to deny
(O Jinn and men)?

³⁹ Then on that Day, neither man nor Jinn will be asked about his sin.
⁴⁰ So which of the blessings of your Lord do you both wish to deny (O Jinn
and men)? ⁴¹ (Instead,) the sinners will be recognized by their marks, and they
will be seized by their forelocks and feet. ⁴² So which of the blessings of your
Lord do you both wish to deny (O Jinn and men)?

⁴³ (Now,) this is Hell, which the sinners (used to) deny. ⁴⁴ They will keep
wandering around (aimlessly) between (the flames of) Hell and scalding water.
⁴⁵ So which of the blessings of your Lord do you both wish to deny (O Jinn
and men)?

Reward that Awaits the Righteous

⁴⁶ But for those who (live their lives righteously because they) fear the
moment when they will have to stand before their Lord, two gardens are
reserved for them. ⁴⁷ So which of the blessings of your Lord do you both wish
to deny (O Jinn and men)? ⁴⁸ Both (gardens that are) abound with (shady trees
and lush) branches. ⁴⁹ So which of the blessings of your Lord do you both wish
to deny (O Jinn and men)?

⁵⁰ In both of them are two springs, flowing. ⁵¹ So which of the blessings of your Lord do you both wish to deny (O Jinn and men)? ⁵² In both of them too are every kind of fruit in pairs. ⁵³ So which of the blessings of your Lord do you both wish to deny (O Jinn and men)? ⁵⁴ And they (who dwell) in these gardens will recline on couches lined with brocade, and the fruits in there will be within their reach. ⁵⁵ So which of the blessings of your Lord do you both wish to deny (O Jinn and men)?

⁵⁶ In the midst of these will be maidens with modest, restrained glances; maidens whom no man or Jinn has ever touched. ⁵⁷ So which of the blessings of your Lord do you both wish to deny (O Jinn and men)? ⁵⁸ (They are as) lovely as rubies and pearls. ⁵⁹ So which of the blessings of your Lord do you both wish to deny (O Jinn and men)? ⁶⁰ Can the reward of goodness be any other than goodness itself? ⁶¹ So which of the blessings of your Lord do you both wish to deny (O Jinn and men)?

⁶² Besides these two, are two other gardens. ⁶³ So which of the blessings of your Lord do you both wish to deny (O Jinn and men)? ⁶⁴ That are dark green in color. ⁶⁵ So which of the blessings of your Lord do you both wish to deny (O Jinn and men)? ⁶⁶ In both of them are two springs gushing forth. ⁶⁷ So which of the blessings of your Lord do you both wish to deny (O Jinn and men)? ⁶⁸ In both of them are fruits, and date-palms and pomegranates. ⁶⁹ So which of the blessings of your Lord do you both wish to deny (O Jinn and men)?

⁷⁰ In each of them, there will be chaste and beautiful maidens. ⁷¹ So which of the blessings of your Lord do you both wish to deny (O Jinn and men)? ⁷² Fair damsels sheltered in their pavilions. ⁷³ So which of the blessings of your Lord do you both wish to deny (O Jinn and men)? ⁷⁴ Whom no man or Jinn has ever touched. ⁷⁵ So which of the blessings of your Lord do you both wish to deny (O Jinn and men)? ⁷⁶ (They will all be) reclining on green cushions and carpets that are most beautiful. ⁷⁷ So which of the blessings of your Lord do you both wish to deny (O Jinn and men)?

⁷⁸ Blessed is the name of your Lord, Owner of (all) Majesty and Glory.

56. Al-Wāqiʻah
[The Inevitable Event : 96 verses]

This is a Makkan chapter. Its main theme here is the inevitability of the Day of Judgment where its name is taken from. On that day, people will be classified into three groups - those gathered on the right are the ordinary believers, those gathered on the left are the disbelievers, and those brought near to God are the best of the believers. Proof is also given in the form of God's wondrous creations that man is asked to ponder and relate to His power and ability to bring about Resurrection.

In the name of God, the Most Gracious, the Most Compassionate.

Three Classes of Men

¹ When the Inevitable Event finally occurs; ² no one can deny (nor prevent) its occurrence. ³ Some will be debased and some exalted. *ᵃ* ⁴ (And so,) when the earth will be shakened to its depths with a violent convulsion; ⁵ and the mountains will be crumbled and crushed into dust; ⁶ and scattered like dust particles; *ᵇ* ⁷ you will be divided into three groups.

⁸ (The first group comprises) the companions of the right. Who are they? (They are those who believe and are truly blessed.) ⁹ And (the second group comprises) the companions of the left. Who are they? (They are those who have lost themselves in evil and will be damned.)

The Foremost

¹⁰ And (the final group comprises) those who were foremost (in striving in God's cause and in performing good deeds during their stay on earth, it is they who) will also be the foremost (to enjoy God's grace in the life to come). ¹¹ They are the ones (who will be drawn) nearest (to God); ¹² in the Gardens of Bliss (on that Day).

ᵃ Things will be put aright and justice will prevail on the Day of Resurrection. Many emperors, kings and leaders of nations who have been adorned in this world and enjoyed the best privileges may be resurrected a pauper and debased if they were oblivious of this fateful day and did not make preparations to face it. At the same time, others who were unknown and undistinguished but abided by the true teachings of the Qur'an and took the Prophet as their role model will be raised and exalted to the loftiest positions on that day.
ᵇ See verses 20:105-107.

[13] (Most of them are) people of earlier times; [14] and a few of later times. [15] They will be seated on decorated couches; [16] reclining, and facing one another. [17] And they will be waited upon by immortal youths; [18] with vessels, jugs and cups filled with drink from a flowing stream; [19] that will neither pain their heads nor take away their senses.

[20] They will also have fruits of their own choice; [21] and the flesh of fowl of what they desire; [22] and fair maidens with lustrous eyes; [23] as lovely as well guarded pearls; [24] as a reward for their good deeds. [25] In (these Gardens), they will neither hear vain talk nor sinful speech; [26] but only the greetings of, "Peace (be upon you)! Peace (be upon you)!"

The Companions of the Right

[27] And the companions of the right. Who are they? [28] They will be amidst Lote trees, stripped of thorns; [29] and banana trees layered (with fruits); [30] and extended shade; [31] and water in constant flow; [32] and abundant fruit; [33] whose season is not limited nor its supply forbidden; [34] and will be reclining on high raised couches.

[35] Indeed, We have produced their spouses in a new creation; [36] and made them virgins, pure and undefiled; [37] devoted and equal in age; [38] for the companions of the right; [39] who are (righteous) people of the earlier times; [40] and also (righteous) people of the later times.

The Companions of the Left

[41] And the companions of the left. Who are they? [42] They will find themselves in the midst of scorching fire and scalding water; [43] and a shade of black smoke; [44] neither cool nor pleasant.

[45] Indeed, they were before that, living in a life that was fully devoted to the pursuit of wealth (and worldly pleasures); [46] and were persistent in heinous sins. [47] And they used to mock, "When we die and become soil and bones, will we really be resurrected; [48] together with our forefathers too?"

[49] Say (to them), "Indeed, the earlier and the later people; [50] will all be (resurrected and) brought together on an appointed time of a known Day (only to God). [51] And then verily, O you who have gone astray and denied the truth! [52] You will surely eat from the tree of *Zaqqum*; [53] then you will fill your bellies with it; [54] and along with it you will drink scalding water; [55] just as thirsty camels do." [56] Such will be their welcome on Judgment Day.

Signs to Ponder

[57] (O mankind!) It is We Who created you. So why do you not (want to believe and) accept the truth (about resurrection when We tell you so)? [a] [58] Have you ever considered (the semen) which you emit? [59] Is it you or We who created it? [60] We have indeed decreed that death will be ever-present among you and there is nothing to prevent Us; [61] from changing the nature of your existence and creating you again in a form that is unknown to you. [62] And (since) you are certainly aware of your first (miraculous) creation, why do you not reflect (and draw any lesson from it)?

[63] Have you considered the seeds you sow (in the soil)? [64] Is it you or We who cause them to grow (from the ground)? [65] If We so wished, We could have reduced your harvest to rubble, and you would have been left wonder-struck (exclaiming); [66] "Indeed, we are laden with debt (and we are surely ruined). [67] In fact, we are now deprived (of our livelihood)."

[68] Did you cast a good look at the water that you drink? [69] Is it you who brought it down from the clouds or is it We? [70] If We wanted, We could have made it salty. So why are you not grateful (to Us)?

[71] Have you considered the fire which you kindle? [72] Is it you or We who created the tree (for use as firewood)? [b] [73] We made it as a reminder (of one of Our favors to you) and (a useful tool as) provision for travelers. [74] So proclaim and glorify your Lord's perfection by mentioning His name (abundantly, for He is indeed) the Greatest.

---

[a] The frequent reminders of resurrection in the Qur'an are not meant as a threat to human civilization or to thwart human progress as understood by those who are ignorant. Rather, they are aimed at breaking man's false pride and egoistic ambitions, and to control his desires and moderate his arrogance. It also serves as a deterrent from committing injustice and causing hardship to others. A normal person with enough common sense will believe in resurrection and the ensuing God's final judgment. He would not forfeit a life of eternal bliss and the rich rewards of the Hereafter in exchange for short-term unrestrained enjoyment in this world. Regrettably, there are more skeptics and disbelievers who completely discard and ignore the belief in the Hereafter. This is a prevalent feature of modern civilization which is the root cause of all the evil and destruction in the world today because the fear of accountability to God and the judgment that awaits people in the Hereafter are not present in them. Therefore, the need to remind people, especially the Muslims who have lost their way, of the certainty of resurrection and the Day of Judgment must never cease. See also the footnote for verse 59:19.

[b] See verse 36:80 and its corresponding footnote.

Judgment is Inevitable

[75] And so! I swear by the setting of the stars. [76] This is indeed a mighty oath, if only you knew (its magnitude)! [77] Verily, this is truly a noble discourse; [78] (conveyed to mankind) in a Book that is well-preserved (in heaven); [79] which none but the pure (of heart) can touch (and derive benefit from). [80] (It is a divine revelation) sent down (part by part) from the Lord of all the worlds. [81] So why do you look down with disdain on a message like this; [82] and (in return for) the provision you are given, you deny (and oppose the Giver)?

[83] (If you think you are not accountable to Us), why don't you (hold back the soul of a dying person) when it reaches his throat? [84] Yet, you (can only) watch (helplessly) at that moment. [85] (The truth is,) We are nearer to him than you, but you are (too stubborn to) see this. [86] So if you still think you are free from Us, why can't you; [87] bring the soul back (to the lifeless body) if you (really think you) are right? [a]

[88] (Verily, all of you are destined to die.) But for the one who is brought close (to God); [89] then for him awaits tranquility, a pleasing atmosphere and a Garden of Bliss (in the life to come). [90] And if he is among the companions of the right; [91] then he will be greeted, "Peace (be upon you)!" from the other companions of the right. [92] But if he is among the deniers (of truth) and those who had gone astray; [93] then the welcome of scalding water (awaits him); [94] together with the burning of the Hellfire.

[95] Indeed, this is surely the absolute truth. [96] So proclaim and glorify your Lord's perfection by mentioning His name (abundantly, for He is indeed) the Most Great.

---

[a] Death is the most profound truth. But being totally preoccupied with day-to-day lives and worldly affairs, the majority of people cannot think beyond their material or physical existence. Because of this, many people are skeptical about resurrection and are quite adamant in their belief that death is the end of their existence. Today's dead are buried by those who will die one day too, and yet the latter continue to ignore death and live as if it will not happen to them. It seldom moves them to think or reflect on their convictions or conduct. By his very nature, man is argumentative, contentious, and stubborn. As generations succeed generations, skeptics and disbelievers throughout the world seem to grow and increase, and become more vociferous. But once they face death, the curtain will fall and nothing will be able to stop it. What lies ahead of them will be the rudest awakening which they had arrogantly rejected and never expected it to come true.

57. Al-Ḥadīd
[Iron : 29 verses]

T his is a Madinan chapter. It starts by mentioning that everything in the heavens and the earth proclaims God's sanctity and glorifies His perfection. It also points out that the worldly life is only a delusion and a fleeting enjoyment which is only temporary in nature. The all-pervasiveness of God's power, knowledge, control, and glory is further affirmed in the chapter to encourage the believers spend in His cause and uphold justice. The chapter is named *Al-Ḥadīd* or The Iron with reference to verse 25 where mention is made of this metal as one of God's special gifts that is of immense importance to man.

In the name of God, the Most Gracious,
the Most Compassionate.

The Dominion of God

¹ Everything in the heavens and the earth (proclaims and) glorifies God's perfection, and He is indeed the Almighty, the All-Wise. ² To Him belongs the dominion of the heavens and the earth, He gives life and causes death, and He has absolute power over everything. ³ He is the First and the Last; the Manifest and the Hidden; and He has full knowledge of everything.

⁴ He is the One Who created the heavens and the earth in six phases, and then firmly established Himslelf on His (Supreme) Throne. He knows everything that enters and comes out of the earth, what descends from the heaven and what ascends to it. He is with you wherever you are and sees everything you do. ⁵ To Him belongs the dominion of the heavens and the earth, and all affairs return to God (for final judgment).

⁶ He makes the night enter into the day and the day into the night, and He fully knows everything that is hidden in the heart. ⁷ (Therefore O mankind,) believe in God and His Messenger and spend in charity out of the wealth that He has entrusted to you. (Verily,) a great reward awaits those who are truly faithful among you and spend (regularly) in charity.

⁸And why should you not have faith in God's (promise) when the Messenger has been (untiringly) calling you to believe in your Lord? Did you not enter into a covenant with Him (during your pre-earthly existence *

ᵃ This reminder is not directed to the disbelievers alone during the time of the Prophet but rather to all mankind too. See verse 7:172 and its corresponding footnote for further explanation.

pledging your faith in Him? So why should you not believe in Him now) if you are able to believe (in other things)? ⁹ He is the One Who sends down upon His servant *a* clear revelations to bring you out from darkness into light. And indeed, God is Most Kind and Most Compassionate to you.

¹⁰ And what is the matter with you that you do not want to spend in God's cause when it is He alone Who will inherit everything that is in the heavens and the earth? Not equal among you are those who spent and fought before the conquest (of Makkah) and those who did so afterwards. They are surely greater in rank. Yet to all, God has promised good reward. And God is All-Aware of what you do.

The Righteous and Their Light

¹¹ Who is it that will lend to God a goodly loan (for His cause) which He will multiply for him and grant a noble reward (on the Day of Reckoning)? ¹² On that Day, you will see the believers - both men women - with their light streaming ahead of them on their right side; (and will be told, "There is) good news for you today! Gardens which rivers flow right beneath them (awaits you) as your permanent home." That is indeed the greatest success!

¹³ On that Day (too), the hypocrites - both men and women - will say to those who believe, "Wait for us! Share with us some of your light." But they will be told, "Go back and seek your own light!" Between them will be a wall with a gate that is erected. Within it is grace and mercy, and outside it is punishment and suffering.

¹⁴ Those (outside the wall) will cry out to those inside it, "Were we not together with you (before)?" They will be told, "Yes, but you brought destruction upon yourselves (by being hypocrites). You were hesitant (in your faith) and doubted (the truth). Indeed, your wishful fancies deceived you until God's command came to pass. Verily, your own deceptive thoughts about God have certainly beguiled you! ¹⁵ So no ransom will be accepted from you today nor from those who had rejected the truth. The Fire of Hell will be your home and it will be your only refuge. How wretched it is as the (final) destination!"

¹⁶ Has the moment not yet arrived for the hearts of believers to become humble at the remembrance of God and at the truth that has been sent down so that they would not become like those who were granted revelation before this whose hearts became hardened with the passing of time? Many of them were

---

a Prophet Muhammad.

indeed disobedient. *^a*

¹⁷ Notice that God restores the earth to life after it is dead (with His grace by sending down rain). Verily, We have made Our signs clear to you so that you may use common sense (to ponder and turn to your Lord in total submission and devotion).

¹⁸ Indeed, as for the men and women who spend in charity and who lend to God a good loan (for His cause), its return will be multiplied for them and they will have a noble reward (in the life to come). ¹⁹ Those who believe in God and His Messengers are people of true words and deeds. They are the witnesses (and upholders) of truth in the sight of their Lord and will be given their reward and light (in the Hereafter). But those who disbelieve and deny Our signs and revelations will be (condemned as) the inmates of Hellfire.

Truth Will be Established

²⁰ (O mankind!) Know that the life of this world is nothing but play and amusement - an adornment and a cause of boasting among you - and rivalry in the quest for greater riches and more children. Like the parable of rain when it produces vegetation, their growth delights the sowers (in the beginning). But then it withers away and you see it turns yellow, and eventually crumbles away as debris. (So be mindful that) in the life to come, there is either grievous punishment (in store for those who ignore and defy their Creator during their sojourn on earth), or forgiveness from Him and the reward of His good pleasure (for those who are always mindful of Him and strive hard in His

---

^a For faith to be genuine and sincere, it must be based on recognition of God together with kindness and compassion to others. In this regard, the behavior of the Israelites is a case in hand which should be taken as a lesson. Verse 5:13 reads, "And because they reneged on their pledge to God, We cursed them and caused their hearts to harden.." Harshness, cruelty, and haughtiness are incompatible to sound faith in God. Even though Muslims are being repeatedly reminded in the Qur'an against following the ways of the Israelites, many do not seem to pay attention and take heed of this advice. Some Muslim preachers who appear pious outwardly, tend to look down on other Muslims. Instead of inviting people to God's path with wisdom, they are loud and harsh, and are also quick to pass judgment on others as though they have been entrusted with the keys to Paradise. This only demoralizes people from practicing Islam properly and from fulfilling their obligations towards the religion. Humility, kindness and wisdom rather than arrogance and self-pride that are manifestations of a hardened heart, are the qualities that are needed to bring people to God's path for the world to be a better place for all.

cause). Indeed, the life of this world is nothing but the mere enjoyment of a delusion. (So, do not be deceived!) **²¹** Hence, vie with one another in seeking forgiveness from your Lord and to (secure for yourself a place in) a garden that its width is (as vast) as the heaven and the earth, prepared for those who believe in God and His Messengers. Such is the bounty of God and He gives it to whomsoever He wills (that submits to Him in true devotion). Verily, God is the Possessor of Great Bounty.

²² (Know that) there is not a single calamity of any kind that ever strikes the earth nor within yourselves except that it is (already inscribed and decreed) in Our Book before We make it manifest (as a means to test one's faith). Surely all this is easy for God (to do). **²³** (Understand this well) so that you will not despair over whatever (good) that has escaped you, nor proudly gloat over what He has given you. Verily, God does not love those who are self-conceited and boastful. **²⁴** They are stingy (with God's bounty) and tell others to be stingy (like them) too. Whoever turns away from the truth, (know that God does not have any need of him, for) God is indeed All-Sufficient, Immensely Praiseworthy.

²⁵ Certainly, We sent Our Messengers with clear evidence, and with them We sent down the Book and the balance (of justice and wisdom) so that men will uphold justice (and fairness among them. *a* As manifestation of Our grace), We sent down iron (to earth) *b* with awesome strength and (great)

---

a As clearly mentioned in this verse, God sent His Messengers and gave revelations commanding men to uphold justice and be fair to one another, regardless of race and religion. Professing faith in Islam is incomplete and meaningless if we allow injustice and double standard practices to prevail and condone this. See verses 5:8, 11:113, 49:13 and 107:4-7. According to the following *hadith* by the Prophet as reported by A'isha (who was one of the Prophet's wives), any nation and society is set for doom if its people allow injustice and double standard practice to prevail : "O people! Your predecessors were destroyed because a person of high social status among them would be spared from punishment if he stole. But when an ordinary and weak one among them committed theft, he was punished." [Sahih Muslim, no.1688].

b In 2005, the findings of a group of space scientists and astronomers were shown in a documentary film in The Discovery Channel titled "Miracle Planet - The Violent Past". The film was jointly produced by The National Film Board of Canada and NHK Japan (Japan Broadcasting Corp.) which explained how the earth took shape. According to the documentary, a continuous rain of meteorites and asteroids pounded the molten earth about 4.5 billion years ago during its infant stage when its size was only a tenth of what it is today. Each strike brought with it more rocks making our planet bigger and at the same time scattering metals over the surface. Then a giant asteroid crashed into the planet and gave earth its massive iron core. It sank towards the centre and attracted all the earth's metals to it as it went down. The lighter debris were cast off into

benefits for mankind so that God may make evident who among you (are grateful to His infinite bounty and) would help Him and His Messengers (in His cause), even though He is unseen. Surely, God is Most Strong, Truly Almighty.

Double Reward for the Believers

²⁶ And indeed We sent forth Noah and Abraham, and bestowed among their descendants Prophethood and the Book. Among them some were guided, but most of them were defiantly disobedient. ²⁷ Then We sent Our Messengers in their footsteps and after them We sent Isa son of Maryam whom We gave the Injeel to. We placed compassion and mercy in the hearts of those who followed his (true teachings) and did not prescribe a monastic life for them. (Some among them) invented this out of their own (misguided) desire for God's goodly acceptance but (erred in it, because) they did not observe what they did with due observance. So We rewarded only the true believers among the followers of Jesus while the rest remained defiantly disobedient .

²⁸ O you who believe! Always be mindful of God (and strive to keep your duty to Him diligently) and believe in His Messenger. Verily, God will give you a two-fold portion of His grace, whereupon He will make for you a guiding light that you will walk in and forgive you (of your past sins and errors). Indeed, God is Most Forgiving, Most Compassionate. ²⁹ (Such is decreed for you) so that the people of earlier revelation (who are in enmity with *Islam*) will know that they do not have the sole right to God's bounty (and favors). Indeed, all bounty is in His hand (alone) and He grants it to whomsoever He wills (among His servants). Verily, God is the absolute Owner of great (and infinite) bounty.

---

space and drawn into orbit around the enlarged planet. These fragments were eventually drawn together by gravity and finally formed the moon. How is it possible for an illiterate man who lived in the plain desert of Arabia during the 7th century knew for a fact that iron did not originate from the earth but was sent down from the sky instead? Another truly amazing fact to consider is why did these huge deadly asteroids suddenly stopped hitting the earth after human beings came into existence and are placed on this planet? Whose mighty power is it that has been protecting all the living beings on earth from these deadly asteroids if not the Ultimate Creator Himself? Is there then any valid reason to not submit to the Owner of the entire universe, reject His revelation of truth in the Qur'an, and refuse to take up the responsibility tasked by Him as His trustee to uphold justice on earth and make this planet prosperous for all of His creations to live in?

58. Al-Mujādalah
[The Petitioner : 22 verses]

This is a Madinan chapter which lays down a number of Islamic rules. It starts by proclaiming that the pre-Islamic custom of *zihar* which is to compare the wife's back with the back of the husband's mother does not constitute a proper divorce. The occasion leading to this ruling was recorded by God when a complaint was made by Khawlah bint Tha'labah to the Prophet against her husband who divorced her through this way. Dissatisfied with the Prophet's advice, she counter-argued and directed her complaint to God who then revealed a divine answer to address this matter conclusively. The chapter's name is taken from this particular occasion which is mentioned in its first verse. Next, the chapter speaks about the scheming of the hypocrites and Jews against the Muslims followed by a rebuke against the hypocrites for taking the Jews and enemies of the Muslims, as friends and allies. The chapter ends by emphasizing that a true believer will not befriend an enemy of God and His Messenger, even if such person is a family member or a close relative.

In the name of God, the Most Gracious, the Most Compassionate.

Safeguarding Women's Rights

¹ Indeed, God has heard the words of the one who pleaded with you concerning her husband's (action) and then directs her complaint to God. Verily, God hears the discourse between both of you. Indeed God is All-Hearing, All-Seeing.

² Those among you who divorce their wives by pronouncing *zihar* (saying, "You are to me like the back of my mother",[a] should know better that) their wives can never be (like) their mother, for none can ever be so except the one who gave birth to them. Indeed, they are surely uttering something despicable. But God is Most Pardoning, Most Forgiving (towards whoever that turns to Him in repentance and mend their ways).

---

[a] This commentary is taken from Muhammad Asad's Qur'an exegesis : "According to classical commentators, this is a reference to the case of Khawlah bint Tha'labah, whose husband Aws ibn as-Samit divorced her by pronouncing the arbitrary pre-Islamic oath known as *zihar* which deprived her of all her marital rights and at the same time made it impossible for her to remarry (as explained in the footnote of verse 33:4). When she pleaded to the Prophet against this divorce, the iniquitous custom of *zihar* was abolished by the revelation of verses 2-4 of this chapter."

³ (So for) those who pronounced *zihar* to their wives and (are then remorseful) and wish to go back on what they have said, (their redemption) is to free a slave before the couple may touch each other again. This is what you are hereby taught, and God is All-Aware of everything that you do. ⁴ Whoever does not have the means (to free a slave), he should fast for two (consecutive) months before he touches his wife again. But if he is not able to fast, then he must feed sixty needy ones. This is (commanded for you) to prove your (remorse in your action and) your true faith in God and in His Messenger, (and also to be more careful in your utterances after this). These are the bounds set by God. Grievous suffering awaits those who defy Him.

⁵ Indeed, those who oppose God and His Messenger will be disgraced like those before them (for stubbornly rejecting) the clear messages that We sent down. A humiliating punishment awaits those who reject the truth; ⁶ on the Day when God resurrects everyone and tell them everything that they have done (during their lifetime. Then, He will fairly requite them for all their deeds. Verily,) God has recorded everything they did even though they may have forgotten it, for God is a witness over all things.

Secret Counsels Condemned

⁷ Are you not aware that God knows all that is in the heavens and the earth? There is no secret talk among three people except He is the fourth, nor among five people except He is the sixth. Whether the number is fewer or more, He is (always) with them wherever they are. Then on the Day of Resurrection, He will tell them everything that they have done (during their lifetime). Indeed, God has full knowledge of everything.

⁸ Are you also not aware of those who have been forbidden from secret talks and yet (always) revert to what they have been forbidden from - which is to conspire in sin, aggression and disobedience against the Messenger? Yet when they come to you (O Prophet), they greet you with a greeting that even God does not greet you with; *ᵃ* and they say to themselves, "(If Muhammad is truly a Prophet,) then why does God not punish us (now) for what we say?" Hell is sufficient for them, in which they will burn forever. That is indeed the worst destination to end a journey!

ᵃ As an expression of disdain for the Prophet and the Muslims, some Jews in Madinah would play on the Arabic word *salām,* meaning "peace" in the greeting "*Assalāmu 'alaykum"* (i.e. Peace be upon you) by replacing it with *sām* instead, which means "death". The Prophet's wife A'ishah was the first to bring this dubious behavior to his attention but he chose to rise above it until the revelation of this verse.

⁹ O you who believe! When you hold private counsels, do not hold it (like the hypocrites do) for sin and aggression or disobedience against the Messenger, but do so for righteousness and piety. And be ever mindful of God, the One Whom you will all be finally gathered to. ¹⁰ Secret talks and scheming are (inspired) by none other than Satan to cause distress to the believers, but it will not harm anyone except by God's will. So let the believers place their full trust in God alone.

¹¹ O you who believe! When you are asked to make room (to accommodate others to join) in assemblies (that are held for noble causes), do so. *ᵃ* In return, God will make room for you (in His grace).*ᵇ* And when you are told to rise (for a good deed), do so too. Indeed, God will elevate the ranks of those among you who are firm in faith and endowed with knowledge, for God is well aware of everything that you do.

¹² O you who believe! Before you consult privately with God's Messenger, offer something in charity (to those who are in need). This will be for your own good and (more conducive to your spiritual) purity. But if you cannot afford, be assured that God is Most Forgiving, Most Compassionate. ¹³ Are you afraid that (you may be sinning if) you cannot offer any charity before you consult (with God's Messenger) privately? If you fail to do it (for lack of means, take comfort in knowing) that God has forgiven you. So attend to your prayer regularly and render the purifying dues (punctually), and (always) obey God and His Messenger, for God is All-Aware of what you do.

The Fate of the Hypocrites

¹⁴ Have you not noticed (how evil) are those (hypocrites) who have taken the people who have incurred God's wrath as their friends and allies? These (hypocrites) are neither with you, nor with those (who openly reject the

---

ᵃ Other than assemblies for that were held for educational or town hall purposes, Fakhruddin Razi - a well renowned Persian scholar who died in 1210 is in the opinion that the plural noun *majalis* or assemblies used here denotes the totality of men's social life. Taken in this sense, the expression "making room for one another" implies the providing of opportunities for a decent life to all members of the community, especially the needy and handicapped.

ᵇ "He who alleviates the suffering of others in this world, God would alleviate his suffering on the Day of Resurrection. He who helps to relieve the burden of someone who is hard-pressed with borrowings, God would make things easy for him in the Hereafter. And he who conceals the embarrassment of another person, God would conceal his embarrassment in the world and in the Hereafter." [Sahih Muslim, no. 2699]

Prophet's call to truth). They (do not have any sense of guilt or remorse when they) knowingly swear to lies and falsehood frequently.[a] 15 (Verily,) God has reserved severe punishment for them (in the life to come). Evil indeed are the things they do; 16 for making their oaths a (guise and) shield for their deceit, and for hindering others from God's path (by sowing doubts in people's hearts). Hence, a shameful punishment awaits them. 17 Neither their wealth nor their children will be able to ever avail (and help) them against God. They will be the Fire's inmates and will remain in it forever.

18 On the Day when God resurrects all of them (from their graves), they will swear to Him just like they swear to you (now pretending to be true believers), thinking that this will save them (from God's punishment). Behold! They are indeed the (greatest) liars.[b] 19 Satan has gained control over them and made them neglect the remembrance of God. Behold! They have indeed become a party of Satan, and the party of Satan will surely be the (greatest) losers.

20 Indeed, those who oppose God and His Messenger will be among the most humiliated (on the Day of Resurrection); 21 (for) God has decreed (and announced that) "Verily, it is I and My Messengers who will most certainly prevail!" Indeed, God is Most Strong, Almighty.

22 You will not find people who believe in God and the Last Day, loving those who are hostile towards God and His Messenger even though they may be their fathers, or their sons, or their brothers, or their close kin. They are the ones in whose hearts God has inscribed faith and whom He has strengthened with His (divine) inspiration. In time, He will admit them into gardens which rivers flow from right beneath them, where they will remain in there forever (as their permanent home). God is pleased with them and they are pleased with Him too. Verily, they are the party of God. Behold! Only those who belong to the party of God will be victorious!

---

[a] Hypocrisy is a vile social disease that poses a great threat to any society. A hypocrite would have no qualms about lying and perjuring himself in court.
[b] Those with a penchant to lie and cheat in this life will try to do the same in the Hereafter too, thinking that they can fool God.

59. Al-Ḥashr
[The Gathering : 24 verses]

This is a Madinan chapter. Its main theme is the expulsion of the Jewish tribe of Bani Nadir from Madinah in the 4th year of Hijra because of their treachery and conspiracy with the enemies of Islam to destroy the Muslims which included even a plot to kill the Prophet. They thought that their strong fortresses, military strength and secret alliance with hypocrites who promised them help will protect them. But God frustrated all their evil scheming and plots and they were rounded by the Muslim forces. With regard to this, rules for the administration of war spoils are also laid down in conjunction with the war spoils that the Muslim side gained from the expulsion of Bani Nadir. The chapter is named *Al-Ḥashr* or The Gathering in reference to its second verse which mentions about the gathering of Bani Nadir outside their fortresses as they were getting ready to leave Madinah. The chapter then draws attention to the Day of Judgment and it ends by mentioning some of the beautiful names and attributes of God.

In the name of God, the Most Gracious, the Most Compassionate.

The Exiled Jews

¹ Everything in the heavens and the earth (proclaims and) glorifies God's perfection, for He alone is the Almighty, the All-Wise. ² He is the One Who brought out those who opposed the truth among the people of earlier revelation *ᵃ* from their homes for the first gathering *ᵇ* (of expulsion because of their act of treason. O believers!) You did not expect them to leave without resistance just as they thought that their strongholds would protect them against God. But God came upon them in a manner they had not expected and cast panic into their hearts. (Hence) they destroyed their homes with their own hands together with the hands of the believers. So take a lesson from this, O people who are endowed with insight!

³ And if God had not decreed exile for them, He would have certainly punished them (with a greater suffering) in this world. Still in the life to come, the (ultimate) punishment of the Fire awaits them. ⁴ That is because they

---

ᵃ The Jewish tribe of Bani Nadir.

ᵇ The second gathering presumably took place during the time of Umar al-Khattab's rule as the second Caliph when he exiled the Jewish tribes of Khaybar and Fadak that lived within the area of Al-Hijaz surrounding Makkah, Madinah and Al-Yamamah to Tayma (about 400 km north of Madinah) and Ariha (which is also known as Jericho in Palestine today).

opposed (and rebelled against) God and His Messenger. Whoever opposes God should know that His retribution is indeed severe.

⁵ (O believers!) Whatever (of their) palm trees that you have cut down or those that you left standing on their roots, it was done by God's will for Him to disgrace those who defiantly disobeyed Him. ⁶ Whatever (spoils) from the enemy that God has turned over to His Messenger (in this case), you did not have to participate in any expedition with your horses or camels (or had to endure great difficulties) to acquire it. But in any case, (be mindful that) God grants authority to whomsoever He wills as His Messengers, for God has the power to will anything.

⁷ (And so,) whatever (spoils) from the people of those villages that God has turned over to His Messenger, (all of it) belongs to God and His Messenger, and the near of kin (of those deceased believers), and the orphans, and the destitute, and the (stranded) traveler so that the gains will not concentrate and circulate only in the hands of those who are rich among you. *ᵃ* Hence, accept whatever the Messenger gives you and refrain from (demanding) anything that he withholds from you. Always be mindful of God; for verily, God is severe in retribution.

⁸ (Part of such spoils are) for the poor emigrants who were deprived of their homes and possessions, and are seeking for the bounty and protection of God; and also for those who aid (the cause of) God and His Messenger. They are the ones who are true (in faith). ⁹ And it is also for those who were already settled in their homes (in Madinah) and have accepted faith before the emigrants arrived. They love those who emigrated to them (for refuge) and do not harbor any desire in their hearts for the spoils given to the emigrants. Instead, they give the emigrants preference over themselves even though they are stricken with poverty. And whoever is saved from the selfishness of his own soul, it is they who are the truly successful ones.

¹⁰ The believers who came after them (fervently) prayed, "O Lord, forgive us and our brothers who preceded us in faith, and do not allow any grudge (or animosity) to set in our hearts against those who have embraced Your religion. Our Lord, indeed You are Full of Kindness, Most Compassionate."

ᵃ The ideal economic model that stresses on equitable distribution of wealth was already expounded and practiced in Islam during the 7ᵗʰ century when powerful nations were blatantly corrupt. It was common for wealth to be concentrated in the hands of a few, namely the feudal rulers and the elites around them while the masses had to endure poverty. Islam dictates that this imbalance must be corrected. Those who are heedless of this decree will face dire consequences in the Hereafter. See Chapter 102.

The Hypocrites Who Fell Short of Their Promise

¹¹ Are you not aware of the hypocrites who say to their friends among the people of the earlier revelation who were faithless, *ª* "If you are driven out, we shall most certainly go together with you and not pay heed to those who are against you. And if you are attacked, we shall most certainly come to your aid (and defend you)." God bears witness that they are indeed liars. ¹² The truth is, if those whom these hypocrites have pledged their loyalty to are driven away, they will not go forth with them. And if they are attacked, these hypocrites will also not aid them. And even if they try to aid them, they will most certainly turn their backs (in flight if you march against them), for they (know that they) will not be able to find any help for themselves. ¹³ Certainly (O believers), you arouse fear in their hearts that is even greater than their fear of God because they are a people who fail to grasp and understand (the truth).

¹⁴ These (exiled) people will not fight you as a united front in an open battlefield except in fortified cities or from behind walls. The enmity among themselves *ᵇ* is great. You think they are united but their hearts are actually divided. That is because they are a people devoid of reason (and fail to understand what truth really is). ¹⁵ (Their case is) like those (Quraysh infidels) who had tasted the evil consequences of their action (in the Battle of Badr) not too long ago. Yet more grievous suffering awaits them (in the life to come).

¹⁶ The parable (of the hypocrites who promised help to the exiled tribe) is like what Satan says to man, "Do not believe in God!" But as soon as man disbelieves (and lands himself in trouble), then Satan says, "I dissociate myself from you because I (actually) fear God, the Lord of all the worlds." ¹⁷ So in the end, both (the deniers of truth and the hypocrites) will find themselves to remain in the Fire forever. Such is the requital for every evil transgressor.

An Exhortation

¹⁸ O you who believe! Be ever mindful of God (and fear His wrath). Let every soul look carefully at the deeds it (has prepared and what it has) sent forth for tomorrow (that will be reckoned on the Day of Judgment. Once again,) be ever mindful of God (and fear His wrath)! Indeed, God is All-Aware of everything that you do. ¹⁹ Do not be like those who are oblivious of God whom He will make them become oblivious of themselves. *ᶜ* They are

---

ª The Jewish tribe of Bani Nadir.

ᵇ In reference to the different Jewish tribes.

ᶜ The Israelite belief in the Hereafter is very fragile. The early books of the Old Testament have very little to say about accountability, reward, and punishment in the

the ones who stubbornly defy and disobey Him. [20] Not equal are the inmates of the Fire and the residents of Paradise. (Surely,) it is the residents of Paradise who will (most certainly) triumph!

[21] Had We sent down this Qur'an on a mountain, surely you would have seen it humbled, breaking asunder from its fear and awe of God. We present these parables to people for them to (think and) ponder.

[22] He is God, Whom there is none except Him alone (Who has the sole right to be worshipped); the All-Knower of the unseen and the manifest. He is the Most Gracious, the Most Compassionate. [23] He is God, Whom there is none except Him (Who solely deserves all worshipped. He is) the King of all Kings, the Most Pure Who is free from all imperfections, the Source of Peace and Tranquility, The One Who Illuminates the Heart with Faith, the Guardian and Protector of all His creatures, the Almighty Who Commands absolute Authority and Respect, the Omnipotent Compeller Who Does as He Wills, the Most Supreme. Glorified is God (Who is free from all imperfections and He is far exalted) above everything that they (falsely) associate Him with. [24] He is God - the Creator, the Originator of all things, the Fashioner of all forms! To Him belong the most beautiful names and perfect attributes. Everything in the heavens and the earth (proclaims and) glorifies His perfection. And He alone is the Almighty, the All-Wise.

Hereafter. Instead, they are mainly a tedious narrative of episodes from the history of a rebellious people who glorify themselves as God's chosen race that are certain to inherit Paradise even if they terrorize people of other races and faiths. Christianity too speaks very little about the concept of accountability in the afterlife. To them, as long as one believes that Jesus is the son of God who was sent to earth to die on the cross to atone for the sins of mankind, then the person is guaranteed Paradise regardless if he has terribly wronged others. However, the confusing Doctrine of Trinity which many Christians find difficult to fathom has caused them to abandon God in multitudes, rejecting the idea of ultimate divine judgment and to regard life after death as mere illusion. As such, Christianity has become part and parcel of today's materialist Western civilization in which people are driven towards greed and immediate gratification. As for other faiths, their concept of afterlife is also based on conjectures instead of proven divine revelation which makes it obscure and false. Some believe that they will be reincarnated as different creatures after they die. All these are the ones who God says are oblivious of Him whom He has caused them to be oblivious of themselves by being lost in their own false beliefs. See also verses 50:19-22. Regrettably, many of those who profess themselves as Muslims are behaving in the same way too - they either do not want to think about the afterlife, or believe in the erroneous assumption that they are entitled to Paradise just because they inherited this faith from their parents and forefathers

60. Al-Mumtaḥanah
[The Tested Woman : 13 verses]

This is a Madinan chapter revealed between the Treaty of Hudaibiyah and the conquest of Makkah. The theme of this chapter is about reminding the Muslim to direct their love, friendship or hatred only for the sake of God and His religion, and that no friendship and alliance should be made with the enemies of God and His religion to the detriment of the wellbeing and security of the Muslim community. In this connection, it is reminded that on the Day of Judgment, neither worldly friendship nor blood relationships will be of any benefit to man. It is also pointed out that the best role model to look-up to is Prophet Abraham and his believing followers who completely severed their connection with their polytheist kinsmen and relatives for the sake of God. The chapter is named *Al-Mumtahanah* or The Tested Woman with reference to verses 10 - 12 where instructions are given on how to deal with women who leave Makkah to join the Muslims in Madinah, and vice versa.

In the name of God, the Most Gracious, the Most Compassionate.

Warning Against Being Friendly with Enemies

¹ O you who believe! Do not take My enemies and your enemies as allies. Even though you may show love (and kindness) to them, they are very much against the belief in (the One and Only) God Who is your true Lord and the way of life that you have embraced, and they have expelled the Messenger and you (out from Makkah) because of this. So if you come forth from your homes to truly strive in My cause longing for My pleasure and goodly acceptance, (then do not) incline towards them in affection and do not confide in them secretly, for I am fully aware of everything that you conceal and reveal. And any of you who do this has certainly strayed from the right path.

² (Know that) if they gain dominance over you, they will become your (ruthless) enemy and employ their hands and tongues against you with every evil (intention) because they desire that you deny the truth (just like them). ³ (So even if they happen to be related to you, be wary - for) never will your kinsfolk nor your children be of any benefit to you on the Day of Resurrection. (On that Day, no one will escape) God (and He) will separate between you (according to your creed and deeds), and then judge all of you (for everything that you have done on your merit alone. Verily,) God sees all that you do.

⁴ Indeed, there is in Abraham and those who followed him an excellent model for you (to learn from and emulate. Take heed of the occasion) when he said to his people, "Indeed, we dissociate ourselves from you and those you

worship besides God. We reject (what) you (believe). Enmity and hatred has come between you and us forever, unless you (repent and) believe in God, the One and Only God." The only exception was what Abraham said to his father, "I shall indeed (pray to God and) ask forgiveness (from Him) for you, but I have no power to obtain anything from God on your behalf." And so he prayed, "O Lord, we place our trust in You and turn to You (alone) in repentance. To You indeed is the final return. ⁵ Our Lord! Do no subject upon us a trial (at the hands) of those who oppose the truth (and hate us). And forgive us (for all our sins and shortcomings) O our Lord. Indeed, You are (truly) the Almighty, the All-Wise."

⁶ Certainly, there is a most excellent example for you in them and for whoever looks forward (with hope) to God and the Last Day. Whoever turns away (from God, then it is he who will suffer a terrible loss), for God is All-Sufficient, Immensely Praiseworthy.

Friendly Relations with Passive Non-Believers

⁷ (O believers!) It may well be that God will bring about (mutual) affection between you and some of those whom you (now) face as enemies, for God is All-Powerful. And (indeed,) God is Most Forgiving, Most Compassionate.

⁸ As for those (among the disbelievers) who do not fight you nor drive you out from your homes because of (your) faith, God does not forbid you from showing them kindness, and acting (courteously and) fairly towards them; for verily, God loves those who are (fair and) just. ᵃ ⁹ God only forbids you from

---

ᵃ How could acts of terrorism that hurt and kill innocent people be justified in Islam when God, in this verse, clearly commands those who believe in Him to be kind and fair towards people of other faiths? It is grossly erroneous and unfair to stereotype and blanketly label Islam as a religion that promotes terrorism when only a fraction of its total 1.8 billion peace-loving adherents are wayward and resort to violence to defend and promote their misguided understanding of Islam just as some sick people of other faiths and ideologies do too (see footnote of verse 5:32). Nowhere in the Qur'an can anyone find a verse that says it is permissible for Muslims to kill another person except in legal retribution (verses 6:151 and 17:32) for the crime of murder or treason, or when in war to retaliate against aggression. Even when in war, God commands Muslims to cease fighting when the enemy ends its hostility (verses 2:192-193). In fact, Muslims are even forbidden from being unfair to those whom they might hate and dislike (verse 5:8). If this is correctly understood, then one can clearly see that Islamophobia has no reason to exist. Isn't it ironic and strange that when systematic atrocities are perpetrated by the Zionists of Israel on the people of Palestine since 1948 until today by cruelly seizing their lands and driving them out of their homes, and killing millions of

making allies with those who fought against you, drove you out from your homes and aided in your exile over matters concerning your religion,. Whoever takes them as allies is committing gross injustice.

Protect Believing Women

[10] O you who believe! Whenever believing women come to you as emigrants (in the cause of faith, examine and) put them to test (first). Verily, God (alone) has knowledge of their faith (whereas you do not). And when you have ascertained them to be believers, do not return them to their former husbands (since) they are no longer lawful for those who do not believe in God, nor are those disbelievers lawful for them. Nonetheless, return to the disbelievers whatever (bridal dues) that they have spent (on these women), and there is no blame on you if you marry these women, provided you give them their bridal dues. On the other hand, do not retain your marriage ties with women who (continue) to reject the truth. Ask for the return of (the bridal dues) that you have spent on them, just as the disbelievers (whose wives have gone over to you) have the right to demand (the return of) what they have spent. Such is the decree of God, and He decides between you (in fairness), for God is All-Knowing, All-Wise. [11] And if any of your women should flee to the disbelievers, then give to those whose wives have fled, the equivalent of (the bridal dues that) they have spent on their wives when your turn of victory comes (and you have a chance to acquire spoils). And always be mindful of God in Whom you believe.

[12] O Prophet! When believing women come pledging to you that they will not associate anything with God, nor steal, nor fornicate, nor kill their children, nor slander others with lies that they have deliberately fabricated, nor disobey you in any lawful matter, then accept their pledge and ask forgiveness from God for them. Indeed, God is Most Forgiving, Most Compassionate.

[13] O you who believe! Do not make friends (and ally yourselves) with those who have incurred God's wrath. Those (who befriend them) are indeed bereft of all hope in the life to come just as the disbelievers are bereft of (ever seeing again) those who are already in their graves.

---

innocent children, women and the old with impunity, they are not called terrorists? Those who are blind and deaf to this blatant transgression of human rights by the Zionists and still choose to regard Islam as a religion of violence are truly devoid of moral conscience. Their double standard hypocrisy which condones injustice and acts of terror while intoxicating themselves with the hype of Islamophobia does not befit them as decent civilized humans.

61. Aṣ-Ṣaff
[The Ranks : 14 verses]

This is a Madinan chapter. Its main theme is *jihad* - fighting in the cause of God to defend His religion and making sacrifices for His sake. The chapter starts by emphasizing that all that is in the heavens and earth proclaim the sanctity and glory of God. It then warns the believers against breach of promises. Next it is stated in verse 4 that God loves those who are united in their *jihad* as if they were a solid structure. The chapter is named *Aṣ-Ṣaff* or The Ranks with reference to this verse. In this context, reference is made to the dealings of the Jews with Prophets Moses and Jesus, and it is specifically mentioned that their Scriptures contained the prophecy about the coming of Prophet Muhammad. The chapter then points out once again that taking part in *jihad* in the cause of God is the most profitable bargain that a believer can ever make and it ends by encouraging the believers to follow the footsteps of the disciples of the Jesus who became his true helpers in God's cause.

In the name of God, the Most Gracious, the Most Compassionate.

Do as You Say

¹ Everything in the heavens and the earth (proclaims and) glorifies God's perfection. He is the Almighty, the All-Wise.

² O you who believe! Why do you say things that you do not do? ³ It is most hateful in the sight of God that you say what you do not do. ⁴ Verily, God loves those who fight in His cause in solid ranks as though they were a unified compact structure. *ᵃ*

⁵ Now behold, when Moses said to his people, "O my people! Why do you cause me grief when you know that I have been sent to you by God?" When they persisted in their (defiance and) deviation (from the truth), God caused their hearts to deviate further, for God does not give guidance to those who are defiantly disobedient. *ᵇ*

ᵃ Empty threats and false claims achieve nothing. This verse condemns those whose actions contradict their words. A believer devotes his whole life to the service of God, proving and manifesting his faith with action. Skeptics, on the other hand, are dissenters who represent an aberration in God's vision of the world.
ᵇ God denounced those communities that rejected His guidance and showed hostility towards His Messengers. At the forefront of such communities were the early Israelites who antagonized Moses and caused him no end of hardship. They lost their nerve when it came to facing their enemies and squandered the Scriptures that were

⁶ And behold too, when Jesus - the son of Mary, said (to his people), "O children of Israel! Indeed, I have been sent to you as a Messenger of God to confirm the (truth in) Torah that was sent before me, and to give you good news of a Messenger after me whose name will be *Ahmad.*" [i.e. The Praised One]. *ª* Yet when he - whose coming Jesus had foretold - came to them with all evidence of the truth, they said, "(O Muhammad!) This (message that you bring) is nothing but a clear evil spell (that has been made up to bewitch and delude us)!"

⁷ Who could be more wicked than he who invents a lie about God when he is invited to submit to Him? Indeed, God does not guide evildoers. ⁸ They hope to extinguish the light of God by (uttering blasphemies) with their mouths. But God wills to perfect His light even if those who reject the truth hate it. ⁹ It is He Who sent guidance and the religion of truth (to mankind) through His Messenger to make it prevail over all other religions (that are false) even if those who worship others besides Him hate it.

---

revealed to them. As a result, they were castigated for their betrayal of Moses and for their refusal to face the enemy when God commanded them so (verses 5:20-25). The Prophet's companions were reminded not to adopt this attitude through the encouragement in verses 10-13.

ª This footnote is to be read in conjunction with the footnote of verse 7:157. According to Muhammad Asad (the renowned Jewish Muslim scholar and Qur'an exegete) regarding this verse in his exegesis of the Qur'an, he said that : "This prophecy is supported by several references in the Gospel of St. John to the *Paraklutos* (usually rendered as The Comforter) who was to come after Jesus. This designation is almost certainly a corruption of the word *Periklytos* (i.e. the Much Praised), an exact Greek translation of the Aramaic term or name *Mawhamana*. It is to be borne in mind that Aramaic was the language used in Palestine at the time of Jesus, and was undoubtedly the language in which the original - now lost - texts of the Gospels were written. In view of the phonetic closeness of *Periklytos* and *Paraklutos*, it is easy to understand how the translator, or more probably a later scribe, confused these two expressions. It is significant to note that both the Aramaic term of *Mawhamana* and the Greek *Periklytos* have the same meaning as the two names of the Last Prophet, which is Muhammad and Ahmad, both of which are derived from the verb *hamida* (i.e. he praised) and the noun *hamd* (i.e. praise)." Therefore, the only way for anyone who insists on claiming that the term *Paraklutos* is being rightfully used in the Bible instead of *Periklytos*, is for him to produce the *Injeel* or Gospel in its original language of Aramaic Hebrew. Until then, it can be safe to argue that the actual Aramaic word mentioned by Jesus was *Mawhamana* which means *Periklytos* in Greek or "The Praised One" in English, but was wrongly translated to Greek as *Paraklutos* or "The Comforter" in English.

The Best Bargain

[10] "O you who believe! Shall I offer you a bargain that will save you from a grievous punishment (in this world and in the life to come)? [11] Have faith in God and His Messenger, and strive hard in God's cause with your wealth and soul. This is best for you, if only you knew (God's reward for it). [12] He will forgive your sins and admit you into gardens which rivers flow right beneath them, and (give you) excellent dwellings in the Garden of Eternity. That is indeed the greatest success! [13] And (He will also grant you) another favor that is dearest to you - His help and an imminent victory!" So give this good news to all who believe (in the message that you are conveying O Muhammad).

[14] O you who believe! Be helpers of God just like the disciples of Jesus - the son of Mary, to whom he said, "Who will be my helpers in God's cause?", whereupon they replied, "We shall be the helpers in God's cause!" Then, a group among the children of Israel became believers (in the Prophethood of Jesus and the Gospel he conveyed) while others denied it. And so We supported those who believed against their enemies and they became victorious. [a]

---

[a] Like Prophet Muhammad's companions, the loyal disciples of Jesus provided him with the strength and support he needed to propagate his true message specifically to the Children of Israel (and not to all mankind) for them to revert to the true teachings of Moses in the Torah, and to also be prepared for the coming of the final Messiah known as *Ahmad* (or *Muhammadim* in Hebrew, *Mawhamana* in Aramaic and *Periklytos* in Koine Greek). However, this true teaching was hijacked and twisted by Paul the Tarsus who invented a new set of belief around 30 to 50 AD which is known as the Pauline Christianity. This was done with the intention to promote the new religion to non-Jews who are called Gentiles, specifically to the Roman occupiers of Palestine who eventually accepted this new religion in place of their centuries-old pagan beliefs. See also verse 19:36. The idea finally led to the official proclamation of the Doctrine of Trinity by The Council of Constantinople in 360 AD at the behest of the Roman Emperor Constantius II, where its final form was formulated and crafted by Gregory of Nyssa in 381 AD. It is simply ironic how this doctrine which is nowhere mentioned in the Bible was only decided to be the fundamental belief of Christianity nearly 400 years after Jesus was gone. If this belief is indeed true, why wait for 400 years to officially announce it? Shouldn't Jesus be proclaiming this himself to his followers while he was together with them? Notwithstanding this, Islam is in greater need for the Muslims of today to understand and appreciate the true meaning of the words "Be helpers of God" mentioned in the beginning of this verse. Muslims must step up to their game and play their roles to the best of their ability to bring justice and peace to the world by embracing the true teachings of Islam.

62. Al-Jumu'ah
[The Friday Congregation : 11 verses]

This is a Madinan chapter. Its main theme is The Friday Congregational prayer mentioned in verses 9 to 11 where its name is taken from. Believers are commanded to attend this congregation promptly when the call for it is made. The chapter also reminds believers of God's grace in sending a Prophet to teach and lead them in the right path. Reference is then made to the Jews who did not act in accordance with the knowledge they have been given but think of themselves as God's chosen and most favored people until today.

In the name of God, the Most Gracious, the Most Compassionate.

God's Bounty

¹ Everything in the heavens and the earth (proclaims and) glorifies God's perfection. (He is) the King, the Most Pure, the Almighty, the All-Wise.

² It is He Who sent a Messenger among the unlettered people, reciting to them His verses, purifying their corrupt faith (and cleansing their souls), teaching them (about the message in) the Book, and (imparting) wisdom (to them through his examples and sayings) - whereas before that they were clearly lost in error; ³ and (to also cause this message to spread) among the disbelievers who have not joined them yet. Verily, He is the Almighty, the All-Wise. ⁴ Such is God's bounty. He gives it to whomsoever He wills (that turns to Him for guidance. Indeed,) God is limitless in His great bounty.

The Parable of a Donkey

⁵ The parable of those who were entrusted with the Torah but ignore it is like a donkey which carries a load of books (but is completely ignorant of what they contain). Wretched is the example of the people who deny God's messages. And God does not guide evil wrongdoers. *ᵃ*

ᵃ Just like the foolish Jewish priests who God likened them to donkeys that are ignorant of the teachings of their own religion even with the Torah in their hands, many Muslim preachers are no different too. They may look pious in their appearance but are actually ignorant of Islam's true teachings. They deliberately limit the scope of their preaching to ritual aspects alone and are not concerned to raise the consciousness of the *ummah* about Islam's emphasis on social justice, let alone encourage Muslims to stand up against injustice as if Islam has nothing to do with this. Worse, some even go

No Escape from Death

⁶ Say (to them), "O Jews! If you claim to be the chosen people of God to the exclusion of all other people and if you are really speaking the truth, then wish for death (now so that you can return to Him quicker and get to enjoy unlimited bounties in the next life)." ⁷ But they will never wish for it because they know very well about the misdeeds that they have committed with their own hands. And God knows everything about these wrongdoers.

⁸ Say (to them further), "Verily, the death that you try to flee from will surely overtake you (one day wherever you are when your time is up). Then you will be sent back to Him Who knows everything about the unseen and the manifest, and He will apprise you about everything that you have done (during your lifetime)."

The Friday Prayer

⁹ O you who believe! When the call for the Friday congregational prayer is made, hasten to the remembrance of God and put aside all worldly commerce. That is better for you, if only you knew! ¹⁰ And after the prayer is concluded, spread out in the land to seek God's bounty, and remember God much so that you will (be rightly guided to) attain success (and prosperity). ¹¹ Yet, when they saw a chance for business transaction or an amusing entertainment, they rushed to it and left you standing (at the pulpit). Say to them, "(Behold!) What is with God is surely better than any entertainment and business transaction, for God is (surely) the Best of Providers."

---

to the extent of manipulating the Qur'an to suit their selfish interests by calling upon others to support corrupt leaders who impoverish and cause hardship to their own people. These religious preachers choose to serve the whims and fancies of despotic leaders instead of speaking up against the wrongdoings that are being committed to protect their worldly interests and also to avoid from falling out of favor with the powers that be. God's curse is upon them for condoning injustice. See verses 5:78-79. Refer also to the story of Bal'am bin Ba'ura in the footnote of verses 7:175-176 who God likened him to a panting dog with its tongue lolling out while serving its master in blind obedience whether it is being scolded or left alone because it cannot tell the difference between a master who is God-fearing or evil as long as it is fed well. Incidentally, we see many Muslims acting in defiance towards Islam today out of confusion as a result of widespread sermons by narrow minded ritual-centric preachers who exaggerate passages from the Qur'an and the Prophet's unauthentic *hadith* to the point where they become absurd, making Islam appear irrelevant and incapable of addressing the challenges of today's modern world. See also the footnote for verses 45:1-6.

63. Al-Munāfiqūn
[The Hypocrites : 11 verses]

This is a Madinan chapter. As its name indicates, the chapter deals with the character and conduct of the hypocrites led by Abdullah ibn Ubayy who professed Islam outwardly but actually despised Islam and had secretly conspired to destroy Islam and the Muslims from within. Their schemes include preventing people from accepting Islam, discouraging financial assistance to the Muslims, and conspiring to oust the Muslims and the Prophet from Madinah. Their evil schemes were exposed in this chapter. The chapter ends by reminding the Muslims to not be lured by wealth and children from the remembrance of God and to spend in the way of God before death overtakes them.

In the name of God, the Most Gracious, the Most Compassionate.

[1] (O Muhammad!) When the hypocrites come to you, they say, "We bear witness that you are surely the Messenger of God." Certainly God knows that you are indeed His Messenger, and He bears witness that the hypocrites are nothing but liars. [2] Behold! They have made their false oaths as a (guise and) shield for their deceit and (strive to) hinder others from God's path (by sowing doubts in peoples' hearts). Evil indeed is what they do!

[3] This is because they (openly declare their) belief in God and His Messenger but they actually do not believe. And so, a seal has been set on their hearts so that they are unable to understand (and discern between truth and falsehood).

[4] And when you see them, their personality captivates you; and if they speak, you are mesmerized by their speech. Yet they are as worthless as hollow pieces of propped up timber; (so do not be fooled by their impressive outward appearance). They (are actually afraid of the truth and) think that every shout made is against them. They are indeed your enemy, so beware of them. May God destroy them! How deluded are they (of the truth).

[5] And when it is said to them, "Come! Let God's Messenger pray for your forgiveness"; they turn aside their heads and you see them turning away in arrogance. [6] (So,) whether you ask forgiveness for them or not, it is all the same because God will not forgive them. Behold! God does not guide those who are defiantly disobedient.

[7] They are the ones who say (to the people of Madinah), "Do not spend on those who are with the Messenger of God so that they will (be forced to) leave

him." To God belong the treasures of the heavens and the earth, but the hypocrites are not able to grasp this truth. ⁸ (On the way home after the battle of Bani Mustaliq,) they also say (out of despise), "Once we return to Madinah, surely the honorable ones among us will drive those abject people out (of our city)." *ᵃ* (The truth is), honor belongs to God, to His Messenger and to the true believers. But the hypocrites are ignorant of this.

An Exhortation

⁹ O you who believe! Let not your wealth and your children divert you from the remembrance of God. Whoever does so will (surely) end up as losers.

¹⁰ Spend in charity out of what We have provided before death comes to any one of you and he cries, "O my Lord! If only You would defer my stay on earth a little longer, I shall (surely) give out alms and charity and be among the righteous." *ᵇ*

¹¹ (Behold!) God will never grant a soul any respite when its time (on earth) reaches its end. God is fully aware of everything that you do.

ᵃ These were the words of Abdullah ibn Ubayy - the leader of hypocrites in Madinah, a troublemaker who wished to divide the Muslim community and undermine its strength out of pure jealousy and hatred towards the Prophet and the Muslims who he held responsible for spoiling his plan and ambition to become the ruler of Madinah. Both Makkan and Madinan Muslims had suffered great trials and tribulations; the former had left their homes and possessions behind in Makkah, while the latter had to receive the emigrants (i.e. *Muhajirun*) and share everything they had with them. Abdullah ibn Ubayy worked very hard to drive a wedge between the Makkan emigrants and the people of Madinah. He also conspired with the Jewish tribes in Madinah to undermine the Prophet's leadership but all his efforts ended in vain.

ᵇ See also verse 23:99-100.

64. At-Taghābun
[Mutual Loss and Gain : 18 verses]

his is a Madinan chapter which draws attention to the fate of previous nations and peoples were punished for their disbelief and rejection towards the divine message that was conveyed to them by the respective Messengers that God had sent to them. It serves as a reminder and warning to those who were rejecting Prophet Muhammad. At the same time, the believers are urged to be wary but forgiving of the enemies they may have within their own families, and warned them to remain steadfast and to spend in God's cause. The chapter is named *At-Taghābun* with reference to verse 9 which speaks about the Day of Resurrection which is also called The Day of Mutual Loss and Gain by virtue of the fact that some people will lose and some others will gain after everyone is judged by God on that day for their beliefs and deeds that they have done during their lifetime on earth.

In the name of God, the Most Gracious, the Most Compassionate.

Disbelievers Warned

¹ Everything in the heavens and the earth (proclaims and) glorifies God's perfection. To Him belong the dominion and all praise. He has absolute power over everything.

² He is the One Who created you (from nothing). Yet some of you (choose to) deny (Him) and some (choose to) believe. *ᵃ* God sees everything that you do (and nothing can be hidden from Him). ³ He is the One Who created the heavens and the earth (to fulfill a purpose that is) in accordance with the truth (which He has decreed). He has formed and shaped you well and to Him is your final return. ⁴ He knows all that is in the heavens and the earth, and He knows what you conceal and what you reveal. Indeed, God has full knowledge of what is in (everyone's) heart.

⁵ (O disbelievers!) Have you not heard of those before you who refused to accept the truth? (Because of their defiance,) they were made to taste the (terrible) consequences of their conduct with even more grievous suffering

---

ᵃ It is highly paradoxical when man shows disrespect towards God Almighty who has created him in the best form and endowed him with all his faculties and provided for him so generously. Some people refused to believe for the simple reason that God's revelation had come to them through other humans, arguing that it should have been brought by Angels.

(that awaits them in the life to come). ⁶ That is because when their Messengers came to them with all evidence of the truth, they said, "Should we take guidance from (mere average) mortals?" *ᵃ* So they disbelieved and turned away. But God is not in need of them, for He is All-Sufficient, Immensely Praiseworthy.

⁷ Those who deny the truth claim that they will not be raised from the dead. *ᵇ* Say (to them), "But why not? By my Lord! You will most certainly be resurrected, and then you will be shown and apprised about everything that you did (during your lifetime). That is easy for God (to do)." ⁸ So believe in God, His Messenger and the light (of revelation) that We have sent down. *ᶜ* And (always be mindful that) God is fully aware of everything that you do.

⁹ (Think of) the Day when He will gather you all on the Day of Assembly which will be the Day of mutual loss and gain (among the people). *ᵈ* Whoever believes in God and does good deeds, God will erase and remove (the sins of) his past misdeeds and admit him into gardens which rivers flow from right beneath them, to remain in there forever. That is the greatest success!

¹⁰ As for those who disbelieved and denied Our signs and revelations, they

---

ᵃ It is in the nature of most people to look down upon those who are regarded as average members of the society that do not have authority, wealth and high social status. The same was also with the Israelites who objected to Saul when God made him their ruler. See verse 2:247.

ᵇ This denial is not new in the history of mankind but it has never been so widespread like it is now. Modern civilization is a materialistic civilization in which living the present life is revered above all else, and life after death is dismissed as absurd nonsense. This attitude is not confined to atheists or pagans alone, but to followers of other divinely-revealed religions too, namely Judaism and Christianity. They are not prepared to accept or tolerate the Qur'anic concept of the Hereafter. See verse 59:19 and its footnote. Hence, a fresh approach is needed to present Islam in a more effective and intelligent manner using scientific evidence to prove the veracity of the Qur'an before people can be drawn to explore Islam and its concept of the Hereafter.

ᶜ That 'light of revelation' is the Qur'an which contains the best advice for an honorable and equitable life for all mankind. Muslims are under obligation to understand their Book and live up to the task defined for them in the Qur'an.

ᵈ Many will regret appeasing certain individuals who were wealthy and powerful, and dismissing others because they were poor and helpless. Wasted opportunities will be recalled and those who disbelieved will wish they had not squandered them. Alas, it will be too late then, for there will be no chance to undo what had already been done, and what is left is only time for reckoning and accountability.

will be the inmates of the Fire forever. How terrible is their final destination!

¹¹ (Verily,) there is not a single misfortune (or calamity) that will ever strike (you) except by God's permission. And whoever truly believes in God (and puts complete trust in Him), God will guide his heart (towards peace and tranquility), for God has complete knowledge of everything. ¹² So obey God and obey His Messenger. But if you turn away (from this reminder), then (know that) Our Messenger's duty is only to convey the message clearly (and he will not be responsible for what you do). ¹³ God, there is no other god except Him. And it is God alone Who all believers should (completely) place their trust in.

Spouses and Children as Trials

¹⁴ O you who believe! Verily, among your spouses and your children, some are bound to be your enemies (who will distract and deviate you from God's path). So be wary of them (and lead them well). But if you pardon, forbear and forgive them (for their shortcomings), then behold! God is indeed Most Forgiving, Most Compassionate. ¹⁵ Verily, your wealth and children are only a test (for you). It is with God where the greatest reward rests. *ᵃ* ¹⁶ So be ever mindful of God (and keep your duty to Him) to the best of your ability. *ᵇ* Pay heed (to His reminders) and obey Him. Spend in charity too. That is good for your own soul. Whoever is saved from his own selfishness and greed are the successful ones.

¹⁷ (Know that) if you lend to God a goodly loan (for His cause), He will multiply (its returns) for you and forgive your sins. And God is Most Appreciative, Most Forbearing; ¹⁸ the Knower of the unseen and the manifest, the Almighty, the All-Wise

---

ᵃ The Makkan Muslims followed Prophet Muhammad to migrate (i.e. *Hijrah*) to Madinah leaving all their possessions behind to free themselves from injustice and oppression in defending their faith and *Taqwa* for the sake of God's pleasure. Not everyone can make such a sacrifice. Some Muslims hesitated, preferring to remain with their wives and children in Makkah, and so they lost out. To these, God responded with verses 14 and 15.

ᵇ Striving against injustice is a part of fulfilling Islam's ideal. It requires unrelenting faith, great sacrifices, courage and tenacity to the best of one's ability. Perpetrators of injustice must not be allowed to have free reign; otherwise peace, security and prosperity will never prevail. Injustice is despised by God and one cannot expect to attain *Taqwa* if he is indifferent to corruption, injustice and oppression. See footnote of verse 2:183 for the definition of *Taqwa*.

65. Aṭ-Ṭalāq
[Divorce : 12 verses]

This is a Madinan chapter. As its name indicates, the chapter lays down the rules regarding the permissible and equitable method of divorce and deals with the questions of *iddah* or the waiting period for the divorced wife, her lodging and cost of maintenance during that period, the suckling and maintenance of infants and other related matters. The chapter warns against transgressing God's rulings and reminds the believers to be ever mindful of Him in all circumstances. The chapter ends by emphasizing God's power and knowledge.

In the name of God, the Most Gracious, the Most Compassionate.

Rulings on Divorce

¹ O Prophet! If (any of you must) divorce your wives, then do so (only) during their prescribed period *ᵃ* and keep count of the waiting period (before she can remarry). *ᵇ* Be mindful of God - your Lord. Do not expel them from their homes, nor should they leave, unless they have become openly guilty of immoral conduct. These are the bounds set by God and whoever transgresses God's bounds, wrongs his own soul. You do not know that perhaps God may bring about a change (in their hearts) later.

² And so, when they are about to reach the end of their waiting term, either retain them honorably or part with them honorably. Take two (fair and) just men among you as witnesses (to this outcome). They will also serve to establish an upright testimony for the sake of God. Whoever believes in God and the Last Day should take heed of this admonition : Anyone who is mindful of God (and strives to keep his duty to Him diligently), God will make for him a way out (of his difficulties); ³ and will provide for him from sources he does not expect and imagine. God is sufficient for those who put their trust in Him, for He will surely accomplish His purpose. And God has indeed set due measure for everything.

⁴ As for your women who no longer menstruate and those whose menstrual courses are doubtful, their prescribed waiting period is three months. The same is also for those who do not menstruate (for whatever physiological reason). And as for those who are pregnant, their prescribed

---

ᵃ Outside their monthly cycle and before any sexual intercourse has taken place.
ᵇ Waiting period before a female divorcee or widow can remarry is known as *'Iddah* in Arabic. See also verses 2:228-237.

period is until the delivery of the child. (Verily), whoever is mindful of God, He will make his affairs easy for him. ⁵ This is God's commandment that is sent down to you (O believers!). God will erase and remove (the sins of) your misdeeds and increase the rewards of those who are always mindful of Him (and keep their duty to Him diligently).

⁶ Lodge your divorced wives wherever you reside according to your means (during their waiting period). Do not harass them and cause distress. If they are pregnant, maintain them well until they deliver (your child). And if they breastfeed your child, compensate them. Settle (this matter) together in a fair manner. But if you find yourselves in difficulty, you may engage a wet-nurse to breastfeed the child on the father's behalf. *ᵃ* ⁷ Let the man of ample means spend according to his means; and he whose provision is limited spend according to what God has given him. *ᵇ* (Verily,) God does not burden a soul beyond what He has given him, and God will bring about ease after hardship.

The Fate of Rebellious Nations

⁸ And how many communities (before you) have rebelled against their Lord's commandments and His Messengers? We called them to account - a stern account, and We punished them severely. ⁹ So they tasted the pain of their own doings and were consequently ruined because of their (evil) deeds. ¹⁰ God has prepared severe punishment for them (in the life to come. So be ever mindful of God, O you who are endowed with insight and wisdom, and you who believe! He has indeed sent down a reminder to you (through this Qur'an); ¹¹ together with a Messenger who recites to you God's clear verses so that He may bring those who believe and do righteous deeds out of darkness into light. And whoever truly believes in God and does righteous deeds, God will admit him into gardens which rivers flow from right beneath them where he will remain forever. Indeed, God has granted a good provision for him.

¹² (Verily,) it is God Who created the seven heavens and He did the same to earth too. His command descends throughout them all. *ᶜ* (This is stated) for you to know that God alone has the absolute power over all things and His knowledge truly encompasses everything.

ᵃ The father is responsibile to ensure that the child's welfare is properly taken care of.
ᵇ See verse 2:233
ᶜ Seven earths could be an allusion to the seven continents that are spread across earth. And God's command that descends throughout them all may possibly be alluded to the universality of revelation where a Messenger was sent to every community to convey the message of God's Oneness. See verse 16:36.

66. At-Taḥrīm
[The Prohibition : 12 verses]

This is a Madinan chapter that speaks about the Prophet's household. It rebukes two of the Prophet's wives for an incident when a confidence was betrayed. In addition, it urges all believers to submit themselves to God and to guard themselves and their families against Hellfire. The chapter closes by giving examples of believing and disbelieving women. The chapter is named *At-Taḥrīm* or The Prohibition in reference to its first verse when the Prophet had accidentally made a wrong move by prohibiting himself from consuming honey from one of his wives' house to please another wife over an incident. His misstep was rebuked by God and he was ordered to retract.

In the name of God, the Most Gracious, the Most Compassionate.

Unlawful Prohibition

¹ O Prophet! Why do you forbid yourself from what God has made lawful for you just because you seek to please your wives? (Behold! Retract this misstep. Verily,) God is Most Forgiving, Most Compassionate.

² (O believers!) Indeed, God has ordained that you revoke your vows (if they run counter to what is right and just), for God is your Patron and He is Full of Knowledge and Wisdom.

³ (Now narrate the story when) the Prophet secretly confided in one of his wives about something but she disclosed it (to another wife), and then God revealed (her disobedience) to him. So he made known to her some of what God had revealed to him, and held back some. And when (the Prophet informed her about this, she asked (in panic), "Who told you this?" He replied, "I was told about this by the All-Knowing, the All-Informed."

⁴ (Now say to both your wives who are at fault), "Your hearts have been impaired. If you both turn to God in repentance, (you will be pardoned). But if you continue to conspire against the Prophet, know that he is protected by God, Gabriel and the righteous among the believers. And besides them, all the other Angels are also his helpers."

⁵ (O wives of the Prophet!) In case he divorces you, (know that) his Lord will give him better wives in return - women who submit themselves to God, who are faithful (to Him), who devoutly obey His will, who turn (to Him) in repentance (whenever they have sinned), who worship (Him alone) and who

regularly fast - be they women who were previously married or who are still virgins. *ᵃ*

Safeguard Families from the Hellfire

⁶ O you who believe! Protect yourselves and your families from a Fire that its fuel is of people and stones, guarded by appointed Angels who are stern and strong. They never disobey what God commands them and always do what they are commanded. ⁷ (And on the Day of Judgment, it will be said to

---

ᵃ Verses 3-6 : The Prophet's wives were virtuous and highly respected women. They accompanied the Prophet during his life and supported him in his mission. They also lived up to the role and expectations defined for them in the Qur'an but were nevertheless criticized on two occasions. The first was over their unhappiness with the Prophet's austere life-style and their collusion to demand from him a higher spending allowance (see verses 33:28-29). However, when he explained to them that his aim in life was not to prosper or become wealthy but to serve God and seek His pleasure and blessings in the Hereafter, they acquiesced and chose to live according to his terms. The second instance was when two of his wives who were driven by jealousy tried to take advantage of his good nature. One of them, reported to be Hafsah, once told him that his breath smelled unpleasant. When he explained that he had eaten some honey at the house of Zaynab - one of his other wives, Hafsah commented sarcastically, "The bees must have been feeding on foul flowers!" The Prophet promised never to eat Zaynab's honey again and asked Hafsah not to relate the episode to anyone else to avoid hurting Zaynab's feelings. However, it soon transpired that out of sheer jealousy, there was collusion between Hafsah and his other wife - A'ishah, aimed at causing the Prophet to lose interest in Zaynab. The Prophet was upset at this behavior and decided to stay away from all his wives to the extent that some people thought he had divorced them all. A'ishah and Hafsah were severely reprimanded for their mistake, and were urged to repent or face castigation. In verse 5, the Prophet's wives were implicitly advised to be considerate, reasonable, and polite in their dealings with him, warning them that God would provide him with better wives than them if he chose to divorce them. The Prophet's laudable qualities should not be abused by his wives, nor should he be maligned for being the good and gentle man he was. His household should not be a place for jealousy and ill will, but rather a haven for the adoration of God and preparation for the Hereafter and devotion in the pursuit of God's pleasure and blessings. By way of severe reprimand to those wives who had upset the Prophet, the closing part of the chapter in verse 10 cites the wives of Prophets Noah and Lot who let their respective husbands down in fulfilling their mission. They had failed to stand behind their husbands and give them the support they needed to fulfill their obligations as Messengers of God who were commissioned for a crucial leadership role among their people. Their shameful attitude caused them to be condemned and to enter the fire of Hell with other wrongdoers.

those who opposed the truth,) "O disbelievers! Do not make excuses today. Verily, you will certainly be requited for what you have done."

⁸ O you who believe! Turn to God in sincere repentance. It may well be that your Lord will erase and remove (the sins of) your past misdeeds and admit you into gardens which rivers flow from right beneath them, on the Day when God will not disgrace the Prophet and those who have believed (and loyally stood by him). Their light will be streaming ahead of them on their right side and they will say, "Our Lord! Make our light perfect for us and grant us forgiveness. Indeed, You have power over everything."

⁹ O Prophet! Strive hard against the (infidels) who openly oppose the truth and the hypocrites (who conceal their hatred for you). Be stern with them, for their final home is Hell - a wretched destination indeed!

A Parable for Disbelieving Women

¹⁰ God sets forth a parable for the disbelievers in (the stories of) the wives of Noah and Lot. They were married to Our righteous servants but both of them betrayed their husbands. Neither of their (husbands) could avail (and help) them against God (on the Day of Judgment). They will be told, "Enter the Fire together with the others!"

¹¹ And as for the (women) of faith, God has set forth the parable of Pharaoh's wife who prayed, "My Lord! Build for me a house near You in Paradise, and save me from Pharaoh and his misdeeds; and save me (too) from the people who are immersed in evil (and sin)." *ᵃ*

¹² And (God has also set forth another parable of God-consciousness in the story of) Mary, *ᵇ* the daughter of Joachim *ᶜ* who guarded her chastity, and into whom We breathed from Our Spirit. She (acknowledged and) confirmed the truth of her Lord's words and His Heavenly Books, and she was indeed among the devoutly obedient.

ᵃ Personal accountability is a fundamental Islamic principle (see verse 53:38). On the Day of Judgment, every man will have to answer for himself - not even a father can fend for his son (see verse 31:33), or a husband for his wife. And in the case of Pharaoh, while he enters the Hellfire, his wife will reside in Paradise unaffected by the consequences of his transgression.

ᵇ Maryam in Arabic.

ᶜ Imrān in Arabic.

67. Al-Mulk
[The Dominion : 30 verses]

This is a Makkan chapter which deals with the fundamentals of faith, mainly the Oneness, Power and Glory of God and the theme of resurrection, judgment, reward and punishment in the Hereafter. It also describes the disbelievers' regret on the Day of Resurrection. The chapter is named *Al-Mulk* or The Dominion after its first verse that declares God's total dominion over everything in this world and the next.

In the name of God, the Most Gracious, the Most Compassionate.

The Kingdom of God

¹ Blessed is He in Whose hand rests all dominion, and Who has power over everything. ² It is He Who has created death and life to test who among you is best in his deeds (and conduct). *ᵃ* And He is the Almighty, the Most Forgiving.

³ He is the One Who has created the seven heavens (in full harmony) one above another. No fault will you see in the creation of the Most Gracious (Lord). Look again - can you see any flaw? ⁴ Then look again. Surely your gaze will return to you, humbled and fatigued.

⁵ And We have certainly adorned the nearest heaven with lamps,*ᵇ* and We have made them as objects (of wild guesses and predictions) for the evil ones *ᶜ* for whom We have prepared the punishment of the Blaze. ⁶ And (let it be no doubt that) those who disbelieve (and pay no heed to the revelation of) their Lord will suffer the punishment of Hell. What a wretched destination it is!

⁷ When they are cast therein, they will hear its terrible roar as it boils; ⁸ almost bursting with rage. Every time a host (of such sinners) is thrown in it, its keepers will ask them, "Did a warner not come to you?" ⁹ They will answer, "Yes indeed, a warner did come to us, but we denied him and said, 'God has not sent down any (revelation as what you claim. Indeed,) you are nothing but someone who is extremely misguided.'" ¹⁰ And they will say (in regret), "If only we had listened (to those warnings) or reasoned (properly), surely we would not have been among the inmates of the Blazing Fire (today)."

ᵃ See verse 18:7. The emphasis is on the quality of deeds, not quantity.
ᵇ Stars.
ᶜ Soothsayers and astrologers.

¹¹ Then they will (realize their errors and) confess their sins (but it will be of no use to them at that time) because these inmates of the Blazing Fire will be very far away (from God's mercy). ¹² But for those who stand in (awe and) fear of their Lord Who is unseen (and strive to get close to Him by diligently following the teachings of His Prophet), for them is forgiveness and a great reward. ¹³ And whether you speak secretly or openly, He has full knowledge of what is in the (deep recesses of everyone's) heart.

¹⁴ How could it be that He Who created (everything) does not know (His own creation)? And He is (indeed) the Most Subtle, the All-Aware. ¹⁵ He is the One Who made the earth manageable for you. So walk in the paths thereof and eat from the (good) things He has provided; and (always be mindful that) it is to Him will you be resurrected.

The Disbelievers Doom

¹⁶ Do you really feel safe (and assured) that He Who (holds authority) in the heaven will not cause the earth to swallow you when it quakes (and trembles)? ¹⁷ Or have you become so sure that He Who is in heaven will not unleash a violent storm to shower stones upon you? Soon you will find out how severe My warning is. ¹⁸ And indeed, those before them had also dismissed (My warning. But look at) how (dreadful) was My wrath (that I unleashed upon them)!

¹⁹ Do they not see the birds flying above them, spreading and folding (their wings with grace)? Nothing holds them (aloft) except (the will and decree of the) Most Gracious (Lord). Indeed, it is He Who watches over (and regulates) everything. ^{*a*} ²⁰ Is there any other power besides the Most Gracious

---

^{*a*} The Golden Plover bird is one of the best examples to illustrate the amazing truth of this verse. This bird hatches in Alaska during the summer months and when winter approaches, it sets off on its epic voyage to Hawaii which is a nonstop flight that takes it across the open sea, where no island punctuates the watery expanse. In addition, the bird cannot swim, so a stop for rest is impossible. The flight is a distance of at least 4,000 km (2,500 miles) across the open sea lasting 88 hours. How then does the Golden Plover carry sufficient fuel to burn enough energy to fly this far nonstop? Consider this : The bird's starting weight is 7 ounces (or 200 grams), and only a maximum of 2.5 ounces can be stored as layers of fat to be used as fuel because its net weight cannot be lesser than 4.5 ounces. The Golden Plover is known to convert 0.5% of its body weight (i.e. 0.035 ounces) per hour into energy. But when this is calculated over a period of 88 hours, it was found that the bird needs about 3 ounces of fuel to complete the journey. This is not possible because it can only carry 2.5 ounces. It also means that the bird will not have enough fuel to reach Hawaii and should crash into the sea about 650km (400 miles) before it reaches its destination. But why is this

(Lord) that can help you (if He does not)? Those who refuse to accept the truth are certainly in a delusion! ²¹ Or is there anyone who could provide you with sustenance if He withholds His provision? Yet they persist in their rebellion and aversion (of the truth). ²² Then, is the one who walks fallen on his face better guided than the other who walks upright on a straight path?

²³ Say (to them), "He is the One Who brought you into being and then endowed you with hearing, sight and heart (with conscience so that you may learn and discern truth from falsehood). Yet how little thanks do you give." ²⁴ Say (further), "He is the One Who multiplied (and dispersed) you all over the earth, and it is to Him will all of you be finally gathered."

²⁵ And they ask (you O Prophet), "When will this promise (of doom) be fulfilled, if you speak the truth?" ²⁶ Say, "Verily, the knowledge is with God alone, and I am only a clear warner." ²⁷ And when they (finally) see it approaching, the faces of those who live in denial of the truth will be in distraught. They will be told, "This is what you used to (mock and) ask for!"

²⁸ Say (to them O Prophet), "Just ponder. Whether God destroys me together with those who follow me, or graces us with His mercy, is there anyone who can protect those who oppose the truth from the grievous suffering (that awaits them in the life to come)? ²⁹ And say (to them too), "He is the Most Gracious (Lord). We believe in Him and in Him alone do we place our trust. Soon you will come to know who is clearly in error." ³⁰ Say (further), "Have you considered that if all the water (that you have in the wells) were to sink down (into the depths of the earth and vanish), who will produce clear flowing water for you (from new sources)?"

---

not the case? The answer is breathtaking. The same Designer and Creator Who gave the bird its aerodynamic shape also gave the bird a vital piece of information, which is to fly in a flock of V-formation that would save about 20% of its energy, just enough to reach its destination safely. Another perplexing question is how does the Golden Plover know the way to get to its destination especially when it has never been there before if it is embarking on a maiden voyage? The answer is : These birds are equipped with an autopilot system which constantly measures its geographical position and then compare this data with its "programmed" destination to ensure an energy-saving flight. Who is it that provides all this crucial information to the Golden Plover and enables it to process if not the Creator of the entire universe Himself Who regulates the affairs of everything? Now ponder this deeply : Is there any valid reason to reject the existence of this Supreme Being Whom we call God and not submit to Him? See also verse 88:17 where God asks us to look at the camels and how they are created.

68. Al-Qalam
[The Pen : 52 verses]

This is an early Makkan chapter. The chapter is named *Al-Qalam* or The Pen in reference to its first verse wherein God swears by the Pen and everything that it has been commanded to write. It then emphasized that the Prophet was not a madman that he was being accused of. The theme of this chapter is about the truth in his Messengership where he is commanded to remain steadfast in carrying out his mission. This is stressed further at the end of the chapter with the story of Prophet Jonah. The chapter also speaks about the general attitude of disbelievers who disregard God in their everyday lives. This is illustrated in a parable about the owners of a garden who regretted their arrogance after God destroyed it when they thought that they had full control over all their affairs.

In the name of God, the Most Gracious, the Most Compassionate.

Not a Madman's Message

¹ *Nūn.* By the pen and what they write! ² By the grace of your Lord, you are not a madman (O Muhammad). ³ And you will surely have an endless reward; ⁴ for you are certainly a man of the most excellent moral character. ⁵ Soon you will see, and they (who deride you now) will also see; ⁶ which of you is actually afflicted (with madness).

⁷ Verily your Lord knows well those who have gone astray from His path, and those who are rightly guided. ⁸ So do not yield to (the likes and dislikes of) those who deny (the truth); ⁹ for they wish that you would compromise (your stand) and they would then soften (their treatment towards you).

¹⁰ And do not yield to any contemptible habitual swearer; ¹¹ the slanderer who goes around with malicious gossip; ¹² the hinderer of good, the transgressor who is lost in sin; ¹³ (and) cruel; and besides all that, was born out of wedlock; ¹⁴ (who behaves in such evil way) simply because he possesses wealth and (many) children. ¹⁵ (Because of this,) whenever Our revelations are recited (and conveyed) to him, he (arrogantly derides by) saying, "These are nothing but (stale) fables of ancient times." ¹⁶ We shall surely (requite his arrogance by) branding his snout (with indelible disgrace)! *ᵃ*

ᵃ The exegesis of *Tafsir Ibn Abbas* and *Tafsir Al-Jalalayn* mention this person as al-Walid ibn al-Mughira, a staunch opponent of the Prophet, who is also the father of one of Islam's most illustrious warrior and military commander - Khalid al-Walid, who embraced Islam sometime between the 6 - 8 Hijra. See also verses 74:11-25.

¹⁷ Indeed (O Prophet), We tested (your people with good fortune) just like We tested the companions of the garden (before this) when they vowed to harvest its fruit in the morning; ¹⁸ but did not make any exception (in believing that nothing can ever happen without God's will). ¹⁹ So a calamity from your Lord struck (their garden) while they were asleep; ²⁰ and it became (barren) as though it was fully harvested. ²¹ And at daybreak, they spoke to one another; ²² "Go to your field early if you wish to harvest the fruit." ²³ So they departed, whispering in low voices; ²⁴ "Hopefully, none of the poor folks will enter the garden today (to steal the fruits) before you arrive." ²⁵ And so they left early, feeling very determined and confident with the thought that they had all the power (to harvest the fruits).

²⁶ But when they (arrived and) saw (the condition of) their garden, they exclaimed, "(This cannot be our garden!) We must have (surely) lost our way. ²⁷ Nay! (But in fact, this is our garden. Woe to us! Indeed,) we have been deprived (of our livelihood)!"

²⁸ Then the most sensible among them said, "Did I not tell you (before this) to glorify God (and always turn to Him in humility)?" ²⁹ (And so) they (finally realized their mistake and) said, "Glory be to our Lord (Who is free from all error and blame)! Indeed, it is we who have wronged ourselves (by forgetting You and brought injustice upon ourselves)."

³⁰ Then they turned upon each other casting blame. ³¹ They said, "O woe to us! Indeed, we have really been unjust (to ourselves)." ³² "Hopefully our Lord will replace something better than this for us. Indeed, it is only to our Lord Whom we (should always) turn with hope."

³³ Such is the (taste of Our small) punishment (and reminder in this world), and surely the punishment that awaits those who (choose to) deny Our message (and persist in their wrongdoings) is greater in the life to come. If only they knew!

The Righteous and Sinners are Not Alike

³⁴ Indeed, for the righteous are Gardens of Delight with their Lord. ³⁵ Should We treat those who truly submit and obey (their Lord) in the same way as those who (ignore Him and) immerse themselves in sin? ³⁶ What is the matter with you (O sinners)? How do you judge?

³⁷ Or do you have a book that you read and learn from (which is superior than this Qur'an); ³⁸ that allows you to choose in it whatever you want? ³⁹ Or do you have a binding promise from Us that extends until the Day of

Resurrection which grants you to have whatever you (think and) judge (as right)? ⁴⁰ Ask them (to tell you) who among them is responsible for this (outrageous belief)? ⁴¹ Or do they have partners (who can defend their beliefs)? If so, then let them bring their partners (to defend them when they are all arraigned before Us on the Day of Reckoning).

⁴² (And so), on the Day when every man's shin will be laid bare ^{*a*} and they will be called to prostrate (before God), they will not be able to do so. ⁴³ Their eyes will be humbled and they will be overwhelmed with disgrace. Indeed, (they had their chance when) they were called to prostrate while they were safe (and sound before this, but they refused).

⁴⁴ So leave Me to deal with those who deny this statement (that you have been tasked to convey O Prophet!). We shall gradually lead them (to ruin, step by step) in unsuspecting ways. ⁴⁵ And (in the meantime,) I shall allow them more time. Indeed, My subtle scheme is exceedingly firm.

⁴⁶ Or did you ask them for a reward that would burden them with debt (if they listened to you O Prophet)? ⁴⁷ Or have they any knowledge of the unseen that they have written it down (for everyone to see)?

⁴⁸ So be patient for your Lord's decision, and do not be like the companion of the fish ^{*b*} who called out (to his Lord) while he was in (its belly in a state of great) distress (after he deserted his mission). ⁴⁹ Had his Lord's grace not reached him, surely (he would have been left to die inside the belly of the fish. But We forgave him after he repented and prayed for Our mercy. And so,) he was cast forth upon a barren shore in a state of disgrace (as a lesson for him to take heed). ^{*c*} ⁵⁰ Thereafter, his (Merciful) Lord chose (to honor) him and counted him among the righteous (and sent him back to complete his mission).

⁵¹ (O Prophet! We know that) when the disbelievers hear this reminder, they look at you as though they would knock you off your feet with their hostile glances and say, "He is surely a madman!" ⁵² (So be patient because) what is being conveyed to them is truly a (clear) reminder to all the worlds (which they will be asked about soon).

---

^{*a*} The expression "when shins are laid bare" in Arabic means "when reality finally sets in."

^{*b*} In reference to Prophet Jonah or Yunus in Arabic. See also verses 37:139-148.

^{*c*} See also verses 37:143-148.

69. Al-Ḥāqqah
[The Inevitable Reality : 52 verses]

T his is a Makkan chapter which deals with the fundamentals of faith. Its main emphasis is on three things : (i) the truth of the Messengership of Prophet Muhammad, (ii) the truth of the Qur'an as a Book sent down by God, (iii) the inevitability of resurrection, judgment, reward and punishment. These themes are brought home by drawing attention to the fate of the previous nations like the Aād, Tsamud and others who disbelieved their respective Messengers and in the truth of resurrection and judgment and were destroyed on account of their disbelief and disobedience to God. Mention is then made of the horrors and circumstances of the end of the world and the resurrection together with reference to the sufferings and punishment of the sinful in the Hereafter and, in contrast to the reward and blissful life of the faithful and the righteous. The chapter ends by once again emphasizing that the Qur'an is sent down by God, that it is neither a poet's composition nor a soothsayer's utterance as alleged by the disbelievers. It goes further by saying that if the Prophet had made up anything and claimed that it is the Qur'an, he would have been severely punished by God and no one could save him from God's wrath. The chapter's name *Al-Ḥāqqah* or The Inevitable Reality is mentioned in the first verse which refers to the event of resurrection.

In the name of God, the Most Gracious,
the Most Compassionate.

The Doom

¹ The Inevitable Reality! ² What is the Inevitable Reality? ³ And do you know what is the Inevitable Reality? *ª*

⁴ Verily, the people of Tsamud and 'Aād denied (all news of) a sudden

---

ª There is very little difference between a disbeliever who outrightly rejects the inevitable reality of the Last Hour and the unseen afterlife, and a Muslim who has weak faith in this. Both are prone to usurp the rights of others, commit cruelty and injustice due to insatiable greed for wealth and worldly pleasures because they do not fear the grievous repercussions that await them in the next life. A weak faith in the afterlife tantamounts to a weak faith or no faith in the existence of God, the infallibility of the Qur'an and the Prophethood of Muhammad because these are the sources that convey the news about the sure existence of Judgment Day in the afterlife. Hence, a Muslim with strong faith in the afterlife will not dare to transgress and commit injustice and usurp the rights of others. He will always be mindful of all his actions that will be recorded for reckoning and requital in the afterlife because he does not want to end up a loser in the Hellfire. See verses 10:61, 34:3 and 99:6-8.

striking calamity. *ᵃ* ⁵ As for the Tsamud, they were destroyed by a thunderous blast. ⁶ And as for the 'Aād, they were destroyed by a storm - violent and furious; ⁷ which He sent to assail them for seven nights and eight days in succession, so that in the end you could see those people laid low (in death) as if they were hollow stumps of date-palms (that have been uprooted). ⁸ Do you see any remnant of them (today)?

⁹ Then came Pharaoh, and those before him whose cities were overturned while they were all lost in sin; ¹⁰ and rebelled against their Lord's Messengers. So He took them to task with an exceedingly severe punishment.

¹¹ And behold! When the water (of Noah's flood) overflowed (beyond all limits), it was We who carried you *ᵇ* in the floating ark; ¹² so that We might make all this a lasting reminder for all of you, and those with heedful ears will forever retain (the lesson they hear from Us).

¹³ Verily, when the trumpet is blown with a single blast; ¹⁴ the earth and the mountains will be lifted and then crushed with a single stroke. ¹⁵ And so on that Day, what has been destined to occur will indeed occur. ¹⁶ The sky will cleave asunder and fall to pieces on that Day. ¹⁷ And on its edges will be the Angels - eight of them, bearing their Lord's Throne aloft. ¹⁸ On that Day, everyone will be exhibited for judgment, so not (even the most hidden of) your secrets will remain hidden.

¹⁹ Then as for him who is given his record in his right hand, he will exclaim (in joy), "Here (everyone)! Read (and see what is in) my record! ²⁰ Indeed, I was certain that I shall be given my account (one day, and here it is now)!" ²¹ And so he will find himself in a pleasant state of life; ²² in an elevated garden; ²³ where clusters of fruits will be hanging near, (within reach). ²⁴ It will be said to them, "Eat and drink in satisfaction as a reward for the good deeds that you have sent forth from your days in the past."

²⁵ But as for him who is given his record in his left hand, *ᶜ* he will exclaim, "O how I wish I had not been given my record; ²⁶ for I have no idea of what has been recorded in it. ²⁷ O how I wish death would put an end to me.

ᵃ The ancient people of Tsamud and 'Aād were destroyed and annihilated because of their disbelief in the news of the striking calamity (i.e. *Al-Qāri'ah*, which is the title of chapter 101) that will be followed with Judgment Day that was conveyed to them by the Prophets who were sent to them. This led them to commit evil transgressions and injustice among themselves

ᵇ In reference to "your forefathers or ancestors".

ᶜ See also verse 84:10 and its footnote.

28 Indeed, my wealth cannot help me today; 29 and my authority has certainly vanished from me."

30 (Then,) it will be commanded, "Seize and shackle him! 31 Now cast him to be burned in Hell; 32 and string him to a chain of seventy cubits long (together with other sinners)!" 33 Indeed, he did not believe in God, the Supreme Lord; 34 nor did he feel the necessity to feed the poor. 35 So today, he is all alone without any friend here; 36 and the only food for him is the filthy discharge of wounds; 37 that only sinners eat.

False Allegations Refuted

38 But nay! I swear by what you see; 39 and what you do not see. 40 Indeed, this (Qur'an) is the (inspired) speech of a noble Messenger. 41 Not the words of a poet (as you claim. Oh,) how little do you believe! 42 Nor are these the words of a soothsayer. (Oh,) how little you take heed!

43 (Instead,) it is (revelation) sent down from the Lord of all the worlds. 44 And if (the Messenger) had fabricated some false sayings against Us; 45 We would have certainly seized him by his right hand; 46 and cut off his aorta.*a* 47 And none of you could have prevented it.

48 Verily, this Qur'an is a reminder for those who are mindful of their Lord (and yearn true salvation). 49 And indeed, We know that among you are such who will always deny the truth; 50 and it will surely become a cause of regret for all who refuse to accept the truth.

51 And verily, this is certainly the ultimate truth! 52 So (proclaim and) glorify your Lord's perfection by mentioning His name (abundantly, for He is indeed) the Most Great!

---

a This is another evidence that the Qur'an was not authored by Prophet Muhammad. Other than the fact that he was illiterate (see verse 7:157), it does not make sense for him to threaten himself with this fierce warning if he ever fabricated any lie about the Qur'an.

70. Al-Ma'ārij
[The Ways of Ascent : 44 verses]

T his is another Makkan chapter. It tells the story of a group of disbelievers in Makkah who derided the Prophet by asking him to hasten the promised punishment to befall them. But God ordered His Prophet to conduct himself with patience towards them and to remind them about The Hour of Doom that is near at hand. When the moment arrives, no friend will be bothered to ask about a friend as everyone is busy saving his own fate even though they are in sight of one another. The name of this chapter is taken from verses 3 and 4 that mention about *Al-Ma'ārij* or The Paths and Ways which Angels ascend to God.

In the name of God, the Most Gracious, the Most Compassionate.

Certainty of Punishment

¹ (O Prophet!) A (mocking) inquirer asked you (to hasten) the torment that you say is bound to befall; ² upon the disbelievers which none can avert. ³ (Behold! Tell them that it will come) from God - Lord of the ways of ascent; ⁴ to Whom the Angels and the Spirit *ᵃ* (regularly) ascend in a period which is equivalent to fifty thousand years of your (earthly) reckoning. *ᵇ* ⁵ And so, be patient (O Prophet), with such beautiful patience (that befits you).

⁶ Indeed, those who are bent on rejecting the truth regard (the Day of Reckoning) as something very far-off; ⁷ but We see it very near. ⁸ (That is) the Day when the sky will be like molten copper; ⁹ and the mountains will be like (scattered) wool; ¹⁰ and no friend will (be interested to) inquire about another friend; ¹¹ (even though) they are within sight of one another. (Verily), the sinner will wish if he could be ransomed from the torment on that Day at the price of his children; ¹² and his wife and his brother; ¹³ and his nearest kin who had sheltered him; ¹⁴ and everyone else on earth, so that he could just set himself free.

ᵃ The Spirit is another name for Angel Gabriel.
ᵇ This verse should not be confused with verses 22:47 and 32:5 that say a day or period in the sight of God is like a thousand years in our reckoning. Both those verses are clearly in reference to the measure of time in relation to the regulation of affairs. On the other hand, the fifty thousand years of our reckoning that is said to be equivalent to a day or period mentioned in this verse relates to the speed the Angels' take to travel and move around in their own realm.

¹⁵ By no means! Indeed, (all that awaits him) is a raging flame; ¹⁶ that would skin the scalp; ¹⁷ summoning him who turned his back and walked away (when Our reminder was conveyed to him); ¹⁸ (because he was too preoccupied) amassing and hoarding (wealth during his stay on earth).

¹⁹ Indeed, man was created with an anxious and restless disposition. ²⁰ Whenever misfortune touches him, he becomes despondent (and laments in self-pity); ²¹ and when blessed with good fortune, he becomes selfish and holds back (stingily). ²² But not so for those who turn (to God) in prayer; ²³ those who are constant in their prayer (regardless of their condition); ²⁴ and those who recognize in their wealth a due share; ²⁵ for the beggar and also for the one who is deprived (of what is good in life but do not beg); ²⁶ and those who truly believe in the Day of Judgment; ²⁷ and are fearful of their Lord's punishment. ²⁸ Verily, no one should ever feel secure from it.

²⁹ And as for those who guard their modesty (and their private parts); ³⁰ except from their spouses or from those who they rightfully possess (through wedlock), then indeed they are free of blame. ³¹ But whoever seeks beyond that are the ones who have clearly transgressed their bounds.

³² And free from blame also are those who honor their trusts and their promises; ³³ and those who (are honest and) stand firm in upholding their true testimonies; ³⁴ and those who are ever vigilant in keeping their prayers. ³⁵ They are the ones who will be in the gardens (of Paradise), graciously honored. ^{*a*}

Leave the Disbelievers by Themselves

³⁶ So what is the matter with the disbelievers who hasten in their scramble towards you (O Prophet); ³⁷ (surging) in crowds from right and left (to get a chance to deride you)? ^{*b*} ³⁸ Do they all wish to enter the Garden of Delight

---

^{*a*} Verses 22-35 : God outlines a number of Islam's great virtues that lead those who practice them to the ultimate success of Paradise. It is a pity to see many Muslims who neglect these fundamental aspects of their great religion, thereby failing to benefit from the numerous advantages it offers. God has also made it clear in the Qur'an that the road to Paradise is littered with hardship and hurdles that would need to be overcome. It is only through trials and tribulations that the caliber and quality of individuals can be tested and determined.

^{*b*} Al-Wahidi mentioned in his *Asbab ul-Nuzul* that the idolaters used to gather around the Prophet in the center of Makkah to listen to his speeches and sermons not with the intention of understanding and accepting the faith, but to mock him. So they happily derided him, running back and forth in a wild rush acting as if they were entering Paradise. Some of them boasted that if there was really such a place called Paradise

(with this behavior)? ³⁹ By no means! Indeed, they know very well about the substance We created them from, *^a* (yet they became arrogant and chose to oppose the truth).

⁴⁰ But nay! I swear by the Lord of the East and the West that indeed We are surely able; ⁴¹ to (easily) replace them with those who are better than them (if We wish so), for there is nothing that can prevent Us (from doing whatever We will). *^b*

⁴² So leave them alone in their vain disputes and amusement until they meet their ill-fated Day which they have been promised; ⁴³ the Day when they will come forth from their graves hastily as though they were rushing toward an erected idol (that they used to sinfully worship during their lifetime). ⁴⁴ (But on that Day,) their eyes will be downcast and humbled, overwhelmed with humiliation. (Behold!) That is the Day that they have been promised!

---

in the afterlife, they would surely enter it first because they were of a higher social status and also wealthier than the Muslims. Verses 36-39 were revealed as God's response to their arrogance.

^a Refers to soil and a clot of semen mentioned in verse 35:11. Knowing this alone will not qualify anyone to secure a place in Paradise. More important to this is he must submit wholeheartedly to God and follow the responsibilities outlined in verses 22–34 above.

^b God asserts that He is fully capable of choosing the right people to carry His message forward. The dithering and the indecisive will be left behind and will occupy a lowly position in the Hereafter.

71. Nūh
[Noah : 28 verses]

T his is a Makkan chapter. It deals with the fundamentals of faith such as monotheism and the Messengership of Prophet Muhammad. This chapter narrates the story of Prophet Noah before the Flood, and the encouragement for him to undertake his mission with patience, and to warn the disbelievers about the consequences of rejecting God's message. The chapter is named after Prophet Noah that is mentioned in its first verse.

In the name of God, the Most Gracious, the Most Compassionate.

Noah Preaches

¹ Indeed, We sent Noah to his people, saying, "Warn your people before a grievous punishment befalls them." ² (And so) he said, "O my people! Verily, I am a plain warner (who is being sent to warn you); ³ that you should only worship God alone, be mindful of Him and obey me. ⁴ He will forgive your sins and grant you respite (by not hastening your punishment) until a specified term (so that you will have time to repent). When the appointed term which God has set for you arrives, it cannot be delayed. If only you knew (and understood this)!"

⁵ (And after a time, Noah) said, "My Lord! Indeed, I pleaded with my people night and day. ⁶ But my calls only increased their aversion. ⁷ Verily, every time I call on them to seek Your forgiveness, they thrust their fingers in their ears, cover their heads with their clothes, become obstinate, and grow ever more arrogant in their false pride. ⁸ Indeed, I have tried calling them openly; ⁹ and also tried preaching to them (in public) and even speaking to them in private. ¹⁰ I said, 'Ask forgiveness from your Lord (for your sins). Indeed, He is Ever Forgiving. ¹¹ He will send down (rain) from the sky for you in abundance; ¹² and give you wealth and children, and also make for you gardens and rivers (that run in their midst).'"

¹³ What is the matter with you that you do not attribute to God due grandeur; ¹⁴ while you truly know that He is the One Who created you in stages? *ᵃ* ¹⁵ Do you not see how God has created the seven heavens (in full harmony) one above the other; ¹⁶ and has made and placed the moon therein as (an illuminating) light and the sun a (radiant) lamp? *ᵇ*

ᵃ See verses 22:5 and 23:14 and their corresponding footnotes.
ᵇ See footnote for verse 10:5.

¹⁷ (Verily,) it is God Who has caused you to grow out of the earth in gradual growth (like a plant); *ᵃ* ¹⁸ and He will return you into it and bring you out from it again (on the day when everyone is resurrected). ¹⁹ And it is God Who has made the earth for you in wide expanse; *ᵇ* ²⁰ so that you may walk along its broad pathways (in search for His bounties).

Destruction of Transgressors

²¹ (And so) Noah continued, "O my Lord! Indeed, they have (persistently) opposed me and chose to follow the one whose wealth and children only added to his ruin. ²² And they contrived an enormous plot (of blasphemy against You); ²³ in which they said (to their followers), 'Do not ever abandon your gods, nor renounce your idols - *Wadd, Suwa, Yaguth, Yauq* and *Nasr.*'ᶜ ²⁴ And indeed, they have misled many. So my Lord, grant nothing good to these evildoers except to let them stray far away (from the right path)."

²⁵ Because of their sins, they were drowned (in the great flood). Then they will be made to enter the Fire where they will not be able to find anyone who can help them, except God. ²⁶ And so Noah prayed, "My Lord! Do not leave on the face of the earth a single dweller from among those who reject the truth. ²⁷ If You spare them, they will lead Your servants astray and beget wicked ungrateful offspring (who will surely corrupt and cause disorder on earth).

²⁸ O my Lord! Forgive me and my parents, and whoever enters my house *ᵈ* in faith, and all-believing men and women (of later times too). But do not give (anything good to) those who are unjust except increase their ruin."

ᵃ There are about twenty other verses in the Qur'an that mention about man being originally created from soil and clay - sometimes describing the clay as sticky, sometimes as dry and extracted from black mud, and also like that of pottery. But this specific verse sums it all by saying that man is made to grow out of the earth in a gradual growth like the plant, which means that man is a product of the earth. It cannot be a sheer coincidence that many elements of earthly minerals are found in our body even at birth, and that We shall experience serious health issues if our body is deficient from any of these natural minerals that are needed to regulate the body's complex biological functions as long as we live. However, although man is originally created from earth, he is given life from water (see verse 21:30) just like how rain gives life to the barren earth and the plants that grow out from it (see the end of verse 22:5 and verses 80:24-32). Hence, there is no contradiction between the verses that say man is created out of the earth and also from water.

ᵇ See verse 15:19 and its corresponding footnote.

ᶜ Names of the five main idols that were worshipped during Noah's time.

ᵈ My place of worship.

72. Al-Jinn
[The Unseen Beings : 28 verses]

This is a Makkan chapter that gives an account of what a group of Jinn said when they listened to the recitation of the Qur'an by the Prophet and realized its truth. The chapter is named after this occasion. It is also mentioned that the higher heaven is protected by God by means of stern guards and flaming fires. It is further emphasized that God does not have any partner and that He alone deserves all worship. Mention is also made regarding the folly of attributing a son or wife to God. In conjunction with this, the duty of His Messenger is only to convey the message which he was tasked with and those who choose to reject it are promised with severe punishment in the Hereafter.

In the name of God, the Most Gracious, the Most Compassionate.

Believers Among the Jinn

¹ (O Prophet!) Inform those around you of the following : 'It has been revealed to me that a group of Jinn listened (to the Qur'an) and said (to their fellow-beings)': "Indeed, we have heard an amazing discourse; ² which gives guidance to the right path. We believe (what we heard) and will never associate anything with our Lord (in divinity). ³ And (we also believe) that He - Exalted is the Majesty of our Lord - has neither taken a spouse nor a son. ⁴ (Now we know) that the foolish one among us has been uttering outrageous lies about God (to mislead us); ⁵ and (we were truly mistaken when) we thought that neither man nor Jinn would tell lies about God."

⁶ "Indeed, some men used to seek refuge with the Jinn, but this only increased their defiance (against God and caused them to be misled further). ⁷ And they thought just as you did that God will never raise anyone from the dead. ⁸ We also sought to reach out towards heaven but found it full with fierce guards and shooting flames. ⁹ Indeed, we used to sit there in hidden stations to steal a hearing. But whoever tries to do that now will find a flaming fire waiting (for him in ambush). ¹⁰ And indeed (with such control in heaven,) we do not know whether misfortune is intended for the dwellers on earth, or whether their Lord intends to guide them aright (to goodness)."

¹¹ Indeed, among us are some who are upright and some who are not. We follow different paths. ¹² And we have come to realize that we can never frustrate God on earth and escape from Him anywhere by running away. ¹³ So as soon as we heard the call to His guidance (through the recitation of this Qur'an), we believed in it. And whoever believes in his Lord will neither fear

suffering any loss nor injustice."

[14] "Among us, some submitted to God while others deviated from the true path. Those who submitted to God have taken the right path"; [15] whereas those who deviated will be the fuel for Hell."

[16] If those (who heard Our call) remained firmly on the right path, We shall certainly give them abundant water (to drink); [17] to test them by this means (whether they will be grateful to their Lord for His generous provision). Whoever turns away from the remembrance of his Lord will suffer severe punishment.

The Prophet's Clear Mission

[18] Indeed, places of worship are only for God alone. So do not pray to anyone else alongside Him. [19] Yet when the servant of God [a] stood up to pray to Him, those (who oppose his teachings) would crowd around him (to harass him). [b] [20] Say to them, "Verily, I worship none but my Lord alone and I do not associate Him with anyone." [21] Say (further), "I do not have the power to bring any harm to you nor force you to accept guidance."

[22] Say, "Verily, (if I disobey God,) no one can ever protect me from His (wrath), nor can I ever find refuge except in Him. [23] (And not is my mission) except to convey (what I receive) from God and (make) His messages (known to all). And whoever disobeys God and His Messenger will be hurled into the Fire of Hell where he will remain forever." [24] (So let them wait) until they see (the doom) that they have been forewarned, then they will know who is actually weaker in aid and fewer in number.

[25] Say, "I do not know whether the doom that you are forewarned is near, or whether my Lord has deferred it for a distant term." [26] He alone is the Knower of all that is hidden and unknown, and He does not divulge His secret to anyone; [27] other than to a Messenger whom He is well pleased with. And verily, He sends forth (Angels as) guards to walk in front of him and another one behind; [28] to ensure that all His Messengers deliver their Lord's messages. His knowledge encompasses everything about them and He keeps count of everything in detail."

---

[a] Prophet Muhammad.
[b] See verses 70:36-39 and the corresponding footnote.

73. Al-Muzzammil
[The Enwrapped One : 20 verses]

his is one of the earliest Makkan chapters. It is named *Al-Muzzammil* with reference to its first verse wherein the Prophet is affectionately addressed as the one enwrapped in clothes. He was commanded to perform prayer at night and to strengthen his soul and have patience over the disbelievers' opposition and ridicule that he was about to face ahead. In addition, the Prophet was also being told by God about the punishment that awaits the Makkan disbelievers in the Hereafter if they do not heed the divine message that he is about to be instructed to convey to them.

In the name of God, the Most Gracious, the Most Compassionate.

Rise and Pray

¹ O you who are enwrapped (with garment)! ² Spend most of the night in prayer; ³ (either) half of it, or a little less; ⁴ or a little more; and recite the Qur'an in calm and measured (rhythmic) tones (with your mind attuned to its meaning). ⁵ Verily, We are about to entrust upon you words of enormous gravity.

⁶ Indeed, getting up at night produces the best effect (in subduing the soul since this is the time when it is) most receptive to the words (of your Lord); ⁷ whereas during the day you are beset with prolonged occupation (of worldly affairs). ⁸ (But whether at night or day, always) remember (and glorify) your Lord's name and devote yourself to Him in full devotion. ⁹ He is the Lord of the East and the West, and there is no other god except Him. So take Him (alone) as your Protector. *ᵃ*

ᵃ Verses 1-9 : In the early days of his mission, Prophet Muhammad was urged to spend most of the night in prayer as he was being prepared by God to receive words of enormous gravity that would charge him with great responsibility and hard work. And so, he would spend most of the night in prayer and by day he had to proclaim the message and confront his detractors. He had only God Almighty to depend on. And so, he devoted his time to God's praise and glorification in order to draw power and strength to face his enemies. His life, unlike any other, was wholly devoted to the service of God and His message. His task was not limited to the confines of Arabia, but to raising a community that would change the direction of humanity altogether, for all time to come. His nation was to carry the banner of truth in the face of all odds. His life was not devoted to reform merely one generation but to establish the tenets of *Tawhid*

¹⁰ Be patient over what those disbelievers say and avoid them courteously. ¹¹ Leave Me alone (to deal) with those deniers of the truth - those who enjoy the blessings of good things in this life (but are utterly ungrateful to the One Who grants those favors to them). So bear with them for a little while; ¹² for behold, We have prepared heavy shackles (for them) and a Blazing Fire; ¹³ and food that chokes as grievous punishment; ¹⁴ on the Day when the earth and the mountains will rock violently, and the mountains will crumble to a heap of pouring sand.

¹⁵ Behold (O men!) We have sent to you a Messenger who will bear witness (to the truth that is being conveyed) to you just as We sent a Messenger to Pharaoh (before this). ¹⁶ But Pharaoh rebelled against the Messenger, so We seized him with a terrible punishment.

¹⁷ If you refuse to acknowledge the truth, how will you protect yourselves on the (dreadful) Day that will turn children's hair grey? ¹⁸ That is the Day when the heaven will split asunder (and) His promise (of resurrection) is fulfilled. ¹⁹ This is indeed a (stern) reminder. So whoever wills, let him make his way to his Lord (by praying to Him in full devotion).

²⁰ Verily (O Prophet), your Lord knows that you stand almost two-thirds of the night, or half of it, or a third of it *^a* with those who are with you. It is God Who determines the (measure of) night and day. He knows that you will never be able to accurately measure it, hence He has turned towards you (in His grace). So recite (as much of) the Qur'an (as you can) with ease. He knows that in time, some among you will be sick, others may be traveling in the land seeking God's bounty, and others may be fighting in God's cause. (All these pose great challenges for you to perform this voluntary prayer). So (sufficient it is for you to) recite what is easy from the Qur'an, remain constant in (your obligatory) prayer, render the purifying dues (punctually) and lend to God a goodly loan (by spending in His cause). Whatever good deed that you send forth, it is for the benefit of your own soul and you will find it safe with God - better and greater in reward! So seek forgiveness from God. Indeed, God is Most Forgiving, Most Compassionate.

(i.e. the indivisible oneness concept of monotheism in Islam) all over the globe forever and to raise the men and women that would carry this forward for posterity.
^a This refers to the supplementary night prayer mentioned in verse 17:79

74. Al-Muddatstsir
[The Enfolded One : 56 verses]

This chapter belongs to the earliest part of the Makkan period at the very beginning of the Prophet's mission. It is believed to be the second chapter that was chronologically revealed after a long break from the time he received the first revelation in the Cave of Hira. But in spite of its early origin and its brevity, the chapter outlines almost all the fundamental concepts to which the Qur'an as a whole is devoted - the oneness and uniqueness of God, resurrection and judgment, life in the Hereafter, man's weakness and utter dependence on God, and his tendency to false pride, greed and selfishness. It ends with exposing the disbelievers' foolish attitude towards divine revelation and the Day of Resurrection. This chapter addresses the Prophet with the affectionate term *Al-Muddatstsir* or The One Enfolded with his cloak in the first verse where the chapter's name is taken from.

In the name of God, the Most Gracious, the Most Compassionate.

Rise and Warn

¹ O you who are enfolded (with a cloak)! ² Arise and warn (mankind); ³ and glorify (the greatness of) your Lord. ⁴ Cleanse (yourself and) your garments; ⁵ and keep away from all filth.*ᵃ* ⁶ And do not do a favor expecting for reward (in return). ⁷ But (do good) for the sake of your Lord and be steadfast (in doing good deeds).

⁸ And warn (all mankind that) when the trumpet (of resurrection) is sounded; ⁹ that very Day will be a Day of anguish; ¹⁰ not of ease - for all who refuse to accept the truth (during their stay on earth).

¹¹ So leave Me to deal with the one whom I created in a state of all alone (and helpless); *ᵇ* ¹² and then I granted vast riches; ¹³ with children who are always present (by his side); ¹⁴ and whose life I have spread much ease. ¹⁵ And

---

ᵃ Filth in this context refers to all forms of idolatry.

ᵇ Having warned the Makkans of the horrors of the Day of Judgment, the chapter makes an implicit reference to one of the most vociferous opponents of the Prophet in Makkah who described the Qur'an as sorcery. He was a man of great wealth and influence, well acknowledged and respected for his literary prowess. According to Al-Wahidi in his *Asbab ul-Nuzul*, this person is one of Makkah's prominent chieftain by name of al-Walid ibn al-Mughira. The contempt leveled against him is of course extended to his followers and supporters. See also verses 68:10-16 and the corresponding footnote.

yet he (greedily) wants Me to still add more.

¹⁶ By no means! Indeed, he is defiant (and rebellious) against Our revelations. ¹⁷ Soon I shall make him endure a painful uphill climb; ^a ¹⁸ because he (put so much) thought and schemed (very hard to oppose the truth). ¹⁹ Woe to him for how he schemed! ²⁰ Again, woe to him for how he schemed!

²¹ Then he looked around; ²² and frowned and scowled; ²³ and then turned his back and gloried in arrogance; ²⁴ and said, "This (Qur'an) is nothing but an evil spell handed down (from ancient times). ²⁵ It is only the words of a mortal (that is not worth listening to)."

²⁶ (Behold!) I shall surely cast him into *Saqar*! ²⁷ And do you know what *Saqar* is? ²⁸ It lets nothing remain and leaves nothing untouched (by Fire); ²⁹ (perpetually) scorching the human skin. ^b ³⁰ Over it are nineteen (Angels).

³¹ Indeed, We have appointed (stern) Angels as guardians of the Fire. And We have not made their (mysterious) number except a trial for those who refuse to accept the truth so that those who were granted earlier revelation will be certain (of this Qur'an's truth), and those who already believe will increase in faith, and that both these groups of people will be freed from all doubt; and so that those in whose hearts is a disease of hypocrisy and those who deny the truth will ask, "What does God mean by this parable?" This is how God lets astray whomsoever He wills (that turns away from His guidance) and guides aright whomsoever He wills (that turns to Him for guidance). And there is no one who knows about your Lord's forces except Him. (Verily,) this (news about *Saqar*) is surely a reminder for all mankind (to take heed).

The Warning

³² Nay! By the moon; ³³ and the night when it departs; ³⁴ and the shining dawn! ³⁵ Indeed, this is surely one of the greatest (signs of God). ³⁶ (So let it be a) warning to all mankind; ³⁷ to each one of you, whether to come forward (and believe in Our message) or to stay behind (and remain in disbelief).

³⁸ (On the Day of Judgment), every soul will be held as hostage for the misdeeds it has committed; ³⁹ except those on the right side. ⁴⁰ They will dwell in gardens (of Paradise), inquiring; ⁴¹ about those who were lost in sin; ⁴² (and then turning their attention to the inmates of the Fire, asking,) "What brought

---

^a Painful uphill climb in this context means an unbearable fate.
^b See the footnote for verse 4:56.

you into the Hellfire?" [43] They will answer, "We were not among those who prayed; [44] nor did we (feel the need to) feed the poor; [45] and we used to indulge in vain discourses along with others (to mock the believers); [46] and we also used to deny the Day of Judgment; [47] until the certainty of death finally came to us." [48] And so, no pleas of intercessors will benefit them (on that Day).

[49] So what is the matter with those around you who (still refuse to listen to the truth and hastily) turn away from the reminder; [50] as though they were terrified donkeys; [51] fleeing from a lion? [52] And yet, each one of them demands Scriptures of his own to be sent down and unrolled before him.

[53] By no means! In fact they do not (even believe in the truth, let alone) fear the Hereafter! (So, what good will the Scriptures do to them?) [54] Nay! Indeed, (sufficient is) this (Qur'an) as a (clear) reminder. [55] So let whoever wills, take heed (and be mindful of it).

[56] But they will not be able to do this unless God wills (to show them the way only if they are receptive to the truth). *a* Verily, He alone is worthy to be feared (and obeyed), for He alone is entitled to grant forgiveness.

---

a See verses 76:29-30, and 81:29 and its footnote.

75. Al-Qiyāmah
[The Resurrection : 40 verses]

This is a Makkan chapter. Its main themes are resurrection, judgment, reward and punishment. Its first fifteen verses describe the inevitability of resurrection. Next, reference is made to the receipt of the Qur'anic revelation by the Prophet and how he used to move his tongue in haste to repeat the recitation of the Qur'an delivered to him by Angel Gabriel. He was asked not to do so and is assured that God will enable him to remember what was delivered to him. These verses very clearly show that what was communicated to the Prophet was in the form of texts, not thoughts or ideas. The chapter then resumes the themes of death and resurrection, pointing out that on the Day of Judgment, the servants of God will be divided into two groups - one is fortunate and happy having a view of their Lord, and the other is unfortunate and distressed awaiting punishment for their rejection of the truth and their sinful deeds. The chapter is named *Al-Qiyāmah* or The Resurrection with reference to its first verse and its main theme.

In the name of God, the Most Gracious, the Most Compassionate.

The Truth of Resurrection

¹ Nay! I swear by the Day of Resurrection! ² And nay! I swear by the self-reproaching soul! ³ Does man think We cannot assemble his bones (again after he is dead)? ⁴ O yes! (In fact,) We are able to even reconstruct and restore his fingertips perfectly. *ᵃ* ⁵ Yet, man still wants to stubbornly deny what lies ahead of him; ⁶ (and) asks (mockingly), "When will the Day of Resurrection come?"

⁷ So when the vision becomes dazzled; ⁸ and when the moon becomes dimmer; ⁹ and when the sun and the moon are gathered together; ¹⁰ on that Day man will ask, "How do I escape from this?" ¹¹ By no means! There is no refuge (on that Day). ¹² It is to your Lord where all journeys will end on that

---

ᵃ The emphasis of Qur'an on fingerprints has an exceptionally unique importance. This is because shapes and details on everyone's fingerprint are unique to each individual. Each individual who has ever lived in this world has an arrangement of exceptional fingerprints. Even identical twins having the very same DNA sequence have their own arrangement of fingerprints that are non-identical. The Qur'an said that on Resurrection Day, God will recreate humans with all details even up to reconstructing their fingertips. How could the Qur'an mention about the uniqueness of fingertips more than 1,450 years ago if it was not a divine revelation?

Day. [13] And on that Day, man will be apprised about everything he has done and left undone too. [14] In fact, man will be called to be a witness against himself; [15] even if he (tries to) offer (a heap full) of excuses (to decline).

[16] (O Prophet!) Do not move your tongue in haste (when reciting the words of the Qur'an). [17] Indeed, We shall gather it (in your heart) and (teach you to) recite it. [18] And when We recite it (through Angel Gabriel), follow its recitation (correctly); [19] then indeed, We shall make (you understand its meaning) clearly.

[20] Nay (O men)! In fact you dearly love the temporary delights (of this fleeting world); [21] and neglect (the eternal nature of) the life to come. [22] Some faces will be radiant (with happiness) on that Day; [23] looking towards their Lord; [24] and some faces will be gloomy on that Day too; [25] in great fear of the painful calamity that is about to befall them.

[26] Nay! When the (last breath) reaches the collarbones (of a dying man); [27] and people ask, "Is there anyone who can cure him?"; [28] then he will realize that it is the time (for his soul) to part away (from the body). [29] And when both his legs are intertwined (in great agony); [30] it is your Lord Whom he will be driven to on that Day (in a state of regret and belated repentance).

The Dead Will be Raised

[31] (But of no use will his repentance be), for neither did he accept the truth nor prayed (for enlightenment while he was alive). [32] Instead, he denied (the message that was conveyed to him) and turned away (from it). [33] Then he went back to his family, swaggering in arrogance.

[34] Alas to you (O men) and woe! [35] Then alas to you (again O men) and woe! [36] Does man (really) think he will be left alone (to do whatever he wants without accountability)? [37] Was he not once a mere (unworthy) clot of fluid from the ejaculated semen; [38] and thereafter was formed into a (leech-like) clinging zygote which God then made it (into a living body with parts that are) well-proportioned; [a] [39] and fashioned out from it either as male or female?

[40] (Now think!) Is God then not able to bring the dead back to life?

---

[a] See verses 22:5 and 23:14 and their corresponding footnotes.

76. Al-Insān
[Man : 31 verses]

This is a Madinan chapter. It deals with life in the Hereafter, particularly the rewards and blessings that await the righteous; and about the Qur'an, emphasizing that God sent it down to the Prophet as a reminder to all. So whoever wills, let him take the right way towards his Lord. The chapter is named *Al-Insān* or Man with reference to its first verse which mentions that he was non-existent for a long time before he was given life.

In the name of God, the Most Gracious, the Most Compassionate.

Man, an Unmentionable Thing in the Past

¹ Was there not a time in the life of man when he was not even a mentionable thing? *ª* ² Indeed, We created man from an intermingled clot of semen (with the female egg) so that We may test him (later) in his life. Hence, We endowed (and equipped) him with the faculties of hearing and sight (together with feelings and reason too). ³ Verily, it is We Who provided him with guidance to the right path, (and it rests with him) whether he chooses to be grateful or not.*ᵇ* ⁴ Indeed, for the ungrateful deniers of truth, We have prepared for them chains, shackles and a Blazing Fire.

The Righteous Will Ultimately Be Well Rewarded

⁵ (And) indeed for the righteous, (they) will drink from a cup that is filled with a mixture of sweet-smelling sepals of blossoming flowers; ⁶ from a gushing spring that flows abundantly for God's servants to drink (and) quench their thirst; ⁷ They (are those who) fulfill their vows (and live righteously), for they are always fearful of the Day when terror is bound to spread far and wide.

⁸ And they give food to the needy, the orphan and the captive in spite of their love for it; ⁹ (saying in their hearts,) "We feed you purely for the sake of God's (pleasure and) countenance, desiring neither reward nor gratitude from you. ¹⁰ Indeed, we stand in awe of our Lord's judgment on a harsh and distressful Day (that is sure to come someday)." ¹¹ And so, God will protect them from the widespread evil of that Day and grant them radiance and happiness; ¹² and reward them for all their enduring patience with a garden (of

---

ª Despite man's insignificance to begin with, he has the audacity to be arrogant on earth during his very short stay on it. See verses 17:37-38..
ᵇ There is connection between this verse and 81:29. Refer to the footnote.

bliss) and (garments of) silk.

¹³ They will be reclining therein on elevated couches and will feel neither the scorching heat nor freezing cold. ¹⁴ And near above them are shades from the trees of Paradise and clusters of fruits (dangling low) within reach; ¹⁵ and vessels of silver and cups of crystal will be circulated among them; ¹⁶ and crystal-like (clear bottles made of) silver which they will determine the measure to fill (according to their wishes). ¹⁷ And they will also be served a cup filled with mixture of sweet ginger; ¹⁸ drawn from a spring there called *Salsabil.* ¹⁹ Immortal youths will wait upon them and when you see them, you would think they are scattered pearls. ²⁰ And whichever direction you look, you will see blessings and the splendor of a great kingdom. ²¹ (Its inhabitants) will wear garments of the finest green silk and rich brocade. And they will also be adorned with bracelets of silver. Their Lord will give them to drink a most pure drink. ²² (And it will be said to them,) "Behold! This is your reward. Your lifetime of striving is hereby (accepted and) appreciated."

Always Keep God in Remembrance

²³ Indeed, We have sent down the Qur'an to you in stages (O Muhammad). ²⁴ So wait for your Lord's judgment patiently and do not yield to any sinner or disbeliever among those (who oppose you). ²⁵ And remember the name of your Lord in the morning and evening. ²⁶ And during a part of the night, prostrate to Him and glorify His perfection throughout the long night.

²⁷ Behold, they (who do not hold God in remembrance are those who) truly love the temporary delights of this fleeting world. They (neglect and) leave behind them (all thought of) a grievous Day. ²⁸ (Because of their overweening arrogance, they conveniently forget that) it is We Who created them and it is We Who strengthened their bones and joints. And if We so wish, We can completely substitute them with better replacement.

²⁹ Indeed, this is a reminder for all. So let whoever wills take the (right) way to his Lord. But you will not be able to do so unless God wills (to show you the way if you believe and accept the truth); *ᵃ* for behold, God is indeed All-Knowing, All-Wise. ³¹ (And so,) He admits to His grace whomsoever He wills (that submits to Him in true devotion). But as for the evil wrongdoers, He has prepared for them a grievous punishment (in the life to come).

ᵃ See verse 81:29 and its footnote.

77. Al-Mursalāt
[Those Sent Forth : 50 verses]

T his is early Makkan chapter. It is named *Al-Mursalāt* or Those Sent Forth with reference to its first verse. Its theme is to impress upon the disbelievers about the inevitability of resurrection, afterlife and personal accountability. One of the dramatic features of this chapter is the repetition of the phrase, " Woe on that Day to those who deny the truth!" which occurs ten times throughout the chapter that serve as a very stern warning to those who stubbornly reject the Qur'an. According to an authentic *hadith* narrated by Imam Muslim (no. 462) on the authority of Ibn Abbas, this chapter could be the last recitation of Prophet Muhammad which he did so in the sunset (i.e. Maghrib) prayer before he passed away.

In the name of God, the Most Gracious, the Most Compassionate.

Consequence of Rejection

[1] By the (winds) sent forth in (swift) succession; [2] blowing with a tempest force; [3] scattering (rain clouds) far and wide.

[4] And by the Angels who (carry divine messages that) separate (right and wrong) with all clarity; [5] delivering a reminder; [6] (to end) excuses or (to give a stern) warning.

[7] Indeed (O men)! What you are promised will surely come to pass. [8] (That is the Day) when the stars are obliterated; [9] and the heaven cleft asunder; [10] and the mountains are blown away (and scattered like dust); [11] and (that is the Day) when the Messengers will (all be gathered) at the appointed time (to testify).

[12] For which Day has all this been set? [13] For the Day of Judgment (of course)! [14] And what will make you realize how (dreadful) will the Day of Judgment be? [15] Woe on that Day to those who deny the truth!

[16] Did We not destroy many earlier generations (for their evil deeds); [17] (and) then succeeded them with those of later times? [18] That is how We deal with habitual sinners. [19] Woe on that Day to those who deny the truth!

[20] Did We not create you from an unworthy (humble) fluid; [21] then We placed it in a safe lodging; [22] for an appointed term (before We brought you into this world)? [23] This is how We determined (the nature of human's creation). How excellent is Our power to determine (the best outcome of

things)! ²⁴ Woe on that Day to those who deny the truth!

²⁵ Have We not made the earth a place to gather; ²⁶ the living and the dead? *^a* ²⁷ And did We not place firm lofty mountains on it (as anchors) and give you fresh sweet water (to drink)? ²⁸ And woe on that Day to those who deny the truth!

²⁹ (On the Day of Judgment, the disbelievers will be told), "Proceed now to Hell which you used to deny! ³⁰ Go to the shadow of smoke (that rises) in three columns; ³¹ that gives neither (cooling) shade nor relief against the flame. ³² Indeed, it throws up sparks (of fire as large as) tree trunks; ³³ as if they were herds of yellow camels (on stampede)." ³⁴ Woe on that Day to those who deny the truth!

³⁵ On that Day, they will not (be able to) utter a word; ³⁶ nor be given permission to offer excuses. ³⁷ Woe on that Day to those who deny the truth! ³⁸ (They will be told,) "This is the Day of Judgment. We have gathered you and everyone before you here (as promised). ³⁹ So if you have any plot (to defeat Me), then use it against Me now." ⁴⁰ Woe on that Day to those who deny the truth!

⁴¹ Indeed, those who diligently kept their duty to God will dwell amidst (cool) shades and springs (of water); ⁴² and will have whatever fruits they desire. ⁴³ It will be said to them, "Eat and drink to your heart's contentment. This is the reward for what you did (on earth before)!" ⁴⁴ Indeed, that is how We reward those who excel in good deeds. ⁴⁵ Woe on that Day to those who deny the truth!

⁴⁶ (For those who refuse to submit to God and perpetrate injustice), eat and enjoy yourselves (on earth) for a short while, for you are truly lost in sin. ⁴⁷ (So) woe on that Day to those who deny the truth! ⁴⁸ And when they are told, "Bow down (in prayer to God)", they refuse to bow. ⁴⁹ Woe on that Day to those who deny the truth! ⁵⁰ (If this is their stance towards God's word,) in what other statement after this will they believe?

---

^a Syaikh Muhammad al-Ghazali interprets this passage from a scientific perspective by alluding it to the mysterious force of gravity which holds everything to the earth. Water covers four-fifths of the earth's surface. Is it not gravity that prevents it from spilling over or shooting up into the atmosphere? It is out of His infinite mercy and grace that God Almighty has made the earth attract things towards it and hold the entire life system together on its surface. He has also placed lofty mountains on it as anchors and give fresh sweet water to drink. Should we not be grateful to God for his blessings that we take for granted?

78. An-Naba'
[The Awesome News : 40 verses]

This is an early Makkan chapter. It starts by calling attention to the Qur'an and the resurrection which is termed as The Awesome News or *An-Naba' al-Azīm* because it appeared as something that is truly unheard-of by the disbelievers who started asking one another about it incredulously and then ridiculed it. This is the chapter's main theme and its name is taken after the initial verses. Then it draws attention to God's power of creation and that He can recreate and resurrect at will. After that, mention is made about the punishment that awaits the disbelievers and transgressors, and the rewards that will be given to the righteous and believers in the Hereafter. The chapter ends by reminding everyone that no one will have power to speak on the Day of Judgment except those who are given permission by God to speak. The disbelievers will wish that they had better remain as dust than be forced to face the everlasting torment that they cannot escape from.

In the name of God, the Most Gracious, the Most Compassionate.

The Day of Distinction

¹ What are they asking each other about? ² Is it about the awesome news (of resurrection); ³ that they are in utter disagreement (and reject)? ⁴ Nay! Soon they will come to know. ⁵ Then, nay! Soon they will come to know.

⁶ Have We not made the earth a resting place for you; *ᵃ* ⁷ and the mountains as its pegs (and anchors)? *ᵇ* ⁸ Verily, We created you in pairs; ⁹ and We made your sleep as a means to rest; ¹⁰ and We made the night as its cloak; ¹¹ and We made the day (bright) for seeking livelihood. ¹² We also built above you seven strong (heavens); ¹³ and placed therein the sun as a lamp, full of blazing splendor. *ᶜ* ¹⁴ And from the clouds We send down rain pouring in abundance; ¹⁵ to bring forth grain and vegetation; ¹⁶ and gardens of thick foliage. *ᵈ*

ᵃ See verse 15:19 and its corresponding footnote.
ᵇ Refer to footnote of 16:15 for a detailed explanation on this.
ᶜ See footnote for verse 10:5.
ᵈ This passage from verse 6 to 16 questioned the Makkan disbelievers that if they are not convinced of what the Prophet is saying, then look at the physical world around them and reflect upon its creation. Did all these come into existence without a Creator or did their lifeless idols create them?

[17] Verily, the Day of Decision is indeed an appointed time. [18] (And so,) on the Day when the trumpet of resurrection is blown, you will come forth in multitudes; [19] and the sky will be opened as gateways; [20] and the mountains made to vanish as if they had been a mirage.

The Disbelievers Will Lament

[21] Verily (on that Day), Hell will lie in wait (for all those who stubbornly reject the truth); [22] a place of return for those who (oppress others and habitually) transgress (the bounds of what is right). [23] They will remain in it for a very long time. [24] They will not taste any coolness nor any thirst-quenching drink in it; [25] except scalding water and pus; [26] as a fitting requital (for their defiance against the truth).

[27] Behold! They did not expect to be called for reckoning; [28] even after they (had wittingly) denied Our messages with (an emphatic) denial. [29] But We have noted every single thing of what they did on record. [30] And We shall say to them, "Taste now (the consequences of your evil doings). Indeed, We shall increase nothing for you except suffering!"

[31] But for those who diligently keep their duty to God, there is supreme fulfillment in store; [32] beautiful gardens and grapevines; [33] and well-matched, splendid companions; [34] and a cup of refreshing drink full to the brim. [35] They will not hear any vain talk nor falsehood in there; [36] as a (fitting) reward from your Lord - a gift according to His reckoning of your (splendid) account; [37] from the Lord of the heavens and the earth, and all that lies between them. He is truly the Most Gracious (Lord. And on the Day when everyone is finally gathered before Him for reckoning,) no one shall say anything without His authority.

[38] (That is) the Day when the Spirit [i.e. Gabriel] and all the Angels will stand in arrays (according to their ranks). And no one is allowed to speak except who is permitted by the Most Gracious (Lord), and he will only speak the truth. [39] That is a Day that is most certain (to arrive). So whoever wills, let him take the (right) path that leads to his Lord (while he is still has the chance to do so).

[40] Indeed, We have warned you of a punishment that is near - the Day when man will see the (evil) deeds that have been sent forth by his own hands. And he who has denied the truth all along will say, "Woe to me! How I wish I can just remain as plain soil (and dust today)!"

79. An-Nāzi'āt
[Those Who Extract Harshly : 46 verses]

T his is also an early Makkan chapter and like the other chapters, its main themes are monotheism, the Messengership of Prophet Muhammad, resurrection, judgment, reward and punishment in the Hereafter. It is named after its first verse wherein God swears by those Angels who He commanded to harshly take the lives of those who rejected Him and did not live a life that is according to the teachings of His Messenger. It then refers to the resurrection and the situation on that day of those who disbelieve in it and to their doubts about it. Then it is pointed that there will be only a single blast and all will be resurrected. Next, reference is made to how Pharaoh disbelieved and rejected Prophet Moses and how God punished him and his followers. This is to remind the disbelievers of the consequences of disbelieving and rejecting the message and guidance delivered by Prophet Muhammad. The chapter ends by once again drawing attention to the Day of Resurrection and the rewards and punishments that await the believers and disbelievers respectively.

In the name of God, the Most Gracious, the Most Compassionate.

The Great Commotion

¹ By the (heavenly Angels) who (are commanded to) harshly extract (the souls of wicked transgressors)! ² And those who gently draw out (the souls of the blessed ones). ³ And those who glide swiftly (in their realm); ⁴ and those who vie with one another in a race (to execute their Lord's commands); ⁵ and those who (have been assigned to) manage the affairs (of all the worlds).

⁶ (Hence O mankind, be mindful of) the Day when the earth will shake with a violent convulsion; ⁷ followed by another violent convulsion. ⁸ Hearts on that Day will tremble (with terror); ⁹ their eyes (downcast and) humbled. ¹⁰ And they will ask (in utter confusion), "Shall we really be restored to our former state; ¹¹ even after we have become crumbled bones?" ¹² They say further, "(In that case,) such a return will surely be a total loss (to us)!" ¹³ Then, all it takes is just a single shout; ¹⁴ and behold! They will suddenly be brought back to life (again) in an open plain.

Pharaoh's Unrivaled Defiance

¹⁵ (O Prophet!) Has the story of Moses reached you; ¹⁶ when his Lord called him in the sacred valley of Thuwa? ¹⁷ (Moses was told,) "Go to Pharaoh! Indeed, he has transgressed (and exceeded all bounds); ¹⁸ and say (to

him), 'Would you like to purify yourself (from sin)? [19] (If so,) then I shall guide you to your Lord Whom you will (surely) stand in awe of.'" [20] Thereupon, Moses (went to Pharaoh and) showed him one of God's great signs. [21] But Pharaoh dismissed it and rebelliously disobeyed. [22] Then he turned his back, getting ready (to challenge); [23] and gathered his people and made a proclamation; [24] "I am your Lord, the Most High!" [25] And so, God seized him and made him an exemplary punishment for the life to come as well as in this world. [26] Indeed, in this is a lesson for all who stand in awe (of God).

A Sign to Ponder

[27] (Now ponder O mankind!) Which is harder to create - you or the (vast) heaven? (Indeed,) He has built the heaven (sturdily). [28] He raised its ceiling (high) and proportioned it (perfectly into seven layers, giving each a task of its own); [29] and He gave (the earth) darkness to its night and brought out its brightness (during the day). [30] And after that, He spread the earth wide [a] (and made it habitable for all living things); [31] and brought forth from it water and pasture; [32] and the mountains He made them firm. [33] (All these) as provision for you and your cattle (to enjoy).

The Final Refuge

[34] And so when the great overwhelming calamity finally arrives; [35] that will be the Day when man will remember what he actually lived his life for; [36] and the Hellfire will be made visible (and clear) for everyone to see. [37] As for him who (did not care about God, habitually) transgressed (the bounds of what is right); [38] and preferred the life of this world (over what is good for his soul); [b] [39] then the Hellfire will indeed be his home. [40] But as for him who feared standing before his Lord and restrained his soul from pursuing vain desires and lusts; [c] [41] then Paradise will indeed be his home.

[42] They ask you about the Hour (O Prophet), "When will it come?" [43] On what (authority can you) say anything about it? [44] Only to your Lord rests its (knowledge and) finality. [45] Indeed, you are only sent to warn those who fear it. [46] (So) on the Day when they finally see (the torment), it will seem as if they had lingered in this world only for a moment in an evening, or at dawn. [d]

---

[a] See verse 15:19 and its corresponding footnote
[b] See verses 25:43, 45:23.and 28:77.
[c] See verse 91:9.
[d] This is an impression of how short life on earth is compared to the eternal nature of the Hereafter. See verse 23:112-114.

80. 'Abasa
[He Who Frowned : 42 verses]

This is an early Makkan chapter. It is named *'Abasa* which means He Who Frowned in reference to the first verse. Further elaboration about this incident is mentioned in the footnote below. Other than this, the chapter also mentions about God's condemnation of man's ingratitude when he thinks he is self-sufficient and quickly forgets his origin and his imminent final return to his Creator.

In the name of God, the Most Gracious, the Most Compassionate.

An Unintentional Mistake

¹ He *ᵃ* frowned and turned away; ² because the blind man came *ᵇ* to (interrupt) him (while he was with some Makkan chieftains).

³ But do you know why (he came to you, O Prophet)? Perhaps he was seeking to purify himself; ⁴ or to be reminded by Our revelation so that it would benefit him.

⁵ But for the one who considers himself free from need (and is aloof towards the message of truth); ⁶ to him you gave attention; ⁷ whereas no blame is upon you if he does not care to purify his (faith). ⁸ Yet to the one who came to you in full eagerness; ⁹ and in awe (of God in his heart); ¹⁰ you paid no attention (and ignored).

ᵃ Prophet Muhammad.

ᵇ Al-Wahidi reported in his *Asbab ul-Nuzul* that this blind man is Ibn Umm Maktum who went to see the Prophet while he was meeting the chieftains of Makkah. He was calling them to God, hoping that they might embrace Islam. Ibn Umm Maktum stood up and said: "O Messenger of God, teach me what God has recently revealed to you." He kept on requesting and repeating his request, not knowing that the Prophet was busy dealing with another party. Signs of annoyance appeared on the Prophet's face because he was being repeatedly interrupted. He said to himself, "These chieftains will surely say that my followers consist of only the blind, the lowly people and also slaves!" So he frowned and turned away from Ibn Umm Maktum, and faced toward the people he was addressing. Then God revealed these verses. After this incident, the Prophet used to honor Ibn Umm Maktum by saying, "Welcome to the one who my Lord rebuked me about!" whenever he saw him. See also verse 6:52 and its footnote.

¹¹ Nay, (you should not have done this O Prophet)! This Qur'an is indeed a reminder (for all). ¹² So let whoever wills, keep it in remembrance. ¹³ (It is recorded) in scrolls that are held in honor; ¹⁴ exalted and kept pure; ¹⁵ (written) by the hands of (heavenly) scribes; ¹⁶ who are noble and virtuous.

It is Man Who Destroys Himself

¹⁷ (But only too often that) man ruins himself (with pride and arrogance). How ungrateful he is! ¹⁸ (Does he ever consider) out of what substance did God create him? ¹⁹ Out of a (humble and unworthy) clot of semen did God create him, fashioned (perfectly) in due proportion; ²⁰ and then makes the way easy for him; ²¹ and in the end causes him to die and lays him in the grave (until an appointed time). ²² And when He wills, He will resurrect him. ²³ But nay! Man (is in the state of loss for) not fulfilling God's commands (because he does not realize that he is being tested with an easy life).

²⁴ Man should reflect about his food; ²⁵ how (it came into existence after) We poured down rain (from the sky) in abundance; ²⁶ then We cleaved the earth, splitting it (with new growth); ²⁷ and then We caused grain to grow out of it; ²⁸ together with grapes and nutritious vegetation; ²⁹ and olive trees and date-palms; ³⁰ with lush gardens of thick foliage; ³¹ and fruits and fodder. ³² (All these) as (Your Lord's grace and) provision for you and your cattle (to enjoy).

No Escape

³³ And so, when the Deafening Blast comes! ³⁴ (That is) the Day when everyone will flee from his brother; ³⁵ his mother and his father; ³⁶ his wife and his children. ³⁷ On that Day, everyone will be too occupied with his own affair (when the Fire is brought close to him, making him oblivious of everything else).

³⁸ Some faces will shine brightly on that Day; ³⁹ laughing and rejoicing. ⁴⁰ But some faces will be covered with dust; ⁴¹ and veiled with darkness. ⁴² They are the ones who rejected the truth ^{*a*} and immersed themselves in deeds (during their short stay on earth).

---

^{*a*} They either rejected God totally or ascribed partners alongside Him in worship.

81. At-Takwir
[The Folding Up : 29 verses]

This is also an early Makkan chapter. It starts by referring to the horrible events that will take place on the eve of resurrection, beginning with the rolling up of the sun termed as *Al-Takwir* which the chapter is named after. It then speaks about the divine revelation and points out that the Qur'an was delivered by the noble Angel Messenger Gabriel to Prophet Muhammad. Next, it points out that the Prophet saw Angel Gabriel in his actual form appearing in the clear horizon. Finally, it emphasizes that the Qur'an is a reminder for all mankind, calling everyone to the straight path.

In the name of God, the Most Gracious,
the Most Compassionate.

An Unimaginable Calamity

¹ When the sun is rolled-up (together with the entire universe like a scroll of parchment); *ᵃ* ² and the stars (start to) fall; ³ and when the mountains are set in motion; ⁴ and full-term pregnant camels are abandoned; ⁵ and all the beasts are brought together.

⁶ And when the seas boil over; ⁷ and souls are reunited (with their bodies); ⁸ and when the (innocent) little girl who was buried alive is asked; ⁹ for what crime was she put to death? *ᵇ*

¹⁰ And when the scrolls (of men's deeds) are laid open; ¹¹ and heaven is stripped bare; ¹² and when the Hellfire is set ablaze; ¹³ and Paradise is brought into view. ¹⁴ (On that Day) each soul will exactly know what it has actually prepared (for itself).

¹⁵ But nay! I swear by the receding (stars and) planets; ¹⁶ that run their courses and hide; ¹⁷ and the night as it departs; ¹⁸ and the rising dawn as it lights up (the day).

ᵃ See verses 21:104 and its corresponding footnote.

ᵇ The barbaric custom of burying female infants alive was widely practiced in pre-Islamic Arabia. The motives were twofold : the fear that an increase of female offspring would result in economic burdens, as well as fear of the humiliation frequently caused by girls being captured by a hostile tribe and subsequently preferring their captors to their parents and brothers. See verses 16:58 and 43:18.

¹⁹ Behold! This (Qur'an that is sent down to the Prophet) is truly the (inspired) words of a (heavenly) noble Messenger; *ᵃ* ²⁰ who has great strength and is held in honor by the Lord of the (Supreme) Throne. ²¹ He is obeyed (in heaven) and is most trustworthy.

Muhammad is a True Messenger of God

²² (O people of Makkah!) This fellow-man of yours *ᵇ* has not gone mad; ²³ for he certainly saw Gabriel in the clear horizon. ²⁴ And never would he withhold (a revelation that he receives) from the realm of the unseen; ²⁵ for this is not the word of an accursed Satan. ²⁶ So which path do you want to take then (O people)?

²⁷ Verily, this (message) is indeed a reminder to all mankind. ²⁸ To those among you who wish to be upright and follow the straight path; ²⁹ (know that) your wish will not avail without God's will, (for He is) the Lord of all the worlds. *ᶜ* (So strive hard in His path and call upon Him to answer your prayers.)

ᵃ Angel Gabriel would recite the divine verses to Prophet Muhammad for him to memorize.

ᵇ Prophet Muhammad.

ᶜ This verse is similar to verses 74:56 and 76:29-30. It implies that the choice of the right way is open to everyone who is willing to avail himself to God's guidance. No one should expect to be guided to the truth by merely relying on wishful thinking without striving towards it with a sincere heart that is accompanied with intellect and reason. There is also a connection between these verses and verse 76:3 which alludes that those who take the true path are considered grateful, while those who do not are ungrateful.

82. Al-Infiṭār
[The Cleaving Asunder : 19 verses]

This is an early Makkan chapter. It starts by drawing attention to the terrible events that will herald the Day of Resurrection, mentioning first the cleaving asunder of the sky i.e. *Al-Infiṭār* which the chapter is named after. Next, it points out how man is deceived about God in spite of the fact that He is the Creator of man Who gives him perfect form and shape. Man is then reminded that he cannot escape by disbelieving in the Day of Judgment, and that Angels are appointed over each individual to keep a record of his deeds that will reckoned on the Day of Judgment. The righteous will be rewarded with a blissful life in the Hereafter while disbelievers will suffer in the Hellfire. The chapter ends by reminding that none will have any power whatsoever on the Day of Judgment and all command will be God's alone.

In the name of God, the Most Gracious, the Most Compassionate.

[1] When the sky is cleft asunder; [2] and when the stars are all scattered; [3] and when the seas burst beyond their bounds; [4] and when the graves are overturned (and laid open)! [5] Each soul will (exactly) know what it has done and left undone (during its sojourn on earth).

[6] O man! What has deceived you about your Most Generous Lord (and lured you away from Him?); [7] (It is He) Who created you, shaped you, proportioned you; [8] in whatever form He chose, and assembled you (perfectly).[a] [9] Nay! But even then you (still choose to) disbelieve in the Judgment (that you will ultimately face one day).

[10] And behold! Over you are ever-watchful guardians; [11] who are noble and they write down (everything). [12] They know everything you do. [13] Behold! The truly virtuous will certainly be in a state of (perpetual) bliss (in the life to come); [14] whereas the wicked will surely be in the Hellfire; [15] which they will enter on Judgment Day; [16] and they will never be able to escape from it.

[17] Do you know what the Day of Judgment is? [18] Once again, do you have any idea about what the Day of Judgment really is? [19] (It is) a Day when (everyone will face the consequences of his own deeds all by himself where) no soul will have the power to help another soul. And on that Day, (it will become manifest that) all command is truly God's alone (which you have chosen to deny all along)!

---

[a] See verses 91:7. 95:4 and 96:1 and their corresponding footnotes.

83. Al-Muṭaffifīn
[Those Who Cheat in Their Measure : 36 verses]

This is a Makkan chapter that emphasizes on honesty and fairness in business dealings, and stern reminders on the inevitability of the Day of Judgment and accountability of all our deeds, the truth of the Qur'an and the Messengership of Prophet Muhammad. It also speaks about the attitude of the disbelievers towards these reminders, and the rewards and punishments in the Hereafter for the believers and the righteous on one hand, and for the disbelievers and habitual sinners on the other hand. The chapter starts with a denunciation of those who defraud others in trade and commerce by cheating their customers in measure or weight. This practice is termed as *Al-Muṭaffifīn* by which the chapter takes its name from.

In the name of God, the Most Gracious,
the Most Compassionate.

¹ Woe to those who skimp in their measure! ² Those who demand on being given full measure when they take from others; ³ but when they measure or weigh for others, they give less (than what is actually due). *ᵃ*

⁴ Do they think that they will not be raised from the dead; ⁵ on a mighty (dreadful) Day? ⁶ (That is) the Day when everyone will stand in front of the Lord of all the worlds (to account for their deeds and actions)!

⁷ Nay! Verily, the record of the wicked is indeed in *Sijjeen*. ⁸ And do you know what is *Sijjeen*? ⁹ It is a register (of the inmates of Hell, indelibly) inscribed. ¹⁰ Woe on that Day to the deniers of the truth; ¹¹ those who deny the (coming of) the Day of Judgment. ¹² No one dares to deny it except those who are immersed in transgression and sin; ¹³ who when Our revelations are recited to him, he says, "These are just fables of ancient people!" ¹⁴ Nay! But the stain of their misdeeds have caused a covering on their hearts. *ᵇ*

¹⁵ Nay! Verily on that Day, they will be blocked from (the grace of) their Lord; ¹⁶ and then behold! They will be herded into the Hellfire; ¹⁷ and told, "This is what you used to deny!"

ᵃ This passage covering verses 1-3 is not limited to commercial dealings alone but also touches upon every aspect of social relations - both practical and moral - which applies to every individual's rights and obligations that must be duly honored and protected.
ᵇ Implying that their persistence in wrongdoing has gradually deprived them of all consciousness of moral responsibility, hence making them oblivious of God's ultimate judgment.

¹⁸ Nay! Verily, the record of the truly virtuous is indeed in *Illiyeen*. ¹⁹ And do you know what is *Illiyeen*? ²⁰ It is a register (of those who will be admitted into Paradise, indelibly) inscribed; ²¹ witnessed (and attested) by those who are nearest to God. ^{*a*}   ²² Behold, the truly virtuous will surely be in state of (perpetual) bliss (in the life to come); ²³ reclining on adorned couches, gazing (at all the splendor) around them. ²⁴ Upon their faces you will see the radiance of bliss.

²⁵ They will be given a drink of pure wine kept sealed; ²⁶ with a sealing of musk which those who aspire (for the best) desire. ²⁷ And its mixture is of *Tasneem*; ²⁸ a spring which those brought near (to God) will drink from.

²⁹ Behold, those who are immersed in sin used to always laugh at the believers. ³⁰ And when the believers passed by them, they would wink at one another (derisively).

³¹ And when they return to their own people, they will return jesting. ³² And when they see the believers, they will say, "Indeed, these people have surely gone astray"; ³³ whereas they have never been appointed as guardians over the believers.

³⁴ But on that Day (of Judgment), those who believe will have their turn to laugh at the deniers of truth; ³⁵ as they recline on couches and gaze (at the splendor around them). ³⁶ (They say to themselves), "Have those who defied God not been paid back for all the evil that they used to do?"

---

^{*a*} The Angels.

84. Al-Inshiqāq
[The Splitting Asunder : 25 verses]

This is an early Makkan chapter dealing with the inevitability of man's meeting with his Lord on the Day of Judgment. It mentions about some of the catastrophic events that will signal the coming of resurrection beginning with the splitting (i.e. *Al-Inshiqāq*) of the sky which the chapter is named after. In addition, the obedience of the sky and earth is contrasted with the disobedience of humans. The reaction of the believers and of the disbelievers on the Day of Judgment is also described.

In the name of God, the Most Gracious, the Most Compassionate.

¹ When the sky splits asunder; ² obeying its Lord's command as it ought to. ³ And when the earth is leveled; ⁴ and throws out all that it contains and becomes empty; ⁵ obeying its Lord's command as it ought to; (then behold, the Final Hour has finally arrived!)

⁶ O mankind! Indeed, if you earnestly strive towards your Lord with great effort, then you will meet Him. ⁷ As for him whose record of deeds is given in his right hand; ⁸ he will have a quick and easy reckoning; ⁹ and will return in happiness to those of his own kind (who are the truly virtuous).

¹⁰ And as for him whose record of deeds is given from his rear; *ᵃ* ¹¹ he will plead for a quick destruction; ¹² but he will be made to endure the Blazing Fire. ¹³ Indeed, he lived happily among people of his own kind (who were all lost in sin during their stay on earth); ¹⁴ and thought that he would never return (to his Creator for accountability). ¹⁵ But of course (he will)! His Lord had indeed kept a close watch (on everything he did).

¹⁶ So behold! I swear by the glow of sunset; ¹⁷ and by the night and what it envelopes (in its darkness); ¹⁸ and by the moon when it grows to its fullness! ¹⁹ Surely your (life) will progress from stage to stage. *ᵇ*

ᵃ At first glance, this seems to contrast with 69:25-26 where it is stated that the record of the unrighteous will be placed in his left hand. In reality however, the present expression alludes to the sinner's horror at his record and his wish that he had never been shown it. In other words, his not wanting to see it is symbolized by the expression "behind his back".

ᵇ This is in reference to the stages of man's life from his initial conception in the womb, to worldly life, to death, to resurrection, and to his eternal life either in the Hellfire or Paradise.

[20] So what is the matter with them that they still do not want to believe (in Our message)? [21] And when the Qur'an is recited to them, why do they refuse to prostrate (and submit themselves to their Creator? Do they think that they can escape Him)? [22] In fact, those who disbelieve (and reject Our message) persist in denial; [23] but God knows everything they conceal (and reveal). [24] So give them news of a grievous (everlasting) punishment.

[25] But those who (repent), believe and then follow through with righteous deeds, for them is a never-ending reward!

85. Al-Burūj
[The Constellations : 22 verses]

This is a Makkan chapter. It refers to an instance of persecution upon the believers by disbelieving tyrants in the past. The believers during that time were thrown into a trench filled with fire because they refused to recant faith and return to disbelief. The story is being is cited here as an encouragement to the Muslims to bear with patience towards the disbelievers' opposition and enmity. The fate of the Tsamud people and the evil forces of Pharaoh were mentioned to bolster the believers' faith further. The chapter also mentions the ultimate reward and punishment in the Hereafter for the righteous and the transgressors respectively and ends by emphasizing that the Qur'an is a guidance given by God that is preserved in a Tablet (i.e. *Lawh al-Mahfuz*) near Him. The chapter is named after its first verse wherein God swears by the sky with its countless number of constellations (i.e. *Al-Burūj*) that He has created as a sign of His Almightiness which only He alone knows their purpose.

In the name of God, the Most Gracious,
the Most Compassionate.

¹ By the heaven and its constellations; ² by the promised Day (of Judgment); ³ and by the Witness and that is witnessed!

⁴ Doomed were the masters of the trench; ⁵ that was blazing with fuel-fed fire; ⁶ while they sat around it; ⁷ to watch what they were doing to the believers; ⁸ whom they hated (and tortured) for no other reason than their faith in God, *ª* the Almighty, the Praiseworthy; ⁹ the One to Whom belongs the dominion of the heavens and the earth. And God is indeed a witness over everything.

ª Based on ancient history, there were several notable incidents regarding the lives of many people who were sacrificed at the stake by their rulers who were people without faith that simply hated to see faith in others. However, the actual identity of the cruel persecutor who is being specifically mentioned in this passage is unknown. Nevertheless, it is worth mentioning a few here for the sake of general knowledge, namely : (i) Nemrod who tried to burn Abraham to death, but by God's grace, the fire became a means of safety for Abraham (verses 21:68-70). (ii) Nebuchadnezzar's attempt to burn three pious Israelites in a fiery furnace (The Book of Daniel 3:19). (iii) The story of Dhu Nuwas, the last Himyarite King of Yemen who by religion is a Jew, that persecuted the Christians of Najran and is said to have burnt them to death. He is reported to have lived during the latter half of the 6th century in the generation immediately preceding the Prophet's birth.

¹⁰ Verily, those who persecute believing men and believing women, and do not repent afterwards, they will have the punishment of Hell and the punishment of the Blazing Fire. ¹¹ As for those who believe and do righteous deeds, they will be admitted into gardens which rivers flow from right beneath them. That is the greatest success! ¹² (So be forewarned that) the seizure of your Lord is indeed very severe.

¹³ Behold! It is He Who originates (man in the first instance,) and it is He Who will repeat it (on the Day of Resurrection). ¹⁴ And He is the Most Forgiving, the Most Loving; ¹⁵ the owner of the Glorious Throne; ¹⁶ Who does as He pleases. .

¹⁷ Has the story of the disbelieving forces (whom God punished) reached you (O Prophet); ¹⁸ (the forces) of Pharaoh and (the people of Tsamud)? ¹⁹ Behold! Those who oppose God are in denial (of His powers). ²⁰ So God encircled them from behind (and destroyed them).

²¹ (Verily,) this (Qur'an) is truly a glorious discourse; ²² inscribed on a Tablet that is well guarded (and preserved). ^a

---

^a The Qur'anic term for "a well guarded tablet" mentioned here is *Lawh al-Mahfuz*. Some commentators take this in its literal sense as an actual "heavenly tablet" upon which the Qur'an is inscribed since all eternity. But to many others, the phrase has always had a metaphorical meaning; namely an allusion to the imperishable quality of this divine writ. They interpret the phrase "upon a well-guarded tablet" as Gods promise that the Qur'an would never be corrupted, and would remain free of all arbitrary additions, diminutions and textual changes. See also verse 15:9 and its corresponding note.

86. At-Ṭāriq
[The Knocker : 17 verses]

This is an early Makkan chapter that deals with matters concerning monotheism. Two amazing phenomena are presented in this chapter to impress upon the stubborn Arab pagans about God's greatness for them to ponder how weak man really is by reflecting on their creation, resurrection and the judgment that all mankind will surely face in due time.

In the name of God, the Most Gracious, the Most Compassionate.

¹ By the heaven and the knocker! ² Do you know what the knocker is? ³ It is the (spinning neutron) star (that flickers in the dark night) with piercing brightness (and produces a knocking sound). *ᵃ*

ᵃ In the first 2 verses of this chapter, the Qur'an mentions *At-Tāriq* which literally means The Knocker and then relates this with the bright piercing star in the 3rd verse. Understandably, it is impossible for anyone to logically relate the relationship between a Knocker and a bright star in the heavens or space to interpret this passage in the absence of accurate scientific information, especially for those who lived in the plain desert of Arabia more than 1,450 years ago. And perhaps because of this, the term *At-Tāriq* has been commonly and widely interpreted as The Night Visitor by other exegetes and commentators. However, recent discovery by space scientists and astronomers ascertained that there are actually fast-spinning bright Neutron stars - some even as fast as 43,000 times per minute - known as Pulsars that produce a knocking sound in space as they spin. The Jodrell Bank Centre for Astrophysics at the University of Manchester in the UK has recorded these sounds that are created by fluctuating electromagnetic waves as the stars spin and translated them into sound waves that we can hear. Neutron stars are essentially remnants of massive stars that are experiencing gravitational collapse after a supernova explosion. Their size is relatively small with a typical radius of about 30 kilometers, and are composed of high-density packed neutrons. These stars are very bright and appear blinking from afar. Once again, the Quran has foretold an astounding scientific phenomenon in the 7th century when no one at that time could make any sense out if it, only to prove its truth 14 centuries later to people in modern times who are now able to witness it with the help of advancement in science and technology. Following this, man is reminded in the next verse (i.e. verse 4) that he has never been left unguarded, which means that everything he does is under the watchful eye of God. As such, man should ponder how weak he is by reflecting upon the fact that he was created from a worthless humble clot of semen which is of no match against the more complex creation of the universe and what it contains (see verse 79:27-29).

⁴ Indeed, there is not a soul that has ever been left unguarded. ⁵ So let man see (and ponder) from what he has been created. ⁶ (Verily,) he is created from a (clot of seminal) fluid that is ejaculated (into the womb); ⁷ coming forth from (the vesicles that are located) between the loin and the pelvic arch. *ᵃ*

⁸ Surely, He (Who originated man the first time) is well able to bring him back (to life again); ⁹ on the Day when all hidden secrets will be laid bare; ¹⁰ and (man) will have neither power of his own nor helper (to save himself from God).

¹¹ And by the heaven with its recurring cycle (of rain); ¹² and the earth which is cracked open (with its flourishing vegetation). ¹³ Indeed, this Qur'an is truly a word of distinction (between truth and falsehood); ¹⁴ and not it is to be taken lightly for amusement.

¹⁵ Behold! They (who refuse to accept the Qur'an) devise evil plots (to refute its truth); ¹⁶ and I too am devising a plot (to bring their worthless effort to nought).

¹⁷ So give respite to those who refuse to accept the truth, and leave them alone (with their fancies) for a little while longer (until I return them back to Me for reckoning).

ᵃ For a very long time, critics of the Qur'an were happy to point out that the Qur'an made a fatal error here because almost everyone assumes that the ejaculated semen emanates from testicles. But the fact is, only sperm is produced in the testicles which accounts for a mere 5% of the semen while 75% of it comes from the seminal vesicles, and the rest 20% comes from the prostate, bulbourethral and urethral glands. Semen is made up of enzymes, flavins, fructose, mucus, phosphorylcholine and prostaglandins, proteins, and vitamin C; and is stored in a pair of sack-like glands called the seminal vesicles located in the male pelvis which sit right exactly between the loins and the pelvic arch just as the Qur'an describes. The purpose of semen is purely for reproduction as a vehicle to carry the sperm into the female reproductive tract; and the sole function of the seminal vesicles is to collect and store semen prior to its expulsion during ejaculation. How could Prophet Muhammad have known about the existence of these seminal vesicles and their exact location in the male's body if it was not divinely revealed to him?

87. Al-A'lā
[The Most High : 19 verses]

his is a Makkan chapter which assured the Prophet that the Qur'an would be made easy for him to propagate. It also speaks about the Hereafter, reward for the believers and punishment for the disbelievers; and it ends by emphasizing that Islam and the message of the Qur'an is the same message which has been communicated through all the previous Messengers of God. The chapter is named after its first verse wherein mention is made of one of God's most beautiful names i.e. *Al-A'lā* or The Most High.

In the name of God, the Most Gracious,
the Most Compassionate.

¹ (Proclaim and) glorify the perfection of your Lord's name Who is the Most High; ² the One Who creates (everything), and makes it perfect (in accordance with what it is meant to be); ³ and Who (determines the nature of everything that exists and) sets its measure precisely, and then guides it (towards its fulfillment). ⁴ (He is also) the One Who brings forth green pasture; ⁵ and then causes it (to decay) into dark stubble.

⁶ (O man! Verily,) We shall teach you to read (and learn) so that you will not forget; ⁷ unless God wills otherwise. *ᵃ* Indeed, He alone knows all that is

---

ᵃ Most commentators opined that the Arabic expression in verses 6 and 7 that reads *"sanuqri u-ka falaa tansaa illaa masyaa Allah"* which means "We shall teach YOU to read (and learn) so that YOU will not forget, unless God wills otherwise" is addressed specifically to the Prophet by virtue of the pronoun *"ka"* or "YOU" which is a second person singular term that is used here. However, the pronoun could also be directed at "man" in general, and not specifically at the Prophet alone since there is no evidence that could be found anywhere in the Qur'an and also in the Prophet's authentic traditions to affirm this. This is substantiated by verse 82:6 where the term *"gharra-ka"* which means "What has lured YOU away.." is addressed to mankind in general. And in 17:23, the term *"rabbu-ka"* that is used in the expression "YOUR Lord has decreed that you worship none but Him alone and to be kind to YOUR parents.." is also directed to all mankind since the verse cannot be specifically meant for the Prophet alone because both his parents have long deceased before the Qur'an this particular verse was revealed. In fact, there are several other verses in the Qur'an which use the term *"ka"* that are addressed to mankind in general instead of the Prophet specifically.

Based on this premise, I am more inclined to interpret the expression *"sanuqri u-ka"* which literally carries the meaning "We shall make you read" as not being specifically directed to the Prophet and not limited to the allusion of reciting, reading and learning about the Qur'an alone, but also includes the phenomenon of man

open to (man's) perception, as well as all that is hidden (from it). [8] And We shall make easy for you the path towards ease (if you turn to Us for guidance in utmost sincerity). [9] So give reminder (about the truth to all, O Prophet); for indeed (some) will surely benefit from it.

---

acquiring the necessary knowledge regarding worldly affairs through whatever means that are being made available to him at any point in time. Essentially, the passage relates to the importance and necessity of seeking knowledge and expertise to manage worldly affairs for the benefit of the society, the *ummah* and for all mankind. The entire process involves mankind's cumulative acquisition of empirical and rational knowledge, handed down from generation to generation and from one civilization to another; and it is to this very phenomenon, in my mind, that this passage refers. See also verse 35:28.

In the same context, the expression ".. so that you will not forget, unless God wills otherwise" in my opinion relates to God's will in making humans to naturally "forget and abandon" certain prevailing ideas, practices, procedures or systems in matters that relate to managing worldly affairs instead of matters that concern true religious doctrines. This is an important function that is critically necessary in the holistic process for the human race to move forward and progress. It is only through this way can new ideas be generated and formed to challenge the prevailing ones for adoption and implementation. If God does not grant the ability for humans to challenge and abandon existing ideas, knowledge and practices, then man will always remain static. As such, the nature and purpose of man's creation with regards to his role as God's emissary on earth to administer worldly affairs cannot be successfully fulfilled. No creativity will ever emerge, hence preventing the world from experiencing any progress.

This alternative interpretation is further substantiated by verse 3 of this same chapter where we are told earlier in an implied fashion that God, Who has perfectly created and formed man in accordance with what he is meant to be, has promised that He will guide man towards the fulfillment of his nature. By connecting all these three verses together (i.e. verses 3, 6 and 7) We shall derive a meaning which implies that as part of fulfilling the nature of man's inherent attributes, man must be enabled to acquire elements of knowledge through the process of accumulating, recording and collectively "remembering" information; except what God may cause man to "abandon and forget" when that knowledge becomes obsolete and redundant by virtue of his new experiences and his acquisition of wider and more differentiated elements of knowledge, including the acquisition of more advanced skills in his quest to bring betterment and progress to his society.

By adopting this interpretation, this passage can be seen to be very closely related to the first Qur'anic revelation, namely verses 1-5 of chapter 96 (i.e. The Clinging Zygote) which commands and encourages man to seek knowledge in all aspects in the name of God who is the Ultimate Creator of everything, where he will be enabled and taught by God about what he does not already know during his learning process.

¹⁰ (Verily,) the one who fears (the Day of Resurrection) will surely pay attention to it; ¹¹ while the wretched one will remain aloof from it. ¹² He will enter the great Fire; ¹³ where he will be in a state of neither dead nor alive (to suffer everlasting torment).

¹⁴ Most certainly, (ultimate) triumph is for the one who purifies himself (from sin and the evils of transgression by always turning to God in repentance); *ᵃ* ¹⁵ constantly glorifying his Lord's name in remembrance and (is ever steadfast) in performing his prayer.

¹⁶ But nay! Most of you prefer (to amuse yourselves with) the life of this fleeting world (and be deceived by it); ¹⁷ whereas the next life to come is better and everlasting.

¹⁸ Indeed, this same message is also inscribed in the earlier scrolls; ¹⁹ the scrolls of Abraham and Moses.

ᵃ See verse 91:9

88. Al-Ghāshiyah
[The Overwhelming Event : 26 verses]

This Makkan chapter describes the overwhelming event on the Day of Judgment where the downcast faces of the disbelievers are contrasted with the radiant faces of the believers on that Day. The title of this chapter is named after this. Then it warns the disbelievers about the punishment that awaits them, encourage the Prophet and the believers to be steadfast in their faith, and absolve him of responsibility for the disbelievers' rejection.

In the name of God, the Most Gracious, the Most Compassionate.

¹ Has the news of the Overwhelming Event reached you? ² On that Day, some faces will be (downcast and) humbled; ³ toiling (under the burdens of sin) and exhausted (by fear). ⁴ They will enter into an intensely hot Fire; ⁵ given to drink from a boiling spring. ⁶ They will have no food except from a bitter thorny plant; ⁷ which neither nourishes nor avails against hunger.

⁸ Some faces on that Day will be joyful; ⁹ well-pleased and satisfied with their effort; ¹⁰ (enjoying themselves) in a lofty garden; ¹¹ where they will not hear any vain talk. ¹² In it is a spring that flows continuously; ¹³ and also adorned couches that are raised high; ¹⁴ and cups put in place before them; ¹⁵ and cushions ranged in order; ¹⁶ with fine carpets spread out.

¹⁷ Do they (who deny resurrection) then not look at the camels, how they are created? *ᵃ* ¹⁸ And at the sky, how it is raised high? ¹⁹ And at the mountains, how (firmly) they are fixed? ²⁰ And at the earth, how (wide) it is spread out? *ᵇ*

²¹ So remind them (O Prophet), for verily your task in only to remind; ²² and not are you given any authority (to compel them to believe). ²³ As for the one who turns away in disbelief; ²⁴ it is he whom God will punish with the greatest punishment (in the life to come). ²⁵ Verily, to Us will be their final return. ²⁶ Then indeed it is upon Us to make them accountable (for everything that they have done).

ᵃ This amazing animal is also known as the "Ship of the Desert". The camel can store water in his stomach for days and live on dry and thorny desert shrubs. Its limbs are made to suit the surrounding environment and it can transport men and goods over very long distances. The camel's flesh can be eaten and hair can be used in weaving. And withal, it is a gentle domesticated animal. How do you then defy and deny the infinite favors of your Lord?
ᵇ See verse 15:19 and its corresponding footnote

89. Al-Fajr
[The Dawn : 30 verses]

This Makkan chapter deals with three main topics. It first alludes to the Messengership of Prophet Muhammad and the opposition and enmity of the disbelievers by mentioning the fate of the peoples of the past, namely the Aād, the Tsamud and Pharaoh and his forces all of whom were punished for their rejection of the truth. Then the chapter speaks about man's love for wealth and how this will destroy him when he resorts to immoral ways to acquire it. Finally the chapter reminds man of his ultimate accountability to God on the Day of Resurrection and Judgment and the reward and punishment that awaits him. The chapter is name *Al-Fajr* or The Dawn with reference to its first verse wherein God solemnly swears by it that He will deal with the tyrants of the Prophet's time like those He dealt with in the past. The chapter closes with a promise by God that He will bestow those who are righteous with a peaceful and serene soul, and that they will return to Him in a state of well pleased with Him and well pleasing to Him for them to be admitted into Paradise.

In the name of God, the Most Gracious, the Most Compassionate.

[1] By the dawn; [2] and by the ten nights (of Dzul-Hijjah); [a] [3] and by (the contrast of) the even and the odd (but yet complements each other); [4] and by the night when it departs! [5] Is there not in these, a solemn evidence (of God's supremacy) for those with sense and reason?

[6] Are you not aware of how your Lord dealt with (the people of) 'Aād; [7] in Iram - (the city) with many lofty pillars; [8] that had never existed in any other land? [9] And (with the people of Tsamud), who had (magnificently) carved (their dwellings) out of rocks in the valley? [10] And Pharaoh, Lord of the stakes (that he had used to impale his victims)?

[11] (Verily, they were those) who transgressed beyond bounds and terrorized the lands; [12] and caused much disorder therein. [13] So your Lord let loose upon them a scourge of grievous punishment. [14] Indeed, your Lord is Ever Watchful.

---

[a] The ten nights mentioned here refers to the first ten nights of the sacred month of Dzul-Hijjah, the twelfth month of the Islamic calendar, which include the Day of Arafat and the Day of Sacrifice. On these days every year, Muslims from all over the world gather at Makkah for pilgrimage, praising God and venerating His sacred House - the Ka'bah.

¹⁵ And as for man, (behold!) Whenever his Lord tests him with generosity by letting him enjoy a life of ease, he (proudly) says, "My Lord has been very gracious towards me!" ¹⁶ But when He tests him by restraining his means of livelihood, then he says, "My Lord has (unfairly) put me to shame (and agony)!" *ᵃ*

¹⁷ Nay (O men)! In fact you do not show kindness to the orphans; ¹⁸ nor do you feel the urge and compassion to feed (and help) the poor and destitute. *ᵇ* ¹⁹ Instead, you consume the inheritance (of the weak, greedily) devouring it altogether; ²⁰ and your love for wealth is simply insatiable (and knows no boundary). *ᶜ*

²¹ Nay! (So how do you think you will fare on the Day of Judgment) when the earth is leveled, pounded and crushed (to dust); ²² and when your Lord (in all His Majesty) will then come with His Angels (standing in ranks), row by row?

²³ (Behold! On that Day,) Hell will be brought in sight! (And) on that Day man will remember the warnings that were conveyed to him earlier. But of what benefit will that remembrance serve him (at that time)? ²⁴ And so he will say, "O woe to me! I should have sent forth deeds that could avail me now (when I had the chance before)."

²⁵ So on that Day, God will severely punish His enemies as none other can punish. ²⁶ And none can bind as severely as He does.

²⁷ (But to the righteous soul, it will be said,) "O serene soul! ²⁸ Return to your Lord well pleased with Him and well pleasing to Him. ²⁹ "So enter together with My (other righteous) servants; ³⁰ enter then (with joy) into My Paradise!" *ᵈ*

ᵃ Man is typically concerned with this world and the promises of what would serve to his immediate advantage. He does not care to think of what will happen after he dies. As such, he regards God's bounty as an entitlement that is due to him. At the same time, he regards the absence or loss of wealth not as a trial, but as an evidence of divine injustice which may lead to the denial of God's existence.

ᵇ The same is mentioned in verse 107:3.

ᶜ See verses 102:1-8.

ᵈ The believer strives for a beautiful death with a rewarding eternal afterlife, while the non-believer strives for a beautiful life in this temporal world without hope of an afterlife. See also footnote of verse 18:29.

90. Al-Balad
[The City : 20 verses]

This chapter is revealed in Makkah. The theme of this chapter is that man is created to work and be judged for his faith and deeds. He should therefore seek to do good deeds rather than indulge in arrogance and wastefulness. The chapter is named after its first verse wherein God swears by the blessed city of Makkah.

In the name of God, the Most Gracious, the Most Compassionate.

¹ Nay! I swear by this city (of Makkah)! ² The city in which you are free to dwell (O Muhammad). ³ And I swear by the parent and his offspring!

⁴ Certainly, We have created man to go through a life of hardship (and pain as a means to educate his soul and test his faith). *ᵃ*

⁵ (As for the one whom We test with ease of life and affluence,) does he think that no one has power over him? ⁶ And so he (proudly) says, "I have spent much of my wealth (as I wish)!" ⁷ Does he really think no one sees what he does?

⁸ Have We not made for him two eyes; ⁹ and a tongue and a pair of lips; ¹⁰ and shown him the two (conspicuous) ways (of good and evil)? ¹¹ But he made no effort to climb the steep path.

¹² And do you know what the steep path is? ¹³ It is (to strive in doing good, like) the freeing of one's neck (from the burden of debt or slavery); ¹⁴ or giving food on a day of great hunger; ¹⁵ to an orphan of near kin; ¹⁶ or to a destitute who is in misery. ¹⁷ And to be among those who believe (in Our message) and counsel one another to persevere in faith and be kind to others. ¹⁸ Verily, they are the companions of the right.

¹⁹ But as for those who reject Our signs (of revelation), they are the companions of the left.*ᵇ* ²⁰ Over them will be the Fire that is closed from all sides (with no way out)!

ᵃ Man is born to strive and struggle. If he encounters hardship, he must exercise patience. God will eventually grant him ease (verses 65:7 and 94:5-6).
ᵇ The companions of the left are described in verses 56:8-9 and 41-56.

91. Ash-Shams
[The Sun : 15 Verses]

This is an early Makkan chapter which points out that just as there is contrast between the sun and moon, the night and day, and the heaven and earth, there is also a big difference between good and evil which is a direct consequence of man's success to purify his soul or allow it to corrupt. In the end, everyone will be judged according to his faith and deeds, and then requited accordingly.

In the name of God, the Most Gracious, the Most Compassionate.

¹ By the sun and its morning splendor; ² and the moon that follows (and rises) after it; ³ and the day when it reveals the world; ⁴ and the night when it veils it (with darkness); ⁵ and the heaven and (He) Who constructed it (in its wondrous marvel); ⁶ and the earth and (He) Who spread it (in great expanse). *ᵃ*

⁷ And by the soul and (He) Who fashioned it well;*ᵇ* ⁸ and then inspired it with the (innate) tendency towards evil and piety (together with the natural disposition to discern between them).

⁹ Indeed, he who (strives to) purify his soul will prosper (and attain a happy state); ¹⁰ while he who corrupts its (natural purity by worshipping his own lusts and treading in evil's path) will certainly be ruined. *ᶜ*

¹¹ (Know that) the people of Tsamud had denied (and rejected God's reminder) with their (rebellion and) transgression; ¹² when the most wicked of them rose up (in rage to kill the she-camel); ¹³ although the Messenger of God had warned them saying, "This is a she-camel that belongs to God. So (leave her alone and) let her drink (as she pleases)." ¹⁴ But they denied him and cruelly slaughtered her. So their Lord destroyed them for their sins and leveled them to the ground! *ᵈ* ¹⁵ And He dreads not its consequences.

ᵃ See verse 15:19 and its footnote.
ᵇ Man is created in the finest form with a pure *fitrah* (i.e. natural disposition). See verses 30:30 and 95:4. Essentially, God has instilled instincts and desires in man that tend to pull him towards immoral and self-indulgement acts and has urged him to resist their power of temptation. Those who tame and overcome such desires will be successful and prosper. This is the essence of faith (i.e. *īmān*) - a force for purification and excellence, and a beacon that leads to God's pleasure.
ᶜ See verses 7:172, 25:43, 45:23, 95:4-6, 102:1-2 and their corresponding footnotes.
ᵈ See also verses 11:61-68.

92. Al-Layl
[The Night : 21 verses]

his is an early Makkan chapter which is named after its first verse wherein God swears by the night i.e. *Al-Layl*. It points out that God provides guidance to man through the Qur'an. Those who reject and turn away from it will be punished in the Hereafter while those who believe and spend their wealth in charity and for the pleasure of God will be saved from the Hellfire and be rewarded with eternal happiness in Paradise.

In the name of God, the Most Gracious, the Most Compassionate.

¹ By the night when it covers (the earth with darkness); ² and the day when it shines (gloriously); ³ and by His creation of male and female! ⁴ Indeed (O mankind), your efforts are certainly diverse (and are directed towards different ends). ᵃ

⁵ As for him who spends in charity and is ever mindful of God; ⁶ and who testifies in goodness (not only in words but also in deeds); ⁷ We shall facilitate his way towards ease.

⁸ But as for him who is stingy and considers himself free of any need (from God); ⁹ and calls the (ultimate) good a lie; ¹⁰ We shall facilitate his way towards hardship. ¹¹ What benefit will his wealth be to him when he goes down (into his grave)?

¹² Indeed (O people!) It is upon Us to grace you with guidance; ¹³ and surely to Us belongs (the dominion over) the life to come and this world.

¹⁴ And so, I warn you now of a Blazing Fire; ¹⁵ in which none will burn except the wretched; ¹⁶ who denies the truth and turns away (from Our reminder).

¹⁷ But the righteous will be kept away from this (dreadful suffering); ¹⁸ (such as) the one who spends in charity so that he might grow in purity; ¹⁹ without expecting any favor in return; ²⁰ except to seek for only the (pleasure and) countenance of his Lord, the Most Exalted. ²¹ And in time, he will surely be pleased (and gratified).

ᵃ Good and bad endings in the afterlife.

93. Aḍ-Ḍuḥā
[The Bright Morning Hours : 11 verses]

This is an early Makkan chapter addressed to the Prophet to reassure him that his Lord had not forsaken him when he had not received revelation for some time. The chapter is named after the first verse in which God swears by the splendor of The Bright Morning Hours i.e. Aḍ-Ḍuḥā to stress His message of optimism for the Prophet to hold on to.

In the name of God, the Most Gracious, the Most Compassionate.

¹ By the glorious morning light; ² and the (still of the) night when it covers (the earth) with darkness!

³ (Verily O Muhammad,) your Lord has not forsaken you, nor is He displeased with you. *ᵃ* ⁴ And surely (the promise of) the life to come is better than the present. ⁵ And soon your Lord will grant you something that you will be well pleased with. *ᵇ*

⁶ Did He not find you as an orphan and sheltered you? ⁷ And were you not lost, then He guided you? ⁸ And did He not find you in need, then gave you sufficiency?

⁹ So towards the orphans, do not be harsh; ¹⁰ and towards those who ask, do not repel. ¹¹ And as for the favors of your Lord, proclaim them.

ᵃ The early years of the Prophet's ministry might have seemed blank. After the first few revelations, there were days and periods of waiting. During this time, his own tribe of Quraysh jeered, taunted and persecuted him and those who followed him. His faith was never shaken. But as a normal human being with feelings and emotions, the sudden lull and feeling of emptiness from the absence of divine revelations and Angel Gabriel's visit did make him feel worried and concerned if he had done anything that might have incurred God's displeasure.

ᵇ According to Ibn 'Abbas, this expression of promise from God refers to the Paradise that has been prepared and guaranteed for the Prophet in the life to come in view of its direct relation with the preceding verse. But Abdullah Yusuf Ali is in the opinion that this promise is also applicable to the life of this world for those who are firm in faith and continuously strive in God's cause, including the Prophet himself, that they will receive God's good pleasure in the form of feeling of complete satisfaction, contentment, and active pleasure when one's will is in consonance with God's will.

94. Ash-Sharh
[The Consolation : 8 verses]

This is another early Makkan chapter addressed to the Prophet. It is a continuation of the reassurance and encouragement given in the chapter before this. The chapter mentions God's special favor of opening the Prophet's heart to the truth and removing from him the burden of all faults where the chapter takes its name from. The Prophet is also reminded that God has raised high his reputation and that he should not be discouraged by any temporary difficulty that come in the way of his mission because with every difficulty comes ease.

In the name of God, the Most Gracious, the Most Compassionate.

¹ (O Muhammad!) Have We not opened your heart; ² and removed your burden; ³ that weighed (heavily) on your back? ⁴ And have We not raised your reputation high?

⁵ So indeed, (remember that) with hardship comes ease. ⁶ Truly, with hardship comes ease. ͣ

⁷ And so when you are freed from your immediate task, resume your toil. ͣ
⁸ And to your Lord, (always) turn in hope.

ͣ The Prophet had endured great hardship while carrying out his prophetic mission, God with his All-Aware and All-Knowing attributes, knew exactly of the difficulties that His Messenger was experiencing. As such, God comforted His Messenger by reminding him of the ease that he has been receiving even before he became a Prophet as mentioned in 93:4-8. Indeed, hardship is never absolute, for it will always be followed by ease. This is strongly emphasized by a literal repetition of the statement: *"With hardship comes ease"* which reaffirmed that the Prophet's hardship was never meant to last, and was unceasingly relieved by inspirational guidance throughout his life. The literal repetition of the statement is also intended to bolster the Prophet's spirits further as a reassurance of God's promise that He would never forsake His beloved Messenger (93:3).

ͣ The gist of this verse means that even though one has been freed from his immediate task, he should not sit back complacently. There are many other tasks that need to be attended to and fulfilled, be it in inviting others to the path of God, or in managing worldly affairs for the society's betterment. Therefore, resume your toil as soon as you finish your immediate task, and vie with one other in performing good deeds. Build yourself a home in the gardens of Paradise in the next life by making the world that we live in today a better place for others while relentlessly inviting mankind to the true path with wisdom.

95. At-Tīn
[The Fig : 8 verses]

T his is an early Makkan chapter which questions how man can ever deny the true religion of monotheism. It also emphasizes on the importance of faith and good deeds.

In the name of God, the Most Gracious, the Most Compassionate.

¹ By the fig and the olive; ² and Mount Sinai; ³ and this secure city! *ᵃ*

⁴ Indeed, We have created man in the best and finest of form.*ᵇ* ⁵ Thereafter, We returned him to the lowest of the low; *ᶜ* ⁶ except those who believe (in Our message) and do righteous deeds. Then for them will be a never-ending reward.

⁷ (O man!) What else would cause you to still deny the religion of God after this? ⁸ Is God not the Most Just of all Judges?

ᵃ According to Muhammad Asad, the fig and the olive in this verse symbolize the lands in which these trees predominate (i.e. Palestine and Syria). It was in these lands that most of the Abrahamic prophets mentioned in the Qur'an lived and preached, culminating in the last Judaic prophet - Jesus. On the other hand, Mount Sinai that is located in the Sinai Desert, stresses specifically the prophethood of Moses, which bears a great significance to the set of religious law that was revealed to him and became valid during his time until the advent of Prophet Muhammad; which was binding upon Jesus as well. Finally, "this secure city" undoubtedly signifies Makkah (as is evident from 2:126), where Muhammad, the Last Prophet, was born and received his divine call. Thus, verses 1-3 draw our attention to the fundamental ethical unity underlying the genuine teachings of all the three historic phases of monotheistic religion that are personified by Moses, Jesus and Muhammad.
ᵇ This refers to the state of pure *fitrah* (see verses 7:172, 17:70, 30:30, 91:7) together with the gift of intellect and reason ready to assume the role as God's emissary and trustee to administer the earth (see verse 2:30) with fairness and compassion that will bring much goodness and prosperity to mankind.
ᶜ Man will need to constantly strive to purify his soul from evil tendencies (verses 91:9-10) that the world presents and apply his reason and intellect according to God's guidance in order to save himself from ruin. Otherwise, he will take his lusts and vain desires as god (verses 25:43 and 45:23) and end up being consigned to the lowest condition of spiritual state with a corrupt and sick soul (see the footnote of verse 7:172) that will prevent him from performing his duty as God's emissary on earth to fulfill the purpose of his creation.

96. Al-'Alaq
[The Clinging Zygote : 19 verses]

The first five verses of this chapter are the earliest passage of the Qur'an that was revealed to the Prophet in the cave of Mount Hira' by the Angel Gabriel, thus marking the beginning of a series of divine revelations that would take place over the next 23 years. The chapter is named after the term *'Alaq* in the second verse which refers to God's creation of man from a clot of leech-like clinging substance. The first five verses also mention God's most important favor to man which is to impart knowledge and teaching him what he does not know. The rest of the chapter was sent down a little later. It refers to the beginning of the truth and the opposition to it by the Makkan chieftains, particularly by Abu Jahl. He and all such persons are reminded of God's retribution and that all of them will ultimately return to Him. The Prophet is told to pay no heed to such opposition and to continue preaching and worshipping God.

In the name of God, the Most Gracious, the Most Compassionate.

¹ Read! In the name of your Lord Who created (everything). *ª* ² He (is the One Who) has created man from a (leech-like) clinging zygote. *ᵇ*

³ Read! For your Lord is the Most Bountiful; ⁴ the One Who taught (man) the use of pen; *ᶜ* ⁵ (and) taught man what he knew not.

ª The Arabic word *Iqra'* may be rendered as "read" or "recite" or perhaps even "learn" depending on the context how this passage may want to be understood. If the passage was to be applied in a context for the reader to draw a lesson from it and put a meaningful use of this lesson in his own life, then *Iqra'* should be understood as a command to "learn" and "acquire knowledge". This is because man would not be fulfilling his basic intellectual nature as a human being that has been created by God as His best and most perfect creature in accordance with what the human race is meant to be if he is without knowledge and does not want to acquire knowledge. Without knowledge too, man will defy his Creator and not be able to play his designated role as God's emissary on earth, and this would defeat the purpose of his creation (2:30, 6:165). The whole concept of why man must endeavor to acquire knowledge is very much in connection with verses 35:28, 41:53, 80:18-20, 82:7 and 87:2-3.

ᵇ See verses 22:5 and 23:14 and their corresponding footnotes

ᶜ For the uninitiated, here is an interesting question to ponder : How many of us have ever thought and realized that man is the only creature in the universe that is endowed with the unique ability to write, read, draw, record, document, analyze and explain his thoughts, experiences and insights, and can then transmit all these from an individual

⁶ Nay! Indeed, man is bound to (defiantly) transgress God's limits; ⁷ when he considers himself self-sufficient. *ª* ⁸ But it is to your Lord Whom you will be finally returned.

⁹ Have you seen the one who tried to prevent; ¹⁰ a servant (of God) from praying? ¹¹ Do you think he is upon guidance; ¹² or encourages true piety? ¹³ Have you seen when he denies the truth and turns away from it (in arrogance)? ¹⁴ Does he not realize that God sees (everything)?

¹⁵ Nay! If he does not desist, We shall surely drag him by his forehead; ¹⁶ his lying, sinful forehead!

¹⁷ So let him call his supporters (for help). ¹⁸ We too shall call the guards of Hell (to deal with him). ¹⁹ Nay! Pay no heed to him. Instead, prostrate (in full devotion to God) and bring yourself closer to Him.

---

to another individual or groups, from generation to generation, and from one cultural environment to another? What makes it interesting is that this phenomenon could not have been carried out without the aid of a simple and often overlooked instrument which we call "The Pen" or other equivalent tools and devices of the modern day that can record and transmit information. This explains the symbolic summons "Read!" or "Learn!" at the beginning of verses 1 and 3 which is repeated twice to emphasize man's utter dependence on God, Who creates him as a biological entity and then implants in him the will and ability to acquire, record and transmit knowledge and information to others. Does this not make man the most special and perfect creature over everything else in the entire universe (95:4), particularly in the area of intellectual faculty as mentioned in verse 2:31?

ª This is such a profound reminder. It is typical of human nature for people to feel proud, arrogant and think that they are always right even to the point of being recalcitrant towards his Creator when he is wealthy and considers himself self-sufficient. A couple of examples to illustrate this are the story of Korah during the time of Pharaoh who thinks that all the wealth that he amassed was because of cleverness (verses 28:76-82) and the parable of a man who was blessed with lush gardens that produced bountiful fruits (verses 18:32-44) that finally ended up in ruin.

97. Al-Qadr
[The Decree : 5 verses]

T his Makkan chapter celebrates the night when the Qur'an - in its original form called *al-Lawh al-Mahuz* or The Well Guarded Tablet (verses 85:21-22) that was kept in the highest point of the 7th heaven which is called *Sidratul Muntaha* (verse 53:14) - was sent down in its entirety to *Baitul Izzah* or The House of Glory in the 1st heaven. This was reported by Ibn Abbas and mentioned by Ibn Kathir in his *Tafsir* of this chapter. No one but God alone knows when this occasion actually took place. Through an authentic *hadith*, the Prophet only informed us that it happened on one of the last 10 nights of Ramadan which is named as *Laylatul Qadr* or the Night of Decree. It was from *Baitul Izzah* that the Qur'an was then sent down in stages to the Prophet through Angel Gabriel over a period of 23 years (verses 17:106 and 76:23).

In the name of God, the Most Gracious,
the Most Compassionate.

¹ Indeed, We have sent this (divine revelation) down *ᵃ* in Its entirety on the Night of Decree.*ᵇ* ² And do you know what the Night of Decree is?

³ The Night of Decree is better than a thousand months. ⁴ Therein descend the Angels and the Spirit *ᶜ* by God's permission to address all affairs. ⁵ That is indeed the night of peace until the break of dawn.

ᵃ The main key in differentiating this verse which says that the Qur'an was sent down in its entirety compared to verses 17:106 and 76:23 which say that the Qur'an was sent down in stages to the Prophet over a period of 23 years is in the word "*Anzalna*" that is used here. Verses 17:106 and 76:23 on the other hand, use "*Wa nazzalnāhu tanzilan*" and "*Nahnu nazzalnā ... tanzilan*" respectively which means "We sent it down in stages". Because of this, The Night of Decree or *Laylatul Qadr* cannot be regarded as the time when the Prophet received his first revelation in the cave of Mount Hira' as presented in Chapter 96. Instead, *Laylatul Qadr* occurred at the time when the Qur'an was sent down in its entirety from *Sidratul Muntaha* to *Baitul Izzah* before it was sent down to the Prophet in stages as mentioned in the chapter's synopsis above.

ᵇ *Al-Qadr* means The Decree. The Qur'an that was sent down from *Sidratul Muntaha* to *Baitul Izzah* on this special night is essentially about God's decree. The Qur'an decrees the right path for man to take in this world and the ultimate fate in the afterlife that awaits those who do so and those who don't. Truth is clearly distinct from falsehood and there is no compulsion in religion. It has been decreed that everyone is given free will to make his choice and will be made accountable for that decision.

ᶜ This Spirit or *Ruh* is another name for Angel Gabriel.

98. Al-Bayyinah
[The Clear Evidence : 8 verses]

T his is a Madinan chapter that takes its title from the clear evidence demanded
by the disbelievers mentioned in the first verse, before they were prepared to
believe in the Qur'an. The chapter further spells out the basic tenets of faith,
and contrasts the Hellfire with the lasting bliss that will be enjoyed by the faithful and
righteous.

In the name of God, the Most Gracious, the Most Compassionate.

[1] (Some of) those who disbelieve among the people of the earlier
revelation and also among the idolaters were not (ready to) depart from their
ways until clear evidence comes to them; [2] (brought by) a Messenger from
God who recites (blessed revelations inscribed on) purified scrolls; [3] that
contain upright principles (and commandments). [a]

[4] And (there were also) those who were given the revelation (in the past)
that became divided after such clear evidence came to them; [5] whereas they
were not commanded except to worship God alone in sincere devotion to His
religion, to be upright, to establish prayer and to spend in charity. That is
surely the true religion.

[6] Indeed, those among the people of earlier revelation and the idolaters (of
Makkah) who (persist in) rejecting the truth (after it has been conveyed to
them, will be cast) in the Fire of Hell where they will remain in it forever.
Such people are the worst of all creatures. [b] [7] But those who believe and do
righteous deeds, they are the best (and noblest) of all creatures. [8] Their reward
with their Lord is Gardens of Eternity which rivers flow beneath, where they
will remain in there forever. God is well pleased with them, and they are well
pleased with Him too. This awaits whoever that fears (incurring the
displeasure of His Lord) and stands in awe of Him.

---

[a] Genuine people of the earlier revelation (i.e. Jews and Christians) welcomed Islam.
They voluntarily and willingly embraced it and understood the Prophet's mission as a
fulfillment of their own Scriptures (verses 17:107-109). Those among the Arab pagans
with pure *fitrah* too (verse 30:30) were the earliest to accept Islam when it was
conveyed to them.
[b] Knowledge is no guarantee of righteousness. Intellectual error or ignorance of the
truth may be forgiven and can be rectified. But the deliberate promotion of evil and
corruption of the soul is unpardonable. This verse makes it clear that the fate of such
greedy, selfish and corrupt people who abuse religion is doomed.

99. Al-Zalzalah
[The Violent Earthquake : 8 verses]

Some scholars are in the opinion that this chapter is a very early Madinan chapter while some say that it is a late Makkan chapter. Regardless of its actual period of revelation, the chapter describes some of the terrible events that will mark the coming of resurrection and the Day of Judgment. It points out that whoever does any good or evil deed even if it is of an atom's weight, he or she will be made accountable for it. The chapter is named after its first verse which mentions about The Violent Earthquake or *Al-Zalzalah* that will happen during the Last Hour.

In the name of God, the Most Gracious, the Most Compassionate.

¹ When the earth is shaken with a violent earthquake; ² and throws out its burdens; *ᵃ* ³ people (will wonder and) cry out "What is happening to the earth?" *ᵇ*

⁴ On that Day the earth will reveal all its history; ⁵ because your Lord commanded it to do so.

⁶ On that Day, people will come forward in separate groups to be shown their deeds.*ᶜ* ⁷ So whoever does an atom's weight of good will see it; ⁸ and whoever does an atom's weight of evil will see it too.*ᵈ*

ᵃ An allusion to the dead being thrown out of their graves as mentioned in verse 100:9.
ᵇ Just like death, the arrival of the Last Hour is not possible to predict and will take people by complete surprise. Its arrival will be swift and decisive while people are going about their normal business (verse 36:48-50).
ᶜ See verses 56:8-12
ᵈ Accountability will be meticulous on that day to the very last atom, and people will wish that their evil deeds had never existed as mentioned in verse 3:30 which reads, "On the Day when every soul will find itself confronted with whatever good and evil it has done, it will wish that the time between itself and that Day were far apart." Indeed, only those who have no faith in the Day of Judgment would dare to cause disorder and corruption on earth, perpetrate injustice, inflict hardship and usurp the rights of others while they are alive.

100. Al-'Ādiyāt
[The War Steeds : 11 verses]

This is an early Makkan chapter where God swears by the warhorses that He has subjected to man's use. The chapter emphasizes man's ingratitude to God's limitless grace and favors, and his obsession with wealth, reminding him of the inevitability of resurrection and judgment which he can never escape from.

In the name of God, the Most Gracious,
the Most Compassionate.

¹ By the snorting horses that charge forward; ² striking sparks of fire (with their hooves); ³ rushing to raid at dawn; ⁴ and raising with it (clouds of) dust; ⁵ penetrating deep into the midst of the enemy.

⁶ Verily, man is most ungrateful to his Lord; ⁷ and he is certainly a witness (of his own ingratitude). *ᵃ* ⁸ Indeed, he is passionately devoted to the love and pursuit of worldly wealth. *ᵇ*

⁹ Does man not know that when whatever lies buried in the graves are thrown out and laid bare (on the Day when he is resurrected); ¹⁰ and all the secrets in everyone's hearts will be fully exposed?

¹¹ Indeed (on that Day), their Lord will show that He is fully aware of all their deeds.

ᵃ On the Day of Judgment, man will be made to testify against himself for the wrongdoings that he has committed. See verses 6:30, 24:24, 36:65 and 41:20.
ᵇ See verses 102:1-2 and 104:2-3.

101. Al-Qāri'ah
[The Striking Calamity : 11 verses]

This is an early Makkan chapter that mentions some of the terrible events when the world comes to an end that mark the coming of resurrection and the Day of Judgment. The chapter also calls attention to the fact that the one whose scale of merit is heavy will have a life of happiness in Paradise and the one whose scale of merit is light will endure suffering in the Hellfire.

In the name of God, the Most Gracious, the Most Compassionate.

¹ The Striking Calamity! ² What is the Striking Calamity? ³ And do you know what the Striking Calamity is?

⁴ It is the Day when people will be like scattered moths (without any sense of direction); *ᵃ* ⁵ and the mountains will be (crushed into bits until they become) like loosened wool.

⁶ Then as for him whose scale (of merit) is heavy; ⁷ he will enjoy a blessed life of (good pleasure and) great satisfaction (in Paradise).

⁸ But as for him whose scale (of merit) is light; ⁹ he will (suffer endless torment) in the womb of the Pit. ¹⁰ And do you know what this is? ¹¹ It is a Fire that blazes fiercely!

ᵃ This is a truly amazing analogy and comparison to ponder. In verse 4 of this chapter, God likens people to moths. But in verse 54:7, He likens people to locusts instead. Why are the analogies different? The answer is because they represent two completely different situations. In this chapter, the scenario is about the day when the world ends; whereas in verse 54:7, the scenario is about the Day of Resurrection that follows. Moths are frail light creatures that do not fly together in a group. Instead they scatter and seem to fly without a proper sense of direction. This is how people will be on the day of great calamity when the world comes to an end. They are in a state of total confusion and will run around aimlessly and helplessly in great distress trying to save themselves from the striking calamity. But everything they do will be in vain because everyone and everything except God, will perish on that day. On the other hand, locusts have a sense of direction as they swarm together in a group. Its analogy is applied here to depict how people will act on the Day of Resurrection. Everyone will come out from their graves at the same time when they are summoned by a Caller, and rush towards him altogether to get ready to face God and be made fully accountable for every bit of their action during their short stay on earth.

102. At-Takātsur
[The Rivalry for Worldly Gains : 8 verses]

T his is another early Makkan chapter. Its name is taken after the first verse, and it is the antithesis of the reminder mentioned in verse 28:77. This chapter criticizes man's preoccupation with their greedy acquisition of worldly gains. It also reminds him of the inescapable accountability that he will face when he is resurrected on the Day of Judgment.

In the name of God, the Most Gracious,
the Most Compassionate.

¹ (O men!) You have (certainly) been distracted by the rivalry (against one another) for the acquisition of worldly gains; ² (and you will never be satisfied with what you greedily amass) until you reach your graves. *ᵃ*

³ Nay! In time you will come to know. ⁴ And once again : Nay! In time you will come to know (how astray you have been). ⁵ Nay! If only you knew this for certain with true knowledge (now); ⁶ surely (you will fear) the Blazing Fire as if you saw it (with your own eyes). ⁷ In the end, you will surely see it with the certainty of your own eyes (when the moment finally arrives).

⁸ Then on that Day, you will surely be asked about all the pleasures that you have enjoyed (and be made accountable for them).

ᵃ Excessive love for the short-lived glittering of this world is caused by the sickness of insatiable greed. It corrupts the soul, makes people worship lusts (verses 25:43, 45:23) and lead a hedonistic lifestyle. It also causes people to perpetrate many acts of evil and injustice while they greedily amass wealth. They succumb to their own lusts (verse 91:7) and the deceits of Satan instead of striving to fulfill the purpose of their creation as God's trustees on earth to serve Him and mankind to the best of their ability. As a result, the Muslim *ummah* and its corrupt leaders become weak and powerless against the transgressions perpetrated by evil forces. See the footnote for verse 22:40. The Prophet has forewarned this 1,450 years ago through the following *hadith* : "People will soon call upon one another to attack you just like those who are eating invite others to share their dish." Then someone asked, "Will that be because our number is small at that time?" The Prophet replied, "No! On the contrary, your number will be large at that time, but you will be like scum and rubbish that is carried down by a torrent. God will take the fear of you away from the breasts of your enemy and at the same time place *Al-Wahn* into your hearts." Then someone asked again, "What is *Al-Wahn*?" The Prophet replied, "Excessive love of the world and dislike of death (which will cause you to be parted from the world that you love so much)." [Sunan Abu Dawud, no. 4297]

103. Al-'Asr
[The Flight of Time : 3 verses]

This is another early Makkan chapter. It concisely points out the fact that the flight of time can never be recaptured and life in this temporary world is extremely short compared to the afterlife which is eternal in nature. And so, every man is by default in a state of loss leading to ruin unless he has faith in the ultimate Creator of the heavens and the earth and submits wholeheartedly to Him, does good deeds to ease the affairs of others, counsels one another to the truth and remains steadfast in this path. Imam Shafi'e - a jurist and traditional scholar of Islam, held that if God had only revealed this chapter alone, it would have been sufficient for the guidance of all humanity. It summarized the very essence of the Qur'anic message. Thus, Imam Shafi'e asserts that if one followed its counsel, it was enough for him to achieve success in this life and the next one to come.

In the name of God, the Most Gracious, the Most Compassionate.

¹ By the flight of time!

² Indeed, man is surely in a state of loss.

³ Except those who believe *a* and do good deeds.*b* They are also those who counsel one another to stay committed to the truth *c* and to remain steadfast (in this path with great patience).

---

a Those who submit wholeheartedly to the One and Only Almighty God with undivided faith in His revelation.

b Good deeds are the result of true faith in God by performing worship rituals that are strictly based on the authentic teachings of the Prophet and emulating his good conduct (see verse 3:31); and to also serve mankind as God's emissary on earth by upholding justice and striving against oppression.

c Truth stands clearly distinct from falsehood (verses 2:256 and 18:29). It is the teachings of the Qur'an as manifested by Prophet Muhammad's practices and conduct in all aspects.

104. Al-Humazah
[The Slanderer : 9 verses]

T his is a Makkan chapter. It condemns those who slander and backbite others, and gives a description of Hell. Further, it warns against being a slave to materialism, devoting solely to the accumulation of worldly wealth which makes him oblivious to the Hereafter and the Hellfire's punishment.

In the name of God, the Most Gracious, the Most Compassionate.

¹ Woe to every slanderer and backbiter! *ᵃ* ² (The one) who hoards wealth and counts it repeatedly; ³ thinking that his wealth will secure him immortality.*ᵇ*

⁴ Nay! He will surely be thrown into a crushing torment. ⁵ And do you know what that crushing torment is? ⁶ It is a Fire kindled by God; ⁷ which will rise up to the hearts (of wicked transgressors).*ᶜ* ⁸ Indeed, it will be securely closed upon them; ⁹ in towering columns.

ᵃ Ibnu Kathir noted in his *Tafsir* that according to Ibn Abbas, the expression *Humazah Lumazah* that is being used here is not only confined to slanderers and backbiters but include those who revile and disgrace others too. This is in direct reference to some wealthy Makkans who did not have to work to earn their livelihood and would normally loiter together to mock the Muslims, scoff at the Prophet and revile Islam to pass their time. Their activity naturally incurred God's displeasure and was rebuked by the revelation of this chapter.

ᵇ The description given here seems to fall within the same category of those who God condemned in verses 100:8 and 102:1-8. It further suggests that those who like to slander and maliciously revile others also have the evil nature of being obsessed with worldly gains at the expense of others because their overweening selfish behavior would lead them to adopt a sense of delusion that they will live forever, and therefore having complete disregard for the Day of Judgment.

ᶜ The Qur'an depicts a horrible scene here which describes the Fire that will rise and burn the hearts of wicked transgressors in Hell first before it consumes the rest of the body. This is because the heart, being the home of all intentions, is the source of every evil thought and action. And when it is not kept in check, it leads to all kinds of wicked actions that will harm the soul and also cause pain to other people. This message also serves as a reminder that we must always strive to purify our hearts to attain *Taqwa* (see verses 2:183 and 29:45) so that our souls will be in the state of serenity in order to be graciously admitted into Paradise (see verses 89:37-39).

105. Al-Fīl
[The Elephant : 5 verses]

T his is an early Makkan chapter. It refers to the invasion of the Ka'bah by Abrahah al-Ashram, the Christian ruler of Yemen in 570 CE, the year of the Prophet's birth. Abrahah came with a huge army of infantry with elephants to destroy the Ka'bah with the intention to divert pilgrims to a new cathedral in Sana'a. But God foiled the attempt and annihilated the invaders by sending successive flights of birds throwing *sijjil* stones on them. The emphasis of this chapter is on the duty to worship God alone and the destruction of Abrahah's army is cited here to encourage the believers and warn the disbelievers of their opposition against the message of truth that was being conveyed to them by the Prophet.

In the name of God, the Most Gracious, the Most Compassionate.

[1] Have you not considered how your Lord dealt with the People of the Elephant?

[2] Did He not frustrate their plot; [3] and send flocks of birds against them; [4] that pelted them with stones of baked clay?

[5] Then He made them become like a field of corn stubble that has been eaten up.

106. Quraysh
[The Tribe of Quraysh : 4 verses]

This is a Makkan chapter that refers to the blessings bestowed by God to the Quraysh inhabitants of Makkah by making the city safe and secured by virtue of the Ka'bah, which made Makkah as a centre of trade in peninsular Arabia. It connects with the previous chapter of how God defeated the threat to Makkah posed by Abrahah, hence allowing the Quraysh to safely continue their two yearly trade journeys to Yemen during winter and to Syria during summer. Essentially, the chapter calls upon them to worship God alone Who is the Lord of the Ka'bah, and to give up their practice of idol worship.

In the name of God, the Most Gracious, the Most Compassionate.

[1] It is the tradition of the Quraysh (tribe and the privilege that God granted them); [2] (to enjoy) the safe passage of their trading caravans (to Yemen) in winter and (to Syria in) summer.

[3] So call upon them to leave idol worship and turn to the Lord of this (sacred) House; [4] Who provides them food against hunger, and security against fear (and danger).

107. Al-Mā'ūn
[Simple Acts of Kindness : 7 verses]

This is a Makkan chapter that describes some characteristics of those who deny God's religion and pay no heed to the promise of resurrection and judgment. The gist of this chapter equates those who are selfish and treat others badly with those who have no faith in God. It goes to show that acts of worship are meaningless and hold no value in the sight of God if they are not complemented with kindness and courtesy to others, and concern for the welfare of the poor. The essence of this chapter clearly demonstrates that Islam is not a religion that is all about rituals alone but is instead a well balanced way of life that places equal emphasis on social justice and establishing good relationship among fellow humans, regardless of race and religion.

In the name of God, the Most Gracious, the Most Compassionate.

[1] Have you seen the one who denies God's religion (and has no fear for the Day of Resurrection)? [2] Such is the one who pushes away the orphan; [3] and does not (care nor) feel the urge (and compassion) to feed the poor.

[4] So woe then to those who pray; [5] but whose (hearts are remote from their) prayer (and) are oblivious (to their moral duties). [6] They are the ones who flaunt (their deeds for show to gain praise); [7] and withhold simple acts of kindness (and assistance to others). [a]

---

[a] Ammar ibn Yasir reported that the Messenger of God (peace be upon him) said, "Verily, a man may complete his prayer without anything good that is written for him except only a tenth (from the full reward) of his prayer, or a ninth, or an eighth, or a seventh, or a sixth, or a fifth, or a fourth, or a third, or a half." [Sunan Abu Dawud, no. 796]. This *hadith* underscores the message of this chapter which tells us that our prayer and other worship rituals may only earn a fraction of their full reward or even be completely nullified if we treat others badly and unjustly (see footnote of verse 2:183). Even worse, when a society condones corruption and injustice and allows double standard practices to prevail, it will incur God's wrath and be cursed with humiliation. See verses 3:112, 6:123, 11:113 and their corresponding footnotes. Now consider this: If those who pray but withhold simple acts of kindness and small assistance to others are cursed by God, what about those who commit violence on innocent people whose lives God hold sacred (verse 17:33)? If this is correctly understood, is it fair to regard Islam as a religion that promotes violence and terrorism?

108. Al-Kautsar
[Pleasure in Abundance : 3 verses]

This is a Makkan chapter and it is the shortest chapter in the Qur'an with only three verses. It tells the story about the Prophet who was taunted by one of the enemies of Islam that he has been cut-off from God's grace as evidenced by the death of his son. The chapter was revealed as a retort to the disbelieving infidel by saying that it is he, and not the Prophet, who is actually being cut-off from all that is good. Further, the Prophet was commanded to be steadfast in making prayers and sacrifices to God alone.

In the name of God, the Most Gracious,
the Most Compassionate.

¹ Indeed, We have bestowed pleasure to you in abundance *ᵃ* (O Muhammad)! ² So pray to your Lord (in full devotion) and make your sacrifice (to Him alone).

³ Verily, (forbear) whoever hates you (for it is he who) has actually been cut-off (from God's grace and mercy).

ᵃ The meaning of *al-Kautsar* or "Pleasure in Abundance" in the context of its mention here refers to the abundant bestowal on the Prophet of all that is good in an abstract and spiritual sense such as revelation, knowledge, wisdom, the doing of good work, and dignity in this world and in the Hereafter. With reference to the believers in general, it signifies the spirit and act to acquire knowledge, to do good work, to be kind towards all living beings that will all lead to the attainment of inner peace and dignity.

109. Al-Kāfirūn
[Those Who Reject The Truth : 6 verses]

This is a Makkan chapter. As a compromise to the Prophet's unequivocal rejection of idolatry practices, some Makkan chieftains suggested to the him that he should worship their gods for a year, and they would alternately worship his for a year in return. This was God's reply.

***In the name of God, the Most Gracious,
the Most Compassionate.***

¹ Say (to the disbelievers), "O you who reject the truth! *ᵃ* ² I do not worship what you worship.³ And you do not worship what I worship."

⁴ "And I shall not worship what you worship. ⁵ And neither will you worship what I worship."

⁶ "For you is your religion, and for me is mine."

ᵃ Even though this chapter is particularly directed towards the Arab Quraysh disbelievers of Makkah during the time of the Prophet in the first instance, it nevertheless commands every Muslim to completely disavow themselves from anything that is being worshipped by the disbelievers which they have ascribed divinity to, besides Almighty God.

110. An-Naṣr
[Divine Help : 3 verses]

A Madinan chapter which is said to be the last whole chapter sent down to the Prophet before his death. It alludes to the impending conquest of Makkah and the completion of his mission with God's help. It is named after first verse wherein mention is made of God's divine help and victory.

*In the name of God, the Most Gracious,
the Most Compassionate.*

¹ When the help of God comes, and victory is granted; ² and you see people embracing the religion of God in multitudes. ᵃ

³ So proclaim the perfection of your Lord by praising Him (immensely) and by asking for His forgiveness. Indeed, He is the ever Acceptor of Repentance.

ᵃ Islam is not a ritual-centric religion for the purpose of self-indulgence. Instead, Islam is a religion of truth that should be actively propagated and shared with others. Many evidence of its divinity are clearly presented in the Qu'ran in the form of irrefutable scientific and historical facts for those who care to use reason, common sense and intellect to analyze and ponder. Hence, Muslims must play an active role to invite others in the best manner to see the truth in Islam through reason by pointing out these evidence in the Qur'an, and also based on Islam's true concept of justice for all. People must be invited to voluntarily submit to God and worship Him alone without compulsion based on facts and reason, instead of exaggeration based on superstitions, myths or weak and false sayings of the Prophet (i.e. *Hadith*). See verses 16:125, 45:4-6 and 62:5 and their footnotes. Notwithstanding this, imagine what would have happened to Islam if the Prophet had kept the religion to himself by only indulging in rituals with an indifferent attitude towards the injustices and oppressions around him? Surely he would have been the only Muslim in this world and Islam would not have grown beyond the four walls of the room in his home! According to this passage, true victory in this world is accomplished when we can successfully invite people to God's religion in multitudes. The least a Muslim can do to contribute towards this is to not behave deplorably and tarnish the image of Islam as this would cause people to form a negative and wrong perception and understanding of Islam and be driven away from it.

111. Al-Masad
[The Palm Fibre Rope : 5 verses]

This is an early Makkan chapter which its name is taken from the last verse. This chapter presents one of the amazing miracles of the Quran. It tells a short story of one of the Prophet's uncles who opposed him fiercely, as did his wife. When many of the most severe opponents in the early days of Islam eventually became devoted followers in later days, this couple persisted in their evil endeavor to oppose, ridicule, and disprove the Qur'an in every possible way they could. According to Islamic scholars, this chapter - which clearly dictated that both Abu Lahab and his wife will dwell in the eternal Fire in the Hereafter - was revealed about 10 years before his death. Theoretically, this means that Abu Lahab and his wife had 3,650 chances (365 days x 10 years) to become Muslims. Not only that, there could have easily been at least 1,000 opponents of Islam around Abu Lahab and none of them had suggested and encouraged Abu Lahab and his wife to claim that they are believers out of false pretense to trick the Prophet. Taking this into consideration, Abu Lahab and his wife actually had close to 3.7 million chances (10 years X 365 days X 1,000 opponents) within every single day of the 10 years that he lived after the revelation of this chapter to prove that the Qur'an is not revealed by God and that the Prophet is a liar. He could have easily done this by pretending to embrace Islam on any of those moments within the 3,650 days, but he did not. Had he done so, then the divine nature of the Qur'an would have surely been doubtful, suspicious and questionable. But he and his wife did not apply this obvious strategy. The logical question is what prevented them, if not the knowledge of God Who knew that they will never believe nor even pretend to believe, and that they would surely die as disbelievers? In fact, God knew exactly that they would never even pretend to embrace Islam to take advantage of the 3.7 million chances to just prove that His public proclamation about them in this chapter made 10 years earlier was wrong. Is this not a clear miracle?

In the name of God, the Most Gracious,
the Most Compassionate.

[1] Doomed are the hands of Abu Lahab, and doomed is he (forever)! [2] Neither his wealth and all that he has earned will benefit him.

[3] (In the life to come,) he will be made to endure a Fire of Blazing Flames; [4] along with his wife - the carrier of thorny firewood (who spreads evil and slanderous tales). [5] (She will have) a palm-fibre rope around her neck!

112. Al-Ikhlāṣ
[Purity of Faith : 4 verses]

This is a Makkan chapter. It is short but a succinct statement of clear monotheism which rebuts the assumptions of all those who set partners with God or with His Attributes, or assign a son or daughter for Him. Nothing is equal to Him, neither in self, nor in names and attributes. The Prophet was reported to have said that this chapter alone represents one third of the Qur'an [Sahih Bukhari, no. 5013] by virtue of its profound message that unequivocally puts the record straight about His indivisible Oneness.

In the name of God, the Most Gracious, the Most Compassionate.

¹ Say, "He is God - The One and only Indivisible God. ᵃ

² God - The Absolute, (Who is never in need of anything but of Whom everything else depends on)."

³ He begets none, nor is He begotten. ⁴ And there is nothing that is ever equivalent and comparable to Him."

ᵃ Rational and sensible contemplation on the very nature of the cosmic structure will tell us that it does not allow for multiple gods. It is nonsensical to believe that there is an independent god for the sun and another for the earth, or one for the animal kingdom another for the plants or one for the African continent and another for Europe or Asia. The cosmic order is in an integrated whole, set up, designed, run, and controlled by a single sufficient power. This power regulates the operation of the human digestive system within us and also the orbiting of the planets and stars in the infinite universe. Plants grow out of the ground, dawn breaks every day and the sun and the moon move in their charted courses in accordance with His will. The Qur'an is abound with strong arguments supporting this principle and a couple of direct references to this can be found in 21:22 and 23:91.

113. Al-Falaq
[The Rising Dawn : 5 verses]

This is an early Makkan chapter. It inculcates monotheism and teaches man to take God as the Only Protector and to seek refuge with Him against any form of evil and harm from any of His creations. It is commonly used as an invocation against evil. It is named after its first verse which mentions *Al-Falaq* or The Rising Dawn.

In the name of God, the Most Gracious, the Most Compassionate.

[1] Say, "I seek refuge in the Lord *ᵃ* of the rising dawn.

[2] From the evil mischief of (the creatures) that He has created; [3] and from the evil of the darkness when it spreads; *ᵇ*

[4] And from the evil of those who blow on knots (that are tied in a string to cast spells); *ᶜ* [5] and from the evil of an envier when he envies." *ᵈ*

ᵃ God answers those who plead with Him and seek His protection. This chapter and the one that follows it teach us how to seek God's protection against all kinds of ill-feelings and evil intentions that we constantly encounter in life.

ᵇ Evil and harm may come from numerous sources that might strike at dawn or at the middle of the night, the latter being a more popular time with thieves and criminals.

ᶜ One should seek refuge in God from the evil of sorcery and witchcraft that involve the mischief of humans acting in cohort with devils and evil spirits to inflict misery on others.

ᵈ And finally, one should always seek God's protection against envy, which reflects hatred for other fellow humans and an evil desire to see them deprived of comfort and success.

114. An-Nās
[Mankind : 6 verses]

T his is an early Makkan chapter. Like the previous chapter, this one also inculcates monotheism and teaches man that God is his only Lord and Protector, and asks him to seek refuge with Him against the evil instigation of man and Jinn. It is named *An-Nās* or Mankind with reference to its first verse where God is mentioned as the Lord of mankind. The chapter is also commonly used as an invocation against evil.

In the name of God, the Most Gracious, the Most Compassionate.

¹ Say, "I seek refuge in the Lord of all mankind; ² the Supreme Ruler of all mankind; ³ the God of all mankind; *ᵃ*

⁴ from the evil intentions of the stalking whisperer; ⁵ who whispers (evil and the feeling of uncertainty) in everyone's heart; ⁶ from among the Jinn and mankind." *ᵇ*

ᵃ Verses 1-3 : Refuge is being sought with God Almighty from the insinuations of the devils of both the jinn and humankind. As humans, we have no knowledge of how jinns act and behave. But we are able to feel their presence and influence in our life. In view of this frailty, it is therefore necessary for us to seek God's help and protection against their potential scheming and ill-will.

ᵇ There is connection between verses 4-6 of this chapter and 6:112. It appears that human devils relish influencing actions, while the jinn devils enjoy confusing people and leading them astray through whisperings. Both devils complement one another. Nevertheless, jinn devils are barred from having any power to force anyone to do anything he does not want to, but the greatest danger lies in their persuasive and inciting skills that could infiltrate the human mind. Having been warned, those who fall for the devils' intrigues would have only themselves to blame. This chapter implicitly warns against adverse psychological and mental influences arising from devils' mischief that can affect human behavior, urging believers to ward against them by seeking protection and safety with God Almighty.

Made in the USA
Middletown, DE
29 July 2023

35869126R00356